AIR PASSENGER RIGHTS

This essential book offers a comprehensive and concise overview of the complex global framework of air passenger rights, examining not only national laws but also regional agreements. From countries that have "copy-pasted" the EU model to those that have significantly enhanced it – such as the Philippines with its tarmac delay provisions, or Canada with its nuanced categorization of disruptions – this book dissects the global landscape.

It reveals how some nations have even surpassed their progenitor, offering unique protections for vulnerable passengers or specifying intricate details down to meal composition. Prior to this book, practitioners faced various issues from language barriers – some laws are not translated into English – to fragmentation. Now there is a consolidated analysis of all these laws in a single accessible resource, making them accessible and comparable for all. The book offers a concise, comparative overview of all distinct national and regional laws in place focusing on delays, cancellations, and denial of boarding. It also contains tables to ensure easier reading access. It can be considered a one-stop shop for understanding the global panorama of air passenger rights.

By meticulously analysing the varied approaches to passenger rights around the world, this book fills a crucial void, offering an invaluable resource for policymakers, legal professionals, airlines, and passengers seeking to navigate the complex world of air travel consumer protection on flight delays, cancellations, and denial of boarding.

Delphine Defossez defended her PhD in Brazil on the topic of liberalization of the Brazilian market. She is currently an assistant professor at Northumbria University. Delphine has published on a range of topics mainly related to aviation law, with an emphasis on passenger protection.

AIR PASSENGER RIGHTS

A GLOBAL PERSPECTIVE

DELPHINE DEFOSSEZ

informa law
from Routledge

Designed cover image: Getty Images© Credit: Michal Krakowiak

First published 2027
by Informa Law from Routledge
4 Park Square, Milton Park, Abingdon, Oxon OX14 4RN

and by Informa Law from Routledge
605 Third Avenue, New York, NY 10158

Informa Law from Routledge is an imprint of the Taylor & Francis Group, an informa business

British Library Cataloguing-in-Publication Data
A catalogue record for this book is available from the British Library

Library of Congress Cataloging-in-Publication Data
Names: Defossez, Delphine author
Title: Air passenger rights : a global perspective / Delphine Defossez.
Description: First. | Abingdon, Oxon [UK] ; New York, NY : Informa Law from Routledge, 2026. | Includes bibliographical references and index.
Identifiers: LCCN 2026008534 (print) | LCCN 2026008535 (ebook) | ISBN 9781041253235 hardback | ISBN 9781041253211 paperback | ISBN 9781003746164 ebook
Subjects: LCSH: Aeronautics, Commercial—Law and legislation | Aeronautics, Commercial—Passenger traffic | Airplane occupants—Legal status, laws, etc.
Classification: LCC K4095 .D44 2026 (print) | LCC K4095 (ebook)
LC record available at https://lccn.loc.gov/2026008534
LC ebook record available at https://lccn.loc.gov/2026008535

ISBN: 978-1-041-25323-5 (hbk)
ISBN: 978-1-041-25321-1 (pbk)
ISBN: 978-1-003-74616-4 (ebk)

DOI: 10.4324/9781003746164

Typeset in Times New Roman
by Apex CoVantage, LLC

CONTENTS

PART II NATIONAL INITIATIVES

DETAILED CONTENTS

PREFACE

This book was born from a simple, yet surprising, discovery. What began as an article on the potential harmonization of passenger rights through an international instrument quickly revealed a significant gap in the literature. I had assumed a comprehensive analysis was readily available, but to my surprise, not only was this information absent in book form, but many of these critical laws had not been discussed in academic articles – at least not in English – despite governing the lives of millions of travellers. This silence surrounding such critically important laws was both surprising and compelling; it transformed my article into a mission.

This book is the fruit of extensive research to fill that void. To make this vast topic manageable and deeply insightful, I have chosen to focus on national and regional laws that sit atop the Montreal Convention and cover the three most common disruptions in air travel: flight delays, cancellations, and denied boarding. These incidents represent the core of passenger grievance and are the areas where harmonization could deliver the most immediate and tangible benefits.

Wherever possible, relevant case law has been incorporated to ground the analysis in practical legal outcomes. These judicial interpretations illuminate how these rights are applied, contested, and enforced in real-world scenarios. It is my sincere hope that this work will not only serve as a valuable resource for practitioners, academics, and policymakers but also open the debate as to whether any harmonization is feasible.

DISCLAIMER

Whenever possible the author has used legal documents in their original language or official translations. However, such official translations are not always available. In those instances, the author has done her best to either request a native speaker to verify the information – for instance for China and Korea – or has had to rely on online translators.

Introduction

In recent years, there has been proliferation in national or regional initiatives and specific legislations granting passengers with greater rights in case of delay, cancellation, or denial of boarding, with Australia among the most recent additions to this list. These initiatives aim at offering a higher level of protection and certainty to passengers than they are afforded by the global regimes, namely the Warsaw Convention of 1929 or the Montreal Convention of 1999. While these international treaties successfully unified certain rules, they left significant gaps, failing to address critical issues like denied boarding and establishing clear compensation standards.[1]

This growing focus on consumer protection is a global phenomenon. The International Civil Aviation Organization (ICAO) reported in 2013 that 55 countries had some form of aviation-specific passenger rights regimes, most of which were adopted in the early 2000s.[2] By 2016, according to the IATA Annual Report, this number had increased to more than 60 countries.[3] However, these reports offer little detail; they neither list the

1 As Aleksandra Puścińska argued "Under the narrow construction of Article 19 of the Warsaw Convention, and now also Article 19 of the Montreal Convention, of the Montreal Convention, denial of boarding falls under the non-performance of contract of carriage rather than delay." See: Aleksandra Puścińska, 'A Fragmented Legal Regime of Air Carrier Liability in International Transportation of Passengers: Delay, Cancellation and Denied Boarding' (McGill University, August 2016) 79. In some countries such as Qatar, the courts have interpreted the conventions broadly to allow passengers suffering from a denial of boarding to get compensated. See: Decision No. 526 year 2018 (Qatari Court of Cassation) as reported in Eman Naboush, 'Evaluating the Rights of Air Consumers Under International and Evaluating the Rights of Air Consumers Under International and Regional Instruments with a Focus on Qatar Regional Instruments with a Focus on Qatar' (2024) 12 International Journal on Consumer Law and Practice <https://repository.nls.ac.in/cgi/viewcontent.cgi?article=1193&context=ijclp> accessed 15 November 2025.

2 International Air Transport Association (IATA), 'A Proposal for a Set of High-Level, Non-Prescriptive Core Principles on Consumer Protection' (ICAO Assembly, 38th Session, Agenda Item 40, Working Paper No 73, Doc A38-WP/73, 5 August 2013) 2.

3 IATA, 'Annual Review 2016, 72nd Annual General Meeting' (June 2016) 27 <https://www.iata.org/contentassets/c81222d96c9a4e0bb4ff6ced0126f0bb/iata-annual-review-2016.pdf> accessed 15 November 2025.

DOI: 10.4324/9781003746164-1

countries nor specify whether their national laws surpass the minimum provisions of the Montreal Convention. These specific legislations are rarely discussed or systematically compared. This book is filling that critical gap by providing a detailed analysis of regional and national initiatives which go beyond the Conventions' provisions and are specially dedicated to air passenger rights. The focus is squarely on laws that follow the model pioneered by the European Union's Regulation 261/2004 and on denied boarding, cancellation, delays, right to care, and compensation or any rule that is unique or enhances passengers' rights.

The undeniable pioneer and leading force in this legislative movement is European Union Regulation 261. After its enactment, the Regulation became an internationally recognized model regulation, spurring the creation of what is now known as "Regulation 261's legacy outside the EU."[4] Some jurisdictions have produced near-replicas, such as the Turkish SHY-PASSENGER, while other EU offspring have actually surpassed their progenitor, such as the Philippines Air Passenger Bill of Rights of 2012 or the Canadian Air Passenger Protection Regulations which can be seen as an upgraded version of EU Regulation 261.[5] These 'updated' versions demonstrate that Regulation 261 is far from perfect.

Unfortunately, as the following analysis will reveal, national rules often vary and sometimes conflict, forming a patchwork of regimes that "are not mutually recognized or coordinated."[6] This book offers a vital overview of this complex landscape, specifically examining countries that have enacted legislation granting passengers additional rights in the spirit of Regulation 261.[7] Consequently, countries where passenger claims are limited to generic consumer or civil aviation laws that lack specific provisions for flight disruptions are excluded. For instance, the author is aware that Madagascar Law No. 2015–014 (consumer protection laws) entitles passengers to receive full information before purchasing a service which include full pricing and that Article L.1.8.1–1 of Law No. 2012–011 (Civil Aviation Code) requires airlines to establish consumer

4 Brian Havel and John Q Mulligan, 'Extraterritorial Application: Exporting European Consumer Protection Standards' in Michal Bobek and Jeremias Prassl (eds), *Air Passenger Rights: Ten Years On* (Hart Publishing 2016) 239.

5 D. Defossez, 'Change Is in the Air in the US and Canada . . . but What about Brazil?' (2020) 19 Issues in Aviation Law and Policy 269.

6 A38-WP/73, 2.

7 For instance, New Zealand Civil Aviation Act 1990 as amended, Part 9 A and B do not afford more rights to passengers. Similarly, the UEA Federal Decree-Law No. 50/2022, also known as the Commercial Transactions Law, Chapter 5 (Articles 353 to 370) includes provisions regarding flight delays or damage to luggage which entitle the passengers to compensation for any inconvenience or loss suffered (Article 357) unless the exception in Article 358 applies. In Indonesia, the law is Aviation Law No. 1 of 2009 and Ministry of Transportation Regulation No. 77 of 2011 on Liability of Air Carriers.

protection policies.[8] Article 78 of the Qatari Civil Aviation law establishes an obligation on carriers to compensate passengers holding a valid ticket.[9] Section 91(2) of Kenyan Consumer Protection Act No. 46 of 2012 (CPA) entitles passengers of long delays or cancelled flights to overnight accommodation or meals. Moreover, in *Ms. Joyce v Skyward Airline Ltd*,[10] an airline's failure to book a passenger on a flight after confirming her reservation was considered a false or misleading representation under section 55(b)(iv)(v) of the Kenyan Competition Act. However, those laws do not provide any further clarifications in case of cancellation, delays, or denied boarding.[11]

Given its status as the pioneer, the sheer number of copycat laws and its influential nature in this field, the European Union's Regulation 261 has been used as the natural benchmark for evaluating the various national laws.

---

8 Loi n°2012-011, portant Code Malagasy de l'aviation civil <https://www.droit-afrique.com/upload/doc/madagascar/Madagascar-Code-2012-aviation-civile.pdf> accessed 15 November 2025.

9 Eman Naboush, 'Evaluating the Rights of Air Consumers under International and Evaluating the Rights of Air Consumers under International and Regional Instruments with a Focus on Qatar Regional Instruments with a Focus on Qatar' (2024) 12 International Journal on Consumer Law and Practice <https://repository.nls.ac.in/cgi/viewcontent.cgi?article=1193&context=ijclp> accessed 15 November 2025.

10 Consumer Protection Cases – Competition Authority of Kenya Case No. 46 <https://www.cak.go.ke/sites/default/files/guidelines/consumer-protection/SampledConsumerProtectionCases.pdf>.

11 Adya Paramita Prabandari and Ramalina Ranaivo Mikea Manitra, 'Need of a Global Aviation Standard Compliance? Air Passenger Rights in Indonesia and Madagascar' (2025) 32 Jurnal Hukum Ius Quia Iustum 207.

PART I

REGIONAL INITIATIVES

While the Warsaw and Montreal Conventions provide a global framework for air carrier liability, they do not comprehensively address passengers' rights in cases of operational disruptions such as denied boarding, cancellations, or delays. Recognizing this gap, several regional and economic communities have developed their own regulatory frameworks to enhance passenger protection beyond what the international conventions provide.

This part explores regional initiatives that have established specific passenger rights regimes, going beyond the Conventions' provisions. The analysis begins with the Andean Community and the Arab Civil Aviation Organization, examining efforts at regional harmonization outside the dominant EU model. A thorough examination of the pioneering EU Regulation 261/2004 follows, deconstructing its scope, core provisions, and the critical 'extraordinary circumstances' defence, while also looking ahead to its forthcoming 2025 revisions. The discussion then turns to the direct influence of the EU model, tracing its extension through the European Common Aviation Area Agreement (ECAA) and the Euro-Mediterranean Aviation Agreements (EMAA) or the Annex 6 of the Yamoussoukro Decision. Finally, the focus shifts to the challenging development of passenger rights frameworks within Africa, the regulations of the Central African Economic and Monetary Community (CEMAC) and the West African Economic and Monetary Union (UEMOA/WAEMU).

The regional approaches vary considerably in their scope, implementation, and effectiveness. Some, like EU Regulation 261 and the ECAA, have created comprehensive and enforceable passenger rights regimes with well-established jurisprudence. Others represent templates or guidance which are non-binding. Nevertheless, all share the common objective of providing passengers with greater certainty, standardized compensation, and clear rights when their travel plans are disrupted.

The landscape of air passenger rights has been profoundly shaped by regional legislation, which has moved beyond the minimalist uniformity of the Conventions to establish more ambitious and passenger-centric regimes.

DOI: 10.4324/9781003746164-2

I.1

Andean Community

Decisión 619 of 2005

The *Decisión 619* of 2005[1] was issued by the Andean Community[2] to promote passenger protection but also to establish rules for the liberalization of air transport services among its member countries. It applies to passengers starting their journey in an airport of a member country. It does share similarities with EU Regulation 261.[3]

The *Decisión* applies to both scheduled and non-scheduled flights.[4] The instrument applies to all carriers departing from a State Party of the Andean Community and to all incoming flights operated by an Andean Community carrier.[5]

Unlike the EU Regulation, the *Decisión* also contains provisions on luggage in its Chapter V. It also establishes a detailed set of obligations to ensure passengers are properly informed which goes further than the one under EU law.[6] The *Decisión* requires air carriers, tour operators, or travel agents to provide detailed information at key points. First, when making a reservation, passengers must be informed about all available flights, specifying whether they are direct, connecting, or code-share flights.[7] They should also receive information about all available fare types from different carriers for that flight, including their validity, restrictions, and terms of refund and the final tariff including taxes.[8] In addition, passengers have the right to know the designated airports

1 *Decisión 619 Normas para la Armonización de los Derechos y Obligaciones de los Usuarios, Transportistas y Operadores de los Servicios de Transporte Aéreo en la Comunidad Andina*, 15 de Julio de 2005, Lima <https://www.comunidadandina.org/StaticFiles/DocOf/DEC619.pdf> accessed 15 September 2025.

2 Colombia, Perú, Bolivia, and Ecuador.

3 Manuel Guillermo Sarmiento García, 'Los derechos del pasajero derivados del convenio de Montreal de 1999 y del derecho comunitario Andino' (2010) Revista Brasileira de Direito Aeronáutico e Espacial 50.

4 Article 1.

5 Article 2.

6 Article 4.

7 Article 4(a).

8 Article 4(b) and (c).

DOI: 10.4324/9781003746164-3

and terminals of departure and arrival, as well as general conditions of carriage, which include terms on reservations, cancellations, baggage allowances, restricted items, and passenger responsibilities.[9] Travel agencies and intermediaries are obligated to provide accurate passenger contact details to the carrier; if they fail to do so and a passenger cannot be contacted regarding a flight change, the intermediary is responsible for any compensation owed.[10] Second, prior to transport, passengers must be notified by the quickest means possible – and at least four hours in advance – of any changes affecting their reservation.[11] In instances of denied boarding due to overbooking, cancellation, or delay, passengers must be informed, preferably in writing, of their rights to compensation and assistance.[12] Finally, during transport, required information includes boarding procedures at the gate, safety instructions before and during flight through demonstrations and announcements, and updates on delays, cancellations, or diversions whenever feasible without impacting crew duties.[13]

The loss of a physical ticket does not invalidate the contract for air transport, and passengers can prove their contract through other means, with the right to a new ticket or a refund if the original was refundable.[14]

In case of denial of boarding, airlines must first call for volunteers and provide them with benefits which they both agree on.[15] Those passengers are also entitled to additional assistance in accordance with Article 8(a) and (e). If not enough volunteers come forward, passengers who have been involuntarily denied boarding have the right to compensation, reimbursement, and assistance.[16] Passengers denied boarding should be re-routed to their final destination on the next available flight on the same date and route. If no flight is available, the air carrier must make the necessary arrangements at its own expense, for the boarding of the user on another air carrier as soon as possible.[17] Similarly, if the re-routing is for another airport than the one originally booked for, the carrier has to bear the transport cost to the original airport selected by the passenger.[18]

The *Decisión* also contains a specific provision on cancellation for reasons within the airline's control or attributable to the carrier (*causas*

9 Article 4(d)–(e).
10 Article 4(f).
11 Article 4(g).
12 Article 4(h).
13 Article 4(i)–(k).
14 Article 5.
15 Article 6.
16 Article 6.
17 Article 8(d).
18 Article 9.

imputables al transportista aéreo).[19] In those cases, passengers have the right to assistance and be re-routed on the next flight or be offered alternative transport (preferably air) or a full ticket refund without penalty.[20] Additionally, they are entitled to compensation in compliance with Article 8(a) and (e). Airlines are exonerated if the passengers were informed at least 15 days in advance or gave shorter notice but offered an alternative flight.[21] The carrier is also exempt if the cancellation resulted from unforeseen circumstances, force majeure, or acts of God, verified by the competent national authority.[22]

In case of cancellation, if the passenger was not reimbursed or re-routed on a flight the same day, airlines will bear the costs of accommodation in which it is necessary to stay overnight and transfer. In addition, if there is a delay before the flight is cancelled, the passenger shall receive the compensation.[23]

The right to compensation is found in Article 8. Interestingly, the article starts with the assistance to passenger; when a flight is delayed between two and four hours, passengers are entitled to a refreshment and a phone call which does not exceed three minutes.[24] For delay exceeding four hours but less than six, passengers are also entitled to a meal. Finally, if the delay exceeds six hours, passengers are entitled to compensation as well as accommodation and transport. In case of interruption of transport, if the passenger does not opt for the return of the proportional part of the price corresponding to the section not covered, he will be compensated for the delay suffered until the travel is resumed.[25]

The passenger could also be entitled to additional compensation with a minimum sum equivalent to 25% of the value of the journey not performed, payable in cash or in any other form accepted by the passenger in case of denial of boarding or delays of more than six hours. The *Decisión* then stipulates that "for the purpose of determining the value of the route subject to compensation, the net value of the ticket paid shall be multiplied by the ratio between the distance of said route over the total distance."[26] Those compensations are also applicable to transit and connection passengers who are unable to continue their journey for reasons attributable to the carrier.[27] As will be discussed, some national legislations, such as in Colombia or Bolivia, provide a better level of protection.

19 Article 7.
20 Article 7(a) and (b).
21 Article 7.
22 Article 7.
23 Article 8(c).
24 Article 8(a).
25 Article 8(b).
26 Article 8(e).
27 Article 8(f).

Event Type	Carrier's Obligations	Compensation (Art. 8.e)
Delay: 2 to 4 Hours	• Refreshments. • One free phone call (max 3 mins).	No.
Delay: 4 to 6 Hours	• All of the above + a full meal.	No.
Delay: Over 6 Hours	• All of the above + Choice of: Hotel/transfers **or** immediate refund (if not at home residence).	**Yes** (25% of segment value).
Interruption (i.e. journey stopped mid-route)	If no refund is taken for unused segment, delay compensation applies until travel resumes (see Delay rules).	Only if delay >6h.
Cancellation (no refund or same-day rebooking)	• Hotel/transfer costs if overnight needed. • Plus any pre-cancellation delay compensation.	Only if delay >6h.
Denied Boarding	• Rebooking on next available flight (own or another airline).	**Yes** (25% of segment value), unless passenger accepts a voluntary deal.

Article 9 establishes the right to assistance for passengers on diverted flights. When, for reasons attributable to the air carrier, an aircraft must operate to or from an airport different from the one for which the reservation was made, the carrier is obligated to cover the passenger's transportation costs to or from this second airport. This transportation can be to the original airport or to another nearby location agreed upon with the passenger.

Right to assistance for passengers with disabilities or special needs, as well as unaccompanied minors is found in Article 10. Carriers must, according to the aircraft type, provide priority and facilitated boarding for these individuals, their companions, or certified assistance dogs. In any event of denied boarding, transport interruption, cancellation, or delays of any duration, these passengers and their companions are entitled to receive priority care and attention.

The *Decisión* also contains a provision on the passengers' obligations as found in the Saudi Regulation such as presenting themselves on time for the check-in.[28] Passengers have a right to withdrawal but are required to inform the airline at least 72 hours in advance. In these instances, the airline may charge an administrative fee that does not exceed 10% of the

28 Chapter IV.

ticket's net value, unless the fare type specifies alternative promotional or non-refundable terms.[29] Passengers are responsible for providing accurate personal information; supplying incorrect data releases the airline from the obligation to notify them about flight changes.[30] The *Decisión* mandates passenger punctual presentation, requiring them to present themselves at the departure airport and complete their check-in within the timeframe indicated by the air carrier or they may lose their seat without compensation being considered a breach of the contract of carriage. However, if upon arrival there are still available seats and the flight has not been closed, the passenger may still be admitted.[31] Article 15 dictates passenger behaviour. It is the user's obligation to follow the instructions of the air carrier's personnel during all phases of the journey: boarding, taxiing, take-off, flight, landing, and disembarkation. The carrier will not be responsible for any adverse effects or damages suffered by a user who fails to comply with these instructions. Any passenger conduct that could affect flight safety, aircraft integrity, or the welfare of others is prohibited, and authorizes the airline to suspend service to individuals not adhering to these guidelines.[32]

The law also contains a chapter dedicated to baggage. A passenger has the right to carry, on the same flight, a quantity and weight of baggage as indicated by the carrier based on the aircraft's capacity and applicable regulations.[33] Carry-on luggage is under the passenger's exclusive custody and does not affect the maximum permissible weight for checked baggage.[34] The law explicitly states that passengers should not include fragile or valuable items like money, jewellery, or electronics in their checked baggage, as the airline will not be held responsible for their loss or damage unless a special declared value is made and an additional fee is paid.[35] Dangerous goods are prohibited.[36]

The *Decisión* also contains the obligations of the airport operators, including adequate flight information communication system, water fountains, and waiting lounges to cite a few.[37] The *Decisión* provides for sanctions to be determined by the State Parties.[38] While both Decision 619 of 2005 and EU Regulation 261 of 2004 share a common core of passenger protections, the Andean Community's framework adopts a distinctly

29 Article 12.
30 Article 13.
31 Article 14.
32 Article 16.
33 Article 17.
34 Article 17.
35 Article 19.
36 Article 20.
37 Chapter VI.
38 Article 25.

broader and more consumer oriented approach. Unlike Regulation 261, the Decision embeds passenger rights within the *Decisión*'s compensation structure (e.g., 25% of the proportional fare for delays exceeding six hours) is less predictable and generally less generous than the EU's fixed-schedule model, and its reliance on national authorities for verification of force majeure introduces variability in enforcement. Ultimately, the *Decisión* offers a model that prioritises transparency and passenger agency over uniform monetary remedies, leaving room for member states like Colombia and Bolivia to surpass its floor of protection.

Bibliography

- *Decisión 619 Normas para la Armonización de los Derechos y Obligaciones de los Usuarios, Transportistas y Operadores de los Servicios de Transporte Aéreo en la Comunidad Andina*, 15 de Julio de 2005, Lima <https://www.comunidadandina.org/StaticFiles/DocOf/DEC619.pdf> accessed 15 September 2025.
- García, M.G.S., 'Los derechos del pasajero derivados del convenio de Montreal de 1999 y del derecho comunitario Andino' (2010) Revista Brasileira de Direito Aeronáutico e Espacial 50

I.2

Arab Civil Aviation Organization (ACAO) Guiding Material

The Arab Civil Aviation Organization (ACAO) has developed guiding material which states can use when developing their own national regulations.[1] The resolution issued by ACAO requested that the Air Transport Committee consider the perspectives of Arab airlines and the Arab Air Carriers Organisation (AACO) throughout the development of these principles.

The guiding principles on passenger rights were derived from two resolutions: the AACO 48th AGM *Resolution* on Passenger Rights of 2015 and the AACO 49th AGM *Resolution* on Passenger Rights of 2016.[2] The 48th AGM *Resolution* also invited Arab States to refer to the Consumer Protection Safety Nets and Caveats template, developed by AACO AWG's Consumer Protection subgroup, when enacting passenger rights regimes.[3] The template reiterated IATA and ICAO's core principles but also includes more general concepts.

First, the Safety Nets and Caveats establishes the prerequisites for a passenger to be eligible for compensation, including being in possession of a valid ticket and necessary travel documents and having presented themselves at check-in in time. The Safety Nets and Caveats does not specify any minimum time the passenger must arrive at check-in. The passenger must also have complied with all airline instructions, security checks, and government requirements for travel, health, and immigration. Crucially, compensation is contingent on the airline being at fault, meaning it could have taken all reasonable measures to avoid the inconvenience but did not do so. There must be proof of fault or damage, and automatic

1 Arab Civil Aviation Organization, 'Passenger Rights' (*Arab Civil Aviation Organization*, 2019) <https://www.aaco.org/policy/passenger-rights> accessed 15 September 2025.

2 Arab Civil Aviation Organization, 'Passenger Rights' (*Arab Civil Aviation Organization*, 2019) <https://www.aaco.org/policy/passenger-rights> accessed 15 September 2025.

3 Arab Air Carrier Organization, 'Safety Nets and Caveats Regarding Consumer Protection Measures (sn)' <https://www.aaco.org/Library/Assets/Safety%20Nets%20and%20Caveats%20Regarding%20Consumer%20Protection%20Measures.pdf> accessed 15 September 2025.

DOI: 10.4324/9781003746164-4

compensation is avoided; instead, the passenger must submit a written complaint within two years to be eligible. Children are eligible for 50% of the adult compensation, while infants are not eligible.

For denied boarding and downgrading, compensation applies if the airline does not provide alternative transportation within three to six hours. The template leaves it to States to decide whether the amount varies based on flight distance. Refreshments should typically be offered after one to three hours, while the threshold for hot meals is set between three and eight hours. Hotel accommodation and transport are provided if the replacement flight departs more than eight hours after the original scheduled departure. Importantly, denied boarding cannot be applied to unaccompanied minors or passengers with special needs. Downgrading requires a reimbursement with no fixed compensation established.

In cases of flight delays, the airline is not liable for compensation if it can prove it took all possible measures to avoid the damage. Unlike some regimes, no financial compensation is explicitly offered for flight delays, though care is mandated, including meals, snacks, hotel accommodation, and communication access, depending on the delay's extent. Airlines must keep passengers updated on the estimated time of departure (ETD). Liability for delays caused by external stakeholders (like air traffic control navigation faults) rests with the source of the fault. While flight diversions are generally not treated as delayed flights, they may be if driven by commercial reasons – such as a transit stop to load/offload passengers or technical faults resulting from poor maintenance.

For cancellations, compensation is typically required only when the passenger was not notified more than seven days before departure or if the passenger was not re-routed and arrived to their final destination within six to eight hours of the originally scheduled arrival time, having departed the origin no earlier than one hour before the departure time of the cancelled flight. Compensation is only required for cancellations due to commercial reasons or technical reasons not covered under extraordinary circumstances. The Montreal Convention governs issues of delayed or lost baggage.

Event Type	**Carrier's Obligations**	**Compensation**
Denied Boarding (if no alternative transport within 3–6 hours)	• Refreshments (after 1–3 hours). • Hot meals (after 3–8 hours). • Hotel accommodation + transport (if replacement flight departs >8 hours after original). • Cannot deny boarding to unaccompanied minors or passengers with special needs.	Yes (left to States to decide).

(*Continued*)

(Continued)

Event Type	**Carrier's Obligations**	**Compensation**
Downgrading	Reimbursement required	No fixed compensation established.
Delay (airline at fault)	• Care mandated (meals, snacks, hotel accommodation, communication access) depending on delay extent. • Keep passengers updated on estimated time of departure (ETD). *Note*: Liability for delays caused by external stakeholders (e.g., ATC) rests with the source, not the airline.	No explicit financial compensation offered.
Delay – Diversion (if driven by commercial reasons or poor maintenance)	Same as Delay above	No financial compensation
Cancellation	Re-routing (implied).	Compensation required if: 1. Passenger **not notified >7 days** before departure; **OR** 2. Not re-routed AND arrived **6–8 hours** late (departing no earlier than 1 hour before cancelled flight).

Finally, the template includes a long list of extraordinary circumstances, which are defined as unpredictable, unavoidable, and external events, exempting airlines from their obligations to compensate. This list includes a broad range of events such as natural disasters, wars and political instability, security reasons, unlawful acts, meteorological reasons, airport closures, medical grounds, bird strikes, manufacturing defects, unexpected flight safety shortcomings, air traffic management issues, and industrial relations issues, including labour and union strikes (both airline staff and other stakeholders) that make operations impossible, as well as technical malfunctions outside the airline's control, such as aircraft manufacturer's defects or technical malfunctions in air navigation systems.

The Consumer Protection Safety Nets and Caveats template establishes a fault-based system where the passenger must prove airline negligence, which greatly differs from other laws such as Regulation 261. Compensation is not automatic and requires a written complaint within two years. For delays, no financial compensation is offered, only care in the form of refreshments and accommodation. For cancellations, compensation is waived if the passenger is rebooked to arrive within a six-to-eight-hour window of the original arrival time. Finally, the list of 'extraordinary circumstances' is very extensive, including aspects which are not recognized under Regulation 261 such as general technical failures and maintenance issues.

Bibliography

- Arab Civil Aviation Organization, 'Passenger Rights' (*Arab Civil Aviation Organization*, 2019) <https://www.aaco.org/policy/passenger-rights> accessed 15 September 2025.
- Arab Air Carrier Organization, 'Safety Nets and Caveats Regarding Consumer Protection Measures' (sn) <https://www.aaco.org/Library/Assets/Safety%20Nets%20and%20Caveats%20Regarding%20Consumer%20Protection%20Measures.pdf> accessed 15 September 2025.

European Regulation 261 of 2004

Regulation (EC) No 261/2004[1] is probably the most hotly debated and criticized legislation on aviation.[2] Since its promulgation, Regulation 261 – repealing Council Regulation 295/91[3] – has been criticized. The Director General of International Air Transport Association (IATA) described the Regulation as "confusing and poorly worded regulation that is adding cost to the European industry."[4] Not only was it criticized by international organizations, but it was also rejected by airlines from being overly in favour of passengers and motivated by a "political obsession for consumer rights."[5] The Regulation has also been overly criticized

1 Regulation (EC) No 261/2004 of the European Parliament and of the Council of 11 February 2004 establishing common rules on compensation and assistance to passengers in the event of denied boarding and of cancellation or long delay of flights, and repealing Regulation (EEC) No 295/91 [2004] OJ L46/1. Hereafter Regulation 261, EU 261 or the Regulation. All of those terms are used to refer to that specific instrument.

For the purposes of homogeneity, Directive (EU) 2015/2302 on package travel and linked travel arrangements has been left aside as well as Regulation (EC) N°1107/2006 concerning the rights of disabled persons and persons with reduced mobility when travelling by air.

2 D. Defossez, 'I Wish My Mum Was Brazilian: The Regulation of Passenger Liability in the EU and Brazil' (2019) Issues in Aviation Law and Policy 333.

3 Council Regulation (EEC) No 295/91 of 4 February 1991 establishing common rules for a denied-boarding compensation system in scheduled air transport, OJ L 36, 8 February 1991, p. 5–7.

4 As quoted by Barry Humphreys, *The Regulation of Air Transport: From Protection to Liberalisation and Back Again* (Routledge 2023).

5 Case C-344/04 *The Queen, on the Application of International Air Transport Association and European Low Fares Airline Association v Department for Transport*, ECLI:EU:C:2006:10; C Van Dam, *Luchtvaartmaatschappijen zijn niet gek op passagiersrechten* (2010) 85 Nederlands juristenblad; George N Tompkins Jr, 'Are the Objectives of the 1999 Montreal Convention in Danger of Failure?' (2014) 39 Air and Space Law 203, 212.

A4E noted that "good intentions do not guarantee good outcomes." See: A4E, IATA and ERA, 'Revision of Regulation 261/2004 Airline Industry Perspectives' (October 2025) 2 <https://www.eraa.org/wp-content/uploads/2025/10/Joint-Industry-Position-EU261-revision_15102025.pdf> accessed 15 November 2025.

DOI: 10.4324/9781003746164-5

in academic writings. As Bernard rightly noted their repulsion for the Regulation and related case law seems to be visceral.[6]

The Regulation was considered superfluous or at best raising serious legal question as both the Warsaw and Montreal Conventions directly address the issue of compensation to passengers for damages suffered.[7] In fact, the Regulation was nearly immediately challenged by the International Air Transport Association (IATA) and the European Low Fares Airline Association (ELFAA) on the ground of inconsistence with the Montreal Convention, a claim rejected by the Court of Justice of the European Union (CJEU).[8] The various judgments of the CJEU seems to touch "a raw nerve" as "they are perceived to be challenging one of the sacred cows of international air transport law, namely the exclusivity of the 1999 Montreal Convention."[9] However, as the Court repeatedly stated, Regulation 261 "operates at an earlier stage than the system which results from the Montreal Convention" and therefore, cannot interfere with the scope of the Montreal Convention.[10] While the distinction has been deemed "artificial,"[11] the Court has perpetuated it in *Adriano Guaitoli and others v easyJet* where it approached the two claims under the two regimes independently even if this could lead to the claims being heard in different forums.[12] Regulation 261 seems to prove that "it is possible to design a scheme of assistance to passengers which is compatible with the Montreal Convention."[13]

6 Nicolas Bernard, 'Taking Air Passenger Rights Seriously: The Case Against the Exclusivity of the Montreal Convention' (2021) International Community Law Review 2 <https://qmro.qmul.ac.uk/xmlui/bitstream/handle/123456789/64713/Bernard%20Taking%20Air%20Passenger%20Rights%20Seriously%3A%20the%20Case%20Against%20the%20Exclusivity%20of%20the%20Montreal%20Convention%202020%20Accepted.pdf?sequence=2&isAllowed=y> accessed 15 November 2025.

7 Paul Stephen Dempsey and Svante O Johansson, 'Montreal v. Brussels: The Conflict of Laws on the Issue of Delay in International Air Carriage' (2010) 35 Air and Space Law 207; Tompkins (n 5).

8 Case C-344/04 *The Queen, on the Application of International Air Transport Association and European Low Fares Airline Association v Department for Transport*; F Rossi dal Pozzo, *EU Legal Framework for Safeguarding Air Passenger Rights* (Springer 2014).

9 Bernard (n 6) 2.

10 Case C-344/04 *IATA and ELFAA* (2006), at 45; Case C-549/07 *Friederike Wallentin-Hermann v Alitalia – Linee Aeree Italiane SpA*, ECLI:EU:C:2008:771, at 32; Cases C-581/10 & C-629/10 *Emeka Nelson and Others v Deutsche Lufthansa AG and TUI Travel plc and Others v Civil Aviation Authority*, ECLI:EU:C:2012:657, at 57; Case C-12/11 *Denise McDonagh v Ryanair Ltd*, ECLI:EU:C:2013:43, at 21; Case C-292/24 *AD v Iberia Líneas Aéreas de España*, ECLI:EU:C:2025:402.

11 Laurent Chassot and Paul S Dempsey, 'Article 29: Basis of Claims' in George Leloudas, Paul S Dempsey and Laurent Chassot (eds), *The Montreal Convention: A Commentary* (Edward Elgar 2023).

12 Case C213/18 *Adriano Guaitoli and others v easyJet Airline Co. Ltd*, ECLI:EU:C:2019:927.

13 Bernard (n 6) 9.

Unlike many of the laws analysed, Regulation 261 has been able to survive the passing of time thanks to the Court of Justice's rulings. Many EU-inspired laws have had to be revised to keep up with some of the changes imposed by the Court. For instance, the interpretation given by the Court in *Sturgeon* which afforded delayed passengers with the same compensation as passengers of cancelled flights on the basis that both groups were suffering from the same inconvenience required an amendment of the Turkish law.[14] The inclusion of right to compensation for delayed passengers has been criticized not only by airlines but also by legal scholars due to the fact that the CJEU went beyond its interpretive role and effectively rewrote the Regulation.[15] The Court's rule has resulted in Regulation 261 being the most-litigated EU regulation ever.[16]

a. The Scope

Regulation 261 applies to all flights departing from a European Union airport or arriving to a European airport when such flight is operated by a community carrier, unless the passenger received compensation in that third country.[17] The issue of whether a flight from a non-EU country to the EU on a non-Community carrier falls within the scope of the Regulation when the travel itinerary originated at an airport within the EU was addressed by the Court of Justice in *Emirates Airlines v Schenkel.*[18] The Court determined that the Regulation should be interpreted as not extending to situations involving round-trip travel where passengers, having initially departed from such an EU airport, return there on a

14 Joined cases C-402/07 and C-432/07 *Christopher Sturgeon, Gabriel Sturgeon and Alana Sturgeon v Condor Flugdienst GmbH and Stefan Böck and Cornelia Lepuschitz v Air France SA*, ECLI:EU:C:2009:716. Confirmed in Cases C-581/10 & C-629/10 *Nelson and others.*

15 Dempsey and Johansson (n 7); R Lawson and T Marland, 'The Montreal Convention 1999, and the Decisions of the ECJ in the Cases of IATA and Sturgeon – in Harmony or Discord?' (2011) 36 Air and Space Law 99; J Balfour, 'Airline Liability for Delays: The Court of Justice of the EU Rewrites EC Regulation 261/2004' (2010) 35 Air and Space Law 71; C Thijssen, 'The Montreal Convention, EU Regulation 261/2004, and the Sturgeon Doctrine: How to Reconcile the Three?' (2013) 12 Issues in Aviation Law and Policy 413; Ricardo Pazos, 'The Carrier's Defence to Liability for Delay under the Montreal Convention and EU Regulation 261/2004' (2024) 49 Air and Space Law 417.

16 Pablo Mendes de Leon, *Introduction to Air Law* (11th edn, Wolters Kluwer 2022) 308.

17 Article 3. See: Commission Notice, 'Interpretative Guidelines on Regulation (EC) No 261/2004 of the European Parliament and of the Council establishing common rules on compensation and assistance to passengers in the event of denied boarding and of cancellation or long delay of flights and on Council Regulation (EC) No 2027/97 on air carrier liability in the event of accidents' C/2024/5687 <https://eur-lex.europa.eu/legal-content/EN/TXT/PDF/?uri=OJ:C_202405687> accessed 15 November 2025.

18 *Case C-173/07 Emirates Airlines – Direktion für Deutschland v Diether Schenkel, ECLI:EU:C:2008:400. Reiterated in Case C-537/17 Claudia Wegener v Royal Air Maroc SA, ECLI:EU:C:2018:361.*

flight originating in a non-member country. The fact that both outbound and return flights are booked as a single itinerary does not alter this interpretation of the Regulation.[19]

The Court ruled that connecting flights on a single reservation, originating from an EU airport, are subject to Regulation 261 even if the journey is operated by different airlines without a formal partnership in place and the delay occurred outside of the EU.[20] Furthermore, the Court clarified that an "operating air carrier," as defined by the Regulation, refers to an entity that enters into a contract with a passenger.[21] This decision carries substantial implications for major airlines engaged in extensive code-share agreements, as they may be held liable not only for their own operations but also for those conducted by their partners. A connecting flight from the EU to a non-EU country operated by a non-EU carrier but booked with an EU airline would still fall within the scope of the Regulation.[22]

In the situation where connecting flights are booked as a single itinerary from a non-EU country to the EU with a stopover in the EU, if a significant delay on the first flight – operated under a code-share agreement by a carrier based outside the EU – occurs, passengers may seek compensation from the EU air carrier operating the second flight.[23] However, a flight with a layover in an EU country is not covered by EU 261 if the initial departure and final destination are both outside the EU.[24]

Flight Route	**EU Airline**	**Non-EU Airlines**
EU–EU	Yes.	Yes.
EU–Third Country	Yes.	Yes.
Third Country–EU	Yes.	No.
EU–Third Country–Third Country (Prague to Bangkok via the UAE)	Yes.	Yes.
Third Country–Third Country–EU (Bangkok to Prague via the UAE)	Yes.	No.
Third Country–Third Country	No.	No.

19 Dempsey and Johansson (n 7).

20 Case C-537/17 *Wegener*, paragraph 18; Case C-502/18 *CS and Others v České aerolinie a.s.*, ECLI:EU:C:2019:604; Case C-191/19 *OI v Air Nostrum Líneas Aéreas del Mediterráneo SA*, ECLI:EU:C:2020:339, paragraph 26; Case C-451/20 *Airhelp Limited v Austrian Airlines AG*, ECLI:EU:C:2022:123, paragraph 25; Case C-436/21 *flightright GmbH v American Airlines, Inc*, ECLI:EU:C:2022:762, paragraph 20.

21 Reiterated in Joined Cases C-146/20, C-188/20, C-196/20 and C-270/20 *AD and Others v Corendon Airlines and Others (Azurair e.a)*, ECLI:EU:C:2021:1038.

22 Case C-561/20 *Q and Others v United Airlines, Inc*, ECLI:EU:C:2022:266, paragraph 44.

23 Case C-367/20 *SP v KLM Royal Dutch Airlines*, ECLI:EU:C:2020:909.

24 Case C-451/20, *Airhelp*.

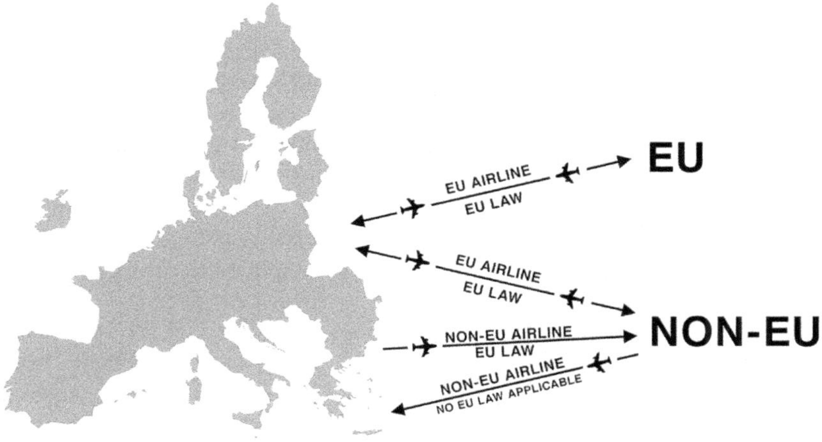

Figure I.3.1 The Scope of Regulation 261

Additionally for the Regulation to apply, the passenger must have a confirmed reservation and present themselves at checking when stipulated or at least 45 minutes before the published departure time or be transferred by the airline.[25] Passengers with a confirmed reservation who have boarded their flight meet check-in requirements and do not need to show a boarding card or other proof of timely presence to claim any benefit under the Regulation.[26]

The Regulation does not apply to special fares unavailable to the general public and free flights.[27] However, passengers on a package tour or third-party financed trips are entitled to the protection under the Regulation as long as they are in possession of a boarding pass, even if they travelled free of charge or on reduced fares.[28] A child travelling for free without a seat, boarding pass, or reservation is not covered by Regulation 261.[29]

25 Article 3(2)(a) and (b). Passengers must adhere to the check-in requirements specified by an airline even if they already checked in online: Case C-474/22 *Laudamotion GmbH v Flightright GmbH*, ECLI:EU:C:2024:73.

26 Case C-756/18 *LC and MD v easyJet Airline Co. Ltd*, ECLI:EU:C:2019:902.

27 Article 3(3). See: Case C-316/20 *VO and Others v SATA International – Azores Airlines SA*, ECLI:EU:C:2020:966 – For tickets that are part of an event sponsorship operation; Passengers on a promotional ticket available to a specific group of people have the right to re-routing: Case C-516/23 *NW and YS v Qatar Airways*, ECLI:EU:C:2025:21.

28 Case C-20/24 *M1.R. and M2.R. v AAA sp. z o.o*, ECLI:EU:C:2025:139.

29 Case C-686/20 *YE and Others v Vueling Airlines SA*, ECLI:EU:C:2021:859.

b. Denial of Boarding, Cancellation, and Delay

The substantive provisions start with passengers' benefits and entitlement in case of denied boarding. The scope of "denied boarding" extends beyond overbooking to include instances driven by operational requirements.[30] Airlines are precluded from evading compensation by citing extraordinary circumstances or by making unilateral assumptions about a passenger's ability to meet a connecting flight schedule.[31] In 2023, the CJEU ruled that Article 4(3) on denial of boarding also applied to pre-emptive denial.[32] The Court, however, refused to apply the principle of equal treatment to denial of boarding.

In the event of denied boarding, airlines must first call for volunteers to surrender their reservations and grant them with benefits.[33] Those volunteers are still entitled to a refund or re-routing at the earliest opportunity or later date.[34] In case an insufficient number of passengers volunteer, the airline may deny boarding to passengers against their will.[35] Under these circumstances, the air carrier must provide care – comprising meals and refreshments – as well as hotel accommodation and airport transfers when required, and access to communication means. Furthermore, the airline must offer the choice between a ticket refund[36] or re-routing to final destination, in addition to paying compensation.[37] Passengers are entitled to compensation if they were informed in advance of the denied boarding and did not present themselves for boarding.[38] Unlike some other national legislation, Regulation 261 is silent regarding

30 Article 2(j).

31 Case C-22/11 *Finnair Oyj v Timy Lassooy*, ECLI:EU:C:2012:604; Case C-321/11 *Germán Rodríguez Cachafeiro and María de los Reyes Martínez-Reboredo Varela-Villamor v Iberia, Líneas Aéreas de España SA*, ECLI:EU:C:2012:609.

The Travel Law Chamber of the Frankfurt am Main Regional Court ruled that airline cannot deny boarding if the aircraft doors are still open and other passengers are still boarding even if the passengers arrived late at their boarding gate. Case number: 2-24 S 93/24.

32 Case C-238/22 *FW v LATAM Airlines Group SA*, ECLI:EU:C:2023:815.

33 Article 4(1).

34 Article 4(1) coupled with Article 8(1). Information on all options must be given by the carrier; passengers are under no obligation to actively contribute to seeking this information. Case C-354/18 *Radu Lucian Rusu and Oana Maria Rusu v SC Blue Air – Airline Management Solutions SRL*, ECLI:EU:C:2019:637, paragraph 56.

35 Article 4(2).

36 Reimbursement must be in cash unless the passenger gave clear and explicit consent to a voucher; a mere registration in a loyalty programme is insufficient: Case C-642/23 *Flightright GmbH v Etihad Airways P.J.S.C*, ECLI:EU:C:2025:12; Case C-76/23 *Cobult UG v TAP Air Portugal SA*, ECLI:EU:C:2024:253.

37 Article 4(3) coupled with Articles 7 to 9.

38 Joined Cases C-650/23 and C-705/23, *E EAD v DW and Flightright GmbH v Condor Flugdienst GmbH*, ECLI:EU:C:2024:903.

no-show and whether such practice would constitute a denial of boarding or not.[39]

Scenario	Passenger Rights
Voluntary Denial	Volunteers get benefits (re-routing/refund) + assistance.
Involuntary Denial	Compensation + re-routing/refund + care/assistance.
Compensation Amounts	€250 for flights under 1,500 km. €400 for intra-EU flights >1,500 km and flights of 1,500–3,500 km. €600 for flights over 3,500 km.

The Regulation defines cancellation as "the non-operation of a flight which was previously planned and on which at least one place was reserved."[40] This definition was refined by the Court of Justice to include flights brought forward by more than one hour.[41] Similarly, when a flight is forced to return to the airport of departure and passengers are transferred to another flight, this would amount to a cancellation.[42] A flight diversion to an airport that is not the booked destination is generally considered a flight cancellation. The exception is if the diversion airport serves the same city or region as the original destination.[43] An unscheduled stopover would not be regarded as a cancellation.[44]

Scenario	Classification	Explanation/Legal Basis
Standard Non-operation	**Cancellation.**	The core regulatory definition.
Flight Brought Forward	**Cancellation.**	When a flight's departure time is scheduled **more than one hour earlier** than the original booking (as refined by the Court of Justice).
Return to Departure Airport	**Cancellation.**	When a flight is forced to return to its origin airport and passengers are transferred to a new flight to continue their journey.

(Continued)

39 Commission Notice (n 17) 11.

40 Article 2(l).

41 Joined Cases C-146/20, C-188/20, C-196/20 and C-270/20 *Azurair and Others*; Case C-263/20 *Airhelp Limited v Laudamotion GmbH*, ECLI:EU:C:2021:1039; Case C-395/20 *EP and GM v Corendon Airlines Turistik Hava Tasimacilik A.S*, ECLI:EU:C:2021:1041.

42 Cases C-83/10, *Aurora Sousa Rodríguez and Others v Air France SA*, ECLI:EU:C:2011:652.

43 Cases C-826/19, *WZ v Austrian Airlines AG*, ECLI:EU:C:2021:318; Case C-253/21 *FI and RE v TUIfly GmbH*, ECLI:EU:C:2021:840.

44 Case C-32/16 *Ute Wunderlich v Bulgarian Air Charter Limited*, ECLI:EU:C:2016:753.

(Continued)

Scenario	Classification	Explanation/Legal Basis
Diversion to a Different Airport	**Cancellation.**	When a flight is diverted to an airport that is **not** the booked destination airport.
Diversion to a Same-Region Airport	**Not a Cancellation.**	The exception: a diversion is **not** considered a cancellation if the new airport serves the **same city or region** as the original destination.

When a flight is cancelled, the passengers are entitled to immediate assistance, which includes a choice between a full ticket reimbursement within seven days or re-routing to their final destination – similarly to denied boarding cases.[45] Furthermore, the airline must provide care, comprising meals and refreshments as well as access to means of communication.[46] Should the re-routed flight depart at least one day after the originally planned departure, the passenger is also entitled to hotel accommodation and transport between the airport and the hotel, provided these are necessary.[47]

Beyond this assistance, passengers are typically entitled to compensation, unless the carrier informed them of the cancellation within a specified timeframe.[48] This notice must be given at least two weeks before the scheduled departure, or alternatively, if given later, the airline must offer a re-routing option that minimizes the passenger's travel disruption, with the acceptable delay varying based on the advance notice provided.[49] Specifically, for notice given between two weeks and seven days before departure, the re-routing must allow the passenger to depart no more than two hours before the original scheduled time and to arrive at the final destination less than four hours after the originally scheduled arrival time.[50] If the cancellation is communicated less than seven days before departure, the re-routing must enable a departure no more than one hour before the original time and an arrival at the destination less than

45 Article 5(1)(a) coupled with Article 8. See Case C-642/23 regarding refund in form of travel vouchers or miles. Case C-642/23 *Flightright (Compte de fidélité)*, ECLI:EU:C:2025:12.
Regarding agency fees: Case C-601/17 *Harms v Vueling Airlines SA*, ECLI:EU:C:2018:702; Case C-45/24, *Verein für Konsumenteninformation v KLM*. This 2026 case establishes that the carrier's liability for the full purchase price persists regardless of whether it possessed prior knowledge of the specific commission fees charged by the intermediary.

46 Article 5(1)(b) coupled with Article 9.

47 Article 5(1)(b) coupled with Article 9.

48 Article 5(1)(c).

49 Article 5(1)(c)(i).

50 Article 5(1)(c)(ii).

two hours after the originally scheduled arrival time.[51] An operating air carrier remains liable for compensation if a passenger was not notified of a flight cancellation at least two weeks prior to the scheduled departure. This applies even when the intermediary – such as a travel agent or online travel agency – contracted by the passenger fails to convey information from the air carrier in a timely manner, unless the passenger has explicitly authorized the intermediary to receive such notifications on their behalf.[52]

An airline can, however, be exempt from the liability to pay compensation if it can successfully prove that the cancellation was caused by extraordinary circumstances – unforeseeable events that could not have been avoided even if all reasonable measures had been taken.[53]

Notice Period	**Compensation Applicable?**	**Amount**
≥14 Days	No.	€0.
7–14 Days	Yes, unless re-routing departs ≤2 hrs earlier and arrives ≤4 hrs later.	€250 for flights under 1,500 km. €400 for intra-EU flights >1,500 km and flights of 1,500–3,500 km. €600 for flights >3,500 km.
<7 Days	Yes, unless re-routing departs ≤1 hr earlier and arrives ≤2 hrs later.	€250 for flights <1,500 km. €400 for intra-EU flights >1,500 km and flights between 1,500–3,500 km. €600 for flights >3,500 km.
Any Time	Exempt if due to *extraordinary circumstances.*	€0.

According to Regulation 261, a delay refers specifically to a delay on arrival. The delay taken into consideration is at arrival, it does not matter whether the delay occurred at the airport of departure or connecting airports if any or only on the second leg.[54] For a diverted flight that lands at an alternative airport serving the same city or region, the total delay is calculated based on when the passenger finally arrives at their booked destination airport, or another nearby agreed-upon location, following any transfer arranged by the airline.[55]

51 Article 5(1)(c)(iii). Case C-130/18 *flightright GmbH v Eurowings GmbH*, ECLI:EU:C:2018:496, paragraph 23.

52 Case C-302/16 *Bas Jacob Adriaan Krijgsman v Surinaamse Luchtvaart Maatschappij NV*, ECLI:EU:C:2017:359; Case C-263/20 *Airhelp Limited v Laudamotion GmbH*.

53 Article 5(3).

54 Case C-11/11 *Air France SA v Folkerts*, ECLI:EU:C:2013:106.

55 Case C-826/19 *Austrian Airlines*.

To calculate a flight delay, the CJEU uses two key moments: the "scheduled arrival time" – the time published in the flight schedule and on the passenger's ticket – and the actual "arrival time" – the moment when at least one aircraft door is opened, indicating that passengers are permitted to disembark. The delay is calculated as the difference between these two times.[56] While the ruling in *Germanwings* has clarified the definition of arrival time, it was always open to interpretation which scheduled time to use. The Court closed this loophole by confirming that the delay must be calculated based on the original scheduled arrival time rather than any revised arrival time found in a new booking confirmation.[57] This ruling shuts the door on the possibility for airlines to officially label the schedule change as "postponement" with a new booking confirmation rather than a "cancellation." The Court noted that any other interpretation, namely allowing airlines to redefine the schedule on their own terms, would render the Regulation effectively meaningless and undermine the protection afford to passengers. In light of the discussion regarding the revision of Regulation 261, the position adopted in this judgment shows clearly which side the Court is on.

Based on the wording of the Regulation itself, passengers on a delayed flight were only entitled to care and assistance based on the length of the delay and the distance of the flight. The assistance starts at two hours or more for flights of 1,500 km or less, three hours or more for intra-Community flights over 1,500 km and all other flights between 1,500 and 3,500 km, or four hours or more for all longer flights. This assistance includes meals and refreshments proportionate to the waiting time, as well as two free telephone calls, telex, fax messages, or emails.[58] Furthermore, if the new expected departure time is at least a day after the original one, the airline must provide hotel accommodation and transport between the airport and the hotel.[59] Should the delay reach at least five hours, passengers have the right to choose between reimbursement of their ticket and re-routing.[60] In all cases, this assistance must be provided within the specified time limits corresponding to each distance bracket.

56 Cases C-452/13 *Germanwings GmbH v Ronny Henning*, ECLI:EU:C:2014:2141; Case C-654/19 *FP Passenger Service v Austrian Airlines AG*, ECLI:EU:C:2020:770; Joined Cases C-146/20, C-188/20, C-196/20 and C-270/20 *Azurair and Others*.

57 Case C-558/24 *Corendon Airlines Turistik Hava Tasimacilik AS v Myflyright GmbH*, ECLI:EU:C:2025:847.

58 Article 6(1).

59 Article 6(1)(c)(ii) coupled with Article 9(1)(b) and 9(1)(c).

60 Article 6(1)(c)(iii), as outlined in Article 8(1)(a).

Flight Distance	Waiting Time	Services
Up to 1,500 km	From 2 hours.	Drinks, meals, communication options.
1,500–3,500 km	From 3 hours.	Drinks, meals, communication options.
Over 3,500 km	From 4 hours.	Drinks, meals, communication options.
All Distances	Overnight required.	Drinks, meals, communication options, hotel accommodation, and transfers between airport and hotel.

All this changed after the landmark *Sturgeon* ruling, in which the Court of Justice determined that an arrival delay of three hours or more is legally equivalent to a flight cancellation.[61] This decision provided a legal basis for passengers to claim compensation for long delays, but a key point of contention remains that a long delay is not truly a cancellation, as all other flight details, such as the flight number, remain unchanged. Indeed, a delayed flight, no matter how long the delay, is not considered cancelled as long as the aircraft operates according to its original flight plan. A flight is only classified as cancelled if the airline rebooks passengers onto a different flight that has a separate and distinct schedule from the one they originally booked.[62] Airlines initially resisted this interpretation.

The legal framework for delays is unique because, unlike denied boarding and cancellations, the issue of delays is regulated by both EU 261 and the international conventions. Airlines have challenged the legality of Regulation 261, arguing that its delay provisions conflict with the compensation rules of the Montreal and Warsaw Conventions. However, European courts have consistently rejected this argument for the following reasons: standardized vs. individual damages and independent application. The Regulation provides a standardized form of compensation that is an identical penalty for all passengers on a given flight. This is considered a form of immediate assistance. In contrast, the Montreal Convention addresses individual damages, which vary from person to person and must be proven on a case-by-case basis. Because they serve different purposes, the two sets of rules are not considered to be in conflict. The European Court of Justice has ruled that passengers can seek compensation under both EU 261 and the international conventions. The standardized amounts under the Regulation 261 are considered legally independent of the Montreal Convention's provisions.

According to the Court, "the right to standardised compensation, calculated on a flat-rate basis and payable by the operating air carrier,

61 Joined Cases C-402/07 and C-432/07 *Sturgeon*. Confirmed in Joined Cases C-581/10 and C-629/10 *Nelson*; Case C-413/11 *Germanwings*. See: Balfour (n 15).

62 Joined Cases C-402/07 and C-432/07 *Sturgeon*.

is among the essential rights conferred on passengers by Regulation No 261."[63] The compensation structure follows a tiered system: 250 euros for flights up to 1,500 km, 400 euros for intra-EU flights over 1,500 km or other flights between 1,500 and 3,500 km, and 600 euros for flights exceeding 3,500 km.[64] This amount can be reduced by 50% when an airline offers passengers re-routing to their final destination on an alternative flight which arrives no later than two hours for flights of 1,500 km or less, three hours for all intra-Community flights over 1,500 km and for all other flights between 1,500 and 3,500 km, or four hours for all longer flights.[65] Where a flight is rescheduled to depart significantly earlier than originally agreed, the flight is considered as cancelled and airlines cannot avail themselves of any provision to reduce compensation by 50% based on the offer of re-routing that enables the passenger to arrive at their final destination without delay.[66]

The compensation is based on the great circle route method.[67] "Double compensation" or "cumulative compensation" is possible when receiving payment for a cancellation and accepting a re-routing, and the subsequent flight operated by the same carrier is delayed to an extent that itself establishes a right to compensation under the Regulation.[68] Passengers are not entitled to compensation when their reservation is amended against their will and the passenger still reaches his or her final destination at the original scheduled time.[69] Similarly, if the passenger re-routes themselves and arrives with a delay of less than three hours, they are not entitled to compensation.[70]

Flight Distance	**Compensation Amount**
All flights of 1,500 km or less	€250.
All intra-EU flights over 1,500 km	€400.
All other flights between 1,500 km and 3,500 km	€400.
All flights over 3,500 km	€600.

63 Case C-11/23 *Eventmedia Soluciones SL v Air Europa Líneas Aéreas SAU*, ECLI:EU:C:2024:194, paragraph 27.

64 Article 7(1)(a)–(c).

65 Article 7(2)(a)–(c).

66 Joined Cases C-146/20, C-188/20, C-196/20 and C-270/20 *Azurair and Others*.

67 Article 7(4). Cases C-559/16 *Birgit Bossen and Others v Brussels Airlines SA/NV*, ECLI:EU:C:2017:644; Case C-939/19 *Flightright GmbH v Eurowings GmbH*, ECLI:EU:C:2020:316; Case C-592/20 *NT and Others v British Airways plc*, ECLI:EU:C:2021:312.

68 Case C-832/18 *A and Others v Finnair Oyj*, ECLI:EU:C:2020:204.

69 Case C-191/19 *Air Nostrum*.

70 Case C-54/23 *WY v Laudamotion GmbH and Ryanair DAC*, ECLI:EU:C:2024:74, paragraph 24.

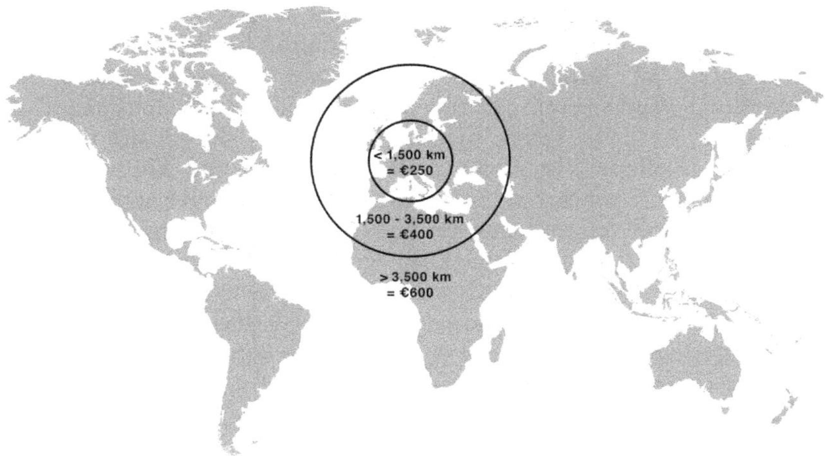

Figure I.3.2 Compensation Under Regulation 261

c. "Extraordinary Circumstances": an Elastic Exemption

The defence of "extraordinary circumstances" under Article 5(3) of Regulation 261 is the principal mechanism by which an air carrier may be absolved from the obligation to compensate passengers for flight cancellations or significant delays under Article 7. This concept – despite its legal and financial implications – is not defined in the Regulation itself but in its preamble as

> where the impact of an air traffic management decision in relation to a particular aircraft on a particular day gives rise to a long delay, an overnight delay, or the cancellation of one or more flights by that aircraft, even though all reasonable measures had been taken by the air carrier concerned to avoid the delays or cancellations.[71]

Point 14 offers a non-exhaustive list of situations which might give rise to an extraordinary circumstance and which includes "political instability, meteorological conditions incompatible with the operation of the flight

71 Point 15 of the preamble. All reasonable measures: Case C-501/17 *Germanwings*, ECLI:EU:C:2019:288. See: Tania Pantazi, '"I Know That I Know Nothing": Extraordinary Circumstances in Air Passenger Rights Regulation' (2020) 28 European Review of Private Law 1093; Ricardo Pazos, 'The Extraordinary Circumstances Defence in Regulation (EC) 261/2004' (2021) 46 Air and Space Law 739.

concerned, security risks, unexpected flight safety shortcomings and strikes that affect the operation of an operating air carrier."

The Court of Justice has established two cumulative criteria for determining whether events qualify as "extraordinary circumstances" in its case law: First, the events, by their nature or origin, are not inherent to the usual operations of the air carrier, and second, they fall outside the actual control of that carrier.[72] Airlines are required to take all reasonable measures to avoid the consequences of extraordinary circumstances. This includes, at the flight planning stage, accounting for the risk of delays linked to such events by building in a reserve of time to complete the flight after the circumstance ends.[73] However, this reserve time should not impose an intolerable sacrifice on the airline given its operational capacities at that time. For example, an airline must demonstrate it deployed all available resources (staff, equipment, financial means) to prevent a tyre change from causing a long delay.[74]

Over time, the Court's decisions have severely reduced the available defence for airlines. The case law distinguishes between events with an "internal" origin, which are part of the airline's normal operational risk, and those with an "external" origin.[75]

As a general principle, the Court has established that a technical problem – which is an internal event – identified during aircraft maintenance or resulting from a failure to maintain an aircraft cannot be considered an "extraordinary circumstance."[76] For instance, a breakdown caused by the premature malfunction of components may be unexpected, but it remains intrinsically linked to the complex operating system of the aircraft, which is operated in often difficult or extreme conditions. This logic also applies to the failure of a part that is only replaced when it becomes defective, known as an "on condition" part.[77] Conversely, a hidden manufacturing defect that is identified by the aircraft manufacturer or a competent

72 Joined cases C-402/07 and C-432/07 *Sturgeon* and others, paragraphs 70–72; Case C-12/11 *McDonagh*, paragraph 29; Case C-394/14 *Siewert v Condor Flugdienst GmbH*, ECLI:EU:C:2014:2377, paragraph 18; Case C-257/14 *van der Lans v Koninklijke Luchtvaart Maatschappij NV*, ECLI:EU:C:2015:618, paragraph 36; Case C-501/17 *Germanwings*, paragraph 20.

73 Case C-294/10 *Andrejs Eglītis and Edvards Ratnieks v Latvijas Republikas Ekonomikas ministrija*, ECLI:EU:C:2011:303.

74 Case C-501/17 *Germanwings*.

75 Case C-28/20 *Airhelp Ltd v Scandinavian Airlines System Denmark – Norway – Sweden*, ECLI:EU:C:2021:226, paragraph 39.

76 Cases C-549/07 *Wallentin-Hermann*.

77 Case C-257/14 *van der Lans v Koninklijke Luchtvaart Maatschappij NV*, ECLI:EU:C:2015:618, paragraphs 40, 41 and 42; Case C-832/18 *Finnair*.

authority, or damage caused by acts of sabotage or terrorism, may be classified as an extraordinary circumstance.[78]

The Court has determined that strikes by an airline's own staff do not constitute extraordinary circumstances. This includes both unofficial ("wildcat") strikes triggered by a sudden company restructuring announcement and strikes formally organized by a trade union to advance worker demands.[79] The fact that prior negotiations with worker representatives may have occurred does not alter this conclusion. In contrast, strikes that are "external" to the airline, such as those by air traffic controllers or airport staff, may be considered extraordinary circumstances.[80] The unexpected absence of a person essential to the operation of a flight due to illness or death is not an extraordinary circumstance.[81]

External events, while sometimes common, are outside the air carrier's control as they stem from natural phenomena or the actions of a third party, such as another carrier or an entity interfering with airport operations. For example, meteorological events such as typhoons, storms, and volcanic eruptions are typically regarded as extraordinary circumstances.[82] Lightning strikes were recognized in 2025 as an extraordinary circumstance.[83] The Court has yet to give a final decision regarding capacity reduction imposed by air traffic control caused by weather conditions in that country, however, at the national level the rulings are inconsistent.[84]

In 2026, the General Court held that a decision relating to air traffic management resulting in a delay may constitute an extraordinary circumstance, irrespective of the length of the delay it causes and the reason for it, if it is established that the decision was beyond the effective

---

78 Case C-411/23 *D. (Vide de conception du moteur)*, ECLI:EU:C:2024:498, paragraph 42.

79 Case C-195/17 *Helga Krüsemann and Others v TUIfly GmbH*, ECLI:EU:C:2018:258; C-28/20 *Airhelp*.

80 Case C-613/20 *CS v Eurowings GmbH*, ECLI:EU:C:2021:820; Shortage of staff providing baggage loading services: Case C-405/23 *Touristic Aviation Services Limited v Flightright GmbH*, ECLI:EU:C:2024:408, paragraph 30.

81 Joined Cases C-156/22, C-157/22 and C-158/22, *TAP Portugal (Décès du copilote)*, ECLI:EU:C:2023:393. See: Cour de cassation 1e civ., 5 February 2020, Bull. civ. I, No. 113 <https://www.legifrance.gouv.fr/juri/id/JURITEXT000041585775/> accessed 15 November 2025; Cyril-Igor Grigorieff, 'The CJEU Confirms its Narrowed Interpretation of the Notion of "Extraordinary Circumstances" in TAP Portugal (Death of Co-Pilot)' (2024) 49 Air and Space Law 111.

82 Case C-12/11 *McDonagh*.

83 Case C-399/24 *AirHelp Germany GmbH v Austrian Airlines AG*, ECLI:EU:C:2025:791.

84 NL: RB Noord-Holland, 3 oktober 2018, ECLI:NL:RBNHO:2018:8187; RB Amsterdam, 27 maart 2018, ECLI:NL:RBAMS:2018:1962.

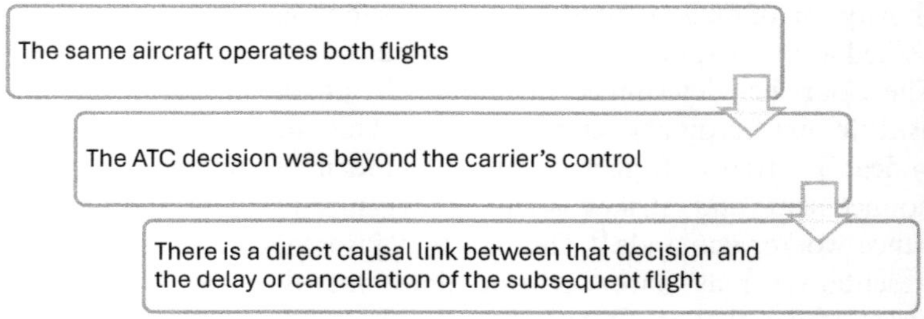

Figure I.3.3 Compensation for delays caused by air traffic management decisions

control of the air carrier concerned, in particular where it can be ruled out that the carrier contributed to the taking of that decision.[85] Moreover, an airline may rely on an extraordinary circumstance defence when the ATC decision affected a previous flight operated by the same aircraft, provided that there is a direct causal link between the occurrence of this circumstance and the delay or cancellation of the flight it subsequently operated. This case is particularly relevant for claims arising from aircraft rotation and knock-on delay. Indeed, when airlines can clearly evidence the link between the ATC decision and the delay, they are not prevented from relying on the extraordinary circumstance defence simply because the initial ATC decision occurred earlier that day. Knock-on delays are, therefore, no longer automatically excluded from the defence.

A bird strike may constitute an extraordinary circumstance, but not if an expert deems the aircraft airworthy, a second check cannot justify a delay.[86] If the bird strike results in an emergency braking manoeuvre damaging the aircraft's tyres, it will be an extraordinary circumstance.[87] The Court also confirmed that delay time caused by the extraordinary circumstance must be deducted from the total delay when assessing compensation. Similarly, the Court of Justice has determined that damage to an aircraft caused by a ground handling contractor shortly before take-off does not constitute an extraordinary circumstance.[88] However, a collision caused by

85 Case T-134/25 *D S.A. v P S.A*, V ECLI:EU:T:2026:35.

86 Case C-315/15 *Marcela Pešková and Jiří Peška v Travel Service a.s.*, ECLI:EU:C:2017:342.

87 Case C-302/22 *YS and RW v Freebird Airlines Europe Ltd.*, ECLI:EU:C:2022:748, paragraph 23.

88 Case C-394/14 *Siewert v Condor Flugdienst GmbH*, ECLI:EU:C:2014:2377.

another airline's aircraft hitting a stationary plane is.[89] In the same vein, damage to an aircraft tyre from foreign object debris on a runway is an extraordinary circumstance as is a runway closure due to a petrol spill not originating from the carrier's own aircraft.[90] The generalized breakdown in the supply of fuel – when such system is managed by the airport – falls within the extraordinary circumstance category.[91] Finally, unruly passenger behaviour necessitating a flight diversion is extraordinary, unless the airline contributed to the behaviour or failed to act on warning signs.[92] Medical emergency would also be covered by the concept of extraordinary circumstance.

An airline may rely on an extraordinary circumstance that affected a previous flight using the same aircraft to be exempt from compensation for a subsequent flight's delay or cancellation. This is permitted provided a direct causal link between the two events is established.[93] However, the General Court decided in *European Air Charter,* that

> an airline may not rely on an extraordinary circumstance which affected an earlier flight if the delay of the subsequent flight is caused by an autonomous decision taken by the airline, provided that that decision is the determining cause of that delay.[94]

Consequently, waiting for late passengers can be deemed an autonomous decision that may trigger compensation.

Finally, re-routing a passenger on a later flight operated by the same carrier due to an extraordinary circumstance, resulting in arrival the next day, is not considered a "reasonable measure" that releases the carrier from compensation.[95] This is unless no other routing option – on its own or another carrier's flights – was available for an earlier arrival, or if implementing such a re-routing would have been an intolerable sacrifice.

89 Case C-264/20 *Airhelp.*

90 Case C-501/17 *Germanwings*, paragraph 34; Case C-159/18 *André Moens v Ryanair Ltd*, ECLI:EU:C:2019:535, paragraph 22.

91 Case C-659/21 *Orbest, SA v CS and Others*, ECLI:EU:C:2022:254, paragraph 26.

92 Case C-74/19 *LE v Transportes Aéreos Portugueses SA*, ECLI:EU:C:2020:460.

93 Case C-74/19 *Transportes Aéros Portugueses*; C-826/19, *Austrian Airline.*

94 Case T-656/24 *European Air Charter, ECLI:EU:T:2026:167.*

95 Case C-74/19 *Transportes Aéros Portugueses*; C-264/20, *Airhelp.*

Category	Generally NOT Extraordinary Circumstances	Generally ARE Extraordinary Circumstances
Technical Problems	General technical failures and maintenance issues (C-549/07, Wallentin-Hermann). Failure of "on condition" parts (C-257/14, van der Lans; C-832/18, Finnair).	Hidden manufacturing defects, sabotage, or terrorism.
Staff Strikes	Internal strikes by airline's own staff (C-195/17, Krüsemann; C-28/20, Airhelp).	External strikes (e.g., air traffic controllers) (C-613/20, Eurowings).
External Events and Damage	Bird strikes (C-315/15, Pešková and Peška). Collision with airport boarding stairs (C-394/14, Siewert).	Collisions caused by another airline (C-264/20, Airhelp). Tyre damage from runway debris (C-501/17, Germanwings). Runway closures from external fuel spills (C-159/18, Moens). Generalized breakdown in the supply of fuel when supplied by airport (C-659/21, Orbest). ATC decisions if it is established that the decision was beyond the effective control of the air carrier concerned (T-134/25, D S.A. v P S.A).
Passenger Behaviour	—	Unruly passenger leading to diversion (C-74/19, Transportes Aéros Portugueses). Medical emergency.
Natural Disasters	—	Volcanic eruption closing airspace (C-12/11, McDonagh). Lightning strikes (C-399/24, AirHelp).
Previous Flight Issues	—	Extraordinary circumstance on a prior flight with a direct causal link (C-74/19, Transportes Aéros Portugueses; C-826/19, Austrian Airlines). ATC decisions if flight operated by the same aircraft with a direct causal link between the occurrence of this circumstance and the delay or cancellation of the flight it subsequently operated (T-134/25, D S.A. v P S.A).

(*Continued*)

(Continued)

Category	Generally NOT Extraordinary Circumstances	Generally ARE Extraordinary Circumstances
Airline Measures	Re-routing on a later same-carrier flight is not 'reasonable' (C-74/19, Transportes Aéros Portugueses; C-264/20, Airhelp). Autonomous decision to wait for passengers (T-656/24, European Air Charter).	Must take all reasonable measures, including reserve time, without intolerable sacrifice (C-294/10, Eglītis and Ratnieks). Must deploy all resources to minimize delays (C-501/17, Germanwings).

Another source of ambiguity stems from the wording that the defence applies when the disruption is caused by circumstances that "could not have been avoided even if all reasonable measures had been taken." A careful reading of this provision reveals two critical nuances: First, the exemption does not strictly require the carrier to have actually implemented every possible measure; rather, it must prove that even the full deployment of all reasonable measures would still have failed to avert the extraordinary circumstances themselves. Second, the legal focus is on the unavoidability of the circumstances, not directly on the resulting cancellation or delay.[96] However, the CJEU's early jurisprudence introduced ambiguity on two fronts: whether the unavoidability had to relate solely to the circumstances or extend to the resulting cancellation/delay, and whether the carrier needed to demonstrate only the theoretical unavoidability or the actual adoption of reasonable measures. Furthermore, the wording of early judgments suggested airlines might have to demonstrate not only theoretical unavoidability but also the actual adoption of all reasonable measures in response. Some commentators viewed this as an overly expansive, or "wrongful stretching," of the Regulation's original intent.[97] The evolution of case law has been complex and at times seemingly contradictory in the specific proof required.[98] Despite these linguistic fluctuations, expert

96 Opinion of the Advocate General in Case C-396/06 Kramme, ECLI:EU:C:2007:555, points 25–26. See: Ricardo Pazos, 'The Extraordinary Circumstances Defence in Regulation (EC) 261/2004' (2021) 46 Air & Space Law 739, p. 755 and following.

97 Jochen Croon, 'Wallentin-Hermann' and a Safe Flight' (2012) 61 Zeitschrift für Luft- und Weltraumrecht 610.

98 In Germanwings, the Court required the carrier to prove two cumulative elements but in Moens and Finnair, the Court used the disjunctive "or," suggesting only one of the two limbs needed to be proven.

consensus and later case law confirm that both preventive and reactive measures are, in fact, required from the carrier. Preventively, airlines must organize their operations with foresight, building in reserve time and contingency plans to absorb the impact of extraordinary events and restart operations thereafter. When extraordinary circumstances do occur, reactive measures must be "appropriate" and not impose further unnecessary inconvenience on passengers. A key reactive duty is re-routing.[99]

A key unanswered question remains how to handle delays with multiple causes: for instance, where a delay is caused by a mix of factors, some within the airline's control (e.g., a technical issue) and others outside of it (e.g., bad weather). While courts have generally focused on a single cause, airlines could potentially exclude their liability by proving that the portion of the delay caused by the extraordinary circumstances would have brought the total delay under the three-hour threshold for compensation.

d. Other Provisions

Should an operating air carrier upgrade a passenger to a class superior to the one ticketed, the carrier is expressly prohibited from requesting any additional payment from the passenger for this enhancement. Conversely, if a passenger is downgraded,[100] the air carrier is obligated to provide a partial reimbursement of the ticket price. This reimbursement must be issued to the passenger within seven days and is calculated based on the flight distance. For flights of 1,500 km or less, the passenger is entitled to 30% of the ticket price; for intra-Community flights exceeding 1,500 km (excluding routes between the European territory of Member States and the French Overseas Departments) and for all other flights between 1,500 and 3,500 km, the reimbursement is 50% of the ticket price; and for all other flights – including those exceeding 3,500 km and flights specifically between the European territory of Member States and the French Overseas Departments – the reimbursement increases to 75% of the ticket price.[101] The relevant price is either the fare of the flight segment where downgrading occurred or a proportion based on the distance of that flight compared to the total entitled journey distance. Taxes and charges

99 Ricardo Pazos, 'The Extraordinary Circumstances Defence in Regulation (EC) 261/2004' (2021) 46 Air and Space Law 739, 755 and following.

100 Not defined in Article 2, but Article 10 provides an indirect definition by stating "air carrier places a passenger in a class lower than that for which the ticket was purchased."

101 Article 10(2)(a)–(c).

shown on the ticket are excluded from this calculation if their payment requirement or amount does not depend on the travel class purchased.[102]

Flight Distance	**Reimbursement Amount**
1,500 km or less	30% of the ticket price.
Intra-Community flights >1,500 km, and all other flights between 1,500 km and 3,500 km (excludes: European territory to French Overseas Departments)	50% of the ticket price.
All other flights	75% of the ticket price.

Operating air carriers are mandated to grant priority handling to persons with reduced mobility, their companions, certified service dogs, and unaccompanied children. In the event of any travel disruption, these individuals have an immediate right to receive the care as soon as practicable.[103]

The rights and compensation established by this Regulation are considered a minimum standard. Passengers retain the full right to pursue further compensation through other legal avenues, with any compensation received under this Regulation being deductible from such subsequent claims. However, this principle does not apply to passengers who have voluntarily surrendered their seats.[104] Unlike other national laws, the Regulation is silent on baggage, so EU passengers must rely on the Montreal provisions.[105]

Airlines have a fundamental duty to inform passengers of their rights.[106] A clearly visible notice must be displayed at check-in, advising passengers of their entitlements in cases of denied boarding, cancellation, or delays of at least two hours. When such disruptions occur, the carrier must provide each affected passenger with a detailed written notice explaining the rules for compensation and assistance, including the contact information of the relevant national enforcement body but not the exact amount of compensation.[107] These provisions must be delivered through appropriate alternative means for blind and visually impaired persons. Any partial,

102 Case C-255/15 *Steef Mennens v Emirates Direktion für Deutschland*, ECLI:EU:C:2016:472, paragraphs 32 and 43.

103 Article 11.

104 Article 12.

105 The Court of Justice decided that pets are not excluded from the scope of baggage within Articles 17(2) and 22(2) of the Montreal Convention. See: Case C-218/24 *Felicísima v Iberia Líneas Aéreas de España SA Operadora Unipersonal and IATA España SLU*, ECLI:EU:C:2025:794.

106 Article 14.

107 Joined Cases C-146/20, C-188/20, C-196/20 and C-270/20 *Azurair and Others*, paragraph 108.

misleading, or wrong information could be considered an infringement of Regulation 261.[108]

Critically, the rights conferred by this Regulation cannot be limited or waived by any clause in the contract of carriage.[109] Any such derogatory clause is legally invalid. This includes any clause prohibiting the assignment of passenger rights is invalid.[110] If a passenger accepts a lower level of compensation due to being misinformed, they retain the full right to initiate legal proceedings to claim the full compensation owed.[111]

Each Member State is required to designate a public body responsible for enforcing this Regulation for flights from its airports.[112] Member States must ensure that the sanctions for violations of these rules are effective, proportionate, and dissuasive.[113] However, very few of such sanctions have been publicized and only regarding very particular events such as Covid or bankruptcy of a travel agency. For instance, the Italian's antitrust authority fined Ryanair and easyJet for failing to offer passengers cash refunds for flights cancelled due to the pandemic.[114] The Dutch Human Environment and Transport Inspectorate (ILT) fined KLM €40,000 for failure to refund passengers who booked cancelled tickets through a bankrupt travel agency.[115]

While Regulation 261 is silent on the limitation period, the CJEU has attempted to clarify this matter.[116] The Court rejected the application of the two-year limitation period similar to the Montreal and Warsaw Conventions as the Regulation is a compensation scheme which differs from those conventions.[117] As a result of the *Moré*, domestic courts in the EU are bound by this decision and ought to apply domestic law on the limitation period to a claim relating to EU Regulation 261 resulting in different periods to sue airlines and a lack of harmonization.

---

108 Commission Notice (n 17) 15.

109 Article 15.

110 Case C-173/23 *Eventmedia Soluciones SL v Air Europa Líneas Aéreas SAU*, ECLI:EU:C:2024:295.

111 Article 15.

112 Article 16(1).

113 Article 16(3).

114 'L'Autorità Garante della Concorrenza e del Mercato' (20 April 2021) <https://www.agcm.it/dotcmsdoc/allegati-news/PS11830_Easyjet%20chiusura.pdf> accessed 15 November 2025.

Appeal was dismissed in February 2025: Sentenza n. 03151 – giustizia-amministrativa.it – 12-02-2025.

115 Dutch News, 'KLM Fined €40,000 for Not Refunding Customers of Bankrupt Tour Operator' (11 May 2022) <https://www.dutchnews.nl/2022/05/klm-fined-e40000-for-not-refunding-customers-of-bankrupt-tour-operator/> accessed 15 November 2025.

116 Case C-139/11 *Cuandrench Moré v Koninklijke Luchtvaart Maatschappij n. V.* ECLI:EU:C:2012:741.

117 Case C-139/11 *Cuandrench Moré v Koninklijke Luchtvaart Maatschappij n. V.* ECLI:EU:C:2012:741, paragraphs 28–29.

e. 2025 Revisions

The role of the Court of Justice also came under hot criticism as Dempsey and Johansson concluded "Brussels' triumphant assertion of power and authority sacrifices global uniformity in the rule of law."[118] It is, therefore, not surprising that the Regulation has been under constant attacks and airlines lobbies have tried, on various occasions, to set its revision on the EU agenda.[119]

The 2025 legislative proposal[120] introduces several pivotal measures designed to strengthen and standardize air passenger rights across the European Union by providing greater clarity and consistency. A central element is the clarification of the right to assistance. While the right to two telephone calls or internet access remains unchanged and would be triggered after a two-hour delay, the other aspects have been revised. The proposed revision is also clarifying that refreshments should be offered every two hours of waiting time and meals after three hours and then every five hours.[121] Accommodation would be available under the same terms as currently, namely when a stay of one or more nights becomes necessary.[122] A provision dedicated to the care and assistance for missed connecting flight under a single contract would be introduced codifying the ruling of the Court.[123]

To increase passenger rights, the proposal also includes a tarmac delay provision entitling passengers to minimum assistance and a mandatory disembarkation after three hours.[124] Moreover, passengers would have the right to adequate cooling or heating as well as receiving water free of charge.[125] However, the provision does not stipulate any minimum threshold nor are passengers entitled to any snacks.

118 Dempsey and Johansson (n 7) 224.

119 D. Defossez, 'Proposed Revisions of Regulation 261/2004: Endangering Passengers' Rights and Going Against the International Trend?' (2021) 91 Journal of Air Transport Management.

120 Proposal for a regulation amending Regulation (EC) No 261/2004 establishing common rules on compensation and assistance to passengers in the event of denied boarding and of cancellation or long delay of flights and Regulation (EC) No 2027/97 on air carrier liability in respect of the carriage of passengers and their baggage by air. Document 10015/2025 <https://data.consilium.europa.eu/doc/document/ST-7503-2025-ADD-1-REV-3/en/pdf> accessed 15 November 2025.

121 Proposed Article 9(a).

122 Proposed Article 9(aa).

123 Proposed Article 6a.

124 Proposed Article 6-2a.

125 Proposed Article 6-2a(1).

Aspect of Care	Current Rules	Proposed 2025 Changes
Communication	2 phone calls/internet access after 2 hours.	Unchanged. Triggered after 2 hours of delay.
Refreshments and Meals	Vague or unspecified intervals.	Refreshments offered every 2 hours. Meals after 3 hours and then every 5 hours.
Accommodation	Provided when a stay of one or more nights is necessary.	Unchanged.
Missed Connections	Based on court rulings.	**Codified into law** for journeys under a single contract.
Tarmac Delays	No specific EU-wide rule.	**New Right:** Minimum assistance and **mandatory disembarkation after 3 hours**.

The major difference relates to the increased period of delay and reduced payout amounts; the proposed revision would apply only to delays of four hours or more for short- and medium-haul routes not exceeding 3,500 km. For long-haul flights, over 3,500 km, the threshold would be moved to six hours – which is shorter than the Commission proposal of 5–9–12 hours. This revised threshold seems to conflict with statistics that the majority of delays are situated between two and four hours on arrival.[126] Moreover, the argument for raising the threshold – namely that the Regulation has not successfully improved on-time performance and passenger protection – does not seem grounded in facts.[127]

The amount of compensation would be reduced from €400 to €300 for flights up to 3,500 km, and from €600 to €500 for longer flights.[128]

126 BEUC, 'The Revision of Air Passenger Rights Regulation' (BEUC-X-2025-021, 25 March 2023) 4 <https://www.beuc.eu/sites/default/files/publications/BEUC-X-2025-021_The_revision_of_the_air_passenger_rights_regulation.pdf> accessed 15 November 2025; Marie-Amandine Stévenin, 'Droits des passagers aériens: Une proposition qui vole bien trop bas!' (*Que Choisir*, 5 March 2025) <https://www.quechoisir.org/billet-de-la-presidente-droits-des-passagers-aeriens-une-proposition-qui-vole-bien-trop-bas-n149616/?utm_medium=email&utm_source=nlh&utm_campaign=nlh20250306&at_medium=email&at_emailtype=retention&at_campaign=nlh20250306> accessed 15 November 2025.

127 See: Hinnerk Gnutzmann and Piotr Śpiewanowski, 'Air Passenger Rights at the Crossroads: Economic Impact of the Proposed EC 261 Reform' (October 2025) <http://www.gnutzmann.info/Air_Passenger_Rights_at_the-Crossroads_Gnutzmann_Spiewanowski_2025.pdf> accessed 15 November 2025.

128 Proposed Article 7(a). "1. In case of disruption, the following compensation amounts shall apply under the conditions defined in Articles 4, 5, 6 or 6a and in this Article: (a)(b) 300 EUR for journeys of 3500 kilometres or less and all intra-Union journeys; 500 EUR for journeys above 3500 kilometres. By way of derogation from the previous subparagraph, for journeys between outermost regions and another territory of a Member State to which the Treaties apply, the compensation amounts shall be determined on the basis of the actual distance of the journeys."

However, it includes a derogation for outermost regions whereby the current compensation amounts would apply, adding a level of complexity to an already quite complex Regulation. Similarly, the compensation for downgrading has been changed to 40% of the flight price for flights of 3,500 km or less or 75% for all other flights.[129]

The new time threshold has been criticized as it could still incentivize airlines to cancel flights in order to minimize the knock-on effects on subsequent services rather than trying to resolve the cause of the delay.[130] Moreover, the limitation on no-show policies by granting those passengers the same rights as someone suffering a denial of boarding has been regarded as unfair.[131]

Flight Distance	**Proposed Compensation (2025 Rules)**	**Downgrading (2025 Rules)**
Up to 3,500 km (short/ medium-Haul)	**4 hours = €300.**	40% of the flight price.
Over 3,500 km (long-Haul)	**6 hours = €500.**	75% of the flight price.

The right to re-routing is also extended in the Council proposal allowing for re-routing on another carrier or another mode of transport.[132] If the passenger self-re-routes, the amount of reimbursement is capped at 400% of the full cost of the ticket.[133]

The proposal also contains a provision obliging certain airports to adopt a contingency plan, which is found in some national laws such as Trinidad and Tobago. This new obligation would be imposed on airports with annual traffic above 5 million passengers to minimize the waiting time and discomfort in case of multiple cancellations or delays.[134]

While the revision of Regulation 261 would have allowed the European Union to increase enforcement by refining the dedicated provision, the legislator has missed the opportunity to mandate a harmonized fine

129 Proposed Article 10(2)(a)–(b).

130 Eurochambres, 'Position on the Revision of the Air Passenger Rights Regulation' (17 September 2025) 3 <https://www.eurochambres.eu/wp-content/uploads/2025/09/250917-Eurochambres-position-on-the-revision-of-the-Air-Passenger-Rights-Regulation.pdf> accessed 15 November 2025.

131 Proposed Article 4(b). Eurochambres, 'Position on the Revision of the Air Passenger Rights Regulation' 6.

Interestingly, the Supreme Court in Spain determined years ago that no-show clauses were abusive: Sentencia 3733/2018, de la Sala de lo Civil del Tribunal Supremo Español (13 November 2018) <https://www.elnotario.es/images/pdf/STS-N83-10.pdf> accessed 15 November 2025.

132 Proposed Article 8(3)(b)–(d).

133 Proposed Article 8(7).

134 Proposed Article 10a(1).

across Member States.[135] As pointed out by the Court of Auditors in a 2018 report, the number of sanctions and their amount "vary greatly among Member States" ranging from "€50 (Poland) to €250 000 per passenger (Ireland), depending on the seriousness of the infringement. In the Netherlands, a cumulative fine for an incident reached as high as €1 million."[136] Additionally, the decision of National Enforcement Bodies should have been made legally binding to ensure better compliance.

Finally, in a move to create legal certainty, the proposal defines "extraordinary circumstances" in proposed Article 2 (e)(m) and includes a non-exhaustive list of specific events that falls within that category in an annex. This list, which includes events such as extreme weather, political instability or war, and air traffic control strikes, delineates the limited conditions under which an airline can be exempted from its obligation to pay compensation to passengers.[137] The proposed text also stipulates that "extraordinary circumstance" can be invoked for an event affecting up to three preceding flights.[138] The Council has also tried to bend a few of the Court's rulings so those specific circumstances could still exempt airlines from their liability. For instance, the preamble also makes it clear that some unexpected technical issues could be regarded as extraordinary circumstances.[139] Similarly, the sudden unexpected absence or death of an essential crew member outside of the home base would fall within this category.[140] Additionally, while the proposed revision recognized that case law of the Court have clearly established that strike by airline staff is not an extraordinary circumstance, point 3(c) of the revision introduces a caveat for certain demands by staff which could only be addressed by public authorities, such as retirement age. In those circumstances, the strike would be an extraordinary circumstance. While this provides courts and passengers with clearer guidelines, the open-ended, non-exhaustive

135 BEUC, BEUC-X-2025-021, 3. Weak enforcement has already pointed as a problem by S Drake, 'Delays, Cancellations and Compensation: Why Are Air Passengers Still Finding it Difficult to Enforce Their EU Rights Under Regulation 261/2004?' (2020) 27 Maastricht Journal of European Law 230.

136 European Court of Auditors, 'EU Passenger Rights Are Comprehensive but Passengers Still Need to Fight for Them' (*European Court of Auditors*, 2018) 27 <https://www.eca.europa.eu/Lists/ECADocuments/SR18_30/SR_PASSENGER_RIGHTS_EN.pdf> accessed 15 November 2025.

137 Annex 1 Proposal for a regulation amending Regulation (EC) No 261/2004 establishing common rules on compensation and assistance to passengers in the event of denied boarding and of cancellation or long delay of flights and Regulation (EC) No 2027/97 on air carrier liability in respect of the carriage of passengers and their baggage by air, 9795/25 ADD 2, issued 6 June 2025 <https://data.consilium.europa.eu/doc/document/ST-9795-2025-ADD-2/en/pdf> accessed 15 November 2025.

138 Proposed Article 5(b) amending paragraph 3.

139 Point 3a of the preamble.

140 Point 3b of the preamble.

nature of this list may not fully resolve the systemic abuse currently seen, where airlines may still attempt to broadly interpret additional events as falling outside of their operational control. However, the Council made it clear in its position in October 2025 that the list should remain non-exhaustive.[141]

In October 2025, the European Parliament's Transport and Tourism Committee (TRAN) voted for an alternative legislative text that keeps the three-hour delay threshold for compensation and signals a broader intent to strengthen air passenger protections.[142] Additionally, an inflation related increase of compensation has been included.[143] To streamline the claims process, the proposal mandates the introduction of a standardized, unified form for both compensation and reimbursement requests, as recommended by the European Court of Auditors.[144] Airlines will be obliged to provide this pre-filled form to affected passengers automatically, or at a minimum, ensure it is made readily available within 48 hours of a flight disruption occurring. The Parliament is also of the opinion that a defined closed list of exemptions is needed which could be kept up to date through delegated acts.[145] Instead of limiting the expansion of case law, the potential introduction of new concepts into the Regulation through delegated acts is likely to provide a foundation for the next decades of CJEU jurisprudence.[146]

141 Position of the Council at first reading with a view to the adoption of a Regulation of European Parliament and of the Council amending Regulation (EC) No 261/2004 establishing common rules on compensation and assistance to passengers in the event of denied boarding and of cancellation or long delay of flights and Regulation (EC) No 2027/97 on air carrier liability in respect of the carriage of passengers and their baggage by air, 10015/25 ADD 1 <https://eur-lex.europa.eu/legal-content/EN/TXT/PDF/?uri=CONSIL:ST_10015_2025_ADD_1> accessed 15 November 2025.

As advocated by BEUC and the Airline industry: BEUC, BEUC-X-2025-021; A4E, IATA and ERA (n 5).

142 TRAN/10/01040; European Parliament, 'MEPs Set Out Their Red Lines for Air Passenger Rights Changes' (*European Parliament*, 13 October 2025) <https://www.europarl.europa.eu/news/en/press-room/20251009IPR30833/meps-set-out-their-red-lines-for-air-passenger-rights-changes> accessed 15 November 2025.

Retaining the three hours threshold is in line with the position of the ECC-Network, 'Towards a More Effective Air Passenger Rights Regulation' (18 March 2025) 15 <https://www.europe-consommateurs.eu/fileadmin/Media/PDF/publications/etudes_et_rapports/Etudes_EN/ECC-Towards_a_More_Effective_Air_Passenger_Rights_Regulation-WHITEPAPER.pdf> accessed 15 November 2025.

143 Hinnerk Gnutzmann and Piotr Śpiewanowski, 'Air Passenger Rights at the Crossroads: Economic Impact of the Proposed EC 261 Reform' (October 2025) 8 <http://www.gnutzmann.info/Air_Passenger_Rights_at_the-Crossroads_Gnutzmann_Spiewanowski_2025.pdf> accessed 15 November 2025.

144 European Court of Auditors (n 126).

145 European Parliament (n 134).

146 There are over 80 judgments by the CJEU reported related to Regulation 261 which might be the record for a single piece of legislation.

The Parliament also took a stronger stand on hand luggage by requesting a provision guaranteeing the right to carry one personal item in addition to one piece of small hand luggage into the cabin free of any charge, with a combined maximum dimension of 100 cm and a weight limit of 7 kg, instead of a mention in the preamble.[147] Such inclusion would avoid fines as imposed by the Spanish consumer right ministry in 2024 on easyJet for €29 million and Ryanair for €108 million for their hand luggage and sitting policies.[148]

Further consumer protections include a prohibition on surcharges applied by airlines for the correction of minor errors in passenger names. Additionally, the Transport Committee MEPs want to ensure that children under the age of 14 are seated next to an accompanying adult at no extra cost, eliminating a previously common fee.[149] The Parliament also seeks to ban no-show clauses practice. The airline industry has already warned that the Parliament position could worsen EU's competitiveness deficit due to the increased cost under the revised Regulation.[150]

One of the major omissions in both positions relates to viable solutions in case of airline bankruptcies. Those passengers are left to national laws and potential collective procedures. Following the controversial judgment that a lost dog was not worth more than a lost luggage under the Montreal Convention, it seems necessary to integrate a specific provision for companion animals into EU passenger rights regulations as found in other national laws.[151] The inclusion of a specific rule would also reflect the fact that in many jurisdictions, pets are no longer considered as objects and have been granted specific rights or status.[152]

---

147 Proposed Points 28 and 28(a) of the preamble would pretty much keep the status quo while the Parliament's position would provide better protection.

European Parliament (n 134).

148 Joanna Partridge and Jack Simpson, 'EasyJet Boss Denounces "Illegal" Fines over Hand Luggage Charges' *The Guardian* (27 November 2024) <https://www.theguardian.com/business/2024/nov/27/fining-budget-airlines-will-make-flying-more-expensive-says-easyjet-boss> accessed 15 November 2025.

149 European Parliament (n 134).

150 Recital 33a of the proposal. See: A4E, IATA and ERA (n 5) 2.

151 Case C-218/24 *Felicísima v Iberia*. See: Marine Lercier, 'Op-Ed: "A Dog Is Still Not a Suitcase: Iberia (C-218/24)"' (*EU LAW Live*, 29 October 2025) <https://eulawlive.com/op-ed-a-dog-is-still-not-a-suitcase-iberia-c-218-24/> accessed 15 November 2025.

152 Various countries have incorporated animal protection into their highest laws, including Switzerland, Germany, Luxembourg, and Austria. For instance, Luxembourg gave animal welfare constitutional value in Article 11bis of the Constitution.

Other EU countries have introduced some form of protective provisions. For instance, Article 515-14 of the French Civil Code recognized that animals are sentient beings. However, they are still subject to the regime of goods.

f. Conclusion

Regulation 261 stands as a monumental, although controversial, pillar of EU consumer law. Conceived as a robust shield for passengers against the operational risks of airlines, it has, through two decades of relentless judicial interpretation and industry pushback, evolved into a unique legal instrument. Despite profound structural challenges, the Regulation has not only survived the passing of time but has also been fundamentally strengthened and expanded over time, primarily through the bold and often controversial jurisprudence of the Court of Justice of the European Union (CJEU). Indeed, the Court of Justice has been the central actor in this drama, not merely interpreting the Regulation but actively shaping its substance. Landmark rulings like *Sturgeon*, which extended cancellation-style compensation to long delays, and a continuous narrowing of the "extraordinary circumstances" defence, have proven the CJEU's unwavering commitment to a passenger-centric reading, even at the cost of being accused of effectively rewriting the law.

The Regulation's ultimate strength and weakness lie in its standardized approach. By creating a system of fixed compensation and immediate assistance, it provides passengers with legal certainty and a clear path to redress, freeing them from the burden of proving individual damages under the more complex Montreal Convention. This has rightfully empowered millions and set a global benchmark for passenger rights. However, this very rigidity has spawned a labyrinth of litigation, making it the most-litigated EU regulation in history. The resulting legal uncertainty for airlines, coupled with the perceived overreach of the CJEU, has fostered deep-seated resentment within the industry and among some legal scholars who see it as a departure from established international law.

The ongoing 2025 revision process highlights the enduring difficulty of striking a balance between passenger protection and airline operational concerns. The proposed changes – such as increasing delay thresholds, reducing compensation amounts, and attempting to codify a definitive list of extraordinary circumstances – represent a clear political compromise aimed at alleviating industry pressure. However, these measures risk diluting the very protections that define the Regulation. The European Parliament's counter-proposal to maintain the three-hour threshold and strengthen enforcement mechanisms underscores the political immovability of core passenger rights.

Regulation 261, forged in controversy and continually shaped by judicial intervention, has cemented the European Union's position as a global leader in airline passenger protection. While for some Regulation 261 is still one of the best models to protect passengers, for others, it is a quintessentially bad piece of legislation whose costs clearly outweigh its benefits as it does not incentivize improving performance enough. All in all, despite the attempt to remodel and amend the Regulation, it would be a political suicide to try to "stuff the genie back in the bottle." However, wobbly or unfit for purpose one thinks the Regulation is, its global influence reflects its success. Its legacy – national and regional laws mirroring its key concepts or wording – demonstrates that overall Regulation is a great piece of legislation in elevating passenger rights to a non-negotiable standard and may be one of the EU masterpieces in setting standards globally.

Bibliography

Case

- 'L'Autorità Garante della Concorrenza e del Mercato' (20 April 2021) <https://www.agcm.it/dotcmsdoc/allegati-news/PS11830_Easyjet%20chiusura.pdf> accessed 15 November 2025.
- Case number: 2-24 S 93/24 (Travel Law Chamber of the Frankfurt am Main Regional Court)
- Cour de cassation 1e civ, 5 February 2020, Bull. civ. I, No. 113.
- Case C-11/11 *Air France SA v Folkerts*, ECLI:EU:C:2013:106.
- Case C-11/23 *Eventmedia Soluciones SL v Air Europa Líneas Aéreas SAU*, ECLI:EU:C:2024:194.
- Case C-12/11 *Denise McDonagh v Ryanair Ltd*, ECLI:EU:C:2013:43.
- Case C-20/24 *M1.R. and M2.R. v AAA sp. z o.o*, ECLI:EU:C:2025:139.
- Case C-22/11 *Finnair Oyj v Timy Lassooy*, ECLI:EU:C:2012:604.
- Case C-28/20 *Airhelp Ltd v Scandinavian Airlines System Denmark – Norway – Sweden*, ECLI:EU:C:2021:226.
- Case C-32/16 *Ute Wunderlich v Bulgarian Air Charter Limited*, ECLI:EU:C:2016:753.
- Case C-45/24 *Verein für Konsumenteninformation v KLM*.
- Case C-54/23 *WY v Laudamotion GmbH and Ryanair DAC*, ECLI:EU:C:2024:74.
- Case C-74/19 *LE v Transportes Aéreos Portugueses SA*, ECLI:EU:C:2020:460.
- Case C-76/23 *Cobult UG v TAP Air Portugal SA*, ECLI:EU:C:2024:253.
- Cases C-83/10 *Aurora Sousa Rodríguez and Others v Air France SA.*, ECLI:EU:C:2011:652.
- Case C-130/18 *flightright GmbH v Eurowings GmbH*, ECLI:EU:C:2018:496.
- Case C-139/11 *Cuandrench Moré v Koninklijke Luchtvaart Maatschappij n. V.* ECLI:EU:C:2012:741.
- Case C-159/18 *André Moens v Ryanair Ltd*, ECLI:EU:C:2019:535.
- Case C-173/07 *Emirates Airlines – Direktion für Deutschland v Diether Schenkel*, ECLI:EU:C:2008:400.
- Case C-173/23 *Eventmedia Soluciones SL v Air Europa Líneas Aéreas SAU*, ECLI:EU:C:2024:295.
- Case C-191/19 *OI v Air Nostrum Líneas Aéreas del Mediterráneo SA*, ECLI:EU:C:2020:339.

- Case C-195/17 *Helga Krüsemann and Others v TUIfly GmbH*, ECLI:EU:C:2018:258.
- Case C-213/18 *Adriano Guaitoli and others v easyJet Airline Co. Ltd*, ECLI:EU:C:2019:927.
- Case C-218/24 *Felicísima v Iberia Líneas Aéreas de España SA Operadora Unipersonal and IATA España SLU*, ECLI:EU:C:2025:794.
- Case C-238/22 *FW v LATAM Airlines Group SA*, ECLI:EU:C:2023:815.
- Case C-253/21 *FI and RE v TUIfly GmbH*, ECLI:EU:C:2021:840.
- Case C-255/15 *Steef Mennens v Emirates Direktion für Deutschland*, ECLI:EU:C:2016:472.
- Case C-257/14 *van der Lans v Koninklijke Luchtvaart Maatschappij NV*, ECLI:EU:C:2015:618.
- Case C-263/20 *Airhelp Limited v Laudamotion GmbH*, ECLI:EU:C:2021:1039.
- Case C-292/24 *AD v Iberia Líneas Aéreas de España*, ECLI:EU:C:2025:402.
- Case C-294/10 *Andrejs Eglītis and Edvards Ratnieks v Latvijas Republikas Ekonomikas ministrija*, ECLI:EU:C:2011:303.
- Case C-302/16 *Bas Jacob Adriaan Krijgsman v Surinaamse Luchtvaart Maatschappij NV*, ECLI:EU:C:2017:359.
- Case C-302/22 *YS and RW v Freebird Airlines Europe Ltd.*, ECLI:EU:C:2022:748.
- Case C-315/15 *Marcela Pešková and Jiří Peška v Travel Service a.s.*, ECLI:EU:C:2017:342.
- Case C-316/20 *VO and Others v SATA International – Azores Airlines SA*, ECLI:EU:C:2020:966.
- Case C-321/11 *Germán Rodríguez Cachafeiro and María de los Reyes Martínez-Reboredo Varela-Villamor v Iberia, Líneas Aéreas de España SA*, ECLI:EU:C:2012:609.
- Case C-344/04 *The Queen, on the application of International Air Transport Association and European Low Fares Airline Association v Department for Transport*, ECLI:EU:C:2006:10.
- Case C-354/18 *Radu Lucian Rusu and Oana Maria Rusu v SC Blue Air – Airline Management Solutions SRL*, ECLI:EU:C:2019:637.
- Case C-367/20 *SP v KLM Royal Dutch Airlines*, ECLI:EU:C:2020:909.
- Case C-394/14 *Siewert v Condor Flugdienst GmbH*, ECLI:EU:C:2014:2377.
- Case C-395/20 *EP and GM v Corendon Airlines Turistik Hava Tasimacilik A.S*, ECLI:EU:C:2021:1041.
- Case C-399/24 *AirHelp Germany GmbH v Austrian Airlines AG*, ECLI:EU:C:2025:791.
- Case C-405/23 *Touristic Aviation Services Limited v Flightright GmbH*, ECLI:EU:C:2024:408.
- Case C-411/23 *D. (Vide de conception du moteur)*, ECLI:EU:C:2024:498.
- Case C-436/21 *flightright GmbH v American Airlines, Inc*, ECLI:EU:C:2022:762.
- Case C-451/20 *Airhelp Limited v Austrian Airlines AG*, ECLI:EU:C:2022:123.
- Cases C-452/13 *Germanwings GmbH v Ronny Henning*, ECLI:EU:C:2014:2141.
- Case C-474/22 *Laudamotion GmbH v Flightright GmbH*, ECLI:EU:C:2024:73.
- Case C-501/17 *Germanwings*, ECLI:EU:C:2019:288.
- Case C-502/18 *CS and Others v České aerolinie a.s.*, ECLI:EU:C:2019:604.
- Case C-516/23 *NW and YS v Qatar Airways*, ECLI:EU:C:2025:21.

- Case C-537/17 *Claudia Wegener v Royal Air Maroc SA*, ECLI:EU:C:2018:361.
- Case C-549/07 *Friederike Wallentin-Hermann v Alitalia – Linee Aeree Italiane SpA*, ECLI:EU:C:2008:771.
- Case C-558/24 *Corendon Airlines Turistik Hava Tasimacilik AS v Myflyright GmbH*, ECLI:EU:C:2025:847.
- Case C-559/16 *Birgit Bossen and Others v Brussels Airlines SA/NV*, ECLI:EU:C:2017:644.
- Case C-561/20 *Q and Others v United Airlines, Inc*, ECLI:EU:C:2022:266.
- Cases C-581/10 & C-629/10 *Emeka Nelson and Others v Deutsche Lufthansa AG and TUI Travel plc and Others v Civil Aviation Authority*, ECLI:EU:C:2012:657.
- Case C-592/20 *NT and Others v British Airways plc*, ECLI:EU:C:2021:312.
- Case C-601/17 *Harms v Vueling Airlines SA*, ECLI:EU:C:2018:702.
- Case C-613/20 *CS v Eurowings GmbH*, ECLI:EU:C:2021:820.
- Case C-642/23 *Flightright GmbH v Etihad Airways P.J.S. C*, ECLI:EU:C:2025:12.
- Case C-654/19 *FP Passenger Service v Austrian Airlines AG*, ECLI:EU:C:2020:770.
- Case C-659/21 *Orbest, SA v CS and Others*, ECLI:EU:C:2022:254.
- Case C-686/20 *YE and Others v Vueling Airlines SA*, ECLI:EU:C:2021:859.
- Case C-756/18 *LC and MD v easyJet Airline Co. Ltd*, ECLI:EU:C:2019:902.
- Case C-826/19 *WZ v Austrian Airlines AG*, ECLI:EU:C:2021:318.
- Case C-832/18 *A and Others v Finnair Oyj*, ECLI:EU:C:2020:204.
- Case C-939/19 *Flightright GmbH v Eurowings GmbH*, ECLI:EU:C:2020:316.
- Case T-134/25 *D S.A. v P S.A, V* ECLI:EU:T:2026:35.
- Case T-656/24 *European Air Charter*, ECLI:EU:T:2026:167.
- Joined Cases C-146/20, C-188/20, C-196/20 and C-270/20 *AD and Others v Corendon Airlines and Others (Azurair e.a)*, ECLI:EU:C:2021:1038.
- Joined Cases C-156/22, C-157/22 and C-158/22 *TAP Portugal (Décès du copilote)*, ECLI:EU:C:2023:393.
- Joined cases C-402/07 and C-432/07 *Christopher Sturgeon, Gabriel Sturgeon and Alana Sturgeon v Condor Flugdienst GmbH and Stefan Böck and Cornelia Lepuschitz v Air France SA*, ECLI:EU:C:2009:716.
- Joined Cases C-650/23 and C-705/23 *E EAD v DW and Flightright GmbH v Condor Flugdienst GmbH*, ECLI:EU:C:2024:903.
- RB Amsterdam, 27 maart 2018, ECLI:NL:RBAMS:2018:1962.
- RB Noord-Holland, 3 oktober 2018, ECLI:NL:RBNHO:2018:8187.
- Sentencia 3733/2018, de la Sala de lo Civil del Tribunal Supremo Español (13 November 2018) <https://www.elnotario.es/images/pdf/STS-N83-10.pdf> accessed 15 November 2025.
- Sentenza n. 03151 – giustizia-amministrativa.it (12 February 2025).

Legislation

- Commission Notice, 'Interpretative Guidelines on Regulation (EC) No 261/2004 of the European Parliament and of the Council establishing common rules on compensation and assistance to passengers in the event of denied boarding and of cancellation or long delay of flights and on Council

Regulation (EC) No 2027/97 on air carrier liability in the event of accidents' C/2024/5687 <https://eur-lex.europa.eu/legal-content/EN/TXT/PDF/?uri=OJ:C_202405687> accessed 15 November 2025.

- Council Regulation (EEC) No 295/91 of 4 February 1991 establishing common rules for a denied-boarding compensation system in scheduled air transport, OJ L 36, 8 February 1991, 5–7.
- Position of the Council at first reading with a view to the adoption of a Regulation of European Parliament and of the Council amending Regulation (EC) No 261/2004 establishing common rules on compensation and assistance to passengers in the event of denied boarding and of cancellation or long delay of flights and Regulation (EC) No 2027/97 on air carrier liability in respect of the carriage of passengers and their baggage by air, 10015/25 ADD 1 <https://eur-lex.europa.eu/legal-content/EN/TXT/PDF/?uri=CONSIL:ST_10015_2025_ADD_1> accessed 15 November 2025.
- Proposal for a regulation amending Regulation (EC) No 261/2004 establishing common rules on compensation and assistance to passengers in the event of denied boarding and of cancellation or long delay of flights and Regulation (EC) No 2027/97 on air carrier liability in respect of the carriage of passengers and their baggage by air. Document 10015/2025. <https://data.consilium.europa.eu/doc/document/ST-7503-2025-ADD-1-REV-3/en/pdf> accessed 15 November 2025.
- Proposal for a regulation amending Regulation (EC) No 261/2004 establishing common rules on compensation and assistance to passengers in the event of denied boarding and of cancellation or long delay of flights and Regulation (EC) No 2027/97 on air carrier liability in respect of the carriage of passengers and their baggage by air, 9795/25 ADD 2, issued 6 June 2025 <https://data.consilium.europa.eu/doc/document/ST-9795-2025-ADD-2/en/pdf> accessed 15 November 2025.
- Regulation (EC) No 261/2004 of the European Parliament and of the Council of 11 February 2004 establishing common rules on compensation and assistance to passengers in the event of denied boarding and of cancellation or long delay of flights, and repealing Regulation (EEC) No 295/91 [2004] OJ L46/1.

Secondary Sources

- A4E, IATA and ERA, 'Revision of Regulation 261/2004 Airline Industry Perspectives' (October 2025) <https://www.eraa.org/wp-content/uploads/2025/10/Joint-Industry-Position-EU261-revision_15102025.pdf> accessed 15 November 2025.
- Balfour, J., 'Airline Liability for Delays: The Court of Justice of the EU Rewrites EC Regulation 261/2004' (2010) 35 Air and Space Law 71.
- Bernard, N., 'Taking Air Passenger Rights Seriously: the Case Against the Exclusivity of the Montreal Convention' (2021) International Community Law Review <https://qmro.qmul.ac.uk/xmlui/bitstream/handle/123456789/64713/Bernard%20Taking%20Air%20Passenger%20Rights%20Seriously%3A%20

the%20Case%20Against%20the%20Exclusivity%20of%20the%20Montreal%20Convention%202020%20Accepted.pdf?sequence=2&isAllowed=y> accessed 15 November 2025.

- BEUC, 'The Revision of Air Passenger Rights Regulation' (BEUC-X-2025-021, 25 March 2023) <https://www.beuc.eu/sites/default/files/publications/BEUC-X-2025-021_The_revision_of_the_air_passenger_rights_regulation.pdf> accessed 15 November 2025.
- Christopher Bisping, 'Analysis: "When Must an Airline Reimburse Intermediary Booking Commissions? Verein für Konsumenteninformation v. KLM (C-45/24)"' (EU Law Live, 21 January 2026).
- Chassot, L. and Dempsey, P. S., 'Article 29: Basis of Claims' in George Leloudas, Paul S Dempsey and Laurent Chassot (eds), *The Montreal Convention: A Commentary* (Edward Elgar 2023).
- Croon, J., 'Wallentin-Hermann' and a Safe Flight' (2012) 61 Zeitschrift für Luft- und Weltraumrecht 610.
- Defossez, D., 'I Wish My Mum Was Brazilian: The Regulation of Passenger Liability in the EU and Brazil' (2019) Issues in Aviation Law and Policy 333.
- Defossez, D., 'Proposed Revisions of Regulation 261/2004: Endangering Passengers' Rights and Going Against the International Trend?' (2021) 91 Journal of Air Transport Management.
- Dempsey, P. S. and Johansson, S. O., 'Montreal v. Brussels: The Conflict of Laws on the Issue of Delay in International Air Carriage' (2010) 35 Air & Space Law 207.
- Drake, S., 'Delays, Cancellations and Compensation: Why Are Air Passengers Still Finding it Difficult to Enforce Their EU Rights Under Regulation 261/2004?' (2020) 27 Maastricht Journal of European Law 230.
- Dutch News, 'KLM Fined €40,000 for Not Refunding Customers of Bankrupt Tour Operator' (11 May 2022) <https://www.dutchnews.nl/2022/05/klm-fined-e40000-for-not-refunding-customers-of-bankrupt-tour-operator/> accessed 15 November 2025.
- ECC-Network, 'Towards a More Effective Air Passenger Rights Regulation' (18 March 2025) <https://www.europe-consommateurs.eu/fileadmin/Media/PDF/publications/etudes_et_rapports/Etudes_EN/ECC-Towards_a_More_Effective_Air_Passenger_Rights_Regulation-WHITEPAPER.pdf> accessed 15 November 2025.
- Eurochambres, 'Position on the Revision of the Air Passenger Rights Regulation' (17 September 2025) <https://www.eurochambres.eu/wp-content/uploads/2025/09/250917-Eurochambres-position-on-the-revision-of-the-Air-Passenger-Rights-Regulation_.pdf> accessed 15 November 2025.
- European Court of Auditors, 'EU Passenger Rights Are Comprehensive but Passengers Still Need to Fight for Them' (*European Court of Auditors*, 2018) <https://www.eca.europa.eu/Lists/ECADocuments/SR18_30/SR_PASSENGER_RIGHTS_EN.pdf> accessed 15 November 2025.
- European Parliament, 'MEPs Set Out Their Red Lines for Air Passenger Rights Changes' (*European Parliament*, 13 October 2025) <https://www.europarl.europa.eu/news/en/press-room/20251009IPR30833/meps-set-out-their-red-lines-for-air-passenger-rights-changes> accessed 15 November 2025.

- Gnutzmann, H. and Śpiewanowski, P., 'Air Passenger Rights at the Crossroads: Economic Impact of the Proposed EC 261 Reform' (October 2025) <http://www.gnutzmann.info/Air_Passenger_Rights_at_the-Crossroads_Gnutzmann_Spiewanowski_2025.pdf> accessed 15 November 2025.
- Grigorieff, C.-I., 'The CJEU Confirms its Narrowed Interpretation of the Notion of "Extraordinary Circumstances" in TAP Portugal (Death of Co-Pilot)' (2024) 49 Air and Space Law 111.
- Humphreys, B., *The Regulation of Air Transport: From Protection to Liberalisation and Back Again* (Routledge 2023).
- Lawson, R. and Marland, T., 'The Montreal Convention 1999, and the Decisions of the ECJ in the Cases of IATA and Sturgeon – in Harmony or Discord?' (2011) 36 Air and Space Law 99.
- Lercier, M., 'Op-Ed: "A Dog Is Still Not a Suitcase: Iberia (C-218/24)"' (*EU LAW Live*, 29 October 2025) <https://eulawlive.com/op-ed-a-dog-is-still-not-a-suitcase-iberia-c-218-24/> accessed 15 November 2025.
- Mendes de Leon, P., *Introduction to Air Law* (11th edn, Wolters Kluwer 2022).
- Pantazi, T., '"I Know that I Know Nothing": Extraordinary Circumstances in Air Passenger Rights Regulation' (2020) 28 European Review of Private Law 1093.
- Partridge, J. and Simpson, J., 'EasyJet Boss Denounces "Illegal" Fines over Hand Luggage Charges' *The Guardian* (27 November 2024) <https://www.theguardian.com/business/2024/nov/27/fining-budget-airlines-will-make-flying-more-expensive-says-easyjet-boss> accessed 15 November 2025.
- Pazos, R., 'The Extraordinary Circumstances Defence in Regulation (EC) 261/2004' (2021) 46 Air and Space Law 739.
- Pazos, R., 'The Carrier's Defence to Liability for Delay Under the Montreal Convention and EU Regulation 261/2004' (2024) 49 Air and Space Law 417.
- Rossi dal Pozzo, F., *EU Legal Framework for Safeguarding Air Passenger Rights* (Springer 2014).
- Stévenin, M.-A., 'Droits des passagers aériens: Une proposition qui vole bien trop bas!' (*Que Choisir*, 5 March 2025) <https://www.quechoisir.org/billet-de-la-presidente-droits-des-passagers-aeriens-une-proposition-qui-vole-bien-trop-bas-n149616/?utm_medium=email&utm_source=nlh&utm_campaign=nlh20250306&at_medium=email&at_emailtype=retention&at_campaign=nlh20250306> accessed 15 November 2025.
- Thijssen, C., 'The Montreal Convention, EU Regulation 261/2004, and the Sturgeon Doctrine: How to Reconcile the Three?' (2013) 12 Issues in Aviation Law and Policy 413.
- Tompkins Jr, G. N., 'Are the Objectives of the 1999 Montreal Convention in Danger of Failure?' (2014) 39 Air and Space Law 203.
- Van Dam, C., 'Luchtvaartmaatschappijen zijn niet gek op passagiersrechten' (2010) 85 Nederlands juristenblad.

I.4

European Common Aviation Area Agreement (ECAA)

The European Common Aviation Area[1] (ECAA) stands as a seminal multilateral agreement designed to extend the liberalized principles of the European Union's Single Aviation Market to non-EU partners, notably the countries of the European Free Trade Association (EFTA) and the Western Balkans. It is rooted in the strategic evolution of the European Union's external aviation policy and as part of the European Neighbourhood Policy (ENP), the European Union strengthened its aviation relations with non-European neighbouring countries.[2] The initiative was a direct response to a series of European Court of Justice "Open Skies" judgments in 2002, which sought to address inconsistencies between bilateral air services agreements and Community law.[3] As Vincent

1 Decision 2006/682/EC of the Council and of the Representatives of the Member States of the European Union meeting within the Council of 9 June 2006 on the signature and provisional application of the Multilateral Agreement between the European Community and its Member States, the Republic of Albania, Bosnia and Herzegovina, the Republic of Bulgaria, the Republic of Croatia, the former Yugoslav Republic of Macedonia, the Republic of Iceland, the Republic of Montenegro, the Kingdom of Norway, Romania, the Republic of Serbia and the United Nations Interim Administration Mission in Kosovo on the Establishment of a European Common Aviation Area (ECAA).

Multilateral Agreement between the European Community and its Member States, the Republic of Albania, Bosnia and Herzegovina, the Republic of Bulgaria, the Republic of Croatia, the former Yugoslav Republic of Macedonia, the Republic of Iceland, the Republic of Montenegro, the Kingdom of Norway, Romania, the Republic of Serbia and the United Nations Interim Administration Mission in Kosovo on the establishment of a European Common Aviation Area, OJ L 285, 16 October 2006, 1–46.

2 Vincent Correia and Noura Rouissi, 'Global, Regional and National Air Passenger Rights – Does the Patchwork Work?' (2015) 40 Air and Space Law 123, 130.

3 Case C-466/98 *Commission v United Kingdom* [2002] ECR I-9427, Case C-467/98 *Commission v Denmark* [2002] ECR I-9519, Case C-468/98 *Commission v Sweden* [2002] ECR I-9575, Case C-469/98 *Commission v Finland* [2002] ECR I-9627, Case C-471/98 *Commission v Belgium* [2002] ECR I-9681, Case C-472/98 *Commission v Luxembourg* [2002] ECR I-9741, Case C-475/98 *Commission v Austria* [2002] ECR I-9797, and Case C-476/98 *Commission v Germany* [2002] ECR I-9855. See: Peter Bombay and Máté Gergely, 'The 2006 ECAA Agreement: Centrepiece of the European Community's Aviation Policy Towards Its Neighbours' (2008) 33 Air & Space Law 214.

DOI: 10.4324/9781003746164-6

Correia and Noura Rouissi noted, "the closer the third country is, the more important the obligation is to integrate the EU 'aviation acquis'."[4]

Established in 2006 between then 27 EU Member States, the European Union itself and a number of external countries, the ECAA liberalizes the air transport industry by creating a single, integrated market, enabling any carrier from a Member State to operate flights between and even within other Member States.[5] This integration is founded on the full adoption of the EU's aviation acquis.[6] The ECAA Agreement officially entered into force on 1 December 2017, marking a pivotal moment for regional integration.

While EU Regulation 261 applies as part of the agreement with the countries which are parties to the European Economic Area (EEA),[7] other countries in the ECAA[8] are only required to harmonize their aviation laws with the EU Regulation.[9] Regulation 261 is not legally binding in the same manner as it is for Member States and EEA's countries.

This agreement mandates that signatory countries, including non-EU states, adopt and apply EU aviation legislation, including rules on passenger rights and competition. This creates a legal obligation to align with the *acquis communautaire*, which includes CJEU's case law, in this specific sector. For instance, Iceland has not transposed Regulation 261 in its national law, instead using the Regulation itself without including the wording of it.[10] That being said, the Icelandic Transport Authority has been quite prolific in issuing decisions regarding any passenger complains.[11]

---

4 Vincent Correia and Noura Rouissi. 'Global, Regional and National Air Passenger Rights – Does the Patchwork Work?' (2015) 40 Air & Space Law 123, 131.

5 Peter Bombay and Máté Gergely, 'The 2006 ECAA Agreement: Centrepiece of the European Community's Aviation Policy Towards Its Neighbours' (2008) 33 Air and Space Law 214.

6 European Commission, 'European Common Aviation Area: Aviation Relations' <https://transport.ec.europa.eu/transport-modes/air/international-aviation/status-aviation-relations-country/ecaa_en> accessed 16 November 2025.

7 Iceland, Norway and Liechtenstein.

8 Albania, Bosnia and Herzegovina, North Macedonia, Kosovo, Macedonia, Montenegro, Serbia, Moldova, Georgia and countries of the European Economic Area.

9 Multilateral Agreement between the European Community and its Member States, the Republic of Albania, Bosnia and Herzegovina, the Republic of Bulgaria, the Republic of Croatia, the former Yugoslav Republic of Macedonia, the Republic of Iceland, the Republic of Montenegro, the Kingdom of Norway, Romania, the Republic of Serbia and the United Nations Interim Administration Mission in Kosovo on the establishment of a European Common Aviation Area, signed in Luxembourg on 9 June 2006, OJ L 285, 16 October 2006, 3–46, Part G of Annex I.

10 Reglugerð 466/2024.

11 See: Icelandic Transport Authority, 'Decisions, Judgements and Rulings' <https://island.is/en/o/transport-authority/rights-of-air-passengers> accessed 16 November 2025.

In essence, the ECAA is the "gold standard" for extending EU passenger rights. It is not merely a trade agreement but a structure that creates a unified legal space for aviation. For passengers, it means that a flight from Berlin to Belgrade is governed by the same consumer protections as a flight from Berlin to Barcelona. It guarantees that the pioneering rights established by EU Regulation 261 are not just a Western European standard but a continental one.

Bibliography

Primary Sources

- Case C-466/98 *Commission v United Kingdom* [2002] ECR I-9427.
- Case C-467/98 *Commission v Denmark* [2002] ECR I-9519.
- Case C-468/98 *Commission v Sweden* [2002] ECR I-9575.
- Case C-469/98 *Commission v Finland* [2002] ECR I-9627.
- Case C-471/98 *Commission v Belgium* [2002] ECR I-9681.
- Case C-472/98 *Commission v Luxembourg* [2002] ECR I-9741.
- Case C-475/98 *Commission v Austria* [2002] ECR I-9797.
- Case C-476/98 *Commission v Germany* [2002] ECR I-9855.
- Decision 2006/682/EC of the Council and of the Representatives of the Member States of the European Union meeting within the Council of 9 June 2006 on the signature and provisional application of the Multilateral Agreement between the European Community and its Member States, the Republic of Albania, Bosnia and Herzegovina, the Republic of Bulgaria, the Republic of Croatia, the former Yugoslav Republic of Macedonia, the Republic of Iceland, the Republic of Montenegro, the Kingdom of Norway, Romania, the Republic of Serbia and the United Nations Interim Administration Mission in Kosovo on the Establishment of a European Common Aviation Area (ECAA).
- Multilateral Agreement between the European Community and its Member States, the Republic of Albania, Bosnia and Herzegovina, the Republic of Bulgaria, the Republic of Croatia, the former Yugoslav Republic of Macedonia, the Republic of Iceland, the Republic of Montenegro, the Kingdom of Norway, Romania, the Republic of Serbia and the United Nations Interim Administration Mission in Kosovo on the establishment of a European Common Aviation Area, OJ L 285, 16 October 2006, 1–46.
- Reglugerð 466/2024 um réttindi flugfarþega <https://island.is/reglugerdir/nr/0466-2024> accessed 16 November 2025.

Secondary Sources

- Bombay, P. and Gergely, M. 'The 2006 ECAA Agreement: Centrepiece of the European Community's Aviation Policy Towards its Neighbours' (2008) 33 Air and Space Law 214.
- Correia, V. and Rouissi, N., 'Global, Regional and National Air Passenger Rights – Does the Patchwork Work?' (2015) 40 Air and Space Law 123.

- European Commission, 'European Common Aviation Area: Aviation Relations' <https://transport.ec.europa.eu/transport-modes/air/international-aviation/status-aviation-relations-country/ecaa_en> accessed 16 November 2025.
- Icelandic Transport Authority, 'Decisions, Judgements and Rulings' <https://island.is/en/o/transport-authority/rights-of-air-passengers> accessed 16 November 2025.

I.5

Euro-Mediterranean Aviation Agreements (EMAA)

The ECAA model has also served as a blueprint for other parallel agreements, such as the Euro-Mediterranean Aviation Agreements (EMAA). EMAA is a series of bilateral aviation agreements between the European Union and countries like Morocco,[1] Jordan,[2] Tunisia,[3] and Israel.[4] These agreements open the market for direct flights for all EU and partner country airlines between the EU and the respective country. They provide a regulatory framework and set standards for aviation safety, security, passenger rights, air traffic management, economic regulation, competition issues, and social aspects. Parties agree to act in accordance with EU legislation on matters relating to passenger rights.

A significant legal complexity arises concerning the territorial scope of the EMAA with Morocco. According to a written response from the

1 Decision 2006/959/EC authorised the signing and provisional application of the agreement while Decision (EU) 2018/146 officially concludes the agreement. Decision 2006/959/EC of the Council and of the representatives of the Governments of the Member States, meeting within the Council of 4 December 2006 on the signature and provisional application of the Euro-Mediterranean Aviation Agreement between the European Community and its Member States, of the one part, and the Kingdom of Morocco, of the other part (Text with EEA relevance), OJ L 386, 29 December 2006, 55–56; Council Decision (EU) 2018/146 of 22 January 2018 on the conclusion, on behalf of the Union, of the Euro-Mediterranean Aviation Agreement between the European Community and its Member States, of the one part, and the Kingdom of Morocco, of the other part, OJ L 26, 31 January 2018, 4–5.

2 Signed on 15 December 2010. Euro-Mediterranean Aviation Agreement between the European Union and its Member States, of the one part, and the Hashemite Kingdom of Jordan, of the other part. <https://assets.publishing.service.gov.uk/media/5a7cc37d40f0b65b3de0b060/8054.pdf> accessed 16 November 2025.

3 Council Decision (EU) 2021/1404 of 28 June 2021 on the signing, on behalf of the Union, of the Euro-Mediterranean Aviation Agreement between the European Union and its Member States, of the one part, and the Republic of Tunisia, of the other part, ST/8455/2021/INIT, OJ L 303, 27 August 2021, 1–2.

4 Signed on 10 June 2013. Euro-Mediterranean Aviation Agreement between the European Union and its Member States, of the one part, and the Government of the State of Israel, of the other part <https://assets.publishing.service.gov.uk/media/5b97d4f840f0b6787a1eb35e/EU_11.2018_Euro_Med_Avia_Israel.pdf> accessed 16 November 2025.

DOI: 10.4324/9781003746164-7

European Commission, the Euro-Mediterranean aviation agreement between the EU and Morocco does not apply to the territory of Western Sahara. This clarification is based on a ruling from the Court of Justice of the European Union (CJEU), which determined that the territory is not part of Morocco's recognized sovereignty under international law.[5] Consequently, a flight to or from a destination in Western Sahara, such as Dakhla, would fall outside the protective scope of the EMAA and its implementation of Regulation 261.[6]

While it has been announced in 2024 that Morocco planned to align passenger rights with European standards, as part of Law No. 40.13 on the Civil Aviation Code, such regulation has not yet been enacted.

The EMAA extend EU-level passenger protection standards to flights between the EU and these Mediterranean countries, meaning that passengers on flights covered by these agreements benefit from similar protections to those provided under EU Regulation 261, including compensation for delays, cancellations, and denied boarding.[7] This dramatically expands the geographical reach of EU 261.[8]

For a passenger flying between the EU and an EMAA partner country, the practical outcome is that the robust protections of EU 261 are guaranteed for flights in both directions, not just those departing the EU. However, the enforcement of the agreement is left to the partner country's national authorities.

Bibliography

- Council Decision 2006/959/EC authorised the signing and provisional application of the agreement while Decision (EU) 2018/146 officially concludes the agreement. Decision 2006/959/EC of the Council and of the representatives of the Governments of the Member States, meeting within the Council of 4 December 2006 on the signature and provisional application of the Euro-Mediterranean Aviation Agreement between the European Community and its Member States, of the one part, and the Kingdom of Morocco, of the other part (Text with EEA relevance), OJ L 386, 29 December 2006, 55–56.

5 Case C-104/16 P *Council v Front populaire pour la libération de la saguia-el-hamra et du rio de oro (Front Polisario)*, ECLI:EU:C:2016:973; Joined Cases C-779/21 P and C-799/21 P *European Commission and Council of the European Union v Front populaire pour la libération de la Saguia el-Hamra et du Rio de oro (Front Polisario)*, ECLI:EU:C:2024:835.

6 Sahrawi Arab Democratic Republic, 'EUC Clarifies: Euro-Mediterranean Aviation Agreement with Morocco Does not Apply to Western Sahara' (20 January 2025) <https://www.sahrawi-emb-au.com/euc-clarifies-euro-mediterranean-aviation-agreement-with-morocco-does-not-apply-to-western-sahara/> accessed 16 November 2025.

7 Article 18 of the EU-Jordan Common Aviation Area Agreement.

8 Also called the horizontal clause.

- Council Decision (EU) 2018/146 of 22 January 2018 on the conclusion, on behalf of the Union, of the Euro-Mediterranean Aviation Agreement between the European Community and its Member States, of the one part, and the Kingdom of Morocco, of the other part, OJ L 26, 31 January 2018, 4–5.
- Council Decision (EU) 2021/1404 of 28 June 2021 on the signing, on behalf of the Union, of the Euro-Mediterranean Aviation Agreement between the European Union and its Member States, of the one part, and the Republic of Tunisia, of the other part, ST/8455/2021/INIT, OJ L 303, 27 August 2021, 1–2.
- Euro-Mediterranean Aviation Agreement between the European Union and its Member States, of the one part, and the Hashemite Kingdom of Jordan, of the other part <https://assets.publishing.service.gov.uk/media/5a7cc37d40f0b65b3de0b060/8054.pdf> accessed 16 November 2025.
- Euro-Mediterranean Aviation Agreement between the European Union and its Member States, of the one part, and the Government of the State of Israel, of the other part <https://assets.publishing.service.gov.uk/media/5b97d4f840f0b6787a1eb35e/EU_11.2018_Euro_Med_Avia_Israel.pdf> accessed 16 November 2025.
- Case C-104/16 P *Council v Front populaire pour la libération de la saguia-el-hamra et du rio de oro (Front Polisario)*, ECLI:EU:C:2016:973.
- Joined Cases C-779/21 P and C-799/21 P *European Commission and Council of the European Union v Front populaire pour la libération de la Saguia el-Hamra et du Rio de oro (Front Polisario)*, ECLI:EU:C:2024:835.
- Sahrawi Arab Democratic Republic, 'EUC Clarifies: Euro-Mediterranean Aviation Agreement with Morocco Does Not Apply to Western Sahara' (20 January 2025) <https://www.sahrawi-emb-au.com/euc-clarifies-euro-mediterranean-aviation-agreement-with-morocco-does-not-apply-to-western-sahara/> accessed 16 November 2025.

I.6

The Economic and Monetary Community of Central Africa/Communauté economique et monétaire de l'Afrique Central (CEMAC) Regulation UEAC N° 06/07-UEAC- 082-CM-15 of 2007

The Economic and Monetary Community of Central Africa, generally referred to by its French acronym CEMAC, is composed by Cameroon, Central African Republic, Chad, the Republic of Congo, Equatorial Guinea, and Gabon. It has enacted Regulation UEAC n° 06/07-UEAC-082-CM-15 in 2007 which lays down the rules on air carrier liability in case of breach of rules of boarding procedures of passengers in the airports of Member States.[1]

Article 2 sets out the scope of the Regulation, which applies in three situations: when an airline refuses to board passengers with valid bookings, when there is an unreasonable delay, and when a flight is cancelled. The Regulation also defines compensation measures in case of damages suffered by a passenger at any Member State's airport, regardless of the passenger's nationality or destination.[2] Airlines are obligated to provide all affected passengers with a notice explaining the rules for financial compensation.[3]

The Regulation stipulates that airlines are required to establish policy regarding overbooking, which must be notified to the competent authority.[4] The policy includes as the first step the request of volunteers.[5] In case of overbooking, passengers are entitled to choose without penalty between reimbursement of the ticket price for the part of the journey

1 Règlement N° 06/07-UEAC-082-CM-15, Fixant le Régime de responsabilité du transporteur aérien enc as de violation des Règles d'embarquement des Passegers dans les Aéroports des Etats members de la CEMAC, N'Djamena, 19 Mars 2007 <https://www.droit-afrique.com/upload/doc/cemac/CEMAC-Reglement-2007-06-responsabilite-transporteur-aerien.pdf>.
The Montreal Convention is found in Regulation n° 10/00-CEMAC-066-CM-04 of 21 July 2000.
2 Article 2.
3 Article 4.
4 Article 3(1).
5 Article 3(3).

DOI: 10.4324/9781003746164-8

not completed, effected at the earliest opportunity, or re-routing to the final destination at the earliest opportunity or later date.[6] Additionally, passengers are entitled to monetary compensation based on the distance of the journey and the category of travel class used. For journeys up to 2,500 km, the reimbursement rate is 100,000 CFA Francs for economy class travel and 200,000 CFA Francs for premium class for the same distance.[7] For longer journeys exceeding 2,500 km, the standard reimbursement for economy class is set at 400,000 CFA Francs. When premium class is used for these long-haul trips, the compensation increases significantly to 800,000 CFA Francs.[8]

Journey	**Category**	**Reimbursement**
Up to 2,500 km	Economy class.	100,000 CFA Francs.
Up to 2,500 km	Premium class.	200,000 CFA Francs.
Over 2,500 km	Economy class.	400,000 CFA Francs.
Over 2,500 km	Premium class.	800,000 CFA Francs.

The compensation amount may be reduced by 50% if the re-routing offered to the final destination results in an arrival time that does not exceed the scheduled arrival time of the original flight by more than three hours for flights up to 2,500 km and five hours for flights over 2,500 km.[9] Compensation amounts shall not exceed the price of the ticket corresponding to the final destination.[10] If the passenger accepts to be downgraded instead, then he is entitled to 50% of the fare.[11] A passenger is not entitled to assistance or compensation if they are travelling for free.[12]

Flight Distance	**Travel Class**	**Full Compensation Amount**	**Reduced Compensation (50%)**
Up to 2,500 km	Economy class.	100,000 CFA Francs.	New arrival time is **less than 3 hours** after the original scheduled arrival time.
Up to 2,500 km	Premium class.	200,000 CFA Francs.	New arrival time is **less than 3 hours** after the original scheduled arrival time.

6 Article 5(1)(i)–(iii).
7 Article 5(2)(i).
8 Article 5(2)(ii).
9 Article 5(3).
10 Article 5(3).
11 Article 5(4).
12 Article 5(4).

Flight Distance	Travel Class	Full Compensation Amount	Reduced Compensation (50%)
Over 2,500 km	Economy class.	400,000 CFA Francs.	New arrival time is **less than 5 hours** after the original scheduled arrival time.
Over 2,500 km	Premium class.	800,000 CFA Francs.	New arrival time is **less than 5 hours** after the original scheduled arrival time.

When an air carrier or tour operator cancels or reasonably expects to cancel a flight, they shall endeavour to contact the affected passengers to agree on terms to waive the confirmed reservation. At a minimum, passengers shall be offered the choice between reimbursement, re-routing at earliest opportunity, or re-routing at passenger's convenience.[13] Passengers who do not reach an agreement with the carrier and present themselves for check-in are entitled to the compensation and assistance offered for involuntary denied boarding.[14] Such obligations do not apply if the cancellation is due to an event of force majeure for which neither it nor its subcontractors shall be held liable. The Regulation does not give any examples of what constitutes an event of force majeure.

Should a flight be delayed at departure by at least three hours for flights up to 2,500 km, or at least five hours for flights exceeding 2,500 km, the passenger is entitled to assistance at the departure airport, including: the cost of a telephone communication and/or a message via telex/fax or electronic mail to the place of destination; sufficient meals and refreshments, relative to the waiting period; and hotel accommodation in the event that a stay of one or more nights becomes necessary.[15] This assistance must be provided no later than three hours (for short-haul) or five hours (for long-haul) following the initial scheduled departure time.

Condition	Assistance Trigger	Entitlements
Flight Delayed at Departure	• **≥3 hours** for flights up to 2,500 km. • **≥5 hours** for flights over 2,500 km.	• Cost of **communications** (phone, email, etc.). • Sufficient **meals and refreshments**. • **Hotel accommodation** if an overnight stay is necessary.

Passengers with disability, unaccompanied minors, or passengers travelling for humanitarian reasons must be given priority.[16]

13 Article 7(1)(i)–(iii).
14 Article 7(2).
15 Article 8.
16 Article 3(4), 8.

To date, the provisions of the CEMAC Regulation have not been interpreted by the CEMAC Court.[17] The CEMAC Regulation, closely modelled on UEMOA Regulation 2003 and EU Regulation 261, is a robust and passenger-friendly instrument offering fixed, distance-based compensation that is not only transparent and predictable but also uniquely differentiated by travel class- a feature absent from its European counterpart. Indeed, the CEMAC framework adds a further layer of differentiation by travel class (economy vs. premium), offering significantly higher sums for premium passengers (e.g., 800,000 CFA for long-haul premium versus 400,000 CFA for economy). However, the CEMAC thresholds for assistance (three hours for short-haul, five hours for long-haul) are simpler but less protective than the EU's graduated system, which triggers assistance at two hours (short-haul) and progressively increases obligations. Moreover, the CEMAC Regulation lacks the EU's extensive case law clarifying core concepts such as "extraordinary circumstances," "cancellation," and "connecting flights," leaving key terms – including force majeure and "unreasonable delay" – uninterpreted by the CEMAC Court. Its effectiveness lags behind the EU's due to under-enforcement and the absence of authoritative interpretation – a gap that no compensation table alone can fill.

Bibliography

- Règlement N° 06/07-UEAC-082-CM-15, Fixant le Régime de responsabilité du transporteur aérien enc as de violation des Règles d'embarquement des Passegers dans les Aéroports des Etats members de la CEMAC, N'Djamena, 19 Mars 2007.
- Regulation n° 10/00-CEMAC-066-CM-04 of 21 July 2000.
- Grigorieff, C. I., 'The Regime for International Air Carrier Liability: To What Extent Has the Envisaged Uniformity of the 1999 Montreal Convention Been Achieved?' (PhD Thesis, Leiden University, 2021).

17 CI Grigorieff, 'The Regime for International Air Carrier Liability: To What Extent Has the Envisaged Uniformity of the 1999 Montreal Convention Been Achieved?' (PhD Thesis, Leiden University, 2021) 154.

I.7

Union Economique et Monétaire Ouest Africaine (UEMOA)/West African Economic and Monetary Union (WAEMU) Regulation N° 03/2003/CM/UEMOA of 2003

The West African Economic and Monetary Union is comprised of Benin, Burkina Faso, Ivory Coast, Guinea-Bissau, Mali, Nigeria, Senegal,[1] and Togo and adopted in 2003 Regulation n° 03/2003/CM/UEMOA which lays down rules in case of denial of boarding, cancellation, and long delays as well as compensation.[2]

The Regulation applies to passengers with a valid ticket departing from an airport within the territory of the State Parties, irrespective of the nationality of the airline or the passengers.[3]

The airline must have procedures in place in case of denied boarding due to overbooking which must be accessible to the public and registered with the Commission.[4] The policy must include rules regarding the asking of volunteers.[5] In the event of a denial of boarding, the passenger has the right to choose between a reimbursement of the ticket or a re-routing at the earliest convenience or later date.[6] In addition, they are entitled to 100,000 CFA Francs for passengers on economy flights and 200,000 CFA Francs for premium class for flights of less than 2,500 km or more.[7] For longer journeys exceeding 2,500 km, the standard reimbursement for economy class is set at 400,000 CFA Francs. When premium class is

1 Interestingly, according to the Air Senegal Passenger Rights document, there must be another Regulation applicable which is not aligned with the WAEMU Regulation. However, such law could not be located. See: Air Senegal SA, 'Passenger Rights' (Form No SZN-ORG-FRM-XX Revision: 00) <https://flyairsenegal.com/wp-content/uploads/2020/01/Passenger-Rights_Air-Senegal.pdf> accessed 16 November 2025.

2 Règlement No. 03/2003/CM/UEMOA du 20 mars 2003 établissant les règles relatives aux compensations pour refus d'embarquement des passagers et pour annulation ou retard important d'un vol.

3 Article 2.

4 Article 3(1)–(2).

5 Article 3(3).

6 Article 4(1).

7 Article 4(2) can also include damages on top of the compensation for denial of boarding see: *Vincent Siliki-Bi Komba and others v Air Cote d'Ivoire*, RGN4270/2018, 22/1/2019.

DOI: 10.4324/9781003746164-9

used for these long-haul trips, the compensation increases significantly to 800,000 CFA Francs.[8]

Journey	Category	Reimbursement
Up to 2,500 km	Economy class.	100,000 CFA Francs.
Up to 2,500 km	Premium class.	200,000 CFA Francs.
Over 2,500 km	Economy class.	400,000 CFA Francs.
Over 2,500 km	Premium class.	800,000 CFA Francs.

The compensation amount may be reduced by 50% if the re-routing offered to the final destination results in an arrival time that does not exceed the scheduled arrival time of the original flight by more than three hours for flights up to 2,500 km and five hours for flights over 2,500 km.[9] Compensation amounts shall not exceed the price of the ticket corresponding to the final destination.[10] If the passenger accepts to be downgraded instead, then he is entitled to 50% of the fare.[11] A passenger is not entitled to assistance or compensation if they are travelling for free.[12] If the passenger is rebooked on a flight departing from another airport, the transport fees must be covered by the airline.[13]

Flight Distance	Travel Class	Full Compensation Amount	Reduced Compensation (50%)
Up to 2,500 km	Economy class.	100,000 CFA Francs.	New arrival time is **less than 3 hours** after the original scheduled arrival time.
Up to 2,500 km	Premium class.	200,000 CFA Francs.	New arrival time is **less than 3 hours** after the original scheduled arrival time.
Over 2,500 km	Economy class.	400,000 CFA Francs.	New arrival time is **less than 5 hours** after the original scheduled arrival time.
Over 2,500 km	Premium class.	800,000 CFA Francs.	New arrival time is **less than 5 hours** after the original scheduled arrival time.

In the event of a flight cancellation, airlines must do their best to contact the affected passengers to agree on terms to waive the confirmed reservation. At a minimum, passengers shall be offered the choice between reimbursement,

8 Article 4(2).
9 Article 4(3).
10 Article 4(4).
11 Article 4(5).
12 Article 4(6).
13 Article 8(2).

re-routing at earliest opportunity, or re-routing at passenger's convenience.[14] Passengers who do not reach an agreement with the carrier and present themselves for check-in are entitled to the compensation and assistance offered for involuntary denied boarding.[15] Such obligations do not apply if the cancellation is due to an event of force majeure for which neither it nor its subcontractors shall be held liable.[16] The Regulation does not give any examples of what constitutes an event of force majeure.

In case of flight delay at departure by at least three hours for flights up to 2,500 km or at least five hours for flights exceeding 2,500 km, the passenger is entitled to assistance at the departure airport, including: the cost of a telephone communication and/or a message via telex/fax or electronic mail to the place of destination; sufficient meals and refreshments, relative to the waiting period; and hotel accommodation in the event that a stay of one or more nights becomes necessary.[17] This assistance must be provided no later than three hours (for short-haul) or five hours (for long-haul) following the initial scheduled departure time, except for disabled passengers or unaccompanied minors. No compensation is available for those passengers. The UEMOA Regulation of 2003 establishes fixed, distance-based compensation that not only offers clarity and predictability but also introduces a premium-class multiplier that doubles the payout- a feature missing in Regulation 261. The Regulation's compensation table (e.g., 800,000 CFA for long-haul premium passengers) provides immediate, quantifiable relief without the complexity of fare calculations. Its assistance regime, triggered at three hours (short-haul) or five hours (long-haul), is straightforward and ensures meals, communication, and accommodation where needed. However, critical weaknesses remain: it offers no definition or examples of force majeure, provides no compensation for delays (only assistance), omits detailed protections for baggage or disabled passengers beyond a passing mention, and has not benefited from interpretative jurisprudence from a regional court, leaving terms like "unreasonable delay" and "volunteer procedures" legally untested.

Condition	Assistance Trigger	Entitlements
Flight Delayed at Departure	• **≥3 hours** for flights up to 2,500 km. • **≥5 hours** for flights over 2,500 km.	• Cost of **communications** (phone, email, etc.). • Sufficient **meals and refreshments**. • **Hotel accommodation** if an overnight stay is necessary.

14 Article 6(1)(a)–(c).
15 Article 6(2).
16 Article 6.
17 Articles 7 and 8.

Bibliography

- Air Senegal SA, 'Passenger Rights' (Form No SZN-ORG-FRM-XX Revision: 00) <https://flyairsenegal.com/wp-content/uploads/2020/01/Passenger-Rights_Air-Senegal.pdf> accessed 16 November 2025.
- Règlement No. 03/2003/CM/UEMOA du 20 mars 2003 établissant les règles relatives aux compensations pour refus d'embarquement des passagers et pour annulation ou retard important d'un vol.

I.8

The Yamoussoukro Decision of 1999

Annex 6

The Yamoussoukro Decision (YD) is a landmark agreement adopted in 1999 aimed at liberalizing air transport across Africa.[1] Annex 6 of this Decision includes Regulations on the Protection of Air Transport Consumers, ensuring fair treatment, compensation for the consumer when their rights are breached by air transport services providers, and establishment of a mechanism for the consumer to seek redress.[2] As Adediran noted, "the de facto non-binding status of the YD poses a challenge to its implementation and that of its regulatory texts especially in relation to consumer protection which is governed by individual domestic laws of Member States."[3] The YD is subordinate to national laws of States Parties; in any conflict, national law takes precedence.[4] Moreover, the YD does not contain any harmonization obligation but rather an alignment of national laws with the Yamoussoukro Decision.

The Realigned Regulations start with a strict prohibition of unfair and deceptive practices, which is a very broad term not only including misleading advertising or failure to disclose ticket conditions but also persistent boarding denials, abuse of free-seating policies,[5] discriminatory

1 Realigned Regulations on the protection of consumers of air transport services, Annex 6 to the Yamoussoukro Decision, adopted by the African Union Specialized Technical Committee on Transport, Intercontinental and Interregional Infrastructures, Energy and Tourism in Lomé, on 13th to 17th of March 2017 which entered into force in January 2018 (Article 25) <https://au.int/sites/default/files/documents/32186-doc-edtd_realigd_consumer.pdf>.

See: William Kiema, *The Air Transport Industry in Africa: A Legal Analysis of the Single African Air Transport Market* (Routledge 2025); Adejoke O Adediran, 'Regulatory Convergence of Consumer Protection in the Single African Air Transport Market: How Far, How Well?' (2022) 47 Air & Space Law 427.

2 Article 3 of the Realigned Regulations.

3 Adejoke O. Adediran, 'Regulatory Convergence of Consumer Protection in the Single African Air Transport Market: How Far, How Well?' (2022) 47 Air and Space Law 427, 430.

4 Adejoke O. Adediran, 'Regulatory Convergence of Consumer Protection in the Single African Air Transport Market: How Far, How Well?' (2022) 47 Air and Space Law 427, 430.

5 Which is based on a first come first served basis allowing passengers to sit anywhere within the class booked.

DOI: 10.4324/9781003746164-10

compensation practices, and chronically delayed flights – a route with over 30 flights in a quarter that are late more than 15 minutes or cancelled more than 50% of the time.[6]

The Regulations contain a rather unique provision prohibiting any discrimination on grounds of nationality, race, sex, age, colour, creed, physical ability, and physical stature.[7] Another odd feature which is found in Rwanda national law is an express requirement for airlines to maintain adequate third-party insurance cover and display proof of insurance visibly.[8] The Regulations also contain a provision on data protection, which obliges airlines and related agents to obtain a reliable means of communication for emergencies and use them only to inform passengers about cancellations, delays, or other essential updates.[9] Airlines must use the passenger's preferred mode of contact and must provide an accessible local office number if the passenger cannot provide contact details.[10] In the event of a notice made less than 12 hours of the departure, the carrier must communicate such notice by phone or messages unless the passenger confirmed they can retrieve their emails on a mobile device.[11]

At the time of ticket purchase or check-in, airlines and ground handling agents must inform passengers in one of the official languages of the African Union about key obligations and rights.[12] This includes the need to supply contact details for emergencies, planned cancellations or delays, the airline's obligations for compensation and assistance in cases of denied boarding or cancellation, and the right to request relevant documents. This includes pre-contractual information on passport, visa, and health formalities.[13] The YD also contains obligations for airport operators including the display of clear notices outlining passengers' rights throughout the airport premises, the provision of adequate restroom facilities, sufficient seating areas, and maintaining a clean and safe environment within the airport.[14]

The Decision allows airlines to overbook flights as long as intelligent market analysis tools are used to understand the loading pattern to limit

6 Article 4(a)–(f).
7 Article 5.
8 Article 6(1).
9 Article 7(2).
10 Article 7(3)–(4).
11 Article 7(4).
12 Article 8(1).
13 Article 14(a).
14 Article 15.

negative effects on passengers.[15] If overbooking is anticipated more than six hours before the flight, the airline must first contact passengers and call for volunteers to surrender their reservations in exchange for benefits, paying attention to passengers travelling from far away.[16] In the event, airlines have to deny boarding at check-in or during boarding, they must first discreetly request for volunteers.[17] When insufficient volunteers come forward at the airport, the airline may deny boarding involuntarily to the smallest practicable number of passengers, who must then be compensated.[18]

Article 11 outlines airline obligations for delayed flights. For delays between two and four hours, airlines must provide regular updates (every 45 minutes), refreshments, two communication credits, and announce the new arrival time.[19] For delays of four hours or more, additional obligations include providing a meal, hotel accommodation, and transport between the airport and hotel.[20] If the delay is at least six hours, passengers have the right to a full ticket reimbursement, re-routing to their final destination at the earliest opportunity, or re-routing at a later date.[21] When an airline offers an alternative flight which departs from another airport, they shall bear the cost of the transfer.[22] The needs of persons with reduced mobility and unaccompanied minors must be prioritized.[23]

Delay Duration	**Airline Obligations and Passenger Rights**
2 to 4 Hours	• Inform passengers every 45 minutes of the new departure time and specific reasons for the delay. • Where the flight duration is less than 3 hours, inform passengers of their right to reschedule without penalty. • Provide refreshments (water, soft drinks, snacks). • Provide two international telephone calls, SMS, or emails. • Announce the new estimated time of arrival at the destination airport.

(Continued)

15 Article 10(1).
16 Article 10(2).
17 Article 10(3).
18 Article 10(4).
19 Article 11(a)(i)–(iv).
20 Article 11(b).
21 Article 11(c)(i)–(iii).
22 Article 11(d)(ii).
23 Article 11(d)(iii).

(Continued)

Delay Duration	Airline Obligations and Passenger Rights
4 Hours or More	• Inform passengers every 45 minutes of the new departure time and specific reasons for the delay. • Where the flight duration is less than 2 hours, inform passengers of their right to reschedule without penalty. • Provide refreshments and a meal. • Provide hotel accommodation and transport between the airport and the hotel. • Provide two international telephone calls, SMS, or emails. • Announce the new estimated time of arrival at the destination airport.
6 Hours or More (from originally announced time)	Passengers have the right to choose one of the following: • **Immediate Reimbursement**[24]**:** Full refund of the ticket price for the unused parts of the journey, plus a return flight to the first point of departure if needed. • **Re-routing**[25]**:** Transport to the final destination at the earliest opportunity. • **Re-routing at a Later Date:** Transport to the final destination at a later date of the passenger's convenience, subject to seat availability.

The regulatory framework establishes a comprehensive and structured approach to managing flight cancellations, delineating clear obligations for air carriers and enforceable rights for passengers. The provisions are primarily contained within Article 12 and are also intrinsically linked to other specific articles on re-routing and compensation. In case of flight cancellation, airlines must inform passengers of the reasons and their rights. The specific obligations depend on whether the cancellation decision is made less than or more than 24 hours before departure. For cancellations made less than 24 hours before the scheduled departure, or affecting passengers already at the airport or in transit, in addition to the prompt information, the passengers have the option to cancel their booking entirely, the right to be re-routed or offered an alternative means of transport, and the right to seek compensation.[26] Furthermore, the airline must provide immediate amenities, including refreshments such as water, soft drinks, and snacks, and grant the right to two international

24 Article 16.
25 Article 17.
26 Article 12(1)(a)(i)–(iv).

telephone calls, SMS, or emails.[27] In contrast, for cancellations made at least 24 hours before departure, the airline's primary duty shifts to proactive and direct communication. They must immediately contact affected passengers, advise them of their core rights (i.e. reimbursement, re-routing, and compensation), and crucially, recommend that they do not travel to the airport if they have not already begun their journey.[28] For all cancellations, regardless of timing, the airline is obligated to provide a clear explanation of the possible alternative transport options available, which may involve travel on a different date, with a different airline, or via another mode of transport, provided it is reasonable and convenient for the passenger.[29]

Passengers have a right to compensation unless they were informed well in advance and offered suitable re-routing, or if the airline can prove the cancellation was due to extraordinary circumstances. If the airline informs the passenger of the cancellation between two weeks and seven days before the scheduled departure and offers re-routing that results in a departure no more than two hours earlier and an arrival less than four hours later than the original time, compensation is not owed.[30] Similarly, if notice is given less than seven days before departure but the offered re-routing allows for a departure no more than one hour earlier and an arrival less than two hours later, compensation is also exempt. The second, and most significant, exemption is for extraordinary circumstances. Article 12.4 explicitly states that an airline is not obliged to pay compensation if it can prove that the cancellation was caused by extraordinary circumstances which could not have been avoided even if all reasonable measures had been taken. However, the term is not further defined, and no examples are given. Furthermore, the compensation amount can be reduced by 50% if the airline offers re-routing that delivers the passenger to their final destination with a delay that does not exceed two hours for short flights, three hours for medium-haul flights, or four hours for long-haul flights.[31]

This right to compensation, found in Article 18, is distinct from the right to reimbursement for the ticket cost and is designed to provide a standardized monetary remedy for the inconvenience and impact of disruptions. The cornerstone of the compensation scheme is Article 18.1, which stipulates fixed monetary amounts based on the total duration of the affected flight. For all flights with an estimated duration of three

27 Article 12(1)(a)(v) and (vi).
28 Article 12(1)(b)(i)–(iii).
29 Article 12(2).
30 Article 12(3)(a) and (b).
31 Article 18(3)(a) and (b).

hours or less, the compensation is set at $250.[32] For flights lasting between three and six hours, the compensation amount is $400.[33] For all flights exceeding six hours in duration, the compensation is fixed at $600.[34] It is crucial to note that the calculation of the flight's duration, as defined in Article 18.2, is not based on a single flight segment but on the passenger's entire journey to their final destination, including all scheduled stopovers or transit points. This ensures that the compensation reflects the full scale of the disruption to the passenger's travel plans.

Circumstance	**Airline Obligations and Passenger Rights**	**Compensation Eligibility**
Cancellation <24 Hours Before Departure	• Inform passengers of specific reasons and their rights. • Provide refreshments and two international telephone calls, SMS, or emails. • **Passenger Rights:** 1. **Reimbursement:** full refund within 30 days. 2. **Re-routing:** to final destination at earliest opportunity or a later date. 3. **Right to Compensation.**	**Yes**, unless • Extraordinary Circumstances.
Cancellation ≥24 Hours Before Departure	• Immediately contact affected passengers and advise them not to travel to the airport. • **Passenger Rights:** 1. **Reimbursement:** full refund within 30 days. 2. **Re-routing:** to final destination. 3. **Right to Compensation.**	**Yes,** unless • Extraordinary Circumstances. • Sufficient notice was given + re-routing.
Compensation Amounts	• **Flights ≤3 hours:** $250. • **Flights 3–6 hours:** $400. • **Flights >6 hours:** $600. *Note: Based on flight duration to final destination. Can be reduced by 50% if re-routing minimizes delay.*	

If an airline places a passenger in a class lower than purchased, they must reimburse the passenger within seven days: 25% of the ticket price

32 Article 18(1)(a).
33 Article 18(1)(b).
34 Article 18(1)(c).

for flights of three hours or less, and 50% for flights of more than three hours.[35] No supplementary payment is due if the passenger is placed in a higher class.[36]

Any service provider that violates these regulations is liable to penalties imposed by the relevant authority. The penalties must be dissuasive, proportionate to the gravity of the case and the economic capacity of the provider, and take the defaulter's compliance record into account. The Executing Agency is tasked with drafting a schedule of penalties for adoption by the African Union.[37]

Bibliography

- Yamoussoukro Decision, adopted by the African Union Specialized Technical Committee on Transport, Intercontinental and Interregional Infrastructures, Energy and Tourism in Lomé, on 13th to 17th of March 2017 which entered into force in January 2018 (Article 25) <https://au.int/sites/default/files/documents/32186-doc-edtd_realigd_consumer.pdf>.
- Adediran, A. O., 'Regulatory Convergence of Consumer Protection in the Single African Air Transport Market: How Far, How Well?' (2022) 47 Air and Space Law 427.
- Kiema, W., *The Air Transport Industry in Africa: A Legal Analysis of the Single African Air Transport Market* (Routledge 2025).

35 Article 13(1)(a) and (b).
36 Article 13(2).
37 Article 22.

PART II

NATIONAL INITIATIVES

The absence of an international convention specifically addressing passenger rights in cases of disruption has prompted a growing number of states to enact their own national legislation. This has resulted in a diverse global landscape where some jurisdictions have closely emulated the European Union's pioneering Regulation 261, while others have developed unique, bespoke regimes.

A striking feature of these national initiatives is the distinct academic and policy discourse that surrounds them. Unlike the significant scholarly criticism directed at Regulation 261 and its associated case-law – often framed as a threat to the uniform application of the Warsaw and Montreal Conventions[1] – many of the national laws discussed in the following have been largely spared such reproach. In fact, several have been praised for proactively filling a critical consumer protection gap. This acceptance is particularly notable given that these domestic laws, much like their European counterpart, inherently challenge the pre-emptive scope of Article 29 of the Montreal Convention and Article 24 of its predecessor. Their legitimacy appears to derive not from international treaty law, but from a perceived imperative to address passenger needs that the global conventions deliberately left unmet.

The national initiatives discussed in this part represent diverse approaches to passenger protection, ranging from comprehensive regulations mirroring EU standards to more limited frameworks addressing specific national challenges to upgraded and very protective standards. They demonstrate that the movement toward enhanced passenger rights is truly global, transcending regional boundaries and

1 Paul Stephen Dempsey and Svante O Johansson, 'Montreal v. Brussels: The Conflict of Laws on the Issue of Delay in International Air Carriage' (2010) 35 Air and Space Law 207.

DOI: 10.4324/9781003746164-11

reflecting a worldwide consensus that passengers deserve better protection than what the international conventions currently provide.

The following analysis explores how these individual states have implemented their own solutions, demonstrating the global acceptance of passenger protection as very divergent although a non-negotiable modern standard.

II.1

Albania

The treatment of passengers in case of flight disruptions is found in Albania's Bylaw No. 1 (also referred to as Regulation no. 1) dated 26 February 2013, "compensation, passenger assistance in cases of denied boarding and cancelation or delay during the flight," which transposes Regulation 261, as required by Article 138/1 of the Albanian Air Code.[1] Aside from the preamble of Regulation No 261, which is not included in the Albanian Bylaw, both acts are otherwise identical in content.

The Bylaw applies to any passengers departing from an airport located in the Albanian territory or the territory of a signatory state to the ECAA Agreement[2] or flights departing from a third country to an airport situated in Albania or the territory within the ECAA Area if the operating air carrier of the flight concerned is an air carrier of a signatory state to ECAA Agreement.[3] In order to invoke the provisions of the Bylaw, passengers are required to hold a confirmed reservation and present themselves for check-in in accordance with the procedures and at the time specified in advance and in writing by the air carrier, tour operator, or authorized travel agent. If no specific check-in time is provided, passengers must check in no later than 45 minutes prior to the

---

1 Air Code of the Republic of Albania, Law No. 10 040, dated 22 December 2008 as amended on 24 November 2011; Agjencia Kombetare e Turizmit, 'Tourist Rights' <https://albania.al/wp-content/uploads/2019/08/TOURIST-RIGHTS-compressed.pdf> accessed 25 November 2025.

2 ECAA Agreement means the Multilateral Agreement between the European Community and its Member States, the Republic of Albania, Bosnia and Herzegovina, the Republic of Bulgaria, the Republic of Croatia, the former Yugoslav Republic of Macedonia, the Republic of Iceland, the Republic of Montenegro, the Kingdom of Norway, Romania, the Republic of Serbia, and the United Nations Interim Administration Mission in Kosovo (pursuant to the Resolution of UN Security Council, UN 1244 of 10 June 1999) on the establishment of a European Common Aviation Area.

3 Article 1(a) and (b).

DOI: 10.4324/9781003746164-12

published departure time.[4] The law is also applicable when the passenger has been transferred by an air carrier or tour operator from the flight for which they held a reservation to another flight, irrespective of the reason.[5] Like other regulations, this law does not apply to passengers travelling free of charge.

In case of denial of boarding,[6] airlines must first request volunteers to surrender their seat in exchange for benefits under conditions they would agree on.[7] The volunteers are still entitled to assistance under Article 8. If an insufficient number of volunteers come forward to allow the remaining passengers with reservations to board the flight, the operating air carrier may then deny boarding to passengers against their will compensating them immediately in accordance with Article 7.[8] Passengers denied boarding against their will should be able either to cancel their flights, with reimbursement of their tickets, or to continue them under satisfactory conditions, and should be adequately cared for while awaiting a later flight.

If a flight is cancelled, passengers have the right to a full refund or re-routing as well as assistance.[9] Passengers are entitled to compensation unless the airline informed them of the cancellation 14 days in advance or it is due to "extraordinary circumstances."[10] Just like Regulation 261, the Bylaw does not define the extraordinary circumstances and since the preamble has not been incorporated in the Bylaw, the definition of this concept is even more uncertain.[11] Compensation is not granted if passengers were informed between two weeks and seven days and they were not offered a route change allowing them to depart not more than two hours before the original departure time and arrive four hours after the original arrival time.[12] Similarly, no compensation is due when passengers are informed less than seven days in advance and not offered a route change allowing them to depart not more than one hour before the original departure time and arrive two hours after the original arrival time.[13]

4 Article 2(a).
5 Article 2(b).
6 Article 2(j) of Bylaw.
7 Article 4(a).
8 Article 4(b) and (c).
9 Article 5(a) and (b).
10 Article 5(c).
11 Elida Shabani–Mezini, 'Passenger Right in Civil Aviation in the Republic of Albania' (2014) 3 Anglisticum Journal 94.
12 Article 5(c)(ii).
13 Article 5(c)(iii).

When Cancelled	Compensation Due?
≥14 days before departure	No.
7–14 days before departure	No, if re-routing allows departure ≤2h earlier and arrival ≤4h later.
<7 days before departure	No, if re-routing allows departure ≤1h earlier and arrival ≤2h later.
<14 days notice + no suitable re-routing	Yes.

An airline is obligated to offer passengers specific assistance if it anticipates a flight will be delayed. What a passenger is entitled to depends entirely on the length of the delay and the flight distance. For short flights of 1,500 km or less, the airline must provide assistance after a two-hour delay. For medium-haul flights between 1,500 and 3,500 km, this assistance is required after three hours. All other, longer flights trigger this right after a four-hour delay.[14] This assistance package includes meals, refreshments, and the ability to make two free phone calls, send emails, or telex messages. Furthermore, if the delay is so significant that the new departure time is on a different day, the airline is also required to provide passengers with hotel accommodation and transport to and from the hotel. Finally, should the delay reach at least five hours, the passenger gains the right to cancel their trip and receive a full refund for any unused parts of their ticket. It cannot be inferred from the law that a flight which is delayed may be classified as a "cancelled flight" merely on the ground that the delay is very substantial.[15]

Passengers are entitled to a compensation of 250 euros for flights of a distance of up to 1,500 km. For flights between 1,500 and 3,500 km, the amount increases to 400 euros as well as flights within the ECAA of more than 1,500 km. Finally for flights over 3,500 km, the compensation is 600 euros.[16] The amount of compensation can be divided by two if passengers are offered an alternative flight which arrives at the final destination no later than two hours for flights of less than 1,500 km, three hours for flights between 1,500 and 3,500 km and all other flights within the ECAA, and four hours for flights longer than 3,500 km.[17]

14 Article 6(a)-c).
15 Elida Shabani–Mezini, 'Passenger Right in Civil Aviation in the Republic of Albania' (2014) 3 Anglisticum Journal 94, 99.
16 Article 7(I)(a), (b), and (c).
17 Article 7(II)(a), (b), and (c).

Situation	Airlines Obligation
Alternative flights less than 1,500 km arriving within 2 hours of the original time	125 euros.
Alternative flights between 1,500 km and 3,500 km or all other flights within the ECAA arriving within 3 hours of the original time	200 euros.
Alternative flights more than 3,500 km arriving within 4 hours of the original time	300 euros.

When an airline is responsible for a flight disruption, passengers are given the right to choose how they wish to proceed. They can either receive a full refund for the unused portions of their ticket within seven days and a return flight to their original departure point at the earliest opportunity, or they can be re-routed to their final destination.[18] This re-routing can happen at the earliest possible time or at a later date that is more convenient for them, depending on seat availability.[19] This right to a refund also applies to passengers who booked their flights as part of a package tour, unless the tour regulations state otherwise.[20] Additionally, if a city or region has multiple airports, the airline may offer a flight to a different, nearby airport, provided the passenger agrees to the change.[21]

During a flight disruption, airlines are obligated to provide passengers with free care.[22] This includes offering meals and refreshments that are appropriate for the length of the waiting time.[23] If the delay extends to the point where an overnight stay becomes necessary, the airline must also cover the cost of a hotel room and transport between the airport and the accommodation.[24] Furthermore, passengers are entitled to two free phone calls or emails.[25] It is also a requirement that the airline gives special consideration and attention to the needs of passengers with reduced mobility and children travelling alone.[26]

If an airline upgrades a passenger to a higher class than what they paid for, they are not allowed to ask for any additional payment. Conversely, if a passenger is moved to a lower class than their purchased ticket, the airline must reimburse a percentage of the ticket cost within seven days.

18 Article 8(1)(a) and (b).
19 Article 8(1)(c).
20 Article 8(2).
21 Article 8(3).
22 Article 9.
23 Article 9(1)(a).
24 Article 9(1)(b) and (c).
25 Article 9(2).
26 Article 9(3).

The refund amount is 30% for flights up to 1,500 km, 50% for flights between 1,500 and 3,500 km, and 75% for all flights longer than that.[27]

Airlines are also under the obligation to inform passengers of their rights. At the check-in area, they must prominently display a notice that tells passengers to ask for a document outlining their rights to compensation and assistance if their flight is denied boarding, cancelled, or delayed by at least two hours. Beyond this general notice, the airline must also provide a written document directly to every passenger affected by such a disruption. This notice must clearly detail the rules for receiving compensation and assistance as outlined in the Regulation, and it must also include the contact information for the official body responsible for handling passenger complaints. For passengers who are blind or visually impaired, the airline must use a suitable alternative method to ensure they receive all the same information.[28] However, there is no provision on potential fixed sanctions for non-compliance with the rules. Instead, it is left to the Civil Aviation Authority to "take all necessary measures to ensure the implementation of the passenger rights" and the "sanctions applied for infringement of these regulation dispositions must be effective, proportional and explanatory."[29]

Unlike Regulation 261, the Bylaw includes a provision on loss of luggage.[30] This article mandates the passengers to report any delay or damages upon arrival and the need to obtain a Property Irregularity Report (PIR). If the luggage is not located within 21 days, it is officially considered lost, at which point a full compensation claim can be submitted to the airline's customer relations or luggage assistance office. For luggage that is simply delayed and then returned within 21 days, passengers are entitled to claim back any reasonable expenses incurred while waiting for their belongings. The maximum compensation a passenger is typically eligible for in cases of luggage loss, delay, or damage is up to 1,100 euros from airlines covered by the Warsaw Agreement, unless the passenger purchased additional insurance.

Albania's Bylaw No. 1 is a direct transposition of EU Regulation 261, meaning its core provisions on compensation, re-routing, and assistance for denied boarding, cancellations, and long delays are the same. Both laws specify the same monetary compensation amounts (€250, €400, €600) based on flight distance and establish the same thresholds for triggering assistance (e.g., a three-hour delay for compensation). However, the omission of the preamble and the lack of inclusion of any definition

27 Article 10(2)(a), (b) and (c).
28 Article 14.
29 Article 16(2) and (4).
30 Article 17.

of the concept of "extraordinary circumstance" makes the Bylaw even more complex. Indeed, without the body of case law from the CJEU, the interpretation of what constitutes an "extraordinary circumstance" may rely on local judicial precedent, leaving passengers in a limbo. the Albanian Bylaw has incorporated specific provisions regarding luggage into its single regulatory document. This consolidates all major passenger rights – from flight disruptions to luggage issues – into one legal text, which is a structural difference from the EU's approach. This provision on luggage, however, aligns with the principles and liability limits of the international Conventions.

Comparison with EU Regulation

Feature	**Bylaw 1**	**EU Regulation 261/2004**
Delay Compensation	≥3h: €250–€600 (by distance).	≥3h: €250–600 (by distance).
Cancellation Notice	<14d notice: Refund + re-routing + compensation.	<14d notice: Refund or re-routing + €250–600 compensation (by distance).
Denied Boarding	Volunteer first; €250–€600 (by distance) if denied boarding.	Volunteer first; €250–€600 (by distance) if denied boarding.
Baggage Liability	€1,100.	Not specified.

Bibliography

- Air Code of the Republic of Albania, Law No. 10 040, dated 22 December 2008 as amended on 24 November 2011.
- ECAA Agreement means the Multilateral Agreement between the European Community and its Member States, the Republic of Albania, Bosnia and Herzegovina, the Republic of Bulgaria, the Republic of Croatia, the former Yugoslav Republic of Macedonia, the Republic of Iceland, the Republic of Montenegro, the Kingdom of Norway, Romania, the Republic of Serbia and the United Nations Interim Administration Mission in Kosovo (pursuant to the Resolution of UN Security Council, UN 1244 of 10 June 1999) on the establishment of a European Common Aviation Area.
- Agjencia Kombetare e Turizmit, 'Tourist Rights' <https://albania.al/wp-content/uploads/2019/08/TOURIST-RIGHTS-compressed.pdf> accessed 25 November 2025.
- Shabani Mezini, E., 'Passenger Right in Civil Aviation in the Republic of Albania' (2014) 3 Anglisticum Journal 94.

II.2

Algeria

Algeria has its own set of passenger rights regulations, which are outlined in Executive Decree No. 16–175 of 2016 (9th Ramadan 1437).[1] The rules apply to both scheduled and non-scheduled flights on fixed-wing aircraft for passengers with a confirmed reservation and check-in on time or at least 45 minutes before the published departure time.[2] The provisions also cover passengers who have been involuntarily transferred to another flight and those holding tickets from loyalty or other commercial programmes. It also extends to any operating air carrier, even if they did not directly contract with the passenger.

In case of denial of boarding,[3] airlines must first request volunteers to surrender their seat in exchange for benefits under conditions they would agree on.[4] The volunteers are still entitled to assistance under Article 8. If an insufficient number of volunteers come forward to allow the remaining passengers with reservations to board the flight, the operating air carrier may then deny boarding to passengers against their will, compensating them immediately in accordance with Article 9.[5] Passengers denied boarding against their will should be able either to cancel their flights, with reimbursement of their tickets for the unused portion of the journey and any parts that have become irrelevant and where possible to return to their initial point of departure. They should also be cared for in accordance with Article 10.

1 Executive Decree No. 16-175 of 9th Ramadan 1437, corresponding to June 14, 2016, establishing the conditions and modalities for the application of the rights of passengers using public air transport. People's Democratic Republic of Algeria, 'Passenger Rights' <https://www.anac.dz/en/passenger-rights/#:~:text=In%20the%20event%20of%20denied%20boarding%20or%20flight%20cancellation%2C%20passengers,compensation%20for%20the%20same%20claim>.

2 Article 3.

3 Article 4.

4 Article 4.

5 Article 4.

DOI: 10.4324/9781003746164-13

In the event of a cancellation, passengers are entitled to reimbursement of the ticket within eight days for the unused portion of the journey and any parts that have become useless, as well as a return flight to their initial point of departure at the earliest opportunity and compensation as specified in Article 9, unless they were informed of the cancellation at least two weeks before the scheduled departure time.[6] The notice period under the Algerian law is much stricter than the nuanced sliding scale in Regulation 261.

The airline does not have to pay compensation if it can prove the cancellation was caused by an event of force majeure, which is not defined in the Decree itself.[7] The EU's "extraordinary circumstances" defence, while still strict, can be slightly wider than the traditional "force majeure" defence found in the Algerian Decree.

If the airline foresees a significant delay, passengers must be offered assistance as outlined in Article 10 after two hours for short-haul flights (under 1,500 km), three hours for flights of 1,500 km–3,500 km, and four hours for long-haul flights (flights over 3,500 km).[8] For delays of at least five hours, passengers can choose to request a full refund of their ticket. Passengers have additionally the right to choose between a re-routing at the earliest opportunity or later date in the event of denied boarding, cancellation, or delays.[9]

In cases of denied boarding or flight cancellation, passengers are entitled to a flat-rate compensation regardless of the distance or delay length of 3,000 DA (Algerian Dinar) for domestic flights and 4,500 DA for international flights.[10] No compensation reduction is mentioned as found in Regulation 261 for instance if the alternative flight's arrival delay is minor.

Aspect	**Rule**
Payable for	Involuntary denied boarding and flight cancellation (if applicable).
Domestic Flight Amount	3,000 DA (Algerian Dinar).
International Flight Amount	4,500 DA (Algerian Dinar).

Passengers are entitled to assistance which includes refreshments and meals appropriate to the waiting time, and hotel accommodation and transport between the airport and the hotel if an overnight stay is

6 Article 5.
7 Article 6.
8 Article 7.
9 Article 8.
10 Article 9.

necessary. In addition, passengers have the right to two free telephone calls, sending two free telex messages, two fax messages, or two electronic messages.[11]

Situation	Right to Refund	Right to Compensation	Right to Assistance (Meals, Hotel, etc.)
Involuntary Denied Boarding	**Yes.** Full refund for unused part within **7 days**.	**Yes.** 3,000 DA for domestic flights and 4,500 DA for international flights.	**Yes.**
Flight Cancellation	**Yes.** Full refund for unused part within **7 days**.	**Yes, unless:** 1. Informed **≥2 weeks** before departure, or 2. Due to **force majeure**.	**Yes.**
Significant Delay (foreseen)	**Yes, if delay is ≥5 hours.** Passenger may request a refund.	**No.** Compensation is not required for delays.	**Yes, if delay exceeds:** • **≥2h** (flights <1,500 km). • **≥3h** (flights 1,500–3,500 km). • **≥4h** (flights >3,500 km).

Similarly to Regulation 261, the Decree contains a provision requiring airlines to accommodate passengers with reduced mobility, their companions, and unaccompanied minors, in full compliance with all applicable regulations.[12] Furthermore, passengers have the right to be informed about the identity of the operating carrier and their rights regarding assistance, reimbursement, and compensation. This information must also be provided to blind and visually impaired passengers through adapted means.[13] Unlike Regulation 261 and other national laws, the Decree does not contain any reference to potential fines for non-compliance.

The Algerian Decree is a good foundational law that mirrors the core principles of the European Union's Regulation 261. It provides passengers with essential protections and a clear legal basis for claims. However, the Algerian law emerges as a notably weaker instrument for passenger protection. The most significant shortcoming is its financial compensation model. The Decree offers only a low, flat-rate compensation amount, which is not proportional to the distance of the flight or the cost of the ticket.

11 Article 10.
12 Article 11.
13 Article 12.

This stands in stark contrast to the EU's tiered system, which mandates substantially higher payments calibrated to the scale of the disruption. It might even be regarded as a symbolic gesture which would not serve as a meaningful deterrent against some airlines' practices such as overbooking. The lack of potential fines reaffirms this weaker positioning. Unlike its EU counterpart, the Decree is stricter, allowing airlines to escape their obligations to compensation only if the notification was made more than 14 days in advance or due to force majeure.

Comparison With EU Regulation 261

Feature	Executive Decree No. 16–175	EU Regulation 261
Delay Compensation	Only assistance.	≥3h: €250–600 (by distance).
Cancellation Rights	<15d notice: Re-routing/ refund + compensation.	<14d notice: Refund + re-routing + €250–600 compensation (by distance).
Overbooking	Volunteers first; 3,000 DA or 4,500 DA if denied boarding.	Volunteers first; €250–€600 (by distance) if denied boarding.
Baggage Compensation	Not specified.	Not specified.

Bibliography

- Executive Decree No. 16-175 of 9th Ramadan 1437, corresponding to June 14, 2016, establishing the conditions and modalities for the application of the rights of passengers using public air transport. People's Democratic Republic of Algeria, 'Passenger Rights' <https://www.anac.dz/en/passenger-rights/#:~:text=In%20the%20event%20of%20denied%20boarding%20or%20flight%20cancellation%2C%20passengers,compensation%20for%20the%20same%20claim>.

II.3

Argentina

In Argentina, air passengers are protected by Decree 809/2024,[1] published in 2024 and entered into force in October 2024,[2] approved the new Regulation on Air Transport Services for Passengers and Baggage, and Protection of Passenger's Rights, thus repealing *Resolución* 1532/98.[3] This new Regulation – an annex to the Decree itself[4] – has been inspired by Regulation 261, the US, Australian, Swiss, Peruvian, and Colombian laws as stipulated in the preamble. It is probably one of the most extensive and comprehensive legislation on passenger transports.

The new Regulation is found in the Annex and applies to both domestic and international scheduled and non-scheduled flights operated in Argentina by both national and foreign airlines.[5] It introduced new obligations such as providing certain information, including the value of the fare, fees, and taxes before the ticket is issued.[6] Interestingly, when tickets are issued by an intermediary, it is only the intermediary which is responsible to comply with the duty to provide information and the carrier cannot be held liable for any errors or omissions of the intermediary.[7] As for the liability for breach of contract, the intermediary will not be responsible for the total or partial breach of the carrier's obligations, as

1 Decreto 809/2024, DECTO-2024-809-APN-PTE <https://www.boletinoficial.gob.ar/detalleAviso/primera/313613/20240910>.

2 Article 7 of the Decree.

3 Elias F Bestani and others, 'Executive Approves Regulation of Commercial Air Transport Services' (*Lexology*, 8 October 2024) <https://www.lexology.com/library/detail.aspx?g=eeeb02d2-d8bb-43ed-81bf-20d74f4314d9> accessed 25 November 2025; Facundo d'Esposito, 'El régimen consumeril en el nuevo Reglamento del Contrato Aéreo' (*PAGBAM*, 13 December 2024) <https://pagbam.com/articulos/el-regimen-consumeril-en-el-nuevo-reglamento-del-contrato-aereo/> accessed 25 November 2025.

4 The Decree is only nine articles long, and most of the detailed provisions are found in the three annexes.

5 Article 2. See Cintia Caserotto Miranda and Horacio Martin Pratto Chiarella, *Mayday en la aviación Argentina: Comentarios sobre las principales reformas al régimen jurídico aeronáutico de la República Argentina* (Tinta Libre Ediciones 2025), Section 11.

6 Chapter 3 Articles 4 and 5.

7 Article 5, 5th sentence.

DOI: 10.4324/9781003746164-14

long as the breach is not caused by an act or omission imputable to the intermediary.[8] Chapter III contains more provisions on information of particular interest is Article 7 which stipulates that the failure to provide an email or telephone number or to check the received e-mails will exonerate the carrier for its information obligation.

Chapter IV is dedicated to the formation of the contract, with Article 14 regulating the "nature of the offer" – which is irrevocable and binds the issuer for as long as it is made. An offer issued by intermediaries and/or third parties which does not comply with the carrier's regulations will only be binding for those who issued it.[9] Article 19 entitles passengers to revoke their contract within ten calendar days from the execution of the contract.

Chapter V regulates the transport contract itself. Interestingly, it contains a provision on data protection which stipulates that the making of a reservation and the issuance of a ticket implies the passenger's consent for some of his information to be shared to the extent that it is necessary or convenient for the execution of the contract of carriage.[10] That chapter also stipulates the rights of minors,[11] passengers with special needs,[12] passengers with medical needs,[13] and pregnant women.[14] Interestingly, the Regulation prohibits pregnant women to travel after their 39th week of pregnancy.[15]

The Regulation lists the situations in which a carrier could refuse the transport of a passenger: for security reasons, to comply with an applicable law or regulation, if any fee has not been paid, or if the passenger lacks proper documentation.[16] A carrier can also refuse on the basis of

> the conduct, age or mental or physical condition of the passenger is such that a. requires special assistance not available by the Carrier's Regulations, or not available by the aerodrome of departure or arrival; b. exhibits disruptive behaviour that may create danger or risk to himself or herself or to other persons or property or jeopardise operational safety, or distract the crew from the normal performance of their duties; c. fails to comply with the instructions of the Carrier; or d. has refused to comply with a security check.[17]

In those cases, airlines have the right to not only terminate the contract but also to deny boarding on future flights.[18] The law also contains a provision

8 Article 5, 6th sentence.
9 Article 14, 2nd sentence.
10 Article 25.
11 Accompanied: Article 29.
Unaccompanied: Article 30.
12 Article 31.
13 Article 32.
14 Article 33.
15 Article 33(c).
16 Article 38.
17 Article 38(IV).
18 Article 38 last sentence.

on no-show which seems to be more of a definition than a substantive provision and which stipulates that the carrier may be entitled to charge for voluntary change of date if the fare so allows.[19]

The Regulation lists the incidental services the carries must provide in cases of cancellations, rescheduling, and delays. Article 41 states that when a flight is cancelled 30 days before the original date of departure, the airline must either re-route the passenger on the "immediate subsequent flight" (el vuelo inmediato posterior) with the same carrier or be re-routed by another route to the destination with either the same or a different carrier or by another means of transport.[20] Article 41 (b) is quite nebulous as it translates as "The endorsement of the contract of carriage in equivalent fare conditions in air Carriers that have an agreement of acceptance in contingencies."[21] It is unclear who can endorse the contract and which contingencies are referred to.

Article 42 refers to the rescheduling attributable to the carrier of either the departure date and/or time. Carriers in those circumstances must comply with Article 43 in relation to the delay except if passengers are informed of the cancellation and/or rescheduling at least two weeks prior to the scheduled departure day, and/or are informed of the cancellation between two weeks and seven days prior to the scheduled departure time and are offered alternative transport to enable them to reach their final destination.[22] If the cancellation results in a loss of connecting flight, the carrier must re-accommodate at its own expenses.[23] According to Article 43, an airline must

> 1) make the necessary arrangements to reallocate passengers whose cancellation results in the loss of a connecting flight; 2) include the passengers on the airline's next immediate flight to their destination; 3) endorse their transport contract, including connections, if acceptable to the passenger; or 4) reroute the passenger to the destination indicated in the contract via another route, using the airline's services, another airline's services, or another means of transportation, subject to availability in the latter cases.

Those passengers who, voluntarily and expressly, accept transportation under any of the conditions just detailed will no longer be entitled to make any type of subsequent claim to the carrier.[24]

Passenger's rights in event of delay (called time alterations in the Regulation) start from the moment the passenger is in the pre-boarding

---

19 Article 39.

20 Article 41(a) and (c).

21 "b) El endoso del contrato de transporte en equivalentes condiciones tarifarias en Transportadores aéreos que tuvieren convenio de aceptación en contingencias."

22 Article 42.

23 Article 43(2)(1).

24 Article 43.

area after completing the administrative formalities.[25] Depending on the length of the delay attributable to the carrier, the airline will be requested to provide different assistance. For instance, if the delay is up to four hours, passengers are entitled to no assistance, unless such delay occurs at night time (between 00:00 hours and 06:00 hours).[26] Those passengers will have the same entitlement as for passengers suffering for a delay between four and eight hours, namely sufficient meals and refreshments.[27] Any delay of more than eight hours entitles the passenger to accommodation and transfer services. Interestingly, the Decree and Regulation do not explicitly mention compensation for flight delays nor do they give the right to phone calls or free internet access.

	Re-routing	**Assistance**	**Compensation**
Delay	No.	Yes (if >8hr delay).	No.
Cancellation more than 30 days	Yes.	No.	No refund only.
Cancellation between 15 and 7 days	Yes.	Yes.	No.
Cancellation less than 7 days	Yes.	Yes.	No.

A carrier is exempted from this obligation when the cancellation, delay, or rescheduling of the flight or a connecting flight is the result of weather circumstances, acts of God or force majeure, or when the passenger is informed of the cancellation, delay, or rescheduling at least 15 days before the departure of the original flight.[28]

Passengers denied boarding due to overbooking are entitled to the compensatory regime provided for in Articles 41, 42, and 43.[29] When there is a situation of overbooking, the carrier must first request for volunteers in exchange for compensation. Carriers will still be required to provide assistance as found in Articles 42 and 43 but will not have the right to file claims against the carrier.[30] In the event that no volunteer passengers are presented, or those presented are not sufficient, the carrier may deny boarding to other passengers, applying the regime established in Articles 41 and 42 of the Regulation.[31]

25 Article 43.
26 Article 43(a).
27 Article 43(b).
28 Article 44.
29 Article 45.
30 Article 46.
31 Article 46.

The right to refund is found in Article 47. The refund must be made within 30 days and with the same means of payment which was used to buy the tickets. The refund shall be made in the same currency received by the carrier, regardless of whether the ticket may have been issued in a different currency. Where applicable, the exchange rate used shall be the rate of exchange corresponding to the date of issue of the contract. The amount of the refund will be calculated in accordance with the fare conditions and/or the causes for which it was requested. Even if the fare conditions do not allow the refund of the ticket, the passenger shall be entitled to a refund of unused taxes and fees.[32] Passengers are entitled to a refund when a carrier cancels a flight, or omits a stopover, or in case of delays of more than four hours or denial of boarding. The refund should be in full when no portion of the journey has been used. If part of the journey has been made, then the amount will be the amount of the fare paid by the passenger from the point of cancellation to the destination aerodrome indicated on the ticket for domestic flights. For international flights, either the one-way fare less applicable discounts from the point of interruption to the point of destination or first stopover or the difference between the fare paid and the fare used, whichever is the highest.[33]

The Regulation also contains a full chapter on baggage and one dedicated to the transport of animals.[34] As already noted this Regulation is extensive in its scope and tries to cover most situations arising out of the air transport. For instance, Article 51 makes it clear that the baggage allowance can be shared amongst passengers travelling together. It, therefore, includes provisions on both service animals and emotional support animals. Article 66 is dedicated to service animals – duly certified – which need to be transported in the cabin and receive a "dignified treatment" (trato digno) free of charge. Article 67 relates to emotional support animals which transport is subject to the provisions of the carrier's regulations. The Regulation allows airlines to require passengers to "demonstrate that the animal has sufficient training, certified by an official public entity, to be used as an emotional support animal on an aircraft for the specific journey to be performed on the aircraft." They are also to be transported free of charge if accompanying a passenger with a medical or psychological certificate requiring such service. Passengers are responsible for the animal.[35]

Article 13 reaffirms the federal jurisdiction in aeronautical matters which "is consistent with the Argentine Supreme Court's precedents of

32 Article 47.
33 Article 48(II)(b)(1) and (2).
34 Chapter VI and VIII.
35 Article 68.

recent years."[36] The prescription to bring a claim is one year for domestic claims and two years for international ones.[37] The Decree also aligns with the Montreal Convention regarding financial relief for victims of aviation accidents and their families.[38]

The Decree also creates a Conciliation Service for Air Transport Passengers and a National Registry of Air Transport Conciliators to settle passengers' claims.[39] The Conciliation Service will be carried out electronically, on a voluntary basis and free of charge for passengers.[40] In November 2025, the National Civil Aviation Administration (ANAC) took steps towards implementing a new mechanism for managing passenger claims through *Resolución* ANAC No. 774/2025.[41]

While the Regulation does not mention any fines for non-compliance, Article 21.6 of Decree 816/2024 makes it clear that cancellation or delay is considered a serious infraction which can be subject to fines and/or temporary suspension of the relevant authorization. However, no fixed fines are mentioned in that Decree. Carriers will be required to submit a corrective plan if the Argentinian National Transportation Agency considers that passenger rights protection is not met or in case of excessive cancellations. This mechanism was used in December 2024 against Flybondi.[42]

Despite being very extensive, the major flaw of the Regulation is the lack of any type of fixed compensation for passengers suffering a delay, cancellation, or denial of boarding. While the Regulation includes a specific limit for damage to luggage of three Argentinian Gold coins per piece, it does not give any fixed limit in case of loss of luggage but instead mentions within the legal limits established for the flight.[43] Those omissions might result in many lawsuits as the Regulation clearly mentions in various articles that the acceptance will then bar passengers to bring a

36 Elias F Bestani and others, 'Executive Approves Regulation of Commercial Air Transport Services' (*Lexology*, 8 October 2024) <https://www.lexology.com/library/detail.aspx?g=eeeb02d2-d8bb-43ed-81bf-20d74f4314d9> accessed 25 November 2025.

37 Article 71.

38 Annex III.

39 Article 4 of the Decree 809/2024 of which the Regulation forms part of the Annex.

40 Article 4 of the Decree 809/2024.

41 Aviacion al dia, 'Argentina Modernizes Complaint System for Air Transport Passengers' (3 November 2025) <https://aviacionaldia.com/en/2025/11/argentina-modernizes-complaint-system-for-air-transport-passengers.html> accessed 25 November 2025.

42 Fl360aero, '48-Hour Ultimatum from Argentine ANAC to Flybondi to Submit a Plan to Reduce Cancellations and Protect Passenger Rights' (*FL360aero*, 5 December 2024) <https://fl360aero.com/detail/48-hour-ultimatum-from-argentine-anac-to-flybondi-to-submit-a-plan-to-reduce-cancellations-and-protect-passenger-rights/1966> accessed 25 November 2025.

43 Article 61(a) and (b).

claim against airlines which then seems to indicate that passengers have another basis for their claim.

Comparison with EU Regulation

Feature	Argentina Decree 809/2024	EU Regulation 261/2004
Delay Compensation	Only assistance.	≥3h: €250–600 (by distance).
Cancellation Rights	<15d notice: Re-routing/refund.	<14d notice: Refund + re-routing + €250–600 compensation (by distance).
Overbooking	Volunteers first; re-routing/refund.	Volunteers first; €250–€600 (by distance) if denied boarding.
Baggage Compensation	3 gold coins (damage).	Not specified.

Bibliography

- Decreto 809/2024, DECTO-2024-809-APN-PTE <https://www.boletinoficial.gob.ar/detalleAviso/primera/313613/20240910>.
- Aviacion al dia, 'Argentina Modernizes Complaint System for Air Transport Passengers' (3 November 2025) <https://aviacionaldia.com/en/2025/11/argentina-modernizes-complaint-system-for-air-transport-passengers.html> accessed 25 November 2025.
- Bestani, E. F., and others, 'Executive Approves Regulation of Commercial Air Transport Services' (*Lexology*, 8 October 2024) <https://www.lexology.com/library/detail.aspx?g=eeeb02d2-d8bb-43ed-81bf-20d74f4314d9> accessed 25 November 2025.
- Miranda, C. C. and Chiarella, H. M. P., *Mayday en la aviación Argentina: Comentarios sobre las principales reformas al régimen jurídico aeronáutico de la República Argentina* (Tinta Libre Ediciones 2025).
- d'Esposito, F., 'El régimen consumeril en el nuevo Reglamento del Contrato Aéreo' (*PAGBAM*, 13 December 2024) <https://pagbam.com/articulos/el-regimen-consumeril-en-el-nuevo-reglamento-del-contrato-aereo/> accessed 25 November 2025.
- Fl360aero, '48-Hour Ultimatum from Argentine ANAC to Flybondi to Submit a Plan to Reduce Cancellations and Protect Passenger Rights' (*FL360aero*, 5 December 2024) <https://fl360aero.com/detail/48-hour-ultimatum-from-argentine-anac-to-flybondi-to-submit-a-plan-to-reduce-cancellations-and-protect-passenger-rights/1966> accessed 25 November 2025.
- ICLG, 'Aviation Laws and Regulations Argentina 2025' (*ICLG*, 7 March 2025) <https://iclg.com/practice-areas/aviation-laws-and-regulations/argentina> accessed 25 November 2025.

II.4

Australia

Australia is one of the latest countries to have started legislation on a consumer protection code for air passengers, Airline Passenger Protections (Pay on Delay) Bill 2024, which aims at overhauling the country's air passenger rights system. The Bill requests the transport minister to enact rules on airline obligations in relation to delayed and cancelled flights and to denied boarding and overbooking claims within 12 months of the commencement of the Act.[1] Those rules would apply to flights to, from, and within Australia, including connecting flights.[2]

The carriers' obligations rules – as named in the Bill – would need to address the airlines' obligation in case of delay, flight cancellation, or denial of boarding including minimum standards of treatment and assistance in the event of a disruption.[3] While the Bill is very vague, leaving a lot of leeway to the transport minister, it also includes more specific rules regarding tarmac delays of over three hours, requiring the rules to address the minimum standards of treatment and obligation to provide timely information and assistance.[4] The new rules are also expected to impose minimum levels of compensation for lost or damaged baggage and delayed or cancelled flights.[5] While the Bill does not provide a fixed time, the draft Aviation Customer Rights Charter of December 2024 suggests that the protections would be applicable after three hours or more delays or disruption.[6]

1 Section 4(1).
2 Section 4(1).
3 Section 4(3).
4 Section 4(3)(f).
5 Section 4(3)(d).
6 Proposed right 3. Australian Government, 'Aviation Customer Rights Charter: Consultation Paper' (December 2024) <https://www.infrastructure.gov.au/sites/default/files/documents/aviation-customer-rights-charter-consultation-paper.pdf> accessed 25 November 2025.

DOI: 10.4324/9781003746164-15

Scenario	Proposed Rules	Notes
Delays/ Cancellations	- After 3+ hours - Full refunds (not vouchers).	Exact amounts TBD by transport minister.
Tarmac Delays	- Food/water, ventilation, lavatories. - Right to disembark after 3 hours.	Aligns with US/EU standards.
Baggage Issues	Fixed compensation for loss/delay.	Likely modelled on Montreal Convention (≈1,288 SDR).

Interestingly, the Bill also contains an obligation to "facilitate the assignment of seats to children under the age of 14 years in close proximity to a parent, guardian or tutor at no additional cost."[7] This is quite unique and will be most certainly welcomed by many parents.

The Bill seems to follow the Canadian example by requiring rules to be enacted to provide minimum standards of treatment for flight disruption within the airline's control, required for safety purposes, and those which are outside the airline's control.[8] From the Bill, it can also be inferred that situations outside of the carrier's control are very limited as the draft only mentions "natural phenomena and security events."[9]

The Bill does not make any mention of an obligation to pay for missed connections but could be included in the later rules. One positive note is that passengers will be able to receive a full refund rather than vouchers in a timely manner.[10]

Currently, passengers are only protected by the Australian Consumer Law which does not impose any specific obligation to provide compensation or assistance. The new rules might, therefore, result in a big change.

The Bill also requires a code of conduct to be drafted to regulate the manner in which airlines deal with passengers and third parties.[11] The Bill mentions that the aviation industry code of conduct would need to include provisions on

> the requirements for a consistent definition of a ticket of carriage to apply to all tickets of carriage issued by carriers, including the minimum rights which passengers and third parties are guaranteed when they purchase a ticket of carriage from a carrier.

7 Section 4(3)(e).

8 Section 4(3)(c)(i) – within the control of the airline; Section 4(3)(c)(ii) – for safety purpose; Section 4(3)(c)(iii) – outside of the control of the carrier.

9 Section 4(3)(c)(iii).

10 Section 4(3)(b).

11 Section 5 of the Bill.

This could mean that the code might include a statutory definition of "minimum rights" which might include any defence available to the airline.

Interestingly, it has been reported that Australia's consumer watchdog has "closely studied the EU scheme in the lead-up to the delivery of a landmark aviation white paper" but did not follow the compensation obligation due to pressure from some airlines.[12]

The draft Aviation Customer Rights Charter also sets out the expectations of fair and reasonable conduct by airlines and airports including the fact of being treated with dignity and respect. It also includes the prompt and fair remedies and support during and after flight disruptions such as cancellations and delays as well as the obligation to provide accurate, timely and accessible information.

Australia's Bill is a modest start but lacks the teeth of stricter regimes, such as the EU or Canada. Its success hinges on the transport minister's final rules. It has been criticized for being weak and confusing. The ministerial discretion may lead to weak rules and low compensation. It is especially worrying as the EU-style fixed compensation was rejected due to airline lobbying.

Passenger Rights Comparison

Feature	**Airline Passenger Protections (Pay on Delay) Bill 2024**	**EU Regulation 261**
Delay Compensation	After 3+ hours - Full refunds (not vouchers).	≥3h: €250–600 (by distance).
Cancellation Rights	After 3+ hours - Full refunds (not vouchers).	<14d notice: Refund or re-routing + €250–600 compensation (by distance).
Overbooking	?	Volunteer first; €250–€600 (by distance) if denied.
Baggage Compensation	Fixed compensation for loss/delay.	Not specified.

Bibliography

- Australian Government, 'Aviation Customer Rights Charter: Consultation Paper' (December 2024) <https://www.infrastructure.gov.au/sites/default/files/

12 Elias Visontary, 'Australia Declines to Follow EU in Forcing Airlines to Pay Passengers for Delayed and Cancelled Flights' *The Guardian* (22 December 2024) <https://www.theguardian.com/business/2024/dec/21/from-delays-to-refunds-how-australias-air-passenger-charter-could-affect-your-travel-rights> accessed 25 November 2025.

documents/aviation-customer-rights-charter-consultation-paper.pdf> accessed 25 November 2025

- Elias Visontary, 'Australia Declines to Follow EU in Forcing Airlines to Pay Passengers for Delayed and Cancelled Flights' *The Guardian* (22 December 2024) <https://www.theguardian.com/business/2024/dec/21/from-delays-to-refunds-how-australias-air-passenger-charter-could-affect-your-travel-rights> accessed 25 November 2025.

II.5

Bahrain

The key legislation governing civil aviation in Bahrain is Law No. 14/2013 on Civil Aviation and its accompanying Executive Regulations.[1] Bahrain has enacted the Aviation Implementing Regulations Law promulgated by Decision No. 21 of 2013 which contains a dedicated chapter to passenger rights, especially flight cancellations and delays.[2]

These Regulations are applicable to passengers arriving and departing from Bahrain in flights operated by aircraft operators registered in Bahrain or those appointed to operate flights to/from Bahrain.[3] It also applies to aircraft operators, airport operators, and ground service providers.[4]

Regarding denial of boarding, national and designated aircraft operators must submit their overbooking policy for approval either to the Air Transport Department (ADT) – for national carriers – or to both the ADT and Civil Aviation Affairs – for international carriers.[5] Those policies must be made clear to passengers "in a prominent way" – a term which is not defined in the Regulation itself – but including in sale and travel office and airport counter, on website and through phone calls.[6] Denial of boarding is not allowed if an alternative seat in a higher class on the same flight is available. In this case, the passenger must be upgraded free of charge.[7]

1 Bahrain Law No. 14/2013 on the Issuance of the Civil Aviation Regulation Law, issued 9 Shaaban 1434 H (corresponding to 18 June 2013) amended by Bahrain Law No. 4/2022 on Amending Some Provisions of the Civil Aviation Regulation Issued in Bahrain Law No. 14/2013, issued 20 Rajab 1443 H (corresponding to 21 February 2022).

2 Chapter 3. See: Practical Guidance, 'Passenger Rights During Flight Cancellations or Delays' (*Lexis Middle East*, 23 August 2024).

3 Article 44(1). See: Zu'bi and partners, 'Passenger Rights: Flight Cancellations or Delays' (Sn) <https://zubipartners.com/2024/08/03/passenger-rights-flight-cancellations-or-delays/> accessed 27 November 2025.

4 Article 44(2).

5 Article 48(1) and (2).

6 Article 48(4).

7 Article 48(5).

DOI: 10.4324/9781003746164-16

If no higher class seats are available and the airline needs to deny travel due to overbooking, the airline may request volunteer passengers to give up their seats in exchange for an offer from the airline.[8] When passengers are involuntarily denied boarding, due to no volunteers or insufficient volunteers, the airline must provide necessary care, attention, support, and compensation. Passengers must be adequately informed in "writing in a clear manner"[9] if any alternative seats are available in a lower class on the *same flight*, and if accepted the airline must compensate total fare difference between the original and downgraded class for that flight segment.[10] Downgrading is not considered a refusal of travel.[11] Passengers have the right to choose travel on another flight by the same or another airline, with the original airline bearing any cost difference.[12] In a situation in which the alternative flight requires the passenger to wait one to eight hours at the airport, passengers are allowed to use hospitality lounges if available.[13] In the event that a passenger is denied boarding for a connecting flight, the airline is obligated to ensure that the passenger reaches their final destination with minimal delay.[14] This may involve arranging travel on alternative airlines or in a higher class of service, with the airline covering any cost differences. The passenger must provide proof of the connecting flight. There is, however, an exemption of compensation if passengers violate ticket terms or if a similar flight is provided within eight hours of the original take-off time.[15]

Interestingly, the article does not mention clearly the amount of compensation but a 50 Special Drawing Rights (SDR) units per day of delay is imposed for late payment.[16] This daily penalty for late compensation is a significant deterrent.

Similarly to provisions found in Saudi Arabian or Omani law, airlines are under an obligation to limit the number of cancelled flights without compromising the safety and security of its passengers.[17] Airlines should inform passengers of cancellations in sufficient time, whenever possible.[18] Like seen in many laws, when the cancellation is notified at least 14 days before travel, the airline is exempt from care, support, and compensation

---

8 Article 48(6).
9 Article 48(7)(a).
10 Article 48(7)(b) and (e).
11 Article 48(7)(e).
12 Article 48(7)(c).
13 Article 48(7)(d).
14 Article 48(7)(f).
15 Article 48(8)(a) and (b).
16 Article 48(9).
17 Article 49(1).
18 Article 49(2).

requirements but must reimburse the ticket value.[19] Interestingly, the next paragraph refers to the same timeframe, 14 days before the date of the flight, but then the airline must offer an alternative flight or reimbursement.[20] The only difference is that paragraph a) is worded as "fourteen days prior to the date of travel" and paragraph b) as "fourteen days before the fixed date of flight" – which does seem a bit odd. If the passenger opts for an alternative flight that extends their residence until the new date, the airline must bear the costs of residence and meals.[21] The Regulations do not seem to include any right for flights cancelled under 14 days and before an unexpected cancellation at the airport.

Article 49(3) regulates unexpected cancellations while the passenger is at the airport and the passenger accepted the alternative flight proposed. In those circumstances, the passenger can be upgraded, on a flight operated by the original airline or a different one, at the airline's cost or downgraded if the passenger receives the full cost difference or 500 SDR units, whichever is higher.[22] Compared to countries that use fixed amount, the Bahraini law is more acting on a case-by-case basis. Quite remarkably, compensation under paragraph 3 could include an open ticket valid for one year, *if the passenger agrees*.[23] Its seems that the wording of Article 49(5) means that if the passengers refused the alternative flight, they will be entitled to full refund, after a declaration form is signed.[24] However, the declaration form does not seem to be a prohibitive element as in case such declaration is missing, the passenger's statement – if different from the airline's – should prevail.[25] The provision on care for delays at airport – Article 50(6) – applies to the period between the cancelled and alternative flight.[26] Any unilateral cancellation by an airline, without the passenger's knowledge, entitles passengers to the rights under Article 49.[27]

While Article 49 provides good protection for passengers facing cancellations, its wording leaves some room for doubt. Firstly, does the rule in paragraph 2 apply to notification of cancellation under 14 days or is it the rule of paragraph 3? Maybe paragraph (2)(b) should be read as cancellation within 14 days prior to the flight date. While specific compensation rules for downgrades are included, no such rule is found for general cancellation. This last point would not have been a problem – and

19 Article 49(2)(a).
20 Article 49(2)(b).
21 Article 49(2)(c).
22 Article 49(3)(a) and (b).
23 Article 49(4).
24 Article 49(6).
25 Article 49(7).
26 Article 49(8).
27 Article 51.

one could have assumed that the provisions on delays would then apply – however, at least one paragraph refers to Article 50 raising the question of whether the assumption is correct or not.

Features	**Bahrain Regulations**
Advance Notice	≥14 days: full refund/rebooking (no extra care).
Short Notice (<14 days)	Refund + rebooking + care (meals/hotel) + case-by-case SDR compensation.
Force Majeure	No compensation; only minimal assistance required.
Downgrading	Full fare difference refunded + compensation.
Compensation Amount	No fixed amount (SDR-based, case-by-case).
Right to Care	Meals/hotel after 3+ hour wait.
Documentation	Passenger must sign cancellation form for refund.

Similar to flight cancellations, the aircraft operator is responsible for taking all necessary measures to minimize the number of delayed flights and to shorten the duration of any delays without compromising passenger safety and security.[28]

Passengers must be informed of any delays before the originally scheduled take-off time. All notifications should clearly state the revised take-off time.[29] When passengers are notified of any delay or schedule change 14 days prior to travel, airlines will be exempt from care, support, and compensation.[30] Moreover, the airline is not responsible for delay damages if it proves all necessary reasonable measures were taken, or it was impossible to take such measures – similar to force majeure principles, but specific to delay damages.[31]

In case the new take-off time cannot be determined, the passengers must be compensated by 15 units of SDR for each hour of delay which may reach up to 100 SDR.[32] While the passenger is at the airport, the airline must provide refreshments after the first hour of delay, a hot meal for any delay exceeding three hours, and a hotel stay for delays exceeding eight hours.[33] Except for refreshments, passengers can choose monetary compensation instead of hot meals (15 SDR) or hotel stay (50 SDR) for

28 Article 50(1).
29 Article 50(4).
30 Article 50(2).
31 Article 50(3).
32 Article 50(5).
33 Article 50(6)(a), (b) and (c).

respective delay durations, which is unheard of.[34] If the flight is delayed for more than eight hours after the announced arrival time, the airline compensates the passenger 10 SDR for each hour of delay, up to a maximum of 100 SDR units. This compensation is additional to other care forms.[35]

Another provision which is rarely found but extremely important is the obligation of airport operators to provide infrastructure and facilities to help airlines offer these care services.[36] If the airline cannot offer care due to a lack of airport infrastructure or other reasons, it must still compensate the passenger (as per paragraph 7). The airline can then claim this amount from the airport operator if the reason was related to airport infrastructure.[37]

In the event of a flight delay occurring prior to the passenger's arrival at the airport, the airline shall bear the cost of extending the passenger's hotel stay until the rescheduled departure time, subject to a maximum limit of 50 SDR units, with proof of costs.[38]

The delay provisions, especially the care and monetary option, apply also in the event of an in-flight diversion.[39] This inclusion is welcomed as it brings legal certainty. Passengers have also the option to treat long delays of more than eight hours as a cancelled flight.[40]

This article thoroughly addresses delays, offering tiered assistance based on the duration of the delay, monetary compensation for significant delays (even if the new time is uncertain), and specific provisions for infrastructure issues and pre-airport delays. The option to treat an extended delay as a cancellation represents a notable passenger right. The only question left unanswered is whether the compensation available to an unknown take-off time also applies to known take-off time. For instance, flight A is delayed by two hours and is announced as such to the passenger, would that then mean the passenger is not entitled to compensation? or what is meant by unknown take-off time is that due to potential roll-over delays, the take-off time is only known at the time of departure of the flight?

34 Article 50(7).
35 Article 50(13).
36 Article 50(8).
37 Article 50(9).
38 Article 50(10).
39 Article 50(11).
40 Article 50(12).

Delay Duration	Airline Obligations	Compensation (if obligations not met)
<1 hour	None.	—
1–3 hours	Provide **refreshments** (e.g., drinks, snacks).	15 SDR/hour (max 100 SDR) if no refreshments provided.
3–8 hours	Provide **hot meals** (or 15 SDR in lieu).	15 SDR for meal replacement.
>8 hours	**Hotel stay** (or 50 SDR in lieu) + rebooking options.	50 SDR for hotel replacement + 10 SDR/hour (max 100 SDR).
Unknown delay duration	Pay **15 SDR/hour** (max 100 SDR) until new departure time is announced.	—
Arrival delay >8 hours	Compensate **10 SDR/hour** (max 100 SDR) *in addition* to care obligations.	Paid regardless of care provided.
Delay due to force majeure	No compensation, but must provide **updates** and **assistance** (e.g., phone support).	—

The only defence available to an airline is force majeure which is defined as "the running of specific flight/flights to a certain destination or destinations, for reasons that the aircraft operator cannot control or avoid" but does not include aircraft technical defects.[41] This definition is not the clearest and would have benefit from further explanation such as what constitutes a technical defect. Even in an event of force majeure, airlines are required, whenever possible, to offer appropriate care and support.[42] However, as already mentioned, airlines can escape their liability if it proves it took all necessary measures or it was impossible to do so.[43] When cancelling or modifying flights due to force majeure, airlines should apply the provisions of Articles 49 (cancellations) and 50 (delays) as much as possible. This implies no liability for compensation compared to non-force majeure events, but care provisions may still apply.[44] Similarly to delays, airport operators have also an obligation to provide assistance

41 Article 54(7).
42 Article 54(1).
43 Article 54(2).
44 Article 54(3).

and infrastructure to airlines.[45] This provision is highly favourable to passengers placing responsibility for any issues firmly on the airlines.

Article 52 addresses the rights and care for passengers with special needs.[46] Airlines cannot refuse transport of a passenger with disabilities unless for genuine security and safety reasons or to preserve the passenger's own health.[47] Airlines, airport operators, and ground service providers must observe the needs of passengers with disabilities including providing wheelchairs and clear guidance signs, provide lifts, provide the necessary care and information, and ensure airport facilities including sale counters are accessible.[48] In case of refusal of service, the refusing party (airline, airport operator, ground service provider) must provide justifications to the passenger within seven days of the refusal or request. Failure to do so is considered an acceptance of the passenger's entitlement to compensation.[49] Such compensation is equivalent to 200% of the total ticket price, in addition to any other applicable compensations.[50] This article demonstrates a strong commitment to accessibility and non-discrimination for passengers with disabilities, with clear requirements for care, facilities, and significant penalties for non-compliance – one of the highest in the world.

The law also contains a provision outlining the airline responsibilities regarding passenger baggage.[51] Compensation is limited to 1,131 SDR for loss, damage, or delay of baggage, which is more or less aligned with the Montreal Convention limit.[52] The same time limit applies, namely 21 days for baggage delay and 14 days for damage.[53] If a passenger wishes to claim more than the standard compensation limit for valuable articles, they must declare these to the airline during baggage examination and confirm it on airline forms.[54]

The Air Transport Department (ADT) is the central authority for passenger rights enforcement, acting as a regulator, mediator, and policy-setter. Indeed, it is responsible for overseeing the implementation of these rules as well as handling complaints.[55] The ADT also has enforcement and

45 Article 54(8).
46 The law itself refers to disabilities.
47 Article 52(1).
48 Article 52(2)(a)–(e).
49 Article 52(3).
50 Article 52(4).
51 Article 53.
52 Article 53(2).
53 Article 53(6) and (7).
54 Article 53(8).
55 Article 46.

investigatory powers.[56] It is also tasked with laying down the minimum terms and conditions for overbooking policies that airlines can follow.[57]

The law also contains articles on transparency and advertising.[58] Airlines must indicate the terms for pet transport to passengers before accepting them and if a pet is not accepted, it must bear the resulting expenses up to a maximum of 100 SDR units.[59] Another interesting provision is that airport operators must ensure clarity and effectiveness of loudspeakers and advertisement boards for guiding passengers.[60]

The Regulations demonstrate a commendable commitment to safeguarding air travellers, encompassing airlines, airport operators, and ground service providers alike. While Bahrain's Regulations provide detailed care protocols for delays, cancellations, and denied boarding, they suffer from a critical flaw: the absence of fixed compensation amounts for most disruptions. For instance, while downgrades and certain types of delays have specific SDR compensation figures, the general provision for "compensation" in some denied boarding scenarios, alongside care and re-routing, might leave room for interpretation. The law's phrasing – particularly regarding "legal limits" for baggage loss and voluntary compensation acceptance – may lead to legal challenges. For instance, passengers may reject settlements and pursue higher claims, as the law suggests that alternative claims are possible. A truly commendable aspect is the dedication to passengers with disabilities. The Regulations unequivocally prohibit refusing transport unless for genuine safety or health reasons; lay down comprehensive requirements for accessible facilities; and impose an exceptionally high penalty of 200% of the total ticket price, in addition to other compensations, for any refusal of transport or necessary services to disabled passengers without proper justification.

Comparison with EU Regulation

Feature	**Bahrain Aviation Implementing Regulations Law (Decision No. 21 of 2013)**	**EU Regulation 261/2004**
Delay Compensation	>8 hrs: 10 SDR/hr (max 100 SDR) + care (meals/hotel).	≥3h: €250–600 (by distance).
Cancellation Rights	<14d notice: Refund + re-routing + care. Force majeure: No compensation.	<14d notice: Refund or re-routing + €250–600 compensation (by distance).

(Continued)

56 Article 46(4).
57 Article 46(6).
58 Articles 55 to 57.
59 Article 55(3) and (4).
60 Article 57(2).

(Continued)

Feature	Bahrain Aviation Implementing Regulations Law (Decision No. 21 of 2013)	EU Regulation 261/2004
Overbooking	Volunteers first; if denied boarding: Upgrade/alternative flight + 50 SDR/day delay.	Volunteer first; €250–€600 (by distance) if denied.
Baggage Compensation	Max 1,131 SDR (loss/damage). Delay: Compensate within 21 days.	Not specified.

Bibliography

- Bahrain Law No. 14/2013 on the Issuance of the Civil Aviation Regulation Law, issued 9 Shaaban 1434 H (corresponding to 18 June 2013) amended by Bahrain Law No. 4/2022 on Amending Some Provisions of the Civil Aviation Regulation Issued in Bahrain Law No. 14/2013, issued 20 Rajab 1443 H (corresponding to 21 February 2022).
- Practical Guidance, 'Passenger Rights During Flight Cancellations or Delays' (*Lexis Middle East*, 23 August 2024).
- Zu'bi and partners, 'Passenger Rights: Flight Cancellations or Delays' (Sn) <https://zubipartners.com/2024/08/03/passenger-rights-flight-cancellations-or-delays/> accessed 27 November 2025.

II.6

Bolivia

Bolivia has its own specific regulations governing air passenger rights, which are outlined in the *Reglamento de Derechos y Deberes de los Usuarios del Transporte Aéreo* (Regulation of Rights and Duties of Air Transport Users), approved by the General Directorate of Civil Aviation (DGAC) and enacted through the *Decreto Supremo N° 0285 of Defensa de los Derechos del Usuario of 2009*.[1]

This Regulation applies to both national and international, regular and non-regular air transport of passengers, baggage, and cargo to and from Bolivia irrespective of the nationality of the airline.[2] The Regulation also stipulates that international conventions ratified by Bolivia will take precedence in case of conflict.[3] The Regulation contains a very exhaustive list of definitions, including extraordinary circumstances but also special needs passengers which includes elderly, children under the age of 5 and pregnant women.[4] Delayed flights are defined as those departing more than 30 minutes after the original departure time.

Chapter II deals with the booking and the information passengers must receive during this process.[5] It contains very classic provisions and includes an article on the possibility for airlines to have waiting lists. Chapter III is dedicated to the air transport contract, containing provisions that the

1 'Reglamento de Proteccion de los Derechos del Usuario de los servicios aéreo y aeroportuario' <https://www.sea.gob.bo/digesto/CompendioII/F/41_REG.pdf>.

2 Article 1.

3 Article 1, 3rd sentence.

4 Article 2 "Todo pasajero con movilidad reducida, sensorial, mental o de locomoción, permanente o temporal, debido a su edad u otra causa; y cuya situación necesita atención especial y la adaptación a sus necesidades de los servicios a disposición de todos los usuarios. Se incluye a personas de la tercera edad, niños menores de cinco (5) años y mujeres embarazadas" translated as "Any passenger with reduced mobility, sensory, mental, or locomotor impairment, whether permanent or temporary, due to age or other causes, and whose situation requires special attention and adaptation of the services available to all users to their needs. This includes senior citizens, children under five (5) years of age, and pregnant women."

5 Articles 3 to 10.

DOI: 10.4324/9781003746164-17

ticket serves as proof of the contract,[6] airline's obligations to transport the passenger safely to their final destination by air according to the schedule, itinerary agreed,[7] the validity period of a ticket which is maximum one year,[8] the extension of the ticket validity when the airline is unable to provide a seat on the requested flight, or when the passenger provides a medical certification of illness or physical incapacity in advance or during the journey.[9] The lack or loss of a ticket does not affect the existence or validity of the transport contract.[10] Errors in the ticket must be corrected immediately. When such error is the fault of the airline or agency, they are obligated to fulfil the conditions of the transport contract and cannot use the error as a reason to evade their responsibility.[11] Passengers can also decide to withdraw from their travel by informing the airline at least 48 hours in advance for domestic flights or 72 hours for international flights without paying any additional charge.[12] If a passenger does not appear at the counter, is late, or voluntarily interrupts their journey, they must pay a fee to change the date of their travel. This fee cannot exceed the amount defined by the competent authority. This penalty will not apply in cases of flight cancellation, a delay of more than four hours, a confirmed reservation being cancelled by the passenger and/or a missed connection due to reasons attributable to the airline, an itinerary change affecting a destination in the transport contract, and/or health reasons supported by a medical certificate.[13]

Chapter IV is dedicated to the rights of air transport service users, especially the information which must be communicated at booking stage,[14] before transportation,[15] and during transport.[16] The passenger has the right to be informed of any changes to their flight or itinerary by the fastest possible means, at least four hours in advance for domestic flights and 12 hours for international flights. In cases of denied boarding due to

6 Article 11.
7 Article 13.
8 Article 15.
9 Article 16(a), (b) and (c). For (b) the validity must be extended for minimum 30 days as well as for any person accompanying that passenger. For (c), When a passenger, who has already begun their journey, provides a medical certificate proving a situation of illness or physical incapacity to continue the trip, the ticket's validity will be extended by the airline for a minimum period of forty-five days.
10 Article 19.
11 Article 18.
12 Article 20(a).
13 Article 20(b).
14 Article 22.
15 Article 23.
16 Article 24.

overbooking, cancellation, or delay, the airline must inform passengers of their rights to compensation and assistance.[17]

As the law tries to be very exhaustive, in addition of the rights included in Chapter IV, Chapter V details more rights passengers are entitled during transport execution such as the issuance of a boarding pass.[18] The treatment of the passengers must be in line with Article 101 of Law No. 2902.[19] Airlines are prohibited to refuse service based on discrimination of any kind and can only refuse service based on legal reasons.[20] The airline must inform a connecting passenger of any delay that would prevent them from reaching their connection on time. The passenger must be given the option to cancel the trip without penalty.[21] Article 30 places an obligation on airlines to comply with published schedules and itineraries unless there is a case of force majeure. Interestingly, this article does not refer to the extraordinary circumstance as defined in Article 2 which covers broader situations than only force majeure.[22]

Rules on special needs passengers with different abilities are found in Chapter VI. Passengers with disabilities, seniors, children under 5, and pregnant women must receive special treatment and priority boarding.[23] For the transport of sick passengers or passengers with mental disabilities, the carrier shall require a medical certificate issued no more than 24 hours prior to the flight, stating the passenger's health conditions and their ability to travel.[24] This requirement might be very cumbersome on the passenger themselves. Depending on the passenger's condition, a doctor or any other person qualified may be required, at the passenger's expense, to assist them during the trip, unless the doctor certifies that it is not necessary. The carrier may charge additional fees if it is necessary to assign personnel to care for the passenger or provide

17 Article 23(a) and (b).

18 Article 26.

19 Article 25.

20 Article 28.

21 Article 27.

22 Article 2 "Circunstancias imprevistas: Son causas de fuerza mayor o caso fortuito, ajenas al normal desenvolvimiento de la actividad del transportista, debidamente comprobadas, que impiden que el vuelo se lleve a cabo o que se retrase su inicio (como ser, y sin estar limitado a causas meteorológicas, fallas técnicas no correspondientes o no atribuibles al mantenimiento programado o rutinario de la aeronave; fallas de los equipos de asistencia en tierra, entre otras)." translated as "Unforeseen circumstances: These are cases of force majeure or unforeseeable events, beyond the carrier's control and duly verified, that prevent the flight from taking place or cause a delay in its departure (such as, but not limited to, weather-related causes; technical failures not related to or attributable to the aircraft's scheduled or routine maintenance; failures of ground support equipment, among others)."

23 Article 32.

24 Article 34.

any other care that involves costs to the carrier. This provision sounds very fair on the airline if they have to assign someone specifically for the care of the passenger.

Carriers may not refuse to transport the passengers, unless it is evident that, under normal flight conditions, their state of health may worsen; that the aircraft does not have the necessary resources for safe transport; and that the condition of such passengers poses a risk or harm to others.[25] This article not only establishes a baseline right for sick passengers but also the three specific conditions for an airline to legally deny boarding to a sick passenger, namely the risk, the lack of resources, or risk to others. It aims to balance the passenger's right to travel with the airline's responsibility for the safety and well-being of all passengers and crew.

As seen in some countries, there is a provision regarding pregnant women. In this case, it is rather strict as it prohibits women who are more than seven months pregnant to travel unless strictly necessary.[26] However, "strictly necessary" is not defined; instead Article 36 requires a medical certificate and a signed document releasing the airline from liability for any issues related to their pregnancy during the flight. Similar exoneration is found regarding damages caused by third parties, the passenger's own fault, or a pre-existing medical condition.[27]

Chapter VII details the airline's obligations during flight disruptions. The Regulation starts with the rights in case of denied boarding due to the airline's fault.[28] When an airline needs to deny boarding to a passenger with a confirmed reservation, it must first ask for volunteers to give up their seats in exchange for benefits. These benefits can include services, communication, food, transportation, airport fees, and lodging until the next flight, as well as a new flight on the same or another airline.[29] Volunteers could also receive a compensation equivalent to 25% of the value of the unfulfilled journey, payable in cash or another form agreed upon by the passenger.[30] If there are not enough volunteers, the involuntarily denied passengers must be immediately compensated and provided assistance.[31] Instead of this compensation being expressed in Article 40, the protection for involuntary denial is found in Article 41. In case of overbooking, in addition to the 25% compensation, the passenger is entitled to a seat on

25 Article 35.
26 Article 36.
27 Article 38.
28 Article 40.
29 Article 40(a) and (b).
30 Article 40(c).
31 Article 40(c).

the next available flight to their final destination, on the same date and on the same route. If no flight is available, the carrier shall make the necessary arrangements, at its own expense, for the passenger to board another carrier as soon as possible.[32]

Scenario	Airline Obligations	Compensation/Assistance
Voluntary Denied Boarding	Seek volunteers to give up seats in exchange for benefits (e.g., services, food, lodging, rebooking).	25% of ticket value (cash/ agreed form) + rebooking.
Involuntary Denied Boarding	Immediate compensation + assistance (rebooking, food, communication, etc.).	25% of ticket value + seat on next available flight.

The Regulation distinguishes between disruptions due to force majeure or unforeseen circumstances, cancellation due to change of itinerary or flight planning and disruptions attributable to the carrier.[33] First, disruptions caused by force majeure or meteorological reasons affecting its safety duly certified and reported by the competent authorities release the airlines from liability. In such cases, passengers may choose to request a refund of the total amount of the ticket, without incurring any charges or wait for the flight to be restarted or completed, in which case the carrier shall be exempt from the compensation.[34] The provision seems to contain two contradicting aspect as it first stipulates that force majeure releases airlines from liability but then allows the passenger to wait which would exempt compensation.

An airline is released from liability when it has informed the passengers of the flight cancellation at least 15 days prior to the scheduled departure date and time, or has informed the user of the cancellation with less than 15 days' notice but has offered another replacement flight to the user's satisfaction.[35] This could be a potential loophole for the airline, allowing them to avoid compensation for a cancellation if they offer a substitute flight that is satisfactory to the user, even if it is offered with little notice. This places the burden of negotiation on the passenger and could lead to them accepting a less-than-ideal rebooking to avoid losing their compensation claim.

32 Article 41(III)–(d).
33 Article 41(I)–(III).
34 Article 41(I)(a) and (b).
35 Article 41(II).

Notification Time	Airline Obligations	Compensation/Refund
≥15 days notice	No liability if passengers are informed.	None (full refund or rebooking allowed).
<15 days notice	Must offer a replacement flight acceptable to the passenger.	No compensation if passenger accepts rebooking. Otherwise, refund + 25% compensation if delay prior to cancellation.
Force Majeure (e.g., weather, safety)	No liability.	No compensation, but full refund allowed.

In cases of cancellations, interruptions, delays, or any other event attributable to the carrier, as well as in cases of overbooking, the carrier shall compensate the passenger. For delays exceeding two hours but less than four hours, the passenger will be provided with a snack and, upon request, a telephone call or the most expeditious means of communication available to the destination or, in the case of connections, to the origin, not exceeding three minutes.[36] For delays between four and six hours, the passenger shall be provided with food – breakfast, lunch, or dinner, depending on the time.[37] For delays exceeding six hours, the carrier must compensate the passenger with a minimum amount equivalent to 25% of the ticket price for the unfulfilled journey. Additionally, after 10 PM (local time), the airline is obliged to offer accommodation – if they are not at home – and transportation expenses, or immediate reimbursement if they are not at their usual place of residence, unless the passenger voluntarily agrees to prolong the wait when it is foreseeable that the flight will take place within a reasonable time.[38]

Delay Duration	Airline Obligations
2–4 hours	Snack + communication (e.g., phone call).
4–6 hours	Full meal (breakfast/lunch/dinner).
>6 hours	25% of ticket value + accommodation/transport if after 10 PM.

In cases of interruption of transport, if the passenger does not opt for a refund of the proportional part corresponding to the uncovered section, they will be compensated for the delay suffered until they arrive at their final destination.[39]

36 Article 41(III)(a)(1).
37 Article 41(III)(a)(2).
38 Article 41(III)(a)(3).
39 Article 41(III)(b).

In cases where the carrier decides to cancel the flight, without having refunded the amount of the ticket for the proportional part of the trip not taken or its entirety if the flight no longer has a reason to exist, nor having found a substitute flight for the same day, the passenger shall be reimbursed for the costs of food, accommodation where an overnight stay is necessary, and transportation between the airport and the hotel.[40] In addition, if there is a delay prior to the cancellation of the flight, the passenger is entitled to the 25% of the ticket compensation. Notwithstanding the foregoing, the passenger may agree with the carrier, where appropriate, on a return flight to the first point of departure as quickly as possible, or a re-routing to their final destination.[41]

The Regulation also covers flight anticipation noting that if the carrier anticipates a flight without notifying the passenger by more than one hour, or if, having notified the passenger, it is impossible for them to travel at the new imposed time, they must be provided with a seat on the next flight that is convenient for their final destination. If the carrier does not have a flight available, it must make the necessary arrangements, at its own expense, for the passenger to board another carrier. In such cases, the passenger shall not pay any excess if the new seat corresponds to a higher fare. If the passenger does not accept any of these alternatives, they may demand a refund of the price paid, without charge.[42] If the disruption results in the passenger missing their connection, they are also entitled to compensation when the event is attributable to the carrier.[43]

When, for reasons attributable to the carrier, the latter must change to an airport other than the one for which the reservation was made, it shall bear the cost of transporting the passenger to the second airport, either from or to the airport for which the reservation was made or from/ to another nearby location agreed upon with the passenger.[44]

Scenario	**Airline Obligations**	**Compensation/Refund**
>1 hour early without notice OR passenger cannot adapt	Rebooking on next convenient flight (same/ another carrier).	Full refund if no alternative accepted.
Missed Connection (carrier's fault)	Rebooking + compensation if attributable to airline.	Calculated compensation (see formula that follows this table).

40 Article 41(III)(c).
41 Article 41(III) (c).
42 Article 41(III)(e).
43 Article 41(III)(f).
44 Article 43.

The law also includes the formula for calculating the compensation which is the Net Ticket Value × [(Unfulfilled Distance)/(Total Distance)] × Compensation Percentage.[45]

Sanctions are found in Chapter VIII. A failure to compensate results in 7% sanctions of the ticket value for the delayed leg for national flights delayed between two and four hours, 10% for the flights delayed between four and six hours, and 40% for flights disruption greater than six hours or cancellation or overbooking.[46] For international flights, a 10% sanctions of the ticket value for delays between two and four hours, 20% for flights delayed between four and six hours and 40% for flights disruption greater than six hours or cancellation or overbooking.[47] Those sanctions must be paid to the passenger. Interestingly, the Regulation does not make any difference in compensation between domestic and international flights but does so for sanction purposes.

Flight Type	**Delay Duration**	**Sanction (% of Ticket Value)**
National (Domestic)	2–4-hour delay.	7%.
	4–6-hour delay.	10%.
	>6 hours/cancellation/overbooking.	40%.
International	2–4-hour delay.	10%.
	4–6-hour delay.	20%.
	>6 hours/cancellation/overbooking.	40%.

Chapter IX is dedicated to the passenger's duties which include the obligation to provide truthful personal information,[48] having the adequate travel document,[49] but also the fact of arriving on time for check-in namely one hour for domestic flights and two hours for international flights.[50] Passengers are required by Article 50 to follow the instructions of the airline, both on the ground, inside the aircraft, and during the flight.[51] Passengers must refrain from any actions that could compromise flight safety, their own safety, or the safety of others, as well as any behaviour that disrupts order, discipline, or causes discomfort to other passengers. If these requirements are not met, the carrier may suspend service and

45 Article 42.
46 Article 45(I)(a)–(d).
47 Article 45(II)(a)–(d).
48 Article 47.
49 Article 48.
50 Article 49.
51 Article 50.

pursue any applicable legal actions. The aircraft captain is authorized to disembark a passenger at the next stop or divert the flight to an alternate airport, and the passenger will be responsible for any resulting consequences regardless of actions by local authorities. If such incidents occur on the ground, the carrier may deny boarding.[52]

Chapter X focuses on baggage, allowing passengers to have hand baggage and bag based on the airlines' policies.[53] Articles 56 to 58 deal with restricted items and valuable objects. If the baggage does not arrive on the same flight as the passenger, the carrier shall take all necessary steps to deliver it as soon as possible so that its owner can verify its condition. If the passenger does not have a residence at the place of arrival, the carrier shall cover the passenger's minimum needs for clothing and hygiene until the baggage is returned. In addition to the preceding, if a passenger's accompanied or unaccompanied baggage does not arrive or arrives on another flight, requiring the owner to wait or return to the airport to claim it, the cost of transportation to and from the airport, if necessary, shall be borne by the carrier. In such cases, the carrier shall also reimburse the passenger for the minimum expenses for toiletries and clothing.[54] While this is a current practice for many airlines, it is good to have it embodied in the law itself. No compensation is included in the law.

Chapter XII relates to the obligations of the airport service provider and includes the minimum facilities that must be provided.[55]

The Bolivian law offers very strong protections and a good framework. It contains many provisions of some common practices in the industry. The most fundamental difference with EU Regulation 261 is the calculation of compensation for disruption. The EU's approach is generally more passenger-friendly because fixed compensation ensures a minimum payout, whereas a percentage-based system could result in very low compensation for cheaper tickets. For cancellation, the key difference is that the EU imposes automatic compensation unless the disruption is beyond the airline's control, whereas Chapter VII allows airlines to avoid compensation simply by rebooking passengers, even at the last minute. For delays, the compensation is only imposed after six hours compared to three in Europe.

A particularly powerful feature of the Bolivian law is its enforcement mechanism. While EU 261 is enforced by national authorities with varying sanctions, the Bolivian regulation explicitly outlines a sanctioning process for non-compliance. The fines, which are also a percentage of the ticket

---

52 Article 51.
53 Articles 52 and 53.
54 Article 62.
55 Article 78.

value, are paid directly to the passenger. This creates a strong incentive for airlines to comply with the compensation requirements, as a failure to do so results in a clear and immediate penalty for them and a benefit for the passenger. The concept of force majeure or unforeseen circumstances is not clearly defined.

Comparison with EU Regulation

Feature	**Bolivia Reglamento de Derechos y Deberes de los Usuarios del Transporte Aéreo**	**EU Regulation 261/2004**
Delay Compensation	>6 hrs: 25% of the ticket + care (meals/hotel).	≥3h: €250–600 (by distance).
Cancellation Rights	<14d notice: refund + re-routing + care. Compensation only if rebooking refused.	<14d notice: Refund or re-routing + €250–600 compensation (by distance).
Overbooking	Volunteers first; if denied boarding: alternative flight + 25% compensation.	Volunteer first; €250–€600 (by distance) if denied.
Baggage Compensation	Not specified.	Not specified.

Bibliography

Reglamento de Proteccion de los Derechos del Usuario de los servicios aéreo y aeroportuario <https://www.sea.gob.bo/digesto/CompendioII/F/41_REG.pdf>.

II.7

Bosnia and Herzegovina

Passenger rights are regulated under the Civil Aviation Contract Law in force since 2015.[1] This law incorporates provisions from the Montreal Convention and EU Regulation 261, which establish rules for compensation and assistance in cases of denied boarding, cancellations, or long delays as well as Regulation 1107/2006 concerning the rights of disabled persons and persons with reduced mobility.

The Civil Aviation Contract Law applies to passengers departing from an airport situated in the territory of Bosnia and Herzegovina or a signatory of the European Common Aviation Area (ECAA) Agreement and to passengers departing from an airport located in a third country to an airport situated in the territory of Bosnia and Herzegovina, unless they received benefits or compensation and were given assistance in that third country, if the operating air carrier of the flight concerned is a carrier from a state signatory of the ECAA Agreement.[2] The law does not apply to flights between two third-party countries. In order to invoke the provisions of the law, passengers are required to hold a confirmed reservation and present themselves for check-in in accordance with the procedures and at the time specified in advance and in writing by the air carrier, tour operator, or authorized travel agent. If no specific check-in time is provided, passengers must check in no later than 45 minutes prior to the published departure time.[3] The law is also applicable when the passenger has been transferred by an air carrier or tour operator from the flight for which they held a reservation to another flight, irrespective of the reason.[4] Like other regulations, this law does not apply to passengers travelling free of charge.[5]

---

1 Bosnia and Herzegovina Civil Aviation Contract Law, Official Gazette of BIH 51/15 of 29 June 2015 <http://www.bhdca.gov.ba/english/dokumenti/contract%20law.pdf>.
2 Article 3(1)(a) and (b).
3 Article 3(2)(a).
4 Article 3(2)(b).
5 Article 3(4).

DOI: 10.4324/9781003746164-18

Comparison of Scope of Application: EU Regulation 261/2004

Flight Scenario	Applies Under EU Regulation 261/2004?	Applies Under Bosnian Law?
Flight within the EU (e.g., Paris to Rome)	Yes.	No (Unless the flight also originates in Bosnia).
Flight departing from an EU country to a non-EU country (e.g., Germany to USA)	Yes.	No (Unless the flight originates in Bosnia).
Flight departing from a non-EU country to an EU country (e.g., USA to France)	Yes, **but with a condition.** Only if the passenger **did not already receive** compensation/benefits for the same disruption in the non-EU departing country.	No (Unless operated by a Bosnian carrier or with a final destination in Bosnia).
Flight departing from Bosnia and Herzegovina to an EU Member State (e.g., Sarajevo to Vienna)	Yes (Departure from an ECAA member).	Yes.
Flight departing from Bosnia and Herzegovina to another ECAA signatory (e.g., Sarajevo to Serbia)	Yes (Departure from an ECAA member).	Yes.
Flight departing from a third country with final destination in Bosnia and Herzegovina (e.g., Türkiye to Sarajevo)	No (Does not depart from an EU/ECAA state).	Yes (Final destination is key).
Flight operated by an EU carrier from a non-EU country to another non-EU country (e.g., Emirates flight from UAE to USA)	No (Neither departs from nor arrives in the EU/ECAA).	No.

As the Civil Aviation Contract Law not only embodies Regulation 261 but also the Montreal Convention of 1999, Chapter II relates to the contract of carriage itself. Chapter III relates to the liability of the carrier in the event of death or injury,[6] or damage to baggage.[7] The limit

6 Article 20.
7 Article 21.

established for delay of baggage is limited to 1,131 SDR.[8] Passengers can also claim for damage caused by delay up to 4,694 SDR in marks (BAM).[9]

In case of denial of boarding,[10] airlines must first request volunteers to surrender their seat in exchange for benefits under conditions they would agree on.[11] The volunteers are still entitled to assistance under Article 8. If an insufficient number of volunteers come forward to allow the remaining passengers with reservations to board the flight, the operating air carrier may then deny boarding to passengers against their will compensating them immediately in accordance with Article 32.[12] Passengers denied boarding against their will should be able either to cancel their flights, with reimbursement of their tickets, or to continue them under satisfactory conditions, and should be adequately cared for while awaiting a later flight. According to Berin Riđanović, an airline is legally justified in denying a passenger boarding without providing compensation if the passenger fails to meet specific requirements. These reasons include a lack of proper travel documents, such as a valid passport or ticket. Furthermore, a carrier may deny boarding on grounds of health or security risks, which includes a passenger's refusal to comply with mandatory public health measures.[13]

If a flight is cancelled, passengers have the right to a full refund or re-routing as well as assistance.[14] Passengers are entitled to compensation unless the airline informed them of the cancellation 14 days in advance or it is due to "extraordinary circumstances."[15] Just like Regulation 261, the law does not define the extraordinary circumstances and since, the preamble has not been incorporated in the law. However, it is clear that courts tend to follow the interpretations given by the CJEU.

Compensation is not granted if they were informed between two weeks and seven days and they were not offered a route change allowing them to depart not more than two hours before the original departure time and arrive four hours after the original arrival time.[16] Similarly, compensation is not due when passengers are informed less than seven days in advance and not offered a route change allowing them to depart not more than

8 Article 26(2).
9 Article 26(1).
10 Article 29.
11 Article 29(1).
12 Article 29(2) and (3).
13 Dr. sc. Berin Riđanović, 'Zaštita prava putnika u međunarodnom vazdušnom saobraćaju u Evropskoj uniji i Bosni i Hercegovini' (2021) LXIV Godišnjak Pravnog fakulteta u Sarajevu 227–70, 233.
14 Article 30(1)(a) and (b).
15 Article 30(1)(c) and (3).
16 Article 30(1)(c)(2).

one hour before the original departure time and arrive two hours after the original arrival time.[17]

When Cancelled	Compensation Due?
≥14 days before departure	No.
7–14 days before departure	No, if re-routing allows departure ≤2h earlier and arrival ≤4h later.
<7 days before departure	No, if re-routing allows departure ≤1h earlier and arrival ≤2h later.
<14 days notice + no suitable re-routing	Yes.

An airline is obligated to offer passengers specific assistance if it anticipates a flight will be delayed. What a passenger is entitled to depends entirely on the length of the delay and the flight distance. For short flights of 1,500 km or less, the airline must provide assistance after a two-hour delay. For medium-haul flights, within the ECAA area, between 1,500 and 3,500 km, this assistance is required after three hours. All other, longer flights trigger this right after a four-hour delay.[18] This assistance package includes meals, refreshments, and the ability to make two free phone calls, send emails, or telex messages. Furthermore, if the delay is so significant that the new departure time is on a different day, the airline is also required to provide passengers with hotel accommodation and transport to and from the hotel.[19] Finally, should the delay reach at least five hours, the passenger gains the right to cancel their trip and receive a full refund for any unused parts of their ticket.[20]

Passengers are entitled to a compensation of 250 euros payable in marks (BAM) for flights of a distance of up to 1,500 km.[21] For flights between 1,500 and 3,500 km, the amount increases to 400 euros as well as flights within the ECAA of more than 1,500 km.[22] Finally for flights over 3,500 km, the compensation is 600 euros.[23] The amount of compensation can be divided by two if passengers are offered an alternative flight which arrives at the final destination no later than two hours for flights of less than 1,500 km, three hours for flights between 1,500 and 3,500 km and

17 Article 30(1)(c)(3).
18 Article 31(1)(a), (b) and (c).
19 Article 34.
20 Article 31(1)(c)(3) in conjunction with Article 33(1)(a).
21 Article 32(1)(a).
22 Article 32(1)(b).
23 Article 32(1)(c).

all other flights within the ECAA and four hours for flights longer than 3,500 km.[24]

Situation	Airlines Obligation
Alternative flights less than 1,500 km arriving within 2 hours of the original time.	125 euros payable in marks (BAM).
Alternative flights between 1,500 km and 3,500 km or all other flights within the ECAA arriving within 3 hours of the original time.	200 euros payable in marks (BAM).
Alternative flights more than 3,500 km arriving within 4 hours of the original time.	300 euros payable in marks (BAM).

When an airline is responsible for a flight disruption, passengers are given the right to choose how they wish to proceed. They can either receive a full refund for the unused portions of their ticket within seven days and a return flight to their original departure point at the earliest opportunity, or they can be re-routed to their final destination.[25] This re-routing can happen at the earliest possible time or at a later date that is more convenient for them, depending on seat availability.[26] This right to a refund also applies to passengers who booked their flights as part of a package tour, unless the tour regulations state otherwise.[27] Additionally, if a city or region has multiple airports, the airline may offer a flight to a different, nearby airport, provided the passenger agrees to the change.[28]

During a flight disruption, airlines are obligated to provide passengers with free care.[29] This includes offering meals and refreshments that are appropriate for the length of the waiting time.[30] If the delay extends to the point where an overnight stay becomes necessary, the airline must also cover the cost of a hotel room and transport between the airport and the accommodation.[31] Furthermore, passengers are entitled to two free phone calls or emails.[32] It is also a requirement that the airline gives special consideration and attention to the needs of passengers with reduced mobility and children travelling alone.[33]

24 Article 32(4)(a), (b), and (c).
25 Article 33.
26 Article 33(1)(c).
27 Article 33(2).
28 Article 33(3).
29 Article 34.
30 Article 34(1)(a).
31 Article 34(1)(b) and (c).
32 Article 34(2).
33 Article 34(3).

If an airline upgrades a passenger to a higher class than what they paid for, they are not allowed to ask for any additional payment. Conversely, if a passenger is moved to a lower class than their purchased ticket, the airline must reimburse a percentage of the ticket cost within seven days. The refund amount is 30% for flights up to 1,500 km, 50% for flights between 1,500 and 3,500 km or flights within the ECAA of over 1,500 km, and 75% for all flights longer than that.[34]

Airlines are also under the obligation to inform passengers of their rights.[35] At the check-in area, they must prominently display a notice that tells passengers to ask for a document outlining their rights to compensation and assistance if their flight is denied boarding, cancelled, or delayed by at least two hours. Beyond this general notice, the airline must also provide a written document directly to every passenger affected by such a disruption. This notice must clearly detail the rules for receiving compensation and assistance as outlined in the regulation, and it must also include the contact information for the official body responsible for handling passenger complaints. For passengers who are blind or visually impaired, the airline must use a suitable alternative method to ensure they receive all the same information.[36] Article 44 lays down the notice that the carrier must provide passengers with which includes the compensation in case of death or injury, for passengers or baggage delays, complaint on baggage and time limit for the action, all based on the Montreal Convention. Such notice might actually be confusing for passengers as it does not include any fixed compensation as referred in the Civil Aviation Contract Law.

Chapter IV is dedicated to passengers with reduced mobility and disabled persons and is a direct adoption of the core provisions from EU Regulation 1107/2006. Air carriers must prioritize passengers with reduced mobility or disabilities, as well as their accompanying persons and unaccompanied children, during transport, boarding, and disembarking.[37] In cases of denied boarding, cancellation, or any length of delay, these passengers have the right to care.[38]

An air carrier or its agent cannot refuse to accept a reservation or deny boarding to a person with reduced mobility or a disability if they hold a valid ticket and reservation. However, they may refuse carriage if doing so

34 Article 35(2)(a), (b) and (c).
35 Article 38.
36 Article 38.
37 Article 53(1).
38 Article 53(2).

is necessary to meet safety requirements or if the size of the aircraft or its doors makes it physically impossible to board the person.[39] In such cases, the airline must try to offer an acceptable alternative.[40] If the person is denied boarding, they have the right to reimbursement or re-routing.[41] An airline may also require a disabled person to be accompanied by another person capable of providing necessary assistance, as long as it aligns with safety requirements.[42] Airlines must make their safety rules and any restrictions on carrying mobility equipment publicly available in accessible formats.

Airport managing bodies, in cooperation with relevant organizations, must designate specific points at the airport where people with reduced mobility can easily request and receive assistance. These points must be clearly marked and provide basic information in accessible formats.[43] Airlines, their agents, and tour operators are responsible for receiving notifications from passengers needing assistance and must transmit this information to the relevant airports and operating carriers at least 36 hours before departure if notified 48 hours in advance. For all other cases, the information should be transmitted as soon as possible.[44] Assistance must be provided even if the passenger did not give 48 hours' notice, although the airport is only required to make all reasonable efforts to provide it in such cases.

Airport managing bodies can charge airlines a fee to fund the assistance provided to passengers with reduced mobility.[45] This charge must be reasonable, cost-related, and transparent, and the funds must be used solely for this purpose, with separate accounting. With a few exceptions for small airports, airport managing bodies must establish quality standards for assistance in cooperation with airport users and disability organizations.[46] All airline and airport personnel who interact directly with the public must be trained on how to meet the needs of people with various disabilities and receive refresher courses as needed.[47] Articles 67 and 68 embody a detailed list of assistance required.

39 Article 55(1)(a) and (b).
40 Article 55(2).
41 Article 55(3).
42 Article 55(4).
43 Article 56.
44 Article 57.
45 Article 59(3) and 60(5).
46 Article 60(1).
47 Article 62.

Journey Stage	Type of Assistance to Be Provided
Arrival and Check-In	• Move from a designated point to the check-in counter. • Check-in and register baggage.
To the Gate	• Proceed from check-in to the aircraft, completing emigration, customs, and security.
Boarding	• Board the aircraft using lifts, wheelchairs, or other needed assistance.
Onboard the Aircraft	• Proceed from the aircraft door to their seat and back. • Store and retrieve carry-on baggage on the aircraft. • Move to the toilet facilities if required. • Efforts must be made to seat a PRM next to their companion.
De-planing	• Disembark from the aircraft using lifts, wheelchairs, or other needed assistance.
Arrival and Baggage	• Proceed from the aircraft to the baggage hall and retrieve checked baggage, completing immigration and customs. • Proceed from the baggage hall to a designated point.
Transit	• Reach connecting flights, with assistance on the air and land sides and between terminals as needed.
Assistance Dogs	• Ground handling and carriage of recognized assistance dogs in the cabin.

The law also contains fixed fines for an offence ranging from BAM 5,000 to 15,000.[48] Like in Montenegro, a tiered system of fines for violations of passenger rights is used. This penalty applies if airlines deny guaranteed rights and assistance to passengers in the event of a flight delay, denied boarding, or flight cancellation.[49] Fines are also issued if a carrier fails to make a compensation payment within 15 days of confirming a person's entitlement or if they do not provide a summary of their liability provisions to passengers during the ticket sale.[50] Additionally, denying rights and assistance to people with disabilities or reduced mobility is a punishable offense.[51] The responsible individual within the company can face a separate fine of BAM 1,000 to BAM 3,000, while a natural person involved can be fined BAM 500 to BAM 3,000.[52] An airport operator or other legal person can be fined from BAM 5,000 to BAM 15,000 for denying guaranteed rights and assistance to people with disabilities or

48 Article 121.
49 Article 121(1)(a).
50 Article 121(1)(b) and (c).
51 Article 121(1)(d).
52 Article 121(2) and (3).

reduced mobility.[53] The responsible person at the airport can be fined between BAM 1,000 and BAM 3,000, and any natural person involved can be fined BAM 500 to BAM 3,000.[54]

Offense Category	**Description of the Violation**	**Fine for the Air Carrier/ Airport Operator (Legal Entity)**	**Fine for the Responsible Person (e.g. Manager)**	**Fine for a Natural Person (e.g. Agent)**
Flight Disruptions and Passenger Rights (Air Carriers – Art. 121)	• Denying rights/ assistance for flight delays, denied boarding, or cancellations. • Failing to make a required advance payment for damages within 15 days. • Failing to inform passengers at sale about liability rules and claim deadlines.	5,000 to 15,000 BAM.	1,000 to 3,000 BAM.	500 to 3,000 BAM.
Rights of Persons With Reduced Mobility (PRMs)	• **Air Carrier (Art. 121):** denying rights/ assistance to disabled persons or persons with reduced mobility. • **Airport Operator (Art. 122):** denying rights/ assistance to disabled persons or persons with reduced mobility.	5,000 to 15,000 BAM.	1,000 to 3,000 BAM.	500 to 3,000 BAM.

Berin Riđanović identifies a significant problem for passengers in Bosnia and Herzegovina who wish to sue a foreign airline; airlines operating in Bosnia and Herzegovina often establish representative offices that, under BiH law, are not considered legal entities. This means they cannot be sued

53 Article 122(1).
54 Article 122(2) and (3).

directly.[55] Consequently, even if a passenger wins a case against a foreign airline in a Bosnian court, it is nearly impossible to enforce the judgment within the country because the airline does not have any assets there that can be legally seized.[56] Enforcement of the judgment would instead have to be sought in the country where the airline is based, which is a complicated and often impractical process for a passenger.

Bosnia and Herzegovina's Civil Aviation Contract Law represents a significant and commendable effort to harmonize national legislation with the European Union's *acquis communautaire* in the field of air passenger rights. The law is a comprehensive legal transplant, incorporating the core principles of both EU Regulation 261 and Regulation 1107/2006 into a single national framework, while also integrating the liability rules of the Montreal Convention of 1999. This creates a robust, self-contained code for air passenger rights. Its core provisions on compensation, re-routing, and assistance for denied boarding, cancellations, and long delays are the same. Both laws specify the same monetary compensation amounts (€250, €400, €600) based on flight distance and establish the same thresholds for triggering assistance (e.g., a three-hour delay for compensation). However, the omission of the preamble and the lack of inclusion of any definition of the concept of "extraordinary circumstance" makes the Civil Aviation Contract Law more uncertain. The law establishes a detailed, tiered system of administrative fines for violations (ranging from BAM 5,000 to 15,000 for legal entities), which applies to both airlines and airport operators. This provides a strong deterrent and a clear enforcement mechanism. In contrast, EU Regulation 261 delegates the setting of penalties to Member States, leading to a less consistent patchwork of sanctions across the EU.

However, its practical effectiveness is critically compromised by the enforcement loophole related to foreign carriers. Without a legal mechanism to easily enforce judgments against these airlines within Bosnia, the rights enshrined in the law risk becoming theoretical for a significant number of passengers. Addressing this jurisdictional and enforcement barrier is the single most important step needed to make this otherwise excellent law fully effective.

55 Dr. sc. Berin Riđanović, 'Zaštita prava putnika u međunarodnom vazdušnom saobraćaju u Evropskoj uniji i Bosni i Hercegovini,' Godišnjak Pravnog fakulteta u Sarajevu, LXIV – 2021., s. 227–270 260 et following.

56 Dr. sc. Berin Riđanović, 'Zaštita prava putnika u međunarodnom vazdušnom saobraćaju u Evropskoj uniji i Bosni i Hercegovini,' Godišnjak Pravnog fakulteta u Sarajevu, LXIV – 2021., s. 227–270, p.260 et following.

Comparison with EU Regulation

Feature	Civil Aviation Contract Law	EU Regulation 261/2004
Delay Compensation	≥3h: €250–€600 (by distance) in marks.	≥3h: €250–€600 (by distance).
Cancellation Notice	<14d notice: refund + re-routing + compensation.	<14d notice: Refund or re-routing + €250–600 compensation (by distance).
Denied Boarding	Volunteer first; €250–€600 (by distance) in marks if denied boarding.	Volunteer first; €250–€600 (by distance) if denied boarding.
Baggage Liability	€1,131.	Not specified.

Bibliography

- Bosnia and Herzegovina Civil Aviation Contract Law, Official Gazette of BIH 51/15 of 29 June 2015 <http://www.bhdca.gov.ba/english/dokumenti/contract%20law.pdf>.
- Riđanović, B., Dr. sc., 'Zaštita prava putnika u međunarodnom vazdušnom saobraćaju u Evropskoj uniji i Bosni i Hercegovini' (2021) LXIV Godišnjak Pravnog fakulteta u Sarajevu 227–70.

II.8

Brazil

Brazilian passenger rights are, in theory, primarily regulated by the National Civil Aviation Agency (ANAC) *Resolução* 400 of 2016[1] which supplements the *Código Brasileiro de Aeronáutica.*[2] In practice, however, passengers seem to rely more on the Brazilian Consumer Protection Code (*Codigo de Defesa do Consumidor*) or CDC[3] than the *Resolução* itself.[4] The sacrosanct prevalence of the Consumer Code could soon change depending on the outcome of the ruling of the Supreme Federal Tribunal (STF), in the so-called Theme 1417 whereby the Tribunal was asked in light of Article 178 of the Federal Constitution, whether air transport regulations prevail over consumer protection norms in governing civil liability for flight cancellations, changes, or delays due to fortuitous

1 Resolution 400/2016 <https://www.gov.br/anac/en/topics/air-services/files/resolution_400_2016_en_us.pdf> accessed 27 November 2025.

2 *Lei no. 7.565, de 19 December 1986. Articles 229–231 Código Brasileiro de Aeronáutica de 1986 contains some general provisions in respect to cancellation or delay. See: Ricardo Bernardi and Lucas Bernardes Augusto, 'Reform of the Brazilian Aeronautical Code' (Lexology, 28 January 2022) <https://www.lexology.com/library/detail.aspx?g=2cc4c97f-6f8e-4455-aa5e-bd521c5849f0> accessed 27 November 2025.*

3 Lei No. 8.078/90 de 11 September 1990. [hereinafter Consumer Code or CDC]. See: Adriana Tayano Fanton Furukawa, 'Responsabilidade civil contratual no transporte aéreo: hipóteses de não incidência à luz do Código de Defesa do Consumidor' 142 <https://www.tjsp.jus.br/download/EPM/Publicacoes/ObrasJuridicas/cdc6.pdf?d=636680533763406696> accessed 27 November 2025.

4 D. Defossez, 'The Excess of Judicialization and the Clinginess of Brazilian Courts to the Brazilian Consumer Protection Code' (2025) (1) Issues in Aviation Law and Policy 287; D Defossez and I Lopes Matos Carneiro de Farias, *Brazilian Civil Aviation Law* (Routledge 2025) ch 3; D Defossez, *The Law and Regulation of Airspace Liberalisation in Brazil: What Is the Way Forward?* (Routledge 2022).

DOI: 10.4324/9781003746164-19

events or force majeure.[5] This mirrors the STF's 2017 precedent, which established the supremacy of the Montreal Convention over the CDC.[6]

The *Resolução* applies to both domestic and international scheduled air transport, irrespective of the passenger nationality, and to non-scheduled flights when the seats are sold individually to the public.[7] However, the *Resolução* does not clarify if its scope covers all flights arriving in and departing from Brazil, irrespective of the carrier's nationality. However, it seems that Brazilian courts have taken the stand that *Resolução* 400 applies to any tickets bought in Brazil irrespective to where the assistance was required. In a 2020 case against Lufthansa, the Tribunal clearly weighed the lack of assistance – according to Brazilian standards – heavily in their final monetary award.[8] Similarly, in a case against Gol, the airline was found liable for not providing assistance while the cancelled flight was operated by KLM from Amsterdam to Stuttgart.[9] In a sense, those judgments highlight an understanding from Brazilian courts that ANAC *Resolução* 400 has an extraterritorial reach.

Airlines have the right to set their own prices and rules for services but must provide clear and easily understandable information about all offered services.[10] Interestingly, the *Resolução* includes a provision requiring airlines to offer passengers at least one ticket option where the penalty for a refund or rescheduling does not exceed 5% of the total air transport service value.[11]

Article 5 lists the minimum information the airline must provide to the passenger before payment is made, including the total fare with

---

5 STF, 'Tema 1417, Prevalência das normas sobre o transporte aéreo em relação às normas de proteção ao consumidor para disciplinar a responsabilidade civil por cancelamento, alteração ou atraso de voo por motivo de caso fortuito ou força maior' (ARE 1560244, Rel. Min. Dias Toffoli) <https://portal.stf.jus.br/jurisprudenciaRepercussao/verAndamentoProcesso.asp?incidente=7313323&numeroProcesso=1560244&classeProcesso=ARE&numeroTema=1417> accessed 27 November 2025.

On 26 November 2025, the STF suspended all judicial proceedings in the country regarding compensation for moral damages in air transport contracts, for domestic and international flights to avoid divergent decisions until the final judgment of the extraordinary appeal. However, a Tribunal in Rio Grande do Sul authorized the continuation of the compensation lawsuit against the airline for unscheduled aircraft maintenance which falls outside the suspension in its opinion. TJ RS/ 5108857-40.2026.8.21.7000/RS 8 April 2026.

6 Peter Macara and Alexandre Lima, 'The Brazilian Supreme Court Upholds the Application of the Warsaw and Montreal Conventions' (2018) 43 Air and Space Law 505.

7 Article 1.

8 Processo: 50001396-04.2020.8.24.0091/SC, Tribunal de Justiça do Estado de Santa Catarina, 27 April 2020.

9 Processo: 005809-83.2019.8.16.0001, Tribunal de Justiça do Estado do Parana, 10 March 2023.

10 Article 2. As reiterated in Article 4 which requires the total price to be paid by the consumer to be displayed only allowing opt-in as an increase on the final price (paragraph 2).

11 Article 3.

a breakdown of its components, rules and penalties for no-show, rescheduling, and refunds, connection times and potential airport changes, baggage rules and fees, and the airlines operating the flight in case of code-sharing.[12] Paragraph 2 prohibits charges for any optional service or product not actively requested by the user (opt-in). Paragraph 3 requires all information to be provided in Portuguese in a clear and objective manner. As found in many jurisdictions, the validity of the ticket is one year from the date of issue.[13]

Any errors in the passenger's name, surname, or alias must be corrected by the airline free of charge, unless it is an international flight involving different carriers and the error is not attributable to the carrier.[14]

Section III addresses Passenger-Initiated Contract Changes. Article 9 stipulates that contractual penalties cannot exceed the value of the air transport services, and airport and governmental fees cannot be included in the calculation of any penalties. Passengers are allowed to cancel the ticket without penalty within 24 hours of receiving the purchase confirmation, provided the purchase was made seven days or more before the departure date.[15]

Section IV deals with Carrier-Initiated Contract Changes. The *Resolução* establishes that passengers should be informed of any scheduled changes with a minimum of 72 hours' notice.[16] Any changes occurring less than 72 hours before the original departure, or if the change is greater than 30 minutes for domestic flights or one hour for international flights, the carrier must offer the passenger a choice of re-booking or a full refund.[17] This has resulted in a parallel business on social media showing passengers how to take advantage of this rule to then rebook the same flight at a date with higher price tag for free. If the passenger shows up at the airport due to a failure in providing this information, the carrier must offer material assistance and, at the passenger's choice, rebooking, a full refund, or execution of the service by another mode of transport.[18]

Chapter II, Section I covers Check-in and Boarding, including an article listing the required identification documents for domestic and international flights.[19] This chapter also contains passengers' obligation including presenting identification on time, adhering to visa or vaccination requirements and obeying carrier instructions. Any non-compliance with

12 Article 5(I)–(V).
13 Article 7.
14 Article 8 for the general rule and Article 8(2) and (3) for the exception.
15 Article 11.
16 Article 12.
17 Article 12(1)(I) and (II).
18 Article 12(2)(I)–(III).
19 Article 16.

such rules authorizes the airline to deny boarding and impose fines.[20] Finally, Article 19 contains a no-show provision allowing airlines to cancel the return segment of a round-trip ticket if the passenger does not use the outbound segment, unless the passenger informed the carrier. Yet again this rule has been bent by the judiciary.[21]

Section II addresses Delay, Cancellation, Service Interruption, and Denied Boarding. It first starts with an obligations on the carrier to immediately inform the passenger of a delay (with new time) or cancellation/interruption, and to provide updates on delays every 30 minutes.[22] The reason for the disruption must be provided in writing upon request. Airlines must offer a rebooking, a refund, or transport by another mode to the passenger in cases of flight delays over four hours, cancellations, service interruptions, denied boarding, or missing a connection due to the carrier's fault.[23] This offer must be offered immediately if the carrier knows in advance that the delay will exceed four hours. The refund must be integral if requested at the origin, stopover, or connection airport with assured return to origin in the latter two cases or proportional for the unused segment if the completed segment benefited the passenger.[24]

Denial of boarding is probably the easiest and less ambiguous aspects of passenger rights as it is regulated by straightforward rules. Denial of boarding is defined by Article 22 of ANAC *Resolução* 400 as "when a passenger shows up for boarding but is not allowed to occupy a seat on the aircraft, except for the cases provided for in *Resolução* No. 280, of 11th of July 2013." In the event of an overbooking, airlines must seek volunteers offering them rebooking with negotiated compensation – those passengers are then not considered denied boarding.[25] Despite being the result of many compromises, denial of boarding is the only disruption which is regulated by provisions mandating an immediate and fixed financial compensation.[26] Article 24 of the *Resolução* states that the airlines must compensate the passengers up to 250 SDR for domestic flights and 500 SDR for international flights.[27]

---

20 Article 18(I)–(III).

21 This rule has been deemed abusive in various cases: TJ-DF Apelaçao Civel no Juizado Especial, 1 December 2005, ACJ 20050110145947 DF; TJ-PR, Processo Civel e do Trabalho, 25 June 2015, Recursos RI 003490039201481601820 PR 003490039.2014.8.16.0182/0(Brazil); TJ-RJ, 14 October 2015, Recurso Inominado RI 00091142820148190208 RJ 0009114-28.2014.8.19.0208 (Brazil). See: D Defossez, 'No-Show Clauses: Are They Abusive under European Law or a Necessary Evil' (2016) XLI Annals of Air and Space Law.

22 Article 20.

23 Article 21.

24 Article 30.

25 Articles 23 and 24.

26 D. Defossez and I. Lopes Matos Carneiro de Farias, *Brazilian Civil Aviation Law* (Routledge, 2025).

27 Article 24(I) and (II).

This *Resolução* obliges airlines to provide means of communications, such as internet, phone calls or others to the passengers after one hour of delay, cancellation, or denial of boarding.[28] After two hours, catering should be offered, which needs to involve at least water and snacks or voucher or other.[29] After four hours, passengers should be taken to another facility or even provided accommodation.[30] The transportation to and from the local of accommodation is at the airlines' expense after four hours. Passengers with Special Needs (PNAE) must be provided accommodation after four hours regardless of whether an overnight stay is required.[31] If the passenger has his/her domicile in the city, the airline may only offer transportation between the passenger residence and the airport.[32] After four hours, passengers have the right to choose between a full refund or an alternative travel plan being with that company or another airline.[33] This *Resolução* also obliges airlines to inform the passengers every 30 minutes about the new estimated departure time.[34]

Hours of delay	**Assistance**
1-hour flight delay	Access to communication.
2-hour flight delay	Free food and refreshments.
4-hour flight delay	Alternative travel plan or refund.
4-hour flight delay (overnight)	Free accommodation + free transfer + alternative travel plan or refund.

Articles 229 to 231 *Código Brasileiro de Aeronáutica de 1986* contain some general provisions in respect to cancellation or delay. Article 229 stipulates that a passenger has the right to be reimbursed of the flight ticket in case of cancellation. Article 230 relates to delay of more than four hours and the obligation for airlines to offer rebooking or reimbursement based on the passenger's choice. Finally, Article 231 relates to delays during connecting flights of more than four hours. Unfortunately, the *Resolução* does not add much to the provisions of the CBA. Indeed, the *Resolução* is silent regarding compensation for delays or cancellations.[35] There is even an understanding that delays less than four hours are not compensable, according to Article 21 IV of *Resolução* 400 (already found in Article 3 of

28 Article 27(I).
29 Article 27(II).
30 Article 27(III).
31 Article 27(2).
32 Article 27(1).
33 Article 21(I).
34 Article 20(1).
35 Article 25 only clarifies that those are contingent on the day of the flight and distinct from planned scheduled changes.

the ANAC *Resolução* 141 of 2010). Airlines are only required to rebook the passengers on a later flight.[36] While some judgments reflect this passive understanding, most tribunals have awarded moral damages in case of delays under four hours.[37]

Responsible Party	**Situation/Condition**	**Key Rules and Passenger Rights**
Passenger	Voluntary cancellation (refund request).	• **24-hour free cancellation:** full refund without penalty. • **After 24 hours:** a cancellation penalty may be applied.
Airline	Cancellation by airline **(>72 hours' notice).**	The airline must immediately offer the passenger a choice of the following alternatives: • Rebooking. • Full Refund. • Alternative Transport.
Airline	Cancellation by airline **(with short or no notice).**	In addition to the standard alternatives (rebooking/refund), the airline must provide **Material Assistance** if the cancellation causes a long wait: • **Meals/Vouchers:** provided if the wait exceeds 2 hours. • **Hotel/Transport:** provided if the wait causes an overnight stay (exemption for passengers residing in the departure city).

36 TJSC, Processo: 0303994-53.2014.8.24.0090, Pedro Mello e Cruz x Gol Linhas Aéreas Inteligentes S.A; TJDFT, Processo nº 0706283-57.2018.8.07.0014. Daniel Duarte Abiorana x Gol Linhas Aereas Inteligentes S.A., julg. 19 February 2019. See: Tadeu Rover, 'Atraso de até 4 horas em voo é tolerável e não gera dever de indenizar' (*Consultor Juridico*, 19 February 2019) <https://www.conjur.com.br/2019-fev-19/atraso-horas-voo-toleravel-nao-gera-indenizacao> accessed 27 November 2025.

37 TJDFT, Processo nº 0706283-57.2018.8.07.0014. Daniel Duarte Abiorana x Gol Linhas Aereas Inteligentes S.A., julg. 19 February 2019. See: Tadeu Rover, 'Atraso de até 4 horas em voo é tolerável e não gera dever de indenizar' (*Consultor Juridico*, 19 February 2019) <https://www.conjur.com.br/2019-fev-19/atraso-horas-voo-toleravel-nao-gera-indenizacao> accessed 27 November 2025. In December 2025, the STJ established that moral damages for flight delays or cancellations are not presumed (*dano in re ipsa*). Passengers must now prove actual damages to receive compensation, moving away from previous automatic compensation practices. Resp 2.232.322, *Latam v Jorge Dalben*, MT (2025/0193367-3), 1 December 2025.

For the awards see: Defossez, D., 'The Excess of Judicialization and the Clinginess of Brazilian Courts to the Brazilian Consumer Protection Code' (2025) (1) Issues in Aviation Law and Policy 287; Defossez, D. and Lopes Matos Carneiro de Farias, I., *Brazilian Civil Aviation Law* (Routledge, 2025).

Resolução 400 is silent regarding downgrading. However, following a rather mediatic case, a Bill – Projeto de Lei 883/2025 – was introduced in March 2025, informally known as the "Lei Ingrid Guimarães," to regulate involuntary downgrading in commercial flights in Brazil.[38] The proposal seeks to guarantee automatic financial compensation and strict sanctions for airlines that fail to comply with the rules, strengthening consumer rights in the airline sector. Moreover, the law would prohibit rebooking without the passenger's prior consent, which would mean that involuntary downgrading would be prohibited by law.[39] This new rule raises the question of the logistics of its application. Indeed, if all passengers are Brazilians and not a sufficient number of them agree to be downgraded, the flight will not be able to depart resulting in a potential cancellation and many more lawsuits claiming moral damages.[40]

Another aspect which is unclear is that Article 1 limits the scope of the law to downgrading on commercial flight in Brazil. However, Article 3 (II) listing the automatic compensation mentions that such compensation must be calculated at 100% of the ticket price for domestic flights and 200% for international flights. The two provisions seem, therefore, at odds; why grant automatic compensation for international flights if the law is supposed to only apply to commercial flights in Brazil?

Instead of automatic compensation, the Bill also allows airlines to offer a flight in the same class within four hours and offer any appropriate material assistance (e.g., food, transport, accommodation) as per National Civil Aviation Agency (ANAC) regulations.[41] However, the law does not exclude any potential claims resulting from the four-hour delay. Due to the current framework in Brazil, it is totally envisioned that passengers could then start a lawsuit for the inconvenience caused by the delay.[42] Non-compliance with this proposed law could result in administrative

38 Article 1.

39 Republicanos, 'Voos: Ely Santos propõe indenização para passageiros rebaixados de classe sem consentimento' (12 March 2025) <https://republicanos10.org.br/republicanos-na-camara/voos-ely-santos-propoe-indenizacao-para-passageiros-rebaixados-de-classe-sem-consentimento/?app=Avant_Empresa_3abfbe32310a3ce3711b848c3f3290e9&ref=null&tipo_1=sim&tipo_2=nao&tipo_3=nao&tipo_4=nao&tipo_5=nao&preferencia_marcada=Salvar+minhas+escolhas&key_avant_valid_preference=96067c3cc56d636f87a2e3d603611a2d> accessed 27 November 2025.

40 D. Defossez, 'Downgrading Passengers in Brazil: or When One Poorly Handled Situation Leads into Potential New Laws' (2025) Annals of Air and Space Law Commentaries <https://www.mcgill.ca/iasl/article/downgrading-passengers-brazil-when-one-situation-leads-potential-new-laws> accessed 27 November 2025.

41 Article 3(I) and (III).

42 Although moral damages must be causa re ipsa, Brazilian courts have interpreted such requirement loosely. D. Defossez, 'The Excess of Judicialization and the Clinginess of Brazilian Courts to the Brazilian Consumer Protection Code' (2025) (1) Issues in Aviation Law and Policy 287.

fines of up to R$50,000 (approximately £8,000) per infraction,[43] suspension of the operating license in cases of serious recidivism,[44] and full reimbursement to passengers if they refuse reaccommodation.[45] ANAC will be responsible for inspecting the companies and applying the penalties.[46] Alongside this proposal, on 20 March 2025, another Bill was presented by Senator Eliziane Gama in the Senate.[47] This complementary Bill seeks to directly amend the *Código Brasileiro de Aeronáutica* (Brazilian Aeronautical Code) to prohibit any involuntary downgrading without the passenger consent.[48] The proposal also includes a fine for airlines that expose passengers to embarrassment by refusing to change seats without stipulating any maximum amount.[49] The Bill also seeks to guarantee passengers the right to compensation when there is a downgrade without giving any specific figure.[50] The major difference between the two proposals is that PL 1149/2025 expressly stipulates that – with the passenger's consent – passengers should be first upgraded.[51]

Chapter IV covers User Service. Article 37 requires the carrier to provide in-person attendance at the airport to handle information requests, complaints, and duties related to flight delays, cancellations, interruptions, and denied boarding. This service must operate for at least two hours before each take-off and two hours after each landing and continue as long as necessary during disruptions. However, smaller carriers transporting less than 1 million passengers in the previous year can offer telephone customer service during business hours on days they operate flights in Brazil.[52]

The *Resolução* is also very generous regarding the timeframe to initiate a claim which is five years for domestic flights and two years for international ones. It also contains a Section on baggage, which provides that passengers are entitled to a minimum free hand baggage allowance of 10 kg per passenger, which can only be restricted for security or aircraft capacity reasons.[53] Unless passengers make a Special Declaration of Value for checked baggage, the standard liability limit of 1,131 Special Drawing

43 Article 4(I).

44 Article 4(II).

45 Article 4(III).

46 Article 5.

47 Projeto de Lei n° 1149, de 2025. This Bill is currently in its initial legislative stages within the Senate.

48 Article 1 which would introduce Article 223-A in Lei 7.565/1986.

49 Proposed Article 223-A(3).

50 Proposed Article 223-A(2).

51 Proposed Article 223-A(1).

52 Article 36.

53 Article 14. There has been major debate regarding the free checked baggage allowance. See: D. Defossez, *The Law and Regulation of Airspace Liberalisation in Brazil: What Is the Way Forward?* (Routledge 2022).

Rights (SDRs) applies – at least in theory as many cases allowed much higher limits through moral damages.[54] In case of loss, the baggage must be returned within seven days for domestic or 21 days for international flights, and if not found, the carrier must pay compensation within seven days.[55] Airlines must reimburse necessary expenses for lost baggage while the passenger is away from home.[56] However, the *Resolução* does not include any limitation or daily maximum amount which is left to airlines to establish but is often disregarded by tribunals.[57]

Non-compliance with the *Resolução* will be characterized as a breach in the meaning of Article 302, item III, subitem "u," of Law No. 7,565, of 19 December 1986.[58] The fine will vary between R$20,000 and R$50,000. The *Resolução* does not include any exemption of liability, although Act of God and force majeure are both accepted defences in the Civil Code[59] and the Brazilian Aeronautical Code (CBA). While the CBA did not define force majeure and Act of God, a definition was included by the new law under Article 256(3) of *Lei* 14.034 amending the CBA. Their application is restricted to four situations: landing or take-off restrictions due to adverse meteorological conditions imposed by an airspace control system agency; restrictions due to unavailability of the airport infrastructure; restrictions to flight, landing, or take-off resulting from a decisions by the civil aviation authority or any other authority or agency of the Public Administration; and finally, pandemic or publication of governmental acts aiming at preventing or restricting air transportation or airport activities.[60]

Infraction Severity	**Fine Value (in Brazilian Reais)**
Minimum Fine	R$20,000.
Intermediate Fine	R$35,000.
Maximum Fine	R$50,000.

Airlines may now also denied boarding or remove unruly passengers-individuals whose conduct undermines flight safety, disrupts public order, or violates the fundamental dignity of crew members and fellow travelers-

54 Article 17 and D. Defossez, 'The Excess of Judicialization and the Clinginess of Brazilian Courts to the Brazilian Consumer Protection Code' (2025) (1) Issues in Aviation Law and Policy 287.

55 Article 32(2)(I) and (II).

56 Article 33.

57 D. Defossez, 'The Excess of Judicialization and the Clinginess of Brazilian Courts to the Brazilian Consumer Protection Code' (2025) (1) Issues in Aviation Law and Policy 287.

58 Article 43.

59 Article 398.

60 One case on the Covid-19 pandemic: TJDFT, 07371615120218070016, Rel: Daniel Felipe Machado, Terceira Turma Recursal dos Juizados Especiais do Distrito Federal, julg. 23 February 2022.

under the new ANAC *Resolução* No. 800 of 2026.[61] The resolution's mandate extends to all domestic scheduled air transport operations, including international flights having a connection in Brazil.[62] Crucially, its jurisdiction encompasses the premises of Brazilian airports, including the processing areas for international flights situated within national territory.[63] This ensures a seamless transition of authority from ground-side security to inflight enforcement.

The framework adopts a progressive enforcement model, categorizing disruptive behaviours and corresponding administrative sanctions based on the severity of the threat. The scale of intervention is ranging from a formal warning, through restraint and removal of the passenger[64], to suspension of the passenger's access to air travel for 6 to 12 months in extremely serious cases such as physical assault[65], bomb threats, or attempted cabin intrusion. In addition to the temporary ban, ANAC may impose administrative fines of up to R$ 17,500.00 depending on the severity of the offense and the passenger's history of recurrence.[66] Airlines can also face fines for failure to maintain records, allow the right to full defence to unruly passengers, maintain a mechanism for the simultaneous sharing of identification data of unruly passengers. The provisions of *Resolução* No. 800 will become enforceable on 14 September 2026.[67]

Description of Conduct	**Provision of Resolution 800**	**Fine (BRL)**
Failure to apply a suspension of access to air transport to a passenger who committed an act of 'extremely serious' indiscipline.	Art. 3, §1, II	70,000 per occurrence.
Failure to inform ANAC.	Art. 4, items I, II, and III	17,500 (if reported late) 35,000 (if the operator fails to report).
Failure to maintain records.	Art. 5	17,500 per occurrence.
Failure to allow the right to full defence (ampla defesa) to the unruly passenger during the application of the suspension of access to air transport.	Art. 6, §2	35,000 per occurrence.

(*Continued*)

61 Article 2 and Annex I.
62 Article 1.
63 Article 1.
64 Article 6.
65 Article 7.
66 Article 9 and Annex II.
67 Article 13 II.

(Continued)

Description of Conduct	Provision of Resolution 800	Fine (BRL)
Failure to establish and maintain a mechanism for the simultaneous sharing of identification data of unruly passengers.	Art. 6, §3	70,000 per month of non-compliance.
Failure to respect the duration of 6 or 12 months.	Art. 7, caput	35,000 per occurrence.
Failure to communicate or present the minimum required information to the unruly passenger when applying the suspension of access to air transport.	Art. 8, §1	35,000 per occurrence.
Failure to respond to an unruly passenger's complaint within the 5-day deadline.	Art. 8, §3	17,500 per occurrence.
Failure to immediately remove a passenger's name from the list of persons with suspended access to air transport.	Art. 8, §4	35,000 per occurrence.

Brazilian passenger rights law, primarily embodied in ANAC *Resolução* 400/2016, reveals a system that is theoretically comprehensive in its scope and detailed in its procedural requirements, yet marked by significant practical and legal ambiguities that create a complex landscape for both passengers and airlines. The framework applies to both domestic and international transport for tickets purchased in Brazil, with Brazilian courts demonstrating a tendency to apply its provisions extraterritorially.

A particularly passenger-friendly feature is the mandate for airlines to offer at least one ticket option with a refund or rescheduling penalty not exceeding 5%, a provision rarely seen in other jurisdictions. The system differentiates clearly between passenger and carrier-initiated changes; passengers benefit from a 24-hour grace period for free cancellation and capped penalties, while airlines are obliged to provide 72 hours' notice for schedule changes or else offer rebooking or a full refund. In operational disruptions, the law mandates a graduated system of care: communication after one hour of delay, meals after two, and accommodation and transport after four hours. For cancellations, denied boarding, or delays over four hours, passengers are granted a choice between rebooking, a full refund, or alternative transport.

However, the system contains critical gaps and inconsistencies compared to Regulation 261. The most significant difference lies in the approach to compensation. Regulation 261 establishes a fixed, automatic compensation ladder for denied boarding, cancellations, and long delays (€250, €400, or €600) based on flight distance and delay length, subject to a narrow exemption for "extraordinary circumstances." In stark contrast, Brazilian law provides no statutory compensation for delays or cancellations, only mandating care and re-routing options. However, this legal vacuum has been filled by Brazilian courts inconsistently, with many awarding moral damages even for delays under four hours despite the regulatory silence.

The legal framework is further complicated by a proposed "Lei Ingrid Guimarães" to address the current silence on involuntary downgrading. This proposal, while well-intentioned, introduces potential logistical nightmares, such as flight cancellations if insufficient passengers volunteer for downgrading, and contains internal contradictions by potentially applying its international compensation rules to a law supposedly limited to domestic flights. Furthermore, the generous five-year limitation period for domestic claims and the lack of a defined daily maximum for baggage expense reimbursements, leaving it to airlines whose limits are often disregarded by courts, contribute to a legally uncertain environment.

Ultimately, Regulation 261 presents a more unified and predictable regime with its automatic compensation scheme, whereas the Brazilian framework, while strong on transparency and immediate care, creates a more litigious environment where passengers must seek redress for operational failures through the courts under the Consumer Protection Code, leading to less predictable outcomes and a heavier reliance on the judiciary to define and enforce passenger rights.

Comparison with EU Regulation

Feature	Resolution 400 of 2016	EU Regulation 261/2004
Delay Compensation	Not stipulated.	≥3h: €250–€600 (by distance).
Cancellation Notice	Not stipulated.	<14d notice: Refund or re-routing + €250–600 compensation (by distance).
Denied Boarding	Volunteer first; 250 SDR for domestic – 500 for international if denied boarding.	Volunteer first; €250–€600 (by distance) if denied boarding.
Baggage Liability	SDR 1,131.	Not specified.

Bibliography

Primary Sources

- *Latam v Jorge Dalben*, MT (2025/0193367-3), 1 December 2025.
- Lei no. 7.565, de 19.12.1986.
- Lei No. 8.078/90 de 11.09.1990.

- Processo: 50001396-04.2020.8.24.0091/SC, Tribunal de Justiça do Estado de Santa Catarina, 27 April 2020.
- Processo: 005809-83.2019.8.16.0001, Tribunal de Justiça do Estado do Parana, 10 March 2023.
- Projeto de Lei n° 1149 de 2025, Altera a Lei n° 7.565, de 19 de dezembro de 1986 (Código Brasileiro de Aeronáutica), para proteger usuários de serviço de transporte aéreo quanto ao remanejamento involuntário de assento adquirido.
- Resolution 400/2016 <https://www.gov.br/anac/en/topics/air-services/files/resolution_400_2016_en_us.pdf> accessed 27 November 2025.
- STF, 'Tema 1417, Prevalência das normas sobre o transporte aéreo em relação às normas de proteção ao consumidor para disciplinar a responsabilidade civil por cancelamento, alteração ou atraso de voo por motivo de caso fortuito ou força maior' (ARE 1560244, Rel. Min. Dias Toffoli) <https://portal.stf.jus.br/jurisprudenciaRepercussao/verAndamentoProcesso.asp?incidente=7313323&numeroProcesso=1560244&classeProcesso=ARE&numeroTema=1417> accessed 27 November 2025.
- TJDFT, 07371615120218070016, Rel: Daniel Felipe Machado, Terceira Turma Recursal dos Juizados Especiais do Distrito Federal, julg. 23/02/2022.
- TJDFT, Processo n° 0706283–57.2018.8.07.0014.
- TJ-DF Apelaçao Civel no Juizado Especial, 1 December 2005, ACJ 20050110145947 DF.
- TJ-PR, Processo Civel e do Trabalho, 25 June 2015, Recursos RI 003490039201481601820 PR 003490039.2014.8.16.0182/0.
- TJ-RJ, 14 October 2015, Recurso Inominado RI 00091142820148190208 RJ 0009114–28.2014.8.19.0208.
- TJ-SC, Processo: 0303994–53.2014.8.24.0090, Pedro Mello e Cruz x Gol Linhas Aéreas Inteligentes S.A.

Secondary Sources

- Bernardi, R. and Augusto, L. B., 'Reform of the Brazilian Aeronautical Code' (*Lexology*, 28 January 2022) <https://www.lexology.com/library/detail.aspx?g=2cc4c97f-6f8e-4455-aa5e-bd521c5849f0> accessed 27 November 2025.
- Defossez, D., 'Downgrading Passengers in Brazil: Or When One Poorly Handled Situation Leads into Potential New Laws' (2025) Annals of Air and Space Law Commentaries <https://www.mcgill.ca/iasl/article/downgrading-passengers-brazil-when-one-situation-leads-potential-new-laws> accessed 27 November 2025.
- Defossez, D., 'The Excess of Judicialization and the Clinginess of Brazilian Courts to the Brazilian Consumer Protection Code' (2025) (1) Issues in Aviation Law and Policy 287.
- Defossez, D., *The Law and Regulation of Airspace Liberalisation in Brazil: What Is the Way Forward?* (Routledge 2022).
- Defossez, D., 'No-Show Clauses: Are They Abusive Under European Law or a Necessary Evil' (2016) XLI Annals of Air and Space Law.
- Defossez, D. and Lopes Matos Carneiro de Farias, I., *Brazilian Civil Aviation Law* (Routledge 2025).

- Macara, P. and Lima, A., 'The Brazilian Supreme Court Upholds the Application of the Warsaw and Montreal Conventions' (2018) 43 Air and Space Law 505.
- Furukawa, A. T. F., 'Responsabilidade civil contratual no transporte aéreo: hipóteses de não incidência à luz do Código de Defesa do Consumidor' <https://www.tjsp.jus.br/download/EPM/Publicacoes/ObrasJuridicas/cdc6.pdf?d=636680533763406696> accessed 27 November 2025.
- Rover, T., 'Atraso de até 4 horas em voo é tolerável e não gera dever de indenizar' (*Consultor Juridico*, 19 February 2019) <https://www.conjur.com.br/2019-fev-19/atraso-horas-voo-toleravel-nao-gera-indenizacao> accessed 27 November 2025.
- Republicanos, 'Voos: Ely Santos propõe indenização para passageiros rebaixados de classe sem consentimento' (12 March 2025) <https://republicanos10.org.br/republicanos-na-camara/voos-ely-santos-propoe-indenizacao-para-passageiros-rebaixados-de-classe-sem-consentimento/?app=Avant_Empresa_3abfbe32310a3ce3711b848c3f3290e9&ref=null&tipo_1=sim&tipo_2=nao&tipo_3=nao&tipo_4=nao&tipo_5=nao&preferencia_marcada=Salvar+minhas+escolhas&key_avant_valid_preference=96067c3cc56d636f87a2e3d603611a2d> accessed 27 November 2025.

II.9

Cabo Verde

Air passenger rights in Cabo Verde are primarily regulated by Decree-Law no. 35/2006, of 26 June 2006, which establishes the rights of air passengers in cases of being denied boarding, flight cancellations, and significant flight delays.[1] The Cabo Verde Civil Aviation Agency (AAC) recently also updated those rules related to transparency in the marketing process and characteristics of a ticket through Regulation No. 1/AAC/2025 of March 2025.[2]

The Decree-Law applies to passengers departing from an airport located in Cabo Verde and passengers arriving in Cabo Verde when the operating carrier is a national carrier – unless those passengers have already received benefits or compensation in that third country.[3] The law applies to passengers with a confirmed reservation who present themselves for check-in as indicated by the carrier or up to 45 minutes before the published departure time – unless the flight was cancelled.[4] Exceptions are made for passengers travelling free or on reduced-fare tickets not publicly available.[5]

Chapter II is central to the law, detailing the rights in specific situations. When an airline anticipates denied boarding, they must first appeal to volunteers to surrender their reservations in exchange for agreed-upon

1 Decreto-Lei n°35:2006 de 26 Junho 2006, Boletim Oficial Numero 18, p.477 <https://passageiro.aac.cv/doc/dl-35-2006-26-jun.pdf>.

The Montreal Convention was implemented through Resolution No. 103/VII/2004, 21st of June 2004 Approves, for Adherence, the Convention for the Unification of Certain Rules for International Carriage by Air, signed at Montreal on 28 May 1999 – Official Gazette No. 19.

2 Agencia da aviaçao civil, Regulamento n° 01/AAC/2025, Aprovando o regulamento que fixa as condições gerais de transporte atinentes à comercialização e às características do bilhete de passage, 6 Março 2025 <https://passageiro.aac.cv/doc/rg-1-aac-25-6-mar.pdf>.

3 Article 3(1)(a) and (b).

4 Article 3(2)(a)(i) and (ii).

5 Article 3(3).

DOI: 10.4324/9781003746164-20

benefits and the assistance.[6] In the event insufficient volunteers are found, the carrier may involuntarily deny boarding but must then provide assistance and reimbursement or re-routing.[7]

In case of flight cancellation, passengers have the right to assistance and, unless informed well in advance with suitable re-routing options, to seek compensation, as per Article 7.[8] When airlines informed passengers at least two weeks before the scheduled departure, they are exempted from the obligation to compensate.[9] Similarly, when passengers were informed between two weeks and seven days before the scheduled departure and were offered re-routing that allowed them to depart no more than two hours before the original time and arrive at their final destination no more than four hours after the original arrival time.[10] Finally, when passengers were informed less than seven days before the scheduled departure and were offered re-routing that allowed them to depart no more than one hour before the original time and arrive no more than two hours after the original arrival time, no compensation is due.[11] Those are exactly the same exemptions as found under Regulation 261. Additionally, the airline is not obligated to pay compensation if it can prove the cancellation was due to extraordinary circumstances that could not have been avoided.[12] However, the term is nowhere defined.

When a carrier anticipates a flight delay of two hours or more it must offer passengers assistance including refreshments and communication.[13] Furthermore, if the reasonably expected time of departure is at least the day after the originally announced departure time, the carrier must also provide hotel accommodation and transport.[14] For delays of at least four hours, the right to a refund or re-routing is activated.[15]

The assistance mandated in these scenarios is detailed in Article 8. This includes free meals and drinks in reasonable relation to the waiting time,

6 Article 4(1).
7 Article 4(2) and (3).
8 Article 5(1)(a)–(c).
9 Article 5(1)(c)(i).
10 Article 5(1)(c)(ii).
11 Article 5(1)(c)(iii).
12 Article 5(3).
13 Article 6(1)(a).
14 Article 6(1)(b).
15 Article 6(1)(c). See: Carla Monterio, 'Civil Liability of Air Carriers in Cape Verde for Flight Delays' (*CMALEX*, 25 November 2021) <https://cmalex.net/civil-liability-of-air-carriers-in-cape-verde-for-flight-delays/> accessed 28 November 2025.

hotel accommodation, airport-hotel transfers if necessary, and two free telephone calls, faxes, or emails. Article 10 reinforces that persons with reduced mobility and unaccompanied minors must be given priority and receive all necessary assistance without delay.

Downgrading entitles the passenger to a reimbursement of the price difference in addition to compensation equivalent to 25% of the ticket price.[16] This provision is definitely a departure from EU Regulation 261. Similarly, the Decree-Law does not stipulate any fixed compensation but instead clarifies that receiving the assistance does not preclude passengers from seeking further damages in court based on general law, except for passengers who voluntarily accepted to surrender their reservations.[17]

The departure from Regulation 261 is even more visible in Chapter III dedicated to breach of contract and rights of air carriers. This chapter establishes that a passenger who does not show up or arrives late for embarkation, unless they cancelled the reservation at least 24 hours in advance, is not entitled to a refund, although an exception applies to same-day domestic return flights.[18] In those circumstances and if the aircraft departs full, the carrier must reimburse 80% of the ticket price.[19]

The Decree-Law contains a detailed list of fines for operating air carriers that violate the law's provisions. Fines are categorized into three tiers based on severity, ranging from $200,000 to $5,000,000.[20] The most severe infractions, listed in Paragraph 1, are punishable by a fine ranging from $500,000 to $5,000,000 and relate to failing to provide required assistance and any violation of passenger rights in case of delays or cancellation. Paragraph 2 outlines infractions subject to a fine of $300,000 to $3,000,000 which includes not calling for volunteers or failure to reimburse the price difference in case of downgrading. Finally, Paragraph 3 specifies infractions related to missed payment deadlines, punishable by a fine of $200,000 to $2,000,000.

16 Article 9(2).
17 Article 11.
18 Article 12(1).
19 Article 12(2) and (3).
20 Article 15.

Fine Amount (CVE)	Description/Potential Violations
$500,000 to $5,000,000	**Tier 1: Serious Violations of Core Passenger Rights** • Denying assistance and benefits to volunteers who give up their seats. • Failing to provide assistance to passengers denied boarding against their will. • Violating passenger rights in case of flight cancellation. • Violating passenger rights in case of flight delay. • Failing to give priority boarding to persons with reduced mobility, their companions, or assistance dogs, and unaccompanied children. • Failing to provide required assistance to persons with reduced mobility and unaccompanied children during any denial of boarding, cancellation, or delay.
$300,000 to $3,000,000	**Tier 2: Procedural and Secondary Violations** • Failing to first call for volunteers before denying boarding. • Not providing detailed explanations on alternative transport after a cancellation. • Failing to provide delay assistance within the stipulated timeframes. • Demanding extra payment when placing a passenger in a higher class. • Failing to reimburse the price difference plus 25% compensation after a downgrade. • Failing to provide a leaflet with the aviation authority's contact details to affected passengers. • Failing to display a visible notice on passenger rights at check-in counters. • Failing to distribute a leaflet with the assistance rules to affected passengers. • Refusing to provide information in accessible formats for blind and visually impaired passengers.
$200,000 to $2,000,000	**Tier 3: Administrative Violations – Missed Deadlines** • Missing the 7-day deadline for the full ticket reimbursement after a cancellation or significant delay. • Missing the 7-day deadline for the reimbursement and compensation payment after a downgrade.

Cabo Verde's Decree-Law No. 35/2006 is a passenger-centric framework, which mainly mirrors Regulation 261 in the core rights. The law's major strength lies in its clarity and comprehensiveness regarding operational assistance, mandating carriers to provide meals, accommodation, and communication and offering the crucial choice between reimbursement and re-routing in cases of cancellation, long delay (four hours or more), or involuntary denied boarding. While the structure of rights is nearly identical, covering assistance, re-routing, reimbursement, the Decree-Law goes a step further by including a provision on no-show of passengers and a remarkably precise list of fines.

The most significant difference is the mandatory financial compensation under EC 261. While both laws require carriers to offer care, assistance, and re-routing/reimbursement, EC 261 goes further by requiring the airline to pay a non-negotiable, fixed sum of money (€250–€600) to the passenger for the mere fact of the significant inconvenience caused by a long delay or cancellation, unless it's due to extraordinary circumstances. In contrast, under DL 35/2006, a Cabo Verdean passenger facing a disruption must rely on Article 11 to seek compensation for damages through the courts, a more cumbersome and uncertain legal process.

In conclusion, Decree-Law No. 35/2006 is a well-crafted and assertive piece of consumer protection legislation. It successfully transplants the core principles of EU Regulation 261 into the Cabo Verdean legal system while introducing refinements, particularly in its detailed sanctioning system.

Comparison with EU Regulation

Feature	Decree-Law No. 35/2006	EU Regulation 261/2004
Delay Compensation	No compensation.	≥3h: €250–€600 (by distance).
Cancellation Notice	Not stipulated.	<14d notice: Refund or re-routing + €250–600 compensation (by distance).
Denied Boarding	Volunteer first; re-routing and care.	Volunteer first; €250–€600 (by distance) if denied boarding.
Baggage Liability	Not specified.	Not specified.

Bibliography

- Decreto-Lei n°35:2006 de 26 Junho 2006, Boletim Oficial Numero 18, p.477 <https://passageiro.aac.cv/doc/dl-35-2006-26-jun.pdf> accessed 28 November 2025.
- Resolution No. 103/VII/2004, 21st of June 2004, Approves, for Adherence, the Convention for the Unification of Certain Rules for International Carriage by Air, signed at Montreal on 28 May 1999 – Official Gazette No. 19.
- Agencia da aviaçao civil, Regulamento n° 01/AAC/2025, Aprovando o regulamento que fixa as condições gerais de transporte atinentes à comercialização e às características do bilhete de passage, 6 Março 2025. <https://passageiro.aac.cv/doc/rg-1-aac-25-6-mar.pdf> accessed 28 November 2025.
- Monterio, C., 'Civil Liability of Air Carriers in Cape Verde for Flight Delays' (*CMALEX*, 25 November 2021) <https://cmalex.net/civil-liability-of-air-carriers-in-cape-verde-for-flight-delays/> accessed 28 November 2025.

II.10

Canada

Canada's Air Passenger Protection Regulations (APPR) came into force in 2019 and were introduced to provide a clear, comprehensive, and consistent set of passenger rights.[1] Its enactment was the result of an increase of 950% in passengers' complaints since 2012.[2] This legislation can be regarded as EU Regulation 261 2.0 as the Canadian legislator has tried to cure some of the defects found in the EU legislation. Unlike its EU counterpart, the APPR have been updated in 2022 with the latest proposed amendments dating back to December 2024 aiming at tightening any loopholes to passenger compensation as well as increase the potential penalties.[3]

Similarly to Regulation 261, questions have been raised as to whether the compensation provided by the APPR was enforceable and in line with the Montreal Convention requiring the Canadian Supreme Court to intervene. The dispute focused on the specific language in the APPR and the Montreal Convention. The Supreme Court came to the same conclusion as the CJEU on the APPR European counterpart, the APPR do not violate the Montreal Convention's exclusive principle.[4] Justice Rowe noted,

1 Air Passenger Protection Regulations, SOR/2019-150. See: Ruwantissa Abeyratne, *Is Air Law International: Perspectives from Practice and Global Regulation* (Ethics International Press 2025) 572.

2 D. Defossez, 'Change Is in the Air in the US and Canada . . . but What about Brazil?' (2020) 19 Issues in Aviation Law and Policy 269–94.

3 Canada Gazette, Part I, Volume 158, Number 51: Regulations Amending the Air Passenger Protection Regulations. See: Diana Klassen, 'Not Yet Cleared for Take-Off: Proposed Changes to the Air Passenger Protection Regulations' (*AHBL*, 7 October 2025) <https://www.ahbl.ca/not-yet-cleared-for-take-off-proposed-changes-to-the-air-passenger-protection-regulations/> accessed 28 November 2025.

4 *International Air Transport Association v Canada (Transportation Agency)* 2024 SCC 30 <https://decisions.scc-csc.ca/scc-csc/scc-csc/en/item/20674/index.do>. See: Wietske Felmore and Darby Heino, 'Supreme Court of Canada Ruling: Air Passenger Protection Regulations Do not Offend the Exclusivity Principle of the Montreal Convention (Mostly)' (*Lexology*, 16 October 2024) <https://www.lexology.com/library/detail.aspx?g=a4801bde-f04a-4493-b649-d290a5dcc175> accessed 28 November 2025.

DOI: 10.4324/9781003746164-21

> The Montreal Convention is exclusive within the scope of the matters that it addresses, but does not deal comprehensively with all aspects of international carriage by air. Pursuant to the text of its Article 29, there must be an "action" that leads to "damages" for the exclusivity principle to apply. The Regulations do not provide for an "action for damages" because they do not provide for individualized compensation; rather, they create a consumer protection scheme that operates in parallel with the Montreal Convention, without trenching on its liability limitation provisions. Accordingly, they do not fall within the scope of the Montreal Convention's exclusivity principle.[5]

Like Regulation 261, the APPR have been criticized by some as "essentially a sham, written by the airlines for the airlines."[6]

Unlike many laws, the APPR's provision regarding the scope of the law might seem less accessible to passengers as it refers to charter flights instead of using a more general wording such as those Regulations apply to x, y, and z.[7] The APPR apply to all flights within, from, or to Canada, whether operated by a Canadian or foreign airline.[8] They impose obligations on carriers in cases of tarmac delays, denial of boarding, and delayed or cancelled flights, and require that the carriers inform passengers of their rights in a timely, clear, and accessible way.[9]

The Regulations start with definition and then introduce some sections on general aspects such as the fact that carriers are jointly liable or that the issuing carrier of the ticket is the one liable for the obligations under sections 5 and 6.[10] Section 5 mandates that carriers communicate their terms and conditions of carriage in simple, clear, and concise language, especially regarding flight disruptions, baggage, and seating for children under 14.[11] It also requires carriers to provide information on passenger treatment, minimum compensation, and recourse options online and at

5 *International Air Transport Association v Canada (Transportation Agency)* 2024 SCC 30.

6 Quote found in Peter Schiefke, 'Strengthening Air Passenger Rights in Canada: Report of the Standing Committee on Transport, Infrastructure and Communities' (April 2023, 44th Parliament, 1st session) 9 <https://www.ourcommons.ca/Content/Committee/441/TRAN/Reports/RP12335393/tranrp10/tranrp10-e.pdf> accessed 28 November 2025.

7 Section 4(1)(a) and (b).

8 Canadian Transport Agency, 'Air Passenger Protection Regulations Highlights' <https://otc-cta.gc.ca/eng/air-passenger-protection-regulations-highlights> accessed 28 November 2025.

9 D. Defossez, 'Change Is in the Air in the US and Canada . . . but What about Brazil?' (2020) 19 Issues in Aviation Law and Policy 269–94.

10 Section 2(2) and (3).

11 Section 5(1)(a), (b) and (c); a 2025 decision from the Québec Court of Appeal imposed punitive damages for misleading 'drip pricing'- although the decision was not based on the APPR but the Law on Consumer protection it is still an important read: *Union des consommateurs and Silas v Air Canada*, 2025 QCCA 480, 22 April 2025 <https://uniondesconsommateurs.ca/wp-content/uploads/2022/11/20250422_JUGEMENT_Cour-appel_Air-Canada.pdf>.

the airport.[12] Section 5 also includes the exact wording of the notice to be displayed on all digital platforms which must be in a format compatible with adaptive technologies.[13] Section 6 mandates that the carrier must take reasonable steps to ensure that all individuals authorized to sell tickets on behalf of the carrier comply with the provisions outlined in Section 5.

The APPR's chapter on delay, cancellation, and denial of boarding starts by setting specific standards in case of tarmac delay.[14] However, they do not set a minimum amount of time to define a "tarmac delay," stipulating instead: "If a flight is delayed on the tarmac after the doors of the aircraft are closed for take-off or after the flight has landed."[15] If there is no possibility to disembark the passengers, airlines must allow access to lavatories,[16] provide proper cooling or heating of the aircraft,[17] food and drink "in reasonable quantities, taking into account the length of the delay, the time of day and the location of the airport,"[18] and the means to communicate with people outside the aircraft free of charge, if feasible.[19] The APPR amendment includes also a provision requiring airlines to facilitate access to assistance to a passenger who requires urgent medical assistance.[20]

If the tarmac delay occurs at a Canadian airport, passengers have the right to disembark three hours after the aircraft doors have been closed for take-off or three hours after landing "or at any earlier time if it is feasible."[21] This obligation will not be imposed if it is likely that take-off will occur fewer than three hours and 45 minutes after the doors are closed, or after landing, provided that the airline can maintain the standard of treatment discussed in the previous paragraph.[22] Airlines are not obliged to comply if disembarking would not be safe or for reasons relating "to air traffic or customs control."[23] Such provisions regarding tarmac delays are not included in the EU Regulation but are a welcome addition.

Another main difference from EU legislation is that the APPR distinguish between small and large carriers regarding denial of boarding,

12 Section 5(3) and Section 7.
13 Section 5(5) and (6).
14 Section 8.
15 Section 8(1).
16 Section 8(1)(a).
17 Section 8(1)(b).
18 Section 8(1)(d).
19 Section 8(1)(c).
20 Section 8(2).
21 Section 9(1)(a) and (b).
22 Section 9(2).
23 Section 9(4).

delays, or cancellations. The idea behind this distinction is to avoid overburdening smaller airlines that operate less popular routes and fly to less populated parts of Canada.[24] Accordingly, a "large carrier" is defined as one that "has transported a worldwide total of two million passengers or more during each of the two preceding calendar years,"[25] while a "small carrier" is one that has transported fewer than two million passengers in the previous two years. However, if a small carrier is carrying passengers "on behalf of a large carrier under a commercial agreement," through codesharing for instance, then it will have the same obligations as a large carrier.[26]

The wish to cure the defects of Regulation 261 is very visible when looking at how the APPR distinguish among three types of situations – those outside the carrier's control; those within the carrier's control but required for safety purposes; and those within the carrier's control – which influences the obligations of the carrier.[27]

First the APPR provides a non-exhaustive list of situations deemed to be outside the carrier's control, such as war or political instability, weather conditions, or natural disasters "that make the safe operation of the aircraft impossible," instructions from air traffic control, medical emergency, airport operation issues, a bird strike or other collision with wildlife, labour disruptions "within the carrier or within an essential service provider," and a manufacturing defect in an aircraft that reduces passenger safety, as identified by the manufacturer or a competent authority and instruction from an official of state or law enforcement agency.[28] Some of these situations also fall within the exception under EU law and as in Europe, the inclusion of bad weather and mechanical problems could lead to abuse with airlines classifying problems under these categories to avoid compensation.

In those circumstances, airlines are required to provide passengers with certain information and, in cases of delay of three hours or more and cancellation, passengers are entitled to alternate travel arrangements or a refund.[29] In case of denial of boarding, the passengers are only entitled to travel arrangements.[30]

24 D. Defossez, 'Change Is in the Air in the US and Canada . . . but What about Brazil?' (2020) 19 Issues in Aviation Law and Policy 269–94.

25 Section 1(2).

26 Section 1(4).

27 D. Defossez, 'Change Is in the Air in the US and Canada . . . but What about Brazil?' (2020) 19 Issues in Aviation Law and Policy 269–94.

28 Section 10(1); in *Geddes v Air Canada*, 2022 NSSC 49 it was held that mechanical malfunction was uncontrollable.

29 Section 10(3)(a), (b) and (c).

30 Section 10(3)(d).

Disruption Type	Passenger Rights
Delays (3+ hours)	• Information. • Alternate travel arrangements or refund. • **No compensation.**
Cancellations	• Information. • Alternate travel arrangements or refund. • **No compensation.**
Denied Boarding	• Information. • Alternate travel arrangements **only**. • **No compensation**.

The second major type of situations – those within a carrier's control but required for safety purposes – is dealt with in another section, which defines "required for safety purposes" as anything "required by law in order to reduce risk to passenger safety."[31] The definition specifically refers to "safety decisions made within the authority of the pilot or any decision made in accordance with the safety management system."[32] The definition explicitly excludes "scheduled maintenance in compliance with legal requirements."[33] In this category, the airline has the same communication obligations as in cases of flight disruptions that are outside its control, and nearly the same obligation to "provide alternate travel arrangements" except that this provision also includes the possibility of a refund.[34] Furthermore, the carrier may have an obligation of care, such as the provision of food, drinks, means of communication, accommodation, and transport,[35] if the passengers were informed less than 12 hours before the original departure time in cases of delay or cancellation. This obligation also applies to denial of boarding but without a minimum time period before the obligation kicks in.

Disruption Type	Passenger Rights
Delays (3+ hours)	• Information. • Alternate travel or refund. • **Care obligations** if informed <12h before departure.
Cancellations	• Information. • Alternate travel or refund. • **Care obligations** if informed <12h before departure.
Denied Boarding	• Information. • Alternate travel or refund. • **Care obligations.**

31 Section 11. *See id.* Section 1(1).
32 Section 1(1).
33 Section 1(1).
34 Section 11(2)(c), (3)(c) and (4)(c).
35 Section 11(2)(b), (3)(b) and (4)(b). As explained in *id.* Section 14.

Finally, situations within the carrier's control – a term which is not clearly defined as the APPR mention situations "within the carrier's control but is not referred to in subsections 11(1) or (2)."[36] Airlines have the same obligations as under the previous section but may also be required to pay minimum compensation to passengers suffering denial of boarding, delays, or cancellation if they were not informed at least 14 days prior to the original departure time in accordance with section 19.[37] In *Fauvel v WestJet*, the decision clarified that auto-cancelling boarding passes and preventing passengers from attempting their connections fall within the airline's control, thereby rendering the airline liable for compensation pursuant to section 19.[38]

The Canadian Transportation Agency APPR Interpretation decision also makes it clear that

> When determining whether a passenger delayed by multiple flight disruptions during their itinerary is entitled to compensation for inconvenience under section 19 of the APPR, it is necessary to take into account all of the flights involved in the delay to the arrival of the passenger's flight at the destination indicated on the original ticket, and to determine the primary reason, or most significant contributing factor, of the overall delay."[39]

In a 2023 case, it was held that such interpretation does not apply to a single flight but only to multiple-leg journeys.[40]

Disruption Type	**Passenger Rights**
Delays (3+ hours)	• Information. • Alternate travel or refund. • **Care obligations** if informed <12h before departure. • Minimum **compensation** if informed <14 days before departure.
Cancellations	• Information. • Alternate travel or refund. • **Care obligations** if informed <12h before departure. • Minimum **compensation** if informed <14 days before departure.
Denied Boarding	• Information. • Alternate travel or refund. • **Full care obligations.** • Minimum **compensation** if informed <14 days before departure.

36 Section 12(1).

37 Section 12(2)(d), (3)(d) and (4)(d).

38 *Fauvel v Westjet Airlines Ltd*, 2024 BCPC 190. Confirmed in *Green v Westjet Airlines Ltd*, 2025 BCCRT 1180.

39 Q6 Decision 122-C-A-2021, applications by multiple applicants against Air Canada, WestJet, Air Transat A.T. Inc. (Air Transat), United Airlines, Inc. (United Airlines), Sunwing Airlines Inc. (Sunwing) and Swoop, Inc. (Swoop), 17 November 2021.

40 *Richardson et al. v WestJet Airlines Ltd*, 2023 NSSM 56.

Similar to the EU situation, any kind of flight disruption obliges airlines to provide specified information to the affected passengers, such as the reason for the disruption, the compensation that passengers may be entitled to receive, the standard of treatment for passengers, and the recourse available against the airline.[41] This last obligation is not found in the EU legislation, but it appears in the other national laws. Interestingly, the obligation to update passengers every 30 minutes in cases of delay,[42] or as soon as the airline obtains new information,[43] is also found in *Resolução* 400/2016 in Brazil. Carriers are required to inform passengers via the "communication method that they have indicated that they prefer,"[44] and must display notices stating passengers' rights in cases of denial of boarding or lost or damaged luggage.[45] This requirement can be found in both the EU Regulation and Brazilian *Resolução*.

Section 14 of the APPR outlines the standard of treatment that air carriers must provide to passengers who are informed of a safety-related delay or cancellation less than 12 hours before their originally scheduled departure time. If a passenger has waited for two hours or more after the original departure time, the carrier must provide the following amenities free of charge. Firstly, passengers are entitled to food and drink in reasonable quantities, taking into account the duration of the wait, the time of day, and the passenger's location. The determination of what constitutes "reasonable quantities" is context-dependent.[46] For instance, a short delay in the mid-afternoon might necessitate a snack and water, whereas a longer delay occurring during a mealtime would reasonably require a more substantial offering. The location of the airport might also influence the availability and types of food and drink that can be provided as well as whether providing such care would further delay the passenger.[47] Secondly, passengers must be provided with access to a means of communication, which is not defined in the Regulations but probably encompasses free Wi-Fi or telephone access.[48]

In situations where a safety-related delay or cancellation necessitates an overnight wait for the original flight or for a flight that is part of alternate travel arrangements, the air carrier has an additional obligation of providing a hotel or other comparable accommodation free of charge

41 *Compare* EU Regulation 261/2004, *article*. 14, *with* Air Passenger Protection Regulations, *section* 13(1)(a)–(d).
42 Section 13(2).
43 Section 13(3).
44 Section 13(5).
45 Section 13(5). Sections 5 and 7.
46 Section 14(1)(a).
47 Section 14(3).
48 Section 14(1)(b).

to the passenger.[49] The accommodation provided must be reasonable in relation to the passenger's location, and the carrier must also provide transportation to and from the accommodation.[50] It is important to note that the carrier may limit or refuse to provide the standard of treatment if providing it would further delay the passenger. This acknowledges the operational realities of flight disruptions and allows carriers to prioritize resuming travel when it is safe and feasible to do so.[51]

There is another interesting aspect to Canada's APPR: the obligation to provide alternate travel arrangements partially depends on whether the flight disruption is within, or entirely outside, the carrier's control. Indeed, if the disruption is within the airline's control and the airline is a large carrier, then it must provide a confirmed reservation on the next available flight on a reasonable air route to each affected passenger, whether the flight is operated by it or by a carrier with which it has a commercial agreement.[52] If the carrier cannot provide such confirmed reservation, it is requested to provide a confirmed reservation for a flight that is operated by any carrier and which "departs within 48 hours of the departure time that is indicated on [the] original ticket."[53] The final alternative is that the carrier transports the passenger to another airport "within a reasonable distance of the airport at which the passenger is located" and provides a confirmed reservation for a flight operated by any carrier.[54] The Superior Court of Ontario ruled in 2026 that airlines are liable for alternative tickets booked by the passengers themselves if it is clear they did not inform the passengers they needed to wait before rebooking.[55] In the case of a small carrier, a confirmed reservation on the next available flight, whether the flight is operated by it or by a carrier with which it has a commercial agreement, must be provided.[56] The concept of a "reasonable air route" is central to these rebooking obligations. However, the APPR does not provide an explicit definition but can be understood as a route that does not cause excessive delays or involve a significantly higher number of connections than the original booking.

In addition to alternate travel arrangements, passengers have the right to choose a refund if the offered rebooking options do not meet their travel needs.[57] If the passenger does not agree with the alternate travel

49 Section 14(2).
50 Section 14(2).
51 Section 14(3).
52 Section 17(1)(a)(i).
53 Section 17(1)(a)(ii).
54 Section 17(1)(a)(iii).
55 *Air Canada v Landry* (2026 ONSC 222).
56 Section 17(1)(b).
57 Section 17(2).

arrangement and the passenger is in transit but does not wish to continue the journey due to the delay, the airline must refund the ticket, provide a confirmed reservation for a flight to the original departure point, and accommodate the passenger's needs.[58] In any other circumstances, the airline is required to refund the unused portion of the ticket.[59] However, the passenger cannot request a compensation for the inconvenience in the change of itinerary.[60] The alternate travel arrangements must, as much as possible, be comparable to those of the original ticket.[61] If the alternative flight does not include additional services purchased by the passenger for the original flight, the airline must reimburse these services.[62] If the alternate travel arrangements provide for a lower class of service, the airline must refund the difference in fare; however, if the alternative arrangements are of a higher class of service, the airline cannot request supplementary payment.[63] While the EU Regulation also requires reimbursement, the EU Regulation is silent regarding the obligation to reimburse additional services.[64] Notably, under the EU Regulation, airlines are not required to pay the actual difference in cases of downgrading, but rather, the difference is calculated according to distance.[65]

The obligation to provide alternate travel arrangements is slightly different where the flight disruption is entirely outside the carrier's control. A large carrier must provide a confirmed reservation on the next available flight operated by it or a carrier with which it has a commercial agreement that "departs within 48 hours of the end of the event that caused the delay, cancellation or denial of boarding."[66] If this is not possible, alternate travel arrangements on any carrier must be provided.[67] A small carrier must provide a confirmed reservation on the next available flight operated by it or by a carrier with which it has a commercial agreement. The main difference between this type of flight disruption and the previous one is that no mention is made regarding the refund of any downgrading or additional services.

58 Section 17(2)(a).
59 Section 17(2)(b).
60 *Lukács v Air Canada Rouge LP*, 2023 FC 1358.
61 Section 17(3).
62 Section 18.1(1).
63 Section 17(5) and 18.1(2).
64 Article 8 of EU Regulation 261/2004.
65 "(a) 30 % of the price of the ticket for all flights of 1500 kilometres or less, or
(b) 50 % of the price of the ticket for all intra-Community flights of more than 1500 kilometres, except flights between the European territory of the Member States and the French overseas departments, and for all other flights between 1500 and 3500 kilometres, or
(c) 75 % of the price of the ticket for all flights not falling under (a) or (b), including flights between the European territory of the Member States and the French overseas departments."
Article 10.
66 Air Passenger Protection Regulations, Section 18(1)(a)(i).
67 Section 18(1)(a)(ii).

Delay Duration	Airline Size	Rebooking Obligations
3+ hours	**Large.**	1. **Next available flight** (same airline or partner) on a reasonable route. 2. **If unavailable within reasonable time**: Any carrier on a reasonable route departing within **48 hours**. 3. **If neither option works**: Next available flight from a **nearby airport** (any carrier), with free transport to that airport.
3+ hours	**Small.**	1. **Next available flight** (same airline or partner) on a reasonable route.

The rebooking option differs slightly if the delay or cancellation was outside of the carrier's control; the carrier must provide an alternative flight, operated by the carrier or a partner carrier departing within 48 hours of the original departure time.[68] If such flight is unavailable, the passenger can either get a refund of any unused portion or an alternative flight.[69] Large carriers can book on any carrier from the same or nearby airport, while small carriers must use their own or partners. Subsection 18(1.2) provides a free return flight if the trip's purpose is lost. Subsection 18(1.3) allows passengers to request a refund before making a new reservation. Similar rules apply if the denial of boarding is caused by an event outside of the carrier's control.[70]

Obligation	Large Carrier	Small Carrier
Rebooking	1. Next available flight (own/partner) on a reasonable route within **48h**. 2. If unavailable: alternate flight on **any carrier** (same route) within 48h, or from a **nearby airport** (free transport provided).	1. Next available flight (own/partner) on a reasonable route within **48h**. 2. If unavailable: alternate flight **only on own/partner carriers** (no third-party flights).
Refund Option	Passenger may choose a refund (unused ticket portion) or alternate travel.	Passenger may choose a refund (unused ticket portion) or alternate travel.
Return to Origin	If trip's purpose is lost, provide: - **Refund** + **free return flight** to origin.	If trip's purpose is lost, provide: - **Refund** + **free return flight** to origin.
Denial of Boarding	Alternate flight on **any carrier** (own/partner or third-party) from same or nearby airport.	Alternate flight **only on own/partner carriers** (no third-party flights).

(*Continued*)

68 Section 18(1).
69 Section 18(1.1)(a) and (b).
70 Section (1.4).

(Continued)

Category	Outside Carrier's Control	Within Carrier's Control but Required for Safety	Within Carrier's Control
Examples	• Weather/natural disasters. • Air traffic control instructions. • Political instability. • Bird strikes. • Labour strikes. • Manufacturing defects (safety-related).	• Pilot's safety decisions. • Safety management system actions. • **Excludes** scheduled maintenance.	• Overbooking. • Staffing shortages. • Operational errors.
Carrier Obligations	• Provide updates. • Alternate travel or refund (for 3+ hour delays/ cancellations). • **No compensation.**	• Alternate travel or refund. • **Care obligations** (food, accommodation) if informed <12h before departure. • Minimum compensation **only** if notified ≤14 days pre-departure (delay and cancellation). Minimum compensation for denial of boarding.	• Full compensation (up to 1,000 for delays/ cancellations, 2,400 for denied boarding). • Refund or rebooking. • Full care obligations (regardless of notice).
Compensation	None.	• If passengers are notified ≤14 days pre-departure (delay and cancellation). • Minimum compensation for denial of boarding.	Mandatory (amount depends on delay length).
Denied Boarding	• Alternate travel only. • No compensation.	• Alternate travel + compensation (no notice required). • Immediate care obligations.	• Highest compensation tier ($2,400). • Full care obligations.

Passengers are entitled to compensation based on the length of delay at arrival at their final destination. Yet again the provisions make a difference between small carriers and large carriers. For delay or cancellation between three and six hours, a large carrier is liable to pay $400 while a small carrier is liable for $125 in compensation.[71] For delay or cancellation between six and nine hours, a large carrier will have to pay $700 in compensation while a smaller carrier must pay only $250.[72] Finally, for delays at arrival destination of more than nine hours, passengers on a large carrier will receive $1,000 while passengers on a smaller carrier get $500.[73] However, if the passenger on the delayed or cancelled flight accepts a refund,[74] large airlines are only liable for $400 in compensation and small carriers for $125, which is the "minimum compensation."[75] A parent company is not automatically liable for its subsidiary's obligation to compensate the passengers.[76]

Length of the Delay (Cancellation and Delay)	**Amount in CAD for Large Airlines**	**Amount in CAD for Small Airlines**
3–6 hours	$400.	$125.
6–9 hours	$700.	$250.
9+ hours	$1,000.	$500.

Passengers have one year to make a compensation claim with the airline that operated the disrupted flight,[77] and the airline has 30 days to respond by issuing a payment or indicating why it believes compensation is not owed.[78] Finally, the Canada Transportation Act prohibits receipt of compensation under the APPR if the claimant has already been compensated for the same event under a different regime.[79] However, the APPR provide that carriers may not refuse compensation on the grounds that the passenger is also eligible for compensation for the same event under a different regime. Compared to the EU Regulation, the amounts are much higher, but the delay is much longer.[80]

Previously, any airline could deny boarding to a passenger in cases of overbooking or for safety reasons. However, the APPR now set out a procedure that airlines must follow in cases of overbooking. A carrier cannot deny boarding to any passenger unless it has first asked all

71 Section 19(1)(a)(i) and (b)(i).
72 Section 19(1)(a)(ii) and (b)(ii).
73 Section 19(1)(a)(iii) and (b)(iii).
74 Section 12(2)(d) or (3)(d).
75 Section 19(2)(a) and (b).
76 *Keung v WestJet Airlines Ltd*, 2025 BCCRT 506 <https://www.canlii.org/en/bc/bccrt/doc/2025/2025bccrt506/2025bccrt506.html>.
77 Section 19(3).
78 Section 19(4).
79 Canada Transportation Act, 1996 S.C., ch. 10, sec. 86.11(3).
80 *Compare* Air Passenger Protection Regulations, Section 19(1), *with* EU Regulation 261/2004 Article 7(1).

passengers if any of them are willing to give up their seats.[81] If the airline offers a benefit in order to encourage volunteers, such benefit must be put in writing before the departure of the flight.[82] To avoid cases as in the United States, the APPR make it clear that airlines cannot deny boarding to anyone who has already boarded the plane unless such denial is for safety reasons.[83] Section 15(4) lists the passengers who should be given priority boarding such as unaccompanied minor, persons with disability and their support person, service animal or emotional support animal, passengers travelling with family members, and passengers previously denied boarding on the same ticket.[84]

Additionally, airlines are obliged to provide passengers who are denied boarding with information, alternate travel arrangements, care or treatment, and monetary compensation, depending on the circumstances.[85] When the denial of boarding results in an overnight stay, the airline must provide reasonable accommodation and transport unless such standard of treatment would further delay the passenger.[86]

If the arrival time at the destination is delayed less than six hours, the passengers have a right to $900, while if the arrival time is delayed by between six and nine hours, the compensation rises to $1,800. Finally, if the arrival time is delayed by more than nine hours, the compensation is $2,400.[87] Where the APPR anticipate an almost immediate payment of compensation in cases of denied boarding with a compensation no later than 48 hours after the denial, passengers must file a request for compensation in cases of delayed and cancelled flights.[88] In the event that the flight arrives later than the expected time, the amount of compensation must be adjusted to reflect the inconvenience suffered.[89] In other words, if the passenger was compensated for an expected delay of six hours but arrival time at destination represents a seven-hour delay, the passenger will be entitled to a higher compensation.

Length of the delay (denial of boarding)	**Amount**
0–6 hours	$900.
6–9 hours	$1,800.
9+	$2,400.

81 Section 15(1).
82 Section 15(3).
83 Section 15(2).
84 Section 15(2)(a)–(d).
85 Section 16(1).
86 Section 16(2) and (3).
87 Section 20(1).
88 Section 20(2).
89 Section 20(5).

The APPR also include a full chapter on assignment of seats to children under the age of 14, requiring them to be placed in close proximity of a parent, tutor, or guardian at no additional costs.[90] For children under 4, the seat must be adjacent to their parent; for children between 5 and 11, the seat must be on the same row and no more than one seat separating them.[91] Finally for children aged 12 or 13, they must not be separated by more than a row from their parents.[92] If that seat assignment results in a downgrading, the airline must reimburse the difference.[93]

The Regulations also contain a chapter on baggage. For lost or damaged baggage, airlines must provide compensation equal to or greater than the sum of the fee paid, the compensation payable under the Carriage by Air Act or the Montreal Convention, depending which is applicable.[94] More peculiar is the provision dedicated to musical instruments and the obligation to carry them unless it is contrary to the airline's terms and conditions.[95] Finally, the APPR also contain a full chapter on advertising.

Penalties range up to $25,000 per violation per carrier which is set to be increased by the modifications to the Act to $250,000.[96] This amount is much higher than under the European approach and might lead to greater implementation of the rules than in Europe, for instance. Indeed, the EU Regulation only stipulates that the penalties must be "effective, proportionate and dissuasive"[97] and are left to Member States to decide. Given the growing number of claim management agencies and the number of cases that are dismissed, it seems that the EU penalties are not that effective.[98]

The APPR represent a significant advancement in air passenger rights, addressing EU Regulation 261's shortcomings with stricter definitions, higher penalties, and tailored obligations. By categorizing disruptions into three distinct tiers (outside carrier's control, safety-related, and within carrier's control), the APPR provide a nuanced approach reflecting the reality of air travel while curbing airlines' ability to evade responsibilities. Its robust

90 Section 22(1).
91 Section 22(2)(a) and (b).
92 Section 22(2)(c).
93 Section 22(3).
94 Section 23(1).
95 Section 24(2).
96 Section 33. See: Michael Pihach, 'New Rules Aim to Clarify Air Passenger Protection Regulations' *PAX News* (21 December 2024) <https://www.paxnews.com/news/airline/new-rules-aim-clarify-air-passenger-protection-regulations>.
97 EU Regulation 261/2004 art. 16(3).
98 For a fascinating discussion of claim agencies and their impact, see Ch Thijssen and L Williams, 'U.K. Court of Appeal Confirms Airlines May Compensate Passengers Directly – the Beginning of the End of Ambulance-Chasing over Passenger Rights Claims in the EU? (2019) 18 Issues in Aviation Law and Policy 275.

compensation framework – coupled with protections for tarmac delays – sets a high bar for passenger rights, particularly if the penalties are increased up to $250,000 per violation. However, challenges remain. The complexity of the APPR's language and structure risks alienating passengers. Although the APPR have been modelled as an improved version of EU Regulation 261, their readability could be improved greatly. Moreover, the distinction between small and large carriers could be quite difficult for passengers to ascertain. Proposed 2024 amendments to tighten loopholes and increase penalties signal Canada's commitment to refining the APPR and maximize their effectiveness, placing Canada as a leader in passenger's rights.

Comparison with EU Regulation

Category	Canada (APPR)	EU Regulation 261/2004
Delay Compensation	- 3+ hours. - Large carriers: $400–$1,000. - Small carriers: $125–$500.	≥3h: €250–€600 (by distance).
Cancellation Rights	- Refund/re-routing. - Compensation only if within carrier's control (same as delay tiers).	<14 days' notice: Refund or re-routing + €250–600 compensation (by distance).
Denied Boarding	Volunteers first; $900–2,400 if denied boarding.	Volunteer first; €250–600 (by distance) if denied boarding.
Baggage Compensation	- Lost/damaged: Up to $2,100 (international) + reimbursement of fees.	Not specified.

Bibliography

Primary Sources

- *Air Canada v Landry* (2026 ONSC 222).
- Air Passenger Protection Regulations, SOR/2019-150.
- Canada Gazette, Part I, Volume 158, Number 51: Regulations Amending the Air Passenger Protection Regulations.
- Decision 122-C-A-2021, applications by multiple applicants against Air Canada, WestJet, Air Transat A.T. Inc. (Air Transat), United Airlines, Inc. (United Airlines), Sunwing Airlines Inc. (Sunwing) and Swoop, Inc. (Swoop), 17 November 2021.
- *Fauvel v Westjet Airlines Ltd*, 2024 BCPC 190.
- *Geddes v Air Canada*, 2022 NSSC 49.
- *Green v Westjet Airlines Ltd*, 2025 BCCRT 1180.
- *International Air Transport Association v Canada (Transportation Agency)* 2024 SCC 30 <https://decisions.scc-csc.ca/scc-csc/scc-csc/en/item/20674/index.do>.

- *Keung v WestJet Airlines Ltd*, 2025 BCCRT 506.
- *Richardson et al. v WestJet Airlines Ltd*, 2023 NSSM 56.

Secondary Sources

- Abeyratne, R., *Is Air Law International: Perspectives from Practice and Global Regulation* (Ethics International Press 2025).
- Canadian Transport Agency, 'Air Passenger Protection Regulations Highlights' <https://otc-cta.gc.ca/eng/air-passenger-protection-regulations-highlights> accessed 28 November 2025.
- Defossez, D., 'Change Is in the Air in the US and Canada . . . but What About Brazil?' (2020) 19 Issues in Aviation Law and Policy 269.
- Felmore, W. and Heino, D., 'Supreme Court of Canada Ruling: Air Passenger Protection Regulations Do Not Offend the Exclusivity Principle of the Montreal Convention (Mostly)' (*Lexology*, 16 October 2024) <https://www.lexology.com/library/detail.aspx?g=a4801bde-f04a-4493-b649-d290a5dcc175> accessed 28 November 2025.
- Klassen, D., 'Not Yet Cleared for Take-Off: Proposed Changes to the Air Passenger Protection Regulations' (*AHBL*, 7 October 2025) <https://www.ahbl.ca/not-yet-cleared-for-take-off-proposed-changes-to-the-air-passenger-protection-regulations/> accessed 28 November 2025.
- Pihach, M., 'New Rules Aim to Clarify Air Passenger Protection Regulations' *PAX News* (21 December 2024) <https://www.paxnews.com/news/airline/new-rules-aim-clarify-air-passenger-protection-regulations> accessed 28 November 2025.
- Schiefke, P., 'Strengthening Air Passenger Rights in Canada: Report of the Standing Committee on Transport, Infrastructure and Communities' (April 2023, 44th Parliament, 1st Session) <https://www.ourcommons.ca/Content/Committee/441/TRAN/Reports/RP12335393/tranrp10/tranrp10-e.pdf> accessed 28 November 2025.
- Thijssen, Ch. and Williams, L., 'U.K. Court of Appeal Confirms Airlines May Compensate Passengers Directly – the Beginning of the End of Ambulance-Chasing over Passenger Rights Claims in the EU?' (2019) 18 Issues in Aviation Law & Policy 275.
- *Union des consommateurs and Silas v Air Canada*, 2025 QCCA 480, 22 April 2025 <https://uniondesconsommateurs.ca/wp-content/uploads/2022/11/20250422_JUGEMENT_Cour-appel_Air-Canada.pdf>.

II.11

Chile

Chilean aviation passenger rights are primarily governed by the Chilean Aeronautical Code and the Consumer Protection Law which establish the rights of passengers and obligations of airlines.[1]

Chapter V is dedicated to air transport contract. Article 127 contains an obligation for a carrier to perform the transport on the date, time, and under the conditions stipulated.[2] A carrier may, however, suspend, delay, or cancel a flight, or modify its conditions, for reasons of safety or unforeseen force majeure,[3] such as meteorological phenomena, armed conflicts, civil disturbances, or threats to the aircraft.[4] In such cases, either party may terminate the contract, with each bearing their own losses.

Passengers have the right to receive clear and timely information regarding their flights, including schedules, potential delays or cancellations, reasons for disruptions, and their rights as passengers.[5]

Article 132 allows a carrier to refuse or impose conditions on the transport of passengers whose condition poses a safety, hygiene, or order risk or requires special care during travel.

In the event of denial of boarding due to overbooking, carriers must first request volunteers in exchange of benefits and compensation to be agreed with the volunteers.[6] If it is necessary to refuse boarding due to insufficient number of volunteers, passengers with confirmed tickets[7]

1 Ley no. 18.916 Codigo Aeronautico, 08 February 1990 as amended on 22 September 2023 by Ley 21610 Modifica el codigo aeronautico para hace exigible el listado de pasajeros en el transporte aéreo nacional and Ley no. 19.496, 7 February 1997, establece normas sobre proteccion de los derechos de los consumidores.

2 Article 127.

3 An event of force majeure or an Act of God is defined in Article 45 of the Chilean Civil Code as an unforeseeable event that is not possible to resist, such as a shipwreck, an earthquake, arrest of enemies, and acts of authority by a public officer.

4 Article 127.

5 Article 127.

6 Article 133(1).

7 As defined in Article 133(4) as "a ticket shall be deemed confirmed for the specified points of departure, destination, and any intermediate connection or stopover points,

DOI: 10.4324/9781003746164-22

may opt between being rebooked on the next flight that the carrier has available, or on an alternate transportation,[8] full reimbursement if the passenger withdraws from the air transportation contract before travel.[9] For connecting flights[10] which have already started, the passenger may elect to either board the next available flight, receive a refund of the unused part, or return to the starting point and receive reimbursement of the ticket price.[11] Additionally, the carrier must offer the affected passenger the economic compensation of an amount equivalent to the terms set forth in the Code.[12]

Flight Distance (Denied Boarding)	**Delay in Arrival Time: 1–3 Hours**	**Delay in Arrival Time: 3–4 Hours**	**Delay in Arrival Time: >4 Hours**
Less than 500 km	2 Unidad de Fomento (UF).[13]	2 UF.	2.5 UF.
500 km–1,000 km	3 UF.	3 UF.	3.75 UF.
1,000 km–2,500 km	4 UF.	4 UF.	5 UF.
2,500 km–4,000 km	8 UF.	10 UF.	10 UF.
4,000 km–8,000 km	12 UF.	15 UF.	15 UF.
More than 8,000 km	16 UF.	20 UF.	20 UF.

If the rebooked flight arrives within three hours of the original arrival time, no compensation is owed.[14] Passengers accepting compensation waive further claims for the same incident – except under consumer protection laws.

In cases of denied boarding due to overbooking, carriers must prioritize boarding for unaccompanied minors, persons with disabilities, elderly passengers or those with fragile health conditions, pregnant women requiring priority boarding due to their condition and any other passengers deemed by the carrier to qualify for humanitarian reasons.[15]

provided that the reservation or ticket has been formally accepted and recorded by the air carrier or its authorized agent."

8 Article 133(1)(a).

9 Article 133(1)(b).

10 As defined in Article 133(5) as "a journey where the arrival at the final destination includes:

- a point of departure,
- One or more intermediate stopover or connection points, provided all segments are part of a single contract."

11 Article 133(1)(c)(i), ii, (iii).

12 Article 133(2).

13 An inflation-adjusted Chilean monetary unit used for legal and financial calculations.

14 Article 133(3).

15 Article 133(6).

Article 133 A, which was introduced in 2015 by Law 20831, lists the assistance a passenger is entitled to receive in the event of a denial of boarding. First, communication access such as phone calls or emails if the difference between the original departure time and the new departure time exceeds one hour.[16] Second, meals and snacks equivalent to at least 0.5 UF if there is a difference in the scheduled time of departure for the flight initially booked of more than two hours. The passenger shall be entitled to a new benefit, and for the same amount, each time an additional three hours of waiting time elapses.[17] The benefits are not cumulative and must be delivered within each corresponding period while the passenger is present at the airport. Accommodation and transport for return and outbound passengers who were denied boarding at a connecting point, who do not reside in the city of the departure airport, in the event that they are offered a new flight, of which the departure is at least on the day following the scheduled departure on the ticket.[18] Overnight stay is understood as time between midnight and 6 AM.[19] Finally, airlines will have to make all necessary arrangements and services for missed connections.[20]

Assistance (Article 133 A)

Condition	**Carrier's Obligation**	**Details**
Communication Access	Provide phone/electronic communication facilities.	Applies if the new departure time exceeds **1 hour** beyond the originally scheduled flight.
Meals/Snacks	Offer meals or refreshments worth **≥0.5 UF** (Chilean Unidad de Fomento).	Required for delays **≥2 hours**; renewed every **3 hours** of additional waiting time.
Accommodation	Provide accommodation for non-local passengers.	Only if rebooking requires an **overnight stay** (from midnight to 6 AM).
Transport	Arrange transfers between airport and lodging/ residence.	Applicable if lodging is provided (e.g., for passengers stranded in a non-home city).
Missed Connections	Assist with rebooking or alternative arrangements.	Covers passengers with confirmed connecting flights missed due to the denied boarding.

16 This was amended by Article 2(3) of Law 21398 of 2021.
17 Article 133(A)(b).
18 Article 133(A)(c) and (d).
19 Article 133(A)(c).
20 Article 133(A)(e).

Delays and cancellations are dealt with together in Article 133B which stipulates that the affected passengers have the right to board the next flight available or alternative transport, assistance as found in Article 133A provided that the cause of the delay or cancellation is attributable to the carrier.[21] Passengers are also entitled to compensation as stipulated in Article 147 – as long as the delay or the cancellation is due to causes imputable to the carrier – for delays exceeding three hours or four hours for aircrafts of a capacity up to 29 seats or at the time of cancellation, unless the passenger is informed and another flight is offered which allows the passenger to arrive with no more than three hours of delay in relation to the expected time.[22] Finally, airlines must reimburse the total amount paid for the ticket or the portion not used if the passenger decides to terminate the contract and the maximum delay terms have expired, regardless of whether the cause of the delay or cancellation is due to the carrier.[23]

The indemnity shall not exceed 250 UF for each of the affected passengers. The indemnity shall not be applicable if the carrier proves that it adopted the necessary measures to avoid the event causing the delay, or that it was impossible for it to adopt them.[24] It is unclear whether the amount scales with flight distance as found in Article 133(2) for denied boarding passengers. Similarly, nothing in the Code clarifies whether the compensations are applicable to both national and international flights or whether another compensation limit applies to international flights.[25]

Rights of Delayed and Cancelled Passengers

Right	Condition	Details	Exceptions/Limits
Rebooking/ Alternative Transport	Applies to all delays/cancellations (regardless of cause).	Passenger may choose: - Next available flight (same carrier). - Alternative transport (e.g., another airline).	None.

(*Continued*)

21 Article 133(B)(a) and (b).
22 Article 133(B)(c)(i) and (ii).
23 Article 133(B)(d).
24 Article 147.
25 This document seems to suggest that compensation for international flights is 4,694 Special Drawing Rights. "VIII. Chile: Passengers' Rights According to the Chilean Aeronautical Code, Applicable to Operations in Chile' (s.n) <https://assets-us-01.kc-usercontent.com/b2956330-c34f-0064-2c6f-27bd5c0147fc/e63e9879-b05f-4130-a2ed-7e2e1f1cefb2/Derechos_pasajeros_US.pdf> accessed 1 December 2025.

(Continued)

Right	Condition	Details	Exceptions/Limits
Assistance (Art. 133 A)	Only if delay/ cancellation is attributable to carrier.	Includes: - Meals/snacks (≥0.5 UF) for delays ≥2h. - Lodging for overnight delays. - Transport to lodging/residence. - Missed connection help.	Assistance not required for force majeure or passenger-caused issues.
Compensation (Art. 147)	Only if delay/ cancellation is carrier's fault **AND**: - Delay >3h (>4h for ≤29-seat aircraft) - Cancellation without timely rebooking (<3h delay offer).	Compensation caps at 250 UF per passenger.	No compensation if carrier proves: - Took all reasonable measures to avoid delay. - Delay was unavoidable.
Full Refund	Passenger opts to terminate contract after delay thresholds expire (regardless of cause).	Refund options: - Total ticket price (if unused) - Unused portion (if travel began).	Refund must be processed within 10 days (30 days for flights booked ≥180d ahead).

Aeronautical fees paid for unused travel (regardless of cause) must be refunded within ten days via the original payment method, with or without an express request by the passenger.[26] Unjustified delays incur 50% penalties in favour of the passenger every 30 days. Once the first 30 days period has expired without the restitution to the passenger, the latter may choose to demand the restitution from the authorized agent who made the sale, or to persist in the restitution and surcharges.[27]

Unlike many laws, the Chilean Code made it clear that carriers may seek reimbursement from third parties responsible for compensation, assistance, or costs incurred.[28] This provision was added by Article 1(2) of Law 20831 of 2015.

Involuntary upgrades cannot be charged if they are due to any cause beyond the passenger's control.[29] The Code does not include any specific

26 Article 133 C.
27 Article 133 C.
28 Article 133 D.
29 Article 133 E.

provision on downgrading nor any compensation for the affected passengers. The Code also expressly allows for collective actions[30] and obliges airlines to seat children under the age of 14 next to a family adult or adult in the same reservation.[31] No specific provision on special needs passengers is found in the Code.

In 2021, the Chilean government issued Law No. 21392, which amends the aeronautical code to allow the endorsement or transfer of airline tickets, as well as withdrawal. The rule allows for the transfer of tickets for one way and/or round trips at no cost. Passengers can endorse or transfer the ticket up to one day prior to the flight.[32] Such transfer can only occur between natural persons and once per ticket. The law also restricts those transfers to twice a year per carrier.[33] Article 131ter gives the right to passenger to unilaterally cancel their ticket within 48 hours of acquisition of the ticket for trips booked at least seven calendar days before the scheduled departure date and flight time, subject to certain conditions. For trips booked 180 days or more before the scheduled flight departure, passengers can withdraw within seven days from the date of purchase of the ticket.[34] The penalty for disregarding this provision is a fine of 11 to 20 monthly tax units and the same penalty shall be imposed on the assignee.[35] In the event of a repeated offence, the penalty may attract a medium-term imprisonment and a fine of 21 to 30 monthly tax units.

Passengers may reschedule or request refunds with a medical certificate proving travel incapacity, submitted within 24 hours of notification. The medical certificate must indicate the reason for the impediment and the period or dates between which he/she is unable to travel by air. Rescheduling is permitted up to one year later, with fare differences payable for higher-value tickets. Spouses, civil partners, parents, and children on the same reservation may invoke this right. Fraudulent certificates are punishable under Article 202 of the Penal Code.[36]

Title IX Chapter 1 is dedicated to the responsibility of the airline and implements the Montreal Convention. Article 148 stipulates that the compensation for loss, damage, or delay of checked baggage shall not exceed 40 UF per passenger. While Article 153 mentions when a claim must be filed, it does not include any fixed damages payable to passengers per day their luggage is delayed as found in Saudi Arabia for instance.

30 Article 133 H.
31 Article 133 I.
32 Article 131bis.
33 Article 131bis.
34 Article 131ter.
35 Article 133 G.
36 Article 133 J.

These laws are complied with by airlines and regularly enforced by the National Consumer Service (SERNAC) and Chilean courts.[37] Infractions to this Code shall result in a written warning or a fine of 5 to 500 monthly minimum wages or a suspension of permits/licenses for up to three years or a permanent revocation of licenses.[38] For breaches of general instructions issued by the aeronautical authority, only sanctions (a) to (c) apply. Before imposing sanctions, the Director General of the DGAC must hear the violator's defence.[39] Fines are immediately enforceable, and any unpaid fines may result in the automatic suspension of licenses until payment.[40] The party has the right to appeal within 15 days to the Commander-in-Chief of the Chilean Air Force for any fines exceeding 20 monthly minimum wages, or license revocations.[41]

Violation	Sanction
Minor Breaches	Written warning.
Moderate Breaches	Fines (5–500 monthly minimum wages).
Severe Breaches	License suspension (up to 3 years) or revocation.
Repeat Offenses	Criminal penalties (medium-term imprisonment + fines).

The Chilean Aeronautical Code offers a strong protection to passengers, although it lags behind global leaders in compensation clarity and disability accommodations. For instance, it does not include specific provisions on downgrading. It contains very strict enforcement rules which could result in penal proceedings.

Comparison with EU Regulation

Feature	Chilean Aeronautical Code	EU Regulation 261/2004
Delay Compensation	≥3h: ≤250 UF (carrier fault).	≥3h: €250–€600 (by distance).
Cancellation Compensation	Re-routing + compensation Or Refund + compensation.	<14d notice: Refund or re-routing + €250–600 compensation (by distance).
Denied Boarding Compensation	2–20 UF based on distance.	Volunteer first; €250–600 (by distance) if denied boarding.
Baggage Liability	40 UF (checked).	Not specified.

37 Articles 183 and 184. More info on the role of SERNAC see: V Andrade, 'Chilean Consumer Law and Policy: A Brief Outlook' (2022) 45 Journal of Consumer Policy 49.
38 Article 185(a), (b), (c) and (d).
39 Article 186.
40 Article 189.
41 Article 188.

Bibliography

- Ley no. 18.916 Codigo Aeronautico, 08 Febreuary 1990 as amended on 22 September 2023 by Ley 21610 Modifica el codigo aeronautico para hace exigible el listado de pasajeros en el transporte aéreo nacional.
- Ley no. 19.496, 7 February 1997, establece normas sobre proteccion de los derechos de los consumidores.
- Andrade, V., 'Chilean Consumer Law and Policy: A Brief Outlook' (2022) 45 Journal of Consumer Policy 49.
- "VIII. Chile: Passengers' Rights According to the Chilean Aeronautical Code, Applicable to Operations in Chile' (s.n) <https://assets-us-01.kc-usercontent.com/b2956330-c34f-0064-2c6f-27bd5c0147fc/e63e9879-b05f-4130-a2ed-7e2e1f1cefb2/Derechos_pasajeros_US.pdf> accessed 1 December 2025.

II.12

China

Chinese air passenger rights are primarily governed by the Provisions on the Management of Flight Regularity,[1] overseen by the Civil Aviation Administration of China (CAAC),[2] which came into effect in 2017.[3] This regulation is a landmark for its system-wide approach, imposing duties on all aviation stakeholders to ensure flight regularity, not just protecting passengers rights.[4] This approach explains that the scope of the legislation is specifically tied to regularity management, targeting the operational handling of delays and cancellations.[5] Other passenger rights issues, such as denied boarding, fall outside its purview and are governed by other civil aviation regulations, CAAC enforcement guidelines, and general contract law under the Civil Code. The Regulation applies to both domestic and foreign airlines operating flights originating from the Peoples' Republic of China (the PRC) or with an agreed stopover in the PRC.[6]

The Regulation enjoins the carrier to schedule crew and aircraft realistically to avoid self-inflicted delays.[7] The core passenger rights are found in Chapter 3 – management of flight delays. Article 17 requires carriers to publish their General Conditions of Carriage, which must explicitly detail the services provided to passengers in the event of delays

1 Order of the Ministry of Transport of People's Republic of China No. 56, 2016.

2 Article 4.

3 Article 75. See: Mert Hifzi, 'Delayed or Cancelled Flights in China – a New Regulation to Affect All Carriers' (*HFW*, 19 December 2016) <https://www.hfw.com/insights/delayed-or-cancelled-flights-in-china-december-2016/> accessed 1 December 2025.

4 For instance, Chapter 2 mandates that all key aviation entities – carriers, airports, air traffic management (ATM), and ground services – must establish systems, procedures, and capabilities to ensure flights operate on time and safely.

5 Article 3(2) defines delays as flights whose actual departure is later than 15 minutes after the scheduled departure time, and Article 3(4) defines cancellation as scheduled flights which are not operated due to a delay or an anticipated delay.

6 Article 2. See: Pablo Mendes de Leon, *Introduction to Air Law* (Wolters Kluwer 2022) point 6.4.

7 Article 8.

DOI: 10.4324/9781003746164-23

and cancellations at time of purchase.[8] Specifically, domestic carriers must specify their policy regarding monetary compensation, including the precise conditions, criteria, and procedures under which such compensation is offered.[9] Most airlines have adopted the Service and Compensation Standards of the Flight Carrier for Anomalies in Aviation Transportation Service Quality (Trial) published by China Aviation Transportation Association (CATA) in 2010 which recommended a cash compensation of RMB200 or RMB300 in credit for flight delays between four and eight hours.[10] For delays exceeding eight hours, the three major airlines, Air China, China Eastern, and China Southern, are willing to pay RMB 400, while other airlines might offer less.

Airline	**Compensation for 4–8-Hour Delay**	**Compensation for Over 8-Hour Delay**	**Key Conditions**
Air China[11]	RMB 200.	RMB 400.	May provide discounts/ mileage instead of cash. May exceed RMB 400.
China Eastern[12]	RMB 200. RMB 20 for infant.	RMB 400.	Cash compensation.
China Southern	RMB 200.	RMB 400.	
Hainan Airlines[13]	RMB 200.	RMB 400.	
Shenzhen Airlines[14]	RMB 200.	RMB 400.	

(*Continued*)

8 As restated in Article 28 and in line with Article 820 of the Civil Law Code.

9 Article 126 of Civil Aviation Law stipulates that the carrier should assume liability for the losses to passengers, baggage, or cargoes caused by delays.

10 Norton Rose Fulbright, 'Developments in Air Passenger Protection in the Peoples' Republic of China' (2017) <https://www.nortonrosefulbright.com/en/knowledge/publications/ac595e81/developments-in-air-passenger-protection-in-the-peoples-republic-of-china>.

11 Point 8.3.1 of Air China, 'General Conditions for Passengers and Baggages' <https://m.airchina.com/c/invoke/ystjnextpage/yunshutianjianZH1@pgenus> accessed 1 December 2025.

12 Point 9.2.5.1 of. China Eastern Airlines Corporation Limited, 'General Conditions for Transportation of Passenger and Baggage' (December 2024) <https://www.ceair.com/global/en_static/Announcement/TravelTips/dsGeneralCondition/chinaEasternLuggageRules/domesticRules/202201/W020241227382639790010.pdf> accessed 1 December 2025.

13 Point 7.5 of Hainan Airlines, 'General Conditions of International Carriage for Passengers and Baggage' <https://www.hainanairlines.com/HUPortal/dyn/portal/DisplayPage?LANGUAGE=GB&COUNTRY_SITE=CN&SITE=CBHZCBHZ&PAGE=GCIC> accessed 1 December 2025.

14 Point 8.3.1 of Air China 'General Conditions for Passengers and Baggages' <https://m.airchina.com/c/invoke/ystjnextpage/yunshutianjianZH1@pgenus> accessed 1 December 2025.

(Continued)

Airline	Compensation for 4–8-Hour Delay	Compensation for Over 8-Hour Delay	Key Conditions
Xiamen Airlines[15]	RMB 200.	RMB 400.	Cash or free tickets.
Sichuan Airline[16]	RMB 200.	RMB 400.	Compensation for child tickets is calculated at the adult rate; compensation for infant tickets is calculated at 10% of the adult rate.
Chengdu Airlines	RMB 200 (Adults).	RMB 400 (Adults).	Children (50%), infants (RMB 50 fixed).
Loong Air[17]	Up to RMB 100 (economy). Up to RMB 200 (Business).	Up to RMB 200 (economy). Up to RMB 400 (Business).	Cash compensation.
No Compensation Airlines[18]	**None.**	**None.**	China United, West Air, Spring Airlines, Urumqi Air, etc.

Carriers are also encouraged to explore other relief such as delay insurance.[19] Throughout the entire disruption process, airlines are required to report flight status, reasons, and estimated times to all parties every 30 minutes.[20] Carriers must not only make the information public on their website but on public information platforms and through telephone calls.[21] Finally, Articles 21 and 23 emphasize preparedness, mandating emergency response plans for alternate flights and overall drills for large-scale delays, ensuring that alternate airports must provide support without excuse if a flight is diverted. The law also mandates for passengers to be "well-

15 Point 1.1.4.2.4 of. Xiamen Air, 'General Conditions of Transportation and Carriage' <https://www.xiamenair.com/brandnew_EN/travel-transport-condition.html> accessed 1 December 2025.

16 Point 15.2.5 of Sichuan Airlines, 'General Conditions for Domestic Transportation for Passenger and Baggage' (July 2025) <https://www.sichuanair.com/pdf/GN0722.pdf> accessed 1 December 2025.

17 Chapter 8, Points 8.3.7.1 and 8.3.7.2 of Loongair, 'General Conditions of Domestic Transportation' <https://www.loongair.cn/#/web/travel/info?code=0.1.3.1> accessed 1 December 2025.

18 See: Xin Yang, Research on Improving Passenger Service Quality After Flight Delay (Haaga-Helia University of Applied Sciences 2025) 11 <https://www.theseus.fi/bitstream/handle/10024/885453/Yang_Xin.pdf?sequence=5&isAllowed=y>.

19 Article 18.

20 Article 22.

21 Article 26(1).

behaved when boarding, and protect their interests in a lawful manner" without really defining those terms.[22]

In case of a flight disruption, passengers have a right to refund or endorsement services as well as services in accordance with the carrier's general conditions of carriage.[23] The Regulation itself is silent with regard to the amount passengers are entitled to if any. Article 29 is the cornerstone of compensation and care. It establishes a core distinction based on the cause of the delay or cancellation. When a delay or cancellation occurs at the departure airport due to reasons attributable to the carrier, such as aircraft maintenance or crew scheduling, the carrier must provide food and accommodation.[24] However, if the disruption at the departure airport is due to non-carrier reasons like weather or air traffic control, the carrier is only obligated to assist passengers in arranging for food and accommodation, but the passengers must bear the costs themselves.[25] Crucially, for delays or cancellations occurring at a stopover on a domestic flight, or for any diverted flight, the carrier must provide food and accommodation regardless of the cause of the disruption.[26] Domestic carriers shall provide food and accommodation for passengers on a diverted flight regardless of the reasons.[27] The phrasing of this article strategically circumvents the core legal battlefield of "extraordinary circumstances" that dominates EU air passenger rights law. The Chinese regulation, through Article 29, sidesteps this legal moratorium by shifting the focus from fault-based compensation to a location- and event-based obligation to provide care. However, it is unclear who determines whether an event is attributable to a carrier as Article 29 seems to only contain examples. Passengers with disabilities, senior citizens, pregnant women, unaccompanied minors, and other passengers who require special care are given priority.[28]

22 Article 24.

23 Articles 27 and 28.

24 Article 29(1).

25 Article 29(2). In a 2006 case, related by Huaping Qin, *Abdul Waheed v China Eastern Airlines Shanghai No.1 Intermediate People's Court (2006) Hu-Yi-Zhong-Min-Yi-Min-Zhong-Zi-609 Judgment*, China Eastern Airlines was held liable for compensation due to the failure to provide full information to the passenger at the point of departure – rather than the point of connection as it occurred – even if the delay was caused by bad weather. It remains to be seen whether this case would still play a role under the new rule. See: Huaping Qin, 'Beyond Litigation: The Use of ADR in Resolving Disputes Between Air Carriers and Passengers: China's Perspective' (2022) 47 Air & Space Law 347, 353.

26 Article 29(3).

27 Article 29(4).

28 Article 30.

Reason for Disruption/Location	At Departure Airport	At a Stopover or on a Diverted Flight
Carrier-Related Reasons (e.g., aircraft maintenance, crew scheduling, operational issues)	**Airline pays.**	**Airline pays.**
External/Non-Carrier Reasons (e.g., weather, air traffic control, security checks, emergency situations)	**Passenger pays.** The carrier must only *assist* in arranging services.	**Airline pays.**

In case of tarmac delay, the Regulation establishes a strict protocol prioritizing information and comfort. Carriers must publish a tarmac delay emergency plan, coordinated with relevant authorities, and report information to passengers every 30 minutes.[29] Throughout the duration of the tarmac delay, lavatory facilities must be accessible.[30] After two hours, the airline must provide drinking water and food to passengers.[31] If a tarmac delay reaches three hours and there is no confirmed take-off time, the carrier must arrange for passengers to disembark provided safety and security regulations allow it.[32]

Elapsed Time	Carrier's Mandatory Obligations
At Start of Delay	• Announce the reason for the delay. • Ensure lavatory facilities are available and functional.
Every 30 Minutes	• Provide dynamic updates on the reason and estimated delay duration.
After 2 Hours	• Provide drinking water and food to all passengers.
After 3 Hours	• If no definite take-off time is available, **arrange for disembarkation** (contingent on safety and security conditions).

The Regulation also contains a provision on large-scale flight delays, namely when a certain number of flights are delayed and a large number of passengers are affected.[33] The Regulation treats large-area delays as a systemic emergency, triggering a coordinated, airport-wide response mechanism that supersedes individual airline handling.[34] Upon initiation, a pre-established coordination mechanism is activated, which centralizes

29 Articles 32 and 33.
30 Article 34.
31 Article 34.
32 Article 35.
33 Article 3(7) and Section 4.
34 Articles 37–38.

information sharing, flight release priorities, and passenger service logistics. The airport authority acts as the command centre, ensuring all entities – airlines, ground handlers, air traffic management (ATM), police, and other support units – work in unison.[35]

The teeth of the Regulation are found in Chapters 4 to 7 which contain the enforcement and penalties. All parties are accountable, with strict legal penalties outlined in Chapter 7 for failure to meet these standards, most notably a fine of up to ¥100,000 for violating the three-hour tarmac disembarkation rule.[36] Unlike some national laws which have divided the penalties by severeness, China has instead divided it depending on the breach itself. If airlines do not use their allocated slots affecting flight regularity, the civil aviation administrative authorities can cancel the slots and impose a fine of up to ¥30,000.[37] Similarly, for non-compliance with the publications requirements – such as compensation in the general terms and conditions – the fine is also capped at ¥30,000 but after a warning was issued.[38] However, a failure to notify passengers of flight information or the general conditions only results in a ¥10,000 fine, unless the issue is of a serious nature then it can be increased to ¥30,000.[39] Fines for failing to provide refunds, written delay certificates, or care services range from ¥20,000 to ¥60,000.[40]

The Chinese framework, primarily embodied in the 2017 Provisions on the Management of Flight Regularity, is best understood as a systemic operational management law with passenger care components. Its primary goal is to ensure the smooth functioning of the entire aviation ecosystem by imposing duties on all stakeholders – airlines, airports, air traffic control, and ground handlers – to prevent and manage disruptions rather than provide passengers with fixed compensation in case such disruption occurs.

Despite this strong mandate for operational excellence through rigorous internal system, the major weakness of the system lies in monetary compensation which is left at the discretion of the airlines in their General Conditions of Carriage. Not only does that result in divergence among airlines, it also leaves passengers to analyse legal terms and conditions to ascertain their right, creating a notable power imbalance. This creates a peculiar regulatory paradox: The law employs a detailed matrix of administrative penalties, with fines calibrated to the specific breach (e.g.,

35 Articles 41–43.
36 Article 60(9).
37 Article 57.
38 Article 58(2).
39 Article 59(1) and (2).
40 Article 60(1) and (2).

¥30,000 for misusing slots, ¥20,000–¥60,000 for failing to provide care) payable to the state, yet it mandates no fixed, standardized compensation payable directly to the passenger for the hardship of a delay. This stands in stark contrast to the EU model, where fixed compensation for the passenger is the central pillar of the redress mechanism.

The Chinese framework, particularly Article 29, is, however, a potential solution to the legalistic battles relating to "extraordinary circumstances" found under Regulation 261. By decoupling the right to essential care from the debate over the cause of the disruption (especially at stopovers), it ensures passengers are not left stranded. The reason for the disruption determines who pays for care, but the passenger's right to receive assistance is constant. Chinese law offers in this regard a much more pragmatic approach.

Comparison with EU Regulation

Feature	Provisions on the Management of Flight Regularity	EU Regulation 261/2004
Delay Compensation	Care + compensation according to airline policy.	≥3h: €250–€600 (by distance).
Cancellation Compensation	Care + compensation according to airline policy.	<14d notice: Refund or re-routing + €250–600 compensation (by distance).
Denied Boarding Compensation	Not part of the Regulation.	Volunteer first; €250–600 (by distance) if denied boarding.
Baggage Liability	Not specified.	Not specified.

Bibliography

- Order of the Ministry of Transport of People's Republic of China No. 56, 2016.
- *Abdul Waheed v China Eastern Airlines* Shanghai No. 1 Intermediate People's Court (2006) Hu-Yi-Zhong-Min-Yi-Min-Zhong-Zi-609 Judgment.
- Air China, 'General Conditions for Passengers and Baggages' <https://m.airchina.com/c/invoke/ystjnextpage/yunshutianjianZH1@pgenus> accessed 1 December 2025.
- China Eastern Airlines Corporation Limited, 'General Conditions for Transportation of Passenger and Baggage' (December 2024) <https://www.ceair.com/global/en_static/Announcement/TravelTips/dsGeneralCondition/chinaEasternLuggageRules/domesticRules/202201/W020241227382639790010.pdf> accessed 1 December 2025.
- Hainan Airlines, 'General Conditions of International Carriage for Passengers and Baggage' <https://www.hainanairlines.com/HUPortal/dyn/portal/DisplayPage?LANGUAGE=GB&COUNTRY_SITE=CN&SITE=CBHZCBHZ&PAGE=GCIC> accessed 1 December 2025.
- Hifzi, M., 'Delayed or Cancelled Flights in China - a New Regulation to Affect All Carriers' (*HFW*, 19 December 2016) <https://www.hfw.com/

insights/delayed-or-cancelled-flights-in-china-december-2016/> accessed 1 December 2025.

- Loongair, 'General Conditions of Domestic Transportation' <https://www.loongair.cn/#/web/travel/info?code=0.1.3.1> accessed 1 December 2025.
- Mendes de Leon, P., *Introduction to Air Law* (Wolters Kluwer 2022).
- Norton Rose Fulbright, 'Developments in Air Passenger Protection in the Peoples' Republic of China' (2017) <https://www.nortonrosefulbright.com/en/knowledge/publications/ac595e81/developments-in-air-passenger-protection-in-the-peoples-republic-of-china> accessed 1 December 2025.
- Qin, H., 'Beyond Litigation: The Use of ADR in Resolving Disputes Between Air Carriers and Passengers: China's Perspective' (2022) 47 Air and Space Law 347.
- Sichuan Airlines, 'General Conditions for Domestic Transportation for Passenger and Baggage' (July 2025) <https://www.sichuanair.com/pdf/GN0722.pdf> accessed 1 December 2025.
- Xiamen Air, 'General Conditions of Transportation and Carriage' <https://www.xiamenair.com/brandnew_EN/travel-transport-condition.html> accessed 1 December 2025.
- Xin Yang, *Research on Improving Passenger Service Quality After Flight Delay* (Haaga-Helia University of Applied Sciences 2025).

II.13

Colombia

In Colombia, passenger rights are governed by the *Reglamentos Aeronáuticos de Colombia* (RAC), which are a vast and complex set of documents which are frequently updated.[1] They are not a single, unified law but rather a comprehensive collection of rules, resolutions, and circulars.[2] RAC 3 is often cited as the key document for passenger rights as they ensure that passengers are entitled to compensation and assistance in cases of flight delays, cancellations, or denied boarding. The rules apply to flights departing from or arriving in Colombia and are enforced by the Civil Aviation Authority of Colombia.[3]

RAC 3 is a very long document, but Section 3.10.1 is dedicated to passenger rights and carrier duties. The first right is that passengers, or a third party acting on their behalf, have the right to receive detailed information from the airline, travel agency, or intermediary during the reservation and ticket purchase process which includes fare types, check-in times, general conditions of carriage among other things.[4] There is also a special duty to inform for internet or distance sales, including complete, clear, and sufficient information about the conditions and consequences for withdrawing from the purchase.[5] Like in Mexico and Venezuela, the

1 For instance, RAC 3 has been updated in 2012, 2015, 2017, 2018, and 2021. Unidad Administrativa Especial de Auronautica Civil, 'Reglamentos Aeronauticos de Colombia: RAC 3' (17 Octubre 2021) <https://www.aerocivil.gov.co/loader.php?lServicio=Tools2&lTipo=descargas&lFuncion=visorpdf&file=https%3A%2F%2Fwww.aerocivil.gov.co%2Floader.php%3FlServicio%3DTools2%26lTipo%3Ddescargas%26lFuncion%3DexposeDocument%26idFile%3D16804%26tmp%3D96ea7ae8cae3dfa8d010dfe89b991546%26urlDeleteFunction%3Dhttps%253A%252F%252Fwww.aerocivil.gov.co%252Floader.php%253FlServicio%253DTools2%2526lTipo%253Ddescargas%2526lFuncion%253DdeleteTemporalFile%2526tmp%253D96ea7ae8cae3dfa8d010dfe89b991546&pdf=1&tmp=96ea7ae8cae3dfa8d010dfe89b991546&fileItem=16804 > accessed 1 December 2025.

2 RAC 3 has been modified by RAC 91, 119, 121, 129, 135, 137, and 138.

3 Daniel Uribe Correa, 'La protección de los pasajeros de transporte aéreo en Colombia' (2019) 21 Revista Estudios Socio-Jurídicos 293.

4 3.10.1.1.

5 3.10.1.1.1. See: Adriana Rocio Rodriguez Cetina, 'La protección al usuario del servicio público de transporte aéreo, abordado desde la perspectiva de la supervisión de

DOI: 10.4324/9781003746164-24

RAC contains a special duty to treat passengers with dignity and respect at all time.[6]

The passenger's ability to exercise withdrawal or retraction is defined in 3.10.1.8.1 and 3.10.1.8.2. A passenger can withdraw from their trip by notifying the airline or travel agency at least 24 hours before the flight. While passengers have the right to a refund, the airline can retain a penalty of up to 10% of the fare value excluding taxes and fees. This right doesn't apply to promotional fares unless specified.[7] For tickets purchased through non-traditional or distance sales (e.g., online), a passenger can retract their purchase within 48 hours of buying the ticket.[8] This right can only be exercised if the flight is at least eight calendar days away for domestic flights and 15 calendar days away for international flights.[9] The airline can retain a fixed amount of $60,000 COP for domestic or $50 USD for international tickets, though this cannot exceed 10% of the fare.[10] However, when the passenger's withdrawal occurs as a consequence of any variation attributable to the airline in the flight time or its conditions, to such an extent that under the new circumstances, they deem it no longer useful or convenient, there shall be no penalty or reduction percentage for the refund.[11]

Feature	**Withdrawal (Desistimiento)** *RAC 3.10.1.8.1*	**Retraction (Retracto)** *RAC. 3.10.1.8.2 (For distance sales)*
Applicability	Applies to **all ticket types** (unless otherwise stated).	Applies **only** to tickets bought via **non-traditional/distance methods** (e.g., online, phone).
Notification Deadline	At least **24 hours** before the scheduled flight departure.	Within **48 hours** of the **purchase** of the ticket.
Flight Deadline	N/A – based on flight time.	The flight must be at least **8 days away** (domestic) or **15 days away** (international) from the date of retraction.
Refund Entitlement	Right to a refund of the paid value.	Right to a full refund of the paid value.

(*Continued*)

la Superintendencia de Transporte' (*LL.M, Universidad Externado de Colombia*, 2024) <https://bdigital.uexternado.edu.co/server/api/core/bitstreams/4d64ab05-9dc2-4987-a9b7-693cfc6ecf93/content>.

6 3.10.2.6.

7 3.10.1.8.1 coupled with 3.10.2.14.1.

8 3.10.1.8.2(a).

9 3.10.1.8.2(b).

10 3.10.1.8.2(e).

11 3.10.2.14.1.

(Continued)

Airline Retention	Airline may retain a **penalty of up to 10%** of the base fare (excluding taxes and fees).	Airline may retain a **fixed amount**: • **$60,000 COP** (Domestic). • **$50 USD** (International). *Cannot exceed 10% of the base fare.*
Promotional Fares	**Does NOT apply**, unless explicitly offered by the airline.	Rules apply unless otherwise stated in the promotion's conditions.
Key Exception	**If the cancellation is due to a significant change** (schedule, conditions) **made by the airline** that makes the trip no longer useful or convenient for the passenger, **the refund is FULL with NO penalty.**	The right is designed for buyer's remorse in distance selling; it is typically not triggered by airline changes.

RAC 3, like Argentinian law, contains a specific provision dedicated to data protection which allows airlines to use personal information only to formalize the reservation and execution of the contract of carriage. Those data cannot be sold or commercialized.[12]

Tickets are valid for a maximum of one year, though this can be extended or determined by the fare's specific terms. If the passenger decides to travel after the validity has expired, they may have to pay additional fees based on the new fare. If they decide not to travel, they have the right to a refund, minus any applicable deductions.[13] The loss of a ticket does not invalidate the contract and passengers have the right to the issuance of a new one or a refund of its value, upon presenting the corresponding report and once it is determined that said lost or destroyed ticket cannot be used by any other person.[14]

RAC 3 contains a specific provision for transport of minor. A child under 2 years old can travel on an adult's lap for free for domestic flights and can be charged a maximum of 10% of the accompanying adult's fare.[15] For children under 12, on domestic flights, they are charged a maximum of two-thirds of the fare and are entitled to their own seat.[16] Unaccompanied minors must travel as "minors recommended to the airline" under the carrier's conditions, which may include additional

12 3.10.1.4.
13 3.10.1.7.1.
14 3.10.2.14.2.
15 3.10.1.9(a)–(b).
16 3.10.1.9(c).

charges for supervision.[17] Moreover, airlines must comply with the Code of Childhood and Adolescence which includes verifying that an unaccompanied minor, or a minor travelling with only one parent or a third party, has the proper legal authorization.[18]

RAC also contains a proactive and comprehensive rule that forces airlines to create and enforce an internal policy to combat the commercial sexual exploitation of children (CSEC).[19] The airline's code of conduct must be included in its corporate policies and must be followed by all legal representatives, directors, administrators, employees, and contractors. The code must include, at a minimum:

- **Prohibition of Promotion and Facilitation:**
  - o Airlines and their personnel must refrain from explicitly or implicitly offering tourism or transport services that in any way include the sexual exploitation of minors.[20]
  - o Airlines must not provide information, directly or indirectly, about places where CSEC is coordinated or practiced.[21]
  - o Airlines must not transport passengers or the public, directly or through third parties, to establishments or locations where CSEC is practiced.[22]
  - o Airlines must not facilitate flights on routes for the purpose of sexual exploitation or abuse of minors.[23]
- **Contractual and Reporting Obligations:**
  - o Airlines must ensure that contracts with their suppliers clearly state the requirement for the supplier to adhere to the same code of conduct.[24]
  - o Airlines must have procedures in place to report any substantiated knowledge of CSEC to the competent authorities, including the existence of related locations. They must ensure their internal procedures comply with reporting obligations.[25]
- **Internal Training and Public Awareness**:
  - o Airlines must design and disseminate measures to prevent all forms of CSEC to their staff and suppliers.[26]

---

17 3.10.1.9.
18 3.10.1.9.1.
19 3.10.1.9.1.1.
20 3.10.1.9.1.1(a).
21 3.10.1.9.1.1(b).
22 3.10.1.9.1.1(c).
23 3.10.1.9.1.1(e).
24 3.10.1.9.1.1(f).
25 3.10.1.9.1.1(g)–(h).
26 3.10.1.9.1.1(i).

- o Airlines must inform all personnel about legal provisions and company measures regarding the prevention of CSEC.[27]
- o Airlines must inform all their clients and users about the legal consequences of the sexual exploitation and abuse of minors in Colombia.[28]
- o Airlines must publish its code of conduct for the prevention of CSEC on its website.[29]

Any promotional information must be real, clear, truthful, and comprehensive. All advertised conditions must be met. Promotional fares must be registered with the Civil Aviation Authority (UAEAC). If they are not registered, the airline cannot withhold any amount from the ticket value in case the passenger uses their rights to withdraw or retract the purchase.[30] For online or distance sales, a double acceptance (double-click) process is mandatory. Before the final confirmation, the passenger must be clearly shown the total price including all taxes, the full itinerary, and the potential deductions if they decide to cancel.[31] When an airline or agency offers a package that includes both airfare and land services, the airline is not liable for any land services it did not directly organize.[32]

Passengers are required to provide complete, accurate, and truthful personal information, including a contact person for emergencies. They must also inform the airline of any special health conditions at least 72 hours before travel. If the information provided is incorrect, the airline is not responsible for failing to notify the passenger of flight changes or for any resulting inconvenience.[33] Passengers are entitled to a refund of the ticket value or the proportional part corresponding to the unused segment or journey, when due to non-compliance with their obligations, improper conduct, or disruptive acts by the passenger, the carrier finds it necessary to refrain from transporting them or to interrupt the transport. In those situations, airlines are entitled to a reduction percentage.[34]

The RAC also limits the reliance on any no-show clause by allowing passengers on a round-trip or connecting ticket to inform the airline no later than one hour after the scheduled departure of that leg of their intent not to use that ticket. If the passenger does not, the airline can cancel the

27 3.10.1.9.1.1(j).
28 3.10.1.9.1.1(k)–(l).
29 3.10.1.9.1.1(m).
30 3.10.1.11.2.
31 3.10.1.11.2.
32 3.10.1.12.
33 3.10.1.13.
34 3.10.2.14.3.

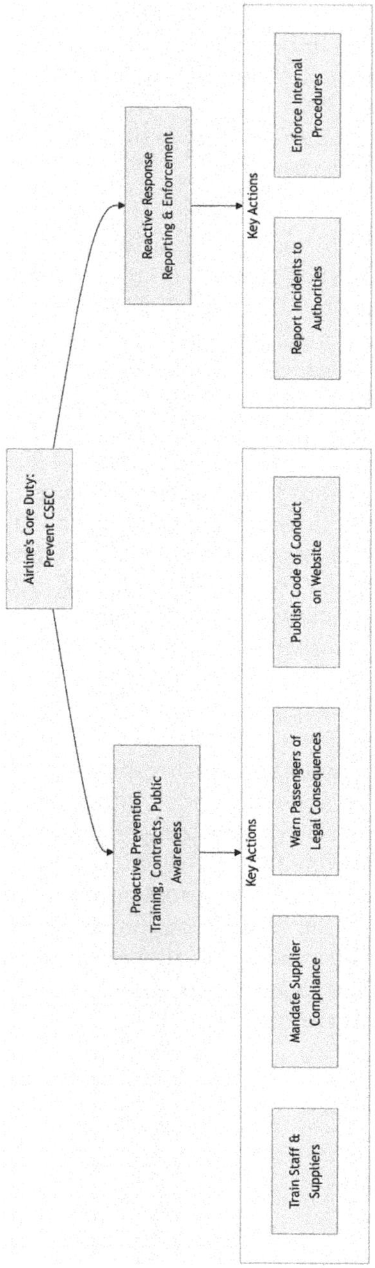

Figure II.13.1 Internal Policy for Airlines to Combat the Commercial Sexual Exploitation of Children (CSEC).

remaining parts of the itinerary.[35] To create a more equal level playing field and reduce no-shows, airlines can require an advance payment in cash or by credit card at the time a reservation is made.[36] Passengers must cancel a reservation at least 24 hours before the flight. Changes to reservations must also be requested with the same lead time, unless the fare has specific restrictions.[37]

Airlines must provide the necessary resources to ensure passengers and their baggage are boarded and disembarked with reasonable comfort, provided the passenger arrives on time and follows instructions.[38]

Passengers requiring special assistance or pet transport should notify the airline during booking or at least 24 hours beforehand. The airline is responsible for ensuring their safety and accommodation.[39] The rights of special needs passengers are detailed across several articles, detailed primarily in Sections 3.10.2.9 to 3.10.2.12, with a primary focus on ensuring their dignity, safety, and priority. The regulations make it clear that airlines have a distinct responsibility to accommodate these passengers and provide them with the necessary assistance. Special passengers, which include persons with disabilities, elderly persons requiring assistance, children under 5 years of age, pregnant women, and their necessary companions are to be given priority for boarding.[40] They should be attended to in a preferential line if airport facilities allow for it. Public Force veterans, as defined by Law 1979 of 2019, are expressly granted the same treatment and rights as all other special passengers.[41] Those passengers should not be placed in an emergency exit row or a seat next to the aircraft's door.[42]

For seriously ill passengers, the airline is also obligated to have the appropriate equipment and logistics to safely board, disembark, and move these passengers, ensuring that no procedure causes them risk, pain, or worsens their condition. In accordance with the Code of Commerce, an airline that knowingly accepts sick, mentally incapacitated, or minor passengers must provide them with ordinary care as required by their condition, within its means.[43] For the transportation of passengers who are ill, the airline may request a medical certificate issued within 12 hours prior to departure, verifying the individual's health status and fitness for travel.

35 3.10.1.14.1.
36 3.10.1.14.2.
37 3.10.1.14.3.
38 3.10.2.4.
39 3.10.1.15.
40 3.10.2.9.
41 3.10.2.9.3.
42 3.10.2.24.1.
43 3.10.2.9.1.

Additionally, the airline may require that a physician or other qualified professional accompany the passenger at the passenger's expense, unless the medical certificate indicates such accompaniment is unnecessary. In instances where supplementary personnel or care is needed, the airline is permitted to levy additional charges, if the assignment of special personnel or any other care implies additional costs.[44] The liability of the airline is not engaged for any damages suffered by passengers when they occur exclusively due to the actions of a third party, the passenger's own fault, or pre-existing organic lesions or illnesses that were not aggravated by facts imputable to the carrier.[45]

Importantly, RAC 3.10.2.11 protects these passengers from arbitrary denial of service. An airline cannot refuse transportation to the passengers covered in Sections 3.10.2.9 and 3.10.2.9.1 unless it is evident that under normal flight conditions their health could worsen, that the aircraft lacks the necessary resources to transport them safely, or that their condition implies risks or harm to others.

Specific provisions for pregnant women are outlined in Section 3.10.2.12. They are advised not to travel by air if their gestation period exceeds 30 weeks, unless the journey is strictly necessary. In all cases, such passengers must sign and present to the carrier a document, backed by a medical certificate issued within the ten days preceding the flight, stating their fitness to travel. This certificate must consider the route and duration of the flight. By signing, the passenger releases the airline from liability for any eventuality arising from their condition during the flight.

RAC 3 is based on the idea that once a reservation is made for one or more segments, the carrier must respect it under the agreed terms, conditions, and itinerary, within a reasonable time and reasonably direct route.[46] This means that airlines must inform passengers of any changes to the flight or itinerary (e.g., time or schedule changes) at least 24 hours in advance by the fastest possible means (phone, email, or messages). This does not apply to sudden changes due to unforeseen circumstances like weather or technical issues, but airlines must still inform passengers as soon as possible.[47] Once a passenger presents themselves at the counter and their reservation and documentation (passport, visa) are verified, the

---

44 3.10.2.9.1.

45 3.10.2.10.

46 3.10.1.5 reiterated in 3.10.2.5 which stipulated that passengers will be transported as according to fare, itinerary, and schedule, provided they comply with their duties. Article 3.10.2.16 mandates the transport of the passenger by air, safe and sound to their place of destination, at the agreed time according to the itinerary schedules and other rules contained in the aeronautical regulations, within a reasonable time and by a reasonably direct route in accordance with Article 982 of the Commercial Code.

47 3.10.1.6.

airline must issue a boarding pass. They must also provide information on the departure time, gate, and boarding conditions, and give the passenger baggage claim tags for any checked luggage.[48]

Carriers are required to furnish adequate, accurate, clear, and prompt information regarding delays, cancellations, and diversions.[49] In the event that a flight delay renders it unlikely for a connecting passenger to arrive at the connection point as scheduled, the airline is required to notify the passenger and provide the option to cancel the journey without incurring any penalties.[50] When passengers cannot continue their journey, they are entitled to 30% of the value of the fare. Otherwise, the passenger must be rebooked on the next flight.[51]

If a flight is cancelled or delayed due to force majeure or weather conditions, the airline is released from liability and must refund the ticket price. If the flight is interrupted mid-journey, the airline must arrange for the passenger to reach their destination by the quickest means possible at its expense, or offer a proportional refund for the unused portion of the trip.[52]

Passengers with a valid ticket or boarding pass cannot be denied boarding without legal cause. Denial based on race, politics, religion, gender, or any other form of discrimination is strictly prohibited.[53] In case of denial of boarding due to overbooking or for any other reason attributable to the airline, the passenger must be rebooked on the next available flight on the same date and on the same route. If no flight is available, the carrier must make the necessary arrangements, at its own expense, to board the passenger on another airline as soon as possible.[54] The passenger is also entitled to 30% of the value of the fare, payable in cash, unless the passenger expressly accepts another form, for involuntary denial of boarding due to overbooking.[55] Interestingly, the RAC 3 is silent on the procedure airlines must adopt in case of overbooking, i.e. required volunteers first.

In instances of delays, cancellations, overbooking without a refund, or any other occurrence attributable to the carrier, RAC 3.10.2.13.2 shall apply. This article mandates that when there is a delay in the initiation of the flight and the scheduled flight time, as authorized by the UAEAC, is

48 3.10.2.1.
49 3.10.2.7.
50 3.10.2.2.1.
51 3.10.2.13.2(g).
52 3.10.2.13.1.
53 3.10.2.3.
54 3.10.2.13.2(d).
55 3.10.2.13.2(f)(1) in the document used it was referred to as g but there was twice a g and no f while f should be referring to compensation.

not met passengers are entitled to a snack and a telephone communication not exceeding three minutes or message to the destination or origin if the delay is greater than one hour and less than three. However, when the cause of the delay has been overcome and the prompt departure of the flight is foreseeable (within the following 15 minutes), the carrier may refrain from providing this compensation if doing so would cause a greater delay.[56] When the delay is greater than three hours but less than five, in addition passengers must be provided with food, e.g. breakfast, lunch, or dinner, depending on the time.[57] For delays exceeding five hours, carriers must compensate the passenger 30% of the value of the fare, payable in cash, unless the passenger expressly accepts another form.[58] When this delay extends past 10 PM (local time), the airline must also provide the passenger with lodging – if they are not in their place of residence – and transportation expenses between the airport and the place of lodging and vice versa, unless the passenger voluntarily agrees to prolong the wait when it is foreseeable that the flight will take place within a reasonable timeframe.[59] Compared to Regulation 261, RAC 3 is more detailed and specific in its requirements, though thresholds are higher.

In cases of transport interruption, if the passenger does not opt for the refund of the proportional part of the price corresponding to the uncovered segment, they will be compensated for the delay suffered until the resumption of the journey.[60]

Delay Duration	**Required Compensation From the Airline**
More Than 1 Hour **Less Than 3 Hours**	• **A snack.** • A **phone call** (max 3 mins) or message to destination/origin.
More Than 3 Hours **Less Than 5 Hours**	• Snack + phone call + a full **meal** (breakfast, lunch, or dinner based on the time of day).
More Than 5 Hours	• Snack + phone call + meal. • **30% of the fare price**.

(*Continued*)

56 3.10.2.13.2(a)(1).

57 3.10.2.13.2(a)(2).

58 3.10.2.13.2(f)(2) in the document used it was referred to as g but there were twice a g and no f while f should be referring to compensation.

For the purpose of determining the compensation value for a single segment, the total price paid for the ticket shall be multiplied by the ratio between the distance of that segment and the total distance.

59 3.10.2.13.2(a)(3).

60 3.10.2.13.2(b).

(Continued)

Delay Duration	Required Compensation From the Airline
Delay Extends Past 10 PM (local time)	Monetary compensation + • **Lodging** (if the passenger is not in their city of residence) and transport.
If the Cause of the Delay Is Resolved and the Flight Is Predicted to Depart Within the Next 15 Minutes	The airline **may refrain from providing** the snack and phone call if distributing them **would cause a further delay.**

In cases where the airline decides to cancel a flight, without the price of the ticket having been refunded, the passenger is entitled to reimbursement for lodging expenses – if outside their place of residence – and transportation costs between the airport and the accommodation. Additionally, should a delay occur prior to cancellation, the passenger will receive the compensations for delayed flights as applicable.[61] If the flight cancellation is not attributable to force majeure or adverse weather conditions affecting safety, the passenger is entitled both to a refund for the segment relating to the cancelled flight and 30% of the value of the fare, payable in cash, unless the passenger expressly accepts another form.[62] In circumstances where a passenger is rebooked on another flight operated by the same or a different airline due to cancellation or other reasons, compensation shall be provided according to the waiting period until the alternative flight departs. If the new flight departs within six hours of the originally scheduled departure time, additional compensation does not apply.[63]

When the airline advances the flight by more than one hour without notifying the passenger, or when, having been notified, it becomes impossible for the passenger to travel at the newly imposed time, the passenger must be provided with travel to their final destination on the next convenient flight of the same airline on the same route.[64] If no flight is available, the carrier must make the necessary arrangements, at its own expense, to board the passenger on another airline as soon as possible. In these cases, the passenger shall not pay any surcharge if the new seat corresponds to a higher fare; if the passenger does not accept any of these alternatives, they may demand a refund of the price paid for the journey or journeys, without any penalty.[65]

61 3.10.2.13.2(c).
62 3.10.2.13.2(f)(3) in the document used it was referred to as g but there was twice a g and no f while f should be referring to compensation.
63 3.10.2.13.2(c).
64 3.10.2.13.2(e).
65 3.10.2.13.2(e).

When food and beverages are supplied on board the aircraft, this does not constitute a duty for the carrier, but it will be responsible for damages to health resulting directly from their poor state of preservation or hygienic conditions when consumed on board.[66]

RAC 3 also includes a section on passenger duties and carrier's rights. Passengers must arrive at the departure airport and check in within the time specified by the travel agency or airline when they purchased their ticket. If no time is indicated, they must do so at least one hour before the departure of domestic flights and two hours before international flights. These times are doubled during peak seasons and are much longer than the minimum threshold found in Regulation 261.[67] If the passenger fails to arrive with the required advance notice, the carrier may dispose of their seat, also called a no-show clause.[68] If there are available seats when the passenger arrives and the flight has not yet been closed, they may be admitted. In the event, the passenger arrives too late to travel or does not show up, the carrier may assign them a seat on another flight and impose an up to 10% penalty, which must be paid as a condition prior to boarding.[69] The RAC 3 also imposes a duty on the passenger to identify and follow all searches and control procedures.[70] While those provisions are pretty standard, the law makes it clear that passengers who declared their valuables can request the search to be conducted in private.[71]

It is the passenger's obligation to comply with instructions from the carrier and its crew regarding safety or behaviour during the flight, given from boarding operations, as well as during taxiing, take-off, flight, landing, and disembarkation. According to the law, the commander is the highest authority on board the aircraft, so other crew members and all passengers are subject to their authority during the journey.[72] Passengers are required to abstain from actions that could compromise flight safety, their own well-being, or the safety of individuals and property on board. This includes any conduct which disrupts order, morals, or discipline, or causes discomfort to fellow passengers – whether on board or at the airport.[73] RAC 3.10.2.25.1 contains a detailed list of prohibited behaviours such as disobeying crew instructions (unfastening seatbelt, using cell phones during the flight); interfering with aircraft systems (stealing life jackets, manipulating any emergency exist, obstructing the fire detection system);

66 3.10.2.15.
67 3.10.2.20.
68 3.10.2.20.1.
69 3.10.2.20.2.
70 3.10.2.21 to 3.10.2.23.
71 3.10.2.23.1.
72 3.10.2.25.
73 3.10.2.25.1.

smoking; assaulting any passengers or crew or unduly causing annoyance to other passengers; being intoxicated or consuming food not supplied by the carrier without authorization; carrying weapons, undeclared valuables, or dangerous goods; causing delays; or engaging in obscene behaviour. Such a level of details is not found anywhere else.

Category	Prohibited Acts
Disobeying Crew	• Unfastening seatbelt/standing while aircraft is moving. • Using electronic devices against instructions. • Disobeying any safety instruction.
Interfering With Safety Equipment	• Misusing life jackets/emergency equipment. • Tampering with emergency exits. • Obstructing alarms/fire detection systems.
Disruptive Behaviour	• Causing annoyance/disturbance to others. • Generating panic. • Physical/verbal assault. • Obscene acts/behaviour.
Prohibited Items	• Carrying weapons or objects that can be used as weapons. • Carrying dangerous goods/prohibited substances. • Carrying undeclared high-value items (>50 min wages). • Carrying pets illegally.
Substance Abuse	• Boarding/being on board under influence of alcohol/drugs. • Bringing illegal drugs on board.
Operational Interference	• Unauthorized entry/refusal to disembark. • Disrupting aircraft weight/balance. • Obstructing aircraft movement. • Causing unnecessary delays/diversions.
Other	• Smoking where prohibited. • Consuming unauthorized food/drink. • Any other act deemed improper by authorities.

Failure to comply with those obligations or engaging in disruptive behaviour could result in a unilateral contract termination or refuse to transport them. In such cases, the carrier may claim or retain from the passenger amounts corresponding to costs or delays incurred due to such behaviour, and any ticket refund will be subject to the reductions.[74] Passengers under special legal conditions travelling under the orders of a judicial, administrative, or police authority, or who are deprived of liberty for being accused of a crime are allowed to travel if special security measures have been adopted prior to the travel.[75]

74 3.10.2.25.2.
75 3.10.2.26.

The RAC 3 also regulates baggage. RAC 3.10.3.1 stipulates that unless otherwise mentioned by the airline, the baggage limit for domestic flights is 20 kg in economy class and 30 kg in business class. For international flights, the limit is 40 kg. These limits may be reduced on smaller capacity aircraft. The airline must also specify what can be transported as carry-on baggage, which must be small enough to fit in the overhead bin or under the seat and does not count toward the checked baggage weight limit. The RAC refers to the international conventions[76] for compensation but includes a twist that any baggage delay exceeding 24 hours results in a sum sufficient to acquire basic clothing, in no case less than 20% of the fare value per day of delay for each affected passenger.[77] Passengers have also important duties to avoid carrying any dangerous goods,[78] safely carrying a weapon if the person is authorized to do so,[79] not to pack fragile items,[80] valuables,[81] money, or electronic devices in their checked luggage. If a passenger fails to fulfil their obligations, the airline is not responsible for any harm suffered by that passenger as a result.[82]

Only small, non-aggressive dogs and cats (max 10 kg including container) may be transported in the cabin, provided that the airline authorized it and the animal is older than 8 weeks.[83] The law specifies that they must be in an approved carrier of max 55×35×25 cm and have all the relevant certificates.[84] There is also a limit on the number of animals per flight – four for planes under 100 seats, six for larger planes.[85] Service animals, including emotional support animals, may be transported in the cabin and the owner might be required to provide a medical or psychological certificate if their disability is not obvious.[86]

---

76 3.10.3.5 to 3.10.3.7.
77 3.10.3.7.1.
78 3.10.3.9.1.
79 3.10.3.9.2.
80 3.10.3.9.3.
81 3.10.3.10.
82 3.10.3.14.
83 3.10.3.11(a)(1)–(3) and (8).
84 3.10.3.11(a)(5) and (9).
85 3.10.3.11(a)(15).
86 3.10.3.11(b)(1).

Pets in Cabin (3.10.3.11)	• **Allowed:** only small, non-aggressive dogs/cats (max 10 kg incl. container). • **Requirements:** 48h notice, health/vaccination certificates, approved carrier (max 55x35x25 cm). • **Limit:** Max 4–6 containers per flight. • **Guide/Support Animals:** permitted with documentation.

While the RAC is extensive and covers many areas in detail, a provision on fines for non-compliance is lacking.

Colombian law on passenger rights is primarily governed by the *Reglamentos Aeronáuticos de Colombia* (RAC) 3. This framework establishes a highly detailed, rule-based system for passenger rights and provides clear guidelines for airlines and sets specific obligations for handling flight disruptions. Obligations for airlines are not left to general principles but are explicitly tiered. For instance, in the event of a delay, the required care is precisely defined: a snack and a phone call after one hour, a full meal after three hours, and a monetary compensation of 30% of the fare value once the delay exceeds five hours or extends past 10 PM, at which point lodging must also be provided. This granularity minimizes ambiguity and provides clear expectations for both passengers and airlines.

Beyond disruption management, the RAC 3 exhibits a proactive stance on consumer protection through unique features like data protection rules, stringent and detailed provisions for the dignified treatment – especially of vulnerable passengers – and a mandate for airlines to adopt and enforce a code of conduct to combat the commercial sexual exploitation of children (CSEC). Furthermore, it establishes one of the most detailed lists of prohibited passenger behaviours, aiding in onboard safety and enforcement.

However, this robust framework has significant weaknesses, primarily in the area of monetary compensation and enforcement. The compensation for a major disruption like a long delay or cancellation is capped at 30% of the ticket's fare value. This is potentially lower than the fixed amounts (€250 to €600) mandated by EU Regulation 261. Furthermore, the threshold for triggering this compensation is a five-hour delay at departure, which is high compared to the EU's model, which bases compensation on a three-hour delay.

In comparison to EU Regulation 261, the philosophical difference is clear. The EU Regulation is fundamentally a compensation-centric model. Colombian RAC 3 is a rule-centric and duty-centric model. Its strength is its incredible detail and breadth, governing not just disruptions but also consumer rights at the point of sale, protections for vulnerable passengers, and social responsibilities. It focuses on obliging the airline to perform specific actions (provide a meal, a phone call, a hotel, a 30% refund) at specific times rather than on a large, standalone compensation for inconvenience. While the EU model is more powerful for securing compensation after a problem, the Colombian model is arguably more proactive and detailed in prescribing how passengers should be treated during a problem and in other aspects of the travel experience. The lack of strong enforcement mechanisms, however, remains a potential critical flaw in the Colombian system.

Comparison with EU Regulation

Feature	RAC 3	EU Regulation 261/2004
Delays Compensation	**Tiered system:** Snack/phone at 1h, meal at 3h, 30% compensation + hotel at 5h/past 10 PM. **30% of fare value if delay at departure is over 5 hours.**	≥3h: €250–€600 (by distance).
Cancellation Rights	30% of fare value (unless force majeure) + care + re-routing/refund.	<14d notice: Refund or re-routing + €250–600 compensation (by distance).
Denied Boarding (Overbooking)	30% of fare value + rebooking on next available flight.	Volunteer first; €250–€600 (by distance) if denied boarding
Baggage Compensations	After 24 hours, 20% fare value per day.	Not specified.

Bibliography

- Unidad Administrativa Especial de Auronautica Civil, 'Reglamentos Aeronauticos de Colombia: RAC 3' (17 Octubre 2021) <https://www.aerocivil.gov.co/loader.php?lServicio=Tools2&lTipo=descargas&lFuncion=visorpdf&file=https%3A%2F%2Fwww.aerocivil.gov.co%2Floader.php%3FlServicio%3DTools2%26lTipo%3Ddescargas%26lFuncion%3DexposeDocument%26idFile%3D16804%26tmp%3D96ea7ae8cae3dfa8d010dfe89b991546%26urlDeleteFunction%3Dhttps%253A%252F%252Fwww.aerocivil.gov.co%252Floader.php%253FlServicio%253DTools2%2526lTipo%253Ddescargas%2526lFuncion%253DdeleteTemporalFile%2526tmp%253D96ea7ae8cae3dfa8d010dfe89b991546&pdf=1&tmp=96ea7ae8cae3dfa8d010dfe89b991546&fileItem=16804 accessed 1 December 2025.
- Cetina, A. R. R., 'La protección al usuario del servicio público de transporte aéreo, abordado desde la perspectiva de la supervisión de la Superintendencia de Transporte' (*LL.M, Universidad Externado de Colombia*, 2024) <https://bdigital.uexternado.edu.co/server/api/core/bitstreams/4d64ab05-9dc2-4987-a9b7-693cfc6ecf93/content> accessed 1 December 2025.
- Uribe Correa, D., 'La protección de los pasajeros de transporte aéreo en Colombia' (2019) 21 Revista Estudios Socio-Jurídicos 293.

II.14

Ecuador

Ecuador's air passenger rights are rooted in a multi-layered legal framework, ranging from the Constitution and international agreements[1] to specific domestic aviation and consumer protection statutes, primarily administered by the *Dirección General de Aviación Civil* (DGAC or General Directorate of Civil Aviation). The national regulations establish the specific obligations of air carriers to consumers in instances of flight disruption, including delays, cancellations, and denied boarding due to overbooking.[2] The latest applicable national law is *Resolución* 009/2024 of June 2024.[3] This comprehensive instrument consolidates and substantially expands the framework governing the rights and obligations of passengers and operators, marking a decisive shift towards a passenger-centric model aligned with international best practices.

According to Article 1, the *Resolución* applies to all international and domestic flights departing from Ecuador. The 2024 *Resolución* considerably extended the scope of the previous *Resolución* 0381 of 2013

1 Ecuador is also a member of the Andean Community of Nations (CAN), and Decision 619 of the CAN is a key piece of regional legislation that sets out common rules for air transport services among member countries.

2 The resolution draws legitimacy from specific aviation and sectoral laws such as Articles 146, 149, Title IX of the Aeronautical Code.

3 Resolución N° 009/2024 'Respecto a Derechos y Obligaciones para los Usuarios de Transporte Aéreo y Operadores del Servicio de Transporte Aéreo' (de 17 Julio de 2024) <https://www.aviacioncivil.gob.ec/wp-content/uploads/downloads/2024/07/resolucion_no._009f-2024.pdf>.

Modifying and unifying previous dispositions on compensation for delays and cancellations such as *Resolución* 046/2012 "Disposiciones complementarias para la compensación a los usuarios por retrasos y cancelaciones de vuelos domésticos regulares por parte de las compañías aéreas" of 5 March 2012 modified by Resolución 318/2013 "Disposiciones complementarias para la Aprobación y Cumplimiento de Itinerarios" of 23 September 2013; Resolución 083/2012 of 23 March 2012; Resolución 024/2013 of 7 August 2013; Resolución 008/2024 of 22 May 2024.

Resolución 0381 of 2013 of the Dirección General de Aviación Civil <https://www.aviacioncivil.gob.ec/wp-content/uploads/downloads/2019/06/res_381_disposiciones_vuelos_domesticos_compress1.pdf>.

DOI: 10.4324/9781003746164-25

which only applied to flights within Ecuador.[4] The territorial scope asserts the state's jurisdiction over the critical first segment of the passenger journey.

The *Resolución* contains an extensive and comprehensive glossary of 23 key terms, including "unforeseen circumstances" and "force majeure." Interestingly, the *Resolución* meticulously distinguishes these two key concepts.[5] Article 3 (e) defines "unforeseen circumstances" in a non-exhaustive list as it stipulates "such as" before providing a full list of potential circumstances. Those situations include meteorological causes, "technical failures not related the scheduled or routine maintenance of the aircraft, or caused by passengers or third parties at the time of the flight, and failures of ground support equipment."[6] "Force majeure" relates to any external, unforeseeable, and inevitable circumstances which absolves contractual liability in line with Article 149 of the Aeronautical Code. This tripartite distinction – between airline-controlled issues, external disruptions, and absolute exonerating events – creates the foundational logic for the entire compensation scheme. While the definitions of force majeure, unforeseen circumstances, and airline-imputable causes are more detailed than in many laws, they are not self-executing. The boundary between an "unforeseen" technical failure and one linked to negligent maintenance will inevitably become a major battleground.

The *Resolución* makes a distinction between overbooking and denial of boarding, explaining that overbooking is not prohibited *per se* but it leads to obligations for the airline. Denial of boarding could be explained by legitimate reasons in which airlines can deny boarding without being liable for compensation for health or security reasons, late check-in, presentation of inadequate travel document.[7]

Type of Disruption	Legal Definition (Art. 3)	Airline Responsibility
Force Majeure (*Fuerza Mayor*)	"An external circumstance that is unforeseen or inevitable, affecting the fulfillment of obligations. It is a reason that releases from contractual or non-contractual liability altered by the event."	**None** – Exonerates airline from liability.

(*Continued*)

4 Article 1 *Resolución* 0381 of 2013 of the Dirección General de Aviación Civil.

5 Article 3(e) and 3(l).

6 As translated by the General Directorate of Civil Aviation in Their Guide for Air Transport Users and Operators' <https://www.aviacioncivil.gob.ec/wp-content/uploads/downloads/2025/04/Guide-for-Air-Transport-Users-and-Operators.pdf>.

7 Article 3(h) for denial and Article 3(q) for overbooking.

(Continued)

Type of Disruption	Legal Definition (Art. 3)	Airline Responsibility
Unforeseen Circumstances (*Circunstancias imprevistas*)	"Causes outside the normal operation of the carrier that prevent the flight from taking place or delay its start, such as weather conditions, technical failures not related to the scheduled or routine maintenance of the aircraft, or caused by passengers or third parties at the time of the flight, and failures of ground support equipment."	**Limited** – Must prove circumstances were unavoidable.
Denial of Boarding	"The refusal to transport passengers on the flight despite having reported for boarding with a confirmed reservation and under the conditions established in the Air Transport Contract, unless there are reasonable grounds to deny boarding, such as health or safety reasons, inadequate travel documents, or the passenger's late arrival at check-in."	**Full** – Presumed responsible unless proves otherwise.
Overbooking (*Sobreventa*)	"A practice that occurs when, on a regular flight, the number of passengers with confirmed reservations who show up for boarding within the stipulated time exceeds the number of seats available on the aircraft."	**Absolute** – Always considered airline's commercial decision.

The text establishes an enforceable right to transparent information which goes much beyond the duty of issuing a ticket found in Article 146 of the Aeronautical Code. The obligations laid down in Article 4 ensure the establishment of a proactive and continuous "duty to inform" and transparency across the entire service chain. Passengers are not only entitled to clear and precise information on available flights, schedules, and fares but also on fare structure – explicitly requiring the disaggregation of the net value from taxes and charges[8] – and all contractual conditions. The duty of information is particularly stringent regarding disruptions: The air operator must inform the user of any change (*cualquier cambio*) to the flight or itinerary in a constant, periodic, and responsible manner, utilizing digital means or text messaging without exception.[9] Crucially, travel agencies or intermediaries are obliged to furnish verifiable user data to the carrier; a failure to do so that prevents timely communication of

8 Article 4(c).
9 Article 4(g).

a disruption holds the carrier liable for corresponding compensations.[10] The most emblematic provision of this empowerment logic is found in Article 4(k), which compels domestic airlines to embed a QR code or hyperlink to the official rights guide within reservation confirmations and at check-in counters, with international airlines required to display it at airport counters.[11] This mechanism transforms the resolution from a static legal text into an accessible tool, operationalizing the "right to know your rights."[12] Unlike previous resolutions, the 2024 version is silent regarding the consequences of a loss of a ticket.[13]

The *Resolución* provides two distinct legal pathways for passengers to dissolve the contract of carriage. Article 5 establishes an unconditional right of withdrawal, granting a 48-hour cooling-off period after purchase, a powerful consumer protection tool modelled on distance-selling regulations. This right is only negated for tickets purchased within 48 hours of departure. Separately, Article 6 governs the passenger's voluntary decision to cancel, which requires 72 hours' notice and permits airlines to retain an administrative fee not exceeding 10% of the ticket's net value, unless a specifically non-refundable promotional fare applies.

Situation	**Time**	**Penalties**
Cooling-off Period	48-hour unconditional withdrawal.	None but not applicable for tickets purchased within 48 hours of departure.
Voluntary Cancellation	72 hours' notice.	Administrative fee of 10% of ticket value (maximum).

The core substantive innovation of *Resolución* 009/2024 is its detailed, graduated, and quantifiable compensation regime for operational failures attributable to the airline, detailed in Chapter I. This system operates on three concurrent levels: care, refund, and monetary compensation. It applies to cancellations, delays caused by the carrier, and case of overbooking.[14]

Article 8 guarantees a full refund of the unused portion, or the entire ticket if the journey is rendered pointless, with strict processing deadlines of 15 days for cash payments and 30 days for card payments. If the journey has commenced and the disruption occurred during a stopover, the airline

10 Article 4(f).

11 Airlines were given two months to implement the mandatory QR code system according to the disposiciones transitorias.

12 Articles 4(h) and (l) mention that passengers must be informed of their rights.

13 Under *Resolución* 0381 of 2013, the loss of a ticket does not invalidate the air transport contract as the validity of the contract can be proven by other means – Article 4.

14 Article 7.

must arrange a return flight to the original departure point at the earliest convenience in addition to issuing a refund.

More significantly, Article 9 introduces an automatic financial penalty for specific carrier-controlled failures: a minimum compensation of 25% of the value of the affected route for overbooking unless the passenger volunteers and for excessive delays defined as over six hours for international flights and over four hours for domestic flights.[15] To determine the value of the compensation, the net value of the ticket paid shall be multiplied by the relation between the distance of the said unused route and the total distance.[16] The compensation also applies to transit or connecting passengers who cannot continue their journey due to reasons attributable to the carrier.[17] Additionally, if the passenger elects to continue the journey (and not take the proportional refund), they are entitled to compensation for the delay suffered until the trip is resumed.[18]

Articles 11 and 12 mandate escalating standards of care and assistance during delays and cancellations, creating a predictable ladder of entitlements. In the event of a cancellation for which the passenger has not received any refund or re-routing on a same day flight, the carrier is obliged to cover lodging and transfer expenses.[19] For domestic delays, the requirements progress from refreshments and communication access equivalent to a phone call of up to three minutes for one-to-two hour delays; to full meals (breakfast, lunch, or dinner) and a future travel discount of 10% on the ticket value for the next trip for two-to-four hour delays; and culminate in hotel accommodation, transfers, an immediate refund option – unless the passenger agreed to wait for a re-routing occurring within five days – and the minimum of 25% monetary compensation for delays exceeding four hours.[20] The structure for international delays is similarly graduated but with higher time thresholds, reflecting the longer-haul context. The right to care kicks in between two and four hours for a snack and free communication, a full meal and a 10% discount is granted for delays between four and six hours with the full suite of care and compensation triggered at the six-hour mark.[21]

15 Article 9(a) and (b). The original text mentioned three hours for domestic flights but has been corrected by a subsequent Fe de Erratas. See: 'General Directorate of Civil Aviation in Their Guide for Air Transport Users and Operators' 9 <https://www.aviacioncivil.gob.ec/wp-content/uploads/downloads/2025/04/Guide-for-Air-Transport-Users-and-Operators.pdf>.

16 Article 9.

17 Article 14.

18 Article 10.

19 Article 11.

20 Article 12(a)–(c).

21 Article 12(a)–(c).

Delay Duration (From Scheduled Departure)	**Domestic Flights**	**International Flights**
>1 Hour to <2 Hours	**Care:** Refreshment + one free communication (≤3 min phone call). **Compensation:** None.	**Not Applicable.**
>2 Hours to <4 Hours	**Care:** Refreshment + communication + **full meal** + **10% discount** on next ticket. **Compensation:** None.	**Care:** Refreshment + one free communication. **Compensation:** None.
≥4 Hours to ≤6 Hours	**Care: All of the above** + **hotel and transfers** (if needed) + **immediate refund** option. **Compensation:** Minimum **25%** of unflown segment's value.	**Care:** Refreshment + communication + **full meal** + **10% discount** on next ticket. **Compensation:** None.
>6 Hours	Same as above.	**Care: All of the above** + **hotel and transfers** (if needed) + **immediate refund** option. **Compensation:** Minimum **25%** of unflown segment's value.

This new provision contrasts a bit with the previous position which entitled passengers right to care after a 30-minute delay.[22] The restrictions on the provision of care due to adverse weather or force majeure are not explicitly mentioned in the 2024 *Resolución*.

If a passenger is denied boarding because of overbooking, the airline is required to provide transportation to the final destination on the next available flight operated by the same airline on the same date and route. If this option is not available, the airline must arrange transportation on an alternative airline at the earliest opportunity.[23] In addition to the re-routing, passengers are entitled to at least 25% compensation.[24] The carrier is expressly prohibited from charging any additional value to the passenger for the re-routing. This removes any financial ambiguity or potential incentive for systematic overbooking. However, unlike its predecessor *Resolución* 0381/2013, the new resolution is silent on the procedure to adopt in case of denial of boarding. Previously it was clearly stipulated that when an airline anticipates the need to deny boarding, it

22 Article 5(a) *Resolución* 0381 of 2013.
23 Article 13.
24 Article 13.

is required to first solicit volunteers from among the passengers. Those who volunteer are provided with additional assistance. If an insufficient number of volunteers come forward, passengers who are involuntarily denied boarding must be compensated, refunded, and assisted.[25]

Furthermore, the protections are expressly extended to the most vulnerable users in transit; Articles 14 and 15 ensure that passengers affected by misconnections or diversions due to the airline's fault receive the same compensation and have their resulting accommodation and transport costs covered to/from the new airport.[26]

Although there are no dedicated provisions on special needs passengers, the *Resolución* reinforces the obligation for preferential treatment for Priority Users, which inclusively covers individuals with reduced mobility, the elderly, pregnant women, and children under 5 years.[27]

Chapter II is dedicated to baggage including rules governing handling, documentation, and liability.[28] Article 21 stipulates that if checked baggage is not delivered on arrival, the airline must cover the minimum cost of essential hygiene products or provide them directly. Critically, if the delay surpasses 24 hours, the airline is obligated to provide funds for basic clothing and pay a daily compensation of 10% of the value of the affected route for each subsequent day of delay. Claims must be presented within seven days of receiving the baggage.

The architecture of rights is consciously balanced by a symmetrical framework of passenger obligations enumerated in Articles 22 through 27. These duties include providing accurate personal data,[29] arriving within stipulated check-in windows of two hours for domestic flights and three for international flights,[30] providing the required documents,[31] and complying with all instructions from crew.[32] Crucially, users must abstain from any act that violates safety, good order, morals, or discipline.[33] On the contrary, airlines are entitled to suspend the provision of services.

25 Article 5(g).
26 Article 15.
27 Article 3(t).
28 Article 16–21.
29 Article 22.
30 Article 23.
31 Article 24. This means "identity card, driver's license, passport, birth certificates for minors, birth registration for newborns, or documents issued by the Civil Registry" for domestic flights and "passport, visa, medical certificate when necessary, current vaccinations (depending on the destination), identity or citizenship card (within the Andean Community), or a blue passport for refugees or stateless persons" for international flights. As translated by General Directorate of Civil Aviation in their Guide for Air Transport Users and Operators' 16 <https://www.aviacioncivil.gob.ec/wp-content/uploads/downloads/2025/04/Guide-for-Air-Transport-Users-and-Operators.pdf>.
32 Article 26.
33 Article 27.

Concurrently, the *Resolución* imposes affirmative organizational duties on operators, mandating in Article 29 the establishment of accessible customer service systems to receive and channel complaints, claims, and suggestions. The ultimate guarantor of this ecosystem is the General Directorate of Civil Aviation, which is tasked with direct oversight and enforcement through dedicated personnel and offices within airport premises.[34] However the *Resolución* does not include any fixed sanctions unlike other national laws.

The major omission is any rule relating to downgrading and potential compensation for passengers.

Travel Phase	Key Rights	Relevant Articles	Passenger Obligations
Booking and Pre-Departure	• 48-hour unconditional withdrawal right. • Transparent fare breakdown (net vs. taxes). • QR code access to rights guide. • Accurate flight information.	Art. 5 (Retracto). Art. 4(c), 4(k). Art. 4(a-d).	Provide truthful personal information (Art. 22).
Check-in and Boarding	• Clear check-in requirements. • Denied boarding compensation for overbooking. • Assistance for passengers with disabilities.	Art. 23, 24. Art. 13. Art. 3(t).	Arrive within stipulated times (2hr domestic/3hr international) (Art. 23).
In-Flight Disruption	• Progressive care during delays. • Re-routing or refund for cancellations. • Information on changes.	Art. 12. Art. 8, 11. Art. 4(g), 4(j).	Comply with crew instructions (Art. 26).
Baggage Handling	• Immediate delivery if delayed. • Daily compensation after 24h delay (10% of route value/day). • Coverage for basic necessities.	Art. 21.	Verify baggage condition upon receipt; file claims within 7 days (Art. 25).
Post-Flight	• Complaint mechanism. • Refund processing timelines (15–30 days). • Follow-up on unresolved issues.	Art. 29. Art. 8. Art. 30.	None specified.

34 Article 30.

Ecuador's *Resolución* 009/2024 reveals a robust and comprehensive framework. While Ecuador's *Resolución* 009/2024 shares some similarities with EU Regulation 261, it differs significantly in scope, compensation structure, and enforcement. First and foremost, the *Resolución* applies only to flights departing from Ecuador, leaving passengers on return journeys to Ecuador from foreign points with potentially weaker protections. This makes the EU Regulation broader in reach, ensuring protections for both intra-EU and international travellers.

The *Resolución*'s foremost strength lies in its comprehensive architecture. It is not a piecemeal set of guidelines but an integrated code that spans the entire passenger journey from the pre-contractual phase of booking to the final resolution of post-flight complaints. By establishing a 48-hour unconditional right of withdrawal, the law intervenes at the very point of sale, granting consumers a powerful cooling-off period rarely included in other national passenger rights law. This pre-emptive protection is complemented by a novel mandate for digital transparency, requiring airlines to provide a scannable QR code that links directly to the full text of the rights guide. This mechanism is a pragmatic and modern solution to the chronic problem of information asymmetry, transforming a complex legal text into an accessible tool meant to empower passengers at the critical moments of booking and check-in.

A notable technical advancement of the *Resolución* is its meticulous definitional framework, which establishes a sophisticated tripartite taxonomy for classifying disruptions. It distinguishes between force majeure, unforeseen circumstances, and airline-imputable causes. This structured approach seeks to provide greater legal certainty than the binary "extraordinary circumstances" test that has fuelled extensive litigation within the European Union, suggesting a regulatory design aimed at pre-empting interpretive disputes.

The Ecuadorian system is inherently value-based, compensating passengers with a minimum of 25% of the net value of the unfulfilled segment of the ticket. The financial compensation is triggered by a severe delay: exceeding four hours for domestic flights and six hours for international flights attributable to the carrier. While this percentage-based approach ensures fairness relative to the fare paid, it can result in lower compensation amounts for inexpensive tickets, even when the disruption is significant. The six-hour threshold for international delays is also notably higher than the EU standard. Moreover, the "net value" concept might result in many complex disputes due to its opacity from a passenger point of view.

Regarding the graduated system of assistance, *Resolución* 009/2024 starts earlier than Regulation 261 and is markedly more prescriptive. Where the EU requires "reasonable" refreshments, meals, and hotel accommodation,

Ecuador's law specifies exact entitlements at precise delay intervals and even mandates a future travel discount. This reduces the discretionary space that has led to variability in service quality across Europe and aligns with a regulatory approach that seeks to eliminate ambiguity in passenger treatment. A notable feature of EU Regulation 261 is its explicit mention of "right to care" (meals, accommodation, communication) as a standalone entitlement, distinct from compensation, applicable in cases of denied boarding, cancellations, and significant delays. While *Resolución* 009/2024 also mandates these assistance measures, they are not seen as a dedicated fundamental right or at least the structure of the *Resolución* does not reflect such status.

The most striking area of divergence relates to baggage delay. Ecuador's creation of a daily percentage-based penalty is a more aggressive and structured intervention, explicitly designed to modify airline behaviour through financial disincentives – a tool absent from the European framework.

Ecuador's framework represents a significant advance in air consumer protection. It is characterized by its high level of detail, strong emphasis on mandatory digital communication, and specific protections (such as the right of retraction and detailed baggage delay compensation) that go beyond the core mandate of Regulation 261. It provides basic protections (assistance, rebooking, partial refunds) but lacks the fixed compensation and stronger enforcement of EU Regulation 261. The *Resolución* addresses several known flaws in the EU system, particularly regarding prescription in care standards and centralization of enforcement, while inevitably creating new challenges around economic calibration and administrative complexity.

Comparison With EU Regulation 261

Feature	*Resolución* 009/2024	EU Regulation 261/2004
Delays Compensation	>4h domestic, >6h international and 25% of segment value (minimum).	≥3h: €250–€600 (by distance).
Cancellation Rights	Lodging/transfer if no same-day rebooking. Delay compensation applies until cancellation time.	<14d notice: Refund or re-routing + €250–600 compensation (by distance).
Denied Boarding (Overbooking)	Rebooking next flight + 25% of ticket value (proportional to unused route).	Volunteer first; €250–€600 (by distance) if denied boarding.
Baggage Compensations	10% of route value per day after 24h.	Not specified.

Bibliography

- Resolución N°008/2024 of 22 May 2024.
- Resolución N° 009/2024 'Respecto a Derechos y Obligaciones para los Usuarios de Transporte Aéreo y Operadores del Servicio de Transporte Aéreo' de 17 Julio de 2024. <https://www.aviacioncivil.gob.ec/wp-content/uploads/downloads/2024/07/resolucion_no._009f-2024.pdf>.
- Resolución N°024/2013 of 7 August 2013.
- Resolución N°046/2012 'Disposiciones complementarias para la compensación a los usuarios por retrasos y cancelaciones de vuelos domésticos regulares por parte de las compañías aéreas' of 5 March 2012.
- Resolución N°083/2012 of 23 March 2012.
- Resolución N°318/2013 'Disposiciones complementarias para la Aprobación y Cumplimiento de Itinerarios' of 23 September 2013.
- Resolución N°0381/2013 of 17 October 2013 <https://www.aviacioncivil.gob.ec/wp-content/uploads/downloads/2019/06/res_381_disposiciones_vuelos_domesticos_compress1.pdf>.
- General Directorate of Civil Aviation in their Guide for Air Transport Users and Operators' <https://www.aviacioncivil.gob.ec/wp-content/uploads/downloads/2025/04/Guide-for-Air-Transport-Users-and-Operators.pdf> accessed 1 December 2025.

II.15

Egypt

Egyptian Civil Aviation Regulation (ECAR) 601, based on the Egyptian Civil Aviation Law N° 28 of 1981 as amended, is the official framework for passenger protection in Egypt in case of delay, cancellation, and denied boarding.[1] It closely mirrors EU Regulation 261.

The ECAR 601 applies to international flights arriving in Egypt from a third country operated by an Egyptian airline and departing from an airport in Egypt, regardless of the airline's nationality.[2] It applies to passengers having a confirmed reservation and presenting themselves on time for check-in as stipulated or at least 45 minutes before the published departure time.[3] Additionally, the passenger must be in possession of the necessary travel documents and abide by the airline's instructions as well as government, immigration, and health requirements.[4]

When an airline expects to deny boarding, it must first call for volunteers to surrender their seat in exchange of benefits.[5] Those passengers are entitled to assistance as an additional benefit to the one airlines will provide.[6] In the event that there are not enough volunteers, the airline may deny boarding to passengers against their will, in which case the passengers are entitled to compensation, assistance, and care.[7]

If a flight is cancelled, passengers are entitled to receive assistance and care if the re-routing departs at least two hours after the planned departure of the cancelled flight and may be eligible for compensation.[8] However, compensation is not required if the airline provides notice of

1 There are two version available online. The author used version 2 of 2019 which seems to be more complete. Egyptian Civil Aviation Authority, Part 601 passengers protection. <https://acrobat.adobe.com/id/urn:aaid:sc:EU:68f25418-db4c-4e08-a013-09cc844f4335>.
2 601–3(a)(1) and (2).
3 601–3(a)(3).
4 601–3(a)(4).
5 601–4(a).
6 601–4(b).
7 601–4(c).
8 601–5(a)(1) and (2).

DOI: 10.4324/9781003746164-26

the cancellation at least two weeks prior to departure, or, if notification occurs within two weeks, offers an alternative routing that enables arrival at the final destination within four hours of the originally scheduled time.[9] Additionally, an operating air carrier must provide each affected passenger with a written notice explaining the rules for compensation and assistance.[10]

Right	**Description**	**Legal Reference**
Right to Information	The operating air carrier must provide each affected passenger with a **written notice** explaining the rules for compensation and assistance. The contact details of the Egyptian Civil Aviation Authority (ECAA) must also be provided.	ECAR 601–14.
Right to Care (Immediate Assistance)	Passengers must be offered free of charge: • **Meals and refreshments** in reasonable relation to the waiting time. • **Hotel accommodation** and transfers between the airport and the hotel if an overnight stay is necessary. • **Two free telephone calls, emails, or fax messages.**	ECAR 601–9.
Right to Assistance (Choice of Remedies)	Passengers have the choice between: • **A full refund** of the ticket cost for the unused part of the journey, to be paid within 7 days, **plus** a return flight to the first point of departure if needed. • **Re-routing** to the final destination at the earliest opportunity on the same or another airline.	ECAR 601–8.
Right to Compen-sation	Passengers are entitled to **fixed financial compensation** unless the cancellation is due to extraordinary circumstances: • **<1,000 km:** EGP 300. • **1,000 km–4,000 km:** EGP 900. • **>4,000 km:** EGP 1,500.	ECAR 601–7.
Exemption From Compen-sation	**No compensation is owed** if the passenger is informed of the cancellation: • **At least 2 weeks** before the scheduled departure, **OR** • **Between 2 weeks and up to the departure** and is offered re-routing that arrives at the final destination **less than 4 hours** after the original scheduled arrival time. • Cancellation is caused by **extraordinary circumstances.**	ECAR 601–5.

9 601–5(a)(2)(i) and (ii).
10 601–14.

The airline is also exempt from compensating passengers if it can demonstrate that the cancellation resulted from extraordinary circumstances that could not have been prevented.[11] While the definitions included in the Regulation define the term "extraordinary circumstances" in vague terms,[12] the Annex contains a non-exhaustive list of instances which are considered extraordinary including natural disasters, certain technical problems not inherent in normal operation, security risks, medical emergencies, air traffic management restrictions, severe meteorological conditions, and labour disputes at essential service providers. Technical problems identified during routine maintenance or shortage of crew members are not considered extraordinary.[13]

Extraordinary Circumstances Under ECAR 601

Category	Specific Circumstances Considered Extraordinary
Natural Events and Disasters	Natural disasters rendering impossible the safe operation of the flight.
Security and Safety Risks	Security risks, acts of sabotage, or terrorism rendering safe operation impossible. Life-threatening health risks or medical emergencies necessitating flight interruption or deviation.
Technical and Airspace Issues	Technical problems not inherent in normal aircraft operation (e.g., a hidden manufacturing defect revealed by the manufacturer that impinges on flight safety). Air traffic management restrictions or closure of airspace or an airport.
Weather and Labour	Meteorological conditions incompatible with flight safety. Labour disputes at essential service providers (e.g., airports, air traffic control).
Aircraft Damage	Damage to the aircraft structure.

In the event of a flight delay by at least two hours, passengers are entitled to care, such as refreshments and meals. If the delay is at least five hours, they are also entitled to assistance which includes reimbursement or re-routing.[14] This also applies to schedule changes that cause a delay of at least two hours, unless the passenger was informed more than 15 days in advance.[15] The ECAR also contains a provision on tarmac delay which entitles passengers to disembark after five hours, unless there are safety or security reasons to prevent it.[16]

11 601–5(b).
12 601–2(f).
13 Annex 601–17.
14 601–6(a).
15 601–6(c).
16 601–6(b).

Passengers can claim compensation within 30 days from the date of the incident based on the flight distance; EGP 300 for all flights under 1,000 km; EGP 900 for all flights between 1,000 and 4,000 km; and EGP 1,500 for all flights above 4,000 km.[17] An airline may reach a different voluntary agreement with the passenger, provided it is signed and reminds the passenger of their rights under this regulation.[18]

Flight Distance	Compensation Amount (EGP)
Under 1,000 km	EGP 300.
1,000 km to 4,000 km	EGP 900.
Over 4,000 km	EGP 1,500.

The right to assistance means that passengers must be offered the choice between a full reimbursement of the ticket price for the unused parts of the journey within seven days, plus a return flight to their first point of departure, or continuation of their travel by re-routing to their final destination at the earliest opportunity subject to seat availability.[19]

The right to care includes free meals and refreshments in a reasonable relation to the waiting time, hotel accommodation if necessary, transport between the airport and the accommodation, and two free telephone calls, telex, fax, or email messages.[20] If the disruption is due to proven extraordinary circumstances, the carrier may limit hotel costs to EGP 500 per night per passenger for a maximum of two nights.[21]

An airline cannot request additional payment if it upgrades a passenger.[22] If an airline downgrades a passenger, it must reimburse a percentage of the ticket price for that segment within seven days, with the amount ranging from 30% for flights of 1,000 km or less, 50% for flights between 1,000 and 4,000 km, to 75% for flights exceeding 4,000 km.[23]

Airlines are required to prioritize the transportation of individuals with reduced mobility, their accompanying persons or service animals, as well as unaccompanied minors. In the event of denied boarding, cancellation, or delays, these passengers are entitled to receive prompt care.[24]

The Egyptian Civil Aviation Regulation (ECAR) Part 601 establishes a robust and clearly defined framework for air passenger rights, drawing

17 601–7(a).
18 601–7(b).
19 601–8(a) and (b).
20 601–9(a)(1)–(3) and (b).
21 601–9(c).
22 601–10(a).
23 601–10(b).
24 601–11.

significant inspiration from the European Union's Regulation 261. ECAR 601 has a narrower scope than Regulation 261. The ECAR does not contain any fixed penalty, nor does it contain any provision relating to baggage. It is a quite faithful copy of Regulation 261 without the changes made by the Court of Justice of the European Union to allow delayed passengers to enjoy the right to compensation. However, ECAR specifically covers tarmac delays. The reduction in compensation under ECAR 601 is also less stringent for passengers than under Regulation 261.

The definition of circumstances that exempt airlines from paying compensation, often termed "extraordinary circumstances," is largely consistent between both regulations. A notable and positive feature of ECAR 601 is its explicit Annex, which provides a non-exhaustive list of what does and does not constitute an extraordinary circumstance, offering greater clarity for both passengers and airlines.

In conclusion, ECAR 601 represents a strong and commendable piece of consumer protection legislation for Egypt, clearly modelled on international best practices. It provides passengers with a clear right to care, re-routing, and refunds. However, when compared directly to EU Regulation 261, its financial compensation levels are considerably lower, its application is narrower in scope, and it imposes a strict time limit for claims. Therefore, while the structure and intent are similar, the practical outcome and level of passenger compensation are distinctly different.

Comparison with EU Regulation

Feature	ECAR 601	EU Regulation 261/2004
Delay Compensation	No.	≥3h: €250–€600 (by distance).
Cancellation Notice	<14d notice: Refund + re-routing + compensation.	<14d notice: Refund or re-routing + €250–600 compensation (by distance).
Denied Boarding	Volunteer first; EGO 300 to 1,500 (by distance) if denied boarding.	Volunteer first; €250–€600 (by distance) if denied boarding.
Baggage Liability	Not specified.	Not specified.

Bibliography

- Egyptian Civil Aviation Authority, Part 601 Passengers Protection <https://acrobat.adobe.com/id/urn:aaid:sc:EU:68f25418-db4c-4e08-a013-09cc844f4335> accessed 1 December 2025.

II.16

Georgia

Georgia rules for passenger rights are found in Order N°122 of the Director of the Civil Aviation Agency of 2012, which transposes the core principles of EU Regulation 261.[1] This was a crucial step that preceded and facilitated Georgia's later integration into the European Common Aviation Area (ECAA), creating a legal framework for modern air passenger rights in the country.

The Order applies to any passengers departing from an airport located in the Georgian territory or flights departing from a third country to an airport situated in Georgia if the operating air carrier of the flight concerned is Georgian.[2] In order to invoke the provisions of the Order, passengers are required to hold a confirmed reservation and present themselves for check-in in accordance with the procedures and at the time specified in advance and in writing by the air carrier, tour operator, or authorized travel agent. If no specific check-in time is provided, passengers must check in no later than 45 minutes prior to the published departure time.[3] Like other regulations, this law does not apply to passengers travelling free of charge.[4]

In case of denial of boarding,[5] airlines must first request volunteers to surrender their seat in exchange for benefits under conditions they would agree on.[6] The volunteers are still entitled to assistance under Article 8 and a re-routing or refund and return to the first point of departure.[7] If an insufficient number of volunteers come forward to allow the remaining

1 Order No 122 of the Director of the Civil Aviation Agency of 17 July 2012 'On the Rules for Compensation and Assistance to Passengers in the Event of Denied Boarding and of Cancellation or Long Delay of Flights' <https://gcaa.ge/wp-content/uploads/2024/05/The-Rules-for-compensation-and-assistance-to-passengers-in-the-event-of-denied-boarding-and-of-cancellation-or-long-delay-of-flights.pdf> accessed 2 December 2025.

2 Article 1(2)(a) and (b).

3 Article 1(3)(b).

4 Article 1(5).

5 Article 4.

6 Article 4(1).

7 Article 3(3).

DOI: 10.4324/9781003746164-27

passengers with reservations to board the flight, the operating air carrier may then deny boarding to passengers against their will compensating them immediately in accordance with Article 7.[8] Passengers denied boarding against their will should be able either to cancel their flights, with reimbursement of their tickets, or to continue them under satisfactory conditions, and should be adequately cared for while awaiting a later flight.[9]

In the event of a flight cancellation, the operating air carrier must notify the passenger and offer a choice of re-routing or a full ticket reimbursement, as well as provide free services and compensation under the conditions specified in Article 7.[10] Compensation is not required if the passenger is informed of the cancellation at least 14 days before departure.[11] Compensation is also not required if the passenger is informed between two weeks and seven days before departure and is offered re-routing that allows them to depart no more than two hours early and arrive less than four hours late.[12] If informed less than seven days in advance, compensation is not due if re-routing allows them to depart no more than one hour early and arrive less than two hours late.[13] An air carrier is also not required to pay compensation if it can prove the cancellation was caused by extraordinary circumstances that could not have been avoided.[14] Order 122 defines "extraordinary circumstances" in Article 2(m) as

> any circumstances such as political instability, meteorological conditions incompatible with the operation of the flight concerned, security risks, unexpected flight safety shortcomings and strikes that affect the activities of an operating air carrier and cause flight delay/cancellation.

This definition mirrors EU Regulation 261, ensuring consistency with European jurisprudence.

When Cancelled	**Compensation Due?**
≥14 Days Before Departure	No.
7–14 Days Before Departure	No, if re-routing allows departure ≤2h earlier and arrival ≤4h later.
<7 Days Before Departure	No, if re-routing allows departure ≤1h earlier and arrival ≤2h later.
<14 Days Notice + No Suitable Re-routing	Yes.

8 Article 4(2).
9 Article 4(2).
10 Article 3(1) and Article 5(a).
11 Article 5(b)(b.a).
12 Article 5(b)(b.b).
13 Article 5(b)(b.c).
14 Article 5(2).

In the event of a long delay, the carrier must provide assistance to passengers.[15] What a passenger is entitled to depends entirely on the length of the delay and the flight distance. For short flights of 1,500 km or less, the airline must provide assistance after a two-hour delay. For medium-haul flights between 1,500 and 3,500 km, this assistance is required after three hours. All other, longer flights trigger this right after a four-hour delay.[16] This assistance package includes meals, refreshments, and the ability to make two free phone calls, send emails, or telex messages. Furthermore, if the delay is so significant that the new departure time is on a different day, the airline is also required to provide passengers with hotel accommodation and transport to and from the hotel. Finally, should the delay reach at least five hours, the passenger gains the right to cancel their trip and receive a full refund for any unused parts of their ticket.[17] The Order has also integrated the right to compensation for delays exceeding three hours, unless such delay was caused by an extraordinary circumstance.[18]

The compensation amounts for denied boarding, delay, and cancellation are a flat rate based on flight distance. Passengers are entitled to a compensation of 250 euros for flights of a distance of up to 1,500 km. For flights between 1,500 and 3,500 km, the amount increases to 400 euros. Finally, for flights over 3,500 km, the compensation is 600 euros.[19] The amount of compensation can be divided by two if passengers are offered an alternative flight which arrives at the final destination no later than two hours for flights of less than 1,500 km, three hours for flights between 1,500 and 3,500 km, and four hours for flights longer than 3,500 km.[20]

Situation	**Airlines Obligation**
Alternative flights less than 1,500 km arriving within 2 hours of the original time	125 euros.
Alternative flights between 1,500 km and 3,500 km or all other flights within 3 hours of the original time	200 euros.
Alternative flights more than 3,500 km arriving within 4 hours of the original time	300 euros.

When an airline is responsible for a flight disruption, passengers are given the right to choose between three options: a full refund for

15 Article 6(1).
16 Article 6(1)(a)–(c).
17 Article 3(4) and Article 6(3).
18 Article 3(4) and Article 6(4).
19 Article 7(1)(a), (b), and (c).
20 Article 7(2)(a), (b), and (c).

the part of the journey not made, re-routing to their final destination as soon as possible under comparable conditions, or re-routing at a later date convenient for the passenger, subject to seat availability.[21] Additionally, if a city or region has multiple airports, the airline may offer a flight to a different, nearby airport, provided the passenger agrees to the change.[22]

During a flight disruption, airlines are obligated to provide passengers with free care.[23] This includes offering meals and refreshments that are appropriate for the length of the waiting time.[24] If the delay extends to the point where an overnight stay becomes necessary, the airline must also cover the cost of a hotel room and transport between the airport and the accommodation.[25] Furthermore, passengers are entitled to two free phone calls or emails.[26] It is also a requirement that the airline gives special consideration and attention to the needs of passengers with reduced mobility and children travelling alone.[27]

If a passenger is upgraded, the carrier cannot require a supplementary payment. Conversely, if a passenger is moved to a lower class than their purchased ticket, the airline must reimburse a percentage of the ticket cost within seven days. The refund amount is 30% for flights up to 1,500 km, 50% for flights between 1,500 and 3,500 km, and 75% for all flights longer than that.[28]

Airlines are also under the obligation to inform passengers of their rights. At the check-in area, they must prominently display a notice that tells passengers to ask for a document outlining their rights to compensation and assistance if their flight is denied boarding, cancelled, or delayed by at least two hours. Beyond this general notice, the airline must also provide a written document directly to every passenger affected by such a disruption. This notice must clearly detail the rules for receiving compensation and assistance as outlined in the regulation, and it must also include the contact information for the official body responsible for handling passenger complaints. For passengers who are blind or visually impaired, the airline must use a suitable alternative method to ensure they receive all the same information.[29] However, there is no provision on potential fixed sanctions for non-compliance with the rules. Instead, it is

21 Article 8(1)(a), (b) and (c).
22 Article 8(3).
23 Article 9.
24 Article 9(1)(a).
25 Article 9(1)(b) and (c).
26 Article 9(1)(d).
27 Article 9(2).
28 Article 10(2)(a), (b) and (c).
29 Article 13.

left to the Civil Aviation Authority to impose liability in accordance with the Code of Administrative Offenses of Georgia.[30] Article 111 establishes that a violation of a normative act applicable in civil aviation results in a fine of GEL 2,000 but any repeat offence within one year after the initial commission would increase the fine to GEL 5,000. If the airline repeats its offence three times within a year, every subsequent commission carries a fine of GEL 10,000.[31]

Georgia's Order 122 is a direct transposition of EU Regulation 261, meaning its core provisions on compensation, re-routing, and assistance for denied boarding, cancellations, and long delays are the same. Both laws specify the same monetary compensation amounts (€250, €400, €600) based on flight distance and establish the same thresholds for triggering assistance (e.g., a three-hour delay for compensation). Unlike other countries, Georgia has not gone a step further. The fixed penalties found in the Administrative Offenses of Georgia increase the level of legal certainty for airlines compared to the EU Regulation. Consequently, the level of protection afforded to passengers in Georgia is, on paper, exactly equivalent to that enjoyed by passengers within the European Union.

Comparison with EU Regulation

Feature	**Order 122**	**EU Regulation 261/2004**
Delay Compensation	≥3h: €250–€600 (by distance).	≥3h: €250–€600 (by distance).
Cancellation Notice	<14d notice: Refund + re-routing + compensation.	<14d notice: Refund or re-routing + €250–600 compensation (by distance).
Denied Boarding	Volunteer first; €250–€600 (by distance) if denied boarding.	Volunteer first; €250–€600 (by distance) if denied boarding.
Baggage Liability	Not specified.	Not specified.

Bibliography

- Order No 122 of the Director of the Civil Aviation Agency of 17 July 2012 'On the Rules for Compensation and Assistance to Passengers in the Event of Denied Boarding and of Cancellation or Long Delay of Flights' <https://gcaa.ge/wp-content/uploads/2024/05/The-Rules-for-compensation-and-assistance-

30 Article 3(7).

31 Resolution of the Supreme Soviet of the Georgian SSR On Putting into Effect the Administrative Offences Code of the Georgian SSR, 15 of December 1984. <https://old.pdps.ge/cdn/2021/02/ADMINISTRATIVE-OFFENCES-CODE-OF-GEORGIA-consolidated-version-23.12.2017-07.03.2018.pdf>.

to-passengers-in-the-event-of-denied-boarding-and-of-cancellation-or-long-delay-of-flights.pdf> accessed 2 December 2025.

- Resolution of the Supreme Soviet of the Georgian SSR on Putting into Effect the Administrative Offences Code of the Georgian SSR, 15 of December 1984 <https://old.pdps.ge/cdn/2021/02/ADMINISTRATIVE-OFFENCES-CODE-OF-GEORGIA-consolidated-version-23.12.2017-07.03.2018.pdf>.

II.17

Ghana

Ghanaian air passenger rights are primarily governed by Part 2 of the Ghana Civil Aviation (Economic) Directives 2019,[1] established by the Ghana Civil Aviation Authority (GCAA) which supplements the Ghana Civil Aviation Act 2004,[2] as repealed by the Civil Aviation Act 2024.[3] While the Schedules of the Civil Aviation Act 2024 provide passengers with important rights in situations such as bodily injury or death, flight delays, damage and loss of baggage or cargo, Part 2 of the Ghana Civil Aviation (Economic) Directives 2019 serves as the core document outlining the specific rights of passengers.

The Directives establish minimum rights for passengers in case of involuntary denial of boarding, cancellation, delays, and baggage damages.[4] Part 2 applies to all passengers departing from an airport located in Ghana or arriving at an airport located in Ghana unless the passenger has already received assistance at the point of departure.[5] The Directive only applies to passengers having a confirmed

1 Ghana Civil Aviation (Economic) Directives, 2019, Part 2- Consumer Protection, June 2019. <chrome-extension://efaidnbmnnnibpcajpcglclefindmkaj/https://www.gcaa.com.gh/web/wp-content/uploads/2018/directives/GCA_ECONOMIC_DIRECTIVES/PART_2_CONSUMER%20PROTECTION.pdf> accessed 3 December 2025.

2 Act 678 of the Parliament of the Republic of Ghana entitled Ghana Civil Aviation Act, 2004 of 11 November 2004. As stipulated in Paragraph 2.1 (2) of the Directive.

3 Act 1120 of the Parliament of the Republic of Ghana entitled Ghana Civil Aviation Act, 2024 of 31 July 2024. The Ghana Civil Aviation Act 2024 expressly stipulates that the Montreal Convention provisions are applicable to both international and domestic air travel. See: Section 36(2)(a) and (b). The Second Schedule pertains to international air travel to and from Ghana, while the Third Schedule addresses domestic air travel within Ghana, irrespective of the nationality of the aircraft. These Schedules provide passengers with important rights in situations such as bodily injury or death, flight delays, damage and loss of baggage or cargo. See: Nana Arhin Assan and Adjoa Owusu-Mintah, 'Consumer Rights Protection: A Case of the Ghanaian Aviation Industry' (*Mondaq*, 1 July 2025) <https://www.mondaq.com/aviation/1644948/consumer-rights-protection-a-case-of-the-ghanaian-aviation-industry#authors> accessed 3 December 2025.

4 Paragraph 2.1(3).

5 Paragraph 2.1(4)(a) and (b).

DOI: 10.4324/9781003746164-28

reservation and who arrived on time at check-in as indicated or 45 minutes before.[6]

In the event that an air carrier can reasonably expect to deny boarding due to overbooking or an emergency change in aircraft type, the airline must first seek volunteers in exchange of benefits. Those volunteers are still entitled to assistance in the form of meals and refreshments or an accommodation.[7] If an insufficient number of volunteers come forward, the airline will be able to deny boarding. Those passengers will then be entitled to care, assistance, and compensation.[8] Operators must have and file a boarding priority procedure with the Ghana Civil Aviation Authority which includes the criteria for determining whose passengers shall be denied boarding in case an insufficient number of volunteers come forward.[9] These criteria and procedures cannot advantage or disadvantage a specific group of people and must be published on the airline's website as well as displayed at their check-in counters.[10] The Directive lists boarding priority factors that airlines may consider, though not in any particular order, which include urgent medical trips, passenger time of check-in, whether a passenger has a seat assignment before boarding, the fare paid, or their frequent-flyer status. Other factors are a passenger's reduced mobility, including unaccompanied minors, and families with at least one child aged 5 or younger (with a maximum of two adults).[11]

The Directive outlines the assistance and compensation passengers are entitled to when their flight is cancelled, distinguishing between international and domestic travel. Regardless of the reason for the cancellation, the airline must immediately offer all affected passengers care and assistance, including accommodation if the alternative flight departs at least one day after the planned departure of the cancelled flight.[12] Passengers have a right to financial compensation unless the airline meets certain conditions related to the timing of the notice and the alternative flight offered. For international flights, airlines can avoid paying compensation if they informed the passengers at least two weeks before the departure, between two weeks and seven days and the new flight departs no more than two hours before the original time and arrives less

6 Paragraph 2.1(5)(a) and (b).

7 Paragraph 2.3(1) and (2). See: Mavis Ekua Enyamah Kwainoe and Caroline Obeng, 'Rights and Responsibilities of Airline Passengers' (*TLOK*, 2024) <https://kwainoelawoffice.com/rights-and-responsibilities-of-airline-passengers/> accessed 3 December 2025.

8 Paragraph 2.3(3) and (4).

9 Paragraph 2.4(1)(b).

10 Paragraph 2.4(3) and (4).

11 Paragraph 2.4(5).

12 Paragraph 2.5(1)(a)–(b) and Paragraph 2.5(2)(a)–(b).

than four hours after the original time, or if passengers were informed less than seven days and the new flight departs no more than one hour before the original time and arrives less than two hours after the original time.[13] For domestic flights, the timing of the notice is much shorter; if the passengers are informed at least three days before the scheduled departure time, no compensation is owed, similarly if passengers were informed less than three days before and the new flight departs no more than two hours before the original time and arrives less than 90 minutes after the original time.[14] Additionally, airlines are exempt from paying compensation if they can prove the cancellation was caused by "extraordinary circumstances" that could not have been avoided even if all reasonable measures were taken.[15]

Condition	International Flights	Domestic Flights
Sufficient Advance Notice	**At least 2 weeks** before the scheduled departure.	**At least 3 days** before the scheduled departure.
Timely Re-routing (shorter notice)	**Between two weeks and seven days** before departure, and offered re-routing that: • Departs **no more than 2 hours before** the original time, and • Arrives **less than 4 hours after** the original time.	**Within three days** of departure, and offered re-routing that: • Departs **no more than 2 hours before** the original time, and • Arrives **less than 90 minutes after** the original time.
Timely Re-routing (minimal notice)	**Less than seven days** before departure, and offered re-routing that: • Departs **no more than 1 hour before** the original time, and • Arrives **less than 2 hours after** the original time.	**Not applicable.**

Air passenger rights for flight delays in Ghana vary based on the duration of the delay and whether the flight is domestic or international. For a domestic flight delay, passengers are entitled water after one hour and phone calls as well as reimbursement or re-routing after two hours.[16] If the airport at the point of departure or final destination is closed, passengers must be offered hotel accommodation and transport. After two hours, the

13 Paragraph 2.5(1)(c).
14 Paragraph 2.5(2)(c).
15 Paragraph 2.5(4). The concept is not further defined by the Directive.
16 Paragraph 2.6.1(1)(a).

full assistance includes refreshments and meals.[17] For international flights, passengers are entitled water after one hour, and meals and refreshments as well as phone calls for delays between two and six hours.[18] Any delays exceeding six hours would entitle the passengers to accommodation and transportation.[19] Damages occasioned by delay are subject to the Second and Third Schedules of the Civil Aviation Act 2024.[20]

Chronically delayed flights – which arrived more than 15 minutes late or cancelled more than 50% of the time over at least 30 flights in a calendar quarter – are considered an unfair and defective practice.[21] This is a significant and proactive measure designed to address persistent poor performance by airlines. By moving the issue from a simple operational hiccup to a potential violation of consumer rights law and opening the door for significant regulatory penalties from the GCAA, the Ghanaian Authority has made it clear that it is the airlines' duty to meet their schedule time.

Duration of Delay	**Domestic Flights**	**International Flights**
>1 Hour	Provision of water.	Provision of water.
>2 Hours	Two phone calls + reimbursement or re-routing.	Two phone calls + Meals/ refreshment.
>6 Hours	N/A	Hotel accommodation + transport.
Airport Closure	Hotel accommodation + transport. After **2 hours,** meals/refreshment.	

The Directive contains also a provision on tarmac delay. Airlines must provide assistance according to their Standard Operating Procedures (SOPs). If no procedure is in place, passengers should be given water and for delays exceeding two hours refreshment and after four hours a meal.[22] Paragraph 2.6.3 then includes another provision stating that passengers must disembark after three hours or more unless the airline's SOPs specify a shorter period for safety or operational reasons.[23] Such obligation to disembark is hard to reconcile with the meal provision after four hours.

17 Paragraph 2.6.1(1)(b).
18 Paragraph 2.6.2(1)(a) and (b).
19 Paragraph 2.6.2(1)(c).
20 Paragraph 2.7(5).
21 Paragraph 2.18(1) and (2).
22 Paragraph 2.6.3(1).
23 Paragraph 2.6.3(2).

Duration of Delay	Assistance and Action Required
Immediately	Water.
>2 Hours	Refreshments.
>4 Hours	Meal.
>3 Hours	**Disembark passengers** unless the airline's SOPs specify a shorter period for safety or operational reasons.

The Directive contains a fixed compensation amount for domestic flights of US$60 while providing a tiered system depending on the distance of the flight for international flights.[24] For international flights up to 1,500 km passengers are entitled to US$200, compensation increases to US$400 for flights of 1,500 km–3,500 km and, finally, US$600 for all other flights in Ghana Cedis equivalent.[25] Those amounts can be reduced by half if an airline offers re-routing and the new arrival time is close to the original schedule, within two hours for domestic flights or three hours for international flights.[26] The final destination that is used to calculate the distance for compensation is the one where the cancellation or denial of boarding caused a delay to the passenger's arrival.[27] The compensation does not seem to apply to passengers suffering from a delay.

Flight Type/Distance	Standard Compensation	Reduced Compensation
Domestic Flights	US$60.	Alternative flight arrived within two hours: US$30.
International ≤1,500 km	US$200.	Alternative flight arrived within three hours: US$100.
International 1,500 km–3,500 km	US$400.	Alternative flight arrived within three hours: US$200.
International >3,500 km	US$600.	Alternative flight arrived within three hours: US$300.

The right to reimbursement and re-routing is similar to the one found in Regulation 261: a full refund for the unused part of the ticket or a re-routing to the final destination at the earliest possible time under comparable travel conditions or at a later date convenient for the passenger, also under comparable conditions.[28] The right to care is also expressed in

24 Paragraph 2.7(1)(a).
25 Paragraph 2.7(1)(b)–(d) and (4).
26 Paragraph 2.7(3)(a)–(b).
27 Paragraph 2.7(2).
28 Paragraph 2.8(1)(a)–(c).

similar wording; meals and refreshment relative to the waiting time, hotel accommodation in case an overnight stay is necessary as well as two phone calls, fax messages, or emails.[29] In cases of denied boarding, cancellation, or delays of any length, persons with disabilities and unaccompanied minor must be cared for as soon as possible.[30]

In case of upgrading, the airline shall not request any supplementary payment from the passenger. In the event of a downgrading, the airline must reimburse the fare difference between the two classes and compensate the passenger the standard compensation (US$60 for domestic flights and US$200–$600 for international flights) or compensate based on the airline's own conditions of carriage, whichever is the highest.[31] Additionally, there is a prohibition for airlines to persistently deny checked-in passengers the specific seat class they paid for and were assigned, even if the airline has a general "free seating" policy.[32]

Scenario	Action Required by the Air Operator
Upgrading	• The airline **shall not request any supplementary payment** from the passenger.
Downgrading	The airline must, within **7 days**: 1. **Reimburse** the fare difference between the two classes. 2. **Compensate** the passenger by paying **the higher** of the following two amounts: • The standard compensation (e.g., US$60 for domestic, US$200–$600 for international flights), **OR** • The compensation amount specified in the airline's own **Conditions of Carriage.**

Airlines are required to give priority to persons with disabilities, those accompanying them, and unaccompanied children.[33] Airlines must display a notice of passenger rights at their check-in counters and on their websites. This notice should be clearly visible and contain specific text provided by the Ghana Civil Aviation Authority (GCAA).[34] In cases of denied boarding, cancellation, or a delay of two hours or more, the airline must provide each affected passenger with a written notice detailing their rights to compensation and assistance. This notice must also include the contact details for the GCAA.[35] For blind or visually

29 Paragraph 2.9(1)(a)–(c) and Paragraph 2.9(2).
30 Paragraph 2.11(2).
31 Paragraph 2.10(2)(a) and (b).
32 Paragraph 2.17.
33 Paragraph 2.11(1).
34 Paragraph 2.14(1).
35 Paragraph 2.14(2).

impaired passengers, any required written information must be provided through appropriate alternative means.[36] Airlines must also prominently display several key pieces of information on their websites, including their contract of carriage, baggage policies and fees, and complaints handling procedures.[37]

The Directive also contains a provision prohibiting airlines from using misleading advertising. All advertised prices for air travel must be the total, entire price the passenger will pay. Any additional taxes, fees, or charges must be included in the headline price.[38] It is illegal for any entity to advertise air transportation without holding the required economic or operating license from the GCAA.[39]

Interestingly, there is no provision on fines but the implementing standards attached to the Directive contain two pages of sanction guidance tables which are very detailed. For instance, an airline can be fined between 5,000 and 300,000 penalty unit (PU) depending on the severity of the offence. A failure to request for volunteers in case of denial of boarding ranges between 100,000 and 199,999 PU while a failure to compensate volunteers for denied boarding can result in a fine between 5,000 and 99,999 PU. Failure to display the boarding priority procedure will lead to a warning letter. Failure to notify passengers of cancellation results in a fine between 5,000 and 99,999 PU, but the fine for failure to compensate such passenger ranges between 100,000 and 199,999 PU. However, as Arhin Assan and Owusu-Mintah noted the major challenge with Part 2 is its enforcement and the fact that many passengers are unaware of their rights.[40]

The Ghanaian passenger rights framework, established by the Ghana Civil Aviation Authority (GCAA) Economic Directives 2019, Part 2, represents a modern, comprehensive, and highly consumer-centric regulatory regime, inspired by Regulation 261. Its principal strength lies in its exceptional specificity in some aspects. It contains a comprehensive set of rules that address a variety of issues beyond just compensation. Its direct bans on misleading advertising and free-seating policy abuse, alongside the chronic delays provision, address gaps that exist in the EU regulation, making it arguably more adaptive to current market practices and consumer grievances. The Directive also contains very detailed fixed penalties depending on the failure which is not found in the Regulation.

36 Paragraph 2.11(4) and 2.14(3).

37 Paragraph 2.14(4)(a)–(d).

38 Paragraph 2.16(1) and (2).

39 Paragraph 2.16(3).

40 Nana Arhin Assan and Adjoa Owusu-Mintah, 'Consumer Rights Protection: A Case of the Ghanaian Aviation Industry' (*Mondaq*, 1 July 2025) <https://www.mondaq.com/aviation/1644948/consumer-rights-protection-a-case-of-the-ghanaian-aviation-industry#authors>.

Compared to Regulation 261, the Ghanaian law also uses a distance-based system but denominates its amounts in US Dollars ($200, $400, $600 for international flights), with a separate, lower category for domestic flights ($60). This domestic flight aspect is not found in the European Regulation. A major distinction lies in compensation for delays. Under EU law, passengers are entitled to fixed compensation for arrival delays of three hours or more, in addition to receiving assistance. Ghanaian law, however, does not provide a fixed compensation for delays, although it does require airlines to offer assistance such as water, meals, and hotel accommodation after certain time thresholds are met.

In conclusion, while EU Regulation 261 has been a pioneering and influential model for passenger rights globally, the Ghanaian framework can be appraised as a significant evolution in certain areas. It not only incorporates the core principles of the EU model but also builds upon them by introducing more precise provisions that tackle systemic airline reliability and transparency, at least on paper.

Comparison with EU Regulation

Feature	Part 2 Directive 2019	EU Regulation 261/2004
Delay Compensation	Not specified.	≥3h: €250–€600 (by distance).
Cancellation Notice	<14d notice: Refund + re-routing + compensation.	<14d notice: Refund or re-routing + €250–600 compensation (by distance).
Denied Boarding	Volunteer first; US$60 for domestic, US$200–$600 for international flights.	Volunteer first; €250–€600 (by distance) if denied boarding.
Baggage Liability	Not specified.	Not specified.

Bibliography

- Ghana Civil Aviation (Economic) Directives, 2019, Part 2- Consumer Protection, June 2019 <chrome-extension://efaidnbmnnnibpcajpcglclefindmkaj/https://www.gcaa.com.gh/web/wp-content/uploads/2018/directives/GCA_ECONOMIC_DIRECTIVES/PART_2_CONSUMER%20PROTECTION.pdf> accessed 3 December 2025.
- Act 678 of the Parliament of the Republic of Ghana Entitled Ghana Civil Aviation Act, 2004 of 11 November 2004 <https://www.gcaa.com.gh/web/wp-content/uploads/2018/Act_678.pdf> accessed 3 December 2025.
- Act 1120 of the Parliament of the Republic of Ghana Entitled Ghana Civil Aviation Act, 2024 of 31 July 2024 <https://www.gcaa.com.gh/web/wp-content/uploads/2025/GHANA%20CIVIL%20AVIATION%20ACT%20%202024%20%20ACT%201120.pdf> accessed 3 December 2025.

- Assan, N. A. and Owusu-Mintah, A., ‘Consumer Rights Protection: A Case of the Ghanaian Aviation Industry’ (*Mondaq*, 1 July 2025) <https://www.mondaq.com/aviation/1644948/consumer-rights-protection-a-case-of-the-ghanaian-aviation-industry#authors> accessed 3 December 2025.
- Kwainoe, M. E. E. and Obeng, C., ‘Rights and Responsibilities of Airline Passengers’ (*TLOK*, 2024) <https://kwainoelawoffice.com/rights-and-responsibilities-of-airline-passengers/> accessed 3 December 2025.

II.18

Iceland

Iceland, as a member of the European Economic Area (EEA), is party to the European Common Aviation Agreement. As a result, Iceland has adopted most European legislation on the field including Regulation 261.[1]

Unlike other countries, Iceland has not really transposed Regulation 261 in its national law,[2] instead the national law refers to the Regulation itself.[3] For instance, Article 8 of Regulation 466/2024 stipulates that the provisions of Regulation 261 apply to compensation for delays, cancellations, or denied boarding as well as assistance, not even including such provisions in the text. This means passengers have to read Regulation 261 itself to know about their rights. The major difference is that it stipulates that passengers on delayed flights might be entitled to compensation.[4]

The Icelandic Air Travel Act no. 80/2022 and Administrative Law no. 37/1993 allow the Icelandic Transport Authority (SGS) to issue decisions and resolve disputes between airlines and passengers.[5] The new Regulation 466/2024 fixes the appeal fee to the Icelandic Transport Authority of ISK 5,000.[6]

The Authority has been quite prolific.[7] For instance, in a denied boarding case, where the passenger received a message that the flight would be delayed by almost two hours, resulting in the passenger getting to the airport later for check-in, the SGS concluded that since the passengers did not receive a notification about a change to the check-in deadline, they were obligated to arrive for check-in by the original, announced deadline, regardless of

1 European Commission, 'Iceland' <https://transport.ec.europa.eu/transport-modes/air/international-aviation/status-aviation-relations-country/iceland_en>.

2 Regulation 261 was given effect by Article 1 of Reglugerð 574/2005 which was repealed by Reglugerð nr. 1048/2012.

3 Reglugerð nr. 1048/2012 repealed by Reglugerð 466/2024.

4 Article 8 Reglugerð 466/2024.

5 Article 208(4) Air Travel Act.

6 Article 4.

7 See: 'Decisions, Judgements and Rulings' <https://island.is/en/o/transport-authority/rights-of-air-passengers>.

DOI: 10.4324/9781003746164-29

the flight delay announcement. No compensation was due.[8] In another instance, a flight was cancelled, and passengers were rebooked on a flight the next day which was also cancelled. The airline claimed it was due to "extraordinary circumstances," in particular adverse weather conditions. The SGS consulted an expert from their flight operations department who concluded that the weather was bad but within the limit and no other flights were cancelled. Passengers were awarded compensation for both cancellations so two times 400 euros, however, the claim for reimbursement of the cost of the separate flight to Paris was rejected as the final destination was Barcelona.[9] According to the SGS a bomb threat and resulting airport closure causing the cancellation of both inbound and outbound flights are extraordinary circumstances. However, the airline did not prove it took all necessary measures to mitigate the disruption – especially considering that the passengers had to wait three days for a new flight – which resulted in an award in favour of the passengers.[10] While Iceland applies Regulation 261, it seems that the Icelandic Transport Authority has taken a narrow approach to "extraordinary circumstances." Ultimately, the SGS ensures that "extraordinary circumstances" is not a blanket defence; airlines must conclusively demonstrate they have taken all reasonable measures to avoid the disruption.

Comparison with EU Regulation 261

Feature	**Reglugerð 466/2024**	**EU Regulation 261/2004**
Delay Compensation	≥3h: €250–€600 (by distance).	≥3h: €250–€600 (by distance).
Cancellation Notice	<14d notice: Refund or re-routing + €250–600 compensation (by distance).	<14d notice: Refund or re-routing + €250–600 compensation (by distance).
Denied Boarding	Volunteer first; €250–€600 (by distance) if denied boarding.	Volunteer first; €250–€600 (by distance) if denied boarding.
Baggage Liability	Not specified.	Not specified.

8 Ákvörðun Samgöngustofu nr. 1/2023 vegna kvörtunar um neitun á fari með flugi Wizz Air nr. W62858 þann 2. apríl 2022.

9 Ákvörðun Samgöngustofu nr. 3/2023 vegna kvörtunar um aflýsingu á flugi Vueling Airlines nr. VY8561 þann 14. og 15. febrúar 2022.

Other adverse weather claims: Úrskurður Samgöngustofu nr. 17/2023 vegna kvörtunar um seinkun á flugi Vueling Airlines nr. VY8561 þann 20. ágúst 2022.

10 Úrskurður Samgöngustofu nr. 11/2023 vegna kvörtunar um aflýsingu á flugi Wizz Air nr. W65054 þann 24. júlí 2022.

Bibliography

- European Commission, 'Iceland' <https://transport.ec.europa.eu/transport-modes/air/international-aviation/status-aviation-relations-country/iceland_en> accessed 3 December 2025.
- Reglugerð 574/2005 um gildistöku reglugerðar EB nr. 261/2004 um sameiginlegar reglur um skaðabætur og aðstoð til handa farþegum sem neitað er um far og þegar flugi er aflýst eða mikil seinkun verður og um að fella úr gildi reglugerð (EBE) nr. 295/91.
- Reglugerð nr. 1048/2012 um skaðabætur og aðstoð til handa farþegum í flugi sem neitað er um far og þegar flugi er aflýst, seinkað eða flýtt eða vegna tapaðs farangurs eða tjóns á honum of 6 December 2012.
- Reglugerð 466/2024 um réttindi flugfarþega of 18 April 2024.
- 'Decisions, Judgements and Rulings' <https://island.is/en/o/transport-authority/rights-of-air-passengers>.
- Ákvörðun Samgöngustofu nr. 1/2023 vegna kvörtunar um neitun á fari með flugi Wizz Air nr. W62858 þann 2. apríl 2022.
- Ákvörðun Samgöngustofu nr. 3/2023 vegna kvörtunar um aflýsingu á flugi Vueling Airlines nr. VY8561 þann 14. og 15. febrúar 2022.
- Úrskurður Samgöngustofu nr. 17/2023 vegna kvörtunar um seinkun á flugi Vueling Airlines nr. VY8561 þann 20. ágúst 2022.
- Úrskurður Samgöngustofu nr. 11/2023 vegna kvörtunar um aflýsingu á flugi Wizz Air nr. W65054 þann 24. júlí 2022.

II.19

India

In India, air passenger rights are primarily governed by the Civil Aviation Requirement (CAR) Section 3, Series M Part IV Revision 4 effective since February 2023 issued by the Directorate General of Civil Aviation (DGCA)[1] and the "Passenger Charter of Rights" of 2019 established by the Ministry of Civil Aviation.[2] The Charter – a soft law instrument[3] – is a simplified and accessible summary of the CAR-specific binding rules.[4] It is unclear whether CAR only applies to domestic flights in India or to international flights also. Indeed, Paragraph 1.1 mentions the "rapid expansion of air services within India and on international routes to/from India." This text seems to suggest that the rules apply to passengers on all flights: domestic, international, scheduled, non-scheduled, and on foreign carriers operating to/from India.[5]

The CAR requires airlines to provide passengers with accurate information about flight details, reservation status, and applicable fare conditions.[6] Airlines must also provide neutral and accurate information about flight details, stops, and aircraft changes at the time of booking.[7]

---

1 Issued under the Aircraft Rules, 1937.

2 The Carriage by Air Act, 1972 as amended in 2009 is the implementation of the Montreal Convention in India. For a case related to this Act see: *Air India Ltd v Tej Shoe Exporters Pvt Ltd RFA* (OS) No. 18/2007 decided on 19 September 2013.

3 Vikrant Pachnanda, 'Is a Dedicated Indian Law for Air Passenger Protection the Need of the Hour Today' (*India Law Journal*) <https://indialawjournal.org/is-a-dedicated-indian-law-for-air-passenger-protection.php>.

4 Bindingness of CAR is found in Paragraph 1.7 Civil Aviation Requirements Section 3-Air Transport Series 'M", Part IV Issue I, dated 6 August 2010, as amended on 15th February 2023.

5 Paragraphs 1.1 and 1.2 Civil Aviation Requirements Section 3-Air Transport Series 'M", Part IV Issue I, dated 6 August 2010, as Amended on 15 February 2023 as found <https://www.dgca.gov.in/digigov-portal/?dynamicPage=CivilAviationReqContent/6/211/viewDynamicRuleContLvl2/html&maincivilAviationRequirements/6/0/viewDynamicRulesReq>.

6 Paragraph 3.1.1.

7 Paragraph 3.1.2.

DOI: 10.4324/9781003746164-30

In the event of denied boarding due to overbooking, the airline must first solicit volunteers to surrender their seats in exchange for benefits.[8] If passengers are denied boarding against their will, the airline is not liable for compensation if an alternate flight is arranged to depart within one hour of the original scheduled departure.[9] Should the alternate flight depart more than one hour later, compensation is mandated. If the alternate flight is scheduled within 24 hours of the original departure, compensation is 200% of the booked one-way basic fare plus fuel charge, up to a maximum of INR 10,000.[10] If the alternate flight is scheduled more than 24 hours after the original departure, the compensation increases to 400% of the fare, up to a maximum of INR 20,000.[11] In cases where the passenger does not accept an alternate flight, they are entitled to a full refund of their ticket and a compensation equal to 400% of the booked one-way basic fare plus airline fuel charge, up to a maximum of INR 20,000.[12] These rules also apply to connecting flights if a passenger is delayed at their final destination by at least three hours due to denied boarding on the first leg of their journey.[13]

Scenario	**Alternate Flight Departure Time**	**Compensation**	**Refund**
Involuntary Denied Boarding	**Within 1 hour** of original schedule.	**No compensation.**	Not applicable.
Involuntary Denied Boarding	Between **1 hour and 24 hours** of original schedule.	**200%** of one-way basic fare + fuel charge (max **INR 10,000**).	Not applicable.
Involuntary Denied Boarding	**More than 24 hours** after original schedule.	**400%** of one-way basic fare + fuel charge (max **INR 20,000**).	Not applicable.
Passenger Opts Out of Alternate Flight	Not applicable.	**400%** of one-way basic fare + fuel charge (max **INR 20,000**).	**Full refund** of the ticket.

However, airlines are allowed to deny boarding if the passenger is considered as unruly and deemed a threat within the meaning of CAR Section 3, Series M Part VI, Issue II of 2017.[14]

8 Paragraph 3.2.1.
9 Paragraph 3.2.2.
10 Paragraph 3.2.2(a).
11 Paragraph 3.2.2(b).
12 Paragraph 3.2.2(c).
13 Paragraph 3.2.3.
14 Paragraph 4.4 CAR Section 3, Series M Part VI, Issue II of 2017. The CAR establishes a three-tier categorization for unruly behaviour in paragraph 4.10:

To ensure minimal inconvenience for passengers due to flight cancellations, airlines are obligated to provide notification at least 14 days prior to the scheduled departure. In such cases, passengers must be offered an alternative flight or receive a full refund.[15] If the airline informs the passenger of the cancellation less than two weeks before departure and up to 24 hours of the scheduled time, an alternate flight or refund must still be offered.[16] However, if passengers receive less than 24 hours' notice, or miss a connecting flight, they are entitled to both a full refund and compensation in addition to being rebooked on an alternate flight.[17] The compensation amounts are INR 5,000 for flights with a block time of up to one hour; INR 7,500 for flights between one and two hours; and INR 10,000 for flights over two hours.[18] These amounts are capped at the one-way basic fare plus fuel charge, whichever is less. Additionally, passengers must be offered care and assistance, including meals and refreshments. Airlines must cover the cost of transferring passengers to an alternate airport or terminal if the change was not communicated at least six hours in advance.[19] These compensations are not payable if the cancellation is due to extraordinary circumstances beyond the airline's control or if the passenger did not provide adequate contact information at the time of booking.[20]

Notification Timeline	Passenger's Options	Compensation	Additional Care and Notes
14 Days or More Before Scheduled Departure	Alternate flight **OR** full refund.	Not applicable.	No.

(*Continued*)

- Level 1: Unruly behaviour (e.g., verbal harassment, physical gestures).
- Level 2: Physically abusive behaviour (e.g., pushing, kicking, sexual harassment).
- Level 3: Life-threatening behaviour (e.g., damaging aircraft systems, physical violence).

Those passengers can be added to the no-fly list with serious repercussions according to paragraph 8.1:

- Level 1: ban up to three months.
- Level 2: ban up to six months.
- Level 3: Minimum of two years, with no upper limit.

For more information see: Shaurya Mehrotra, 'Unruly Passenger and Air Rage: Legal Framework and Challenges in Indian Aviation' (2025) 5 Indian Journal of Legal Review 264.

15 Paragraph 3.3.1 Civil Aviation Requirements Section 3-Air Transport Series 'M", Part IV Issue I, dated 6 August 2010, as amended on 15 February 2023.

16 Paragraph 3.3.1.

17 Paragraph 3.3.2.

18 Paragraph 3.3.2(a)–(c).

19 Paragraph 3.10.1.

20 Paragraph 3.3.4 and 3.3.3.

(Continued)

Notification Timeline	Passenger's Options	Compensation	Additional Care and Notes
Less Than 14 Days up to 24 Hours Before Scheduled Departure	Alternate flight **OR** full refund.	Not applicable.	No.
Less Than 24 Hours' Notice (or missed connection)	Alternate flight **AND** full refund.	**Yes.** The amount is based on flight block time: • **≤1 hour:** INR 5,000. • **1–2 hours:** INR 7,500. • **>2 hours:** INR 10,000. *Compensation is the lower of the stated amount or the one-way basic fare + fuel charge.*	Meals and refreshments must be provided.

Airlines are not obligated to offer compensation for disruptions resulting from "extraordinary circumstances" or "force majeure," which refer to events outside the control of the airline. Such events may include political instability including civil war and insurrection, natural disasters and flood, explosion, labour strikes "causing cessation, slowdown or interruption of work," government regulation or order affecting the aircraft and matters associated with air traffic control (ATC), or adverse meteorological conditions.[21]

Category of Event	Specific Examples
Political and Civil Unrest	Political instability, civil war, insurrection, riot.
Natural Disasters	Natural disaster, flood, explosion.
Labour Disputes	Strikes that cause a cessation, slowdown, or interruption of work.
Government and Regulatory Actions	A specific government regulation or order that affects the aircraft.
Air Traffic Management	Decisions made by air traffic control (ATC) leading to delays/cancellations.
Weather and Security	Adverse meteorological conditions, security risks.

21 Paragraphs 1.4 and 1.5 Civil Aviation Requirements Section 3-Air Transport Series 'M', Part IV Issue I, dated 6 August 2010, as amended on 15 February 2023.

With respect to flight delays, airlines are required to provide meals and refreshments commensurate with the waiting period when a delay exceeds certain thresholds: two hours for flights up to two and a half hours in duration; three hours for flights between two and a half and five hours; and four hours for flights with block time[22] of more than five hours.[23] For domestic flights delayed by more than six hours, airlines must offer passengers either an alternative flight scheduled to depart within the next six hours or a full refund.[24] Additionally, if the total delay exceeds 24 hours, or if a delay of more than six hours affects a flight originally scheduled to depart between 8 PM and 3 AM, the carrier is obligated to provide complimentary hotel accommodation, including airport transfers.[25] These obligations do not apply if the delay results from extraordinary circumstances outside the airline's control.[26]

Delay Duration/Flight Condition	**Entitlements/Actions**
2+ Hours for Flights **up to 2.5 Hours**	Meal and refreshments.
3+ Hours for Flights **Between 2.5 and 5 Hours**	Meal and refreshments.
4+ Hours for Flights **More Than 5 Hours**	Meal and refreshments.
Delay Exceeds **6 Hours**	Choice of an **alternative flight within 6 hours** or a **full refund**.
Delay Exceeds **24 Hours** AND Passenger Was Informed **>24 Hours Before** the Original Flight	Free hotel accommodation.
Delay Exceeds **6 Hours** for Flights Scheduled to Depart **Between 20:00 (8 PM) and 3:00 (3 AM)**.	Free hotel accommodation.

The DGCA issued new guidelines in November 2024 which require airlines to provide water for delays up to two hours, snacks with tea or coffee for delays of two to four hours, and meals if the delay exceeds four hours.[27] However, a point of ambiguity remains regarding how these

22 Defined as "the total time from the moment an aircraft first moves for the purpose of taking off until the moment it finally comes to rest at the end of the flight." Paragraph 2.9 1 of the Civil Aviation Requirements Section 3-Air Transport Series 'M', Part IV Issue I, dated 6 August 2010, as amended on 15 February 2023.

23 Paragraph 3.4.1.

24 Paragraph 3.4.2.

25 Paragraph 3.4.3.

26 Paragraph 3.4.4.

27 This was shared on X as reported in Dhanusha Gokulan, 'Flight Delayed? You Are Now Entitled to a Free Meal Indian Civil Aviation Watchdog Has Issued New Rules for Airlines' *Gulf News* (22 November 2024) <https://gulfnews.com/business/aviation/flight-delayed-you-are-now-entitled-to-a-free-meal-1.1732285232536>.

Reference are also found in this document: Government of India, Ministry of Civil Aviation, Rajya Sabha, Unstarred Question N°1122 <https://sansad.in/getFile/annex/267/AU1122_m6EA5O.pdf?source=pqars>.

new provisions interact with the existing regulations. Indeed, it is unclear whether the original tiered system based on flight duration (e.g., specific provisions for flights up to two and a half hours, between two and a half and five hours, etc.) has been superseded or if it still applies in conjunction with these new, more specific guidelines.

Delay Duration/Flight Condition	**Entitlements/Actions**
Delay of 0–2 Hours	Bottled water.
Delay of 2–4 Hours	Snacks + tea or coffee.
4+ Hours	Full meal.
Delay Exceeds **6 Hours**	Choice of an **alternative flight within 6 hours** or a **full refund**.
Delay Exceeds **24 Hours** AND Passenger Was Informed **>24 Hours Before** the Original Flight	Free hotel accommodation.
Delay Exceeds **6 Hours** for Flights Scheduled to Depart **Between 20:00 (8 PM) and 3:00 (3 AM)**	Free hotel accommodation.

Additionally, airlines will be permitted to deplane passengers if a flight is delayed by more than two hours because of adverse weather conditions in Delhi and reboard them without requiring new security checks.[28]

The Regulation 261 influence on Indian law is very visible in the downgrading provision.[29] If a passenger is involuntarily downgraded, the airline is required to reimburse them a portion of the ticket cost. For domestic flights, the reimbursement is 75% of the ticket cost, including taxes. For international flights, the reimbursement is tiered based on the flight distance: 30% of the ticket cost for flights of 1,500 km or less; 50% for flights between 1,500 km and 3,500 km; and 75% for flights of more than 3,500 km.[30]

Domestic Flights	**International Flights**
A flat reimbursement of **75%** of the ticket price (including taxes).	Reimbursement is based on flight distance: • **1,500 km or less:** 30% of ticket price. • **1,500 km to 3,500 km:** 50% of ticket price. • **More than 3,500 km:** 75% of ticket price.

28 As reported in Dhanusha Gokulan, 'Flight Delayed? You Are Now Entitled to a Free Meal Indian Civil Aviation Watchdog Has Issued New Rules for Airlines' *Gulf News* (22 November 2024) <https://gulfnews.com/business/aviation/flight-delayed-you-are-now-entitled-to-a-free-meal-1.1732285232536>.

29 As pointed out by Havel and Mulligan, when the rules were first adopted, they closely followed Regulation 261. See: Brian F Havel and John Q Mulligan, 'Extraterritorial Application: Exporting European Consumer Protection Standards' in Michael Bobek and Jeremias Prassl (eds), *Air Passenger Rights Ten Years On* (Hart Publisher 2016) 252.

30 Paragraph 3.5.

Foreign carriers must follow either their country's regulations or the compensation amounts specified in this CAR.[31] Airlines must display their compensation and refund policies on their websites as part of their Passenger Charter of Rights.[32] The CAR does not include any fixed penalty in case of non-compliance.

Interestingly, the Passenger Charter of Rights contains a dedicated section on passengers with disability and no-charge cancellation or amendment within 24 hours. However, the rules regulating those situations are not found in CAR Section 3, Series M Part IV Revision 4 but in CAR Section 3, Series M Part I and II respectively.

CAR Section 3, Series M Part I, Issue III of 2022 is titled "Carriage by Air of Persons with Disability and/or Persons with Reduced Mobility." Recent changes were implemented following an incident involving IndiGo, in which the airline denied boarding to a distressed teenager on the grounds that he posed a risk to other passengers. The Directorate General of Civil Aviation subsequently imposed a fine of 500,000 rupees on IndiGo and established new guidelines to help prevent similar incidents in the future.[33] The rules for passengers with disabilities apply to all Indian airlines (scheduled and non-scheduled, domestic and international), all foreign airlines operating to/from India, and all airport operators within India.[34] This CAR places specific obligations on airlines, airport operators, and other service providers to ensure non-discriminatory and accessible air travel for persons with disability and reduced mobility. For airlines, the fundamental principle is that they shall not refuse carriage to a person on the basis of their disability or reduced mobility.[35] This extends to their assistive devices, escorts, and guide dogs, provided the airline is informed of their requirements at the time of booking.[36] Airlines must make their booking websites accessible, allowing passengers to specify their needs, and must provide all safety information in an accessible format.[37] While a 48-hour advance notice is recommended for optimal planning, airlines must make all reasonable efforts to assist passengers travelling on short

---

31 Paragraph 3.6.1.

32 Paragraph 3.10.2.

33 Syed Tamjeed and Rakhee Biswas, 'Boarding for People with Disabilities: Analysis of DGCA's New Rules' (*Lexology*, 6 July 2022) <https://www.lexology.com/library/detail.aspx?g=0cbe8519-ea2f-45fb-89c7-7f559938163d>.

34 Paragraph 2(a)–(c) of Civil Aviation Requirements Section 3-Air Transport Series 'M", Part I Issue III, dated 28 February 2014 as amended on 21 July 2021.

35 Paragraph 4.1.1 of Civil Aviation Requirements Section 3-Air Transport Series 'M", Part I Issue III, dated 28 February 2014 as amended on 21 July 2021.

36 Paragraph 4.1.1 of Civil Aviation Requirements Section 3-Air Transport Series 'M", Part I Issue III, dated 28 February 2014 as amended on 21 July 2021.

37 Paragraph 4.1.2 of Civil Aviation Requirements Section 3-Air Transport Series 'M", Part I Issue III, dated 28 February 2014 as amended on 21 July 2021.

notice or in emergencies.[38] Airlines must assign accessible seats with extra legroom free of charge and make every effort to seat passengers next to their escorts. In situations of overbooking, persons with disability and their escorts are to be given the highest priority to avoid offloading.[39] For safety, the number of non-ambulatory persons permitted on a flight is limited to the number of cabin crew unless they have a trained escort.[40] This rule is directly linked to the stringent emergency evacuation standards that aircraft must meet, namely a full evacuation within 90 seconds under simulated emergency conditions. Airlines must have procedures for carrying guide dogs and must include emergency evacuation plans for persons with disabilities in their manuals, with cabin crew responsible for briefing these passengers before take-off.[41] Boarding and disembarking should be separate to ensure a smooth process.[42] Airlines cannot insist on a medical certificate unless they have reason to believe the passenger's health could pose a risk during the flight, such as having a communicable disease, or if they require medical attention and/or special equipment.[43] If a certificate is required, it must confirm that the passenger is fit to fly without extraordinary medical assistance.[44] A critical requirement for all personnel from airlines, airport operators, and ground handling agencies is to undergo mandatory disability awareness and assistance training based on modules provided by the Ministry of Social Justice and Empowerment.[45]

Passengers have the right to cancel or amend their booking within the first 24 hours after purchase if the flight departs more than seven days from the booking date according to the CAR, which is a binding document.[46] Any cancellation charges must be expressly indicated at the time of booking which cannot be more than the basic fare plus fuel charge.[47] The CAR does not deal with any compensation for delay, cancellation, or

38 Paragraph 4.1.5 of Civil Aviation Requirements Section 3-Air Transport Series 'M", Part I Issue III, dated 28 February 2014 as amended on 21 July 2021.

39 Paragraph 4.1.13 and 4.1.15 of Civil Aviation Requirements Section 3-Air Transport Series 'M", Part I Issue III, dated 28 February 2014 as amended on 21 July 2021.

40 Paragraph 4.1.12 of Civil Aviation Requirements Section 3-Air Transport Series 'M", Part I Issue III, dated 28 February 2014 as amended on 21 July 2021.

41 Paragraph 4.1.16 and 4.1.17 of Civil Aviation Requirements Section 3-Air Transport Series 'M", Part I Issue III, dated 28 February 2014 as amended on 21 July 2021.

42 Paragraph 4.1.22 of Civil Aviation Requirements Section 3-Air Transport Series 'M", Part I Issue III, dated 28 February 2014 as amended on 21 July 2021.

43 Paragraph 4.1.25 and 4.1.26.

44 Paragraph 4.1.28.

45 Paragraph 4.3.

46 Paragraph 3(e) of Civil Aviation Requirements Section 3-Air Transport Series 'M", Part II Issue I, dated 22 May 2007 as amended on 27 February 2019.

47 Paragraph 3(h) and (i) of Civil Aviation Requirements Section 3-Air Transport Series 'M", Part II Issue I, dated 22 May 2007 as amended on 27 February 2019.

denial of boarding but rather any delay in refund of unused tickets, the amount to be refunded, and the refund policies.

Finally, the Charter contains a rule on lost, delayed, or damaged baggage which stipulates that in those situations, the carrier's liability is limited to 20,000 Rupees for domestic flights and 1,131 SDR for international flights.[48]

The Indian legal framework for air passenger rights, while comprehensive in substance, is characterized by a structural complexity that creates a significant challenge for accessibility and enforcement. The system is built on a two-tiered foundation: the non-binding, user-friendly "Passenger Charter" that summarizes key rights and a set of binding but CARs that contain the actual legal force. This structure means that while it is easy for a passenger to learn their basic rights from the Charter, understanding the full scope, nuances, and exceptions of the law requires navigating multiple technical documents. This structure can make it confusing for a passenger to find the exact legal text governing a specific issue, as the Charter references different CARs for different topics without ever giving the full reference.

Substantively, the influence of Regulation 261 on the Indian CARs is visible, particularly in the principles of care and compensation. Although the latest revisions tend to move away from Regulation 261 and refining passenger rights by stipulating the passenger's entitlement, such as bottled water within the first two hours. The provisions on involuntary downgrading, with reimbursement calculated as a percentage of the ticket price based on flight distance, are directly comparable. However, the Indian rules often introduce modifications. Compensation for denied boarding and cancellation is calculated as a percentage of the fare with absolute caps, unlike the EU's fixed amounts, and is only triggered for cancellations with less than 24 hours' notice. Furthermore, the Indian law provides an extensive and explicit list of what constitutes "extraordinary circumstances" that exempt airlines from paying compensation, a clarity that contrasts with the EU's reliance on case law to define this concept.

Despite these substantive strengths, the Indian framework has critical weaknesses. A major omission is the lack of a fixed penalty for airline non-compliance within the CARs themselves, potentially weakening enforcement. Additionally, recent updates have introduced ambiguity;

48 Rule 22 of the Carriage by Air Act, 1972 as amended by the Carriage by Air (Amendment) Act, 2009. For the domestic part see: Notification regarding application of the Carriage by Air Act, 1972, to carriage by air which is not international (After Montreal Convention) – S. O. 142(E) dated 17 January 2014 <https://www.dgca.gov.in/digigov-portal/?baseLocale=en_US?page=jsp/dgca/InventoryList/RegulationGuidance/NationalLegislation/natconv_ind.html&mainundefined>.

the new November 2024 guidelines on refreshments during delays have created uncertainty over whether they replace or coexist with the previous tiered system based on flight duration. This regulatory uncertainty is problematic.

In conclusion, the Indian system has successfully imported the protective principles of international standards but delivers them through a fragmented structure that can hinder practical access to justice. Consolidating these rules into a single CAR – or at least pinpointing in the Charter which CAR is applicable – would bridge the gap between the simplified Charter and the complex legal reality, significantly strengthening the framework for the benefit of passengers.

Comparison with EU Regulation

Feature	**CAR Section 3, Series M**	**EU Regulation 261/2004**
Delay Compensation	No.	≥3h: €250–€600 (by distance).
Cancellation Notice	<24 hours' notice: Refund + re-routing + compensation.	<14d notice: Refund or re-routing + €250–600 compensation (by distance).
Denied Boarding	Volunteer first; alternate flight arriving within 24 hours: 200% of one-way, **(max INR 10,000)** alternate flight arriving after 24 hours: 400% of one-way **(max INR 20,000).**	Volunteer first; €250–600 (by distance) if denied boarding.
Baggage Liability	1,131 SDR (international) or 20,000 Rupee (domestic flights).	Not specified.

Bibliography

Primary Sources

- Aircraft Rules, 1937 as amended in 2019 <https://www.dgca.gov.in/digigov-portal/?dynamicPage=aircraftRules1937/1/0/viewDynamicRulesReq>.
- *Air India Ltd v Tej Shoe Exporters Pvt. Ltd RFA* (OS) No. 18/2007 Decided on 19 September 2013.
- The Carriage by Air Act, 1972 as amended in 2009, Act N° 69 <https://prsindia.org/files/bills_acts/bills_parliament/2007/bill100_20070906100_Carriage_by_Air_Act__1972.pdf>.
- Civil Aviation Requirements Section 3-Air Transport Series 'M", Part IV Issue I, dated 6 August 2010, as amended on 15 February 2023 <https://www.dgca.gov.in/digigov-portal/?dynamicPage=CivilAviationReqContent/6/211/viewDynamicRuleContLvl2/html&maincivilAviationRequirements/6/0/viewDynamicRulesReq> accessed 3 December 2025.

- Civil Aviation Requirements Section 3-Air Transport Series ‘M”, Part I Issue III, dated 28 February 2014 as amended on 21 July 2021.
- Notification Regarding Application of the Carriage by Air Act, 1972, to Carriage by Air Which Is Not International (After Montreal Convention) – S. O. 142(E) dated 17 January 2014 <https://www.dgca.gov.in/digigov-portal/?baseLocale=en_US?page=jsp/dgca/InventoryList/RegulationGuidance/National Legislation/natconv_ind.html&amainundefined> accessed 3 December 2025.

Secondary Sources

- Gokulan, D., ‘Flight Delayed? You Are Now Entitled to a Free Meal Indian Civil Aviation Watchdog Has Issued New Rules for Airlines’ *Gulf News* (22 November 2024) <https://gulfnews.com/business/aviation/flight-delayed-you-are-now-entitled-to-a-free-meal-1.1732285232536> accessed 3 December 2025.
- Havel, B. and Mulligan, J., ‘Extraterritorial Application: Exporting European Consumer Protection Standards’ in Michael Bobek and Jeremias Prassl (eds), *Air Passenger Rights Ten Years On* (Hart Publisher 2016).
- Mehrotra, S., ‘Unruly Passenger and Air Rage: Legal Framework and Challenges in Indian Aviation’ (2025) 5 Indian Journal of Legal Review 264.
- Pachnanda, V., ‘Is a Dedicated Indian Law for Air Passenger Protection the Need of the Hour Today’ India Law Journal <https://indialawjournal.org/is-a-dedicated-indian-law-for-air-passenger-protection.php> accessed 3 December 2025.
- Government of India, Ministry of Civil Aviation, Rajya Sabha, Unstarred Question N°1122 <https://sansad.in/getFile/annex/267/AU1122_m6EA5O.pdf?source=pqars> accessed 3 December 2025.
- Tamjeed, S. and Biswas, R., ‘Boarding for People with Disabilities: Analysis of DGCA’s New Rules’ (*Lexology*, 6 July 2022) <https://www.lexology.com/library/detail.aspx?g=0cbe8519-ea2f-45fb-89c7-7f559938163d> accessed 3 December 2025.

II.20

Indonesia

Passenger rights are primarily regulated by Minister of Transport Regulation 89 of 2015 (MT89/2015) Concerning Handling of Flight Delays in Scheduled Commercial Air Transport Business.[1] As Ridha Aditya Nugraha and Lalin Kovudhikulrungsri noted, "The regulation is aimed to protect airline passengers' rights travelling on domestic routes by establishing a delay management standard."[2] The Regulation explicitly stipulates that flight delays in scheduled commercial air transport also apply to denied boarding and flight cancellation issues.[3]

Article 3 of Regulation 89 contains a list of six categories of flight delays:

> a. Category 1, delay 30 minutes to 60 minutes; b. Category 2, delay 61 minutes to 120 minutes; c. Category 3, delay 121 minutes to 180 minutes; d. Category 4, delay 181 minutes to 240 minutes; e. Category 5, delay of more than 240 minutes; and f. category 6, flight cancellation.

While it may be surprising that cancellation is regarded as the 6th category of flight delay, the definition of delay in Article 1(6) is very much a standard definition in the industry.[4]

The delay time is calculated based on the time difference between the scheduled departure or arrival time and the actual departure or arrival time which is when the aircraft is off-block leaving its parking position or when it is on-block and parks at its parking position.[5] The inclusion of such definition facilitates the calculation for passengers, unlike under

1 Pada Badan Usaha Angkutan Udara Niaga Berjadwal di Indonesia (Minister of Transportation Regulation regarding Delay Management on Scheduled Commercial Airline in Indonesia), Permenhub No. 89 Tahun 2015, BNRI No. 716 Year 2015 (Minister Regulation No. 89 Year 2015, SG No. 716 Year 2015).

2 Ridha Aditya Nugraha and Lalin Kovudhikulrungsri, 'Aviation Legal Issues in Indonesia and Thailand: Towards Better Passenger's Rights in ASEAN' (2017) 7 Indonesia Law Review 23, 28.

3 Article 2 of the Regulation.

4 It would translate as "Flight Delay is the time difference between the scheduled departure or arrival time and the actual departure or arrival time."

5 Article 4.

DOI: 10.4324/9781003746164-31

Regulation 261 when the Court of Justice of the European Union had to intervene.[6]

In line with Article 146 of Law Number 1 of 2009 concerning aviation, airlines are liable for losses suffered by passengers due to delays unless the event was caused by specific factors. Article 5 (1) contains a list of factors which may cause delay including "a. airline management factors; b. operational technical factors; c. weather factors; and d. other factors." Airline management factors are defined in the second paragraph as including "a. delays in pilots, co-pilots, and cabin crew; b. delays in catering services; c. delays in handling on the ground; d. waiting for passengers, whether they have just reported (checked in), transferred or connecting flights; and e. unpreparedness of aircraft." Operational technical factors are defined in paragraph 3 as airport closure or disruptions to airport access or runway functionality, such as cracks, flooding or fires, queuing for take-off, landing, or allocation of departure slot time at the airport or delay in refuelling. Weather factors are listed in paragraph 4 and relate to "heavy rain, flooding, lightning, storms, fog, smoke, visibility below minimum standards or wind speeds exceeding maximum safety limits for aviation." Other factors referred to in paragraph 1 (d) relate to factors beyond airline management, operational technical issues, and weather, such as riots and/or demonstrations within the airport area.

Cause	**Airline Liability?**	**Proof Required**
Airline Management (e.g., crew delays, catering issues)	Yes (compensation for Category 5).	None.
Operational Technical (e.g., runway closures, fuel delays)	No.	Official airport authority proof.
Weather (e.g., storms, fog)	No.	Meteorological agency proof.
Riots/Demonstrations	No.	Police/airport authority proof.

Airlines are exempted from their compensation obligation for any delay caused by force majeure or airport operational factors as defined in Article 5 or strikes or riot.[7] Airlines are required to provide an official proof from the relevant authorities before relying on operational technical, weather, or other factors.[8] Compensation is only due when the delay is caused by the airline management's fault.[9] The reliance on a fault-based regime

6 Case C-452/13 *Germanwings GmbH v Ronny Henning*.
7 Article 6(2).
8 Article 5(6).
9 Article 5(1).

places the burden of proof on the passengers which might make it harder to get compensation.[10]

Passengers are entitled to receive information regarding their flight delay which includes clear and accurate information on the reason for the delay no later than 45 minutes before the scheduled departure or once the delay is known.[11] Failure to give passengers sufficient information regarding the management of flight delays could result in a lawsuit for both material and immaterial losses.[12]

Article 9 refers to compensations but in most countries, those would be called care and assistance. It lists the different rights for the different categories as summarized in the following table.[13]

Category	**Delay Duration**	**Assistance**	**Refund/ Re-routing**	**Compensation**
1	30–60 mins.	Light refreshment.	No.	No.
2	61–120 mins.	Refreshment + snack.	Optional.	No.
3	121–180 mins.	Refreshment + full meal.	Optional.	No.
4	181–240 mins.	Snack + meal.	Optional.	No.
5	>240 mins (4+ hrs).	Accommodation (if necessary) for a delay of more than 6 hours.[14]	Optional.	**IDR 300,000** (cash, voucher or bank account transfer).
6	Cancellation.	None.	**Yes.**	No.

When a passenger is being assigned to another flight, regardless of the category, the airline shall bear any difference in price if such reassignment results in a downgrading of the passenger.[15] With regard to the 5th delay category, the compensation must be insured.[16] As Ridha Aditya Nugraha

10 See: Stepani Rahmawati Dewi and others, 'Liability of Airlines that Unilaterally Cancel Flights in Indonesia' (2025) 2 Jurnal Legisci 350.

11 Article 7(3).

12 See: Stepani Rahmawati Dewi and others, 'Liability of Airlines That Unilaterally Cancel Flights in Indonesia' (2025) 2 Jurnal Legisci 350 355.

13 Also found in Muhammad Arief Ramadhan and Dina Normanza Sibagariang, 'Flight Delay: Know Your Passenger Rights' (*MNL*, 12 August 2025) <https://mnllaw.co.id/flight-delay-know-your-passenger-rights/#:~:text=Article%201%20point%2030%20of,actual%20time%20of%20departure%20or> accessed 4 December 2025.

14 Article 10(4).

15 Article 10(3).

16 Article 12(1). See: Wetria Fauzi, 'Airline Customers Conflict Resolution in the Framework of Legal Protection for Consumers in Indonesia' (2023) 6 UNES Law Review 35, 40.

and Lalin Kovudhikulrungsri argued, "It is thus quite evident that numerous preventive measures are being established by the government with a view to protecting passengers' rights."[17] It is, however, interesting to note that only delays above four hours entitle the passenger to compensation, which compared to other legislations does not seem to offer a great protection to passengers. Article 12(3) establishes that compensation must be given to passengers within 72 hours of the delay or cancellation.[18]

Airlines can be sanctioned for not complying with the Regulation. The sanctions will be based on assessment carried out by the Director General and could vary in format but are not dealt in financial terms.[19] A written warning is issued if the airline has an assessment score below 60% ("Unsatisfactory") for three consecutive months.[20] If the airline maintains a score below 60% for three consecutive months after receiving the written warning, the Director General could impose a suspension of new routes.[21] If the unsatisfactory scores continue for three consecutive months after the route suspension sanction, the airline will face route reduction.[22] Finally, the Director General could revoke the business licence.[23] While on paper those sanctions can be very serious, it seems that in practice sanctions are rarely applied with Ridha Aditya Nugraha and Lalin Kovudhikulrungsri referring to Lion Air failing to fulfil its obligations under the Regulation but no sanctions were taken.[24] They even noted, "Questions have arisen as to whether there is a link between sanctions and the airline owner's position within the government, which ultimately dulls the law enforcement that should have taken place."[25]

Violation	**Sanction**
<60% Compliance Score (3 months)	Written warning.
Continued Non-compliance (3+ months)	Suspension of new routes.
Further Non-compliance (3+ months)	Route reduction or license revocation.

17 Ridha Aditya Nugraha and Lalin Kovudhikulrungsri, 'Aviation legal issues in Indonesia and Thailand: Towards better passenger's rights in ASEAN' (2017) 7 Indonesia Law Review 23, 29.

18 The Regulation mentions 3 × 24 hours for an unknown reason.

19 Article 16.

20 Article 16(a).

21 Article 16(b).

22 Article 16(c).

23 Article 16(d).

24 Ridha Aditya Nugraha and Lalin Kovudhikulrungsri, 'Aviation Legal Issues in Indonesia and Thailand: Towards Better Passenger's Rights in ASEAN' (2017) 7 Indonesia Law Review 23, 30–1.

25 Ridha Aditya Nugraha and Lalin Kovudhikulrungsri, 'Aviation Legal Issues in Indonesia and Thailand: Towards Better Passenger's Rights in ASEAN' (2017) 7 Indonesia Law Review 23, 31.

Interestingly, Chapter IV on handling passengers stipulates that airlines must appoint an authorized staff, such as a general manager, who can make on-field decisions in handling delayed passengers.[26] Article 8(2) stipulates that the person must show "empathy, attention, and care" and must assist passengers.[27]

Similar to many national laws, the Regulation provides a time limit for refund and compensation. It also makes it clear that any conflicting provisions in prior regulations are repealed.[28] However, the Regulation does not mention its scope and whether it applies to international flights or only to domestic ones. It seems from the definition of air transport business in Article 1(2) that it is limited to Indonesian legal entities or state-owned enterprises which would indicate the Regulation does not apply to foreign airlines.

Indonesia's framework provides basic protections but lacks the teeth of stricter regimes such as the EU, Oman, or Saudi Arabia. The global trend toward enhanced passenger rights such as fixed compensation highlights gaps in Indonesia's approach. Its limited compensation, only for category 5, and broad exemptions limiting compensation make it a more airline-friendly regulation. Moreover, the Regulation has a domestic focus which leaves questions as to its applicability to foreign airlines and international flights. Finally, while the sanctions are severe on paper, it can be wondered if they are applied in reality.

Comparison with Regulation 261

Feature	**MT89/2015**	**EU Regulation 261**
Delay Compensation	≥4h: IDR 300K.	≥3h: €250–€600 (by distance).
Cancellation Compensation	Full refund.	<14d notice: Refund or re-routing + €250–600 compensation (by distance).
Denial of Boarding Compensation	Treated as delay.	Volunteer first; €250–600 (by distance) if denied boarding.
Baggage Compensation	Not specified.	Not specified.

Bibliography

- Pada Badan Usaha Angkutan Udara Niaga Berjadwal di Indonesia (Minister of Transportation Regulation regarding Delay Management on Scheduled Commercial Airline in Indonesia), Permenhub No. 89 Tahun 2015, BNRI No. 716 Year 2015 (Minister Regulation No. 89 Year 2015, SG No. 716 Year 2015).
- Case C-452/13 *Germanwings GmbH v Ronny Henning*, ECLI:EU:C:2014:2141.

26 Article 8(1).
27 Article 8(2)(a), (b), (c).
28 Article 18.

- Nugraha, R. A. and Kovudhikulrungsri, L., 'Aviation Legal Issues in Indonesia and Thailand: Towards Better Passenger's Rights in ASEAN' (2017) 7 Indonesia Law Review 23.
- Ramadhan, M.A. and Sibagariang, D.N., 'Flight Delay: Know Your Passenger Rights' (*MNL*, 12 August 2025) <https://mnllaw.co.id/flight-delay-know-your-passenger-rights/#:~:text=Article%201%20point%2030%20of,actual%20time%20of%20departure%20or> accessed 4 December 2025.
- Fauzi, W., 'Airline Customers Conflict Resolution in the Framework of Legal Protection for Consumers in Indonesia' (2023) 6 UNES Law Review 35.
- Dewi, S.R. and others, 'Liability of Airlines that Unilaterally Cancel Flights in Indonesia' (2025) 2 Jurnal Legisci 350.

II.21

Israel

Israeli air passenger rights are governed by the Aviation Services Law (Compensation and Assistance for Flight Cancellation or Change of Conditions), 5772–2012 (ASL), a pro-consumer legislation.[1] This law is similar in many ways to the EU's Regulation 261, providing passengers with rights in the event of flight disruptions. However, it also includes some innovations such as the possibility for courts to impose exemplary damages for any non-compliance with the ASL.[2]

The ASL applies to passengers having a confirmed reservation for a flight purchased at a fare available directly or indirectly to the general public, if they have presented themselves to the airport at the time provided by the carrier or at least 90 minutes before the flight time, unless the flight has been cancelled.[3] It applies to flights departing from an airport in Israel or a flight arriving at an airport in Israel, unless the passenger received benefits or compensation and was given assistance in another country and those benefits, compensation, and assistance directly correspond to their entitlement under ASL.[4]

ALS starts with the various benefits a passenger may receive.[5] These include assistance services including food and drink in accordance with the waiting time,[6] hotel accommodation, travel between the hotel and

1 Aviation Services Law (Compensation and Assistance for Flight Cancellation or Change of Conditions), 5772-2012 <https://www.aeroflot.ru/media/aflfiles/docs/legal/aviation_services_law_eng1.pdf>.

This pro-consumer approach is also found in the interpretation of the Montreal Convention with the Israeli Supreme Court being one of the rare courts which allows moral damages to be recoverable. See: Chen Shalem, 'The Israeli Supreme Court Rules Non-Material Losses Are Recoverable Under Montreal Convention' (2023) 48 Air and Space Law 225.

2 Eyal Doron and Hugh Kowarsky, 'Air Passenger Rights in Israel' (*Lexology*, 6 September 2019) <https://www.lexology.com/library/detail.aspx?g=00ed940b-53d8-4078-9ac4-ef780be640df> accessed 4 December 2025.

3 Clause 2(a).

4 Clause 2(a) coupled with the definition of 'flight' in Clause 1.

5 Clause 3.

6 Clause 3(a)(1)(a).

DOI: 10.4324/9781003746164-32

airport if an overnight stay or longer,[7] and communication services like phone calls,[8] as well as financial benefits. The law stipulates the right to a reimbursement of the consideration (ticket price, fee, and charges),[9] which must be paid within 21 days of a written request.[10] It also specifies the right to a replacement flight ticket to the final destination at the earliest possible time or a later date.[11] Additionally, passengers are entitled to monetary compensation, as detailed in the First Schedule of the law, which must be paid within 45 days.[12] Finally, the law provides for monetary compensation for any downgrading to a lower class of service, as outlined in the Second Schedule.[13]

For a flight with a stopover, if a disruption occurs and the passenger does not reach their final destination, they are entitled to a full refund even if the flight did actually occur.[14] However, no compensation is due and the airline can charge a rebooking fee if the passenger does not present themselves on time at the gate as ruled by the Tel Aviv Magistrates Court.[15]

For a return ticket, a disruption on the outbound flight entitles the passenger to a full refund, while a disruption on the return flight entitles them to a 50% refund.[16] The law also clarifies that a passenger who accepts a replacement flight ticket is generally not entitled to a refund.[17]

In case of denial of boarding, the carrier must first ask for volunteers to give up their seats for a mutually agreed-upon consideration.[18] If a passenger is involuntarily denied boarding, they are entitled to assistance services and monetary compensation, as well as the choice between a reimbursement or a replacement flight ticket.[19] The law allows for a 50% reduction in compensation if the airline offers a replacement flight that arrives at the final destination within a certain timeframe, depending on the flight distance. For flights up to 2,000 km, the alternative flight must arrive no more than four hours after the originally scheduled arrival

7 Clause 3(a)(1)(b) and (c).

8 Clause 3(a)(1)(d).

9 Keren Marco, 'Consumers' Aviation Claims the Israeli Perspective' (January 2019) <https://www.aerosociety.com/media/10486/3-keren-marco.pdf>.

10 Clause 3(a)(2).

11 Clause 3(a)(3).

12 Clause 3(a)(4).

13 Clause 3(a)(5).

14 Clause 3(b)(1).

15 Levitan, Sharon and Co, 'Passenger's Responsibility to Arrive at Departure Gate on Time' (*Lexology*, 25 July 2018) <https://www.lexology.com/library/detail.aspx?g=90c4e270-1efb-434f-a384-4f17eec09dfa> accessed 4 December 2025.

16 Clause 3(b)(2).

17 Clause 3(b)(4).

18 Clause 5(a).

19 Clause 5(b).

time.[20] For flights between 2,000 km and 4,500 km, the alternative flight must arrive no more than five hours after the originally scheduled arrival time.[21] For flights over 4,500 km, the alternative flight must arrive no more than six hours after the originally scheduled arrival time.[22] The distance is calculated based on the shortest route between the points of departure and arrival on the surface of the globe and not the great circle route as under Regulation 261.[23] However, these provisions do not apply if a passenger is denied boarding due to security concerns, health issues, or a lack of proper travel documents.[24] There is an exception for security-related denials, where a passenger who is found to be compliant with security checks is still entitled to compensation if the passenger arrived at the airport at least three hours before the scheduled departure, had valid travel documents, and fully cooperated with the security check.[25] In those cases, the airline cannot use security concerns as an excuse to avoid paying compensation.

Scenario	Monetary Compensation (NIS)	Assistance Services
Voluntary Denial	Mutually agreed consideration (e.g., travel voucher, cash, miles) from the airline.	Not explicitly stipulated.
Involuntary Denial	**Full Compensation:** • ≤2,000 km: 1,350 NIS. • 2,000–4,500 km: 2,025 NIS. • >4,500 km: 3,040 NIS. **Reduced Compensation (50%):** Applies if the airline offers a replacement flight that arrives within a specified delay: • ≤2,000 km: ≤4 hours late. • 2,000–4,500 km: ≤5 hours late. • >4,500 km: ≤6 hours late.	Right to care, including: • Meals and refreshments. • Hotel accommodation (if overnight stay required). • Transport to/from hotel. • Two phone calls/emails.

In the event of a flight cancellation, a passenger on a cancelled flight is entitled to assistance services, a choice between a reimbursement or a replacement flight ticket, and monetary compensation.[26] The airline may reduce compensation by 50% if an alternative flight arrives within set

20 Clause 5(c)(1).
21 Clause 5(c)(2).
22 Clause 5(c)(3).
23 Clause 12.
24 Clause 5(d).
25 Clause 5(e)(1)–(3).
26 Clause 6(a)(1)–(3).

times: up to two hours late for flights under 2,000 km, three hours for flights up to 4,500 km, and four hours for flights over 4,500 km.[27]

A passenger is not entitled to monetary compensation if the airline notified them of the cancellation at least 14 days in advance.[28] Compensation is also not required if the airline provided notice between seven and 14 days in advance and offered an alternative flight that departed no more than two hours before the original time and arrived at the final destination no more than four hours after the original arrival time. Similarly, passengers cannot request a compensation if they were notified fewer than seven days before the scheduled departure, and offered an alternative flight that departs no more than one hour before the original time and arrives at the final destination no more than two hours after the original arrival time.[29] The wording is similar to the EU Regulation, however, the ASL contains a clause that these exemptions do not apply if a passenger refuses the alternative flight for reasons of security, religion, or medical limitations or if the alternative flight offer was not extended to a person travelling with the passenger.[30]

Notice Period Provided to Passenger	Required Alternative Flight Offered
At Least 14 Days Before the Original Flight	No specific alternative flight requirements.
Between 7 and 14 Days Before the Original Flight	A flight that departs ≤2 hours earlier **and** arrives ≤4 hours later.
Fewer Than 7 Days Before the Original Flight	A flight that departs ≤1 hour earlier **and** arrives ≤2 hours later.

The passengers are not entitled to monetary compensation if the airline proves the cancellation was caused by extraordinary circumstances beyond its control, which could not have been avoided even if all reasonable measures had been taken.[31] The ALS lays down explicit examples such as circumstances not within the airline's control or that "even if It would have done whatever was under its control – it could not have prevented the cancelation due to those circumstances,"[32] which includes severe weather, political instability, air traffic restrictions, and security risks. Technical malfunctions usually don't fall under this category unless they are really

27 Clause 6(b)(1)–(3).
28 Clause 6(c)(1).
29 Clause 6(c)(2)–(3).
30 Clause 6(d).
31 Clause 6(e).
32 Clause 6(e)(1).

extraordinary.[33] Other reasons are strike or protected industrial action or cancellations undertaken to prevent the desecration of the Sabbath or a Jewish holiday.[34] However, it was determined that the pilot's medical condition, significant technical malfunctions, and lightning strikes do not constitute special circumstances.[35] As Doron and Kowarsky noted, "in the spirit of the pro-consumer nature of the ASL, the Israeli courts have given a narrow interpretation to the provision in the ASL exempting the carrier from the obligation to compensate passengers."[36]

Upon cancelling a flight, the airline is obligated to present the passenger with available alternative options for reaching their final destination.[37] The minister of transport, with consent, holds the authority to adjust the delay timeframes stipulated in the law. Any increase or reduction may not exceed four hours from the originally stated figures. Should the minister reduce these timeframes, corresponding provisions will be established to adjust the benefits owed for significantly delayed flights.[38]

The ASL provides a tiered system of benefits for delayed flights, based on the length of the delay. A flight that is delayed by at least two hours entitles the passenger to immediate assistance services, which include food, drink, and communication services.[39] For longer delays, the law provides for additional benefits. If a flight is delayed by five hours but less than eight hours, the passenger is given a choice between a full refund of their ticket price or an alternative flight. If the alternative flight requires an overnight stay, the passenger is also entitled to accommodation and travel services to and from the hotel. However, if the delay is caused by a strike, the passenger is only entitled to a refund, along with the standard food, drink, and communication services.[40] Delays over eight hours are considered as cancelled flights.

33 C.F. 69167-11-17 *Regev v EL-AL* (29.3.17–Magistrates Court). Keren Marco, 'Consumers' Aviation Claims the Israeli Perspective' (January 2019) <https://www.aerosociety.com/media/10486/3-keren-marco.pdf> accessed 4 December 2025.

For severe weather condition: SC (Tel Aviv) 12644-03-23 *Muzlebet & Others v Aegean Airlines* (1 September 2023).

34 Clause 6(e)(2) and (3).

35 Peggy Sharon and Keren Marco, 'Court Considers Extreme Weather Conditions "Special Circumstances" for Flight Cancellation' (*Lexology*, 1 November 2023) <https://www.lexology.com/library/detail.aspx?g=fb057207-8920-4e48-b110-787a9e59863e> accessed 4 December 2025.

36 Eyal Doron and Hugh Kowarsky, 'Air Passenger Rights in Israel' (*Lexology*, 6 September 2019) <https://www.lexology.com/library/detail.aspx?g=00ed940b-53d8-4078-9ac4-ef780be640df> accessed 4 December 2025.

37 Clause 6(f).

38 Clause 6(h).

39 Clause 7(a).

40 Clause 7(b).

Length of Delay	Passenger Entitlements	Conditions and Exceptions
2 Hours +	**Right to care:** Food, drink, and communication services.	Applies to all delays meeting the minimum threshold.
5 to 8 Hours	1. A **full refund** of the ticket price, or 2. A **replacement flight ticket** to the final destination. **Additional care:** If the replacement flight departs the next day, the airline must also provide accommodation and travel services to and from the hotel.	**Strike exception:** If the delay is due to a strike or protected labour action, the passenger is **only** entitled to a refund and care services (food, drink, communication), **not** to a replacement flight or accommodation.
8 Hours +	Flight is considered **cancelled.**	

When a carrier changes a flight's departure to an earlier time, passenger rights are triggered based on the scale of the change and the notice provided. If the take-off time is brought forward by more than five but not more than eight hours, and the passenger receives notice of this change less than 14 days before the original departure time, they are entitled to choose between a full reimbursement of the ticket price or a replacement flight.[41] If the departure is brought forward by more than eight hours and the passenger receives less than 14 days' notice, the passenger is entitled to a refund or a replacement flight ticket, as well as monetary compensation, save for the extraordinary circumstances.[42]

The law also governs changes to the ticket conditions, while the passengers' rights regarding buying and cancelling flight tickets is regulated by the Israeli Consumer Protection Law 1981 (CPL). If an airline decides to transfer a passenger to a class higher than the one stipulated on their ticket, the passenger cannot be asked to pay any additional sum for this upgrade.[43] Conversely, if a passenger is involuntarily transferred to a class lower than the one they purchased, the carrier must pay them monetary compensation. This compensation is calculated as a percentage of the ticket price paid, proportionate to the flight distance on which the downgrade occurred.[44] Specifically, compensation is set at 60% of the price paid for the flight in the case of a transfer from first class to business class. A transfer from business class to economy class confers a right to compensation of 80% of the flight price. A transfer from first class directly

41 Clause 8(a).
42 Clause 8(b)(1) and (2).
43 Clause 9(a).
44 Clause 9(b).

to economy class confers a right to compensation of 90% of the flight price. Furthermore, in the case of a transfer from either first class or business class to economy class on a flight whose distance was over 4,500 km, the passenger is entitled to full compensation of 100% of the price paid for the flight.[45] For flights involving a stopover, the compensation is calculated based on the ratio of the downgraded flight distance to the total travel distance. A specific method of calculating the ticket price for this purpose applies when the ticket was part of a purchased tourist package.[46] Those rules are much more specific than under Regulation 261.

Original Class	**Downgraded To**	**Flight Distance**	**Compensation (% of Leg's Ticket Price)**
First class.	Business class.	Any distance.	60%.
Business class.	Economy class.	Any distance.	80%.
First class.	Economy class.	Any distance.	90%.
First class.	Economy class.	Over 4,500 km.	100%.
Business class.	Economy class.	Over 4,500 km.	100%.

An airline is prohibited from issuing a flight ticket that stipulates a departure time which has not been pre-approved by the relevant Airport Authority, unless one of two conditions is met.[47] First, the passenger must have received notice of the officially approved flight time from an authorized entity at least three months in advance.[48] Second, the Airport Authority must have granted retrospective approval for the flight time printed on the ticket.[49] This regulatory provision is specifically targeted at carriers and does not apply to travel agency service providers who are not themselves the organizers of the flight.[50]

The ASL also contains a very unique and strong provision which allows courts to award exemplary damages to passengers, independent of any actual damages they may have suffered up to 11,540 New Israel Shekels.[51] These damages can be awarded if the court finds that the airline or organizer "knowingly" committed one of several breaches, including but not limited to the failure to provide mandated benefits for denied boarding, cancellations, delays, or brought-forward flights, as well as the failure to

45 Second Schedule.
46 Clause 9(b).
47 Clause 10(a).
48 Clause 10(a)(1).
49 Clause 10(a)(2).
50 Clause 10(b).
51 Clause 11(a) stipulates 10,390 New Israel Shekels, however that amount has been increased.

pay compensation for involuntary downgrades or the issuance of a ticket for an unconfirmed flight that results in a cancellation or a delay of over two hours.[52] In determining the amount, the court must consider factors such as the need to enforce the law, encourage passengers to realize their rights, the severity and circumstances of the breach, and whether it was a repeat offense.[53] Crucially, the actual extent of the passenger's personal damage is not a factor in this calculation. This right to exemplary damages exists in addition to the passenger's right to claim the standard benefits owed under the law.[54] This article could be equated to the fixed fines for non-compliance but is receivable by the passengers themselves.

A core principle of the law is transparency. Airlines and organizers are required to prominently display a notice detailing passenger rights at their public reception areas and on their websites. Airport operators must also display this information in visible locations within the airport. Furthermore, when a flight is disrupted, the airline must provide the affected passenger with a document explicitly outlining their entitlements. Airlines and the travel agents who sell their tickets must also inform passengers of the location and contact details of the airline's appointed representative at the airport who is responsible for assisting passengers with their rights.[55]

The Israeli ASL provides a generous four-year statute of limitations from the date the cause of action arose.[56]

While the Israeli Aviation Services Law is fundamentally modelled on EU Regulation 261, it has been adapted to its specific legal and operational environment. Its approach is characterized by a strong emphasis on procedural clarity, precise definitions, and a structured system of remedies. The most notable differences are the higher delay threshold for compensation (eight hours vs. three hours) and the inclusion of exemplary damages, which offers a unique and powerful enforcement mechanism. A central strength of the Israeli law is its meticulous granularity. It provides exceptionally clear, mathematical rules for reducing compensation by 50% if a suitable alternative flight is offered, with specific delay thresholds (e.g., two, three, or four hours, depending on distance) that create predictability for both airlines and passengers. This contrasts with the EU regulation's

52 Clause 11(a)(1)(a)–(e) See: Keren Marco, 'Consumers' Aviation Claims the Israeli Perspective' (January 2019) <https://www.aerosociety.com/media/10486/3-keren-marco.pdf> for examples.

53 Clause 11(b)(1)–(5).

54 Clause 11(c).

55 Clause 14.

56 Clause 19.

more general concept of a "re-routing" arriving within a certain time, which can lead to more interpretive disputes.

Perhaps the most significant philosophical difference lies in the scope of exemptions from compensation. The Israeli law carves out a specific and substantial exception for cancellations made to prevent the desecration of the Sabbath or Jewish holidays. This culturally and religiously specific provision has no equivalent in EU Regulation 261 and reflects the law's adaptation to its national context. In terms of enforcement, the Israeli law possesses a powerful and unique tool: exemplary damages of up to approximately 11,540 NIS. This provision allows courts to penalize airlines for knowingly violating the law, with the explicit aim of encouraging passenger claims and deterring breaches. This is a more aggressive enforcement mechanism than the EU system, which relies on national enforcement bodies and the compensation amounts themselves as a deterrent.

While the Israeli amounts are indexed for inflation – a smart feature the EU lacks – the starting point is lower. The heavy reliance on advance notice rules also creates a larger loophole for airlines to avoid paying compensation compared to the EU's narrower focus on truly extraordinary circumstances. Under the ASL, a passenger who is initially denied boarding for security reasons can still be entitled to compensation if they cooperated with the check and were ultimately cleared to fly. This addresses the specific security environment in Israel and offers passengers a clear recourse in a situation that might be less regulated elsewhere.

In conclusion, the Israeli Aviation Services Law is a sophisticated and well-structured legal framework that successfully translates core principles of passenger protection into a precise, legally operable system. It excels in its procedural clarity, its adaptation to national specificities, and its innovative enforcement via exemplary damages.

Comparison with EU Regulation 261

Feature	**Aviation Services Law (Rights of Passengers) 5772–2012**	**EU Regulation 261/2004**
Delay Compensation	≥8h: 1,350–3,040 NIS (by distance).	≥3h: €250–€600 (by distance).
Cancellation Compensation	<14d notice: Full refund + re-routing + compensation.	<14d notice: Refund or re-routing + €250–600 compensation (by distance).
Denial of Boarding Compensation	Volunteer first; 1,350–3,040 NIS (by distance) if denied boarding	Volunteer first; €250–600 (by distance) if denied boarding.
Baggage	Not specified.	Not specified.

Bibliography

- Aviation Services Law (Compensation and Assistance for Flight Cancellation or Change of Conditions), 5772-2012 <https://www.aeroflot.ru/media/aflfiles/docs/legal/aviation_services_law_eng1.pdf>.
- C.F. 69167-11-17 *Regev v EL-AL* (29.3.17– Magistrates Court).
- SC (Tel Aviv) 12644-03-23 *Muzlebet & Others v Aegean Airlines* (1 September 2023).
- Doron, E. and Kowarsky, H., 'Air Passenger Rights in Israel' (*Lexology*, 6 September 2019) <https://www.lexology.com/library/detail.aspx?g=00ed940b-53d8-4078-9ac4-ef780be640df> accessed 4 December 2025.
- Levitan, Sharon and Co, 'Passenger's Responsibility to Arrive at Departure Gate on Time' (*Lexology*, 25 July 2018) <https://www.lexology.com/library/detail.aspx?g=90c4e270-1efb-434f-a384-4f17eec09dfa>.
- Marco, K., 'Consumers' Aviation Claims the Israeli Perspective' (January 2019) <https://www.aerosociety.com/media/10486/3-keren-marco.pdf> accessed 4 December 2025.
- Shalem, C., 'The Israeli Supreme Court Rules Non-Material Losses Are Recoverable Under Montreal Convention' (2023) 48 Air and Space Law 225.
- Sharon, P. and Marco, K., 'Court Considers Extreme Weather Conditions "Special Circumstances" for Flight Cancellation' (*Lexology*, 1 November 2023) <https://www.lexology.com/library/detail.aspx?g=fb057207-8920-4e48-b110-787a9e59863e> accessed 4 December 2025.

II.22

Japan

Unlike regions with a unified set of regulations like the European Union (EU Regulation 261), Japan does not have a comprehensive, government-mandated law for air passenger rights that is similar in scope. Instead, passenger rights are primarily governed by a combination of international conventions and, most importantly, the individual airline's Conditions of Carriage. As Kamiya and Kamimura noted, "Although it is not a legal obligation, Japanese carriers typically provide compensation for delay and cancellation of flights and carriage of disabled passengers on a voluntary basis."[1]

Under Japan's Civil Aeronautics Act, airlines are required to establish their own conditions of carriage and get them approved by the Ministry of Land, Infrastructure, Transport and Tourism (MLIT). These conditions must include provisions on liability and fares.

Passengers are entitled to a full refund if their flight is cancelled by the airline rather than by themselves. This rule still applies even if the airline cancels the flight due to external factors, such as government prohibition orders.[2] For instance, Rule 24 of Japan Airlines mentions that the carrier will ensure the passenger is either re-routed to their final destination on the next available flight being from the airline or a competitor without any additional fees or grant a full refund.[3] The carrier could also extend

1 Miki Kamiya and Tomohiko Kamimura, 'Air Passenger Rights in Japan' (*Lexology*, 6 September 2019) <https://www.lexology.com/library/detail.aspx?g=1d08ba8f-46aa-4166-a45c-8fd4fdbe3b25> accessed 5 December 2025.

However, in the terms and conditions of Japan Airlines such voluntary compensation was not included <https://www.jal.co.jp/jp/en/dom/yakkan/240326/> nor in ANA's <https://www.ana.co.jp/en/jp/guide/terms/dom-conditions-of-carriage/>.

2 Paragraph 1 of Article 536 of the Civil Code.

3 The exact same rule is found in Rule 26 of ANA's condition of carriage. <https://www.ana.co.jp/en/jp/guide/terms/dom-conditions-of-carriage/> or Article 7(B) of Air Japan <https://www.flyairjapan.com/pdfs/policy/conditions-of-carriage/en/airjapan-conditions-of-carriage.pdf>.

Article 22 of Air Do conditions of carriage <https://www.airdo.jp/en/corporate/info/conditions-of-carriage/>.

DOI: 10.4324/9781003746164-33

the period of validity of the unused sector. This rule will not apply if the change of scheduled time is due to reasons beyond the carrier's reasonable control.[4] If the passenger cancels the ticket, they might be obliged to pay cancellation fees unless such fee is excessive.[5]

While there is no single law on passenger rights, Japan presents a critically important alternative model: a system where passenger compensation is driven by proactive carrier practice and regulatory expectation rather than reactive legal compulsion. For major Japanese carriers, maintaining trust and social harmony (wa) is paramount. Proactively offering compensation, even when not legally mandated, is a matter of corporate responsibility and brand preservation. Analysing Japanese aviation requires a deep dive into contract law and the specific provisions airlines file. This contrasts with regions like the EU, where the regulation sits above and supersedes the contract.

Bibliography

- Civil Code Act No. 89 of 27 April 1896 as amended <https://www.moj.go.jp/content/000056024.pdf> accessed 5 December 2025.
- Air Do, 'Conditions of Carriage – Domestic Passengers and Baggage' (until 18 May 2026) <https://www.airdo.jp/en/corporate/info/conditions-of-carriage/> accessed 5 December 2025.
- Air Japan, 'Conditions of Carriage- International Passengers and Baggage' (effective 28 October 2025) <https://www.flyairjapan.com/pdfs/policy/conditions-of-carriage/en/airjapan-conditions-of-carriage.pdf>.
- Amakusa Airlines, 'Conditions of Carriage' <https://www.amx.co.jp/en/provision/> accessed 5 December 2025.
- ANA, 'Conditions of Carriage- Domestic Passengers and Baggage' (until 18 May 2026) <https://www.ana.co.jp/en/jp/guide/terms/dom-conditions-of-carriage/> accessed 5 December 2025.
- Japan Airlines, 'Domestic Flights Conditions of Carriage' <https://www.jal.co.jp/jp/en/dom/yakkan/240326/> accessed 5 December 2025.
- Kamiya, M. and Kamimura, T., 'Air Passenger Rights in Japan' (*Lexology*, 6 September 2019) <https://www.lexology.com/library/detail.aspx?g=1d08ba8f-46aa-4166-a45c-8fd4fdbe3b25> accessed 5 December 2025.

4 Rule 43 of the Japan Airlines condition of carriage and Rule 44 of ANA.

5 Article 9 of the Consumer Contract Act. For Japan Airlines, the fee is 430 yen per sector of the ticket as the refund charge according to Rule 22 of their condition of carriage. For ANA, the amount is 440 yen per sector. It is 400 yen per sector of the ticket for Amakusa Airlines (Rule 19) <https://www.amx.co.jp/en/provision/>.

II.23

Jordan

In Jordan, air passenger rights are primarily regulated by Consumer Protection Instructions (Part 209) of 2020 Issued under the Provisions of Article 55 of the Civil Aviation Law No. 41 of 2007 as amended.[1] The Instructions apply to flights departing from any airport in the Kingdom by a Jordanian or international airline, including stopovers, and to flights arriving in the Kingdom by a national airline.[2] Part 209 does not apply when the passenger has already received compensation or benefits outside of Jordan for the same issue.[3] The Instructions do not apply to passengers travelling free of charge or on reduced fares not available to the public (except for frequent flyer tickets) or in cases of Air Travel Package cancellations for reasons other than flight cancellation.[4]

The law details the obligations of the passenger, which include having a confirmed reservation, being at check-in at the announced time (or 45 minutes before departure if no specific time is announced), possessing necessary travel documents, following up with the airline for flight changes, and disclosing any special needs at the time of booking.[5]

Interestingly, the Instructions start with the right to care, assistance, and monetary compensation before discussing delay, cancellations, and denial of boarding. Those articles are often found the other way around.

Article 6 outlines the rights of passengers to receive care from operating air carriers free of charge in situations of delays, cancellations, or denied boarding. This care includes refreshments and meals proportional to the delay, accommodation until an alternative flight is available, transportation to the accommodation, and access to free communication methods. In

1 Consumer Protection Instructions (Part 209) of 2020 Issued under the Provisions of Article 55 of the Civil Aviation Law No. 41 of 2007 as amended.

2 Article 3a and b.

3 Article 14(b).

4 Article 22(d) and (e).

5 Article 5(a)–(e).

DOI: 10.4324/9781003746164-34

cases of force majeure,[6] the care provided should be reasonable and customary within the industry. The vagueness of the law regarding the care and support in case of force majeure makes it open to lawsuits and abuse.

Passengers may choose the right to assistance, which forfeits their right to care.[7] The right to assistance includes either the reimbursement of the unused portion of the ticket within 30 days along with a return flight to the origin if the original purpose is no longer met and the journey has commenced, or re-routing to the final destination under comparable conditions, including land transport to the original final destination airport.[8]

The Instructions contain a right to monetary compensation for passengers on international flights in cases of delays, cancellations, or denial of boarding.[9] The Regulation follows a distance-based approach for compensation but increases the distance compared to the EU Regulation; namely, 100 SDR for flights not exceeding 1,500 km, 150 SDR for flights between 1,500 km and 4,000 km, and 200 SDR for flights exceeding 4,000 km.[10] The compensation can be reduced by 50% if the passenger accepts an alternative flight with arrival times within two hours for flights of less than 1,500 km, three hours for flights with a distance between 1,500 km and 4,000 km, or four hours for flights exceeding 4,000 km.[11] The calculation method is the same as in the European Regulation, namely the great circle route method.[12] Article 8 d makes it clear that the compensations listed do not apply to domestic flights.

Flight Distance	**Compensation (SDR)**	**Reduction if Alternative Flight Arrives Within**
≤1,500 km	100 SDR.	≤2 hours later → 50 SDR.
1,500–4,000 km	150 SDR.	≤3 hours later → 75 SDR.
>4,000 km	200 SDR.	≤4 hours later → 100 SDR.

6 As defined in Article 2 as "Exceptional or unusual events which are by nature or origin beyond the actual control of the air carrier."
7 Article 7(b).
8 Article 7(a)(1) and (2).
9 Article 8.
10 Article 8(a).
11 Article 8(b).
12 Article 8(c).

Article 9 is dedicated to flight delays and stipulates that no care or assistance is required for delays under two hours.[13] Passengers are entitled to right to care for delays exceeding two hours. However, the right to care would not include providing accommodation.[14] For delays of five to seven hours, airlines must not only comply with the right to care but also with the right to assistance, i.e. refund or re-routing.[15] Finally, only passengers suffering from a delay exceeding eight hours will be entitled to monetary compensation in addition to right to care and assistance.[16] Compared to other laws, the delay time is very long before a passenger could claim any compensation. The provision could have been made clear by expressly mentioning accommodation for delays above five hours, which seems to be how the rules must be interpreted.

Flight Delay Compensation

Delay Duration	**Passenger Rights**
<2 Hours	No compensation.
≥2 Hours	Right to **care** (meals, refreshments, communication).
5–7 Hours	Right to **care + assistance** (refund/re-routing).
≥8 Hours	Right to **care + assistance + monetary compensation**.

Article 10 addresses flight cancellations. Passengers informed less than seven days prior to the flight are entitled to care, assistance, and monetary compensation. No monetary compensation is due if the passenger was informed at least seven days prior.[17] Airlines must inform passengers of alternative transport options when notifying of the cancellation.[18] Airlines are not liable for monetary compensation if the cancellation is due to force majeure that could not be avoided or passenger non-compliance with Article 5.[19] The burden of proof for informing passengers lies with the airline (or travel agency for chartered flights).[20] Passengers whose flight is brought forward by more than five but less than eight hours are entitled to assistance.[21] If the departure time is moved forward by eight hours or

13 Article 9(a).
14 Article 9(b).
15 Article 9(c).
16 Article 9(d).
17 Article 10(a).
18 Article 10(c).
19 Article 10(d)(1) and (2).
20 Article 10(e).
21 Article 10(f).

more with at least seven days' notice, care, assistance, and compensation are due.[22]

Notice Period	Passenger Rights	Exceptions
<7 Days	- Right to **care.** - Right to **assistance.** - **Monetary compensation.**	**No compensation if:** - Force majeure (e.g., extreme weather). - Passenger fails obligations (Article 5).
≥7 Days	Only **care + assistance** (no monetary compensation).	Flight brought forward by 8 hours + → monetary compensation.

Article 11 deals with denied boarding. Airlines must first ask for volunteers to give up their seats in exchange for agreed benefits.[23] In those circumstances, the passengers are entitled to right to care and right to assistance.[24] In the event that no sufficient volunteers come forward,

Airlines may start denying boarding. Those non-volunteering passengers are entitled to care, assistance, and monetary compensation immediately, provided they complied with Article 5.[25] Unlike many laws, Part 209 does not include a list of passengers who cannot be denied of boarding such as passengers with special needs within the article dedicated to denial of boarding. Instead, Article 13 mandates airlines to give priority to persons with special needs and their accompanying assistants. This provision is not clear whether it applies to denial of boarding or to general boarding.

Article 12 prohibits airlines from charging extra when a passenger is involuntarily upgraded.[26] In the event that a passenger is downgraded, they are entitled to compensation, either the price difference or 50% of the ticket price excluding taxes.[27] Part 209 also requires the entity issuing the ticket to indicate the ticket price, duties, and taxes at the time of purchase (excluding GIT and FIT prices).[28]

Airlines can seek reimbursement from any third party responsible for damages that led to compensation payment to passengers.[29]

Similarly to EU Regulation 261, airlines are under the obligation to inform passengers of their rights by displaying signage at boarding gates,

22 Article 10(g).
23 Article 11(a).
24 Article 11(c).
25 Article 11(b) and (d).
26 Article 12(a).
27 Article 12(b)(1) and (2).
28 Article 16.
29 Article 15.

on their website, and at sales offices.[30] Any agreement releasing the air carrier from liability under these instructions is null and void.[31] Airlines must inform passengers of their liability limits for death, injury, lost or damaged baggage, and delay or cancellation claims.[32]

Unlike many laws, Part 209 sets a two-year time limit for bringing compensation claims "from the date of arrival at the destination, or from the date on which the aircraft ought to have arrived, or from the date on which the carriage stopped."[33] This is a very welcomed addition as it makes it clear on all parties as to when a claim would become time barred. Similarly, Article 22 specifies that the relationship between contracting air carriers is governed by relevant international agreements and contracts.[34] It also requires compliance with international baggage rules.[35]

Part 209 does not include specific sanctions but empowers the Chief Commissioner to take necessary actions to enforce these instructions.[36] Interestingly, Article 23 allows the Board to adjust the compensation amounts in Article 8 every three years based on the Jordanian inflation rate reported by the Department of Statistics.[37] This inclusion is a welcomed addition as it futureproofs this piece of legalization in a way.

The Euro-Mediterranean Aviation Agreement between Jordan and the European Union is resulting in a gradual alignment of Jordan's legislation with European standards in areas such as consumer protection and passenger rights.[38]

Jordan's framework for air passenger rights, established by the Consumer Protection Instructions (Part 209) of 2020, represents a deliberate and structured incorporation of international consumer protection standards into national law. As an instrument issued under the Civil Aviation Law, it provides a legally enforceable foundation for passenger claims, moving beyond mere guidelines. The law's core architecture mirrors the influential European Union model, establishing the trilogy of passenger rights: the right to care, the right to assistance, and the right to monetary compensation for operational disruptions. This alignment is no accident but a direct consequence of the Euro-Mediterranean Aviation Agreement,

30 Article 17.
31 Article 19(b).
32 Article 20.
33 Article 21.
34 Article 22(a).
35 Article 22(b).
36 Article 23(a).
37 Article 23(b).
38 European Commission, 'EU-Jordan Aviation Relations' <https://transport.ec.europa.eu/transport-modes/air/international-aviation/status-aviation-relations-country/jordan_en>.

which fosters a gradual harmonization of legislation, including in the realm of consumer protection.

Part 209 reveals a legal text with notable procedural strengths but substantively limited protections. Among its most commendable features are several forward-thinking provisions that provide clarity and adaptability. The establishment of a clear two-year limitation period for claims, calculated from the date of arrival or scheduled arrival, offers crucial legal certainty for all parties – a detail often omitted in similar regulations. Furthermore, the innovative clause mandating the Civil Aviation Regulatory Commission to adjust compensation amounts every three years in line with Jordanian inflation is a significant step towards futureproofing the legislation, ensuring its financial remedies do not erode over time.

However, these administrative virtues are offset by substantive limitations that consciously narrow the scope of passenger compensation. The most striking is the exceptionally high threshold for delay compensation: passengers are only entitled to monetary redress after a delay of eight hours or more at their final destination. This stands in stark contrast to the three- and four-hour thresholds common in other jurisdictions and significantly restricts eligibility. Similarly, the explicit exclusion of monetary compensation for all domestic flights creates a major gap in the protection of a key segment of air travel within the Kingdom. While the care and assistance obligations apply, the absence of a financial consequence for airlines in cases of cancellation or long delay on domestic routes weakens passenger leverage. The compensation amounts themselves, though structured sensibly using Special Drawing Rights and a distance-based formula, are set at modest levels, approximately half of the equivalent sums in EU Regulation 261.

The law's drafting also introduces ambiguities that may lead to litigation. The standard of care required during a force majeure event is defined only as "reasonable and customary within the industry," a subjective standard open to wide interpretation. Furthermore, the provisions detailing rights during long delays are awkwardly phrased, particularly regarding the provision of hotel accommodation, necessitating interpretive effort to reconcile the articles.

When directly compared to its European inspiration, Regulation 261, the Jordanian Instructions emerge as a more minimalist version. The EU Regulation offers more robust substantive protection: compensation is triggered for delays of three hours, cancellation notice must be given if less than 14 days (versus seven in Jordan) to avoid compensation, and the payout amounts are considerably higher. Both frameworks share core principles of care and assistance, but the EU Regulation provides a stronger compensatory safety net for passengers.

In conclusion, Jordan's Part 209 successfully establishes a formal, enforceable regime for air passenger rights, integrating key global norms and incorporating several commendable procedural mechanisms. It marks a definitive step towards the modernization of consumer protection in Jordanian aviation. Nevertheless, the Regulation reflects a calibrated policy choice to prioritize the operational concerns of the airline industry within its regional context. By setting high thresholds for compensation, excluding domestic flights, and maintaining modest compensation levels, the law offers a baseline of protection that, while functional, falls short of the more passenger-centric standards seen in other jurisdictions.

Comparison with EU Regulation 261

Feature	**Part 209**	**EU Regulation 261/2004**
Delay Compensation	≥8-hour: 100–200 SDR (by distance).	≥3-hour: €250–€600 (by distance).
Cancellation Notice	<7 days notice: Full compensation.	<14 days notice: Refund or re-routing + €250–600 compensation (by distance).
Denied Boarding	Volunteers first; non-volunteers get 100–200 SDR (by distance).	Volunteers first; €250–€600 (by distance) if denied boarding.
Baggage Compensation	Not specified.	Not specified.

Bibliography

- Consumer Protection Instructions (Part 209) of 2020 Issued under the Provisions of Article 55 of the Civil Aviation Law No. 41 of 2007 as amended.
- European Commission, 'EU-Jordan Aviation Relations' <https://transport.ec.europa.eu/transport-modes/air/international-aviation/status-aviation-relations-country/jordan_en> accessed 5 December 2025.

II.24

Kazakhstan

Kazakhstan has specific regulations in place to protect air passenger rights, primarily outlined in the Law of the Republic of Kazakhstan "On the use of the Airspace of the Republic of Kazakhstan and aviation activities" Article 86.[1] The Law on Aviation Activities covers a wide range of aspects related to aviation, not just passenger rights, and applies to users of the air space of the Republic of Kazakhstan.[2] It is, therefore, a bit unclear whether it only applies to flights departing from Kazakhstan or also flights to Kazakhstan operated by domestic carriers.

Airlines are obliged to inform passengers about flight status changes such as delays, cancellations, and rescheduling, including the reasons for the change, new departure times, and any new routes.[3]

Changes in a flight status[4] due to the fault of the carrier or late arrival of the aircraft entitles passengers to care and assistance. Article 86 is the first law which explicitly mentions that passengers travelling with a child under the age of 7 should be given access to a room for mothers, if such a room is available.[5] In addition, the passengers should be given two phone calls, including international communication, of no more than five minutes or two emails for any disruption exceeding two hours.[6] Cold drinks must be given for any waits exceeding two hours, while hot meals are to be granted after four hours and then every six hours during day time and eight hours during night time.[7] Hotel accommodation should be

1 As amended by the Law of the Republic of Kazakhstan dated 4 July 2013 № 132-V; Law of the Republic of Kazakhstan dated 10 May 2017 № 64-VI; Law of the Republic of Kazakhstan dated 29 December 2022 № 174-VII <https://adilet.zan.kz/eng/docs/Z100000339_>.

2 Article 4.

3 Article 86(1) and (2).

4 Defined in Article 1 (66–4) as "a change in the route of the planned direction, flight delay, change in the flight schedule, flight cancellation or other change that affects the departure (arrival) time of the flight or the route."

5 Article 86(1)(1).

6 Article 86(1)(2).

7 Article 86(1)(3) and (4).

DOI: 10.4324/9781003746164-35

provided after eight hours of wait during day time and six hours at night time as well as transportation to and from the airport.[8] These services are provided by the airline at no additional charge.

Service	Conditions	Details
Mother's Room Access	If available.	For passengers travelling with children **under 7 years old** (Art. 86).
Communication	**>2 hours.**	- Two phone calls (incl. international, max 5 mins each) **OR** two emails.
Refreshments	**>2 hours.**	
Hot Meals	**>4 hours.**	Then every **6 hrs (day)/8 hrs (night).**
Accommodation	**>8 hours (day).** **>6 hours (night)**.	Includes airport transfers.

In case of a delay or cancellation of a flight due to the fault of the carrier for a period exceeding five hours, the passenger has the choice between re-routing on the next available flight or a refund for the full cost of the ticket.[9]

In the event that a flight is delayed as a result of the airline's responsibility, passengers are entitled to compensation in the form of a fine amounting to 3% of the fare value for the affected segment for each hour of delay, unless the delay was caused by force majeure. In addition, any losses incurred by the passenger due to the delay must be compensated.[10] However, the amount of the fine cannot exceed the cost of the purchased fare. Such compensation is only paid at the passenger's request through a written application online or at the ticket sales points.[11] This percentage-based model risks inconsistency in addition to making it hard on passengers to know how much they are due. Indeed, a passenger might not be aware of the value of the route on which the delay occurred.

Scenario	Passenger Rights	Compensation
Delay <5 Hours	- Care services + Reimbursement of proven losses (e.g., missed connections).	- **3% of fare value per hour** (max 100% of fare).
Delay ≥5 Hours	Choice of: Refund **OR** re-routing.	- Additional compensation for losses (e.g., hotel, meals).

8 Article 86(1)(5) and (6).
9 Article 86(2)(1) and (2).
10 Article 86(3).
11 Article 86(4).

Despite the very extensive list of definitions found in Article 1, force majeure is not defined in the law itself, but according to SCAT Airlines, it includes adverse weather conditions, closure of airports, and air traffic control strikes.[12]

Claims are time barred after two years which starts from the day after the occurrence of the event.[13] There are no fines in case of non-compliance.

Interestingly, the law is silent regarding denial of boarding or cancellation. However, denial of boarding is regulated by the Rules for the carriage of passengers, baggage, and cargo by air transport.[14] The Rules indicate that passengers must arrive on time for check-in, no later than 40 minutes, otherwise the airline is entitled to cancel the ticket and deny boarding to the passenger according to the airline's terms and conditions.[15] Airlines are allowed to terminate unilaterally the contract and deny boarding if the passenger refuses to undergo inspections as mandated by Article 107 of the law, violates the Rules or threatens the safety of the aircraft, is intoxicated (drugs or alcohol) and potentially posing a threat to the health of the passenger or the safety of persons and property on board the aircraft, as well as being an inconvenience to other passengers.[16] The intoxication of the passenger will then need to be confirmed by a medical examination as prescribed by law. The failure to fulfil their duties or passengers with restricted air transport are also other reasons for denial.[17] In those cases, the passenger will be refunded the amount of the unused ticket.[18]

Scenario	**Airline Action and Passenger Rights**
Late Check-In	- Denial if passenger arrives **<40 mins** before departure (per airline terms).
Safety/Security Violations	- Refuses security checks (Art. 107). - Violates airline rules or threatens safety. - Intoxicated (alcohol/drugs) – requires medical confirmation.
Other Reasons	- Failure to fulfil duties or restricted air transport status.

12 SCAT Airlines, 'Passenger's Rights' <https://www.scat.kz/en/passenger-rights/> accessed 5 December 2025.

13 Article 86–1(2) and (3).

14 Order of the Minister of Investment and Development of the Republic of Kazakhstan dated 30 April 2015 No. 540. Registered in the Ministry of Justice of the Republic of Kazakhstan on 25 September 2015 No. 12115.

15 Clause 12 in conjunction with Clause 17.

16 Clause 22(1)–(3).

17 Clause 22(4)–(5).

18 Clause 23.

The Rules also deal in some depth with regard to tickets, the validity of open tickets up to one year, but also that in the event a ticket is lost or damage, the airline must duplicate the ticket.[19] "In case of loss or damage of a ticket (or any part thereof) issued by a foreign airline, a written request from the passenger to the airline must be sent with a receipt attached to issue a duplicate."[20] Such a requirement seems quite burdensome on the passenger. Stopovers are only permitted if they have been agreed with the airline and it is mentioned on the ticket.[21]

In case of downgrading, the airline must reimburse the difference. However, the airline cannot charge extra in case of upgrading due to its fault.[22] Clause 21 stipulates that when airlines downgrade passengers, passengers must first agree to the downgrade. If the passenger accepts, he or she is still entitled to the free baggage allowance and meals according to the higher class as purchased. In the event the passenger refuses, the airline must bear expenses within the limits of the actual costs of accommodating this passenger in a hotel, meals, using communications equipment, and ground transportation until the passenger can be carried according to the class bought.[23] This Clause seems vaguely drafted and could easily be subject to abuses.

The Rules also contain provisions on minor passengers and unaccompanied minors, allowing birth certificates to be checked and requiring written authorization from the parents for unaccompanied minors.[24] Unaccompanied minors cannot be younger than 6 and cannot travel from 11 PM to 6 AM in accordance with paragraph 5 of Article 36 of the Law of the Republic of Kazakhstan dated 8 August 2002 "On the Rights of the Child in the Republic of Kazakhstan."[25] This is a particularly strong and protective measure. It acknowledges the vulnerability of children, especially at night, and aims to ensure they are not travelling during hours when supervision might be less stringent or when they might be more distressed. This shows a holistic approach, linking aviation regulations to broader child protection laws. It also aligns with reasonable international standards on children's age as younger children typically require a higher level of care that airlines are not equipped to provide.

Airlines cannot charge for minor passenger under the age of 2 travelling on an international flight if they do not occupy a separate seat but are

19 Clauses 4–15.
20 Clause 13.
21 Clause 18.
22 Clause 20.
23 Clause 21(2).
24 Clause 25.
25 Clause 26.

not allowed any baggage allowance. This is a very common international practice. If the minor under 2 occupied a seat, then the fare should be 50% of the accompanying adult passenger fare. Similarly, for each minor passenger between the ages of 2 and 12 travelling with an adult on an international flight, a fee equal to 50% of the applicable or special fare for the accompanying adult is charged.[26] The same rule of thumb applies on domestic routes.[27] The 50% discount seems generous which would encourage families to travel.

Category	Rules	Exceptions/Notes
Unaccompanied Minors	Minimum age: **6 years.**	Written parental authorization required.
	No travel from 11 PM–6 AM.	Airlines may verify birth certificates.
Infants (<2 Years)	**Free** if no separate seat (international/domestic). **50% fare** if occupying a seat.	**No baggage allowance**.
Children (2–12 Years)	**- 50% of adult fare** (international/domestic).	Applies to "accompanying adult" fares (not special promotions).

The Rules also lay down the conditions for transporting a patient on a stretcher and that the passenger can be accompanied by a person providing care.[28] There are also provisions dedicated to pregnant women who can travel until 34 weeks for singleton pregnancy and 32 weeks for multiple pregnancy as long as the health of the mother so allows.[29] Derogations can be issued by the medical advisory commission.[30] However, airlines can still refuse transportation, despite the derogation, if the birth is expected within the next seven days.[31] Those provisions reflect common practice while also allowing for expert medical assessment to override general rules when safe to do so, accommodating individual medical circumstances.

New mothers and newborn children cannot fly within the first seven days after birth.[32] For the transportation of children born prematurely in multiple pregnancies, the children's parents or accompanying adults must present a medical certificate for each child, which confirms the

26 Clause 27.
27 Clause 28.
28 Clauses 30–31.
29 Clause 32.
30 Clause 33.
31 Clause 34.
32 Clause 35.

child's ability to be transported by air.[33] Those rules are highly specific and essential to protect newborns against vital health and safety risks.

These provisions demonstrate a commendable effort by Kazakh aviation authorities to provide detailed and specific regulations for various categories of vulnerable passengers, going beyond just general consumer protection. This level of detail helps create clarity for both passengers and airlines, aiming to ensure safety and appropriate care. They reflect a regulatory framework which considers not just commercial aspects but also the human element of air travel.

The Rules also contain an in-flight service standard, Clauses 41 to 51, which go beyond just handling disruptions and delve into the expected quality of service on board. For instance, in addition to the cleanliness of the cabin, working toilets, and functional seats, airlines must maintain the cabin temperature not lower than 18 degrees and not higher than 25.[34] Clause 44 is dedicated to the specific mandatory requirements for passengers with special needs and limited mobility, such as priority boarding, seat allocation, and assistance.

There is also a part dedicated to baggage transportation procedure, Clauses 52 to 79, including the maximum weight limit (32 kg) but also the dimension (158 cm).[35] Clause 59 clearly stipulates that the weight, dimensions, and free allowance for carry-on luggage are established by the carrier. In case of delayed baggage, the airline pays 10% of the air ticket cost for each day of delay, up to a maximum of 50% of the ticket cost.[36] Animal transport is dealt with in Clauses 75–79. Guide dogs are to be transported free of charge and within the cabin provided they have a collar and muzzle and are next to the owner.[37]

Kazakhstan's regulatory framework for air passenger rights, anchored in Article 86 of the law "On the use of the Airspace and aviation activities" and elaborated in the detailed "Rules for the carriage of passengers, baggage and cargo by air transport," presents a distinctive and domestically focused approach to consumer protection. Unlike the EU's Regulation 261, which is a specialized, self-contained instrument, Kazakh law embeds passenger rights within a broader aviation statute, resulting in a system that is both highly prescriptive in service standards and somewhat fragmented in its remedial structure. The law's primary strength lies not in its compensation regime but in its exhaustive, granular regulation of service quality and its exceptionally detailed provisions for

33 Clause 36.
34 Clauses 45–46.
35 Clause 54.
36 Clause 74.
37 Clause 79.

vulnerable passengers, reflecting a paternalistic legislative style that seeks to dictate minimum service standards across the travel experience.

Its most commendable feature is the remarkable depth of its protective provisions for specific passenger categories. The law goes far beyond the typical scope of passenger rights regulations by integrating stringent child protection measures, such as prohibiting unaccompanied minors from travelling between 11 PM and 6 AM, and establishing clear, medically informed rules for pregnant women, new mothers, and premature infants. Similarly, its provisions for passengers with disabilities, including requirements for trained staff to assist individuals with autism spectrum disorders, demonstrate a progressive and inclusive intent rarely codified with such specificity. The in-flight service standards, mandating cabin temperature ranges and cleanliness, further illustrate a regulatory philosophy aimed at governing the entire passenger experience, not merely managing disruptions.

However, the core mechanisms for addressing flight irregularities – delays, cancellations, and denied boarding – are less robust and clear. The compensation model for delays, based on 3% of the fare per hour (capped at 100% of the fare), is unique. While theoretically proportional, it creates uncertainty for passengers, who may not know the applicable fare value for their flight segment, and can lead to inconsistent compensation outcomes compared to fixed-sum models. The five-hour threshold for triggering the right to a refund or re-routing in case of a carrier-caused delay is reasonable, but the law's silence on explicit compensation for cancellations is a glaring omission, creating a significant gap in protection. The rules on denied boarding are primarily defensive, outlining the airline's right to deny boarding for late check-in, security violations, or intoxication, but lack the proactive, compensatory framework found in other jurisdictions for involuntarily denied boarding due to overbooking. Furthermore, key concepts like force majeure are not defined in the law, leaving a critical area of airline liability open to interpretation and potential dispute.

When juxtaposed with EU Regulation 261, the Kazakh framework reveals a fundamentally different regulatory philosophy. Kazakhstan's aviation passenger law represents a sophisticated but idiosyncratic system. It excels in setting detailed, protective service standards and safeguarding vulnerable groups, demonstrating a holistic concern for passenger welfare that extends beyond mere compensation. However, its core financial protection mechanisms for operational disruptions are less coherent, predictable, and comprehensive than those under EU Regulation 261. It provides a strong safety net of care and detailed service protocols but a weaker and more uncertain shield of monetary compensation. For passengers, it offers exceptional clarity on what service to expect but less clarity and potency on what redress to receive when things go wrong, positioning it as a detailed code of conduct rather than a powerful compensatory tool.

Comparison with Regulation 261

Feature	Kazakhstan's Law	EU Regulation 261/2004
Delay Compensation	3% of fare/hour (max 100% of fare) for airline-caused delays.	≥3h: €250–€600 (by distance).
Cancellation Notice	No explicit notice period.	<14d notice: Refund or re-routing + €250–600 compensation (by distance).
Denied Boarding	No explicit compensation (regulated by airline rules). Refund for unused ticket.	Volunteer first; €250–€600 (by distance) if denied boarding.
Baggage Liability	10% of ticket cost/day for delays (max 50%). Covers loss/damage post-check-in.	Not specified.

Bibliography

- 'On the Use of the Airspace of the Republic of Kazakhstan and Aviation Activities' Law of the Republic of Kazakhstan dated 15 July 2010 № 339-IV <https://adilet.zan.kz/eng/docs/Z100000339_> accessed 5 December 2025
- Law of the Republic of Kazakhstan dated 4 July 2013 № 132-V.
- Law of the Republic of Kazakhstan dated 10 May 2017 № 64-VI.
- Law of the Republic of Kazakhstan dated 29 December 2022 № 174-VII.
- Order of the Minister of Investment and Development of the Republic of Kazakhstan dated April 30, 2015 No. 540. Registered in the Ministry of Justice of the Republic of Kazakhstan on 25 September 2015 No. 12115.
- SCAT Airlines, 'Passenger's Rights' <https://www.scat.kz/en/passenger-rights/ > accessed 5 December 2025.

II.25

Korea

Until 2016, Korea did not have any specific legal framework addressing passenger rights specifically.[1] While South Korea still does not have a single legislation on passenger protection, consumer rights are protected through a combination of several laws and regulations. The primary legal framework is the Aviation Business Act,[2] which requires airlines to create their own procedures and plans for providing remedies to passengers in cases of delays, cancellations, overbooking, and baggage issues.[3] This ensures that a fundamental level of protection is built into each airline's operations. However, airlines are not liable for any reasons beyond their control, so-called force majeure events, which include worsening weather conditions, natural disasters, unforeseen maintenance necessary to ensure the safe operation of the aircraft, and unavoidable flight connections.[4] As noted by Seo Il-won, "Airlines do not disclose compensation regulations for flight cancellations and delays." Instead, each has a different statement.[5]

Furthermore, the Consumer Protection Act provides a general legal basis for consumer rights, and the Consumer Dispute *Resolution* Standards offer a baseline for settling conflicts.[6] The Korean Commercial Act also includes provisions that govern compensation for delays and baggage, especially for flights to countries that are not signatories to the

---

1 Korea had only a limited set of aviation-related laws, such as the Aviation Act and the Air Transport Business Promotion Act. The 'Carriage by Air' as Part VI of the Commercial Act 2011 was a first attempt to fill the gap. See: Ji-Min Sur, 'The Regulatory Standards of Extraordinary Circumstances in Carriage of Passengers by Air: An Analysis of EU Law and Implications for Korea' (2023) 5 Journal of International Trade and Commerce 89.

2 Act No. 14550, 17 January 2017 <https://elaw.klri.re.kr/eng_service/lawView.do?hseq=43253&lang=ENG> accessed 5 December 2025.

3 Article 61(1)(2)–(4).

4 Article 61(1) coupled with Article 12(1)(1)–(5).

5 Seo Il-won, 'Airlines in Korea Lack Clear Delay Compensation Policies, Unlike European Counterparts' (*Chosun Biz*, 1 May 2025) <https://biz.chosun.com/en/en-industry/2025/05/01/KHLQMKBAFNHLNMFTYZNTXYZFEU/> accessed 5 December 2025.

6 Regulations on Consumer Dispute Resolution (KFTC Notification N° 2011-10) <https://www.kca.go.kr/down/eng/coun_02_1.pdf> accessed 5 December 2025.

DOI: 10.4324/9781003746164-36

Montreal Convention or for compensation of psychological damages.[7] Finally, air traffic user protection standards in Korea are established under the Aviation Safety Act and enforced by the Korea Office of Civil Aviation (KOCA), which requires the airlines to administer a plan for the compensation of damages pursuant to the standard and be accessible online.[8]

If a passenger is unable to reach their destination due to a flight cancellation by the airline, or if boarding is denied as a result of overbooking, the air carrier is obligated to provide compensation to the affected passenger.[9] The Fair Trade Commission issues compensation recommendations for domestic and international flight delays or cancellations, determined on a case-by-case basis according to Consumer Dispute *Resolution* Standards.[10] Air Transport User Protection Standards of 2016[11] apply to air transport business operators, foreign airlines, and airports.[12]

According to those Standards, when a passenger with a confirmed ticket is unable to board a flight due to the airline's overbooking, the airline is now obligated to provide compensation of 20% of the fare for domestic flights and $100 for international flights when an alternative flight is provided. If no alternative flight is provided, the airline must refund the fare and provide compensation for the affected flight segment for domestic flights and $400 in compensation for international flights.[13]

For domestic flights if an alternative flight is provided within three hours, the passenger is entitled to a compensation equivalent to 20% of the fare, and if the alternative flight is provided after four hours, the compensation increases to 30%. The Standard was revised to include a compensation for delays between one and two hours for 10% fare compensation.[14] In the event that no alternative flight, within 12 hours, is provided, the

---

7 Pablo Mendes de Leon and Jin Choi, 'Opening Pandora's Box: Comparing Airline Passenger Protection in Korea and Europe in Light of Global Treaties' (2023) 88 Journal of Air Law and Commerce 105, 114 referring to Seoul East District Court decision of July 2019.

8 Article 10. See Finnair, 'Air Traffic User Service Plan (Korea)' <https://www.finnair.com/kr-en/info/conditions-of-carriage-and-notices/air-traffic-user-service-plan--korea-> accessed 5 December 2025.

9 Article 4(1) Air Transport User Protection Standards amended by Notice of the Ministry of Land, Infrastructure and Transport No. 2020-383, 27 May 2020.

10 Regulations on Consumer Dispute Resolution (KFTC Notification N° 2011-10) 143.

11 고시 제2016–471호.

12 Article 3.

13 Article 4 Korea Transport DataBase, 'Press Release: Establishing "Air Transport User Protection Standards" to Prevent Consumer Damage' (12 July 2016) <https://www.ktdb.go.kr/www/selectBbsNttView.do?key=46&bbsNo=3&nttNo=2891&searchCtgry=&searchCnd=all&searchKrwd=&pageIndex=7&integrDeptCode=> accessed 5 December 2025.

14 "현행) 2~3시간 지연 운임의 20%, 3시간이상 지연 운임의 30% 배상 → (개정안) 1~2시간 지연운항 시에도 운임의 10% 배상토록 하는 규정이 추가될 예정"

passenger shall be refunded and receive another ticket for the same route. For any domestic delays between two and three hours, the compensation is equivalent to 20% of the fare while for delays of above three hours, the compensation is 30% of the fare.[15]

Scenario	**Condition**	**Recommended Compensation**
Flight Cancellation/ Denied Boarding	• Alternative flight provided **between 1 and 2 hours.** • Alternative flight provided **within 3 hours.** • Alternative flight provided **after 4 hours.** • **No alternative flight provided within 12 hours.**	• **10%** of the ticket fare. • **20%** of the ticket fare. • **30%** of the ticket fare. • **Full refund + a new ticket** for the same route.
Long Delay at Departure	• Delay of **2 to 3 hours** • Delay of **more than 3 hours**	• **20%** of the ticket fare • **30%** of the ticket fare

For international flights, cancellation and overbooking can result in a compensation of $100 if the alternative flight is provided within four hours from original and $200 if the alternative flight is provided after four hours.[16] The Regulations on Consumer Dispute *Resolution* KFTC Notification N° 2011–10 then relies on a strange wording by providing different compensations for "an alternative flight provided after the lapse of four hours." The wording seems to suggest that if an airline cannot get the passenger on a new flight within four hours, then the compensation remains at $200 and $400 for any longer delays. This was quite confusing and has been clarified as flights under four hours entitle passengers to $200 for alternative flights departing within four hours, and if the alternative flight departs after, then it increases to $400. For flights over four hours, passengers receive $300 if a replacement flight leaves within four hours of the original departure, or $600 plus a refund if it departs more than four hours later due to overbooking or cancellation.[17]

If no alternative flights are provided, the passenger is entitled to a refund as well as an additional $400 as compensation. In the event the passenger refuses to use the alternative flight, they must receive a refund as well as compensation based on the earliest available time of alternative flights.

15 Regulations on Consumer Dispute Resolution (KFTC Notification N° 2011-10) 144.

16 Regulations on Consumer Dispute Resolution (KFTC Notification N° 2011-10) 148.

17 "[정책] 공정거래위원회, 정비로 인한 항공기 지연 운항을 보상하는 방향의 '소비자분쟁해결기준' 개정안 검토 중" (Fair Trade Commission Is Reviewing a Revision to the 'Consumer Dispute Resolution Standards' to Compensate for Aircraft Delays Due to Maintenance) <https://www.kca.go.kr/home/board/download.do?menukey=4083&fno=10020239&bid=00000018&did=1002576437> accessed 5 December 2025.

Any international flight delays between two and four hours result in a 10% of the fare compensation while longer delays would result in compensation of 20% of the fare.[18] Those measures only apply if the carrier offers an alternative flight and are tied to the promptness of an alternative flight. These compensations are not due if the delay or cancellation is due to a force majeure event.[19] Finally, passengers are not entitled to compensation to cover the price of a new ticket if they refuse the alternative flight and have been refunded for the unused ticket.[20]

Scenario	Condition	Compensation
Alternative Flight IS Provided (flights under 4 hours)	• Provided **within 4 hours** of the original flight time. • Provided **after 4 hours** have passed from the original flight time.	• $200. • $400.
Alternative Flight IS Provided (flights over 4 hours)	• Provided **within 4 hours** after the original flight time. • Provided **after 4 hours** after the original flight time.	• $300. • $600.
No Alternative Flight	The airline fails to provide any alternative flight.	**Full refund** for the affected section **+ $400.**
Passenger Refuses Alternative Flight	The passenger chooses not to take the flight offered by the airline.	**Full refund** for the affected section + **compensation.**

Passengers are also entitled to "expenses for room and board of a reasonable level, if needed" in case of delays or cancellation on both domestic and international flights due to the business's accidental or intentional fault.[21] Passengers also have the right to free calls and emails as well as refreshments.

Korea also has guidelines on tarmac delays since 2016. Article 7 imposes strict limits on extended tarmac delays and mandates care for passengers during such events. The delay is kept at four hours for international flights and three hours for domestic flights with mandatory care after two hours comprising of food and water. In 2024, various airlines have been fined for

18 Regulations on Consumer Dispute Resolution (KFTC Notification N° 2011-10) 149.

19 Article 61(1) coupled with Article 12(1)(1)–(5).

20 Pablo Mendes de Leon and Jin Choi, 'Opening Pandora's Box: Comparing Airline Passenger Protection in Korea and Europe in Light of Global Treaties' (2023) 88 Journal of Air Law and Commerce 105, 114, 119.

21 Regulations on Consumer Dispute Resolution (KFTC Notification N° 2011-10) 144 and 147.

violating the Aviation Business Act for non-compliance with the tarmac delay rules.[22]

Passengers must be proactively notified of any significant schedule changes including delays of above 30 minutes and flight cancellations.[23] The Montreal liability applies for baggage lost in international transport. For domestic flights, the Consumer Dispute *Resolution* Standards provide that in case a baggage is delayed, airlines may be required to pay for "daily necessities." Unlike the EU Regulation, the Standards establish that a failure to comply with the guidelines can result in a fine of up to KRW5 million.[24]

South Korea's approach to air passenger protection represents a sophisticated yet complex hybrid model, born from a deliberate shift away from a previously unregulated space. Unlike jurisdictions with a single, overarching statute, Korea has constructed its framework through a deliberate layering of general consumer law, specific aviation regulations, and quasi-administrative standards. The cornerstone is the Aviation Business Act, which imposes a unique "meta-obligation" on airlines: rather than dictating specific remedies, it mandates that each carrier establish and publish its own internal procedures for handling delays, cancellations, overbooking, and baggage issues. This structure is then operationalized and given concrete form by the Air Transport User Protection Standards (enforced under the Aviation Safety Act) and the Consumer Dispute *Resolution* Standards issued by the Fair Trade Commission (KFTC). The resulting system is one of delegated specificity, where the law sets the requirement for a compensation plan, and subordinate standards define the quantitative benchmarks for what that plan should contain. The system has significant procedural strengths and innovative incentives but is inherently more challenging for passengers to navigate than unified models, creating a degree of opacity in favour of airlines. As noted in the assessment, airlines often do not proactively disclose their compensation policies, placing the burden of knowledge and claim initiation squarely on the passenger.

Its most commendable feature is its powerful incentive structure for airlines to minimize disruption times. The compensation model, particularly for international flights, is ingeniously tied not just to the fact of a cancellation or overbooking, but to the promptness of the rebooking.

22 David Hughes, 'Delta, Korean Air Fined over Tarmac Delays by Korea MLIT' (19 December 2024) <https://aviationa2z.com/index.php/2024/12/19/delta-korean-air-fined-over-tarmac-delays/#:~:text=Passengers%20were%20forced%20to%20remain,(%2417%2C221)%20on%20Korean%20Air>.

23 Article 8 in Korea Transport DataBase (n 12).

24 Article 3 Korea Transport DataBase (n 12).

Compensation escalates sharply if an alternative flight is provided more than four hours after the original departure (e.g., from $200 to $400 for shorter flights). This creates a direct financial imperative for airlines to re-accommodate passengers swiftly, a policy goal that aligns closely with passenger interests in reaching their destination. Furthermore, Korea's tarmac delay rules are exceptionally strong, imposing hard limits (three hours domestic, four hours international) and mandating care after two hours, with recent fines demonstrating active enforcement – a standard that meets or exceeds global best practices.

The Korean system, particularly post-2016, represents a significant and commendable step forward in consumer protection. However, when directly compared to the EU's Regulation 261, it emerges as a more complex, less uniform, and generally less passenger-friendly system. The core weakness of the Korean system lies in its fundamental structure. The Korean system for compensation is complex and heavily dependent on how quickly the airline provides a new flight. It is based on a mixture of USD amounts (for international flights) and percentage-of-the-fare model (for domestic flights). While the framework can provide a good incentive for airlines to act as quickly as possible, it might be a bit of a gymnastic for passengers to figure out whether their replacement flight left within the four hours threshold or not. Despite these weaknesses, the Korean framework has notable strengths that align with or even exceed global standards. Its rules on transparency are exemplary, mandating proactive notification for delays over 30 minutes and clear pre-purchase disclosure of cancellation fees and baggage policies. The right to care (meals, accommodation) during disruptions is also firmly established, mirroring the EU's strong standards in this area.

In conclusion, South Korea's framework is a deliberate and cleverly engineered system that seeks to govern airline conduct through economic incentives and layered regulation rather than through blunt, uniform passenger entitlements. It represents a major advancement from a previously unregulated environment and excels in specific, targeted areas like preventing tarmac imprisonment and forcing rebooking speed. However, its very sophistication renders it less accessible and predictable for the average passenger compared to the EU's model. It is a system that protects the informed and persistent consumer adequately but may fail the passive or confused one. The framework functions effectively as a regulatory tool for modifying airline operational behaviour, whereas the EU regulation functions more powerfully as a consumer rights guarantee. For the passenger, the EU system offers the clarity of a straightforward insurance policy; the Korean system offers the potential for tailored redress but requires navigating a complex claims process.

Comparison with EU Regulation 261

Feature	Korean Standards	EU Regulation 261/2004
Delay Compensation	Domestic: % of fare (20%–30%) based on delay of alternative flight.	≥3h: €250–€600 (by distance).
Cancellation Notice	• Domestic: % of fare (10%–30%) based on delay of alternative flight. • International: Fixed USD amounts ($200–$600) based on delay of alternative flight.	<14d notice: Refund or re-routing + €250–600 compensation (by distance).
Denied Boarding	• Domestic: 20% of fare (new flight provided)/Full refund + new ticket (no flight). • International: $100 (new flight provided)/Full refund + $400 (no flight provided).	Volunteer first; €250–€600 (by distance) if denied boarding.
Baggage Liability	1,288 SDRs.	Not specified.

Bibliography

- Act No. 14550, 17 January 2017 <https://elaw.klri.re.kr/eng_service/lawView.do?hseq=43253&lang=ENG> accessed 5 December 2025.
- Air Transport User Protection Standards amended by Notice of the Ministry of Land, Infrastructure and Transport No. 2020-383, 27 May 2020.
- Regulations on Consumer Dispute Resolution (KFTC Notification N° 2011-10) <https://www.kca.go.kr/down/eng/coun_02_1.pdf> accessed 5 December 2025.
- Finnair, 'Air Traffic User Service Plan (Korea)' <https://www.finnair.com/kr-en/info/conditions-of-carriage-and-notices/air-traffic-user-service-plan-korea> accessed 5 December 2025.
- Hughes, D., 'Delta, Korean Air Fined Over Tarmac Delays by Korea MLIT' (19 December 2024) <https://aviationa2z.com/index.php/2024/12/19/delta-korean-air-fined-over-tarmac-delays/#:~:text=Passengers%20were%20forced%20to%20remain,(%2417%2C221)%20on%20Korean%20Air> accessed 5 December 2025.
- Il-won, S., 'Airlines in Korea Lack Clear Delay Compensation Policies, Unlike European Counterparts' (*Chosun Biz*, 1 May 2025) <https://biz.chosun.com/en/en-industry/2025/05/01/KHLQMKBAFNHLNMFTYZNTXYZFEU/> accessed 5 December 2025.
- Korea Transport DataBase, 'Press Release: Establishing "Air Transport User Protection Standards" to Prevent Consumer Damage' (12 July 2016) <https://www.ktdb.go.kr/www/selectBbsNttView.do?key=46&bbsNo=

3&nttNo=2891&searchCtgry=&searchCnd=all&searchKrwd=&pageIndex=7&integrDeptCode=> accessed 5 December 2025.

- Mendes de Leon, P. and Choi, J., 'Opening Pandora's Box: Comparing Airline Passenger Protection in Korea and Europe in Light of Global Treaties' (2023) 88 Journal of Air Law and Commerce 105.
- Sur, J.-M., 'The Regulatory Standards of Extraordinary Circumstances in Carriage of Passengers by Air: An Analysis of EU Law and Implications for Korea' (2023) 5 Journal of International Trade Commerce 89.
- "[정책] 공정거래위원회, 정비로 인한 항공기 지연 운항을 보상하는 방향의 '소비자분쟁해결기준'개정안 검토 중" (Fair Trade Commission Is Reviewing a Revision to the 'Consumer Dispute Resolution Standards' to Compensate for Aircraft Delays Due to Maintenance) <https://www.kca.go.kr/home/board/download.do?menukey=4083&fno=10020239&bid=00000018&did=1002576437> accessed 5 December 2025.

II.26

Kosovo

Kosovo's air passenger rights are largely aligned with European Union regulations, specifically Regulation 261 which was implemented through Ministry of Infrastructure Regulation 2008/5 as part of Kosovo's commitment to the Agreement on the European Common Aviation Area (ECAA).[1] Regulation 2008/5 establishes common rules on compensation and assistance to passengers in the event of denied boarding and of cancellation or long delay of flights.[2] Another relevant Regulation is Regulation 2008/4 which implements the Montreal Convention with regard to carrier's liability for passengers and baggage.[3]

Regulation 2008/5 applies to all passengers departing from an airport located in the territory of Kosovo or passengers departing from a third country to an airport situated in the territory of Kosovo if operated by an ECAA licensed carrier, unless they have already received compensation or assistance in that third country.[4] Interestingly, the Ministry of Infrastructure itself noted that the Regulation applies to "all passengers departing from EU/EEA/ECAA airports or all passengers departing from outside of the EU/EEA/ECAA but arriving at an EU/EEA/ECAA airport on an EU/EEA/ECAA licensed carrier" which is broader than the scope of the Regulation itself.[5] The Regulation only applies to passengers having a confirmed reservation and presenting themselves for check-in in

1 Such implementation was possible due to Article 93.4 of the Constitution of the Republic of Kosovo and Article 6.1 of Law No. 03/L-051 on Civil Aviation Civil Aviation of 4 June 2008, official gazette 28/2008.

See: Republic of Kosovo Ministry of Infrastructure, 'Air Passenger Rights' <https://www.mit-ks.net/en/civil-aviation/air-passenger-rights-861> accessed 10 December 2025.

2 Article 1.

3 Article 1 of Regulation N°2008/4 on Air Carrier Liability in Respect of the Carriage of Passengers and Their Baggage by Air <https://www.mit-ks.net/repository/docs/Regulation_2008-4_Liability1430731936.pdf> accessed 10 December 2025.

4 Article 3(1)(a) and (b).

5 Republic of Kosovo Ministry of Infrastructure (n 1).

DOI: 10.4324/9781003746164-37

accordance with the procedures and at the time specified in advance and in writing by the air carrier, tour operator, or authorized travel agent. If no specific check-in time is provided, passengers must check in no later than 45 minutes prior to the published departure time.[6] The Regulation is also applicable when the passenger has been transferred by an air carrier or tour operator from the flight for which they held a reservation to another flight, irrespective of the reason.[7] Like other regulations, this law does not apply to passengers travelling free of charge.[8]

In case of denial of boarding,[9] airlines must first request volunteers to surrender their seat in exchange for benefits under conditions they would agree on.[10] The volunteers are still entitled to assistance under Article 8. If an insufficient number of volunteers come forward to allow the remaining passengers with reservations to board the flight, the operating air carrier may then deny boarding to passengers against their will, compensating them immediately in accordance with Article 7.[11] Passengers denied boarding against their will should be able either to cancel their flights, with reimbursement of their tickets, or to continue them under satisfactory conditions, and should be adequately cared for while awaiting a later flight. This includes meals and refreshments offered free of charge and in reasonable relation to the waiting time, and a choice between reimbursement of the cost if the passenger decided not to travel or re-routing to their final destination at the earliest opportunity. Hotel accommodation may be provided if a stay of one or more nights becomes necessary as well as two telephone calls, telex or fax messages, or emails.[12] Passengers are entitled to a compensation of 250 euros for flights of a distance of up to 1,500 km when the denial of boarding results in a delay of more than two hours, and 125 euros for a delay of less than two hours. For intra-Community flights or all flights between 1,500 and 3,500 km, the amount increases to 400 euros for denial of boarding resulting in delays of over three hours or 200 euros if the delay is less than three hours. Finally for all flights over 3,500 km, the compensation is 600 euros when the delay is over four hours or 300 euros when the delay does not exceed four hours.[13]

6 Article 3(2)(a).
7 Article 3(2)(b).
8 Article 3(3).
9 Article 4.
10 Article 4(1).
11 Article 4(2) and (3).
12 Articles 8 and 9.
13 Article 7(1)(a), (b), and (c) and 7(2)(a), (b), and (c).

Flight Distance	Delay Time	Compensation Amount
1,500 km or Less	Less than 2 hours.	€125.
	2 hours or more.	€250.
Intra-Community >1,500 km **or** **Other Flights 1,500 km–3,500 km**	Less than 3 hours.	€200.
	3 hours or more.	€400.
All Other Flights (e.g., >3,500 km)	Less than 4 hours.	€300.
	4 hours or more.	€600.

If a flight is cancelled, passengers have the right to a full refund or re-routing as well as assistance.[14] Passengers are entitled to compensation unless the airline informed of the cancellation 14 days in advance or it is due to "extraordinary circumstances."[15] Just like Regulation 261, the Regulation 2008/5 does not define the extraordinary circumstances and since the preamble has not been incorporated in the Regulation 2008/5, the definition of this concept is even more uncertain. However, the Kosovar Ministry of Infrastructure offers examples of extraordinary circumstances which includes "meteorological conditions, air traffic control restrictions, security risks and strikes that affect the operation of the flight"[16] which are identical to those found under Regulation 261.

Compensation is not payable if the passengers were informed at least two weeks in advance and were offered a full refund or an alternative flight at the earliest opportunity or at a later date based on the passenger choice.[17] If passengers were informed between two weeks and seven days and they were offered a route change allowing them to depart not more than two hours before the original departure time and arrive four hours after the original arrival time, then compensation is not due.[18] Similarly, no compensation is due when passengers are informed less than seven days in advance and offered a route change allowing them to depart not more than one hour before the original departure time and arrive two hours after the original arrival time.[19]

14 Article 5(1)(a) and (b).
15 Article 5(3).
16 Republic of Kosovo Ministry of Infrastructure (n 1).
17 Article 5(1)(c)(i).
18 Article 5(1)(c)(ii).
19 Article 5(1)(c)(iii).

When Cancelled	Compensation Due?
≥14 Days Before Departure	No.
7–14 Days Before Departure	No, if re-routing allows departure ≤2h earlier and arrival ≤4h later.
<7 Days Before Departure	No, if re-routing allows departure ≤1h earlier and arrival ≤2h later.
<14 Days Notice + No Suitable Re-routing	Yes.

If a flight is cancelled without prior notification, the airline must provide a written notice outlining a passenger's rights, particularly regarding compensation and assistance.[20] The airline is also required to display a sign at the check-in area with text informing passengers of their rights if a flight is cancelled, delayed, or if they are denied boarding. While waiting for a re-routed flight, care and assistance are to be offered free of charge. This includes meals and refreshments in reasonable relation to the waiting time, along with hotel accommodation and transportation if an overnight stay becomes necessary. Additionally, two free telephone calls, emails, faxes, or telexes are to be provided. Passengers are to be offered an alternative flight to their final destination at the earliest opportunity. As an alternative, a full refund of the ticket is to be provided for the parts of the journey not made. If a flight no longer serves a purpose due to the cancellation, a full refund for the entire journey and a return flight to the first point of departure are to be offered at the earliest opportunity. Additionally, passengers are entitled to compensation based on the distance of the flight and the reason for the cancellation.[21]

An airline is obligated to offer passengers specific assistance if it anticipates a flight will be delayed. What a passenger is entitled to depends entirely on the length of the delay and the flight distance. For short flights of 1,500 km or less, the airline must provide assistance after a two-hour delay. For medium-haul flights between 1,500 and 3,500 km, this assistance is required after three hours. All other, longer flights trigger this right after a four-hour delay.[22] This assistance package includes meals, refreshments, and the ability to make two free phone calls, send emails, or telex messages. Furthermore, if the delay is so significant that the new departure time is on a different day, the airline is also required to provide passengers with hotel accommodation and transport to and from the hotel. Finally, should the delay reach at least five hours, the passenger gains the right to cancel

20 Article 14(2).
21 Article 7.
22 Article 6(1)(a), (b) and (c).

their trip and receive a full refund for any unused parts of their ticket.[23] It cannot be inferred from the wording of Regulation 2008/5 that delayed passengers are entitled to compensation. However, the Kosovar Ministry of Infrastructure clearly stipulates that the outcome of the *Sturgeon* case applies.[24]

Passengers are entitled to compensation of 250 euros for flights of a distance of up to 1,500 km. For flights between 1,500 and 3,500 km, the amount increases to 400 euros as well as intra-ECAA flights of more than 1,500 km. Finally, for flights over 3,500 km, the compensation is 600 euros.[25] The amount of compensation can be divided by two if passengers are offered an alternative flight which arrives at the final destination no later than two hours for flights of less than 1,500 km, three hours for flights between 1,500 and 3,500 km and all other flights within the ECAA, and four hours for flights longer than 3,500 km.[26]

One aspect that remains unclear is the interaction between Regulation 2008/4 and 2008/5. Indeed, a single event (like a long delay) can trigger rights and claims under both regulations simultaneously.

Scenario	Governing Regulation	What It Covers
Flight is cancelled 3 hours before departure.	**Regulation 2008/5.**	Passengers entitled to care (refreshments, hotel if needed), re-routing/refund, and potentially €250/€400/€600 in compensation for the disruption.
Fight arrives, but your suitcase is damaged.	**Regulation 2008/4.**	Passengers entitled to compensation for the value of the damaged items, up to a limit of 1,000 SDR (approx. €1,100), provided you complain in writing within 7 days.
Flight is delayed for 5 hours, causing you to miss a crucial business meeting.	**Dual Application.**	1. Regulation **2008/5**: For the delay itself (if over the threshold), passengers get care and a fixed compensation. 2. Regulation **2008/4**: For any *financial losses*, passenger could sue for proven damages up to 4,150 SDR (approx. €4,560).

23 Article 6(1)(c)(iii).
24 Republic of Kosovo Ministry of Infrastructure (n 1).
25 Article 7(I)(a), (b), and (c).
26 Article 7(II)(a), (b), and (c).

When an airline is responsible for a flight disruption, passengers are given the right to choose how they wish to proceed. They can either receive a full refund for the unused portions of their ticket within seven days and a return flight to their original departure point at the earliest opportunity, or they can be re-routed to their final destination.[27] This re-routing can happen at the earliest possible time or at a later date that is more convenient for them, depending on seat availability.[28] This right to a refund also applies to passengers who booked their flights as part of a package tour, unless the tour regulations state otherwise.[29] Additionally, if a city or region has multiple airports, the airline may offer a flight to a different, nearby airport, provided the passenger agrees to the change.[30]

During a flight disruption, airlines are obligated to provide passengers with free care.[31] This includes offering meals and refreshments that are appropriate for the length of the waiting time.[32] If the delay extends to the point where an overnight stay becomes necessary, the airline must also cover the cost of a hotel room and transport between the airport and the accommodation.[33] Furthermore, passengers are entitled to two free phone calls or emails.[34] It is also a requirement that the airline gives special consideration and attention to the needs of passengers with reduced mobility and children travelling alone.[35]

Upgrading made by the airline must be done without any additional payment. Conversely, in the event of downgrading, the airline must reimburse a percentage of the ticket cost within seven days. The refund amount is 30% for flights up to 1,500 km, 50% for flights between 1,500 and 3,500 km, and 75% for all flights longer than that.[36]

Airlines are also under the obligation to inform passengers of their rights. At the check-in area, they must prominently display a notice that tells passengers to ask for a document outlining their rights to compensation and assistance if their flight is denied boarding, cancelled, or delayed by at least two hours. Beyond this general notice, the airline must also provide a written document directly to every passenger affected by such a disruption. This notice must clearly detail the rules for receiving compensation and assistance as outlined in the regulation, and it must

27 Article 8(1)(a) and (b).
28 Article 8(1)(c).
29 Article 8(2).
30 Article 8(3).
31 Article 9.
32 Article 9(1)(a).
33 Article 9(1)(b) and (c).
34 Article 9(2).
35 Article 9(3).
36 Article 10(2)(a), (b) and (c).

also include the contact information for the official body responsible for handling passenger complaints. For passengers who are blind or visually impaired, the airline must use a suitable alternative method to ensure they receive all the same information.[37]

Like Regulation 261, there is no fixed penalty amount provided in Regulation 2008/5. Instead, the Regulation refers to Article 97.2 of Law No. 03/L-051 on Civil Aviation which stipulates that the fine might not exceed 1,000,000 euros for each such violation. "If any such violation is a continuing one, each day of such violation shall constitute a separate violation." This provision is clearer than the one in Regulation 261.

Unlike Regulation 261, Regulation 2008/4 includes a provision on loss of luggage which specifies in the Annex that the liability for delay of baggage is limited to 1,000 SDRs (approximately 1,100 euros).[38]

Kosovo's Regulation 2008/5 is a direct transposition of EU Regulation 261, meaning its core provisions on compensation, re-routing, and assistance for denied boarding, cancellations, and long delays are the same. Both laws specify the same monetary compensation amounts (€250, €400, €600) based on flight distance and establish the same thresholds for triggering assistance (e.g., a three-hour delay for compensation). However, the omission of the preamble and the lack of inclusion of any definition of the concept of "extraordinary circumstance" makes the Regulation 2008/5 even more complex. Such complexity is eased by the information provided by the Ministry of Infrastructure, which made it clear that the law is entirely aligned with the EU case law. While there is no fixed sanctions in the Regulation itself, the Civil Aviation includes a maximum penalty amount.

Comparison with EU Regulation

Feature	**Regulation 2008/5**	**EU Regulation 261/2004**
Delay Compensation	≥3h: €250–€600 (by distance).	≥3h: €250–€600 (by distance).
Cancellation Notice	<14d notice: Refund or re-routing + €250–€600 (by distance).	<14d notice: Refund or re-routing + €250–600 compensation (by distance).
Denied Boarding	Volunteer first; €250–€600 (by distance) if denied boarding.	Volunteer first; €250–€600 (by distance) if denied boarding.
Baggage Liability	€1,100.	Not specified.

37 Article 14.
38 Article 5.

Bibliography

- Constitution of the Republic of Kosovo <https://mapl.rks-gov.net/wp-content/uploads/2017/10/1.CONSTITUTION_OF_THE_REPUBLIC_OF_KOSOVO.pdf> accessed 10 December 2025.
- Law No. 03/L-051 on Civil Aviation of 4 June 2008, official gazette 28/2008 <https://gzk.rks-gov.net/ActDetail.aspx?ActID=2532&langid=2> accessed 10 December 2025.
- Republic of Kosovo Ministry of Infrastructure, 'Air Passenger Rights' <https://www.mit-ks.net/en/civil-aviation/air-passenger-rights-861> accessed 10 December 2025.
- Regulation N°2008/4 on Air Carrier Liability in Respect of the Carriage of Passengers and Their Baggage by Air <https://www.mit-ks.net/repository/docs/Regulation_2008-4_Liability1430731936.pdf> accessed 10 December 2025.

II.27

Libya

Passenger rights in Libya are governed by the Passenger Rights Protection Regulation approved by Decision No. 84 of 2024, which started being effective as of 22 January 2024.[1] This legislation represents a transformative step for consumer rights and the aviation sector in Libya, systematically establishing the legal relationship between air carriers and passengers, particularly during operational failures. It aligns with international frameworks but is tailored for the Libyan context.

The Regulation applies to all flights departing from airports located within Libya, regardless of the operating airline. Furthermore, it applies to passengers arriving in Libya on flights operated by Libyan airlines, unless the passenger has already received compensation.[2] The airline is responsible for the passenger throughout the duration of the flight and any services provided.[3]

The Passenger Rights Protection Regulation establishes passenger obligations including adhering to the ticket conditions including the baggage policies, disclosing any special additional services required before completing the reservation, notifying the carrier of any special services required, having a valid passport, and informing the carrier about valuable items in checked or carry-on baggage that require additional insurance.[4] Similarly, the Regulation provides for the airline's obligations including to provide transparency, give all necessary information about a passenger's booking promptly, provide service to high standards, and adhere to the Regulation.[5]

1 Hadi Naser, 'Libya's Ministry of Transport Issues New Passenger Rights Protection Regulation' (*The Law Society of Libya*, 6 February 2025) <https://lawsociety.ly/en/libyas-ministry-of-transport-issues-new-passenger-rights-protection-regulation/#:~:text=84%20of%202024%2C%20approving%20the,treatment%2C%20transparency%2C%20and%20accountability> accessed 10 December 2025.

2 Article 2(1) and (2).

3 Article 3.

4 Article 4.

5 Article 5.

DOI: 10.4324/9781003746164-38

If a flight is delayed, cancelled, or if boarding is denied, the airline must provide care and assistance to passengers. This includes refreshments and drinks for delays of three hours or more, appropriate meal for delays exceeding four hours and hotel accommodation and transportation if the delay exceeds six hours.[6] The Regulation is silent regarding access to email and phone calls. Even in the event of force majeure, the airline is required to provide appropriate care and assistance and continuous and real-time information.[7] Force majeure is broadly defined in Article 1 with Article 15 listing what it is not such as technical failures, operational issues, or negligence by the airline, ensuring the exemption is applied narrowly and fairly.[8]

Triggering Event	**Required Care and Assistance**
Delay ≥3 Hours	• Refreshments and drinks.
Delay ≥4 Hours	• Appropriate meal service.
Delay ≥6 Hours/Cancellation/ Denied Boarding	• Hotel accommodation. • Free transport between hotel and airport.
Any Disruption	• Continuous, real-time information and updates.
Force Majeure Event (e.g., severe weather, political instability)	• **Appropriate care and assistance** (e.g., refreshments, information, accommodation if needed). • **Exemption from financial compensation.**

Article 7 imposes a primary obligation on the air carrier to minimize such incidents. A critical consumer-friendly provision mandates that if seats are available in a higher class, the airline must upgrade denied boarding passengers free of charge rather than refuse them carriage.[9] When denial is unavoidable, the carrier must immediately provide written guidance on rights and offer a choice between rebooking on another class or airline, with the original carrier covering any fare difference.[10] The most significant financial deterrent is the requirement for a full refund plus compensation equal to 100% of the ticket value for the affected segment if the passenger chooses to cancel.[11] The obligation to compensate does not apply if the denial of boarding was mandated by authorities or was due to the passenger's failure to adhere to his obligations.[12] Moreover, the airline

6 Article 6(1)–(3).
7 Article 15(1).
8 Article 15(2).
9 Article 7(2).
10 Article 7(3)(A) and (B).
11 Article 7(3)(C).
12 Article 4(8) coupled with Article 7(3)(D) which states Article 5 but Article 5 is the carrier's obligation.

is exempted if it provides an alternative flight within a six-hour window.[13] Airlines are allowed to seek volunteers to give up their seats in exchange for compensation, a common industry practice to resolve overbooking issues amicably.[14]

Downgrading is not considered denied boarding.[15] The Regulation forbids denying a passenger boarding if lower-class seats are available; instead, the carrier must inform the passenger and seek agreement.[16] If a passenger accepts a downgrade, the airline must refund the fare difference for the affected segment and provide an additional 50% compensation of that fare difference.[17] If the passenger chooses to cancel the contract due to the downgrade, they are entitled to a refund of the unused ticket portion plus 100% compensation of the ticket value for the affected segment.[18] The carrier must also provide care and assistance.[19] Crucially, these compensations do not prevent passengers from claiming other damages resulting from the downgrading.

Airlines cannot deny boarding to passengers with special needs except for security reasons.[20] They must provide free special assistance, including wheelchairs and communication for the hearing or visually impaired.[21] In cases of denied boarding or downgrading, the carrier must secure the next best alternative flight that "closely matches the schedule of the original booking."[22] A severe penalty of 200% of the total ticket value is imposed in case of failure to provide a suitable alternative or required services.[23]

Scenario	Passenger's Options	Compensation and Refunds
Denied Boarding	1. Be re-routed on another flight, another class, or with another airline. 2. Cancel the booking and receive a full refund.	**If cancelling:** Full refund of the ticket + **100% of the ticket value** as additional compensation for the affected segment. 200% for special needs passengers.

13 Article 7(3)(D).
14 Article 7(3)(E).
15 Article 8(1).
16 Article 8(2).
17 Article 8(2)(A).
18 Article 8(2)(B).
19 Article 8(2)(C).
20 Article 11(1).
21 Article 11(2).
22 Article 11(3)(1).
23 Article 11(3)(2).

Scenario	Passenger's Options	Compensation and Refunds
Downgraded (passenger agrees to a lower class)	Accept the available seat in a lower class.	**Refund:** The full fare difference between your original ticket and the lower class. **Compensation:** An additional **50% of that fare difference**.
Downgraded (Passenger refuses the lower class and cancels)	Cancel the booking and receive a full refund.	**Full refund** of the ticket + **100% of the ticket value** as additional compensation for the affected segment.

Except for force majeure,[24] airlines cannot cancel flights – which is a strong obligation as found in Saudi Arabia.[25] The obligations of the airline vary significantly based on the notice period. If the cancellation is notified at least 14 days in advance for international flights and seven days for domestic flights, the airline is exempt from providing care and assistance but must refund the ticket.[26] If notified between 14 days and 24 hours for international flights and seven days and 24 hours for domestic flights, the airline must offer a replacement flight within 24 hours or contract termination.[27] Stricter rules apply for cancellations within 24 to four hours, where failure to provide an alternative within six hours triggers a full refund plus 100% compensation, on top of necessary care and assistance.[28] If a replacement flight leads to an extended hotel stay, the airline must cover the costs of accommodation, meals, and transportation.[29] If a flight is cancelled at the airport, the carrier must secure an alternative flight which might result in mandatory upgrades or compensation for downgrades of the fare difference as well as 50% compensation.[30] Passengers can elect to cancel and receive a refund of the unused portion and 50% compensation.[31]

Special rules apply to airports with limited flights, including the option of ground transportation to the final destination or a nearby airport, coupled with proportionate refunds and compensation.[32] In those cases, the airline

24 Defined in Article 1 as "An event or extraordinary circumstance that the air carrier could not foresee, predict, or avoid despite taking all reasonable measures necessary for the regular operation of the flight and damage prevention or where the air carrier couldn't take such measures." It does not include technical failure, operational issue, misjudgement by air carrier, and negligence or misconduct. Article 15(2).

25 Article 9.

26 Articles 9(A)(1) and Article 9(B)(1).

27 Articles 9(A)(2) and Article 9(B)(2).

28 Article 9 paragraph 2.

29 Article 9 paragraph 3.

30 Article 9 paragraph 4.

31 Article 9 paragraph 5.

32 Article 9 paragraph 6.

must secure an alternative flight within six hours. Passengers have the right to assistance if the delay between the cancelled flight and alternative flight exceeds six hours.[33] Passengers are entitled to compensation of the value of the ticket for the affected segment and 50% compensation if they agree to ground transportation.[34] If the passenger decides to cancel, then he is entitled to a full refund and 100% compensation.[35]

Airlines are not permitted to delay flights unless for security and safety reasons.[36] The airline must notify passengers of delays at least 45 minutes before departure.[37] If the delay occurs when the passenger is still at the hotel, the airline must cover costs of extending the stay until the new departure time.[38] A delay exceeding six hours grants the passenger the right to have their flight treated as cancelled, invoking all the rights and compensation, as well as care and assistance.[39]

Scenario	Notice Period	Passenger's Rights and Options	Compensation
Flight Cancellation (international)	More than 14 days.	Full refund of the ticket.	None.
	Between 14 days and 24 hours.	Choice between: 1. A replacement flight within **24 hours**. 2. A full refund.	None.
	Between 24 and 4 hours.	Full refund of the ticket + mandatory care and assistance.	**100% of ticket value** if the airline **fails to provide an alternative flight within 6 hours**.
Flight Cancellation (domestic)	More than 7 days.	Full refund of the ticket.	None.
	Between 7 days and 24 hours.	Choice between: 1. A replacement flight within **24 hours**. 2. A full refund.	None.

(Continued)

33 Article 9 paragraph 6(2).
34 Article 9 paragraph 6(3).
35 Article 9 paragraph 6(4).
36 Article 10(1).
37 Article 10(2).
38 Article 10(3).
39 Article 10(4) and (5).

(Continued)

Scenario	Notice Period	Passenger's Rights and Options	Compensation
	Between 24 and 4 hours.	Full refund of the ticket + mandatory care and assistance.	**100% of ticket value** if the airline **fails to provide an alternative flight within 6 hours**.
Long Delay (more than 6 hours)	N/A	Right to have the flight treated as **cancelled**.	As per cancellation rules.

Article 12 outlines compensation for lost baggage, setting a floor of 350 SDRs and a ceiling of 1,131 SDRs for lost or damaged checked baggage.[40] For higher-value items, a formal declaration and additional insurance purchase are required. Compensation for delayed baggage is specified as a daily allowance of 20 SDRs for domestic and 40 SDRs for international flights up to a maximum of 100 SDRs for domestic flights and 200 SDRs for international flights, payable upon the baggage's return.[41]

Issue	Compensation
Lost or Damaged Baggage	• Minimum: 350 SDR. • Maximum: 1,131 SDR.
Delayed Baggage (domestic)	20 SDR per day (max 100 SDR).
Delayed Baggage (international)	40 SDR per day (max 200 SDR).

As found in various national laws, the Regulation mandates transparency in advertising and pricing.[42] All prices must be final and inclusive of all fees, and any additional fees must be explicitly stated in the advertisement. All conditions and any post-booking change fees must be clearly disclosed upfront. Article 18 contains general provisions and imposes on the carrier a full responsibility for ensuring passengers have the necessary travel documents, holding them liable for return costs and accommodation if a passenger is denied entry due to missing documents.[43]

Article 19 explicitly states that the compensations to passengers are separate from and additional to any administrative penalties and fines that the minister of transport will levy on the airline for violating the Regulation. However, the article does not include any fixed penalty.

40 Article 12(1).
41 Article 12(4).
42 Article 17.
43 Article 19(2).

The Libyan Passenger Rights Protection Regulation represents a remarkably robust and progressive piece of consumer protection legislation that marks a significant leap forward for the country's aviation sector. Its importance is multifaceted. Firstly, it signifies a monumental shift from a previously unregulated or discretionary environment to one where passenger rights are clearly codified, enforceable, and aligned with international best practices. The Regulation has comprehensively detailed the passenger's choices as well as their compensation. The law's most significant strength is the robust nature of its compensation and refund policies. The Regulation's use of a combination of refunds, percentages of ticket value, and compensation in Special Drawing Rights (SDRs) can result in a more equitable financial remedy for the passenger, particularly for high-priced tickets. It also includes a severe consequence for denial of boarding of someone with special needs.

The law exhibits a strong consumer-focused philosophy through several standout provisions. It mandates free upgrades for passengers in cases of overbooking if seats are available in a higher class, a feature that places passenger convenience above airline revenue. Perhaps most crucially, it defines "force majeure" or extraordinary circumstances in an exceptionally narrow and passenger-friendly manner, explicitly excluding technical failures, operational issues, and airline negligence from this exemption. This pre-emptively closes loopholes that airlines in other jurisdictions have frequently exploited. Furthermore, the Regulation demonstrates thoughtful adaptation to the local context through specific rules for airports with limited flight availability, proving it is not merely a copied text but a law designed for practical application within Libya's unique infrastructure. A key distinction is that the Libyan law explicitly includes detailed rules and compensation for lost, damaged, or delayed baggage within its text. The true test of its success, however, will lie in the consistent enforcement by the Civil Aviation Authority and the awareness among passengers to actively claim these newly established rights.

Comparison with EU Regulation

Feature	**Passenger Rights Protection Regulation 2024**	**EU Regulation 261/2004**
Delay Compensation	≥6h: Full refund + 100% of fare.	≥3h: €250–€600 (by distance).
Cancellation Rights	Full refund + 100% of fare (if cancelled between 24 and 4 hours).	<14d notice: Refund or re-routing + €250–600 compensation (by distance).
Denial of Boarding	Volunteers first; refund + 100% of fare.	Volunteer first; €250–600 (by distance) if denied boarding.
Baggage Liability	Between 350 and 1,131 SDR.	Not specified.

Bibliography

- Decision No. 84 of 2024 issued by Minister of Transport Regarding the Approval of the Passenger Rights Protection Regulation <https://lawsociety.ly/en/legislation/decision-no-84-of-2024-issued-by-the-minister-of-transport-regarding-the-approval-of-the-passenger-rights-protection-regulation/> accessed 10 December 2025.
- Naser, H., 'Libya's Ministry of Transport Issues New Passenger Rights Protection Regulation' (*The Law Society of Libya*, 6 February 2025) <https://lawsociety.ly/en/libyas-ministry-of-transport-issues-new-passenger-rights-protection-regulation/#:~:text=84%20of%202024%2C%20approving%20the,treatment%2C%20transparency%2C%20and%20accountability> accessed 10 December 2025.

II.28

Malaysia

In 2016, Malaysia introduced the Malaysian Aviation Consumer Protection Code 2016 to protect the rights and interests of passengers in Malaysia.[1] The Code comprehensively details the rights of passengers in Malaysia in relation to flight delay and cancellation, denied boarding, air fare, and compensation for mishandled baggage. It establishes clear guidelines to enable passengers to make an informed choice but also provides remedies in case of disruption.

The Code applies to all airlines that have been granted a licence or air service permit by the Malaysia Aviation Commission and to all airlines operating into and out of Malaysia.[2] In 2024, the Code was amended – for the second time[3] – to provide greater protection to passengers by the so-called enhanced Malaysian Aviation Consumer Protection Code (MACPC) with most changes taking effect from 1 September 2024.[4]

The protection starts to kick in after two hours of delay – except for communication of change in flight status which must be communicated "as soon as practicable after the operating airline becomes aware of such change."[5]

After two hours, passengers must be offered compensation and care according to the First Schedule. For a flight delay, passengers must be offered "free of charge, meals, refreshments, limited telephone calls and internet access."[6] Before the enhancements to the Code, when a flight was

1 Malaysian Aviation Consumer Protection Code 2016, P.U.(B) 305/2016 of 20 June 2016.

2 Paragraph 2, definition of airline.

3 The MACPC was amended in 2019 through the Aviation Consumer Protection (Amendment) Code 2019, Code P.U.(B) 250/2019 of 10 May 2019.

4 Article 1(2) except for Paragraph 8A which came into force on 1 January 2025 – Article 1(3).

Key Changes (2024): – Extended passenger rights (refunds, disclosures). – Higher baggage compensation (1,288 SDR). – Stricter penalties (fines up to RM200,000).

5 Paragraph 8(1) of the 2016 Code. Change of flight status is defined by paragraph 8(3) as cancellation or a delay of 30 minutes or more.

6 Point 3 of First Schedule.

DOI: 10.4324/9781003746164-39

delayed by five hours or more, the operating airline was only obliged to offer passengers free of charge meals, refreshments, limited telephone calls and internet access, as well as hotel accommodation where necessary and transport between the airport and place of accommodation.[7] Full refund or alternative flight was only available to passengers whose flight had been cancelled. Following the amendments, if a passenger no longer wishes to continue with the flight, the operating airline is now obliged to offer a full refund in the original mode of payment within 30 days.[8] The new rules also cover passengers who decide not to take the delayed flight and instead choose to book another flight. Those changes are a great improvement for consumers by offering the option for passengers to walk away and get a full refund. As made clear through the illustration in Paragraph 10 of the MACPC, passengers' rights are cumulative; airlines have to provide assistance after two hours and if the delay is rolling on totalling five hours delay at the end of the trip, then the airline is also required to offer passengers the choice between refund or hotel accommodation.[9]

Delay Duration	**Airlines Must Provide**
2+ Hours	Meals, refreshments, phone calls, internet access.
5+ Hours	Hotel + transport **or** full refund (passenger's choice).

According to the First Schedule, in the event of a flight cancellation, passengers can choose between a full refund within 30 days or a re-routing. It is not clear if the passenger is entitled to any compensation as the compensation article only refers to flight delays but then the limitation of liability refers to both delay and cancellations.[10] No minimum cancellation period notice is mentioned.

7 Point 4 of First Schedule.

8 Item No. 4 of the First Schedule read with new paragraph 15B of the Malaysian Aviation Consumer Protection (Amendment) Code 2024, P.U.(B) 345/2024 of 30 August 2024.

9 The illustration is as followed: "A consumer purchased a ticket for a journey from KUL to MEL with Airline A and the flight is scheduled to depart at 2000 hours. On the day of departure, after check-in at the airport, consumer received a notification from Airline A informing consumer of a delay of the flight from 2000 hours to 2200 hours. At 2230 hours, another flight delay notification was received by the consumer from Airline A stating that the flight is further delayed to 0100 hours the next day.

The consumer's rights are cumulative, namely:

(a) for the delay of two hours from 2000 hours to 2200 hours, Airline A is required to offer consumer meals, refreshments, telephone calls and internet access; and

(b) for the total delay of five hours until 0100 hours, Airline A is required to offer consumer the choice between refund, or hotel accommodation (where a stay of one or more nights becomes necessary) and transport between the airport and place of accommodation (hotel or other)."

10 Paragraph (3) and (5).

While the Code does not provide any fixed amounts of compensation as in other countries, it contains a provision on the maximum liability for an airline fixed at 4,694 Special Drawing Rights (SDR) per passenger which was increased to 5,346 SDR per passenger.[11] Although paragraph 12(2) is quite clearly worded "the airline is liable for damage occasioned by delay in flight," there seems to be some contradicting information as the MAVCOM noted that passengers are not entitled to any additional compensation for the inconvenience caused by a delay exceeding five hours.[12]

Scenario	Compensation	Notes
Delay	None (only care/ refund).	MAVCOM states no compensation for "inconvenience."
Baggage Loss/ Damage	Up to 1,288 SDR (was 1,131 SDR).	Aligns with Montreal Convention.
Max Liability	5,346 SDR/passenger (was 4,694 SDR).	Covers delays, cancellations, denial of boarding.

Airlines can escape their liability if they can demonstrate that they took "all measures that could reasonably be required to avoid the damage or that it was impossible for the airline to take such measures."[13] Airlines could also rely on the "extraordinary circumstances" defence found in subparagraph 5 of paragraph 12 and defined as "circumstances that may, in particular, occur in cases of war, meteorological conditions incompatible with the operation of the flight concerned, security risks, unexpected flight safety shortcomings and strikes that affect the operation of an operating airline."[14] This definition resembles the European one and just like with Regulation 261, the definition is very vague. It can be assumed that unforeseen weather conditions might be included as well as wildcat strikes. However, it is not clear whether planned strikes will fall within the definition.

If the flight disruption is caused by an extraordinary circumstance which is beyond the airline's control, the operating airline is required to offer a refund in the original mode of payment, but they can also offer a full refund in alternative forms of refunds such as travel vouchers or credit

11 Paragraph 12(3) of the Code, Paragraph 12(3) of the Amended Code and Third Schedule.

12 Answer to question 13. Malaysian Aviation Commission, 'Malaysian Aviation Consumer Protection Code 2016 (MACPC) Enhancement FAQ' (2 September 2024) <https://www.mavcom.my/wp-content/uploads/2024/09/ENG-MACPC-2024-FAQ.pdf> accessed 11 December 2025.

13 Paragraph 12(2) of the Code.

14 Paragraph 12(7) of the Code.

shells.[15] However, "the consumers retain the right to choose their preferred mode of refund."[16]

Airlines are also required to remove cancelled flights from all booking platforms immediately. This rule has been included to ensure passengers cannot purchase tickets for unavailable flights. Any change to the scheduled departure time must be notified to the passenger at least two weeks in advance unless such change was due to extraordinary circumstances or technical reasons which could not have been avoided by taking reasonable measures.[17] In the event of a rescheduling of three hours or more – before or after the scheduled time of departure – the airline is required to notify the passengers about "the new departure time when the new timing has been determined or at least twenty-four hours from the scheduled time of departure."[18]

Regarding route cessation and flight rescheduling, the enhancement introduced new obligations in points 6 and 7 of the First Schedule to the Code obliging airlines to offer a full refund in the original mode of payment within 30 days, or to re-route the consumer's flight under comparable circumstances to the consumer's final destination at the earliest opportunity or at a later date to the consumer's convenience at no extra charge. If the re-routing flight arrives to an alternative airport, the airline must bear the cost of transferring the consumer from the alternative airport to that for which the reservation was made.[19] In the event that a passenger does not board a flight and a full refund is not available, the airline must at least refund the "fuel surcharge, taxes, fees, and charges referred to in subsubparagraphs (1) (c), (d), (e) and (f)."[20]

To avoid situations as seen in the US, the MACPC makes it clear that denial of boarding can only occur before the consumer boards the aircraft and that such denial must be done at the check-in counter or departure gate. Denial of boarding is only available after airlines have first requested for volunteers to surrender their reservation.[21] Those passengers must be offered compensations as established in the First Schedule such as meals, limited telephone calls and internet access, hotel accommodation where a stay of one or more nights is necessary, and transport between the airport and place of accommodation.[22]

Passengers can also claim for baggage delay, loss, or damage, which was increased under the amended paragraph 13(5) of the Code from 1,131

15 New paragraph 12(5A) read with existing paragraph 12(8) of the Code.

16 Malaysian Aviation Consumer Protection Code 2016 (MACPC) Enhancement FAQ (n 12).

17 Paragraph 8A of the Amendment.

18 Paragraph 8(6)(b) the Amendment.

19 Point 6(2) of the First Schedule.

20 Paragraph 15A(2) of the Amended Code.

21 Paragraph 11(1) of the Code.

22 Point 2 of the First Schedule.

to 1,288 SDR per passenger.[23] The MACPC also contains guidelines and standards regarding the handling of complaints through the Complaints Management System (CMS).[24] According to a report, 65.4% of the total number of requests related to complaints and the main categories of complaints related to flight cancellation, refund, mishandled baggage, online booking, and flight delay.[25]

The enhanced Code also extended the time for submission of complaint to the Malaysian Aviation Commission (MAVCOM) from one to two years.[26] Airlines violating the MACPC can face fines of up to 200,000 ringgit, with the possibility of higher penalties for repeat offenses.[27] As of 2024, "the Commission has fined AirAsia Berhad, AirAsia X Berhad, and Batik Air a total of RM4.76 million for breaches of the MACPC – failing to disclose the final price of airfares and failing to communicate flight status changes to consumers."[28]

Interestingly, the longest provision of the Code relates to passengers with disability. Paragraph 9 is more than two pages long and mandates some strict obligations on airlines, such as the prohibition to deny boarding on the ground of disability.[29] The Enhanced Code introduced a new paragraph 10A relating to "reasonable accommodation of persons with disability." The Code also contains a full disclosure of air fare and provisions on the prohibition on automatic adding on services. In addition to the existing requirements to disclose base fare, taxes, and fees, the MACPC requires airlines to include any other fees or charges.[30] This

23 As stipulated in the Third Schedule.

24 Paragraphs 17 and 18 of the Code.

25 Malaysian Aviation Commission, 'Aviation Consumer Protection in Malaysia' (UN Trade and Development Intergovernmental Group of Experts on Consumer Protection Law and Policy, 8th Session Geneva, Switzerland, 1–2 July 2024), 21 and 23.

26 Paragraph 18 of the Amended Code.

27 Paragraph 22 of the Code based on section 69(4) of the Malaysian Aviation Commission Act (MAVCOM Act) 2015.

28 Malaysian Aviation Commission (n 25) 30.

29 Paragraph 9(1)(b) of the Code.

30 Paragraph 3(1) of Amended Code reads as "(a) the base fare, including all charges payable to the airline;

(b) any taxes and fees imposed by the Government;

(c) any fees and charges prescribed under any written law;

(d) fuel surcharge;

(e) such other fees and charges as determined by the Commission to be imposed on consumers by providers of air services."

The previous version mentioned "(a) government imposed taxes and fees;

(b) fees and charges imposed by the Commission;

(c) passenger service charges;

(d) security charges;

(e) baggage fees; and

(f) fuel surcharge."

revision is aimed at preventing airlines from advertising the base fare only as the Enhanced Code makes clear that any advertisements must not be false, misleading, or deceptive.[31]

While this law can be seen as a step towards the right direction, the fact that it was amended recently shows the flaws of the initial code. The lack of any kind of compensation for delays, as prescribed by Regulation 261, is also a missed opportunity. Malaysia might be reluctant to agree on an international convention on passenger rights which includes fixed compensation for delayed or cancelled flights as it will not be in line with their national legislation.

Finally, although MAVCOM will be dissolved very soon, the MACPC still refers to it which will potentially require another review. The legislator could have avoided this by including a sentence MAVCOM "or any of its successors."[32]

The evolution of the Malaysian Aviation Consumer Protection Code (MACPC), culminating in its 2024 enhanced iteration, represents a deliberate and sophisticated legal engineering of passenger rights within the Asia-Pacific region. The Enhanced MACPC is, in many respects, a strong instrument for managing operational disruptions from a consumer's standpoint. Its core mechanics are both logical and passenger-centric. The Code's strength lies in its meticulous detailing of passenger entitlements in the event of flight delays, cancellations, denied boarding, and mishandled baggage, applying to all airlines licensed or operating within, into, or out of Malaysia. The recent 2024 amendments notably bolster passenger protection by introducing the right to a full refund in the original mode of payment within 30 days for delays exceeding five hours, an option not previously mandated. The enhancement further ensures that the obligation for care, such as meals and communication, begins after a two-hour delay and that rights are cumulative, meaning care is continuous even when the delay reaches the refund-triggering five-hour mark. Other commendable improvements include stricter rules on communication of flight status changes and the immediate removal of cancelled flights from booking platforms. Furthermore, the MACPC contains one of the region's most detailed provisions for passengers with disabilities and ensures transparency through full disclosure of airfares and prohibition of automatic add-on services. This system's governance structure is backed by financial penalties of up to 200,000 ringgit for

31 Paragraph 3(2) of the Amended Code.

32 Shannon Rajan, Eric Gabriel Gomez and Foong Wai Leong, 'Clear Skies Ahead: Navigating Your New Air Travel Rights – the Malaysian Aviation Consumer Protection (Amendment) Code 2024' (*SKRINE*, 10 October 2024) <https://www.skrine.com/insights/alerts/october-2024/clear-skies-ahead-navigating-your-new-air-travel-r> accessed 11 December 2025.

airline non-compliance. Despite these clear steps in the right direction, the need for a second set of amendments highlights initial flaws in the 2016 Code, and a key area of divergence from international best practice remains.

The most significant omission is the complete absence of a fixed compensation scheme for inconvenience caused by delay or cancellation. The Malaysian framework is built upon a foundation of contractual restitution and compensatory damages for proven loss, capped at a Montreal Convention-aligned liability limit (now 5,346 SDR). As clarified by the Malaysia Aviation Commission (MAVCOM), passengers are not entitled to additional compensation for the "inconvenience" itself. This stands in stark contrast to the philosophical underpinning of EU Regulation 261, which is rooted in consumer protection law with a strong deterrent element but is aligned with the Montreal Convention's liability paradigm.

The definition and application of the "extraordinary circumstances" defence bear resemblance in both codes. The MACPC's definition mirrors the European concept, including war, meteorological conditions, and security risks. However, the legal and judicial clarity established through decades of European Court of Justice rulings interpreting EC 261 – for instance, definitively classifying unforeseen technical problems as not extraordinary circumstances – is absent in the MACPC. This vagueness in the Malaysian Code offers airlines greater flexibility in avoiding liability compared to the rigorously interpreted European Regulation.

In conclusion, the Enhanced MACPC of 2024 is a commendable and recently upgraded instrument that places a strong emphasis on service recovery, transparency, and consumer protection in the face of disruption. It successfully addresses many of the most acute consumer pains – opaque pricing, stranded passengers without options, inadequate care – and does so with clarity and enforceable teeth. However, in the international landscape of passenger rights, it is fundamentally disadvantaged by its reluctance to adopt a fixed monetary compensation model for significant delays and cancellations.

Comparison with EU Regulation

Feature	**Malaysia MACPC 2024**	**EU Regulation 261/2004**
Delay Compensation	Care/refund only.	≥3h: €250–€600 (by distance).
Cancellation Rights	Full refund in 30 days or re-routing.	<14d notice: Refund or re-routing + €250–600 compensation (by distance).
Denial of Boarding	Volunteers first; no fixed compensation.	Volunteer first; €250–600 (by distance) if denied boarding.
Baggage Liability	1,288 SDR.	Not specified.

Bibliography

- Malaysian Aviation Commission Act 2015 (MAVCOM Act), Act 711 as amended on 1 August 2018 <https://www.caam.gov.my/wp-content/uploads/2025/07/MALAYSIAN-AVIATION-COMMISSION-ACT-2015-ACT-771.pdf> accessed 11 December 2025.
- Malaysian Aviation Consumer Protection Code 2016, P.U.(B) 305/2016 of 20 June 2016 <https://www.caam.gov.my/wp-content/uploads/2025/07/pub_20160630_P.U.-B-305.pdf> accessed 11 December 2025.
- Aviation Consumer Protection (Amendment) Code 2019, Code P.U.(B) 250/2019 of 10 May 2019 <https://www.caam.gov.my/wp-content/uploads/2025/07/Malaysian-Aviation-Consumer-Protection-Amendment-Code-2019.pdf> accessed 11 December 2025.
- Malaysian Aviation Consumer Protection (Amendment) Code 2024, P.U.(B) 345/2024 of 30 August 2024 <https://www.caam.gov.my/wp-content/uploads/2025/07/MACPC-Enhancement-PUB345_2024.pdf> accessed 11 December 2025.
- Malaysian Aviation Commission, 'Malaysian Aviation Consumer Protection Code 2016 (MACPC) Enhancement FAQ' (2 September 2024) <https://www.mavcom.my/wp-content/uploads/2024/09/ENG-MACPC-2024-FAQ.pdf> accessed 11 December 2025.
- Malaysian Aviation Commission, 'Aviation Consumer Protection in Malaysia' (UN Trade and Development Intergovernmental Group of Experts on Consumer Protection Law and Policy, 8th Session Geneva, Switzerland, 1–2 July 2024).
- Rajan, S., Gomez, E. G. and Leong, F. W., 'Clear Skies Ahead: Navigating Your New Air Travel Rights – the Malaysian Aviation Consumer Protection (Amendment) Code 2024' (*SKRINE*, 10 October 2024) <https://www.skrine.com/insights/alerts/october-2024/clear-skies-ahead-navigating-your-new-air-travel-r> accessed 11 December 2025.

II.29

Mexico

Mexico does not have per se a regulation, instead passenger rights are governed by the Civil Aviation Law[1] and the Federal Consumer Protection Law.[2] These laws are enforced by the Mexican Civil Aeronautic Authority (DGAC) and the Federal Consumer Protection Agency (Profeco).

Article 47 Bis of the Civil Aviation Law states that airlines are obligated to provide efficient, high-quality service to all travellers. To do so, they must comply with rights that are also found in the Federal Consumer Protection Law (LFPC). It also mandates airlines to establish mechanisms to guarantee the transportation of persons with disabilities, in accordance with operational safety measures.[3] Those passengers have the right to travel with their equipment.[4] Infants under 2 years old can travel for free with the child having their own boarding card which then entitles the passenger to transport a stroller at no additional charge.[5]

Passengers have the right to dignified treatment and a high level of information, which allows them to know their options and take alternatives if required. Airlines are required to quickly and efficiently notify passengers of any changes to their itinerary, whether it is a delay, cancellation, or other circumstance that could affect their service. According to Article 47 Bis III, airlines must do so via phone calls, emails, or text messages with at least 24 hours' notice before the scheduled departure. If changes occur within that 24-hour window, the airline is obligated to inform the passenger as soon as it becomes aware of the change and the airline is certain the changes are inevitable. Such notification does not exempt airlines from their responsibility. This proactive communication ensures

1 Ley de Aviación Civil de 1995, as modified in 2017 <https://www.profeco.gob.mx/politicasaviacion/pdf/LAC.pdf>.

2 Ley Federal de Protección al Consumidor de 1992, as amended in 2012. <https://www.profeco.gob.mx/juridico/pdf/l_lfpc_ultimo_camdip.pdf>.

3 Article 47 Bis I.

4 Article 47 Bis 1.

5 Article 47 Bis II.

DOI: 10.4324/9781003746164-40

travellers can adjust their plans, accordingly, avoiding unnecessary stress. The law also guarantees that passengers having purchased a round-trip or connecting ticket, are able to use each segment independently, so an airline cannot deny boarding a flight just because the passenger missed an earlier part of their journey.[6] Passengers must, however, inform the airline within 24 hours from the scheduled time of the unused segment, that they will use the subsequent segments, through the means that the concessionaire or licensee has for this purpose. The scope of any no-show clause is, therefore, very much restricted.

In case of a delay attributable to the airline, passengers are entitled to compensation. The type of compensation depends on the duration of the delay. For delays between one and four hours, the airline's compensation policies will apply, which must include at least discounts on future flights, and/or food and beverages.[7] For delays over two hours but less than four, the discount must be at least 7.5% of the ticket price and such compensation policies must be registered with the Profeco every six months and be made available publicly. If the delay extends beyond four hours, the airline must offer compensation and offer the same options as a flight cancellation, which includes a full refund or a substitute flight.[8] In all circumstances, the service provider must make available to waiting passengers access to phone calls and email.

Duration of Delay	**What the Airline Must Provide**	**Additional Notes**
>1 Hour	Compensation according to the airline's own policy. Phone and email access.	Policies must: • Be registered and public. • Include, at a minimum, discounts on future flights and/or food and beverages.
>2 Hours (but <4)	Compensation according to the airline's policy. Phone and email access.	The discount on future flights **cannot be less than 7.5%** of the price of the original ticket.
>4 Hours	Compensation as per the airline's policy + the passenger gains the right to the same options and indemnities as for a **flight cancellation**. Phone and email access.	This is a major escalation. The passenger can now choose a full refund + indemnity or to be rebooked + indemnity.

6 Article 47 Bis IV.
7 Article 47 Bis V(a).
8 Article 47 Bis V(b).

For flight cancellations attributable to the airline, passengers have several choices as outlined in Article 47 Bis VI. They can choose to receive a full refund for their ticket or for the portion of the trip that was not completed.[9] Alternatively, they can request substitute transportation on the first available flight and receive additional support like access to phone calls and emails, food according to the waiting time until boarding another flight, and, if an overnight stay is necessary, accommodation and transportation.[10] Another option is to be rebooked on a later flight to the same destination.[11] If the passengers decide for a full refund or a rebooking at a later date, they are entitled to additional compensation of at least 25% of the ticket price or the unflown part of the journey.[12] Any clause from the airline that tries to avoid this responsibility is null and void.[13] Interestingly, the Civil Aviation Law does not include any prior notice period to exempt airlines from their liability.

Passenger's Choice	What the Airline Must Provide	Additional Indemnity
Option A: Full Refund	Reimburse the full price of the ticket (or the value of the unused segment(s) of the journey).	**Yes.** The airline must also pay an indemnity of **no less than 25%** of the ticket price (or unused segment value).
Option B: Re-routing	1. Provide transport on the next available flight. 2. Provide, **free of charge**: - Phone and email access. - Food and beverages according to wait time. - Hotel accommodation + transport if an overnight stay is required.	**Yes.** The airline must also pay an indemnity of **no less than 25%** of the ticket price (or unused segment value).
Option C: Later Travel	Transport the passenger on a future date that is convenient **for the passenger**.	**Yes.** The airline must also pay an indemnity of **no less than 25%** of the ticket price (or unused segment value).

In case of overbooking, airlines must first request for volunteers in exchange for benefits which cannot be less advantageous than the

9 Article 47 Bis VI(a).
10 Article 47 Bis VI(b).
11 Article 47 Bis VI(c).
12 Article 47 Bis VI.
13 Article 47 Bis X.

ones available to involuntary denial.[14] The passenger can request a reimbursement of the price of the ticket or request a re-routing on the first available flight as well as telephone and email communication, food in accordance with the waiting time, and hotel accommodation if an overnight stay is required.[15] Passengers could also opt for a rebooking at a later date.[16] In addition, the passengers who opted for a reimbursement or a rebooking at a later date are also allowed to receive a compensation of at least 25% of the ticket price. This was slightly modified by the Supreme Court (SCJN) in 2023 which held that airlines must compensate passengers who are denied boarding due to overbooking, irrespective of other alternatives provided as per the Civil Aviation Law.[17] This means that airlines must compensate at least 25% of the ticket price even if the passenger chooses a rebooking on the next available flight.[18] The law is silent on downgrading.

In May 2025, a Bill amending the Civil Aviation Law was introduced to the Chamber of Deputies which has among its objectives a potential increase of compensation for passengers impacted by overbooked flights from 25% to 35%.[19] This project's purpose is to align the statute with the Supreme Court's ruling and solidify it. Indeed, as pointed out by José Antonio Cervantes Acosta because the decision was decided by a three-justice majority of the First Chamber, it does not constitute a binding precedent for other courts, and instead a legislative amendment is necessary to uniformly enforce these protections.[20]

---

14 Article 52 Bis.

15 Article 52 I and II.

16 Article 52 III.

17 Suprema Corte de Justicia de la Nación, Case 401/2023, of 8 August 2023. See: MND Staff, 'Supreme Court Rules Airlines Must Partly Refund Overbooked Flights' *Mexico News Daily* (17 July 2023) <https://mexiconewsdaily.com/news/supreme-court-airlines-must-partly-refund-overbookings/#:~:text=Lifestyle-,Supreme%20Court%20rules%20airlines%20must%20partly%20refund%20overbooked%20flights,$51%2C000%20pesos%20(US%20$3%2C000)> accessed 11 December 2025.

18 José Antonio Cervantes Acosta, 'Airlines Must Compensate Passengers, in Any Case, for Overbooking a Flight: Mexican Supreme Court' (8 November 2023) <https://irglobal.com/article/airlines-must-compensate-passengers-in-any-case-for-overbooking-a-flight-mexican-supreme-court/#:~:text=According%20to%20the%20Mexican%20law,missed%20leg%20of%20the%20trip>.

19 Iniciativa con Proyecto de decreto por el que se reforma el articulo 52 y se adiciona el articulo 52 Bis de la Ley de aviación civil. <https://ceglegal.mx/wp-cgelegal/uploads/2025/05/Inic_PVEM_Dip_Quiroga_art_52_aviacion_civil-1-2.pdf>.

20 José Antonio Cervantes Acosta, 'The Increase in Compensation for Overbooked Flights: An Effective Measure or a Regressive Burden for Passengers?' (*IRGlobal*, 25 July 2025) <https://irglobal.com/article/the-increase-in-compensation-for-overbooked-flights-an-effective-measure-or-a-regressive-burden-for-passengers/>.

Another project aims at including a 5,000 UMA fine for denied boarding due to overbooking.[21]

In the event the aircraft must land at a place other than the destination due to an act of God or force majeure, the airline must transport the passenger by the fastest available means of transportation to the destination.[22] However, those two concepts are not defined in the law. In case of connecting flights, the airline is responsible for any damages caused to the passenger or their baggage in transit or by delay, if the connection is part of the contract.[23] In the 2023 case, the passenger argued that the unconstitutionality of Article 54 and the denial of boarding led to unforeseen out-of-pocket expenses due to missing the connecting flight but it failed.[24]

Passengers can also withdraw from the travel and request a refund provided they notify the airline within 24 hours from the time of ticket purchase.[25] Passengers have the right to know the terms of the contract and their rights.[26] Article 47 Bis 4 includes the passengers' obligations such as to provide truthful information at the time of purchase, present official documentations at airport, comply with the airport security and operational rules, occupy the assigned seat unless the crew requested or authorized a change of seat, and abide by any other obligations established by law.

Finally, Article 47 Bis IX specifies that passengers have the right to a luggage allowance for both domestic and international flights. For flights with aircraft that can hold 20 or more passengers, the baggage allowance is 25 kilograms of luggage free of charge provided the suitcases comply with the instructions of the airlines regarding the number of pieces and volume restrictions.[27] For smaller aircraft, the minimum is 15 kilograms. Furthermore, the passenger may carry up to two pieces of carry-on baggage in the cabin, as long as they meet the size (up to 55 centimetres long by 40 centimetres wide by 25 centimetres high) and weight restrictions of 10 kilos each. The transport of domestic animals on aircraft of public

21 Iniciativa con Proyecto de decreto por el que se adiciona un parrafo al articulo 52 de la Ley de aviación civil. <https://sil.gobernacion.gob.mx/Archivos/Documentos/2025/07/asun_4912565_20250716_1752679029.pdf>.

22 Article 47 Bis VII.

23 Article 54.

24 José Antonio Cervantes Acosta, 'Airlines Must Compensate Passengers, in Any Case, for Overbooking a Flight: Mexican Supreme Court' (8 November 2023) <https://irglobal.com/article/airlines-must-compensate-passengers-in-any-case-for-overbooking-a-flight-mexican-supreme-court/#:~:text=According%20to%20the%20Mexican%20law,missed%20leg%20of%20the%20trip>.

25 Article 47 Bis VIII.

26 Article 47 Bis X.

27 Article 47 Bis IX.

passenger air transport service will be carried out by the airline, observing humane treatment at all times. Humane treatment shall be understood as the set of measures that seek to reduce tension, suffering, pain, and the production of trauma during the mobilization of animals.[28] In case of lost or damaged carry-on luggage, airlines must compensate up to 80 Units of Measurement and Updating (UMAs) while loss or damage of checked baggage shall be equivalent to 150 UMAs unless it is due to an inherent defect of the goods or inadequate packaging.[29]

The Civil Aviation Law does not contain any fixed sanction but allows Profeco to sanction in accordance with the Federal Consumer Protection Law.[30] In 2017, Profeco fined five airlines a total of 22.4 million pesos for charging an extra fee for the first piece of checked luggage on flights to the US and Canada.[31]

The Mexican legal framework for passenger rights, as established in its Civil Aviation Law, is a comprehensive and robust system that prioritizes remedial care and clear, actionable obligations for airlines. Its core philosophy is to ensure passengers are not stranded without assistance and are compensated for breaches of contract. However, its financial compensation model is based on a percentage of the ticket price, which can result in relatively modest sums. Mexican law stipulates that for delays over four hours, or for cancellations, a passenger is entitled to a refund or re-routing plus a mandatory indemnity of no less than 25% of the ticket price. This means the compensation is variable which might create some uncertainty for passengers as well as differences between airlines. Mexican law does not contain any "extraordinary circumstance" escape clause, but rather airlines are liable if the cause is attributable to them. While on paper this might sound stricter than the "extraordinary circumstance" loophole in Regulation 261, it might be harder for passengers to argue that the cause was attributable to an airline. The limitation on the scope of the no-show clause is a unique feature.

The Mexican passenger rights framework is a strong, detailed, and passenger-centric set of regulations that excels in ensuring immediate care and assistance. Its weakness lies in the potential for low financial compensation and very short deadlines to file a claim.

28 Article 50.

29 Article 62 coupled with Article 67.

30 Article 47 Bis 3.

31 Michael J Shapiro, 'Mexican Consumer Agency Fines Airlines, Establishes Passenger Rights' (28 June 2017) <https://www.meetings-conventions.com/News/Travel/Mexican-Consumer-Agency-Fines-Airlines#:~:text=The%20laws%20were%20enacted%20to,%E2%80%A2>.

Comparison with EU Regulation

Feature	Ley de aviación civil	EU Regulation 261/2004
Delay Compensation	Care/refund ≥4h: 25% of the fare.	≥3h: €250–€600 (by distance).
Cancellation Rights	25% of the fare.	<14d notice: Refund or re-routing + €250–600 compensation (by distance).
Denial of Boarding	Volunteers first; 25% of the fare.	Volunteer first; €250–600 (by distance) if denied boarding.
Baggage Liability	80 UMAs (carry on). 150 UMAs (checked baggage).	Not specified.

Bibliography

- Iniciativa con Proyecto de decreto por el que se reforma el articulo 52 y se adiciona el articulo 52 Bis de la Ley de aviación civil <https://ceglegal.mx/wp-cgelegal/uploads/2025/05/Inic_PVEM_Dip_Quiroga_art_52_aviacion_civil-1-2.pdf> accessed 11 December 2025.
- Iniciativa con Proyecto de decreto por el que se adiciona un parrafo al articulo 52 de la Ley de aviación civil <https://sil.gobernacion.gob.mx/Archivos/Documentos/2025/07/asun_4912565_20250716_1752679029.pdf> accessed 11 December 2025.
- Ley de Aviación Civil de 1995, as Modified in 2017 <https://www.profeco.gob.mx/politicasaviacion/pdf/LAC.pdf> accessed 11 December 2025.
- Ley Federal de Protección al Consumidor de 1992, as amended in 2012 <https://www.profeco.gob.mx/juridico/pdf/l_lfpc_ultimo_camdip.pdf> accessed 11 December 2025.
- Suprema Corte de Justicia de la Nación, Case 401/2023, of 8 August 2023.
- Acosta, J. A. C., 'Airlines Must Compensate Passengers, in Any Case, for Overbooking a Flight: Mexican Supreme Court' (8 November 2023) <https://irglobal.com/article/airlines-must-compensate-passengers-in-any-case-for-overbooking-a-flight-mexican-supreme-court/#:~:text=According%20to%20the%20Mexican%20law,missed%20leg%20of%20the%20trip> accessed 11 December 2025.
- Acosta, J. A. C., 'The Increase in Compensation for Overbooked Flights: An Effective Measure or a Regressive Burden for Passengers?' (*IRGlobal*, 25 July 2025) <https://irglobal.com/article/the-increase-in-compensation-for-overbooked-flights-an-effective-measure-or-a-regressive-burden-for-passengers/> accessed 11 December 2025.
- MND Staff, 'Supreme Court Rules Airlines Must Partly Refund Overbooked Flights' *Mexico News Daily* (17 July 2023) <https://mexiconewsdaily.com/news/supreme-court-airlines-must-partly-refund-overbookings/#:~:text=Lifestyle-,Supreme%20Court%20rules%20airlines%20must%20partly%20refund%20

overbooked%20flights,$51%2C000%20pesos%20(US%20$3%2C000)> accessed 11 December 2025.

- PROFECO, 'Derechos y obligaciones de los pasajeros del servico publico de transporte aéreo' (2020) <https://www.profeco.gob.mx/politicasaviacion/pdf/DERECHOS%20Y%20OBLIGACIONES%20VIAJAR%20EN%20AVI%C3%93N%20QR%20(vf).pdf> accessed 11 December 2025.
- Shapiro, M. J., 'Mexican Consumer Agency Fines Airlines, Establishes Passenger Rights' (28 June 2017) <https://www.meetings-conventions.com/News/Travel/Mexican-Consumer-Agency-Fines-Airlines#:~:text=The%20laws%20were%20enacted%20to,%E2%80%A2> accessed 11 December 2025.

II.30

Moldova

In the Republic of Moldova, air passenger rights are outlined in the Regulation on Compensation and Assistance for Passengers in the Event of Denied Boarding, Flight Cancellation, or Long Delays, approved by Government Decision No. 836 of 8 November 2012, as amended in 2018,[1] which is the transposition of EU Regulation 261.

Decision No. 836 applies to all passengers departing from an airport located in the territory of the Republic of Moldova or passengers departing from a third country to an airport situated in the territory of the Republic of Moldova if operated by a Moldovian carrier, unless they have already received compensation or assistance in that third country.[2] Decision No. 836 only applies to passengers having a confirmed reservation and presenting themselves for check-in in accordance with the procedures and at the time specified in advance and in writing by the air carrier, tour operator, or authorized travel agent. If no specific check-in time is provided, passengers must check in no later than 45 minutes prior to the published departure time.[3] Like other regulations, this law does not apply to passengers travelling free of charge.[4]

Chapter II is dedicated to denial of boarding and establishes that airlines must first request volunteers to surrender their seat in exchange for benefits under conditions they would agree on.[5] The volunteers are still entitled to assistance under Chapter VI. If an insufficient number of volunteers come forward to allow the remaining passengers with reservations to board the flight, the operating air carrier may then deny boarding to passengers against their will, compensating them immediately

1 Article 939 Republica Moldova, Guvernal, Hotarare Nr. HG 889 of 12.09.18, MO347-357/14.09.18.
2 Item 2(a) and (b).
3 Item 3(a) and (b).
4 Item 4.
5 Item 9.

DOI: 10.4324/9781003746164-41

in accordance with Chapter V.[6] Passengers denied boarding against their will should be able either to cancel their flights, with reimbursement of their tickets, or to continue them under satisfactory conditions, and should be adequately cared for while awaiting a later flight. This includes meals and refreshments that shall be offered free of charge and in reasonable relation to the waiting time, and a choice between reimbursement of the cost if the passenger decided not to travel or re-routing to their final destination at the earliest opportunity.[7] Hotel accommodation may be provided if a stay of one or more nights becomes necessary as well as two telephone calls, telex or fax messages, or emails.[8] Passengers are entitled to a compensation of 250 euros for flights of a distance of up to 1,500 km.[9] For flights between 1,500 and 3,500 km, the amount increases to 400 euros. Finally, for all flights over 3,500 km, the compensation is 600 euros.[10] However, if the re-routing allows the passenger to arrive at their final destination no later than two hours for all flights of 1,500 km or less, three hours for flights between 1,500 and 3,500 km, and four hours for all other flights, then the compensation can be reduced by half.[11]

Chapter III regulates flight cancellation and establishes that passengers have the right to a full refund or re-routing as well as assistance.[12] Passengers are entitled to compensation unless the airline informed them of the cancellation 14 days in advance or it is due to "exceptional circumstances which could not have been avoided despite the adoption of all possible measures."[13] Compensation is not payable if the passengers were informed at least two weeks in advance and were offered a full refund or an alternative flight at the earliest opportunity or at a later date based on the passenger choice.[14] If passengers were informed between two weeks and seven days and they were offered a route change allowing them to depart not more than two hours before the original departure time and arrive four hours after the original arrival time, then compensation is not due.[15] Similarly, no compensation is due when passengers are informed less than seven days in advance and offered a route change allowing them

6 Item 11.
7 Item 25(a)–(d).
8 Item 26.
9 Item 18(a).
10 Item 18(b) and (c).
11 Item 19(a)–(c).
12 Items 12(a) and (b).
13 Items 12(c) and Item 14.
14 Item 12(c).
15 Item 12(c).

to depart not more than one hour before the original departure time and arrive two hours after the original arrival time.[16]

Just like Regulation 261, Decision No. 836 does not define the exceptional circumstances and since the preamble has not been incorporated in the Decision, the definition of this concept is left to national courts to decide. The Supreme Court of Justice of Moldova in a landmark case of *Aliona Armaş v ÎS Compania Aeriană "Air Moldova"* overturned an appeals court's decision and upheld the original ruling of the first instance court.[17] The Supreme Court confirmed that technical failure was not an "exceptional circumstance," and the airline did not prove it took all reasonable measures to avoid the delay. For the court it was clear that technical failures discovered during maintenance or due to deficiencies in those maintenances cannot constitute, by themselves, an exceptional circumstance. Such problems are inherent in the airline's operation and are part of its normal business risk. They are considered imputable to the carrier, not exceptional. To reach its conclusion, the Supreme Court cited established jurisprudences of the Court of Justice of the European Union (CJEU). The Moldovan Supreme Court's explicit citation and application of CJEU case law is a very strong indicator of judicial alignment, but it does not, in itself, create a binding precedent for all future cases. Unless proven otherwise, it seems that Moldova follows the narrow interpretation of "exceptional circumstances" as interpreted by the CJEU.

When Cancelled	**Compensation Due?**
≥14 Days Before Departure	No.
7–14 Days Before Departure	No, if re-routing allows departure ≤2h earlier and arrival ≤4h later.
<7 Days Before Departure	No, if re-routing allows departure ≤1h earlier and arrival ≤2h later.
<14 Days Notice + No Suitable Re-routing	Yes.

If a flight is cancelled without prior notification, the airline must provide a written notice outlining a passenger's rights, particularly regarding compensation and assistance.[18] The airline is also required to display a sign at the check-in area with text informing passengers of their rights if a flight is cancelled, delayed, or if they are denied boarding. While waiting for a re-routed flight, care and assistance are to be offered free of

16 Item 12(c).

17 Dosarul nr. 2ra-1483/2019 Prima instanţă, Judecătoria Chişinău, Instanţa de apel, Curtea de Apel Chişinău, Decision of 2 October 2019.

18 Chapter XII.

charge. This includes meals and refreshments in reasonable relation to the waiting time, along with hotel accommodation and transportation if an overnight stay becomes necessary. Additionally, two free telephone calls, emails, faxes, or telexes are to be provided. Passengers are to be offered an alternative flight to their final destination at the earliest opportunity. As an alternative, a full refund of the ticket is to be provided for the parts of the journey not made. If a flight no longer serves a purpose due to the cancellation, a full refund for the entire journey and a return flight to the first point of departure are to be offered at the earliest opportunity. Additionally, passengers are entitled to compensation based on the distance of the flight and the reason for the cancellation.[19]

An airline is obligated to offer passengers specific assistance if it anticipates a flight will be delayed. What a passenger is entitled to depends entirely on the length of the delay and the flight distance. For short flights of 1,500 km or less, the airline must provide assistance after a two-hour delay. For medium-haul flights between 1,500 and 3,500 km, this assistance is required after three hours. All other, longer flights trigger this right after a four-hour delay.[20] This assistance package includes meals, refreshments, and the ability to make two free phone calls and send emails or telex messages. Furthermore, if the delay is so significant that the new departure time is on a different day, the airline is also required to provide passengers with hotel accommodation and transport to and from the hotel. Finally, should the delay reach at least five hours, the passenger gains the right to cancel their trip and receive a full refund for any unused parts of their ticket.[21]

Unlike Regulation 261, Decision 836 clearly stipulates that delayed passengers are entitled to compensation in accordance with Chapter V.[22] Interestingly, there was a project to exclude Item 17 based on the fact that such provision is not clearly established in Regulation 261. However, it was rejected based on the principle of equal treatment and the case laws of the Court of Justice of the European Union.[23] In *Aliona Armaş v ÎS Compania Aeriană "Air Moldova"* the Supreme Court agreed with the

19 Chapter V.

20 Item 16(a), (b) and (c).

21 Items 25 and 26 and Item 16.

22 Item 17.

23 Raport de expertiza anticoruptie 'asupra nivelului coruptibilităţii proiectului de hotărâre a Guvernului cu privire la modificarea Hotărârii Guvernului pentru aprobarea Regulamentului privind compensarea şi asistenţa pasagerilor în eventualitatea refuzului la îmbarcare şi anulării sau întârzierii prelungite a zborurilor' (13 October 2015) <https://old.cna.md/public/files/raport_expertiza/rea_compensare_calatori_avia.pdf> accessed 11 December 2025.

first-instance court's decision to deny moral damages on top of the fixed compensation due to the lack of sufficient evidence to support the claim.[24]

Passengers are entitled to compensation of 250 euros for flights of a distance of up to 1,500 km. For flights between 1,500 and 3,500 km, the amount increases to 400 euros. Finally, for flights over 3,500 km, the compensation is 600 euros.[25] The amount of compensation can be divided in half if passengers are offered an alternative flight which arrives at the final destination no later than two hours for flights of less than 1,500 km, three hours for flights between 1,500 and 3,500 km, and four hours for flights longer than 3,500 km.[26] The distance is measured through the great circle route method.[27]

Flight Distance	**Standard Compensation**	**Reduced Compensation (50%) Conditions and New Arrival Time**
Up to 1,500 km (e.g., Chişinău to Istanbul)	250€.	If alternative flight arrives at destination **less than 2 hours** later than original arrival time.
1,500 km to 3,500 km (e.g., Chişinău to Paris)	400€.	If alternative flight arrives at destination **less than 3 hours** later than original arrival time.
Over 3,500 km (e.g., Chişinău to New York)	600€.	If alternative flight arrives at destination **less than 4 hours** later than original arrival time.

When an airline is responsible for a flight disruption, passengers are given the right to choose how they wish to proceed according to Chapter VI. They can either receive a full refund for the unused portions of their ticket within seven days and a return flight to their original departure point at the earliest opportunity, or they can be re-routed to their final destination.[28] This re-routing can happen at the earliest possible time or at a later date that is more convenient for them, depending on seat availability.[29] This right to a refund also applies to passengers who booked their flights as part of a package tour, unless the tour regulations state otherwise.[30] Additionally, if a city or region has multiple airports, the

24 Dosarul nr. 2ra-1483/2019.
25 Item 18(a), (b), and (c).
26 Item 19(a), (b), and (c).
27 Item 21.
28 Item 22(a) and (b).
29 Item 22(b) and (c).
30 Item 23.

airline may offer a flight to a different, nearby airport, provided the passenger agrees to the change.[31]

During a flight disruption, airlines are obligated to provide passengers with free service.[32] This includes offering meals and refreshments that are appropriate for the length of the waiting time.[33] If the delay extends to the point where an overnight stay becomes necessary, the airline must also cover the cost of a hotel room and transport between the airport and the accommodation.[34] Furthermore, passengers are entitled to two free phone calls or emails.[35] It is also a requirement that the airline gives special consideration and attention to the needs of passengers with reduced mobility and children travelling alone.[36]

Upgrading made by the airline must be done without any additional payment. Conversely, in the event of downgrading, the airline must reimburse a percentage of the ticket cost within seven days. The refund amount is 30% for flights up to 1,500 km, 50% for flights between 1,500 and 3,500 km, and 75% for all flights longer than that.[37]

Airlines are also under the obligation to inform passengers of their rights, as found in Chapter XII. At the check-in area, they must prominently display a notice that tells passengers to ask for a document outlining their rights to compensation and assistance if their flight is denied boarding, cancelled, or delayed by at least two hours. Beyond this general notice, the airline must also provide a written document directly to every passenger affected by such a disruption. This notice must clearly detail the rules for receiving compensation and assistance as outlined in the regulation, and it must also include the contact information for the official body responsible for handling passenger complaints. For passengers who are blind or visually impaired, the airline must use a suitable alternative method to ensure they receive all the same information.[38]

Like Regulation 261, there is no fixed penalty amount provided in Decision 386. Instead, the Decision requires the Ministry of Economy and Infrastructure to adopt the necessary measures to ensure respect for passenger rights.[39]

Interestingly in 2025, the Civil Aviation Authority of the Republic of Moldova launched a national information campaign to raise public

31 Item 24.
32 Chapter VII.
33 Item 25(a).
34 Item 25(b) and (c).
35 Item 26.
36 Item 27.
37 Item 29(a), (b) and (c).
38 Chapter XII.
39 Item 43.

awareness about passengers' rights.[40] There is also a Bill amending the Law on Civil Liability and Insurance Requirements for Air Operators and Aircraft Operators and providing an increase in civil liability for damages caused by delays from 5,346 SDR to 6,303 SDR per passenger and an increase in case of delay or damage to luggage from 1,288 SDR to 1,519 SDR per passenger.[41] The interaction between this proposed legislation and Decision 386 regarding delays is not at all clear, however, it might be clarified within the legislative process.

Moldova's Decision 386 of 2012 is a direct transposition of EU Regulation 261, meaning its core provisions on compensation, re-routing, and assistance for denied boarding, cancellations, and long delays are the same. Both laws specify the same monetary compensation amounts (€250, €400, €600) based on flight distance and establish the same thresholds for triggering assistance (e.g., a three-hour delay for compensation). However, the omission of the preamble and the lack of inclusion of any definition of the concept of "exceptional" renders the Decision less accessible to passengers. Based on the Supreme Court case it seems that Moldovan law is entirely aligned with the EU case law and a narrow interpretation of "exceptional" circumstances is applicable. The major positive aspect of this law is the express inclusion of compensation for passengers suffering from a long delay, which strengthens passengers' rights.

Comparison with EU Regulation

Feature	**Decision N°836**	**EU Regulation 261/2004**
Delay Compensation	≥3h: €250–€600 (by distance).	≥3h: €250–€600 (by distance).
Cancellation Notice	<14d notice: Refund or re-routing + €250–600 compensation (by distance).	<14d notice: Refund or re-routing + €250–600 compensation (by distance).
Denied Boarding	Volunteer first; €250–€600 (by distance) if denied boarding.	Volunteer first; €250–€600 (by distance) if denied boarding.
Baggage Liability	1,519 SDR.	Not specified.

40 Civil Aviation Authority, 'The Civil Aviation Authority Launches the Awareness Campaign "Know Your Rights, Claim Them!"' (10 July 2025) 1 <https://www.caa.md/index.php/en/press-releases/civil-aviation-authority-launches-awareness-campaign-know-your-rights-claim-them> accessed 11 December 2025.

41 Eliza Mihalache, 'Airline Passengers Will Receive Higher Compensation for Baggage and Delays' (*Moldova 1*, 20 February 2025) <https://moldova1.md/p/44378> accessed 11 December 2025.

Bibliography

- Republica Moldova, Guvernal, Hotarare Nr. HG 889 of 12.09.18, MO347-357/14.09.18 <https://www.legis.md/cautare/getResults?doc_id=109063&lang=ro> accessed 11 December 2025.
- Dosarul nr. 2ra-1483/2019 Prima instanţă, Judecătoria Chişinău, Instanţa de apel, Curtea de Apel Chişinău, Decision of 2 October 2019 <https://jurisprudenta.csj.md/search_col_civil.php?id=53051> accessed 11 December 2025.
- Civil Aviation Authority, 'The Civil Aviation Authority Launches the Awareness Campaign "Know Your Rights, Claim Them!"' (10 July 2025) <https://www.caa.md/index.php/en/press-releases/civil-aviation-authority-launches-awareness-campaign-know-your-rights-claim-them> accessed 11 December 2025.
- Raport de expertiza anticoruptie 'asupra nivelului coruptibilităţii proiectului de hotărâre a Guvernului cu privire la modificarea Hotărârii Guvernului pentru aprobarea Regulamentului privind compensarea şi asistenţa pasagerilor în eventualitatea refuzului la îmbarcare şi anulării sau întârzierii prelungite a zborurilor' (13 October 2015) <https://old.cna.md/public/files/raport_expertiza/rea_compensare_calatori_avia.pdf> accessed 11 December 2025.
- Mihalache, E., 'Airline Passengers Will Receive Higher Compensation for Baggage and Delays' (*Moldova 1*, 20 February 2025) <https://moldova1.md/p/44378> accessed 11 December 2025.

II.31

Montenegro

The Law on Obligations and Basics of Proprietary Right in Air Transport[1] (*Zakon o obligacionim i osnovnim svojinskim odnosima u vazdušnom saobraćaju*) is the main piece of legislation in Montenegro that governs key legal aspects of air travel. Originally published in 2011, it has been amended in 2014 and 2018. It is heavily influenced by international conventions, primarily the Chicago Convention of 1944 and the Montreal Convention of 1999, which Montenegro is a party to as well as Regulation 261 through the ECAA agreement.[2]

Article 1 lays out the purpose and scope of the law. It clarifies that the law regulates both contractual obligations and proprietary rights in air transport. The general provisions on contract are found in Part 2 which defines the contract of air carriage,[3] its forms, and the application of international conventions. Article 5 addresses a passenger's right to cancel their trip and receive a refund. A passenger can receive a full refund if they cancel at least 24 hours before a domestic flight or 48 hours before an international one.[4] The airline can retain a small 10% of the fare for this service.[5] However, if a passenger is unable to travel due to a serious illness or death of the passenger or an immediate family member or companion without whom the passenger cannot travel, they are entitled to a full refund with only a minimal 2% fee, provided they notify the airline before the flight.[6] If the impediment to travel arises during the transport, the

1 'Law on Obligations and Basics of Property Right in Air Transport', SI.I CG br (Official Gazette of Montenegro) No. 18/2011, with amendments by SI.I. CG br. N° 46/2014 and 43/2018.

2 'Law on amendments to the Law on ratification of the Multilateral Agreement on establishing the European Common Aviation Area (ECAA Agreement)' SI.I CG br. (Official Gazette of the Republic of Montenegro) No 62/2007 and "Official Gazette of Montenegro – international treaties" No 1/2011.

3 Article 3.

4 Article 5(2).

5 Article 5(3).

6 Article 5(4) and (5).

DOI: 10.4324/9781003746164-42

transport fee shall be refunded in proportion to the unused part of the journey.[7]

Part 2 is the most critical part of the text, setting out passenger protections in case of denied boarding, cancellations, and delays. This part only applies to passengers travelling from or arriving at airports located on the territory of Montenegro.[8] For flights arriving at a Montenegrin airport, they must be operated by Montenegrin air carriers and the passengers must not have obtained compensation in the other territory.[9] The law only applies to passengers having a confirmed reservation and those having presented themselves for check-in in accordance with the procedures and at the time specified in advance and in writing by the air carrier, tour operator, or authorized travel agent. If no specific check-in time is provided, passengers must check in no later than 45 minutes prior to the published departure time.[10] It also applies if they are transferred by the air carrier or tour operator from the flight for which they had reservations to another flight, regardless of the reason.[11] Like other regulations, this law does not apply to passengers travelling free of charge.[12]

When an airline expects to deny boarding, it is required to first request volunteers to give up their seats in return for a negotiated benefit.[13] Those passengers are entitled to the rights set out in Article 11, namely a right to refund or re-routing. If there are insufficient volunteers, the airline may proceed to involuntarily deny boarding to some passengers and must promptly provide compensation and additional assistance, such as meals and alternative travel arrangements.[14]

In the event of a cancellation, passengers are entitled to a refund or re-routing, compensation, as well as care and assistance.[15] Article 7 contains a similar wording as Regulation 261, namely an airline is not required to pay compensation if it notifies passengers in advance, at least two weeks before the scheduled departure time.[16] If passengers were informed at least seven days in advance and they were offered a route change allowing them to depart not more than one hour before the original departure time and arrive within two hours after the original arrival time, then compensation

7 Article 5(6).
8 Article 3 of the 2014 amendment, amending Article 9(2).
9 Article 3 of the 2014 amendment.
10 Article 9(2)(a).
11 Article 9(2)(b).
12 Article 9(5).
13 Article 6(1).
14 Article 6(3) and (4).
15 Article 7(1)(a), (b) and (c).
16 Article 7(1)(c).

is not due.[17] Unlike Regulation 261, the law did not include any possibility to cancel a flight less than seven days before the original departure time without paying any compensation. In the event of flight cancellation, the air carrier shall inform passengers of alternative transport options.[18] The airline is also not liable for compensation if the cancellation was caused by extraordinary circumstances, and it is the airline's burden to prove that it informed the passengers of the cancellation.[19] The law itself does not provide an exhaustive list but defines these extraordinary circumstances by their core characteristic: They are events that are beyond the control of the air carrier and could not have been avoided even if all reasonable measures had been taken.

The law details the assistance an airline must provide for a delayed flight. This includes meals and refreshments as well as two free phone calls, fax, messages, or emails for flights with a delay of two hours or more for flights under 1,500 km.[20] For delays of three hours or more for flights between 1,500 km and 3,500 km in addition to the meals and refreshment and phone calls, the passenger is entitled to hotel accommodation when the actual expected departure time is at least one day after the previously announced departure time.[21] For four hours or more and all other flights, passengers are entitled to all the care in Article 12.[22] In the event of a delay of at least five hours, they are also entitled to a refund of the fare.[23]

Article 10 sets out the specific amounts of compensation that passengers are entitled to for denied boarding or cancellations, which are based on flight distance: 250 euros for flights up to 1,500 km, 400 euros for flights between 1,500 km and 3,500 km, and 600 euros for all other flights.[24] This amount may be reduced by 50% if the airline offers an alternative flight whose actual arrival time does not exceed the originally scheduled arrival time by two hours in the case of flights of up to 1,500 km, by three hours in the case of flights between 1,500 km and 3,500 km, and by four hours for all other flights.[25] The distance is to be determined using the great circle route method.[26]

17 Article 7(1) (c).
18 Article 7(2).
19 Article 7(3) and (4).
20 Article 8(a) coupled with Article 12, paragraph 1, point a, and paragraph 2.
21 Article 8(b) coupled with Article 12, paragraph 1, point a, b, c, and paragraph 2.
22 Article 8(c).
23 Article 8(c).
24 Article 10(1)(a), (b) and (c).
25 Article 10(3)(a)–(c).
26 Article 10(5).

Flight Distance	Standard Compensation	Reduced Compensation (50%) Condition
Up to 1,500 km.	250€.	If alternative flight arrives **less than 2 hours** after the original arrival time.
1,500 km to 3,500 km.	400€.	If alternative flight arrives **less than 3 hours** after the original arrival time.
Over 3,500 km.	600€.	If alternative flight arrives **less than 4 hours** after the original arrival time.

In case of downgrading, the airline must refund a specific percentage of the ticket price within seven days. This amount is based on the flight's distance: 30% for short-haul, 50% for medium-haul, and 75% for long-haul flights.[27] The law also includes provisions for the rights of passengers with reduced mobility,[28] the right to seek additional compensation,[29] and the airline's right to seek reimbursement from other parties.[30] Article 17 places a clear obligation on airlines to inform passengers of their rights. Airlines must post a written notice at check-in desks and hand out a written notice to passengers who are denied boarding, or whose flights are cancelled or delayed by two hours or more. Overall, this section of Montenegro's law provides a clear and comprehensive framework for protecting air passenger rights, demonstrating a strong alignment with the standards established by the European Union's Regulation 261.

Interestingly, in the 2014 amendment a full section on rights of persons with disabilities and reduced mobility was added. Article 36a states that persons with disabilities or reduced mobility have the right to assistance at any airport in Montenegro, whether they are arriving, departing, or in transit.[31] This right is supplementary to, and does not replace, other passenger rights for denied boarding or cancellations.[32] Airlines or their agents are explicitly forbidden from refusing a reservation or boarding to a person with a disability.[33] Article 36c outlines the only acceptable reasons an airline can deny a reservation or boarding to a person with a disability which can be divided into two categories: safety and physical constraints.[34] In these cases, the airline must offer an alternative transport option and

27 Article 13(2)(a), (b) and (c).
28 Article 14.
29 Article 15.
30 Article 16.
31 As reiterated in Article 36(i).
32 Article 36a(3).
33 Article 36b(1) and (2).
34 Article 36c(1) and (2).

provide a written explanation for the refusal upon request. The airline can also require an able-bodied escort to travel with the person if safety demands it.[35] Airports must designate clear, accessible, and marked points for passengers to announce their arrival and request assistance.[36] Airport management is required to provide assistance free of charge, as long as the airline is informed of the person's special needs for such assistance at least 48 hours before the published departure time of the flight.[37] This includes: assistance with check-in and baggage drop-off, to proceed to custom control and security check, boarding and de-planing using lifts or wheelchairs, collecting baggage and moving from the baggage claim area, and with movement within the aircraft cabin to their seat.[38]

Responsible Party	Key Obligations
Airline	• **Non-discrimination:** Cannot refuse booking/boarding to a PRM with a valid ticket. • **Notification:** Must inform the airport of a PRM's need for assistance **at least 36h** before the flight. • **Onboard:** Must carry guide dogs and mobility equipment (up to 2 pieces, including electric wheelchairs). • **Seating:** Must make reasonable efforts to seat a PRM with their companion.
Airport Management	• **Free Assistance:** Must provide all assistance **free of charge** to the passenger. • **Designated Points:** Must have clear, accessible points where PRMs can request help. • **Full Journey Help:** Must assist from curb to gate (and vice versa), including check-in, security, boarding (with lifts if needed), de-planing, baggage claim, and transit. • **Equipment:** Must provide a temporary replacement if a wheelchair is damaged or lost.

Aspect of Assistance	What Is Provided?	Key Conditions
Designated Points	Clearly marked, accessible points **inside and outside** terminal buildings to announce arrival and request assistance.	Must be clearly signed and readily available.
Check-In and Baggage	Assistance with the check-in process and dropping off baggage.	Assistance is provided free of charge.

(Continued)

35 Article 36c(2) and (4).
36 Article 36d.
37 Article 36f.
38 Article 36m.

(Continued)

Aspect of Assistance	What Is Provided?	Key Conditions
Through the Terminal	Help to proceed through customs, immigration (border control), and security checkpoints.	Assistance is provided free of charge.
Boarding the Aircraft	Assistance with boarding the plane, which may include the use of wheelchairs, lifts, or ambulifts.	The airline must be notified of the need **at least 48 hours** before the flight's departure.
Onboard the Aircraft	Help to move within the aircraft cabin to reach their assigned seat.	
De-planing	Assistance with leaving the aircraft upon arrival, using necessary equipment.	
Baggage Reclaim	Help with collecting baggage and moving from the baggage claim area to a designated point.	
Transit Assistance	Full assistance for passengers who are transiting through a Montenegrin airport.	Applies to arriving, departing, and transiting passengers.
Cost	**All assistance is provided free of charge.**	The passenger must **not** be charged for this mandatory assistance.

If a wheelchair, other mobility equipment, or aids are lost or damaged during the provision of services at the airport or during air transport, the passenger shall be entitled to compensation in accordance with this law and the relevant international agreement.[39] For airports with over 150,000 annual passengers, the law mandates the establishment of quality standards for assistance, which must align with international best practices.[40] This amendment showcases Montenegro's alignment with EU regulations (particularly EC Regulation 1107/2006).

Part 3 is dedicated to the execution of the passenger transport contract and implements rules from the Montreal Convention such as the liability of the transport contractor. Part 4 deals with the air carrier liability and includes the compensation limits as found in the Montreal Convention. For instance, the limit of 4,150 SDRs per passenger for damages caused by delays to be converted into local currency.[41]

39 Article 36k.
40 Article 36h.
41 Article 27(4).

The law contains provisions on baggage and personal items expressly stipulating that passengers can bring carry-on baggage free of charge, but they are personally responsible for it. The airline sets the size and weight limits and can refuse items that are dangerous or unsuitable for the cabin.[42] The airline is only liable for damage, loss, or destruction of carry-on baggage if the passenger can prove it was caused by the airline's fault. However, if the damage occurs due to a plane crash, the airline is liable unless it can prove it took all necessary measures to prevent it.[43] While such rules are found in other countries, such as Kazakhstan, it is a positive step for a country to include a specific rule on carry-on baggage allowance. The law includes a similar rule for checked baggage and establishes the compensation threshold capped at 1,000 SDRs per passenger, unless the passenger made a special declaration of a higher value.[44]

The text also contains a part on the legal responsibilities of ground handling service and how the liability is divided between airlines and third-party ground handling companies.[45] A ground handling company is only responsible for higher liability than required by law if it has expressly agreed to it in the airline's contract.[46] Any clause in a ground handling contract that attempts to reduce the ground handler's liability as defined by this law is null and void.[47]

Specific time limits for different types of claims are set out in Article 131, ranging from one year for claims from commercial air activities to five years for insurance contract claims. Claims arising from a transport contract and related claims for recourse expire after two years.

Fixed penalties were imposed by the 2014 amendment in Article 182a. The fines are tiered based on who is held responsible: The air carrier itself, as a legal entity, faces the highest fines: €2,000 to €10,000 for violation such as failure to offer re-routing or compensation in case denial of boarding, cancellations, and delays.[48] A responsible person within the airline or another legal entity (e.g., a manager) can be personally fined €300 to €1,000,[49] an entrepreneur can be fined €300 to €3,000,[50] and finally, a natural person, such as an individual agent, can be fined €150 to €1,000.[51]

42 Article 34.
43 Article 35.
44 Article 38.
45 Articles 89 and 90.
46 Article 91.
47 Article 92.
48 Article 182a(1).
49 Article 182a(2).
50 Article 182a(3).
51 Article 182a(4).

Category	Offense Numbers	Description of the Offense
Denied Boarding (Overbooking)	1, 2	• Failure to first call for volunteers to give up their seats when overbooking is expected. • If involuntary denial occurs, failure to immediately pay compensation (Art. 10), provide re-routing/refund (Art. 11), and care (Art. 12).
Flight Cancellation	3, 4, 5, 6	• Failure to provide a refund or re-routing (Art. 11). • Failure to provide care (meals, hotel, etc.) (Art. 12). • Failure to pay compensation (Art. 10). • Failure to inform passengers about alternative transport options.
Long Delay	7, 8, 9	• For delays of 2+ hours on flights up to 1,500 km, failure to provide meals, refreshments, as required by the length of delay and flight distance. • For delays of 3+ hours on flights 1,500 km–3,500 km, failure to provide meals, refreshments, and hotel accommodation as required by the length of delay and flight distance. • For delays of 4+ hours on flights exceeding 3,500 km, failure to provide meals, refreshments, and hotel accommodation if the delay stretches into the next day. • For very long delays (5+ hours on long-haul), failure to also offer a refund.
Downgrading	10	Failure to reimburse 30–75% of the ticket price within 7 days if a passenger is moved to a lower class.
Priority and PRM Rights	11, 15, 17, 18, 19, 20, 21	• Failure to give priority boarding to PRMs, companions, guide dogs, and unaccompanied children. • Refused reservation or boarding to a person with a disability who has a valid ticket. • Failure to allow a guide dog in the cabin. • Failure to transport mobility equipment (up to 2 pieces per PRM), provided they were notified 48h in advance and safety rules are met. • Failure to provide accessible information, adequate seating, toilet access, and a seat for a companion, if possible.
Passenger Communication	12, 14	• In case of disruption, failure to provide a written notice explaining rights and how to claim them. • At the point of sale, failure to inform passengers about the airline's liability and deadlines for complaints.

(Continued)

(Continued)

Category	Offense Numbers	Description of the Offense
Claims and Advance Payments	13	After an accident, failure to make an advance payment (within 15 days) to cover immediate economic needs.
PRM Coordination	16	Failure to notify the airport (at least 36h before departure) of a PRM's need for assistance.

Article 182b deals with airport management or other legal entities which can face fines ranging from 2,000 to 10,000 euros for failing to meet their obligations to passengers with disabilities or reduced mobility.[52] Similar to the airline penalties, responsible individuals within airport management can also be fined between 300 and 1,000 euros and natural persons from 150 to 1,000 euros.[53]

Offense Category	Offense Numbers	Description of the Offense
Assistance Points and Information	1, 18	• Failure to designate clear, accessible **assistance points** inside/outside terminals. • Failure to allow **guide dogs** and provide **accessible flight information**.
Full Journey Assistance	2, 3, 4, 5, 11, 12, 14	Failure to provide assistance for PRMs throughout their entire airport journey, including: • From **arrival point to assistance request point**. • From **assistance point to check-in** and **through check-in/baggage drop**. • From **check-in to the gate** (through security, border control). • From **baggage claim to a meeting point** (including baggage retrieval and arrival formalities). • Access to **toilet facilities**.
Aircraft Boarding and De-planing	6, 7, 8, 9, 10	Failure to provide assistance for PRMs related to the aircraft, including: • **Boarding** and **de-planing** using lifts/equipment. • Moving from **aircraft door to seat** and back. • **Stowing and retrieving** carry-on baggage onboard.

(Continued)

52 Article 182b(1).
53 Article 182b(2) and (4).

(Continued)

Offense Category	Offense Numbers	Description of the Offense
Transit Assistance	13	Fail to provide assistance for PRMs in **transit** to reach connecting flights (including between terminals).
Specific Situations and Equipment	15, 16, 17	• Failure to assist a **person accompanying a PRM**. • Failure to provide **ground handling with mobility equipment** (e.g., electric wheelchairs). • Failure to provide a **temporary replacement** for damaged/lost mobility equipment.

Fine amounts

Violator	Fine Range
Air Carrier (Legal Entity).	**€2,000 to €10,000.**
Airport Management (Legal Entity).	**€2,000 to €10,000.**
Responsible Person (e.g., Manager).	**€300 to €1,000.**
Entrepreneur (Preduzetnik).	**€300 to €3,000.**
Natural Person (e.g., Agent).	**€150 to €1,000.**

Montenegro's Law on Obligations and Basics of Proprietary Right in Air Transport represents a comprehensive and ambitious piece of legislation that closely mirrors the European Union's Regulation 261, especially regarding passenger rights. While the law faithfully adopts the core entitlements for denied boarding, cancellation, and long delays such as the right to care (refreshments and accommodation), re-routing or refund, and compensation, it also includes a detailed inclusion of rights for persons with reduced mobility (PRMs), which goes beyond the core focus of Regulation 261. By integrating principles from EU Regulation 1107/2006 directly into its national text, Montenegro has created a more holistic passenger rights framework. The most significant divergence lies in the conditions for exemption from compensation in case of cancellation. While Regulation 261 allows for exemption with notice of less than two weeks if passengers are re-routed and arrive within a specific time window (e.g., less than two hours for short-haul flights), the Montenegrin law is arguably more passenger-friendly. It explicitly states that no exemption from compensation is possible if passengers are notified less than seven days before the scheduled departure time, removing the airline's ability to avoid payment through last-minute re-routing. This creates a stricter liability regime for late cancellations than exists in the EU.

Another key difference lies in the specific and very structured financial penalty regime. The Montenegrin law imposes fines on airlines and airport managers for non-compliance, with specific monetary values assigned to different violations. These fines are levied by the Montenegrin Civil Aviation Agency, whereas Regulation 261 holds airlines directly accountable to passengers and allows passengers to pursue claims through national enforcement bodies or courts.

In conclusion, Montenegro's law is not a mere copy of Regulation 261 but a sophisticated legal adaptation that successfully integrates its core principles while making deliberate enhancements. It is, in several aspects, more detailed and passenger-friendly, particularly regarding last-minute cancellations and the rights of persons with reduced mobility. By combining the tenets of Regulation 261 with those of Regulation 1107/2006 and elements of the Montreal Convention, Montenegro has established a robust, self-contained, and modern legal framework for air passenger rights that stands up favourably to comparison with the EU's own regulations.

Comparison with EU Regulation

Feature	Law on Obligations and Basics of Proprietary Right in Air Transport	EU Regulation 261/2004
Delay Compensation	≥3h: €250–€600 (by distance).	≥3h: €250–€600 (by distance).
Cancellation Notice	<14d notice: Refund or re-routing + €250–600 compensation (by distance).	<14d notice: Refund or re-routing + €250–600 compensation (by distance).
Denied Boarding	Volunteer first; €250–€600 (by distance) if denied boarding.	Volunteer first; €250–€600 (by distance) if denied boarding.
Baggage Liability	1,000 SDR.	Not specified.

Bibliography

- 'Law on Obligations and Basics of Property Right in Air Transport', SI.I CG br. (Official Gazette of Montenegro) No. 18/2011.
- 'Law on amendments to the Law on ratification of the Multilateral Agreement on establishing the European Common Aviation Area (ECAA Agreement)' SI.I CG br. (Official Gazette of the Republic of Montenegro) No 62/2007 and "Official Gazette of Montenegro – international treaties" No 1/2011.
- 'Decree on the proclamation of the law on amendments to the Law on Obligations and Basics of Property Right in Air Transport' SI.I. CG br. N° 46/2014, adopted 16 October 2014 <https://www.caa.me/sites/default/files/zakon_o_izmjenama_i_dopunama_zakona_o_obligacionim.pdf> accessed 11 December 2025.

- 'Decree on the Proclamation of the Law on Amendments to the Law on Obligations and Basics of Property Right in Air Transport' SI.I. CG br. N° 43/2018, adopted on 26 June 2018 <https://www.caa.me/sites/default/files/zakon_o_izmjenama_zakona_o_obligacionim_odnosima_i_osnovama_svojinsko-pravnih_odnosa_u_vazdusnom_saobracaju_2.pdf> accessed 11 December 2025.

II.32

Morocco

Law No. 40.13 on the Civil Aviation Code, adopted by Parliament in 2016, is a cornerstone instrument for civil aviation in Morocco.[1] It provides the overarching legal structure for nearly all civil aviation activities in Morocco, from air navigation and safety to personnel licensing and passenger rights. It is the fundamental national law that governs the sector.

The Moroccan Civil Aviation Code includes provisions for passenger compensation and assistance in cases of denied boarding, flight cancellations, or significant delays in its Title VIII. It aims to align Moroccan regulations with international standards, particularly those of the European Union, to meet the requirements of the Euro-Mediterranean Aviation Agreement.[2] The Code contains general provisions on the contract of transport, as well as the implementation of the Montreal Convention.[3] However, the limits found in the Convention are not implemented in the Code itself.

While the Civil Aviation Code contains provisions on delays, cancellations, and denial of boarding, it makes it clear that the specific and detailed rules for passenger rights, including compensation for flight disruptions, must be introduced by subsequent regulatory texts.[4] However, such a regulation has not yet been enacted.[5]

1 Loi n°40-13 portant Code de l'aviation civile, Royaume du Maroc, Bulletin Officiel N° 6474, 16 hija 1438 (7 September 2017). See: Aeronautique.ma, 'Maroc: Le code de l'aviation civile fait peau neuve' (*Aeronautique.ma*, 26 June 2016) <https://www.aeronautique.ma/Maroc-Le-code-de-l-aviation-civile-fait-peau-neuve_a4266.html> accessed 11 December 2025.

2 Samira Benboubker, 'Les droits des passagers aériens: la transposition du droit européen adaptéee au secteur du transport aérien marocain' <https://samirabenboubker.com/les-droits-des-passagers-aeriens-la-transposition-du-droit-europeen-adaptee-au-secteur-du-transport-aerien-marocain/> accessed 11 December 2025.

3 Article 206 and following.

4 L'observateur, 'Passagers aériens. Bientôt de nouvelles règles d'indemnisation' (4 June 2024) <https://lobservateur.info/article/110922/economie/passagers-aeriens-bientot-de-nouvelles-regles-dindemnisation> accessed 11 December 2025.

5 L'observateur, 'Passagers aériens. Bientôt de nouvelles règles d'indemnisation' (4 June 2024) <https://lobservateur.info/article/110922/economie/passagers-aeriens-bientot-de-

DOI: 10.4324/9781003746164-43

Article 222 regulates denial of boarding in a similar manner as Regulation 261/2004. First, the airline must call for volunteers to give up their reservations in exchange for certain benefits, according to terms to be agreed between the passengers concerned and the air carrier. In addition to those benefits, volunteers shall receive assistance under the conditions set out in Article 223, including meals, accommodation, and communications. Where the number of volunteers is not sufficient to allow the other passengers with reservations to board, the air carrier may refuse to board passengers without their agreement. In this case, the air carrier shall immediately compensate them in accordance with Article 230 and provide them with assistance under the conditions and in accordance with the procedures laid down by regulation.[6] This is a literal transposition of Regulation 261.

Flight cancellation and delays are found in Article 223. Unfortunately, the Code itself does not clearly define cancellation or delays.[7] In the event of flight cancellation or delay, passengers are entitled to compensation and assistance as established in a subsequent regulation. However, according to Samira Benboubker, there is a discrepancy between the Arabic and French versions, whereby the word "compensation" has been omitted in the Arabic version.[8] This discrepancy creates a legal uncertainty as to the application of Article 223. In her opinion, the French version prevails due to its anterior nature as well as its conformity with Regulation 261.

The care and attention given to passengers with special needs or reduced mobility or unaccompanied children must be adequate for their needs.[9] The law also mandates the exact text that must be printed and displayed in the check-in area, along the lines of

> If you are denied boarding or if your flight is cancelled or delayed by at least two hours, ask at the check-in counter or boarding gate for the text setting out your rights, in particular with regard to compensation and assistance.[10]

When passengers are informed of the cancellation of a flight by the carrier, they shall be provided with information on other possible flights at no additional cost.[11] The obligation to compensate does not apply when the event was caused by an "extraordinary circumstance."[12] Extraordinary

---

nouvelles-regles-dindemnisation> accessed 11 December 2025; Zineb Jazouli, 'Un nouveau texte réglementaire en préparation pour indemniser les voyageurs aériens' (2 June 2024) <https://fr.hespress.com/370604-un-nouveau-texte-reglementaire-en-preparation-pour-indemniser-les-voyageurs-aeriens.html> accessed 11 December 2025.

6 Article 222.

7 Benboubker (n 2).

8 Benboubker (n 2).

9 Article 227.

10 Article 217(3).

11 Article 224.

12 Article 225.

circumstances for the purposes of Article 225 include events that may occur in particular in the event of public order measures, weather conditions incompatible with the performance of the flight concerned, risks related to flight safety, and unforeseen technical failures that may affect flight safety. The same applies in cases where administrative measures are taken or if the necessary means for carrying out flights under appropriate conditions are not provided.[13]

Category of Extraordinary Circumstance	**Examples**
Political and Security	Public order measures, security risks.
Meteorological	Weather conditions incompatible with the safe operation of the flight.
Technical and Safety	Unforeseen technical failures that affect flight safety.
Operational	Administrative measures or failure to provide necessary means for carrying out flights.

Chapter II contains the rules on upgrading and downgrading which mirror the EU Regulation; no additional payment can be required in case of upgrading.[14] In case of downgrading, the airline must refund a specific percentage of the ticket price within seven days. This amount is based on the flight's distance: 30% for short-haul, 50% for medium-haul, and 75% for long-haul flights.[15] Interestingly, Article 222 on denial of boarding refers to Article 230 for indenization which seems to suggest that instead of adopting the European approach of fixed-amount compensation (e.g., €250, €400, €600) for all eligible disruptions, the Moroccan legislation has chosen more flexibility by offering compensation based on the price of the ticket and the flight distance. This selective transposition reflects a deliberate policy choice to balance robust passenger protection with the economic realities and development goals of the national aviation industry.

Flight Distance	**Refund Required**
1,500 km or less (short-haul).	30% of the ticket price.
1,500 km–3,500 km (medium-haul).	50% of the ticket price.
More than 3,500 km (long-haul).	75% of the ticket price.

The provision on the imposition of fines in the Civil Aviation Code is much more detailed than under Regulation 261. Article 231 mentions

13 Article 226 paragraph 2.
14 Article 230 paragraph 1.
15 Article 230 Paragraphs 2(1), (2) and (3).

that the fines vary depending on the type and gravity of the violation. Low-class violation only attracts a warning, then an administrative fine between 10,000 and 50,000 dirhams per violations.[16] In more serious cases, the licence of the airline might be revoked temporarily or definitively in case the airlines commit three violations within the same year.[17] Finally, Article 217 requires the airlines to inform passengers of their rights as well as the available procedures.[18]

The Moroccan Civil Aviation Code (Law 40.13) represents a significant and deliberate effort to modernize the kingdom's aviation sector and align its passenger protection standards with international benchmarks, particularly the European Union's Regulation 261. However, there is a fundamental dichotomy between the two frameworks: while the Moroccan law is inspired by the European model and shares its protective aspirations, it remains a nascent and incomplete system that currently offers a notably lower level of practical certainty and enforceable passenger rights. The most critical distinction lies in the legal nature of the two instruments. EU Regulation 261 is a directly applicable and self-executing regulation. Its provisions are precise, detailing exact compensation amounts, clearly defined delay thresholds, and specific procedures, which creates uniform legal certainty across all Member States. In stark contrast, the Moroccan Code is an enabling framework law. It successfully establishes broad principles and outlines a structure for rights similar to the EU's – such as obligations of care in the event of denied boarding, cancellation, or delay – but it consistently defers the crucial specifics to future implementing regulations. These detailed rules, particularly those defining the exact compensation amounts and the precise conditions for their application, have not yet been enacted. This absence creates a state of legal limbo, rendering the core promise of compensation vague and largely unenforceable for passengers, thereby significantly weakening the law's practical effectiveness.

Moroccan law, through its reference to Article 230, suggests a move towards a flexible model based on a percentage of the ticket price. While this may offer adaptability to the local economic context, it risks resulting in derisory compensation sums for passengers holding low-cost fares and undermines the financial deterrent effect on airlines that the EU's fixed sums create. Adding to this uncertainty is a significant legal discrepancy within the Moroccan Code itself, where the Arabic and French versions

16 Article 231(1) and (2).

17 Article 231(3) and (4).

18 See: Association Régionale des Agences de Voyages de Casablanca, 'Guide du passager aérien' (2018) <https://aravcs-travel.com/ittaki_allah_meda/Droits-Passager-Aerien.pdf> accessed 11 December 2025.

of Article 223 conflict on the very existence of a right to compensation for cancellations and delays. This law is a good step forward but in desperate need for further clarifications.

Comparison with EU Regulation

Feature	**Law 40.13**	**EU Regulation 261/2004**
Delay Compensation	Not specified.	**≥3h:** €250–€600 (by distance).
Cancellation Notice	Not specified.	<14d notice: Refund or re-routing + €250–600 compensation (by distance).
Denied Boarding	Volunteer first; compensation if denied boarding.	Volunteer first; €250–€600 (by distance) if denied boarding.
Baggage Liability	Not specified.	Not specified.

Bibliography

- Loi n°40-13 portant Code de l'aviation civile, Royaume du Maroc, Bulletin Officiel N° 6474, 16 hija 1438 (7 September 2017) <https://archive.gazettes.africa/archive/ma/2017/ma-bulletin-officiel-dated-2017-09-07-no-6602.pdf> accessed 11 December 2025.
- Aeronautique.ma, 'Maroc: Le code de l'aviation civile fait peau neuve' (*Aeronautique.ma*, 26 June 2016) <https://www.aeronautique.ma/Maroc-Le-code-de-l-aviation-civile-fait-peau-neuve_a4266.html> accessed 11 December 2025.
- Association Régionale des Agences de Voyages de Casablanca, 'Guide du passager aérien' (2018) <https://aravcs-travel.com/ittaki_allah_meda/Droits-Passager-Aerien.pdf> accessed 11 December 2025.
- Benboubker, S., 'Les droits des passagers aériens: la transposition du droit européen adaptéee au secteur du transport aérien marocain' <https://samirabenboubker.com/les-droits-des-passagers-aeriens-la-transposition-du-droit-europeen-adaptee-au-secteur-du-transport-aerien-marocain/> accessed 11 December 2025.
- Jazouli, Z., 'Un nouveau texte réglementaire en préparation pour indemniser les voyageurs aériens' (2 June 2024) <https://fr.hespress.com/370604-un-nouveau-texte-reglementaire-en-preparation-pour-indemniser-les-voyageurs-aeriens.html> accessed 11 December 2025.
- L'observateur, 'Passagers aériens. Bientôt de nouvelles règles d'indemnisation' (4 June 2024) <https://lobservateur.info/article/110922/economie/passagers-aeriens-bientot-de-nouvelles-regles-dindemnisation> accessed 11 December 2025.

11.33

New Zealand

New Zealand's approach to air passenger rights is primarily based on a combination of specific provisions within the new Civil Aviation Act 2023, which comes into force on 5 April 2025,[1] alongside the broader Consumer Guarantees Act (CGA) 1993, the Fair Trading Act 1986, and the Contract and Commercial Law Act 2017, as well as international conventions for international flights.

The Civil Aviation Act 2023, which replaces the previous Civil Aviation Act 1990[2] and the Airport Authorities Act 1966, is the new cornerstone of New Zealand's civil aviation regulatory system, aimed at consolidating and modernizing the legal framework. While it was hoped that the Civil Aviation Act 2023 would be a significant modernization,[3] the new Act is lacking in terms of passengers' rights and protection. As Macey deplored, "protections were not strengthened in the replacement of the Civil Aviation Act 1990 with the Civil Aviation Act 2023."[4]

While the 2023 Act is primarily focused on safety, security, and the efficient operation of the aviation system, it does continue and refine provisions related to passenger redress, similar to the previous 1990 Act. Part 8, along with schedules 4 to 6, provide protection for air passengers. Most of those provisions are in fact the enactment of the Montreal Convention. Part 8 is structured into two distinct regimes, determined by whether the carriage in question is classified as international or domestic. According to section 270(1), Subpart 3 on domestic carrier applies to any carriage which has its origin and destination in New Zealand without any agreed stopping place outside of New Zealand. This means that an

1 Section 3 of the Civil Aviation Act 2023.

2 For more details on previous Act see: Pablo Mendes de Leon, *Introduction to Air Law* (Wolters Kluwer 2022).

3 According to the Government. See: 'Civil Aviation Bill and Civil Aviation Amendment Bill – Third Readings' (28 March 2023) <https://www.parliament.nz/en/pb/hansard-debates/rhr/combined/HansDeb_20230328_20230329_68> accessed 12 December 2025.

4 James Macey, 'Navigating Towards an Airworthy Protection Regime for New Zealand's Airline Passengers' (2024) 55 Victoria University of Wellington Law Review 173.

DOI: 10.4324/9781003746164-44

internal flight which is part of an international itinerary will be considered as international carriage[5] for the purpose of the Act. However, passengers flying this route only, not part of a longer journey, will fall within section 270(1).[6]

The Civil Aviation Act only applies when the delay or cancellation is within the airline's control. The carrier will not be liable if the damage is caused by meteorological conditions; compliance with instructions, advice, or information given by an air traffic control service; obedience to orders or directions given by a lawful authority; force majeure; or "was necessary for the purpose of saving or attempting to save life."[7] Like many laws, airlines are presumed liable for damages occasioned by delay unless they prove that such delay was caused by an exception.

Compensation is capped at ten times the price of the ticket or the actual proven costs, whichever is lower.[8] From the wording of the Act, it seems that it is for the passenger to demonstrate the quantum of damage. As Macey noted "in practical terms, making a claim will necessitate the collation of receipts for expenses caused by delays, such as meals, accommodation and ground transport."[9] Section 276 exempts airlines from liability if they have taken all measures necessary to avoid the damage or that such measure could not have been taken. However, the limit does not apply if damages resulted from an act or omission of the carrier done "with intent to cause damage or recklessly as to whether damage would result."[10]

For international travel, the liability and its limit is the same as found in the Montreal[11] Convention, namely passenger delay is limited to 5,346 SDR and for baggage delay to 1,288 SDR per passenger.[12] Interestingly, the Act is silent with regard to damage to delays of baggage for domestic flights. Section 410 introduces a regulatory authority mandating airlines to inform passengers of their rights and entitlements, in addition to requiring the publication of operational statistics.

5 As defined in Section 270(3) as "The international carriage referred to in subsections (1) and (2) is carriage in which, according to the contract between the parties, the place of departure and the place of destination, whether or not there is a break in the carriage or a transhipment, are –

(a) within the territories of 2 countries; or

(b) within the territory of a single country if there is an agreed stopping place within the territory of another country."

6 Section 270(2).

7 Section 274(2)(a)–(c).

8 Section 277(1).

9 James Macey, 'Navigating Towards an Airworthy Protection Regime for New Zealand's Airline Passengers' (2024) 55 Victoria University of Wellington Law Review 173, 175.

10 Section 279(a) and (b).

11 Section 260(2).

12 Schedule 6 Article 22(1) and (2).

Any misleading or deceptive information would be caught under the Fair Trading Act 1986, especially section 13(i). This means that if airlines mislead passengers or do not provide correct information regarding refunds and compensations, they will be able to rely on this specific provision. Charges were filed against Jetstar in September 2024 regarding some allegations of misleading passengers on their compensation rights in case of delays.[13] In 2023, New Zealand's Dispute Tribunal found an airline liable for misrepresentation and awarded 13,555 NZD in damages to a passenger, setting a precedent for inflight marketing.[14] The judge noted that the Fair Trading Act applied as "the advertising of a service that Emirates knew would unlikely be delivered is misleading and deceptive." Moreover, the Consumer Guarantees Act also applied as the provided services were not as described to the passenger.[15]

The ACA does not include any provision on care and assistance, denial of boarding, or an obligation of re-routing. This makes it one of the least stringent laws analysed in this book.

Like the Montreal Convention, the Act does not deal with cancellation or denial of boarding. Similarly, there is no care and assistance mentioned in the Act. Passengers might rely on the Consumer Guarantees Act (CGA) 1993, New Zealand's principal consumer protection law, to claim for damages. Indeed, section 28 stipulates that the services must be carried out with reasonable care and skill, so any failure to comply would lead to a breach of the guarantee. This section also applies to sub-contractors who fail to exercise reasonable care and skill.[16] Section 29 mandates for the service to be reasonably fit for a particular purpose. Such section might also be used in case of long delays or cancellation mid-journey as then the particular purpose might be lost. Finally, section 30 requires the service to be completed within a reasonable time, however, this section might not be of such help as airlines' contracts mention the timing of flights is not guaranteed. However, it could still be used in case of cancellation. In case of breach of guarantee, section 32 stipulates that the faulty party must

---

13 Commerce Commission, 'ComCom Alleges Jetstar Misled Consumers About Compensation for Flight Delays and Cancellations' (18 September 2024) <https://comcom.govt.nz/news-and-media/news-and-events/2024/comcom-alleges-jetstar-misled-consumers-about-compensation-for-flight-delays-and-cancellations> accessed 12 December 2025.

14 *Dr Mark Morgan v Emirates*, referee Laura Mueller, March 2023. See: Chrystel Erotokritou and Sofia Mateou, 'Air Passenger Rights Case Law Developments from 1 January to 25 November 2023' (2024) 49 Air and Space Law 59.

15 As reported by Rob Stock, 'Emirates Pays Tauranga Man $13,555 over "Misleading and Deceptive' Advertising of Business Class Seats' (*Stuff*, 11 March 2023) <https://www.stuff.co.nz/business/131468446/emirates-pays-tauranga-man-13555-over-misleading-and-deceptive-advertising-of-business-class-seats> accessed 12 December 2025.

16 James Macey, 'Navigating Towards an Airworthy Protection Regime for New Zealand's Airline Passengers' (2024) 55 Victoria University of Wellington Law Review 173, 181.

remedy the breach within a reasonable time or allow the passenger to cancel the contract and obtain a refund. Passengers could also use this section to claim reimbursement for arranging another ticket in case of denial of boarding or cancellation, for instance.[17] In case of a breach of "substantial character" or which cannot be remedied, passengers can cancel the contract or obtain compensation for any reduction in the value of the flight.[18] In both cases, the passenger will be entitled to reasonably foreseeable damages caused by the breach.[19] Such liability is however not unlimited and the right of redress is limited if the breach occurs because of a cause independent of human control or an act or default or omission of a third party not related to the supplier.[20] However, it is unclear who will fall within the definition of servant or agent.[21] Moreover, there are some uncertainties regarding delays. The CAA 2023 clearly expresses that an airline will be liable for the omission of their sub-contractors; however, under the CGA those sub-contractors might not be considered "agent or servant" of the airlines as they might not provide a direct service to the passenger. For instance, the late arrival of the catering company which has a knock-on effect would under the CAA fall within the CAA 2023 but would not fall under the CGA if the knock-on effect is the flight being cancelled.

The New Zealand approach is characterized by a fragmented and largely reactive legal architecture. Its cornerstone, the Civil Aviation Act 2023 represents a consolidation and modernization of safety and operational regulation but, as noted by Macey, constitutes a missed opportunity for strengthening passenger rights and is, therefore, a bit of a disappointment. Indeed, the Act is mainly the enactment of the Montreal Convention's principles extended with some modifications to domestic carriage. Part 8 of the Act establishes separate regimes for international and domestic flights, with a critical distinction: a domestic leg that is part of an international itinerary is treated as international carriage, thereby applying the Montreal Convention limits. For purely domestic travel, the Act imposes liability for delays within the airline's control, capping compensation at ten times the ticket price or proven costs, whichever is lower. This structure places a significant evidentiary burden on the passenger, requiring them to collate and demonstrate their actual losses, such as receipts for accommodation and meals.

17 Section 32(a)(i) and (ii) of the Consumer Guarantees Act.

18 Section 32(b)(i) and (ii). Section 36 sets out when a breach of a guarantee is of a "substantial character."

19 Section 32(c).

20 Section 33(a) and (b).

21 Kate Tokeley, 'Consumer Guarantees Act 1993: Remedies' in Kate Tokeley and Victoria Stace (eds), *Consumer Law in New Zealand* (3rd edn, LexisNexis 2023) 166.

The CAA reveals a fundamental divergence in regulatory philosophy and passenger protection compared to Regulation 261. New Zealand's Civil Aviation Act 2023, while replacing the 1990 Act to modernize the regulatory system, notably lags behind in terms of direct passenger protection for common disruptions. In essence, while the Civil Aviation Act 2023 modernizes New Zealand's aviation regulatory structure, its approach to passenger rights is fundamentally conservative. It maintains a system of seeking proven damages, which can be burdensome for passengers, and relies heavily on other general consumer protection laws for comprehensive coverage that the EU integrates directly into its aviation-specific regulation.

This gap forces passengers and adjudicators to turn to New Zealand's horizontal consumer protection statutes. The Consumer Guarantees Act 1993 becomes a critical, though imperfect, tool. Passengers may argue that a severe delay or cancellation constitutes a failure to provide services with reasonable care and skill (section 28), that the service was not fit for its particular purpose (section 29), or, more challengingly given common carriage contract terms, that it was not completed within a reasonable time (section 30). However, the Act's exclusions for events beyond human control or caused by third parties create uncertainty, particularly regarding whether subcontractors (e.g., catering or ground handling companies) are considered agents of the airline. This creates a potential conflict with the Civil Aviation Act, which holds airlines liable for their subcontractors' omissions.

While powerful, this patchwork of legislation – the Civil Aviation Act, the Consumer Guarantees Act, and the Fair Trading Act – creates a complex, layered system where passengers must navigate multiple legal avenues to ascertain their rights, which are often focused on redress after the fact rather than on-the-spot support like Regulation 261 has. New Zealand's framework is essentially a fault-based, compensatory model rooted in general contract and consumer law principles, augmented by a limited aviation statute. It requires passengers to be litigants, gathering evidence to claim back proven expenses. The system is reactive, is legally complex, and places a higher burden of engagement on the traveller. Regulation 261, conversely, is a rights-based, preventative model. It imposes affirmative, standardized duties on airlines to mitigate inconvenience immediately and provides automatic financial compensation for the non-performance of the travel contract, irrespective of individual loss. It is proactive, simple in its application for the passenger, and designed to deter disruptions by internalizing their costs to carriers.

In conclusion, while New Zealand's Civil Aviation Act 2023 updates the regulatory superstructure, its passenger rights provisions remain anchored in a minimalist, damage-recovery paradigm. It effectively transplants the

Montreal Convention's philosophy into domestic law, relying on a web of general consumer statutes to fill its considerable gaps. This stands in opposition to the EU's unified, prescriptive approach, which prioritizes immediate passenger welfare and standardized compensation as a matter of right. For the everyday traveller, the difference is profound: Under Regulation 261, rights are clear, upfront, and enforceable at the airport; under New Zealand's regime, they are often deferred, contingent on proof, and require navigation through a labyrinth of legislative instruments. The New Zealand model offers flexibility and ties redress directly to proven harm, but at the cost of certainty, immediacy, and a robust, aviation-specific safety net for passengers.

Comparison with EU Regulation

Feature	**Civil Aviation Act 2023**	**EU Regulation 261/2004**
Delay Compensation	Domestic: Max 10 times the ticket price. International: Max 5,346 SDR.	≥3h: €250–€600 (by distance).
Cancellation Rights	Not specified.	<14d notice: Refund or re-routing + €250–600 compensation (by distance).
Overbooking	Not specified.	Volunteer first; €250–€600 (by distance) if denied boarding.
Baggage Compensation	1,288 SDR.	Not specified.

Bibliography

- Civil Aviation Act 2023, Act N°10 of 5 April 2023 <https://www.legislation.govt.nz/act/public/2023/0010/latest/LMS49346.html>.
- Consumer Guarantees Act 1993, Act N°91 of 20 August 1993 <https://www.legislation.govt.nz/act/public/1993/0091/latest/dlm311053.html>.
- Contract and Commercial Law Act 2017, Act N°5 of 1 March 2017 <https://www.legislation.govt.nz/act/public/2017/0005/21.0/DLM6844033.html>.
- Fair Trading Act 1986, Act N° 121 of 17 December 1986 <https://www.legislation.govt.nz/act/public/1986/0121/latest/DLM96439.html>.
- *Dr Mark Morgan v Emirates*, referee Laura Mueller, March 2023.
- Civil Aviation Bill and Civil Aviation Amendment Bill – Third Readings (28 March 2023) <https://www.parliament.nz/en/pb/hansard-debates/rhr/combined/HansDeb_20230328_20230329_68> accessed 12 December 2025.
- Commerce Commission, 'ComCom Alleges Jetstar Misled Consumers About Compensation for Flight Delays and Cancellations' (18 September 2024) <https://comcom.govt.nz/news-and-media/news-and-events/2024/comcom-alleges-jetstar-misled-consumers-about-compensation-for-flight-delays-and-cancellations> accessed 12 December 2025.

- Erotokritou, Ch. and Mateou, S., 'Air Passenger Rights Case Law Developments from 1 January to 25 November 2023' (2024) 49 Air and Space Law 59.
- Macey, J., 'Navigating Towards an Airworthy Protection Regime for New Zealand's Airline Passengers' (2024) 55 Victoria University of Wellington Law Review 173.
- Mendes de Leon, P., *Introduction to Air Law* (Wolters Kluwer 2022).
- Stock, R., 'Emirates Pays Tauranga Man $13,555 over "Misleading and Deceptive' Advertising of Business Class Seats' (*Stuff*, 11 March 2023) <https://www.stuff.co.nz/business/131468446/emirates-pays-tauranga-man-13555-over-misleading-and-deceptive-advertising-of-business-class-seats> accessed 12 December 2025.
- Tokeley, K., 'Consumer Guarantees Act 1993: Remedies' in Kate Tokeley and Victoria Stace (eds), *Consumer Law in New Zealand* (3rd edn, LexisNexis 2023).

II.34

Nigeria

The absence of relevant laws on passengers' protection has resulted in flight delays being the norm in Nigeria.[1] To solve the issue and to ensure a better compliance with the Montreal Convention, the Nigerian authorities have enacted various laws and regulations.[2] Section 4 of the Civil Aviation Act 2022 (CAA 2022) designates the Nigerian Civil Aviation Authority (NCAA)[3] as the regulatory agency responsible for overseeing the Nigerian Aviation Industry and empowers it to enact regulations and rules, whenever necessary.[4] As a result of those powers, the Nigerian Civil Aviation Regulations (NCARs or Nig. CARs) were promulgated in 2006 and amended several times.[5] The latest and fourth amendment was introduced in 2023.[6]

The Civil Aviation Act 2022 provides that air carriers are generally liable for damages occasioned by delay and works in tandem with the Montreal Convention.[7] The Act is complemented by the Nigerian Civil Aviation Regulations 2023 (NCARs 2023) and more precisely Part 19 – effective since July 2023.[8] Part 19 lays down certain rights and responsibilities

1 Chidimma Stella Nwakoby and Adinnu Elton Chukwujekwu, 'Impact of Consumer Protection Laws on Aviation Industry in Nigeria' (2020) 2 International Journal of Comparative Law and Legal Philosophy 38.

2 The Montreal Convention was domesticated into Nigerian law by virtue of Section 55 of the Civil Aviation Act 2022 which repealed and replaced Civil Aviation Act 2006 (CAA 2006). The 2022 Act incorporated the 2006 Act.

3 "It was originally established by Decree 49 of 1999, as the regulator for technical and safety issues in the industry." See: ICLG, 'Aviation Laws and Regulations Nigeria 2024–2025' (2 April 2024) <https://iclg.com/practice-areas/aviation-laws-and-regulations/nigeria>.

4 Section 4 of the Nigerian Civil Aviation Act 2022.

5 Nigeria Civil Aviation Authority Regulations, Federal Republic of Nigeria Official Gazette, S.I. No. 36 of 2015, B771-910. Hereafter Nigerian Civil Aviation Regulations 2015.

6 Pursuant to Section 8(1)(f) of the Civil Aviation Act 2022. Nigeria Civil Aviation Authority Regulations Part 19 consumer Protection (2023). See: Bariyima Silvester Kokpan, 'A Critical Analysis of Air Passengers' Protection in the Nigeria Civil Aviation Authority Regulations (NCARs) 2023' (2024) 11 Journal of Commercial and Property Law 1.

7 Section 55.

8 Under the previous Nigerian Civil Aviation Regulations 2015, passenger protection is also found under Part 19. See: Esther Inko Abili, 'Litigating Air Passengers' Rights in

DOI: 10.4324/9781003746164-45

of passengers and airlines. These rights can be broadly categorized into right to reimbursement and re-routing, right to accommodation and care, and financial compensation to air passengers. Unlike any other laws, the NCARs covers instances of "no show"[9] and allow airlines to rely on overbooking.[10] It also contains a specific provision allowing the correction of misspelt names free of charges up to 48 hours before the flight.[11]

The NCARs 2023 applies to domestic flights, international flights, and travellers on international airlines having a layover in Nigeria.[12] The scope of application of Part 19 is, therefore, not limited by the nationality of the air carrier. However, passengers on an international flight departing from outside of Nigeria will only be able to avail themselves of the Regulations if they have not been compensated under the law of the country of origin.[13] This rule is to avoid double benefit on the part of the passenger. Passengers travelling free of charge or at reduced fare which is not directly or indirectly available to the public cannot avail themselves of Part 19 protection.[14]

Similarly to most existing regulations and as provided for in the Annex 6 of the Yamoussoukro Decision, air carriers have a duty to give passengers necessary assistance in case of delays which includes refreshment and two telephone calls, SMS, or emails.[15] Unlike other laws, the NCARs distinguishes and provides different protections depending on whether the delay relates to a domestic flight, international flights, or tarmac delay. For instance, on domestic flights passengers are entitled to assistance after two hours in the form of refreshments and telephone calls.[16] For international flights this protection is extended until four hours, at which point passengers are also entitled to a meal as specified in 19.10.1.1(b).[17] Passengers suffering a tarmac delay are entitled to both food and drink "no later than 2 hours after the start of the delay."[18] Similarly, while the provisions on delays in an international flights context request a delay of at least six hours for the passenger to qualify for a hotel accommodation

Nigeria: A Reflective Analysis of the Relevant Laws and Institutions' (2025) 2 UAI Journal of Arts, Humanities and Social Sciences 5.

9 Section 19.3.1.1.

10 Section 19.3.1.2.

11 Section 19.16.1.1.

12 Section 19.2.1.1.

13 Section 19.2.1.1(b).

14 Section 19.2.1.3.

15 Section 19.10.1(a) for refreshment, (b) meal and Section 19.10.2 for telephone calls, and emails.

16 Section 19.6.1.1 referring to section 19.10.1.1(a) and Section 19.10.1.2.

17 Section 19.6.2.1.

18 Section 19.6.3.1(d).

and transport,[19] in the domestic flight context, the provision is much more vague "at a time beyond 10pm till 4am, or at a time when the airport is closed at the point of departure or final destination, the assistance specified in sections 19.10.1.1(c) and 19.10.1.1(d) (hotel accommodation and transport)."[20] It could potentially mean that a passenger will have to spend a whole day before being entitled to this assistance on domestic flights.

The division of the provisions between domestic and international flights in delay situations might raise some questions regarding the lack of consistency. For example, for domestic flights, Section 19.6.1.1 stipulates that airlines are expected to inform passengers of the reason(s) for the delay within 30 minutes after the scheduled time of departure. However, no such provision is found regarding international flights. Equally, while Section 19.6.1.1(b) is very clear as to when passengers could request for a reimbursement or re-routing in a delayed domestic flight context – after three hours – and compensation after six hours,[21] the delayed international flights do not entail any re-routing or reimbursement – which seems odd.[22]

Entitlements	**Delayed Domestic Flights**	**Delayed International Flights**	**Tarmac Delay**
Refreshment	2 hours.	Not specified.	No later than 2 hours.
Meal	Not specified.	4+ hours	No later than 2 hours.
Hotel + Transport	At a time beyond 10 PM till 4 AM, or at a time when the airport is closed.	6+ hours	Not available.
Phone Calls, Emails, and SMS	2 hours.	Between 2 and 4 hours.	Not specified.
Reimbursement	3 hours.	Not specified.	Not specified.
Compensation	6+ hours + 25% of the ticket price.	Between 2 and 4 hours = 30% of the ticket price.	Not specified.

Another discrepancy is that the section on domestic flights clearly excludes liability of carrier for six hours and more delays if the operating

19 Section 19.6.2.1(b).
20 Section 19. 6.1.1(c).
21 Section 19. 6.1.1(d).
22 Section 19.6.2.1.

airline can prove that the "delay is caused by extraordinary circumstances which could not have been avoided if all reasonable measures had been taken."[23] Extraordinary circumstance is defined broadly in Section 19.1.2.1 as "any mechanical, technical, operational, climatic, socio-political or any other conditions beyond the actual control of the party involved." This definition is very broad and raises many questions such as whether strikes or technical problems identified during routine maintenance will fall under the definition.

Part 19 does not include a specific amount of compensation with regard to the time or distance but rather a percentage of the ticket price. For domestic flights, delayed passengers are entitled to claim 25% of their ticket price as compensation after six hours.[24] On international flights, for delays between two and four hours, passengers are entitled to a 30% refund of the ticket price.[25] Airlines might reduce the compensation by half if the passenger's new flight arrives no later than one hour after the original time for domestic flights and three hours for international flights.[26] It remains to be seen whether the limit in relation of delay (US$4,150) found in Article 22 of the Civil Aviation Act 2022 would cap the compensation entitlements found in the NCARs.

Similarly to other regulations, the NCARs does not prejudice the right of passengers to claim further compensation.[27] Part 19 also contains a provision on upgrading and downgrading. While the former must be done free of charge, the latter grants passengers the right to claim reimbursement of the difference as well as compensation amounting to 30% of the price of the ticket for domestic flights and 50% for international flights.[28]

	Domestic Flights	**International Flights**
Compensation	25% of the ticket price.	30% of the ticket price.
If Re-routing	1 hour of the original time = compensation reduced by 50%.	3 hours of the original time = compensation reduced by 50%.
Downgrading	Reimbursement + 30% of the price of the ticket.	Reimbursement + 50% of the price of the ticket.

The Regulations place the burden of proof regarding whether and when the passenger has been informed of the cancellation or delay of the flight

23 Section 19.6.1.2.
24 Section 19.6.1.1(d) and Section 19.8.1.1(a).
25 Section 19.6.2.1(b) and Section 19.8.1.1(b).
26 Section 19.8.1.2(a) and (b).
27 Section 19.14.
28 Section 19.11.1.1(a).

upon the air carrier.[29] As reported by Oluwaseun Adedayo Omotoso, the Federal High Court "held that the failure of an airline to provide adequate reasons for prolonged delays violated Part 19 of the NCARs and entitled the passengers to compensation."[30]

Part 19 contains equivalent provisions to those found in Malaysia or Saudi Arabia regarding denial of boarding; airlines are under the obligation to request volunteers and to ensure the least number of passengers are denied boarding.[31] However Part 19 does not mandate airlines to identify early and contact passengers for volunteers as mandated by Annex 6 of the Yamoussoukro Decision.[32] Passengers voluntarily or involuntarily denied boarding are entitled to compensation in accordance with Section 19.8.1.1.[33] Interestingly, the provision on denial of boarding does not reflect the ruling in *Aziz v Arik Air*[34] in which the court granted passengers with additional damages for the inconvenience caused as well as compensation for the breach of contract. Those additional damages are in fact not found in the NCARs.[35] In a recent case, the Federal High Court has ruled that denial of boarding is a fundamental breach of contract and airlines cannot rely on an exclusionary clause.[36]

Compared to the 2015 Regulations, the 2023 included a clear provision on tarmac delay and the obligations of airlines towards passengers such as allowing disembarking before the delay exceeds three hours.[37] Passengers are also entitled to receive food and drink, proper ventilation and heating and access to lavatories alongside being informed of the reason

29 Section 19.7.1.4.

30 *Aero Contractors Nigeria Ltd v Nigerian Civil Aviation Authority & Ors*, Unreported case, Federal High Court of Nigeria, 2020 as reported by Oluwaseun Adedayo Omotoso, 'Flight Delays, Cancellations, and the Rights of Air Travelers in Nigeria' (S.D) <https://lawcentriole.com/flight-delays-and-cancellations-the-rights-of-air-travelers-in-nigeria/#_ftnref4> accessed 25 February 2025.

31 Section 19.4.1.1(a) and (b).

32 Adejoke O Adediran, 'Regulatory Convergence of Consumer Protection in the Single African Air Transport Market: How Far, How Well?' (2022) 47 Air and Space Law 427, 440.

33 Section 19.4.1.2.

34 *Federal High Court of Nigeria, Lagos Division, Suit No. FHC/L/CS/142/2017.*

35 In *Miss Promise Mekwunye v Emirates Airlines* (2019) CLR 2(d) (SC) the Supreme Court also allowed for additional damages in addition to the refund of her ticket.

36 Suit No. FHC/L/CS/240/2017 – *Mrs. Andrea Ajibade & Ors v Ethiopian Airlines & Anor* decided on 16 May 2023. For a summary see: Olaoye Olalere, 'Recent Judicial Restatement on Jurisdiction and the Utility of Exclusionary Clauses in Contracts of Carriage of Passengers By Air' (*Mondaq*, 19 June 2023) <https://www.mondaq.com/nigeria/aviation/1331008/recent-judicial-restatement-on-jurisdiction-and-the-utility-of-exclusionary-clauses-in-contracts-of-carriage-of-passengers-by-air> accessed 25 February 2025.

37 Section 19.6.3.2. See: B. Silvester Kokpan, 'A Critical Analysis of Air Passengers' Protection in the Nigeria Civil Aviation Authority Regulations (NCARs) 2023' (2024) 11 Journal of Commercial and Property Law 1.

for the delay.[38] Interestingly, the three-hour period could be extended by 45 minutes "if it is likely that it will take off within that period."[39] The NCARs establishes the disembarking order in Section 19.6.3.5. Airlines must also submit a report to the relevant authorities on the tarmac delay.[40]

Where a flight is cancelled, the airline is obligated to offer assistance to the passengers, in addition to re-rerouting and reimbursement.[41] Passengers are also entitled to compensation, unless the cancellation is communicated to the passenger 24 hours prior to the time of the scheduled flight in the case of a domestic flight and seven days for an international flight or the airline can prove the cancellation was due to an extraordinary circumstance.[42] No compensation is due on international flights if the cancellation occurs between three and seven days and the re-routing option allows the passengers to reach their final destination no later than four hours after the original scheduled arrival time and does not depart more than two hours before the original time.[43] The third option is

> they are informed of the cancellation less than seven days before the scheduled time of departure and are offered re-routing, allowing them to depart not more than one hour before the scheduled time of departure and to reach their final destination less than two hours after the scheduled time of arrival.[44]

This last provision will need interpretation as it seems to directly conflict with Section 19.7.1.1(d)(2). It might in fact be that paragraph 3 should have read as less than three days, which would have then made a lot more sense. As it stands, there is a potential of many lawsuits with airlines relying on paragraph 2 and passengers relying on paragraph 3.

Passengers are given the right to retract from their contracts by cancelling their ticket "no later than 24 hours after purchasing it, for tickets bought at least seven days before the flight's departure."[45] In those circumstances, passengers have the choice between receiving a refund or placing the ticket on hold for six months. Such addition aims at clarifying the position – which was unclear under the previous Regulations – but might also help reduce the no-show instances.

---

38 Section 19.6.3.1.

39 Section 19.6.3.3.

40 Section 19.6.3.7.

41 Section 19.7.1.1(a) and (b).

42 Section 19.7.1.1(c) and (d)(1) + Section 19.7.1.3.

43 Section 19.7.1.1(d)(2). See: E. Inko Abili, 'Litigating Air Passengers' Rights in Nigeria: A Reflective Analysis of the Relevant Laws and Institutions' (2025) 2 UAI Journal of Arts, Humanities and Social Sciences 5, 11.

44 Section 19.7.1.1(d)(3).

45 Section 19.9.2.

Concerning reimbursement or re-routing, passengers are to be reimbursed immediately and in cash for domestic flights and within 14 days for international flights.[46] The reimbursement must cover the total flight cost or the part of the journey not made in the case of connecting flights. Passengers could also elect a re-routing which must be under comparable transport conditions to their destinations at the earliest opportunity or at a later date at the passenger's convenience, subject to the availability of seats.[47] If the passenger accepts a flight to an alternative airport, the carrier must bear the cost of transferring the passenger from the alternative airport to the airport for which the booking was made.[48]

Notice Period	**Passenger Rights**
Domestic (<24hrs)	Re-routing + 25% compensation (unless due to extraordinary circumstances).
International (<7 days)	Re-routing + compensation (exempt if alternative flight arrives ≤4 hrs late).
Force Majeure	No compensation (but refund/re-routing allowed).

As found in the Saudi Arabian Regulation or the Malaysian law, Part 19 contains special provisions for persons with reduced mobility or special needs.[49] Section 19.12.4.1 prohibits discriminatory practices on ground of disability by the air carrier but not on ground of race as found in the Yamoussoukro Decision. Additionally, the NCARs 2023 includes a novel obligation on managers of airports to facilitate the movement of persons with reduced mobility.[50] Those safeguards are aligned with section 42 of the Constitution of the Federal Republic of Nigeria, 1999.[51] However, the entitlement to transport a passenger with a disability on a commercial flight is subject to certain conditions and is not unconditional. Indeed, NCARs includes provisions specifying circumstances under which refusal or prevention of carriage due to disabilities or reduced mobility may be justified. For instance, Section 19.12.5 regulates situations in which it is unsafe or impossible to provide such transportation and their entitlement to reimbursement or re-routing.[52] Additionally, the passenger might be entitled to compensation if they are denied boarding due to their disability due to the size of the aircrafts or its doors.[53]

46 Section 19.9.1.1(a).
47 Section 19.9.1.1(b) and (c).
48 Section 19.9.1.3.
49 Section 19.12.
50 Section 19:12.
51 See: Silvester Kokpan (n 6).
52 Section 19.12.5(a) and (b).
53 Section 19.12.5(b)(2).

Passengers have the right to receive clear information, including notices about refusal of carriage as outlined in Section 19.12.6. Air carriers and their representatives must ensure that safety regulations and important passenger information are accessible to the public, offered in alternative formats, and available in all languages provided to other travellers. This covers flight specifics, arrangements for persons with reduced mobility, and any restrictions on passengers or mobility equipment due to aircraft size.[54] In short, everyone must be made aware of all necessary safety guidelines and areas subject to restrictions. If no such notice is given, the carrier must take reasonable steps to provide assistance so the individual can board the flight for which they have a reservation, including right of care and re-routing.[55]

The NCARs also requires the establishment of a Family Assistance Programme (FAP) to "provide succor to aircraft accident victims and their families."[56] Such obligation is in line with section 55(3) of the Nigeria CAA 2022 which imposes a duty of air carriers to make an advance payment of US$30,000 each to bereaved families in the event of aircraft accident within 30 days. This subsection applies only to situations of aircraft accident.

Section 19.21.1.1 stipulates that prior to the purchase of any ticket for air carriage, whether from the carrier or its agents, passengers must be provided with full, fair, and clear disclosure of all applicable terms and conditions. This disclosure should include, but is not limited to, information regarding required documents for check-in, check-in deadlines, refund and rebooking policies, as well as procedures and responsibilities concerning delayed or cancelled flights. Additional terms may address liability limitations, claim-filing deadlines, and other essential conditions. Moreover, travel agents and/or tour operators involved with airlines must provide passengers with information regarding passport and visa requirements, total price of the package, and terms and conditions amongst other things.[57] Furthermore, there is a section dedicated to misleading advertising, as found in other national laws and the Yamoussoukro Decision, which requires the full price to be stated and prohibits the charging of additional fees not expressly displayed.[58] Those requirements are in line with the obligations under the Federal Competition and Consumer Protection Act which prohibits the use of hidden terms.[59]

54 Section 19.12.6.2.
55 Section 19.12.6.3.
56 Section 19.13.
57 Section 19.21.1.2.
58 Section 19.20.1.1 and 19.20.1.2.
59 See: Silvester Kokpan (n 6).

In situation where a check-in baggage is delayed, the airline must tender an amount of 10,000 Naira in cases of domestic flights and US$170 in cases of international flight to the passenger as compensation for the inconvenience suffered.[60] Should such baggage be lost or damaged, the passenger shall be compensated in accordance with the provisions of the Nigeria Civil Aviation Act which limits such damage to US$1,000.[61] A domestic flight baggage is deemed lost after seven days, while for international flights, 21 days are required.[62] NCARs 2023 introduced a new provision related to mobility equipment and assistive devices. In the event such devices are lost or damaged while under the care of the airline, whether during handling or transport on the aircraft, the airline is fully responsible for covering the cost of repair or replacement.[63] For compensation purposes, mobility equipment is presumed lost if not delivered within seven days from the scheduled delivery date for domestic flights or within 21 days for international flights.[64] As pointed out by Silvester Kokpan, a notable gap exists within the NCARs; while provision expressly refers to "delayed" equipment, it remains silent on the practical consequences of such a delay for the passengers who depend on it.[65] This omission is critical, as equipment like wheelchairs or mobility scooters – distinct from ordinary baggage – are essential extensions of personal mobility. Logically, delays are not only possible but likely to cause significant inconvenience, underscoring the urgent need for regulations to explicitly account for these real-world scenarios.

Issue	Compensation	Notes
Delay	10,000 Naira (domestic)/ US$170 (international).	Paid for inconvenience.
Loss/Damage	Up to US$1,000 (aligned with Montreal Convention).	Domestic: Lost after 7 days; international: 21 days.
Carry-On Damage	Not specified (likely falls under general liability).	Airlines exempt for passenger negligence/force majeure.
Mobility Equipment	Full repair + Up to US$1,000 if lost.	Not expressed compensation for delays.

There are no defined fines in the NCARs. Instead, the NCAA has power at the conclusion of the hearing to make directives.[66] Where the

60 Section 19.18.2.1(a).
61 Section 19.18.2.1(b) in conjunction with Article 22(2) of the CAA 2022.
62 Section 19.18.2.1(c).
63 Section 19.12.7.1.
64 Section 19.12.7.2.
65 Silvester Kokpan (n 6).
66 Section 19.27.

affected passenger is not satisfied by the decision of the body, he/she has a right to institute an action against the body and the carrier in a competent court of law, which is usually the Federal High Court that has exclusive jurisdiction,[67] or employ another alternative dispute resolution mechanism.

Part 19.27 also requires passengers to attend the administrative hearing physically or by a duly authorized representative. This requirement is not only cumbersome but also unrealistic and might explain that the enforcement of the NCARs is rare.[68] Indeed, passengers will have to incur an additional financial burden to attend the hearing of their complaint, such amount will not be reimbursed, and the compensation granted under Part 19 might not give a sufficient incentive for the passenger to pursue his or her case. Such a procedure is even more inadequate for passengers suffering a delay or cancellation while visiting Nigeria. For instance, a Nigerian living in London in holidays in Nigeria who took a flight from Lagos to Abuja would not go back to Nigeria for his hearing. The NCARs could have given the possibility for remote or virtual hearings.

The Nigerian regulatory landscape governing air passenger rights is principally constructed upon the Civil Aviation Act 2022, which serves as the foundational statute, and its operational counterpart, the NCARs, most recently amended in 2023. Within this framework, Part 19 of the NCARs 2023 constitutes the core of passenger protection, delineating specific rights and airline responsibilities across a spectrum of disruptions including delay, cancellation, denial of boarding, and tarmac confinement.

A defining, and perhaps complicating, feature of Part 19 is its stratified approach, which creates distinct entitlements contingent upon whether the flight is domestic or international. This dichotomy, while aiming for contextual relevance, introduces inconsistencies that challenge regulatory coherence. For instance, the right to refreshments and communication arises after two hours for domestic delays, while for international delays, similar assistance is specified within a two-to-four-hour window. More strikingly, the entitlement to hotel accommodation and transport for international delays triggers unambiguously after six hours, whereas for domestic delays, it is nebulously tied to flights occurring "at a time beyond 10pm till 4am, or at a time when the airport is closed." This vagueness

67 Based on Section 251(1) k of the Constitution of the Federal Republic of Nigeria 1999 and *KLM Royal Dutch Airline v Idehen* (2017) LPELR 4357 CA; *KLM Royal Dutch Airlines v Taher* (2014) 3 NWLR (1393) 137.

68 Chidimma Stella Nwakoby and Adinnu Elton Chukwujekwu, 'Impact of Consumer Protection Laws on Aviation Industry in Nigeria' (2020) 2 International Journal of Comparative Law and Legal Philosophy 38, 44.

could, in practice, oblige a domestic passenger to endure a prolonged daytime delay without such care, a disparity that lacks clear justification.

The compensation mechanism itself further entrenches this divide, employing a percentage-of-ticket-price model rather than one based on distance or a fixed sum. For domestic delays exceeding six hours, compensation is set at 25% of the ticket price. For international delays between two and four hours, it is 30%. Airlines may reduce this compensation by half if re-routing achieves arrival within one hour of the original time for domestic flights or within three hours for international flights. This structure exists in a potential tension with the Civil Aviation Act's liability cap of US$4,150, leaving an unresolved question as to whether this ceiling applies to the percentage-based compensations under the NCARs.

A critical shield for carriers is the defence of "extraordinary circumstances," defined broadly as conditions beyond the airline's control, including mechanical, technical, operational, climatic, or socio-political events. This expansive definition, mirroring debates in other jurisdictions, risks being over-relied upon by airlines, potentially diluting the Regulations' protective intent if interpreted to include routine technical issues identified during maintenance. The burden of proof, however, rests squarely on the airline to demonstrate both the existence of such circumstances and that they informed passengers of delays within stipulated timeframes – a procedural duty upon which courts have shown willingness to penalize non-compliance. There also seems to be relatively little case law on the interpretation of the NCAR's provisions despite their vagueness regarding time which has not been cured by the various amendments. In fact, some newer cases do not seem to refer to the Regulations. The aim of the Regulations is commendable but, like Regulation 261, might be too complex for the average passengers and result in an abuse of the "extraordinary circumstances" defence.

A significant and welcome addition in the 2023 amendment is the detailed regime for tarmac delays, mandating disembarkation opportunities after three hours (extendable by 45 minutes under certain conditions) and ensuring access to necessities. Further progressive elements include specific protections against discrimination for persons with reduced mobility, a mandated Family Assistance Programme for accident victims, and clear provisions on delayed, lost, or damaged baggage. For delayed baggage, a fixed inconvenience payment is required (₦10,000 domestically, US$170 internationally), while loss or damage is aligned with the Montreal Convention limit of US$1,000.

Despite its commendable comprehensiveness, the enforcement mechanism of Part 19 presents a formidable practical barrier. The requirement for aggrieved passengers – including international visitors –

to attend administrative hearings in person, without provision for remote participation, is both cumbersome and economically disincentivizing. The costs of such attendance are not recoverable, and the modest compensation amounts may not justify the expense and effort. This procedural hurdle, coupled with a relative scarcity of clarifying case law due to the Regulations' complexity and the airlines' frequent invocation of extraordinary circumstances, suggests that while Nigeria has constructed a legally sophisticated passenger rights edifice on paper, its full and consistent translation into everyday passenger experience remains an ongoing challenge. The framework thus stands as a potent yet imperfect instrument, whose ultimate efficacy will depend on subsequent judicial interpretation, regulatory oversight, and perhaps future amendments to streamline its application and accessibility.

Comparison with EU Regulation 261

Feature	**Nigeria NCARs 2023**	**EU Regulation 261/2004**
Delay Compensation	25–30% of ticket price.	≥3h: €250–€600 (by distance).
Cancellation Rights	<24 hrs notice (domestic): Re-routing + 25% compensation (unless due to extraordinary circumstances). <7d notice(international): Re-routing + compensation (exempt if alternative flight arrives ≤4 hrs late).	<14d notice: Refund or re-routing + €250–600 compensation (by distance).
Overbooking	Allowed (volunteers first).	Volunteer first; €250–€600 (by distance) if denied boarding.
Baggage Compensation	Up to US$1,000 (aligned with Montreal Convention).	Not specified.

Bibliography

Primary Sources:

- Civil Aviation Act 2022, Federal Republic of Nigeria Official Gazette, Act N°30, A903-994 <https://ncaa.gov.ng/media/sxxn42yu/civil-aviation-act-2022-publi9cation.pdf>.
- Constitution of the Federal Republic of Nigeria, 1999 <https://nigeriarights.gov.ng/files/constitution.pdf>.
- Nigeria Civil Aviation Authority Regulations, Federal Republic of Nigeria Official Gazette, S.I. No. 36 of 2015, B771-910 <https://sabilaw.org/wp-content/uploads/2021/03/NCAA-Regulations-2015.pdf>.

- Nigeria Civil Aviation Authority Regulations Part 19 consumer Protection (2023) <https://ncaa.gov.ng/media/co1nbi24/nig-cars-part-19-consumer-protection.pdf>.
- *Aero Contractors Nigeria Ltd v Nigerian Civil Aviation Authority & Ors*, Unreported case, Federal High Court of Nigeria, 2020.
- *Mrs. Andrea Ajibade & Ors v Ethiopian Airlines & Anor*, Suit No. FHC/L/CS/240/2017 – decided on 16 May 2023.
- Federal High Court of Nigeria, Lagos Division, Suit No. FHC/L/CS/142/2017 (Unreported).
- *KLM Royal Dutch Airline v Idehen* (2017) LPELR 4357 CA.
- *KLM Royal Dutch Airlines v Taher* (2014) 3 NWLR (1393) 137.
- *Miss Promise Mekwunye v Emirates Airlines* (2019) CLR 2(d) (SC).

Secondary Sources:

- Adedayo Omotoso, O., 'Flight Delays, Cancellations, and the Rights of Air Travelers in Nigeria.' (S.D) <https://lawcentriole.com/flight-delays-and-cancellations-the-rights-of-air-travelers-in-nigeria/#_ftnref4> accessed 12 December 2025.
- Adediran, A. O., 'Regulatory Convergence of Consumer Protection in the Single African Air Transport Market: How Far, How Well?' (2022) 47 Air and Space Law 427.
- ICLG, 'Aviation Laws and Regulations Nigeria 2024–2025' (2 April 2024).
- Inko Abili, E., 'Litigating Air Passengers' Rights in Nigeria: A Reflective Analysis of the Relevant Laws and Institutions' (2025) 2 UAI Journal of Arts Humanities and Social Sciences 5.
- Olalere, O., 'Recent Judicial Restatement on Jurisdiction and the Utility of Exclusionary Clauses in Contracts of Carriage of Passengers by Air' (*Mondaq*, 19 June 2023) <https://www.mondaq.com/nigeria/aviation/1331008/recent-judicial-restatement-on-jurisdiction-and-the-utility-of-exclusionary-clauses-in-contracts-of-carriage-of-passengers-by-air> accessed 12 December 2025.
- Stella Nwakoby, Ch. and Elton Chukwujekwu, A., 'Impact of Consumer Protection Laws on Aviation Industry in Nigeria' (2020) 2 International Journal of Comparative Law and Legal Philosophy 38.
- Silvester Kokpan, B., 'A Critical Analysis of Air Passengers' Protection in the Nigeria Civil Aviation Authority Regulations (NCARs) 2023' (2024) 11 Journal of Commercial and Property Law 1.

II.35

North Macedonia

The Republic of North Macedonia has harmonized its national legislation with the EU law with regard to protection of passenger rights in air transport by transposing Regulation 261 in its Law on Contractual and Real Right Relations in Respect of Aviation Transport of 2008 as amended.[1] Regulation 1107/2006 has been transposed in the Regulation on measures and procedures for facilitation of civil aviation.[2]

The legal framework for air travel is designed to be binding and non-negotiable. The compulsory application of the provisions of Regulation 261 is made clear in Article 3 of the Law on Contractual and Real Right Relations in Respect of Aviation Transport. Article 3 makes it clear that air carriers cannot exempt themselves from liability, restrict a passenger's rights, or shift the burden of proof as defined by the law. Carriers are also obligated to publish and make their general terms of transport accessible to the public. The law itself does not stipulate its scope. However, it is clear that it applies to all flights departing from North Macedonia and all flights arriving in the country operated by an ECAA's carrier.

Chapter 1 of the Second Part of the law is dedicated to the contract of transport. A contract for passenger transport is established between the air carrier and the passenger or a transport ordered.[3] The air carrier's primary duty is to transport the passenger from the departure point to the destination on time, in exchange for a fare.[4] This contract is confirmed by a travel ticket, which must include the price, locations, and flight times. While a ticket can be a physical or electronic document, it serves as proof of the contract's existence.[5]

---

1 Law on Contractual and Real Right relations in respect of Aviation Transport, Official Gazette of the Republic of Macedonia, N°85/08, from 11 July 2008, as amended by N°148/2011; 10/2015; 150/15; 173/15.

2 Official Gazette of Republic of Macedonia, No. 50/2011, 36/2013, 26/16; 37/18.

3 Article 5(1).

4 Article 5(2).

5 Article 5(6).

DOI: 10.4324/9781003746164-46

Passengers have the right to cancel their travel before the trip begins. For domestic flights, a cancellation at least 24 hours in advance allows for a refund, with the carrier retaining a 10% fee.[6] For international flights, this period is extended to 48 hours. In cases of "force majeure," such as the death or serious illness of a passenger or a close family member, a full refund is due if the carrier is notified before departure, with a minimal 5% retention fee.[7]

The law then refers directly to Regulation 261 for compensation and assistance for flight cancellations, denial of boarding, and long delays.[8] According to the Civil Aviation Agency, the *Sturgeon* ruling is also applied in North Macedonia.[9] Article 11 refers to the obligations to inform passengers of their rights by referring directly to Regulation 261.

Article 12 establishes that the transport orderer is liable to the air carrier for obligations from the contract, and passengers may need to seek claims directly from the orderer. Article 13 permits a contractual air carrier to use an actual air carrier to perform the transport, provided similar terms are offered. It also mentions that their mutual relations are governed by Regulation 261.

When it comes to liability for death or injury, the Montreal Convention and Regulation (EC) 2027/97 govern the air carrier's responsibilities and the extent of their financial compensation. Articles 18 to 21 are based on the Montreal Convention and relate to the liability of the air carrier in case of death or injury to a passenger. Articles 22 to 25 are dedicated to luggage transport and the fact that passengers are entitled to carry hand luggage for free but the weight, size, and number must be set out by the carrier.[10]

This framework also mandates that carriers carry compulsory insurance and make advance payments for damages to affected individuals. It also includes sections on the transport of goods, specialized service with aircraft, aircraft lease contract, responsibility for damages on the ground, and real rights of the aircraft. Interestingly, any reference to special needs passengers found in Regulation 261 has not been included but are found

6 Article 7(2) and (3).

7 Article 8(1) and (2).

8 Articles 9 and 10. Article 9 reads as follow: "The compensation of damages and assistance to passengers in the event of flight cancelation shall be regulated pursuant to Regulation (EC) 261/2004."

9 CAA, 'Long Delay of Flight' <https://www.caa.gov.mk/en/passengers/2-long-delay-of-flight/>.

10 Article 22.

in a different law.[11] While this means the rights are technically provided for elsewhere in the national legal system, this separation creates a potential risk of fragmentation and could make it less straightforward for passengers to identify the full spectrum of their rights compared to the EU's more consolidated approach in a single regulation.

The Law on Contractual and Real Right Relations in Respect of Aviation Transport of the Republic of North Macedonia is a curious piece. Its architecture reveals a deliberate, albeit bifurcated, strategy for aligning with EU air passenger rights regimes, particularly Regulation (EC) 261.

However, the methodology of transposition is where the North Macedonian approach markedly diverges from the EU's legislative technique. Rather than a substantive transposition that rewrites the provisions of Regulation 261 into national legal language and structure, the law opts for a technique of direct incorporation by reference. For the critical matters of compensation and assistance in cases of denied boarding, cancellations, and long delays, the law does not articulate these rights within its own text. Instead, it directs passengers, airlines, and adjudicators to consult the EU Regulation directly. This creates a notable peculiarity: the heart of the modern air passenger rights regime in North Macedonia is governed by a foreign legal text, albeit one granted direct effect through national law. While the Civil Aviation Agency's confirmation that the *Sturgeon* ruling is applied mitigates some interpretative uncertainty, this technique places a significant burden on all parties to navigate a regulation not originally designed for the national legal context. It is a minimalist transposition that achieves formal compliance but potentially at the expense of legal clarity and accessibility for the ordinary citizen, a gap partially filled by the Agency's commendable efforts to provide clear online summaries. The law functions effectively as a bridge to EU law but falls short of being a fully realized, autonomous codification of air passenger rights.

The transposition is not a perfect carbon copy and exhibits a hybrid structure. The North Macedonian law chooses to elaborate on certain procedural aspects that Regulation 261 leaves to airlines or national authorities. The specific national refund rules for voluntary cancellations (10% fee for 24-hour notice on domestic flights, 5% in cases of force majeure) provide clarity but exist outside the scope of the EU regulation, which focuses exclusively on involuntary denials of boarding, cancellations,

11 The Regulation on measures and procedures for facilitation of the civil aviation, which implements Regulation 1107/2006.

and delays. This adds a layer of national consumer law alongside the transposed EU rights.

A significant point of substantive divergence, rather than just methodological difference, lies in the treatment of passengers with reduced mobility. The text correctly observes that the specific non-discrimination and assistance provisions for PRMs found in Regulation 261 are not integrated into this law. While these rights may be provided elsewhere in the national legal system, their excision from this central statute creates a risk of fragmentation. This contrasts with the EU's consolidated approach in Regulation 261, which aims to provide a single, comprehensible source of key passenger rights. The North Macedonian model thereby requires passengers to consult multiple legal sources to assemble the full picture of their entitlements, a process less straightforward than the EU's aspirational model of coherence.

Conversely, the law exhibits a more traditional, detailed legislative approach in areas where the EU regulation is silent or less prescriptive. The provisions governing the formation of the transport contract, the issuance of tickets, and notably, the specific national rules on voluntary cancellation refunds demonstrate a capacity for detailed national rule-making. These refund rules, with their precise timeframes and percentage-based fees for domestic and international flights, including compassionate provisions for force majeure, introduce a layer of national consumer contract law that exists in parallel to, but separate from, the transposed EU rights. This results in a hybrid structure: a detailed national contract law framework for the initiation and voluntary termination of travel, coupled with a referenced EU-derived regime for when the journey is involuntarily disrupted by the carrier.

The North Macedonian law thus presents a study in selective integration. On liability for death, injury, and baggage, it faithfully transposes the principles of the Montreal Convention and related EU regulations, embedding them into discrete articles. Yet, for the operational disruptions that most commonly affect passengers, it builds a legislative bridge to the EU regulation rather than importing its bricks. It leaves the national legal system with a central statute that is incomplete without its annexed EU counterpart. Ultimately, the law is less a self-contained codification and more a sophisticated conduit. It effectively channels EU passenger rights into national legal force and complements them with specific national contractual provisions, but it stops short of achieving the autonomous comprehensiveness that characterizes a fully realized transposition. It is a functional, if imperfect, legal hybrid that secures compliance while revealing the practical challenges of integrating a detailed supranational acquis into a national civil law system.

Comparison with EU Regulation

Feature	**Law on Contractual and Real Right Relations in Respect of Aviation Transport**	**EU Regulation 261/2004**
Delay Compensation	≥3h: €250–€600 (by distance).	≥3h: €250–€600 (by distance).
Cancellation Notice	<14d notice: Refund or re-routing + €250–600 compensation (by distance).	<14d notice: Refund or re-routing + €250–600 compensation (by distance).
Denied Boarding	Volunteer first; €250–€600 (by distance) if denied boarding.	Volunteer first; €250–€600 (by distance) if denied boarding.
Baggage Liability	Not specified.	Not specified.

Bibliography

- Law on Contractual and Real Right Relations in Respect of Aviation Transport, Official Gazette of the Republic of Macedonia, N°85/08, from 11 July 2008, as amended by N°148/2011; 10/2015; 150/15; 173/15 <https://caa.gov.mk/wp-content/uploads/2019/11/85_08-1.pdf>.
- Regulation on Measures and Procedures for Facilitation of the Civil Aviation, Official Gazette of Republic of Macedonia, No. 50/2011, 36/2013, 26/16 and 37/18.
- Civil Aviation Agency, 'Long Delay of Flight' <https://www.caa.gov.mk/en/passengers/2-long-delay-of-flight/> accessed 15 December 2025.

II.36

Norway

Norwegian Regulation No. 141 of 17 February 2005 is the domestic implementation of the EU regulation on common rules for compensation and assistance to passengers in the event of denied boarding and of cancellation or long delay of flights, known as EU Regulation 261.[1] This Norwegian regulation, also known as Air Passenger Regulation, established the framework for passenger rights in the Norwegian aviation sector, ensuring that passengers are protected and compensated according to the standards set by the EU legislation.

The Norwegian Regulation No. 141 is very short with only five provisions. The Regulation stipulates when it enters into force[2], and that its scope extends to Svalbard, despite Svalbard's general exemption from the EEA Agreement under Protocol 40.[3] Regulation 261 is attached in the Annex.

The Norwegian Civil Aviation Authority is responsible for supervising compliance with the regulation for flights from Norwegian airports and flights from third countries to Norwegian airports, utilizing enforcement powers under the Civil Aviation Act, including the imposition of violation fines for infringements.[4] On the Norwegian Dispute *Resolution* Board (Transportklagenemnda),[5] there is a clear statement that cases cannot be submitted if the country where the incident occurred is not Norway. So if

1 Section 1 of the Regulation. By Form 1 of 14 April 2005 (Doc No 316132), Norway notified the implementing measure as 'Regulation [of 17 February 2005 No 141] implementing Regulation (EC) No 261/2004 of the European Parliament and the Council of 11 February 2004 establishing common rules on compensation and assistance to passengers in the event of denied boarding and of cancellation or long delay of flights, and repealing Regulation (EEC) No 259/91.' The Regulation has since been amended by the following amending regulations: FOR-2008-10-31-1168, FOR-2009-07-03-969, and FOR 2012-09-03-849.

The transposition was possible through section 10-44 and Section VIII of the Aviation Act.

2 Section 5.

3 Section 4.

4 Section 2.

5 Established through Aviation Act, Section 10-44 and Section VIII.

DOI: 10.4324/9781003746164-47

passengers suffered a delay in a flight from Germany to Norway, the claim must be submitted to the German NEB.[6]

In 2020, the Supreme Court was faced with a case regarding whether a claim submitted in excess of three months after the event under the Air Passenger Regulation would render the action time barred. The Supreme Court rejected the Court of Appeal argument that it did.[7] Justice Thyness noted, “my conclusion is that there is no sufficient reason on a non-statutory basis for establishing a requirement to give notice of claims for standard compensation under the Air Passenger Regulation in a timely manner.”[8]

In November 2022, the EFTA Surveillance Authority received a complaint regarding Norway’s implementations of Regulation 261, especially the wrongful interpretation of Article 5(3) of the Regulation.[9] The complainants “allege that the interpretation applied is outdated and cannot be reconciled with the interpretation upheld by the Court of Justice of the European Union (CJEU) in its recent case law.”[10] While the EFTA Surveillance Authority found that in that particular case, the Oslo District Court’s interpretation was hard to reconcile with the CJEU’s related case law, it did not find any generalized failure.[11]

Norwegian Regulation No. 141 of 17 February 2005 serves as the domestic implementation of EU Regulation 261, incorporating its provisions directly into national law by reference. This approach results in a notably concise legal instrument, with the EU Regulation attached in an annex. The enforcement mechanism is clearly delineated, vesting supervisory authority in the Norwegian Civil Aviation Authority. Like North Macedonia, the Norwegian method of implementation creates a significant practical hurdle for passengers seeking to understand their rights. By embedding the core rules in an annexed EU regulation (which is not written with a Norwegian audience in mind) and using a very short domestic law to handle administrative details, the system places a burden on the individual. This law is arguably less user-friendly than the approach of some other states, such as Bosnia or Montenegro, which have fully transposed the regulation into a dedicated, self-contained national law.

6 NRF, ‘Complaint on an Air Travel’ <https://www.reiselivsforum.no/web/klageinformasjon/fly/> accessed 15 December 2025.

7 HR-2020-2401-A, (case no. 19-186250SIV-HRET), Svenn Nilsen, *The Norwegian Consumer Council (intervener) v Finnair Oyj and The Federation of Norwegian Aviation Industries* (intervener), 14 December 2020 <https://www.domstol.no/globalassets/upload/hret/translated-rulings/hr-2020-2401-a.pdf>.

8 Paragraph 59.

9 Case: 89545, decision 076/24/COL of 29 May 2024.

10 Case: 89545, decision 076/24/COL of 29 May 2024, p. 2.

11 Case: 89545, decision 076/24/COL of 29 May 2024, p. 6.

Comparison with EU Regulation

Feature	Norwegian Regulation No. 141	EU Regulation 261/2004
Delay Compensation	≥3h: €250–€600 in marks (by distance).	≥3h: €250–€600 (by distance).
Cancellation Notice	<14d notice: Refund or re-routing + €250–600 compensation (by distance).	<14d notice: Refund or re-routing + €250–600 compensation (by distance).
Denied Boarding	Volunteer first; €250–€600 (by distance) in marks if denied boarding.	Volunteer first; €250–€600 (by distance) if denied boarding.
Baggage Liability	Not specified.	Not specified.

Bibliography

- Forskrift om flypassasjerers rettigheter ved nektet ombordstigning og innstilt eller vesentlig forsinket flyging (Regulations on air passengers' rights in the event of denied boarding and cancelled or significantly delayed flights), Norwegian Regulation No. 141 of 17 February 2005, FOR-2005-02-17-141 <https://lovdata.no/dokument/SF/forskrift/2005-02-17-141/%C2%A71#%C2%A71>.
- Regulations on amendments to the regulations on the rights of air passengers in the event of denied boarding and cancelled or significantly delayed flights and regulations on the rights of disabled persons and persons with reduced mobility in connection with air transport, FOR 2012-09-03-849 <https://lovdata.no/dokument/LTI/forskrift/2012-09-03-849>.
- ESA, Case: 89545, decision 076/24/COL of 29 May 2024 <https://www.eftasurv.int/cms/sites/default/files/documents/gopro/College%20Decision%20076_24_COL%20-%20Norway%20-%20Complaint%20regarding%20Regulation%20%28EC%29%20No%20261_2004%20-%20Flyhj%C3%A6lp%20v%20KLM.pdf> accessed 15 December 2025.
- HR-2020-2401-A, (case no. 19-186250SIV-HRET), Svenn Nilsen, *The Norwegian Consumer Council (intervener) v Finnair Oyj and The Federation of Norwegian Aviation Industries (intervener)*, 14 December 2020 <https://www.domstol.no/globalassets/upload/hret/translated-rulings/hr-2020-2401-a.pdf> accessed 15 December 2025.
- NRF, 'Complaint on an Air Travel' <https://www.reiselivsforum.no/web/klageinformasjon/fly/> accessed 15 December 2025.

II.37

Oman

Oman's Civil Aviation Authority (CAA) issued the Passenger Rights Protection Regulation (PRPR), based on Royal Decree No. 65/2006, through the Ministerial Decision N°757 of 2024.[1] The Regulation aims to enhance protections for passengers travelling from, to, or within Oman.[2] It applies regardless of the nationality of the carrier for flights departing from the Sultanate and only to national carriers for flights arriving to Oman unless the passenger was compensated in the country of departure.[3] Article 3 makes it clear that flights operated by foreign carriers arriving to Oman are subject to the country of departure laws or international conventions.

The PRPR demonstrates the desire of the CAA to render this Regulation as effective as possible but also airtight to potential conflicts. For instance, Article 4 defines the point of contract, i.e. when the ticket is issued, which then could avoid some conflicts. Article 5 reinforces passenger protection by ensuring that when multiple airlines are involved in a single journey based on a code-sharing agreement, they are jointly responsible for fulfilling the obligations outlined in the Regulation, while the passenger has the right to claim compensation from either. Nonetheless, "in the event of a dispute between the two carriers, the marketing carrier will be responsible for compensation." Airlines must include the rights in the PRPR on their website.[4]

Like Saudi Arabia, the PRPR stipulates in its Article 8 the obligations of the passengers which include providing correct personal data and details, complying with the safety and discipline instructions of the aircrew on

1 Ministerial Decision No. 757/2024 Issuing the Passenger Rights Protection Regulation, 20 Safar 1446 AH (corresponding to 25 August 2024) translation available at chrome-extension://efaidnbmnnnibpcajpcglclefindmkaj/https://c.ekstatic.net/ecl/documents/rules-and-notices/oman-passenger-rights-protection-regulation-en.pdf; CAA, 'Passenger Rights' <https://www.caa.gov.om/en/passenger-rights-1>.

2 Article 2. The PRPR does not apply to passenger travelling free of charge.

3 Article 2(1) and (2).

4 Article 7.

DOI: 10.4324/9781003746164-48

board, disclosing any special needs before confirming reservation, reading the terms and conditions or complete travel procedures, and having valid travel documents. In the event the passenger fails to comply with those obligations, the airline will not be liable for any compensation.[5]

Article 10 contains the airlines' obligations such as providing passengers with all the terms and conditions or refraining from accepting passengers lacking the valid travel documents but also ensuring transparent pricing in advertising ticket fares, flights, and services. Airlines must avoid adding any hidden or undisclosed fees to tickets or services.[6] Article 11 makes it clear that if airlines accept passengers who do not satisfy the travel requirements, any consequence is on them and they will have to refund the full value of the ticket as well as provide the necessary care and support.

While the PRPR specifically addresses air passenger rights, Oman also has broader consumer protection laws under the Consumer Protection Authority (CPA), established by Royal Decree No. (66/2014). The CPA safeguards consumer rights against unfair trade practices, misleading advertisements, and substandard goods and services across various sectors.

According to the Regulation, carriers are obligated to limit overbooking.[7] Carriers may prevent some passengers from travelling if the flight is overbooked. However, "Passengers with disabilities, special-needs passengers, first-degree relatives, unaccompanied minors and accompanying housemaids, are exempt from the travel ban." An airline cannot deny boarding if there are seats available in a lower class on the same flight.[8] In those circumstances, either the passenger accepts the downgrading and is entitled to the difference in price and a 50% compensation of that difference or the passenger can terminate the contract and receive a refund for the unused portion plus compensation equal to 50% of that value and is entitled to care and support.[9]

In the event a passenger is denied boarding involuntarily, airlines must provide written rights information and allow the passenger to choose between alternative flights (with the same or another carrier) or upgrade for free.[10] Passengers are eligible for compensation equivalent to 50% of the unused sector's ticket value when the alternative flight departs between two and six hours after the original time, in addition to providing care and support.[11] When the alternative flight departs after more than six

5 Article 9.
6 Article 10(5).
7 Article 12.
8 Article 34.
9 Article 34(2).
10 Article 13(2) and (3).
11 Article 15.

hours from the original time, passengers are eligible for compensation available for cancelled flights.[12] Passengers can also choose to terminate the contract due to denial of boarding. In this case, airlines must fully refund any unused ticket to its full value and offer compensation equal to 100% of that value. If the ticket was already partially used, passengers are entitled to a refund for the unused portion of the ticket plus compensation equal to 50% of the total ticket value.[13]

Passengers are not eligible for compensation for denied boarding if the passenger failed to adhere to the obligations in Article 8, or when the airline offers a comparable flight that departs within two hours of the original schedule, the right to care and support remains applicable.[14]

Denial of boarding

Timeframe	Care and Assistance	Compensation
<2-Hour Delay	- Refreshments and beverages.	N/A
2–6-Hour Delay	- Full meal. - Communication access.	50% of ticket value.
>6-Hour Delay	- Hotel accommodation + transport.	Full cancellation compensation (Art. 16).
Passenger Chooses to Cancel	Right to terminate contract.	100% of ticket value for unused tickets. 50% of the ticket value for partially used tickets.

The Regulation is very strict and only allows cancellation or delays in case of force majeure and for safety and security requirements.[15] In case of a delay while the passenger is in paid accommodation, the airline must bear the accommodation extension cost until the alternative departure time.[16] Delays or cancellations due to force majeure might allow airlines to limit care and support to a maximum three nights while relieving airlines from any compensation requirement.[17]

Passengers experiencing delays of less than six hours are entitled to care and support as stipulated in the Regulation. The airline is also liable for financial expenses incurred by the passenger due to the delay,

12 Article 16.
13 Article 17(1) and (2).
14 Article 14(1) and (2).
15 Article 18. Force majeure is defined in Article 1 as "An extraordinary event or circumstance that is unexpected or unanticipated by the air carrier." Further guidance is given in the annex of the PRPR.
16 Article 19.
17 Article 42.

in accordance with the Montreal Convention.[18] Any delay exceeding six hours entitles the passenger to compensation under the Regulation's flight cancellation provisions unless it is due to a force majeure event.[19]

The PRPR distinguishes between cancellations which have been notified to the passengers at least 14 days in advance and notifications not exceeding 14 days. Unlike many regulations, compensation does not increase the shorter the notice is. No compensation is due when passengers are informed of an international flight cancellation more than 14 days before departure. Passengers have the right to an alternative flight or to terminate the contract, receiving a refund for the unused sector and any additional fees.[20] The airline is not required to provide care and support in these circumstances.[21]

The Regulation also makes a distinction between domestic and international flights. When the notification of the cancellation is within 14 days of departure of an international flight, airlines must inform the passenger of their rights to care and support and offer available alternative flights.[22] The PRPR mirrors EU Regulation 261 as the compensation is based on flight distance, namely 108 Omani Riyals for flights not exceeding 1,500 km, 173 Omani Riyals for flights between 1,500 and 3,500 km, and 260 Omani Riyals for flights above 3,500 km.[23] Compensation is based on the air distance between origin and final destination and not the great circle route method as found in the EU Regulation.[24] No compensation is due if the alternative flight arrives to the final destination no more than two hours later than the originally scheduled time.[25] The compensation can also be reduced by half if the arrival time does not exceed three hours for all international flights of less than 1,500 km, four hours for flights between 1,500 and 3,500 km, and five hours for flights exceeding 3,500 km.[26]

Article 23 grants a right to terminate the contract upon cancellation and non-acceptance of the alternative flight. Passengers will then receive a full refund for the unused ticket sector including additional fees and compensation. Airlines are exempted from providing care and support.[27]

18 Article 20.

19 Article 21 in conjunction with Article 42.

20 Any refund must be made within 14 business days from the date the airline acknowledges the passenger's right in cash, bank transfer, bank draft, or exchange vouchers (at the passenger's choice). Article 40.

21 Article 24.

22 Article 22(1) and (2).

23 Article 22(2).

24 Article 22.

25 Article 26.

26 Article 28(1)–(3).

27 Article 23.

For cancellation of connecting flights, the airline must inform the passenger. The passenger can request to reschedule the flight or terminate the contract, with compensation provided according to the flight cancellation provisions.[28] Any early departure or re-routing of international flights within 14 days of the original schedule which results in damages should be compensated by the airline in accordance with the Montreal Convention.[29]

Compensation for cancellation of domestic flights is regulated by Articles 30 to 33. In the event a domestic flight is cancelled within 24 hours of departure and the airline is unable to offer an alternative flight within four hours of the original time, the airline must compensate the passenger with an amount equal to the unused ticket portions' value and an additional 100% of that value, in addition to providing care and support.[30] When the passenger is notified of the cancellation between 24 hours and seven days before departure, the airline must provide an alternative flight and compensation equivalent to 50% of the total ticket value. Should the passenger choose to terminate the contract, not only should they be refunded for the unused portion but also receive 50% of the total ticket value as compensation. In those circumstances, the airline is relieved of care and support obligations.[31] The airline is relieved of any care and support or compensation when the passenger is notified more than seven days before the departure and the alternative flight departs within 24 hours of the original time.[32] When the alternative flight departs more than 24 hours after the original time, airlines must compensate the passenger with 50% of the total ticket value. Passengers can terminate their contract at any time and receive a refund for the unused portion.[33] Interestingly, no maximum period was fixed for the alternative flight when the notice is given within 24 hours and seven days. Could it exceed 24 hours or the same limit applies as for notice over seven days?

The PRPR also includes a provision on handling domestic cancellation at airports. Article 33 makes it clear that any upgrading costs are on the airline. Any downgrading on the alternative flight results in an obligation for airlines to refund the difference between the original ticket value and the lowest reservation booking designators (RBD) in the cabin in addition to compensation equivalent to 50% of the original ticket value.[34] Airlines also have a care and support duty.

---

28 Article 25.
29 Article 29.
30 Article 30.
31 Article 31.
32 Article 32.
33 Article 32.
34 Article 33(2).

Flight Cancellation

Criteria	Domestic Flights	International Flights
Care and Assistance	- Meals/refreshments (after 2h delay). - Hotel if >6h delay.	Same as domestic.
Compensation	**100% refund + 100% ticket value.**	Distance-based: • ≤1,500 km: **108 OMR**. • 1,500–3,500 km: **173 OMR**. • >3,500 km: **260 OMR**.
Alternative Flight	- Within 4h for notice within 24 hours of departure time. - Within 24h for notice more than 7 days of departure time.	Next available flight (same/other airline).
Passenger Opts to Cancel	**100% refund + 50% compensation.**	**100% refund + compensation.**
Reduced Compensation	- ≥7 days notice and alternative flight exceeding 24 hours.	Alternative flight: • ≤1,500 km and 3 hours: **54 OMR**. • 1,500–3,500 km and 4 hours: **86.5 OMR**. • >3,500 km and 5 hours: **130 OMR**.
No Compensation Cases	- ≥7 days notice and alternative flight within 24 hours. - Force majeure.	- ≥14 days notice. - Alternative flights arrive within 2 hours → **no compensation**. - Force majeure.

Any diversion of international flights to another airport than the agreed destination which caused damages to the passengers should be compensated in accordance with the Montreal Convention.[35]

Passengers may request compensation of 100 Special Drawing Rights (SDR) for each undeclared stopover at the time of reservation as it will be contrary to the obligations set in Article 35.[36] This compensation is in addition to any compensation for flight delays. Stops added for security, safety, or onboard emergencies (properly documented and approved by the competent authority) are excluded.[37] When stopovers are added after

35 Article 27.
36 Article 36.
37 Article 36.

the ticket is issued, it gives the right to the passenger to terminate the contract and receive a full ticket refund.[38]

Passenger Compensation Requirements (Oman PRPR)

Scenario	Compensation	Conditions and Exceptions
1. Denied Boarding (Art. 12–17)	**Option 1:** Rebooking on next flight + compensation: • **50% of ticket value** (if 2–6 hrs delay, Art. 15) • **Full cancellation compensation** (if >6 hrs) **Option 2:** Terminate contract + **100% refund + 100% compensation**	- **Exemptions**: Disabled/ minors/families - No compensation if passenger violated rules
2. Flight Cancellation (Art. 22–24, 30–33)	**International Flights (Art. 22):** • ≤1,500 km: **108 OMR•** 1,500–3,500 km: **173 OMR** • >3,500 km: **260 OMR**. **Domestic Flights (Art. 30–31):** • **100% refund + 100% compensation** (if <24 hrs notice). • **50% compensation** (if 24 hrs–7 days notice).	- **No compensation** if notified ≥14 days (int'l) or ≥7 days (domestic) - Exempt for force majeure.
3. Flight Delay (Art. 20–21, 38)	**>6 hrs delay**: Same as cancellation compensation.	- **No monetary compensation** if delay ≤6 hrs (only care). - Force majeure exempt.
4. Downgrading (Lower class, Art. 34)	**If accepted**: • Refund **price difference + 50% of difference.** **If rejected**: • **100% refund + 50% compensation.**	

The right to care comprises refreshments and beverages after the second hour of delay, appropriate meals if the delay exceeds three hours, and a hotel accommodation and transportation to or from the airport if the delay exceeds six hours.[39] Any failure to comply with the care and support obligation would result in a compensation of 10 SDR for lack of refreshments and drinks, 30 SDR for not providing a proper meal, and

38 Article 37.
39 Article 38(1), (2), (3).

100 SDR for not providing hotel accommodation and transportation.[40] This compensation is in addition to any other compensations found in the Regulation. Interestingly, the PRPR does not mention communication access as a care and support mechanism.

Time	Required Support	Potential Compensation for Failure
2+ Hours	- Refreshments and beverages.	10 SDR.
3+ Hours	- Appropriate meal.	30 SDR.
6+ Hours	- Hotel accommodation + transport.	100 SDR.
Overnight	- Extended hotel stay (if already in one).	N/A
Force Majeure	- Max 3 nights' accommodation.	No monetary compensation, but basic care provided.

The Regulation also contains a full chapter dedicated to passengers with disabilities and special needs. The provisions within Chapter III are pretty much standard provisions except for the compensation for failing to provide an alternative flight or necessary services which should be equal to 200% of the total value of the ticket.[41] Airlines cannot ask passengers to waive their rights and must permit the transport of essential mobility devices and service animals, subject to approval.[42]

In a similar vein, Chapter IV concerning baggage does not introduce any revolutionary regulations. Passengers are permitted to transport baggage in accordance with the terms of the contract, which specify the permissible number, size, and weight.[43] Valuable items must be declared before being handed over.[44] In the event that such baggage is lost or damaged, compensation will be determined based on the declared value.[45] If baggage does not arrive within 21 days, it is deemed lost, necessitating compensation. Passengers are required to report any damage within 24 hours of arrival.[46] As found in Saudi Arabia, a fixed compensation is provided in the PRPR for baggage delay but only with regard to the first

40 Article 39(1), (2), (3).
41 Article 53.
42 Article 49.
43 Article 54.
44 Article 55. See: Vinod Nair, 'Oman: CAA 'Passenger Rights' Specifies Compensation if Baggage Is Delayed or Lost' (*Zawya*, 11 September 2024) <https://www.zawya.com/en/business/aviation/oman-caa-passenger-rights-specifies-compensation-if-baggage-is-delayed-or-lost-r8xcckrs> accessed 15 December 2025.
45 Article 57.
46 Article 57.

day, namely 148 SDR for the first day. The maximum compensation for financial costs incurred is 1,288 SDR.[47]

The Civil Aviation Authority can impose penalties for any violation of the regulations.[48] Those penalties must be in line with Article 62 of the Civil Aviation Law (Royal Decree 76/2019) which lists the potential penalties; the CAA can issue a warning or temporary withholding or cancelling of exemptions and approval, and it can also ban or limit the operating privilege temporarily or permanently. The CAA could also stop or restrict any flight operated by the airline. Finally, an administrative penalty of no more than 30,000 Omani Rials can be imposed. That amount can be doubled in case of recurrence.[49]

As mentioned, this Regulation is very extensive and includes a long table of potential force majeure incidents. However, some of the categories are still vague, such as meteorological factors. It mentions potential damages caused by "other meteorological events (for example lightning strikes, hailstones, thunderstorms, severe turbulence, etc.)" which seems to suggest those will not be considered bad weather. Similarly, airport closure seems rather difficult to comprehend. Whether it includes technical failure is up in the air. For strikes, the Regulation mentions "Strikes that affect the operation of an air carrier, such as strikes carried out by air traffic controllers." It remains unanswered whether pilots or crew strike would also fall within this definition.

Category	Examples
1. **War/Political Unrest**	Armed conflict, travel advisories, political instability.
2. **Fuel Shortage**	Unexpected unavailability of aircraft fuel.
3. **Unlawful Acts**	Terrorism, threats to airport/aircraft safety.
4. **Sabotage**	Deliberate damage to aircraft.
5. **Security Reasons**	Bomb alerts, hijacking, airport closures, removal of unaccompanied baggage, unruly passengers.
6. **Meteorological factors**	Bad weather conditions, weather-related airport closures, damages to aircrafts due to other meteorological events.
7. **Airport Closure**	Non-weather/non-security shutdowns.
8. **Medical Emergencies**	Passenger/crew illness or death mid-flight.
9. **Bird Strikes**	Collisions causing immediate aircraft checks and potential repair.

(*Continued*)

47 Article 59.
48 Article 62.
49 Article 62d. of the Royal Decree 76/2019 promulgating the Civil Aviation Law, published in Official Gazette No 1317 on 11 November 2019.

(Continued)

Category	Examples
10. Manufacturing Defects	Hidden defects in properly maintained aircraft parts.
11. Unanticipated Shortcomings Affecting Flight Safety	Damage to the aircraft caused by 3rd parties, in-flight damage, technical issues requiring the aircraft to turn around or divert, failure of the bleed air system/environmental control system on an aircraft, premature failure of life-limited parts, failure of necessary or required aircraft systems, smoke, fire, or fumes on board the aircraft.
12. Strikes	Air traffic controller strikes.
13. ATC Restrictions	Airspace blocks or operational suspensions.
14. Load Issues	Weight/balance restrictions for safety.

The document available to the public is extremely well structured, with a table of contents. It has five chapters, each separated by a page, and detailed guidelines on force majeure. The font is also relatively large, making it easier for the reader. Overall, it is quite an enjoyable experience to read the document.

Oman's newly introduced Passenger Rights Protection Regulation (PRPR 2024) represents a significant step forward in air traveller protections in the Sultanate's aviation governance, blending elements of the EU's robust Regulation 261 with innovative local adaptations. The PRPR's architecture mirrors the EU Regulation in its core scenarios – denied boarding, cancellation, and delay – and even adopts a similar distance-based compensation matrix for international flight cancellations, albeit with fixed amounts in Omani Riyals rather than euros. However, the Omani framework introduces distinctive features, such as its exceptionally detailed and expansive catalogue of force majeure events, which provides greater ex ante clarity than the EU's more general "extraordinary circumstances" doctrine, though it leaves some ambiguity around categories like "airport closure" and strikes beyond air traffic controllers.

Another notable divergence is the compensation trigger threshold for delays, set at six hours in Oman compared to the EU's three or four hours depending on distance, representing a more carrier-friendly standard. The Regulation also uniquely differentiates compensation rules for domestic and international flights, offering robust, value-based compensation for domestic cancellations – including a 100% refund plus 100% of the ticket value as compensation for short-notice cancellations – which in some cases exceeds the EU's fixed amounts for short-haul flights.

The PRPR exhibits several sophisticated procedural and enforcement mechanisms that, in certain aspects, surpass the EU model. The provision for joint liability in code-share agreements, with a clear dispute resolution rule favouring the marketing carrier, strengthens passenger recourse. The establishment of specific financial penalties for failures in the duty of care (10 SDR for lacking refreshments, 30 SDR for meals, and 100 SDR for hotel accommodation) adds a layer of enforceability that the EU Regulation lacks. Furthermore, the dedicated chapter on passengers with disabilities, which includes a potent compensation of 200% of the ticket value for service failures, alongside the CAA's broad authority to impose administrative fines up to 30,000 OMR and operational restrictions, creates a formidable deterrent against non-compliance. This enforcement rigour is complemented by consumer-friendly transparency obligations, such as requiring airlines to publish rights on their websites and prohibiting hidden fees.

In conclusion, Oman's PRPR 2024 is a meticulously drafted, modern regulation that successfully transplants the core principles of advanced passenger rights regimes while tailoring them to regional legal and operational contexts. It balances passenger protection with operational realities through its high delay threshold and detailed force majeure list. While the Regulation demonstrates notable strengths – particularly in domestic flight protections and enforcement mechanisms – it retains some limitations when measured against global gold standards.

Comparison with EU Regulation

Feature	Oman PRPR (2024)	EU Regulation 261/2004
Delay Compensation	>6h: full cancellation compensation. ≤6h: care only.	≥3h: €250–€600 (by distance).
Cancellation Compensation	<14d notice **International Flights**: **108–260 OMR.** **Domestic Flights:** • <24 hrs notice: **100% refund + 100% compensation** (if <24 hrs notice). • 24 hrs–7 days' notice: **50% compensation** (if 24 hrs–7 days' notice).	<14d notice: Refund or re-routing + €250–600 compensation (by distance).
Denied Boarding	Volunteer first; **Option 1:** Rebooking on next flight + compensation: • **50% of ticket value** (if 2–6 hrs delay, Art. 15). • **Full cancellation compensation** (if >6 hrs). **Option 2**: Terminate contract + **100% refund + 100% compensation**.	Volunteer first; €250–600 (by distance) if denied boarding.
Baggage Liability	• 148 SDR 1st day. • Max 1,288 SDR total.	Not specified.

Bibliography

- Ministerial Decision No. 116/2023, issuing the Executive Regulation of the Civil Aviation Law, Published in Official Gazette 1479 issued on 5 February 2023. Translation available at <https://decree.om/2023/caa20230116/>.
- Ministerial Decision No. 757/2024 Issuing the Passenger Rights Protection Regulation, 20 Safar 1446 AH (corresponding to 25 August 2024). Translation available at <https://c.ekstatic.net/ecl/documents/rules-and-notices/oman-passenger-rights-protection-regulation-en.pdf>.
- Royal Decree 76/2019 promulgating the Civil Aviation Law, published in Official Gazette No 1317 on 11 November 2019. Translation available at <https://www.caa.gov.om/upload/files/regulations/civil-aviation-law_en.pdf>.
- CAA, 'Passenger Rights' <https://www.caa.gov.om/en/passenger-rights-1> accessed 15 December 2025.
- Nair, V., 'Oman: CAA "Passenger Rights" Specifies Compensation if Baggage Is Delayed or Lost' (*Zawya*, 11 September 2024) <https://www.zawya.com/en/business/aviation/oman-caa-passenger-rights-specifies-compensation-if-baggage-is-delayed-or-lost-r8xcckrs> accessed 15 December 2025.

II.38

Peru

Air passenger rights in Peru are protected by the Civil Aeronautics Law No. 27261,[1] which implements the Montreal Convention, and the Supreme Decree N° 050–2001-MTC,[2] which approves the "Regulation of the Civil Aeronautics Law" – the legal framework that develops and complements Law N° 27261. The legal framework is overseen by the National Institute for the Defense of Competition and the Protection of Intellectual Property (INDECOPI) and aligns with the Andean Community Decision No. 619. It is also supplemented by the Peruvian Consumer Protection Code (*Código de Protección y Defensa del Consumidor*).[3] These regulations determine air passenger rights in case of denied boarding, delays, cancelled flights, and luggage issues.

As a member of the Andean Community of Nations (CAN), Peru is subject to its legal framework, which is designed to be supranational,[4] specifically Decision 619. It was incorporated into Peruvian law not through a domestic legislative process but by the automatic operation of the Andean Community legal system. Decision 619 specifically governs international air travel between Andean member countries and sets the liability regime for those journeys. Peruvian Law 27261 and its regulations govern domestic air travel within Peru. Despite no incorporation, it seems

1 As modified by Law N° 32325 of 2024, Ley que modifica la Ley 27261, Ley de Aeronáutica Civil del Perú, con el fin de fortalecer los derechos de los usuarios de transporte aéreo de pasajeros, published 9 May 2025.

2 Decreto Supremo N° 050-2001-MTC, Reglamento de la Ley de Aeronáutica Civil.

3 Law No. 29571, Código de protección y defensa del consumidor. See: Indecopi, 'Código de protección y defensa del consumidor' (2023) <https://cdn.www.gob.pe/uploads/document/file/4265044/Co%CC%81digo%20de%20Proteccio%CC%81n%20y%20Defensa%20del%20Consumidor%20-%202023%20%281%29.pdf.pdf?v=1678981494> accessed 15 December 2025.

4 Article 4 of the Treaty of Creating the Court of Justice of the Andean Community (Treaty of Cochabamba).

DOI: 10.4324/9781003746164-49

that the same compensation and obligations apply to domestic flights.[5] The rules apply when the airline is responsible for the disruption and not for any events outside of the airlines' control.

In cases of a delayed flight, based on Decision 619, passengers are entitled to a tiered level of care based on the length of the wait. For a delay of between two and four hours, the airline is obligated to provide passengers with a snack and the opportunity to make a telephone call. When the delay extends between four and six hours, passengers are due a snack and a full meal (breakfast, lunch, or dinner, as appropriate), in addition to a phone call. For a delay exceeding six hours, the airline's obligations escalate to include food and a cash compensation equivalent to 25% of the ticket's remaining value. If the delay necessitates an overnight stay, the airline must also cover the cost of accommodation and transport to and from the airport.[6] Meanwhile, Civil Aeronautics Law No. 27261 Article 122 is very vague on the right in case of delay and Article 269 of the Supreme Decree N° 050–2001-MTC implements the Montreal Convention limiting the damage to 1,000 SDR per passengers.

In the event of a cancelled flight, passengers have a choice between a full refund of the ticket's remaining value or an alternative flight scheduled for the same day.[7] During the waiting period, the airline must provide care – including snacks and meals – in accordance with the rules for delayed flights. Should a substitute flight not be available on the same day, the airline's duty of care expands to include providing accommodation, all necessary meals, and transportation until a new flight can be secured. Any delays incurred before the cancellation are subject to additional compensation under the delayed flight regulations.[8] Under Article 125.1 of Law 27261 in case of cancellation, passengers are only entitled to a full refund. Additionally, passengers may choose between re-routing on the next available flight on the same or a similar route, operated by the carrier or any other airline.[9] According to Article 274 of Supreme Decree N° 050–2001-MTC, passengers are also entitled to re-routing on the next available flights being operated by the carrier and entitled to reimbursement of the ordinary costs of accommodation, meals, communications, and transport

5 See poster by INDECOPI, 'Derechos de los pasajeros en el transporte aéreo' <https://cdn.www.gob.pe/uploads/document/file/6571050/5719990-a3-derecho-de-pasajeros-2024.pdf?v=1724786457> accessed 15 December 2025; Lima Easy, 'Air Passenger Rights in Peru' (10 March 2025) <https://www.limaeasy.com/peru-guide/legal-stuff/air-passenger-rights-in-peru#google_vignette> accessed 15 December 2025.

6 Article 8(a) Decision 619.

7 Article 8(c) Decision 619.

8 Article 8(c) Decision 619.

9 Article 126.1(c).

that may be necessary. When the flight is interrupted, the passenger has the right to reimbursement of the part of the fare not travelled or ordinary expenses for accommodation, food, communication, and travel necessary for the duration of the interruption.[10]

Decision 619 is also much more detailed regarding denied boarding, where a distinction is made between voluntary and involuntary situations. An airline can deny boarding to a passenger who poses a health, safety, or security risk; such circumstances include intoxication, possession of prohibited items, violent behaviour, or travelling with invalid documentation.[11] In these specific scenarios, the airline's sole obligation is to refund the net value of the ticket. In comparison, the provisions related to denial of boarding in Peru's Civil Aviation Law are very brief and mainly refer to overbooking.[12]

Aviation regulations did not prohibit flight overbooking, as they expressly contemplated the possibility of overbooking or overselling. Thus, both Article 125 of Law 27261, Peru's Civil Aviation Law, and Article 8(d) of Andean Decision 619 provided for the possibility of overbooking or overselling. However, the rights of the passengers differ slightly depending on which instrument is applicable. Based on the Decision, in cases of overbooking, airlines often seek volunteers to give up their seats in exchange for benefits.[13] Passengers who volunteer forfeit any claim to standardized legal compensation, so negotiation is key. However, if a passenger is involuntarily denied boarding due to overbooking, the airline must provide compensation equivalent to 25% of the remaining ticket value and rebook the passenger on the next available flight on the same route the same day. If this is not possible, the airline must arrange a flight with another carrier at the earliest opportunity.[14] Article 125.4 of the Civil Aeronautics Law does not refer to any fixed compensation but rather grants involuntarily denied passengers the right to immediate reimbursement of the full or part of the ticket as well as the reimbursement of any expenses such as meals, hotels, or communication.

Passengers are entitled to claim damages.[15]

10 Article 125.2.

11 Chapter IV Decision 619.

12 Articles 125 and 126.

13 Reiterated in case of Corte Superior de Lima, la Quinta Sala especializada en lo contencioso administrative Expediente N° 12081-2015.

14 Article 6 Decision 619.

15 Article 125.5.

Event Type	Carrier's Immediate Obligations (Care and Rebooking)	Monetary Compensation (Art. 8.e Decision)	Law 27261
Delay	**>2h to <4h:** Refreshments and free communication. **>4h to <6h:** Above + a full meal. **>6h:** Above + **choice of:** hotel/transfers **or** full refund.	**Yes.** Minimum 25% of the value of the affected route segment.	**No real right. 1000SDR as per** Article 269 of the Supreme Decree N° 050–2001-MTC.
Cancellation	• Full refund **or** re-routing. • Hotel/transfer costs if overnight stay is necessary (if re-routing is for the next day).	**Yes,** if the alternative flight offered arrives at the final destination with a delay exceeding **6 hours** compared to the original scheduled time.	• Full refund **or** re-routing. • Expenses such as food, hotel/ transfer.
Denied Boarding (Overbooking)	• Compensation and assistance **without delay**. • Offer of re-routing to final destination at the earliest opportunity **or** a refund.	**Yes.** Minimum 25% of the ticket value for the affected route. **Double** the compensation (50%) if the new arrival time is delayed by more than **6 hours**.	• Full refund **or** re-routing. • Expenses such as food, hotel/ transfer.

When a flight departs before its officially scheduled time and the passenger was not informed of this change in a timely manner, resulting in them missing the flight despite arriving at the airport on time, the passenger can either request a full refund of the ticket's value or choose to be rebooked on the next available flight with any airline. Should this rebooking necessitate an overnight wait, the operating airline is responsible for providing accommodation, meals, and associated transport.[16]

While Decision 619 contains some rules regarding luggage,[17] the major part of those rules is found in Law 27261 and the Regulation of the Civil

16 Article 125.3.
17 See Andean Community.

Aeronautics Law. Title XII of Law 27261, complemented by Title XII of the Regulation, establishes the responsibility of the carrier. The liability of air carriers operating in Peru is governed by a hierarchical legal structure that clearly differentiates between international and national travel, with each domain having specific rules, limits, and procedures. This framework is established primarily by Law No. 27261 and its implementing Regulation, which provides the necessary detail and updated financial amounts to operationalize the broader principles set forth in the law. Peru operates under two distinct liability systems for air transport: one for international flights and another for domestic flights.

For international air transport, the Peruvian legal framework defers to international agreements. The responsibility of the carrier is governed by international instruments to which Peru is a party, such as the Montreal Convention. As stated in Article 264 of the Regulation, the specific rules for liability in international air transport are not defined in this Peruvian law but are found in the international treaties themselves.

For domestic flights, a specific and detailed liability system is in place, with clear monetary limits. For passenger liability (death or injury), the carrier is responsible for damages, and the maximum amount of liability is 45,000 SDRs per passenger.[18] In the case of death, the carrier is obligated to pay an advance of 20% of this amount to the victim's heirs within 15 calendar days of a request.[19] For liability for delays, the carrier is responsible for damages resulting from a delay in the air transport of passengers, and this responsibility is limited to 1,000 SDRs per passenger.[20] For checked baggage and cargo, the compensation is 17 SDRs per kilogram, while for hand luggage or personal effects carried by the passenger, the compensation is a fixed amount of 300 SDRs in case of loss or destruction.[21] Passengers can declare a special value for their baggage or cargo and pay an additional fee; in such a case, the carrier must compensate up to the declared value.

The procedural requirements for filing a claim, known as the "protesta" or notice of claim, are strict. The law and Regulation establish deadlines that must be met to pursue a claim: five business days from delivery for damage to or partial loss of checked baggage, ten business days for cargo, and five business days from the passenger's arrival for issues with personal effects.[22] For cases of total loss or destruction, the deadline is calculated

18 Article 114 of the Law and 265–267 of the Regulation.
19 Article 267 of the Regulation.
20 Article 269 of the Regulation.
21 Articles 270–271 of the Regulation.
22 Article 120.3 of the Law and 273 of the Regulation.

from the date the carrier notifies the passenger or the date the items should have been delivered. The consequence of failing to file a timely protesta is severe, as it renders the items presumed delivered in good condition and makes any subsequent legal action against the carrier inadmissible, except in cases of fraud. A key exemption from liability exists under the Regulation, which states that a carrier is not liable for denying boarding to a passenger who lacks the necessary documentation, such as a visa or passport, required for the destination.

Baggage Type	**Law 27261**	**Regulation of the Law**
Checked Baggage	Amount set by respective regulations (Art. 118).	**Specifies the amount (Art. 270):** 17 SDR per kilogram.
Personal Effects (Carry-On)	Treated under general baggage rules.	**Creates a specific category (Art. 271):** A fixed limit of **300 SDR** for loss, destruction, or damage.
Delay	Carrier is liable for damages (Art. 122).	**Sets a specific limit for passenger delay (Art. 269):** 1,000 SDR per passenger.

While those look very similar to the Montreal Convention's liability system, the two systems are not identical. For instance, the carrier for death or bodily injury is much lower in Peru (45,000 SDR) compared to the strict liability for proven damages up to 128,821 SDRs per passenger in the Montreal Convention. Similarly, the non-refundable advance payment is much lower. The Peruvian law also contains a fixed limit for hand luggage which is not found in the Convention.

Aspect	**National Transport (Peruvian Regulation)**	**International Transport (Montreal Convention 1999)**
Death/Bodily Injury	45,000 SDR limit.	~128,821 SDR limit for strict liability.
Advance Payment	9,000 SDR (20%) within 15 days.	Advance payment to meet immediate economic needs.
Checked Baggage	1,131 SDR.	1,288 SDR per passenger (approx.).
Carry-On Baggage	300 SDR (fixed).	Typically falls under "Checkable Baggage" limit.
Delay (Passenger)	1,000 SDR limit.	4,694 SDR per passenger (approx.).
Protesta Required?	Yes, strict deadlines (5/10 days).	Yes, written complaint required (21 days for damage).

INDECOPI can fine airlines up to 450 Unidad Impositiva Tributaria (UIT).[23] For a minor infraction, the fine is up to 50 UIT, serious infraction can lead to a fine of up to 150 UIT and very serious infraction to 450 UIT. INDECOPI regularly sanctions airlines for a variety of offenses such as failure to provide correct compensation or assistance following a denial of boarding or delay or cancellation.[24]

Peruvian air passenger law, a modern and consumer-centric framework, stands as a robust system for protecting travellers' rights. It is primarily built upon the Andean Community's Decision 619, the Peruvian Civil Aeronautics Law, and the Consumer Protection and Defense Code, creating a comprehensive legal structure. INDECOPI acts as the key enforcement body, ensuring that airlines adhere to their obligations. However, Regulation 261 is more user-friendly and standardized. For instance, the applicability of Decision 619 to national flights is based on INDECOPI's posters but not based on the law itself.

The most significant divergence is in the approach to monetary compensation for delays and cancellations. EU Regulation 261 mandates fixed, standardized monetary compensation that is not tied to the ticket price. While the Peruvian system ensures fairness relative to the ticket cost, it makes it harder on the passengers especially as the compensation is also tied to a longer waiting time.

The Peruvian system's strength lies in its detailed and escalating care obligations (refreshments, meals, communications, hotel accommodation) which are clearly defined based on the duration of the delay, a structure that is just as detailed, if not more so in its initial stages, as the EU's. Both systems exonerate airlines from paying monetary compensation if the disruption was caused by "extraordinary circumstances" without defining the concept in detail.

While the Peruvian system excels in its clarity on certain procedural and care aspects and contains clear rules on passengers' behaviour, EU Regulation 261 is generally considered to be a more powerful tool for consumers due to its straightforward and generous compensation model.

23 Article 110 of the *Código de Protección y Defensa del Consumidor*.

24 Daniel Martinez Garbuno, 'Peru Fines LATAM' (25 November 2020) <https://simpleflying.com/peru-latam-flight-cancelation-fine/#:~:text=According%20to%20Indecopi%2C%20LATAM's%20Peruvian,fine%20LATAM%20for%20canceling%20flights%3F> accessed 15 December 2025; Nathalie Newman, 'Peru's Indecopi Fines Six Airlines for Delays' (6 January 2017) <https://www.ch-aviation.com/news/52168-perus-indecopi-fines-six-airlines-for-delays#:~:text=The%20Cuzco%20office%20of%20Peru's,for%20violations%20of%20consumer%20protections> accessed 15 December 2025.

This simplicity makes it easier for passengers to understand their rights and pursue their claims without a complex calculation.

Comparison with EU Regulation

Feature	Peru	EU Regulation 261/2004
Delay Compensation	1,000 SDR (national law). >6h: 25% of the fare (Decision).	≥3h: €250–€600 (by distance).
Cancellation Compensation	Refund and re-routing (national law). <15 days notice: 100% refund or re-routing (Decision).	<14d notice: Refund or re-routing + €250–600 compensation (by distance).
Denied Boarding	Refund (national law). Volunteer first; 25% of fare or 50% if arrived after 6 hours (Decision).	Volunteer first; €250–€600 (by distance) if denied boarding.
Baggage Compensation	300 SDR hand luggage. 1,131 SDR checked luggage.	Not specified.

Bibliography

Primary Sources

- Corte Superior de Lima, la Quinta Sala especializada en lo contencioso administrative Expediente N° 12081-2015
- Decreto Supremo N° 050-2001-MTC, Reglamento de la Ley de Aeronáutica Civil <https://cdn.www.gob.pe/uploads/document/file/474866/395507-reglamento-de-la-ley-de-aeronautica-civil-n-27261.pdf?v=1697838617>.
- Law N° 27261, Ley de Aeronáutica Civil del Perú, published 10 May 2000 <https://cdn.www.gob.pe/uploads/document/file/474863/Ley_de_Aeronautica_Civil_27261.pdf?v=1617630949> accessed 15 December 2025.
- Law No. 29571, Código de protección y defensa del consumidor <https://www.gacetajuridica.com.pe/boletin-nvnet/img_bol08/COdigo%20de%20protecciOn%20y%20defensa%20del%20consumidor.pdf>.
- Law N° 32325 of 2024, Ley que modifica la Ley 27261, Ley de Aeronáutica Civil del Perú, con el fin de fortalecer los derechos de los usuarios de transporte aéreo de pasajeros, published 9 May 2025 <https://cdn.www.gob.pe/uploads/document/file/8042353/6752434-ley-32325.pdf?v=1746799446>.
- Treaty of Creating the Court of Justice of the Andean Community (Treaty of Cochabamba) <https://wits.worldbank.org/GPTAD/PDF/annexes/Cartagena%20justicetreaty.pdf>.

Secondary Sources

- Indecopi, 'Código de protección y defensa del consumidor' (2023) <https://cdn.www.gob.pe/uploads/document/file/4265044/Co%CC%81digo%20de%20Proteccio%CC%81n%20y%20Defensa%20del%20Consumidor%20-%202023%20%281%29.pdf.pdf?v=1678981494> accessed 15 December 2025.
- INDECOPI, 'Derechos de los pasajeros en el transporte aéreo' <https://cdn.www.gob.pe/uploads/document/file/6571050/5719990-a3-derecho-de-pasajeros-2024.pdf?v=1724786457> accessed 15 December 2025.
- Lima Easy, 'Air Passenger Rights in Peru' (10 March 2025) <https://www.limaeasy.com/peru-guide/legal-stuff/air-passenger-rights-in-peru#google_vignette> accessed 15 December 2025.
- Martinez Garbuno, D., 'Peru Fines LATAM' (25 November 2020) <https://simpleflying.com/peru-latam-flight-cancelation-fine/#:~:text=According%20to%20Indecopi%2C%20LATAM's%20Peruvian,fine%20LATAM%20for%20canceling%20flights%3F> accessed 15 December 2025.
- Newman, N., 'Peru's Indecopi Fines Six Airlines for Delays' (6 January 2017) <https://www.ch-aviation.com/news/52168-perus-indecopi-fines-six-airlines-for-delays#:~:text=The%20Cuzco%20office%20of%20Peru's,for%20violations%20of%20consumer%20protections> accessed 15 December 2025.

II.39

Philippines

In 2012, the Department of Trade and Industry (DTI) and the Department of Transportation and Communication (now the Department of Transportation or DOTr) approved the Air Passenger Bill of Rights, also known as the Joint DOTC-DTI Administrative Order No.1 Series of 2012 as a result of the mounting pressure from dissatisfied passengers.[1] Francisco Ashley L. Acedillo noted,

> The Joint Administrative Order (JAO) was merely an executive issuance without the force of law, and was perceived as a stopgap measure to placate the increasing number of discontented airline passengers. But, in general, the JAO was still welcomed with joy and relief as, finally, the riding public has something to push back to the airlines in terms of better airline service.[2]

In 2013, more prescriptive rules protecting air passengers were adopted under the House Bill N°23 named An Act Ensuring the Rights of Airline Passengers by Providing Standards for Airline Carrier Services.[3] The Air Passenger Bill of Rights (APBR) was amended by subsequent Civil Aeronautics Board (CAB) resolutions and circulars.[4] In January 2024, the CAB approved Economic Regulation N°9 amended for A Bill of Rights for Passengers and Air Carriers Obligations.[5]

The APBR has a broad scope as it applies to

1 Joint DOTC-DTI Administrative Order No.1 Series of 2012, Passenger Bill of Rights. Article 1 mentions the name as Air Passenger Bill of Right. See: Francisco Ashley L Acedillo, 'A Truly Relevant and Responsive Air Passenger Bill of Rights' (2017) 61 Ateneo Law Journal 782, 784.

2 Acedillo (n 1) 785.

3 Vincent Correia and Noura Rouissi. 'Global, Regional and National Air Passenger Rights – Does the Patchwork Work?' (2015) 40 Air and Space Law 123, 142.

4 Respicio and Co, 'Passenger Rights for Delayed Flights in the Philippines' (3 December 2025) <https://www.respicio.ph/commentaries/passenger-rights-for-delayed-flights-in-the-philippines> accessed 16 January 2026.

5 Republic of the Philippines, Civil Aeronautics Board Economic Regulation N°9, as amended providing for A Bill of Rights for Passengers and Air Carriers Obligations, adopted 30 January 2024.

DOI: 10.4324/9781003746164-50

> all aspects of contracts of carriage for flights or portions of a flight into, from, and within the territory of the Philippines operated by Philippine air carriers, and flights or portions of a flight from the territory of the Philippines operated by foreign air carriers.[6]

The Regulation, therefore, applies to both domestic and international flights operated by Philippine airlines or by international airlines when departing from the Philippines but not to inbound international flights operated by foreign carriers which originate outside of the Philippines. However, if the laws of the country of origin provide similar or higher compensation, the Regulation will not apply.[7]

The APBR is divided into three chapters, each embodying one of the main principles governing the Regulation, namely the right to be provided with accurate information before purchase of the ticket,[8] the right to receive the full value of the service purchased,[9] and the right to compensation.[10]

The right to accurate information relates to the right of passengers to receive a complete, clear, and fair disclosure of terms and conditions before purchasing which includes the documents to be presented at check-in, the check-in deadlines, refund and rebooking policies as well as procedures and responsibilities for delayed and/or cancelled flights.[11] The APBR even suggests the wording of the clause – which if printed must be in bold letters – in Section 4.4 as follows.

> NOTICE:
>
> The ticket that you are purchasing is subject to the following conditions/restrictions:
>
> 1.
> 2.
> 3.
>
> Your purchase of this ticket creates a binding contract that is subject to the terms and conditions attached to the ticket and of the flight. Depending on the fare rules applicable to your ticket, non-use of the same may result in forfeiture of the fare or may subject you to the payment of penalties and additional charges if you wish to change or cancel your booking.
>
> For more choices and/or control in your flight plans, please consider other fare types.

Airlines will have fulfilled their obligation if they sent the information to a travel agency or third person, in the event of the tickets being

6 Section 3 of both the 2012 Administrative Order and 2024 Economic Regulation N°9.
7 Section 3.
8 Chapter II.
9 Chapter III.
10 Chapter IV.
11 Section 4.

brought by such travel agency or third person which only contains their information.[12] The carrier will not be held liable in the absence of any contact information. Similarly, Section 4.6 clarifies that airlines can use the passenger data to inform them of any delays, cancellation, or irregular operations.

Section 5 relates to the right of clear and non-misleading advertisements while Section 6 relates to the right against misleading and fraudulent sales promotion practices. AirAsia Move was fined 6 million Php for "excessive and unreasonable" airfares on it booking platform by the Civil Aeronautics Board.[13] Section 7 grants the passengers the right to have access to on-time performance (OTP) information during booking. OTP should consist of "a flight's aggregate arrival OTP during the immediately preceding month."[14]

The right to full value of purchased service includes the right to be processed for check-in found in Section 9. This rule stipulates that a passenger, holding a confirmed ticket, will not be considered late or no-show and should not be denied check-in if they are already within the air carrier's designated check-in area or cordoned zone at least one hour prior to the estimated time of departure (ETD) or within the air carrier's prescribed time.[15] Any dispute regarding this provision must be resolved on-site through the use of closed-circuit monitor recordings or number slips or any available means which demonstrate that the passenger was not on time.[16]

Passengers have also the right to sufficient processing time before the published ETD to undergo airport procedures, such as check-in and security inspections.[17] This means that check-in counters for international airports and other airports designated by the DOTr should be open at least three hours before the ETD – which was increased compared to the previous version. For other airports, the counters must be opened at least one hour before the ETD. When the passenger opts to check-in online, they must arrive at the airport at least one hour before for international flights and 45 minutes for domestic flights – which is the time when the baggage drop counters will close.

---

12 Section 4.6.

13 Carlo Caoile, 'DOTr Backs ₱6-M Fine vs AirAsia MOVE over "Excessive and Unreasonable" Airfares' *Bilyonaryo News Channel* (27 June 2025) <https://bnc.bilyonaryo.com/dotr-backs-%e2%82%b16-m-fine-vs-airasia-move-over-excessive-and-unreasonable-airfares/news/> accessed 16 December 2025.

14 Per last paragraph of Section 7.

15 Section 9.

16 Section 9.

17 Section 10.

Airlines, operating at international airports or designated airports, should also provide a separate dedicated counter for flights nearing the check-in deadline to facilitate the check-in of passengers at least one hour before the published ETD.[18] Persons with disabilities (PWDs), senior citizens, or passengers requiring special assistance must have their own priority check-in counter, as found in Brazil for instance.[19] Passengers can be accompanied by one companion, unless two or more companions are needed to provide care, there is no queue at the counter, or the booking was made for a group.[20] The airline will only be held liable if the PWD had informed them of their special needs or assistance upon booking.[21]

Scenario	**Requirement**
Check-In Deadline	Passenger not denied if in check-in area ≥1hr before ETD or carrier's time.
Dispute Resolution	Use CCTV/number slips to verify timeliness.
Counter Opening Times	- International/DOTr-designated airports: ≥3hrs before ETD. - Other airports: ≥1hr before ETD.
Online Check-In	Arrive ≥1hr (international). Arrive ≥45mins (domestic) before baggage drop closes.
Priority Counters	Dedicated counters for: - PWDs/seniors (with 1–2 companions). - Flights nearing check-in deadline.

Section 10 of the JAO and 11 of the 2024 Order are named the right to board aircraft for the purpose of flight which contains a prohibition of denial of boarding without the passenger's consent, unless one of the exceptions applies. Such exceptions include immigration issues, safety and security, health concerns, non-appearance at the boarding gate at boarding time, or government requisition of space.[22]

While the practice of overbooking is accepted, any expense, consequence, or inconvenience caused to the passengers must be borne by the airline.[23] In those situations, the airline must announce the flight is overbooked and look for volunteers in exchange of compensation.[24] There is a difference between the APBR 2012 and the proposed 2024 version; in the original document, airlines must increase their compensation

18 Section 10.1.
19 Section 10.2.
20 Section 10.2(a),(b), –(c).
21 Section 10.2 last paragraph.
22 Section 10.2 or 11.3.
23 Section 10.1 JAO or 11.1 2024 Order.
24 Section 10.1(b) JAO or Section 11.1(a) and (b) 2024 Order.

package until the required amount of volunteers is met, the so-called auction system.[25] There is also no safeguards for priority list passengers. In the 2024 version, if there is an insufficient number of volunteers, after ensuring that passengers from the boarding priority list[26] will be able to board, the airline can start denying boarding to other passengers.[27] Unlike the JAO "auction system," this new provision is much clearer in stating the potential "compensation package" must contain a list of offers and amenities from which volunteers can choose from. The package must either be the carrier's best offer or a package comprising of a refund of the ticket or a compensation of 5,000 Php for domestic flights and 10,000 for international flights whichever is the highest, priority in the next flight operated by the airline and accommodation if necessary, or access to an airport lounge if available.[28] In the event the passenger fails to make a choice or refuses to do so, the airline shall decide which package to provide the passenger.

The CAB Regulation N°9 also includes a prohibition of overbooking to exceed 10% of the total seat capacity – which was not found in the previous regulation. In the contrary, the airline will be considered as acting in bad faith.[29] There is, however, an exception for change of aircraft to a smaller one which then also exempts airlines from compensation.[30] Passengers can also be placed on standby lists as long as they are informed and board the intended flight or the next available flight which shall not exceed two immediately succeeding flights from the intended flight.[31] If the passenger cannot board the next two immediately succeeding flights, they may request a refund. Section 11.3 deals with the government agencies and/or official requisitioning seats for official government purpose.

Chapter IV on compensation starts with cancellation or change of aircraft which caused a displacement of passengers. Again, the two documents diverge. Under Section 11 of the JAO, when a flight cancellation

25 Section 10.1(d) of the Order N° 01. See: 'Summary of the Rights of Air Passengers' <https://dtiwebfiles.s3.ap-southeast-1.amazonaws.com/Laws+and+Policies/JAO/Summary+of+The+Rights+of+Air+Passengers.pdf> accessed 16 December 2025.

26 Article 11(1)(d).

"(i) Unaccompanied minors;
(ii) Senior Citizens, PWD and their companion/s;
(iii) Passengers travelling with children under four (4) years old;
(iv) Passengers with scheduled non-elective medical procedures;
(v) Passengers who were previously denied boarding on the same ticket;
(vi) Passengers who have outward connecting flights."

27 Section 11.1(e).

28 Section 11.1(c)(i), (ii) and (iii).

29 Section 11.1(f).

30 Section 11.1(g).

31 Section 11.2(a) and (b).

is attributable to the carrier, the passengers have the right to be notified via public announcement, be provided with care and assistance if the passengers are at the airport such as sufficient refreshments or meals, hotel accommodation, and free phone calls and first-aid, if necessary.[32] Passengers have the right to be reimbursed of the value of the fare or a rebooking on the next available flight operated irrespective of which airline operates it.[33]

Aspect	**Provisions Under JAO**
Applicable Situation	Attributable to the air carrier.
Notification	Public announcement.
Immediate Care and Assistance (When passengers are at the airport)	• Refreshments/Meals: Sufficient provisions. • Accommodation: Hotel accommodation. • Communication: Free phone calls. • Medical: First aid, if necessary.
Passenger Options	Passengers are entitled to choose between: 1. Full Reimbursement of the ticket fare's value. 2. Rebooking on the next available flight, irrespective of which airline operates it.

The CAB Regulation N°9 is much more detailed by differentiating between when the passenger was notified of the cancellation. When the cancellation or change of aircraft is made more than seven days prior to the Scheduled Time of Departure (STD), passengers have the right to be notified by public announcement or text and to a full refund made in the original form of payment[34] or a rebooking at no cost for the first rebooking, but fare difference may apply.[35]

In the event of a cancellation or change of aircraft made seven days or less caused by force majeure or reasons not attributable to the airline, passengers have the right to be notified and the airline has a duty to clearly explain to the affected passengers the reason for the cancellation or change of aircraft. The Regulation goes a step further by noting that "mere pronouncement that the flight has been cancelled or that the change of aircraft is due to force majeure or for reasons not attributable to the air carrier shall not be substantial compliance with the aforementioned requirement."[36]

32 Section 11.1(b) JAO.
33 Section 11.1(c)–(e) JAO.
34 Section 12.8.
35 Section 12.1(a), (b) and (c).
36 Section 12.2(a).

When the cancellation occurs 24 hours or less from the STD and the passengers are already at the airport for check-in, the airline is under the obligation to provide sufficient refreshments or meals or voucher if the circumstances permit it. They are also entitled to "reasonable assistance in coordinating with hotels or ground transportation providers (cost of lodging and/or transportation shall be on the account of the passenger)."[37] Airlines must offer free phone calls, text, internet access, and first aid, if necessary.[38] Additionally, passengers are entitled to choose within 30 days or the validity period of the passenger ticket, whichever is longer, between a full refund, a rebooking, or a special replacement flight operated or organized by the carrier at no additional costs for the passenger.[39] For the rebooking, no fare difference or rebooking fee is payable if rebooking is made on a flight 30 days or less from departure date of passenger's first flight, otherwise fare difference, rebooking, or other fees may apply.[40] Any subsequent rebooking made by the passenger after the first rebooking will be subject to fare difference and rebooking fees.[41]

If the flight cancellation or change of aircraft is made in seven days or less and is not caused by force majeure, in addition to notifying the passengers, airlines will also have to provide those passengers with refreshments, meals, free phone calls, and first aid if necessary. Accommodation is only available if the flight is cancelled 24 hours or less from STD and the passenger was already at the airport.[42] Passengers can also choose between a full refund, a rebooking, or a special replacement flight operated or organized by the carrier at no additional costs for the passenger as well as endorsement by another airline or alternative modes of transport.[43] Passengers could also request the airline to purchase a one-way ticket for the cancelled sector directly from a third-party airline, subject to conditions such as available space or that the third-party flight is scheduled not less than four hours earlier than the scheduled time of the next available flight from the initial carrier or that the price of the one-way does not exceed the total full value of the initial round-trip.[44] The value condition differs if the original ticket was a one-way, in which case, the total cost of the third-party ticket cannot exceed twice the full value of the original ticket.[45] Any optional service items purchased should be

37 Section 12.2(b)(2).
38 Section 12.2(b)(3) and (4).
39 Section 12.2(c)(i), (ii) and (iii).
40 Section 12.2(c)(ii).
41 Section 12.2(c) (ii).
42 Section 12.3(a).
43 Section 12.3 + 12.3(b).
44 Section 12.3(c)(i), (ii), and (iii).
45 Section 12.3(c)(iv).

included in the replacement ticket when possible.[46] Moreover, passengers with connecting flights must be rebooked to their final destination.[47]

If the airline is unable to offer reasonable alternative transportation, a passenger may purchase a ticket from another airline and/or other transport provider subject to the airline's consent and then seek reimbursement under conditions set by the airline, which should not be stricter than those in the APBR.[48] Passengers will still be able to seek reimbursement from the Board if they are able to prove the airline "unreasonably conditioned, delayed or withheld its consent."[49]

In the event the airline has pre-selected an option, they still must expressly inform the passengers that they have the right to reject the option and be informed about all options provided under Section 12.[50] The carrier must allow passengers a reasonable amount of time to accept or reject the pre-selected option. In case the passenger fails to express their choice or did not do so before the deadline set by the carrier, the passenger will be deemed to have accepted the pre-selected option. Nowhere is "reasonable amount of time" defined, which could lead to disputes.

Cancellation according to CAB Regulation

Cancellation or Change of Aircraft That Causes Displacement of Passengers	**Passenger Rights**
More than 7 calendar days prior to the Scheduled Time of Departure (STD)	Notification; and □ Refund; or □ Rebooking (no fee for 1st rebooking; fare difference may apply).
7 calendar days or less prior to the STD caused by force majeure or reasons not attributable to the airline	Notification; and □ Refund; or □ Rebooking (no fare difference or fee if new flight 30 days or less from original departure date); or □ Special replacement flight (no additional cost).
24 hours or less from STD caused by force majeure or reasons not attributable to the airline	Notification; and □ Refund; or □ Rebooking (no fare difference or fee if new flight 30 days or less from original departure date); or □ Special replacement flight (no additional cost).

(*Continued*)

46 Section 12.6.
47 Section 12.7.
48 Section 12.3(e).
49 Section 12.4.
50 Section 12.5(a), (b), (c) and (d).

(Continued)

Cancellation or Change of Aircraft That Causes Displacement of Passengers	Passenger Rights
	☐ If the circumstances permit, and the passenger is already at the airport: o Sufficient refreshments or meals or voucher; o Reasonable assistance in coordinating with hotels or ground transportation providers (cost of lodging and/or transportation shall be on the account of the passenger); o Free phone calls, text, internet access; and o First aid.
7 calendar days or less from the STD and due to a cause other than force majeure	Notification; and ☐ If the flight is cancelled 24 hours or less from STD and the passenger is already at the airport: o Sufficient refreshments or o Meals; o Free phone calls, text, and internet access, and o First aid; and ☐ Hotel accommodation and transportation; and ☐ To choose among: o Refund; or o Rebooking (no fare difference; rebooking fees and other fees shall not apply to the first rebooking); or o Special replacement flight (no additional cost); or o Endorsement to another airline and alternative modes of transportation (no fees or fare difference); or o Purchase by the airline of a one-way ticket for the cancelled sector directly from a third-party airline, subject to conditions; or o If the airline is unable to offer reasonable alternative transportation, passenger may purchase a ticket from another airline and/or other transport provider and require its reimbursement.

Section 12.8 regulates the refund which should be made in the original form of payment. The APBR specifies that airlines may verify the identity of the person filling the refund request or deny such refund request if they were unable to verify the identity. Nonetheless, such denial or delay may then result in the passenger filing a complaint with

the Board. Refund in credit to a travel wallet or miles must "remain valid for the lifetime of the named account holder of such travel wallet of mileage account."[51]

Section 12.11 of the 2024 version stipulates that replacement tickets "may include stop-overs, flights operated by multiple air carriers, and/or transportation combining air and other modes of transportation." The next available flight is defined as a "flight scheduled to depart or arrive up to two (2) calendar days earlier than the time of departure or arrival of the passenger's original flight."[52] Carriers are also invited to provide more generous amenities.[53] This provision is much more extensive than in the JAO.

The rights of delayed passengers are found in Section 12 of the JAO and Section 13 of CAB Regulation. According to the JAO, if a flight is delayed by at least three hours beyond the ETD, regardless of whether the delay is attributable to the carrier, passengers are entitled to certain amenities. These include complimentary refreshments or meals; free access to phone calls, text messages, or emails; and first aid assistance if necessary. Additionally, passengers may choose to rebook or refund their ticket, or be endorsed to another carrier.[54] If a flight is delayed by at least six hours beyond the ETD, passengers may treat the flight as cancelled for the purpose of exercising the rights and amenities applicable in cases of actual cancellation. In such circumstances, passengers are entitled to additional compensation equal to at least the value of the affected sector. Passengers who have not chosen to rebook or request a refund retain the option to board the rescheduled flight within six hours of the initial departure time.[55] Furthermore, if a tarmac delay occurs while passengers are already on board the aircraft, they are entitled to adequate provisions of food and beverages after two hours.[56] There is no fixed or automatic monetary compensation under the APRB.

Hours of Delay	Rights of Passengers
Terminal Delay of at Least 3 Hours (whether or not attributable to the carrier)	- Refreshments or meals. - Free phone calls, text, or e-mails, and first aid, if necessary. - Rebooking or refund.

(*Continued*)

51 Section 12.9.
52 Section 12.15.
53 Section 12.12.
54 Section 12.1(a) and (b) JAO.
55 Section 12.2 JAO.
56 Section 12.3 JAO.

(Continued)

Hours of Delay	Rights of Passengers
Terminal Delay of at Least 6 Hours (for causes attributable to the carrier)	- Flight considered cancelled → cancellation rights and amenities. - Additional compensation equivalent to at least the value of the sector delayed. - To board the rescheduled flight within 6 hours if the affected passenger has not opted to rebook and/or refund.
Tarmac Delay of at Least 2 Hours After the ETD	- Sufficient food and beverage.

Section 13 of CAB Regulation is divided between delays exceeding two hours, exceeding four hours, and tarmac delay. Delays exceeding two hours, whether or not attributable to the airline, grant the passengers the right for sufficient refreshment or meals, free phone calls and internet access and first-aid if necessary.[57]

Delays exceeding four hours attributable to the carrier can be treated by the passenger as cancelled with passengers being entitled to all the protection for cancelled flights. Passengers can also elect to continue with the flight which results in an entitlement to a "compensation equivalent to at least the value of the sector delayed"[58] as well as the right to board the flight if such boarding takes place more than four hours after the STD.[59] Unlike the section on cancellation which is quite extensive and provides its own definitions, nothing is said regarding the meaning of the "value of the sector delayed."

The provision on tarmac delay only refers to the Guidelines on Deplaning of Passengers and Promoting their Convenience without providing much more information.[60] Connecting passengers are entitled to a rebooking if they miss the connection due to the airline's fault. However, such protection is expressly not applicable to passengers performing a self-connection or transfer.[61]

57 Section 13.1.
58 Section 13.2(a).
59 Section 13.2(b).
60 Section 13.3.
61 Section 13.4.

CAB Regulation 9

Delay >2 Hours	Delay >4 Hours for Causes Attributable to the Airline	Tarmac Delay
Sufficient refreshments or	Passengers who choose to continue with the flight: compensation equivalent to at least the value of the sector delayed;	Adequate food and potable water, satisfactorily working air conditioning, operable lavatory facilities, and medical attention, if needed.
Meals.	Right to board the flight if it takes place more than 4 hours after the STD.	Timely and accurate announcements.
Free phone calls, text, and internet access.		Immediate deplaning unless impossible if after 3 hours.
First aid if necessary.		After deplaning, accommodation when necessary; food and communication services (JMC No. 001 s. 2023 – Guidelines on Long Tarmac Delays).

A passenger who is forcibly downgraded from the original class will receive the fare difference, and as compensation a penalty equal to 50% of the fare difference.[62] Such penalty cannot be less than 5,000 pesos. Airlines are also responsible for the failure to provide an in-flight service normally and customarily available as part of the in-flight service on a particular class. The APBR does not specify the compensation but mentions that the airlines had to provide a list to the Board.[63]

The APBR also contains provisions on the right to compensation for delayed, lost, or damaged baggage or death and bodily injury.[64] While Section 14 of the JAO and Section 16 of CAB resemble the Warsaw and Montreal Conventions on the subject, they also include a specific daily rate of 2,000 Php as compensation for the inconvenience caused by the delayed baggage. The Regulation also expressly provides that "a fraction of day shall be considered as one day for purposes of calculating the compensation."[65] The 24-hour period commences one hour from the

62 Section 14.
63 Section 14.
64 Section 14 JAO and Sections 16 and 17 CAB.
65 Section 14.1 JAO and Section 16.1 CAB.

arrival of the flight.[66] In the event the baggage is lost or suffered any damage attributable to the carrier, the compensation is found in the Montreal Convention for international flights and maximum 50% of such amount for domestic flights.[67] The deadline is, however, very short as a luggage will be consider lost after seven days.[68]

While there are mentions of force majeure or "reasons not attributable to the airline" in various provisions, the Bill of Rights for Passengers and Air Carriers Obligations does not include any definition. Annex A only provides a non-binding and non-exhaustive list of scenarios which could be considered force majeure. This list is divided into circumstances deemed to affect the safe operation of the flight – such as natural disasters, meteorological conditions, security risks, acts of sabotage, war or political instability, disruptive passenger behaviour, and damage to the aircraft – and other circumstances such as health risks, hidden manufacturing defect revealed by the manufacturer or the competent authority which impede flight safety. Partial or full closure of the airport and air traffic management restriction or closure of the airspace are also potential force majeure. More uncommon is the addition of the collision with birds which requires immediate compulsory checks and repairs. Unexpected technical defects when they are discovered after or during the pre-flight check and the maintenance have been executed in accordance with approved maintenance programme. On paper, the APBR seems to provide fair protection to passengers. However, the very long list of potential force majeure scenarios might result in a toothless and worthless regulation.

Similarly, there is no timeline for the payment of compensation; Section 19 mentions that compensation must be done promptly at the airport counter or airline's main office or branch without giving a strict deadline for payment.[69]

The JAO does not contain fixed penalties but refers to the provisions in the Civil Aeronautics Act, except violations of sections 5 and 6 which are subject to the Consumer Act of the Philippines.[70] Non-compliance with the CAB Regulation 9 can have far-reaching consequences according to Section 29. False and/or misleading advertisement of fare and/or promotional fares can result in a fine of 50,000 Php for each passenger proven to have relied on that advertisement.[71] Similarly, any violation of

66 Section 14.1 JAO and Section 16.1 CAB.
67 Section 14.2(a) and (b) JAO and Section 16.2(a) and (b).
68 Section 16.3.
69 Section 19.
70 Section 23 of JAO. Republic Act N°776 of 20 June 1952.
71 Section 29.1(a).

Section 8 can result in a fine of 50,000 Php.[72] For any unjustified loss, damage, or delay in baggage, airlines can incur a fine of 10,000 Php.[73] Equally, a failure to designate a dedicated counter for senior citizens, PWDs, and special assistance results in a 10,000 Php fine.[74] Any deliberate overbooking is fined at 50,000 Php.[75] For each unjustified denial of a passenger to check-in or board a 20,000 Php fine can be imposed.[76] Finally, non-compliance with the reportorial requirements rules concerning flight delays and cancellation can result in a fine ranging from 50,000 Php to 180,000 Php depending on whether the airline is a repeated offender.[77]

10,000 Php	**20,000 Php**	**50,000 Php**
Unjustified loss, damage or delayed in baggage.	Denial of passenger to check-in or board.	False and/or misleading advertisement.
Failure to designate a dedicated counter for senior citizens, etc.		Violation of Section 8.
		Any deliberate overbooking.
		Non-compliance with the reportorial requirements rules.

Moreover, for any non-deplaning upon three hours of tarmac delay, airlines will be fined unless deplaning was not possible. For first offence the fine is 1,000 Php per passenger, then the amount is doubled (second 2,000 Php, third 4,000 Php, any succeeding is 8,000 Php).[78] The penalty can, however, not exceed 2 million pesos. Any non-compliance with the duties of care results in similar fines.[79]

The Regulation also contains a peculiar but highly useful separability clause which clarifies that even if some provisions are declared unconstitutional, the remaining sections shall remain effective.[80] There is also a periodic review obligation every three years.[81]

The Philippine APBR, especially the Civil Aeronautics Board Economic Regulation No. 9 (2024), represents a sophisticated and ambitious attempt to create a robust domestic framework for air passenger protection. Its

72 Section 29.1(b).
73 Section 29.1(c).
74 Section 29.1(g).
75 Section 29.1(e).
76 Section 29.1(f).
77 Section 29.1(h).
78 Section 29.2(a).
79 Section 29.2(b).
80 Section 27.
81 Section 26.

development from a non-binding administrative order in 2012 to a detailed regulation reflects a conscious effort to respond to passenger discontent and systematize carrier obligations.

Structurally, the Philippine regulation is organized around three core principles: accurate information, full value of service, and compensation. Its granularity is immediately apparent, extending to mandating specific bold-font warning clauses for tickets and detailed check-in counter opening times differentiated by airport type. This level of operational prescription is largely absent from the EU Regulation, which sets outcome-based standards rather than dictating specific operational procedures.

A cornerstone of the APBR is its elaborate governance of overbooking, an area where it arguably surpasses the EU regime in detail. It explicitly permits the practice but caps it at 10% of seat capacity. The prescribed "compensation package" for volunteers, which must be the carrier's "best offer" or a defined minimum package including cash compensation (5,000/10,000 Php), priority rebooking, and amenities, introduces a structured flexibility. This replaces a previous "auction system" and creates a more predictable, though potentially less passenger-empowering, mechanism.

The Philippine APBR employs a complex, multi-tiered matrix based on the notice period (more than seven days, seven days or less, 24 hours or less) and the cause (attributable to the airline, force majeure, or reasons not attributable). Crucially, the APBR does not mandate a fixed monetary compensation for cancellations within the carrier's control; instead, it emphasizes re-routing, refunds, and care amenities. Compensation equivalent to the sector's value is only specified for delays over four hours where the passenger chooses to continue the journey, a provision whose ambiguity contrasts sharply with the EU's clear compensation tables. Furthermore, the APBR's annex providing a non-exhaustive list of potential force majeure events, including "unexpected technical defects" discovered during pre-flight checks, could be interpreted more expansively than the CJEU's strict interpretation of "extraordinary circumstances," potentially creating a wider exemption window for carriers.

The regulation shines in its attention to specific passenger categories and procedural justice. Its mandates for dedicated check-in counters for persons with disabilities and seniors, complete with companion allowances, and its explicit on-site dispute resolution protocol using CCTV evidence, demonstrate a commitment to accessible and fair process. The inclusion of a daily 2,000 Php inconvenience fee for delayed baggage, accruing by the hour, is a consumer-friendly innovation beyond the Montreal Convention's provisions. However, these strengths are counterbalanced by systemic weaknesses. The absence of statutory deadlines for the payment of owed compensation or refunds, merely requiring "prompt" action, is a significant enforcement gap compared to the EU's mandated timelines. The penalty structure, while detailed, imposes fines on a per violation basis that may not scale effectively to deter systemic failures by large carriers, relying on a maximum cap of 2 million Php for tarmac delays.

In conclusion, the Philippine APBR is a remarkable document of its kind, reflecting a highly prescriptive, procedurally oriented approach to passenger rights. It excels in regulating operational conduct, protecting vulnerable passengers, and managing overbooking with innovative detail. However, when compared to the EU's paradigm, its compensatory framework for the core disruptions of cancellation and delay is less direct, more legally complex, and potentially less potent due to its cause-based matrix and broad force majeure catalogue. Thus, the APBR establishes the Philippines as a jurisdiction with one of Asia's most detailed passenger rights frameworks, one that prioritizes structured re-routing and care but leaves the ultimate financial consequence for airline operational failures more ambiguous than its European counterpart. Its effectiveness will hinge on vigilant enforcement by the Civil Aeronautics Board and the judiciary's interpretation of its many open-textured terms, such as "reasonable amount of time" and "value of the sector delayed."

Comparison with EU Regulation

Feature	Philippines APBR 2024	EU Regulation 261/2004
Delay Compensation	>4h = sector value (undefined).	≥3h = €250–600 (by distance).
Cancellation Compensation	<24h notice: 100% refund or re-routing.	<14d notice: Refund or re-routing + €250–600 compensation (by distance).
Denied Boarding	Volunteer first; 5,000–10,000 Php or best offer.	Volunteer first; €250–€600 (by distance) if denied boarding.
Baggage Compensation	2,000 Php/day.	Not specified.

Bibliography

- Republic of the Philippines, Civil Aeronautics Board Economic Regulation N°9, as amended providing for A Bill of Rights for Passengers and Air Carriers Obligations, adopted 30 January 2024 <https://c.ekstatic.net/ecl/documents/rules-and-notices/philippines-passenger-bill-of-rights-july-2024.pdf>
- Joint DOTC-DTI Administrative Order No. 1 Series of 2012, Passenger Bill of Rights <https://dtiwebfiles.s3.ap-southeast-1.amazonaws.com/Laws+and+Policies/JAO/DOTC+DTI+JAO+No+1+s+2012+-+Air+Passenger+Bill+of+Rights_10+December+2012.pdf>.

- Acedillo, F. A. L., 'A Truly Relevant and Responsive Air Passenger Bill of Rights' (2017) 61 Ateneo Law Journal 782.
- Caoile, C., 'DOTr Backs ₱6-M Fine vs AirAsia MOVE over "Excessive and Unreasonable" Airfares' *Bilyonaryo News Channel* (27 June 2025) <https://bnc.bilyonaryo.com/dotr-backs-%e2%82%b16-m-fine-vs-airasia-move-over-excessive-and-unreasonable-airfares/news/> accessed 16 December 2025.
- Correia, V. and Rouissi, N., 'Global, Regional and National Air Passenger Rights – Does the Patchwork Work?' (2015) 40 Air and Space Law 123.
- Respicio and Co, 'Passenger Rights for Delayed Flights in the Philippines' (3 December 2025) <https://www.respicio.ph/commentaries/passenger-rights-for-delayed-flights-in-the-philippines> accessed 16 January 2026.
- 'Summary of the Rights of Air Passengers' <https://dtiwebfiles.s3.ap-southeast-1.amazonaws.com/Laws+and+Policies/JAO/Summary+of+The+Rights+of+Air+Passengers.pdf> accessed 16 December 2025.

II.40

Russia

Passengers rights in case of delays, cancellation, and denial of boarding in Russia are governed by the Order of the Ministry of Transport of the Russian Federation No. 82 of 2007 on General Rules of Air Carriage of Passengers, Baggage and Cargo and Requirements for Servicing Passengers, Consignors and Consignees, last amended in 2024.[1] The Rules were established under the authority of the Federal Air Code of the Russian Federation. The General Rules are applicable to both domestic and international flights of Russian operators and can be supplemented by the carrier's own rules as long as those rules do not contradict the General Rules.[2]

Section VII, "Passenger Services," mentions that airlines must provide passengers with visual and acoustic information including the reason for the delay or cancellation.[3] The Russian Federal Aviation Regulations also detail the specific service obligations of air carriers once a flight is underway. These rules ensure a standardized level of passenger safety, comfort, and care. They include in-flight safety briefing, first aid, and food and beverage. The regulations establish clear requirements for meal service based on the duration of the flight. For any flight lasting longer than three hours, a hot meal must be served. Subsequent hot meals must be provided on a structured schedule: every four hours during the daytime and every six hours at night. These provisions create a clear set of responsibilities for Russian carriers, extending passenger protection beyond ticketing and check-in to cover the entire in-flight experience.[4] Such obligation is

1 Order of the Ministry of Transport of Russia dated June 28, 2007 No. 82 (as amended on December 25, 2024) "On approval of the Federal Aviation Rules "General rules for the air transportation of passengers, baggage, cargo and requirements for servicing passengers, consignors, consignees" (Registered with the Ministry of Justice of Russia on 27 September 2007 No. 10186) <https://cis-legislation.com/document.fwx?rgn=18809>.

2 Paragraphs 2 and 4.

3 Paragraph 92.

4 Paragraph 95.

DOI: 10.4324/9781003746164-51

excluded if the passenger is informed about the conditions of service prior to the conclusion of the contract.[5]

Paragraph 99 outlines the range of services that Russian air carriers are obligated to provide passengers during flight disruptions, such as delays, cancellations, or route changes. These complimentary protections are applicable irrespective of the underlying cause – whether the carrier's fault, technical malfunction, or adverse weather conditions. The airline's responsibilities commence at specific intervals calculated from the scheduled departure time. Passengers travelling with children under 7 years of age receive immediate access to a mother and child room, while luggage storage is available to all affected travellers. This reflects a strong state policy of supporting families and mothers, which was also found in Kazakhstan.

For delays exceeding two hours, carriers must offer refreshments and facilitate two telephone calls or emails per passenger. Should the delay extend beyond four hours, a hot meal is required, with additional meals provided every six hours during the day and every eight hours overnight. In cases of prolonged disruption, the carrier must arrange hotel accommodation for passengers if delays surpass eight hours during the day or six hours at night, including necessary transportation between the airport and hotel. These comprehensive regulations are designed to ensure the welfare and support of travellers during unanticipated interruptions to their journey. The carrier may provide additional services of increased comfort based on the procedure established by the carrier.[6]

Elapsed Time Since Scheduled Departure	**Services and Amenities Obligated by the Airline**
Immediately Upon Disruption	• **For passengers with children under 7:** Immediate access to a **mother and child room.** • **For all passengers:** Access to **luggage storage**.
After 2 Hours	• Provision of **refreshments.** • Facilitation of **two telephone calls or two emails** per passenger.
After 4 Hours	• Provision of a **hot meal.** • Refreshments and communication access continue.
For Prolonged Delays (ongoing)	• **Meals are repeated:** Every **6 hours** during the daytime, and every **8 hours** overnight.

(*Continued*)

5 Paragraph 98.
6 Paragraphs 100 and 101.

(Continued)

Elapsed Time Since Scheduled Departure	Services and Amenities Obligated by the Airline
After 8 Hours (daytime) **After 6 Hours (nighttime)**	• Provision of **hotel accommodation.** • **Transportation** to and from the hotel and airport.
Additional Carrier Discretion	The carrier may choose to provide **additional services of increased comfort** based on its own established procedures.

The General Rules contain a chapter dedicated to certain categories of passengers which includes children, passengers with disabilities, and other specific cases. The provisions reveal a system that is both highly protective and conditional, often diverging from Western models in significant ways. The regulations governing infants and children are fundamentally structured around the principle of safety through accompaniment. Children under 2 years old, as well as disabled children under 12, must be accompanied by an adult.[7] For a domestic flight, a single child under 2 travelling with a parent without a separate seat flies for free. On international flights, this child receives a discount of at least 90%.[8] Any additional children under 2 must have a separate seat. For domestic flights, Russian citizens between 2 and 12 years old are entitled to a 50% discount. This does not apply to first-class or business-class fares, or on certain government-subsidized routes.[9]

Children between 2 and 12 years of age can travel as unaccompanied minors under the carrier's supervision, provided their parent or legal guardian submits a written application. This service may be extended to children up to 16 years old upon request. Children over 12 may travel unaccompanied.[10]

The regulations address the needs of passengers with various disabilities, making a distinction between those who require accompaniment and those who do not. A person who is legally declared incompetent must be accompanied by a guardian.[11] Similarly, a passenger with both hearing and vision impairments must travel with an assistant.[12] In contrast, a passenger with a general disability, or who is deaf, blind, or uses a

7 Paragraph 104.
8 Paragraph 106.
9 Paragraph 106.1.
10 Paragraph 106.2.
11 Paragraph 109.
12 Paragraph 111.

wheelchair, is permitted to travel without an accompanying person.[13] Patients who require a stretcher must purchase additional seats for their transport.[14] Visually impaired passengers can travel with a guide dog, which is transported free of charge and in addition to the standard baggage allowance. The dog must have a muzzle and a collar, and must remain at the passenger's feet.[15]

Category	Condition	Regulatory Provision
Infants and Children Under 2	General rule.	Must be accompanied by an adult or emancipated minor.
	Fare (domestic).	One infant per adult travels free (lap infant). Additional infants require a separate seat.
	Fare (international).	Lap infant fare: ≥90% discount. Separate seat: Discount at carrier's discretion.
	Fare (Russian citizens).	**50% discount for a separate seat on domestic flights** (excl. first/business and state-subsidized routes).
2–12 Years	Unaccompanied.	Permitted only under carrier's supervision **if** provided for in the carrier's rules, and with a mandatory written application.
12+ Years	General rule.	May travel without any accompaniment.
Passengers With Disabilities		
Incompetent (court-decided)		Transport only upon request of guardians and **must be accompanied** by a capable adult.
Stretcher Patient		Requires the **purchase of additional seats** at a carrier-defined cost.
Deaf and Blind		**Must be accompanied** by an assistant.
Wheelchair User, Deaf, or Blind		**May travel unaccompanied.**
Visually Impaired With Guide Dog		**Permitted with documentation.** Dog travels free in cabin. Must be muzzled and secured.

13 Paragraph 112.
14 Paragraph 110.
15 Paragraph 113.

For passengers with connecting flights, the transportation and baggage handling are governed by agreements between the different carriers involved. Baggage that is subject to customs inspection is handled in accordance with the customs laws of the countries through which the journey passes.[16]

Russian Federal Aviation Regulations provide detailed rules governing both checked baggage and carry-on luggage in Chapter X. A foundational principle of the system is the establishment of mandatory minimum allowances. The carrier is granted the authority to set its own free checked baggage allowance, which can be based on a piece or weight system. However, this corporate policy is constrained by law; the allowance cannot be less than ten kilograms per passenger.[17] If a passenger checks in baggage that is less in weight, size, or number of pieces than what was booked and pre-paid, the passenger is eligible for a refund of the difference in the carriage fee between the paid amount and the actual baggage presented.[18] Similarly, for carry-on luggage, the carrier-defined free allowance must be at least five kilograms.[19] For groups of passengers travelling together for the same purpose on the same flight, carriers must allow them to combine their free baggage allowances upon request. While each piece must be checked in individually, the combined weight cannot exceed 30 kilograms per piece without incurring an extra fee.[20] This establishes a critical consumer safeguard, ensuring that even on the most basic fare, a passenger is entitled to a minimum capacity for their belongings without incurring additional fees. In the event of a forced downgrade, passengers maintain their original baggage allowance.[21]

The regulations also set strict rules for baggage condition. Each piece must have proper packaging to ensure its safety during transport and to prevent harm to others or damage to the aircraft. The maximum weight for a single piece of checked baggage is 50 kilograms, with the exception of wheelchairs for passengers with disabilities.[22] A comprehensive list of prohibited items is also outlined, barring anything that could endanger the aircraft, its occupants, or which is forbidden by Russian law or the laws of any relevant country.[23]

The regulations also specify a list of items that can be carried in addition to the standard carry-on allowance at no extra charge. This includes a

16 Paragraphs 115 and 116.
17 Paragraph 122.
18 Paragraph 125.
19 Paragraph 133.
20 Paragraph 127.
21 Paragraph 137.
22 Paragraphs 128 to 131.
23 Paragraphs 138 and 140.

backpack, a briefcase, a bouquet of flowers, outerwear, baby food, medications, and items purchased from duty-free shops in a sealed bag. Importantly, it also includes assistive devices like crutches, walkers, and folding wheelchairs used by passengers with disabilities.[24] This delineation ensures that passengers are not penalized for carrying essential personal effects.

While there is a chapter described as "claim of checked baggage," the provisions within that chapter does not include any compensation but rather the procedure to claim.[25]

The Rules establish a precise legal dichotomy between passenger-initiated actions and carrier-initiated actions, each with distinct financial consequences. Under Paragraph 227 of Russia's Federal Aviation Regulations, passengers are granted specific rights to a "forced refusal" of air transportation, which entitles them to a full refund. This means that if any of the conditions listed are met, the passenger is legally entitled to refuse to fly and receive a full refund for their ticket. This provision protects travellers from a range of circumstances beyond their control, holding the carrier accountable for disruptions and ensuring passengers are not financially penalized. The key grounds for a forced refusal are multifaceted. Passengers can refuse a flight and receive a refund if the flight is cancelled, significantly delayed, or its route is changed. This also applies if the carrier fails to provide a seat as indicated on the ticket or fails to deliver services corresponding to the ticket class. The provision also covers logistical failures, such as the carrier issuing an incorrect ticket or failing to ensure a single-ticket connection. Furthermore, it addresses personal emergencies, allowing a passenger a refund in the event of a sudden illness or death of themselves or a family member travelling with them, provided it is supported by medical documentation. Uniquely, the law allows a refund if a passenger misses their flight due to a prolonged security inspection, as long as no prohibited items are discovered. In all such cases, the airline is legally required to provide documentation confirming the passenger's right to a refund, a crucial step for the reimbursement process.[26] The law also gives carriers discretion to recognize other situations as a valid basis for a refund, allowing for flexibility in unforeseen circumstances. This framework provides robust legal protections for Russian air travellers, ensuring they have recourse when their plans are disrupted by carrier error or personal crisis.

24 Paragraph 135.
25 Chapter XIII.
26 Paragraph 227.

Conversely, a voluntary refusal encompasses any situation not explicitly listed as a forced refusal. This typically includes a simple change of plans by the passenger. In such cases, the contract is terminated under the terms of the applied tariff.[27]

Paragraph 230 of the General Rules stipulates when a carrier can unilaterally terminate the contract based on the violation by the passenger of passport, customs, sanitary, and other requirements established by Russian law; the refusal by the passenger to comply with requirements imposed by the federal aviation regulations, for health reasons; if the passenger refuses to pay for baggage in excess of the baggage allowance; refusal to pay for a child unless the child is under 2; violation of the onboard rules of conduct which results in a threat to the safety of the flight; and the carrying of any prohibited substance in baggage.

Termination Type	Grounds for Termination	Key Examples and Notes	Financial Consequence for Passenger
Forced Refusal (*Vynuzhdennyy Otkaz*)	**Circumstances attributable to the carrier or external factors beyond passenger control.**	• Flight cancellation, delay, or schedule change. • Change of route by the carrier. • Failure to provide a confirmed seat. • Missing connection due to carrier's fault. • Denied boarding due to lengthy security screening (if no violations found). • Failure to provide the paid class of service. • Incorrect ticket issuance by carrier/agent.	**Full refund** of the fare paid. The carrier must document the circumstance.
	Grave Personal Circumstances	• Illness of passenger or accompanying family member (with medical proof of contraindication for flight). • Death of a family member (with documentation).	**Full refund** of the fare paid upon presentation of required documentation.

(*Continued*)

27 Paragraph 228.

(Continued)

Termination Type	**Grounds for Termination**	**Key Examples and Notes**	**Financial Consequence for Passenger**
		• *Note:* Requires notification to carrier before check-in closes. Family is legally defined (spouses, parents, children, grandparents, grandchildren, siblings).	
Unilateral Termination	**Passenger Violations of Safety, Security, or Legal Requirements.**	• Violation of passport, customs, sanitary, or other legal requirements. • Refusal to comply with federal aviation regulations. • Presence of prohibited items or substances in baggage/cargo.	**No refund.** The passenger is in breach of contract.
	Passenger Conduct or Condition Threatening Safety/Order	• Disruptive or threatening behaviour on board. • Failure to obey the lawful orders of the aircraft commander. • A health condition that threatens the safety of the passenger or others, or creates "irreparable inconvenience" (medically documented).	**No refund.** The action is taken to uphold safety and order.
	Financial/ Contractual Breach by Passenger	• Refusal to pay for excess baggage or pre-agreed services. • Refusal to pay for the transportation of a child (except where legally exempt).	**No refund.** The passenger has failed to meet their financial obligations under the contract.

Unlike EU Regulation 261, the General Rules do not seem to include any exception such as extraordinary circumstances. It is clear that passengers can obtain a full refund for any disruptions caused by the carrier or extraordinary personal circumstances. The General Rules do not contain any fixed automatic compensation. Passengers have to claim under the Russian Air Code[28] which establishes a compensation of 100 Rubles for each hour of delay, but this amount cannot exceed 50% of the ticket fare. The carrier is exempt from paying this penalty if it can prove that the delay was due to circumstances beyond its control, such as an act of God or a technical issue that threatened the life or health of passengers.[29] For baggage without declared value, the compensation is 600 Rubles per kilogram of the baggage's weight. The compensation for lost or damaged carry-on luggage is capped at 11,000 Rubles.[30] Additionally, the Law of the Russian Federation No. 2300–1 "On Protection of Consumer Rights" does apply to air travel.[31] There is also no fixed penalty in case of non-compliance with the General Rules. The law is also silent about the procedure to adopt in case of denial of boarding due to overbooking.

Russian air passenger rights are governed by a comprehensive and detailed regulatory framework, primarily established by the Order of the Ministry of Transport of the Russian Federation No. 82, known as the General Rules of Air Carriage, which derive their authority from the Federal Air Code. These rules apply uniformly to domestic and international flights operated by Russian carriers and set forth extensive obligations. Unlike the EU's system, which is built around a dichotomy of carrier liability and a core principle of monetary compensation, the Russian model is characterized by its unconditional care obligations and a nuanced, often conditional, approach to financial redress. This system reflects a broader philosophy of state-mandated provision and consumer protection within a clearly defined legal hierarchy. The provision of a 50% discount on domestic fares for children who are Russian citizens is a unique feature. It effectively functions as a state-sponsored social benefit, integrating aviation policy with broader national welfare objectives. This creates a clear, legally enforced price advantage for Russian families.

The Russian General Rules, while also regulating passenger rights, cover a much broader range of topics from baggage weight and special passenger handling to in-flight service standards. When it comes to disruptions, the Russian law focuses on providing services and a penalty to the passenger, rather than the fixed, predetermined compensation model of Regulation 261. While the right to a full refund is robust, financial redress beyond

28 Air Code of the Russian Federation of 19 March 1997, № 60-FZ (as amended on 28 February 2025) <https://cis-legislation.com/document.fwx?rgn=1552>.

29 Article 120 of the Russian Air Code.

30 Article 119 of the Russian Air Code.

31 Passengers can claim penalty and moral damages under that law. The penalty is 3% of the ticket price for each hour of delay, capped at a maximum of 50% of the total ticket cost unless caused by force majeure or fault of the passenger themselves.

that is not a guaranteed entitlement. Instead, passengers must seek penalties under the law "On Protection of Consumer Rights," a process that requires filing a claim and often necessitates litigation, with success contingent on proving carrier fault. The system places the onus on the passenger to enforce their rights. The law is silent on specific procedures for overbooking, and the concept of "extraordinary circumstances" operates as a potential carrier defence against delay penalties rather than as an exemption from care obligations.

In essence, the Russian legal framework represents a model of detailed, state-mandated provision and conditional financial redress, emphasizing carrier duties of care and consumer protection within a national context. The EU system, conversely, prioritizes a harmonized, compensatory approach across Member States, creating more predictable financial rights for passengers but with a narrower regulatory focus on disruption management. Both systems offer protection, but their philosophical underpinnings and mechanisms diverge significantly, with one emphasizing care and the other compensation.

Comparison with EU Regulation

Feature	General Rules (as amended in 2024)	EU Regulation 261/2004
Delay Compensation	Not mentioned (potentially 100 Rubles for each hour of delay, but this amount cannot exceed 50% of the ticket fare).	≥3h: €250–600 (by distance).
Cancellation Compensation	Care and assistance.	<14d notice: Refund or re-routing + €250–600 compensation (by distance).
Denial of Boarding	?	Volunteer first; €250–€600 (by distance) if denied boarding.
Baggage Compensation	600 Rubles per kilogram of the baggage's weight. The compensation for lost or damaged carry-on luggage is capped at 11,000 Rubles.	Not specified.

Bibliography

- Order of the Ministry of Transport of Russia dated 28 June 2007 No. 82 (as amended on 25 December 2024) 'On Approval of the Federal Aviation Rules "General Rules for the Air Transportation of Passengers, Baggage, Cargo and Requirements for Servicing Passengers, Consignors, Consignees"

(Registered with the Ministry of Justice of Russia on 27 September 2007 No. 10186)' <https://cis-legislation.com/document.fwx?rgn=18809> accessed 17 December 2025.

- Air Code of the Russian Federation of 19 March 1997, № 60-FZ (as amended on 28 February 2025) <https://cis-legislation.com/document.fwx?rgn=1552> accessed 17 December 2025.

II.41

Rwanda

Air passenger rights in Rwanda are primarily governed by the country's Civil Aviation Regulations, especially Rwanda Civil Aviation Regulations (RCARs) Part 36 Subpart C.[1] This regulation outlines the obligations of air carriers operating in Rwanda concerning the treatment of passengers in cases of disruption. While Subpart A should relate to the applicability of the RCARs, there is no provision regarding the scope of the Regulations.

Subpart C starts with the rights and obligations of the passengers including the right to receive clear and complete information about rates and terms, have their personal information protected, and be protected from unfair practices and false advertising.[2] In turn, the passenger shall not abuse air carrier services, must familiarize themselves with and honour their ticket's terms and conditions, must make reasonable decisions when exercising choice, and must abide by safety and security requirements.[3] A consumer must notify the air carrier of any special needs during booking or at least 48 hours before departure, detailing the assistance required, any mobility equipment, and if an escort is needed.[4]

For their part, air carriers are required to issue a ticket and boarding pass with clear travel information or a link to its conditions of carriage.[5] In case of service disruption, the carrier must keep passengers informed at the earliest opportunity.[6] The carrier must take reasonable measures to provide the service as sold and ensure all advertising is complete and

1 Law 20 establishing Regulations Governing Civil Aviation of 2018, Published in Official Gazette 18 on 30 April 2018. For Rwanda Civil Aviation Regulations (RCARs) Part 36 Subpart C <https://www.caa.gov.rw/index.php?eID=dumpFile&t=f&f=72963&token=21f74fcddca0a619683edcf8b72a46d9b76707f2>.

2 Article 36.080(a)(1), (3) and (5).

3 Article 36.080(b)(1), (2), (3), (4).

4 Article 36.080(b)(5).

5 Article 36.085(2). This includes a transparency requirement to give all essential information before purchase under Article 36.140.

6 Article 36.085(3).

DOI: 10.4324/9781003746164-52

accurate.[7] It must make safety and carriage rules for persons with disability available in an accessible format.[8] The carrier must keep passenger personal information confidential and safeguard its security.[9] In case of insolvency, the airline must require administrators to prioritize consumers who hold tickets.[10]

The regulations prohibit several unfair and deceptive practices.[11] Misleading advertising includes increasing the price of air transportation after it has been purchased or charging any fees not expressly disclosed at the time of initial inquiry.[12] It is also a violation to fail to disclose the name of the operating air carrier before a ticket is purchased.[13] Other prohibited practices are the persistent involuntary denial of boarding without first seeking volunteers,[14] the persistent abuse of a free-seating policy that denies passengers the seat class they paid for,[15] the discriminatory application of compensation that is less than what is required under the Montreal Convention[16] and operating chronically delayed flights, defined as flights that arrive more than 15 minutes late or are cancelled more than 50% of the time in a calendar quarter.[17] This protection against chronically delayed flights and persistent abuse of free-seating are identical to those found in Ghana. Additionally, airlines, tour operators, and agents are also obliged to obtain and hold a passenger's contact information to be used for emergencies and essential information relevant to the flight following the passenger's preferred mode of communication.[18] For notifications of cancellations or delays made less than 12 hours before departure, the airline must communicate by phone or SMS unless the passenger has confirmed they can retrieve emails on a mobile device.[19]

A more peculiar provision is found in Article 36.089 which requires airlines to maintain adequate third-party liability insurance as required by law and visibly display the insurance certificate in a location accessible to consumers. They must be able to demonstrate compliance with this requirement to Authority officials upon request.

7 Article 36.085(4) and (5).
8 Article 36.085(6).
9 Article 36.085(7).
10 Article 36.085(9).
11 Article 36.086.
12 Article 36.086(a)(1)(i) and (ii).
13 Article 36.086(a)(2).
14 Article 36.086(a)(3).
15 Article 36.086(a)(4).
16 Article 36.086(a)(5).
17 Article 36.086(a)(6).
18 Article 36.087(a) and (b).
19 Article 36.087(d).

In addition to these general provisions, the regulations specify detailed rules for handling various disruptions. For denied boarding, an airline can overbook flights[20] provided it has an Authority-approved overbooking policy and makes it known to consumers.[21] If an airline anticipates denied boarding due to overbooking more than six hours before a flight, it must contact affected passengers by phone, SMS, or email to first seek volunteers to surrender their reservations in exchange for benefits that meet or exceed the standard compensation scheme.[22] Special consideration should be given to passengers travelling from farthest away to prevent hardship.[23] On the day of travel, the airline can make discrete requests for volunteers at check-in or during boarding.[24] If insufficient volunteers come forward, the airline may involuntarily deny boarding to the smallest practicable number of passengers, who must then be compensated according to the regulations.[25]

Before denying boarding, airlines must first verify there is no seat in a higher class available, if not then they must first call for volunteers to surrender their seats in exchange for compensation.[26] If a passenger is involuntarily denied boarding, they are entitled to a written notice and necessary care.[27] If a seat is available in a lower fare class, the passenger has the right to accept the downgrading with a refund of the fare difference as downgrading is not regarded as denied boarding or rebooked on a later flight and be provided with care for flights departing within one hour to six hours.[28] For passengers with connecting flights, the airline must ensure they reach their final destination with minimal delay, bearing any extra cost.[29] The airline must pay compensation within 30 days of confirming the passenger's entitlement. A penalty of 20% of the ticket price per day is applied for late payment.[30] Interestingly, the law does not mention when compensation is due but the scenarios in which it is not due: if the passenger failed to comply with check-in or ticketing rules, if the airline arranges alternative transport that arrives at the final destination within

20 Provision on overbooking is found in Article 36.121. Airlines must utilize intelligent market analysis to minimize negative effects on passengers, such as by offering online boarding.

21 Article 36.090(a)–(e).

22 Article 36.121(b).

23 Article 36.121(b).

24 Article 36.121(c).

25 Article 36.121(d).

26 Article 36.090(f)–(g).

27 Article 36.090(h)(1).

28 Article 36.090(h)(3), (4), (5).

29 Article 36.090(h)(6).

30 Article 36.090(j) and (k) as repeated in (l) and (m).

three hours of the original time or for volunteers, provided the airline fully disclosed all restrictions on the compensation offer.[31]

Category	**Requirements** and **Passenger Rights**
Pre-conditions	- Airlines may overbook if they have an Authority-approved policy. - Policy must be clearly communicated to consumers.
Procedure Before Denial	1. First, check for available seats in a **higher class** (may offer upgrade). 2. If no higher class, **request volunteers** to surrender seats for compensation.
Involuntary Denial Rights	If involuntarily denied boarding, passengers are entitled to: - **Written notice** of their rights. - **Necessary care.**
Rebooking Options	Passenger may be offered: - **Downgrading** (with refund of fare difference) – *not considered denied boarding*. - **Rebooking on later flight** (with care if wait is 1–6 hours).
Compensation Exceptions	No compensation required if: - Passenger failed check-in/ticketing rules. - Alternative transport arrives within **3 hours** of original time. - Passenger was a **volunteer** (with full disclosure of offer restrictions).

For flight cancellations, in case of a flight cancellation less than 24 hours before departure, the airline must inform passengers of the specific reasons and their rights, which include the right to cancel for a refund, to be re-routed, and to compensation.[32] Passengers have the right to compensation unless they were informed of the cancellation between two weeks and seven days in advance and were offered re-routing departing no more than two hours before the scheduled departure time and arriving less than four hours after the original time. When passengers are notified less than seven days in advance, the alternative flight must depart no more than one hour in advance and arrive less than two hours after the original scheduled arrival time.[33] Compensation amounts vary depending on the duration of the flight; $250 for flights of three hours or less, $400 for

31 Article 36.090(i)(1)–(3).
32 Article 36.095(a)(1)(i)–(iii).
33 Article 36.095(c)(1) and (2).

flights between three and six hours, and $600 for flights over six hours.[34] If re-routing is offered and the arrival delay is minimal (two hours for short flights, three hours for medium flights, four hours for long flights), the compensation may be reduced by 50%.[35]

Flight Duration	Standard Compensation	Reduced Compensation (50%)
3 Hours or Less	$250.	Re-routing arriving with 2 hours' delay.
Between 3 and 6 Hours	$400.	Re-routing arriving with 3 hours' delay.
Over 6 Hours	$600.	Re-routing arriving with 4 hours' delay.

Compensation is not required if the cancellation was caused by extraordinary circumstances that could not have been avoided.[36] Extraordinary circumstance is vaguely defined in Article 36.005 as including acts of sabotage or terrorism, Acts of God or nature, political or civil unrest, latent manufacturing defects, wars or acts of foreign enemies, strikes or lock-outs.

When a flight is delayed, the airline's obligations increase with the duration of the delay. For delays between two and four hours, the airline must provide refreshments which might include snacks or confectioneries, two phone calls/SMS/emails, and updates every 45 minutes.[37] For delays exceeding four hours, the airline must also provide a meal and hotel accommodation with transport if needed.[38] If the delay is six hours or more, passengers have the right to a full refund of the ticket price or to be re-routed to their final destination.[39] Airlines might offer a flight departing from an alternative airport.[40] The airline must prioritize persons with reduced mobility and unaccompanied minors.[41]

Delay Duration	Passenger Rights and Airline Obligations
2 to 4 Hours	The airline must provide: - Refreshments (e.g., snacks, confectioneries, water). - Two telephone calls, SMS, or emails. - Regular updates every 45 minutes on the delay's status.

(*Continued*)

34 Article 36.157(a)(1)–(3).
35 Article 36.157(c)(1) and (2).
36 Article 36.095(d).
37 Article 36.100(a)(1)(i)–(iii).
38 Article 36.100(a)(2)(iii) and (iv).
39 Article 36.100(a)(3)(i)–(iii).
40 Article 36.100(a)(4)(ii).
41 Article 36.100(a)(4)(iii) as reinforced by Article 36.125.

(Continued)

Delay Duration	Passenger Rights and Airline Obligations
Exceeding 4 Hours	The airline must provide all of the above, plus: - A meal. - Hotel accommodation if necessary (including transport between the airport and the hotel).
6 Hours or More	Passengers have the right to choose between: - A full refund of the ticket price. - Being re-routed to their final destination at the earliest opportunity or later date.

The Regulations also provide specific protections for persons with disabilities or special needs, prohibiting airlines from denying them boarding unless it's for security or safety reasons.[42] Airlines must make advance arrangements to assist these passengers and, if an airline fails to provide the necessary services, the passenger is entitled to compensation of 150% of the ticket value.[43] The RCARs also contain a no-show clause which entitles passengers to be considered for wait-listing on another flight subject to seat availability.[44]

If an airline places a passenger in a class lower than what was purchased, it must reimburse the passenger 25% of the ticket price for flights of three hours or less, and 50% for flights longer than three hours.[45] In the event a passenger is upgraded to a higher class, the airline is not entitled to any supplementary payment.[46]

Finally, the law also contains provisions on baggage handling. Airlines are liable for lost, damaged, or delayed baggage up to a maximum of 1,000 Special Drawing Rights (SDRs).[47] RCARs do not lay down any fixed penalties but only that those penalties must be "dissuasive, proportionate to both the gravity of the case, and the economic capacity of the service provider. The defaulter's compliance record shall also be taken into consideration."[48]

RCARs Part 36 Subpart C establishes a robust and detailed framework for air passenger rights that is clearly modelled on the consumer-centric approach of international regulations like the European Union's Regulation 261. However, while the structure and intent are similar, there are key differences in compensation metrics and level of details. The

42 Article 36.110.
43 Article 36.110(h).
44 Article 36.105(a).
45 Article 36.123(a)(1) and (2).
46 Article 36.123(b).
47 Article 36.115(b).
48 Article 36.176(b).

core principles of care, re-routing or refund, and financial compensation for disruptions are fully embedded within the Rwandan law. Similarly, the fixed compensation amounts for cancellations – \$250, \$400, and \$600 based on flight duration – and the 50% reduction clause if re-routing minimizes the arrival delay, are conceptually directly aligned with the European approach, albeit using flight duration as a metric instead of flight distance.

Rwanda's law demonstrates significant innovation and, in some areas, potentially greater specificity is in its provisions against systemic airline malpractices. The explicit prohibitions of "chronically delayed flights" and the "persistent abuse of a free-seating policy" are powerful consumer protection tools not explicitly found in Regulation EC 261. These provisions allow regulators to address patterns of poor service rather than just individual incidents. Furthermore, Rwanda's law includes notably strong protections for persons with disabilities, stipulating compensation of 150% of the ticket value if an airline fails to provide the required services, a deterrent that exceeds the norms in many other jurisdictions. The detailed communication protocols, requiring contact via SMS or phone for last-minute disruptions, also reflect a practical and consumer-centric design.

However, the law has also several weaknesses such as the vague definition of "extraordinary circumstances." This vagueness in the Rwandan law could be exploited by airlines to deny claims. Similarly, the penalty provision does not include any fixed amount. This lack of specificity may lead to inconsistent enforcement and could weaken the law's deterrent effect.

In conclusion, RCARs Part 36 Subpart C represents a sophisticated and largely consumer-friendly legal transplant of the EU's air passenger rights regime. It successfully incorporates the core elements of Regulation EC 261 and, in several key areas, introduces more progressive and specific protections.

Comparison with EU Regulation

Feature	**RCACs Part 36**	**EU Regulation 261/2004**
Delay Compensation	Care and assistance.	≥3h: €250–600 (by distance).
Cancellation Compensation	<24 hours' notice: Refund or re-routing + €250–600 compensation (by distance).	<14d notice: Refund or re-routing + €250–600 compensation (by distance).
Denial of Boarding	Volunteer first; care + rebooking or downgrading + compensation(?).	Volunteer first; €250–€600 (by distance) if denied boarding.
Baggage Compensation	1,000 SDR.	Not specified.

Bibliography

- Law 20 Establishing Regulations Governing Civil Aviation of 2018.
- Rwanda Civil Aviation Regulations (RCARs) Part 36 Subpart C <https://www.caa.gov.rw/index.php?eID=dumpFile&t=f&f=72963&token=21f74fcddca0a619683edcf8b72a46d9b76707f2> accessed 17 December 2025.

II.42

Saudi Arabia

In Saudi Arabia, the General Authority of Civil Aviation (GACA)[1] plays a pivotal role in safeguarding the interests of air travellers. To ensure those interests are safeguarded, the GACA has published a comprehensive set of regulations and policies. In 2023, a new set of regulations was issued which abrogated the 2017 regulations.[2] The Customer Protection Rights Regulations entered into force within 90 days from their date of issuance.[3] The Regulations place a paramount emphasis on upholding the passengers' rights and have been viewed as a key component to reach Saudi Aviation Strategy targets. The law can also be amended at any time by the board of directors of the GACA.[4]

The Passenger Rights Protection Regulations cover ticketing, boarding, in-flight services, baggage handling, and helping passengers with special needs,[5] including those with reduced mobility. It applies to flights departing from the Kingdom of Saudi Arabia operated by both national or foreign carriers as well as flights operated by a national carrier arriving to the Kingdom airports, "unless the passenger is compensated according to the regulations of the country of departure."[6] It also applies to passengers

1 Issued by the Board of Directors of the General Authority of Civil Aviation Resolution No. (20/380) dated 26 May 1438 H (corresponding to 23 February 2017), Based on the Civil Aviation Law issued by the Royal Decree No. M/44 dated 18 July 1426, and the Statute of the General Authority of Civil Aviation issued by the Council of Ministers Resolution No. (33) dated 11 February 1426H.

Version used: <https://www.saudia.com/pages/-/media/Project/SA/SC/Advanced-Artical/How-Can-We-Help/More-Information/Passenger-Rights/CP_Regulation_English_Version.pdf>.

2 Article 30 of the 2023 version.

3 Article 30.

4 Article 29.

5 The GACA Regulations place specific emphasis on protecting the rights of special needs passengers see Article 18 Regulations.

6 Article 3.

DOI: 10.4324/9781003746164-53

who are travelling as part of a package and claims relating to baggage for flights arriving to the Kingdom on a foreign airline.[7]

The passenger protection starts kicking in after one hour similarly to Brazil. After one hour of delay, cancellation, or denial of boarding, passengers are entitled to refreshments or beverages – which is not defined in the Regulation.[8] After three hours of delay, passengers are entitled to an appropriate meal – again no definition is provided.[9] Finally, any delay exceeding six hours entitles the passengers to a hotel accommodation and transport to and from the airport.[10] Interestingly, nothing is mentioned regarding granting the consumers access to internet or a phone call. Compared to the original version, the amendment also includes compensation in case the airline does not comply with its obligations of care and support. According to the 2023 version, carriers are liable to compensate

> a. (10) Special Drawing Rights Units when refreshments and beverages are not provided. b. (30) Special Drawing Rights Units when the appropriate meal is not provided. c. (100) Special Drawing Rights Units when failing to offer hotel accommodation and transportation to and from the airport are not provided.

Timeframe	**Passenger Rights**	**Compensation (SDR)**
1–3 Hours	Refreshments/beverages.	10 SDR if not provided.
3–6 Hours	Meal + refreshments.	30 SDR if not provided.
>6 Hours	Hotel + transport.	100 SDR if not provided.

The Regulation is rather strict regarding the situations in which carriers could deny boarding, delay, or cancel a flight. Article 13 on denial of boarding starts by requesting airlines to take "all necessary efforts to minimize" the number of passengers denied boarding due to overbooking.[11] For instance, airlines cannot deny boarding if there are higher class seats available on the same flight. In those circumstances passengers must be upgraded to the higher class free of charge.[12] If no alternative seats are available on the same flight, the airline must immediately provide passengers with "clear information in writing" and provide the "necessary care and support."[13] Passengers have also the right

7 Article 3(4) and (5).
8 Article 17(1).
9 Article 17(2).
10 Article 17(3).
11 Article 13(1).
12 Article 13(2).
13 Article 13(5)(a).

to decide between travelling with the same airline on a different flight or travelling with another carrier free of charge.[14] While airlines are subject to strict restrictions, the law could have gone a step further by banning overbooking policy altogether.

Passengers have also the option to terminate the contract. In that case, the passenger is entitled to a full refund for any unused section and a compensation equal to 200% of that amount – which is an increase compared to the 2017 Regulation.[15] Volunteers have also a right to compensation, however, the amount is not stipulated in the Regulation itself.[16]

Similarly, the exclusions of liability for carriers have been restricted to only situations in which the airline arranges comparable air travel within two hours of the scheduled departure time.[17] The time has also drastically decreased as previously the alternative flight had to depart within six hours of the original. In the 2017 version, the other exclusion related to passengers who had failed to comply with the requirements in Article 5.[18] Interestingly, the 2023 version also excludes some passengers from being denied boarding, such as persons with disability, special needs passengers, first-degree relatives and their accompanying domestic workers, unaccompanied minors, and travel groups.[19]

The Regulation also contains a specific article on downgrading which does not classify as a denial of boarding as clearly mentioned in Article 14(1). In that situation, the airline must inform the passenger who then has the choice between accepting and receiving a partial refund of the difference between the original fare paid and the replacement fare as well as a compensation or refusing and terminating the contract which would entitle the passenger to a full refund as well as a compensation equivalent to 200% of the refund.[20] Interestingly, the new Article 14 no longer mentions that downgraded passengers should be provided assistance and support. The law has now made it clear that carriers are

14 Article 13(5)(b).

15 Article 13(7).

16 Article 13(4).

17 Article 13(8).

18 Article 5 of the 2017 Regulation reads as follow "The Customer is required to:

1. Read the terms and conditions of the carriage contract before the Confirmed Reservation process has been finalized.

2. Disclose any of his/her needs (if any) before the Confirmed Reservation process has been finalized.

3. Show up at the airport at the time specified by the Air Carrier to finalize travel formalities and follow the Air Carrier's instructions issued to that effect.

4. Provide all documents and fulfill all legal requirements necessary for traveling."

19 Article 13(9).

20 Article 14(2) and (3).

not permitted to downgrade passengers without their prior agreement. Interestingly, the Regulation also makes it clear that the compensation in case of downgrading "shall not be considered as compensation for any consequential damages resulting from the downgrade in class."[21] This sentence could open the door to many lawsuits.

Interestingly, all the provisions relating to compensations are expressed in SDR rather than in Saudi Riyals.

Situation	Carrier Obligation
Seat in higher class available.	Upgrade passenger free of charge.
Downgrading.	1. If passenger accepts, refund of the difference between the original fare and the replacement fare + 50% compensation. 2. If passenger refuses, full refund + 200% compensation.
Passenger wants to travel with another airline.	Carrier must pay.
Termination of contract by passenger.	Reimbursement of the unused part of the flight + 200% compensation.
Volunteers.	Offer compensation.
Failure to comply with Article 5.	No longer applicable.
New air travel within 2 hours of the scheduled departure time.	No compensation.

The Passenger Rights Protection Regulations also contain a provision prohibiting airlines to bring flights forward "unless it is required for security and safety reasons based on reports approved by GACA."[22] In those limited situations in which airlines are allowed to bring the flight forward, passengers will still have the choice to accept the new flight or request an alternative flight.[23] If the passenger elects to terminate the contract, then the flight will be "deemed cancelled" and the passenger will be entitled to the compensation for cancelled flights.[24]

Delays are regulated by Article 10 which provides that airlines must notify passengers about a delay 45 minutes before take-off time and then update the flight status every 30 minutes.[25] The airlines are under the obligation to offer care and support found in Article 17 or pay for the cost

21 Article 14(2).
22 Article 9(1).
23 Article 9(2).
24 Article 9(4).
25 Article 10(2) and (3).

of extending the passenger's accommodation until the new flight time.[26] Delayed passengers are entitled to compensation which is only based on the duration of the delay and not the distance nor the nature of the flight (domestic or international). Passengers are entitled to 50 SDR for delays between three and six hours. For delays above six hours, they are entitled to 150 SDR.[27] After two hours, passengers can request the termination of the contract and are entitled to a full refund.[28] The Regulation also allows passengers to consider their flight as cancelled if the delay is more than five hours and they are entitled to the protection for cancelled flights.[29] The earlier restriction of delays to safety or security reasons has been removed.[30]

Delay Duration	**Passenger Rights**
3–6 Hours	50 SDR.
>6 Hours	150 SDR.
>5 Hours	Treat as cancellation.

Article 11 relates to tarmac delays and obliges airlines to provide access to toilet, "adequate ventilation and air conditioning or heating," food, and drink and grant passengers the ability to contact people outside the aircraft.[31] If the tarmac delay exceeds three hours, passengers can request to disembark the aircraft – unless prohibited for security and safety reasons.[32] In case of disembarking, passengers with disabilities and special needs should disembark first alongside their assistants or companions – "whether persons or animals."[33] If the passenger elects to disembark, then the flight will be considered as cancelled for the purpose of the Regulations.[34] As Mahmoud Abdelgawwad Abd Elhady noted, "The regulations impose responsibilities on airlines regarding passengers during runway delays, which are often due to airport authorities, causing both the carrier and passengers to suffer as a result of these delays."[35]

The GACA Regulations set a high standard for flight reliability, prohibiting cancellations except under very limited situations, namely

26 Article 10(5) and (4).
27 Article 10(6)(a) and (b).
28 Article 10(7).
29 Article 10(8).
30 Old Article 11(1) of 2017 Regulations.
31 Article 11(1).
32 Article 11(2).
33 Article 11(3).
34 Article 11(4).
35 Mahmoud Abdelgawwad Abd Elhady, 'The Saudi Passenger Rights Regulation of 2023 "A Critical Analytical Study"' (2023) 12 Journal of Law and Sustainable Development 1, 13.

"Force Majeure or for safety and security reasons based on reports approved by GACA."[36] In case of permissible cancellations, extensive passenger rights are set out in the regulation. Not only do passengers on cancelled flights have the right to care and support but they have the option to either accept the alternative flight or refuse.[37] If they accept the alternative flight, they will not be entitled to compensation.[38] However, the protection for delay will be applicable which then raises the question as to whether compensation for delay is also available for passengers suffering a cancellation and who accept an alternative flight.[39]

If the passenger decides to terminate the contract, the airline will be relieved from their care and support obligation but the passenger would still be entitled to a full refund including additional baggage fees or seat selection fees.[40] Compensation due to passengers vary depending on when the cancellation notice was given to passengers; if the passenger is informed of the cancellation between 60 and 14 days before the departure time, they are entitled to a refund of the remaining part of the flights and 50% of the value of that remaining part as compensation.[41] If the notice is given between 14 days and 24 hours prior to departure time, the carrier is liable for the same refund and an additional 75% of the value of that remaining part as compensation.[42] Finally, airlines will need to offer a refund and 150% of the of the value of that remaining part as compensation for any cancellation occurring within 24 hours of the departure time.[43] For discounted tickets, the compensation should be granted in accordance with "the highest price value of the class that was booked."[44] In situations where there are no daily flights, the airlines must provide passengers with an alternative method of transportation.[45] The emphasis on advanced notice, restrictive situations in which cancellation is permitted, and the penalty structure aims to incentivize airlines on time performance. This robust set of protections for flight cancellations establishes Saudi passengers' rights as among the strongest globally.

---

36 Article 12(1).
37 Article 12(2).
38 Article 12(3).
39 Article 12(3). "In case the passenger accepts the alternative flight, the passenger is not entitled to compensation, and the provisions related to flight delays mentioned in this Regulation shall apply to the time difference between the original flight and the alternative flight."
40 Article 12(4) and (5).
41 Article 12(6)(a).
42 Article 12(6)(b).
43 Article 12(6)(c).
44 Article 12(7).
45 Article 12(8).

Notice Period	Compensation (% of Remaining Ticket Value)	Passenger Options
60–14 Days	Refund of remaining part + 50%.	Alternative flight **or** terminate.
14–24 Hours	Refund of remaining part + 75%.	Alternative flight **or** terminate + care and support.
<24 Hours	Refund of remaining part + 150%.	Alternative flight **or** terminate + care and support.
Force Majeure	No compensation (but care obligations remain).	Terminate after 3hrs (domestic)/6hrs (international).

Passengers can also claim for consequential damages – which is not clearly defined in the Regulations. Such damages are left to the discretion of the court.[46]

	Delay	Cancellation (Refusal of Alternative Flight)	Cancellation (Acceptance of Alternative Flight)	Denial of Boarding (Refusal of Alternative Flight)	Denial of Boarding (Acceptance of Alternative Flight)
Care and Support	Yes.	No.	Yes.	?	Yes.
Full Refund	Yes if passenger terminates the contract.	No.	No.	Yes.	No.
Partial Refund	No.	Yes of the remaining part.	No.	No.	No.
Compensation	<6 hours: 50 SDR. >6 hours: 150 SDR.	• 50% of the value if notified between 60 and 14 days. • 75% of the value if notified between 14 days and 24 hours. • 150% of the value if notified within 24 hours of the flight departure.	No but rules on delays apply.	Equivalent to 200% of the value as compensation.	compensation as if delay flights. BUT not if flight alternative flight is within 2 hours.

46 Article 26.

Force majeure is broadly defined in Article 20 in a negative manner making it quite hard to know which situations will fall within the definition. Article 20(2) reads as follows"

> The air carrier shall not claim Force Majeure if any breach of the provisions of the Regulations is due to a technical failure of the aircraft, operational conditions, scheduling, or underestimation caused by the air carrier or its employees or due to negligence or default of the air carrier or its agents.

From that paragraph, it is clear that strike and technical failures will not be considered as force majeure. Scheduled or unscheduled maintenance will probably fall within the definition as well as adverse meteorological circumstances. Force majeure does not relieve the airline for their support and care obligations but does exempt them from compensation.[47] Passengers are also given the option to terminate their contract due to force majeure and receive a refund after three hours for national flights and six for international ones.[48]

While the Regulations regulate stopovers and successive carriage, they do not address the potential responsibility of intermediaries.[49] Interestingly, Saudi Arabia took a similar position as Brazilian judges by treating successive carriage as "one and indivisible carriage" even if it is subject to a series of contracts.[50] Passengers can request a compensation of 100 SDR for each stopover that was not mentioned at time of reservation.[51]

To establish a uniform standard, the Regulations stipulate the airlines' liability for baggage delay based on the time it took for the passenger to be reunited with their suitcase but also provide a maximum compensation in line with international Conventions. The carrier is liable for 148 SDR for the first day and then 60 SDR daily to a maximum compensation of 1,288 SDR.[52] For baggage loss, defect, or damage, compensation is 1,288 SDR unless the defect or damage was "caused by underlying or inherent defect in the baggage."[53] A baggage is considered as lost if it does not arrive within 21 days.[54] Passengers can make special declarations before checking their baggage to be entitled to a higher level of compensation.[55] However, if the damage relates to a special equipment or supporting tools for special needs passengers, then the airline is requested to compensate

47 Article 20(1)(b) and 20(4).
48 Article 20(3).
49 Article 16.
50 Article 16(1).
51 Article 16(6).
52 Article 15(4).
53 Article 15(5)(a), (b) and (c).
54 Article 15(5)(d).
55 Article 15(6).

for the value of the caused damage.[56] Airlines are also required to provide an alternative wheelchair – if the passenger's wheelchair does not arrive on the same flight – or 100 SDR if such alternative is not provided. The GACA Regulations set passengers expectations in different situations by providing detailed rules.

Baggage Rules

Issue	**Compensation (SDR)**	**Notes**
Delay	148 (Day 1) + 60/day (max 1,288).	Reunion time considered.
Loss/Damage	1,288 (unless inherent defect).	Lost if not delivered in 21 days.
Special Needs Equipment	Full repair/replacement cost.	Wheelchair: Alternative or 100 SDR.

A peculiarity of the GACA is that it includes an article dedicated to passengers' obligations – Article 6 (previously Article 5). Those obligations include reviewing the terms and conditions before booking but also coming to the airport on time and having all the required documents.[57] Article 6(6) also imposes on passengers the obligation to "commit to public decency and avoid any action that would affect the safety of the flight or disrupt its take-off at the scheduled time, or any action that could result in considering the passenger as a unruly passenger." It is rare to find any passenger rights laws or regulations which include an obligation on passengers but also target unruly passengers. Similarly, the GACA contains the airlines' obligations in Article 7. Finally, it also contains a provision dedicated to the transport of animals making it one of the most complete laws.[58]

Airlines can face fines up to 50,000 Saudi Riyals for non-compliance with those Regulations.[59] The Regulations do not include any appeal procedure nor the possibility to increase the fine for repeat offences, as is the case in Malaysia for instance. Airlines must compensate or refund passengers within 15 days of the event.[60] While the Regulations contain a clause on submitting a complaint, the maximum time period to submit such a claim is not clearly mentioned in the text.[61]

The GACA Regulations have been criticized for the lack of consideration and specific provisions which "adequately address issues that occur during

56 Article 18(5).
57 Article 6(1), (3) and (4).
58 Article 27.
59 Article 25.
60 Article 21.
61 Article 22.

peak times in Saudi Arabia, both for domestic and international flights."[62] Indeed, "as a significant religious destination for Muslim pilgrims," Saudi Arabia attracts many tourists during the Hajj season and puts an immense pressure on the aviation sector.[63] Moreover, there is no mention in the Regulations of any international Convention which might increase the likelihood of conflicts between those rules and the Montreal Convention to which Saudi Arabia is party since 2003.[64]

The 2023 Saudi Customer Protection Rights Regulations represent a formidable and uniquely structured legal framework for air passenger rights that, while drawing inspiration from global standards like the EU's Regulation 261, establish a distinct and often more rigorous regime tailored to the Kingdom's strategic and social context. Indeed, if the European Regulation 261 was viewed as too passenger-friendly, the GACA Regulations can be regarded as Regulation 261 on steroids by affording passengers many rights and restricting airlines' ability to limit their liability, strict cancellation and downgrading rules, and high compensations.

A distinctive feature is its incorporation of clear passenger obligations alongside carrier liabilities, intertwining consumer rights with expected social conduct, a synthesis less common in other national laws. Similarly, the provisions for baggage delay are uncommonly precise, mandating fixed, daily compensation accruing from the first day of delay, which provides passengers with predictable remedies often absent in other jurisdictions. The regulations further narrow the circumstances under which airlines can avoid liability, offering a restrictive definition of force majeure that explicitly excludes technical failures and operational shortcomings, thereby placing a high burden of reliability on carriers. There are some minor gaps which remain, such as limited arrival coverage. Travelers benefit from unparalleled refund guarantees, though airlines face stricter operational constraints.

In synthesis, the 2023 GACA Regulations represent a purposeful and assertive advancement in passenger rights law. They surpass the EU benchmark in several areas of financial recompense and procedural specificity, particularly for cancellations and baggage issues, crafting one of the most protective regimes on paper. This reflects a deliberate policy

62 Mahmoud Abdelgawwad Abd Elhady, 'The Saudi Passenger Rights Regulation of 2023 "A Critical Analytical Study"' (2023) 12 Journal of Law and Sustainable Development 1, 5.

63 Mahmoud Abdelgawwad Abd Elhady, 'The Saudi Passenger Rights Regulation of 2023 "A Critical Analytical Study"' (2023) 12 Journal of Law and Sustainable Development 1, 4–5.

64 ICAO, 'Parties' <https://www.icao.int/sites/default/files/secretariat/legal/CurrentListofParties/Mtl99_EN.pdf>.

choice to elevate service standards and consumer confidence within the Kingdom's aviation strategy. The comparison with EU law ultimately highlights a dichotomy of legal philosophy: The EU system provides a broad, harmonized baseline of protection across a common market, while the Saudi system establishes an intensive, centrally administered code of conduct for its sovereign airspace. The efficacy of the Saudi model will ultimately be determined by the consistency of its administrative enforcement and its evolving interface with the established norms of international aviation law.

Comparison with EU Regulation

Feature	GACA (2023)	EU Regulation 261/2004
Delay Compensation	50–150 SDR based on duration of delay.	≥3h: €250–600 (by distance).
Cancellation Compensation	Up to 150% of ticket value.	<14d notice: Refund or re-routing + €250–600 compensation (by distance).
Denial of Boarding	Volunteer first; full refund + 200% of ticket value.	Volunteer first; €250–€600 (by distance) if denied boarding.
Baggage Compensation	148 (Day 1) + 60/day. Max 1,288 SDR.	Not specified.

Bibliography

- Issued by the Board of Directors of the General Authority of Civil Aviation Resolution No. (20/380) dated 26 May 1438 H (corresponding to 23 February 2017), Based on the Civil Aviation Law Issued by the Royal Decree No. M/44 dated 18 July 1426, and the Statute of the General Authority of Civil Aviation issued by the Council of Ministers Resolution No. (33) dated 11 February 1426 H. Version used: <https://www.saudia.com/pages/-/media/Project/SA/SC/Advanced-Artical/How-Can-We-Help/More-Information/Passenger-Rights/CP_Regulation_English_Version.pdf> accessed 17 December 2025.
- Abd Elhady, M. A., 'The Saudi Passenger Rights Regulation of 2023 "A Critical Analytical Study"' (2023) 12 Journal of Law and Sustainable Development 1.
- ICAO, 'Parties' <https://www.icao.int/sites/default/files/secretariat/legal/CurrentListofParties/Mtl99_EN.pdf> accessed 23 March 2026.

II.43

Serbia

As a signatory of the European Common Aviation Area (ECAA) Multilateral Agreement, Regulation 261 has been implemented in the legislation of the Republic of Serbia.[1] According to the domestic Law on Obligations and the Basics of Property Relations in Air Transport, all passengers in Serbia have the same rights as passengers within the European Union.[2] Passengers are guaranteed minimum rights in case of denial of boarding, cancellation, and delays. The Law on Obligations and the Basics of Property Relations in Air Transport is, however, not limited to the implementation of Regulation 261 and also contains the implementation of the Montreal Convention. The list of definitions is also much longer.

Unlike many laws, the Serbian Law does not start or end with the scope of the Law. Rather it is found within Article 8, which is actually transcribing Regulation 261. The Law applies to all flights departing from a Serbian airport or arriving at a Serbian airport as well as flights departing from airports in countries part of the ECAA Agreement such as Albania, Bosnia and Herzegovina, North Macedonia, Kosovo, and Montenegro or arriving at such airports from a third country.[3] It applies only to passengers who have a confirmed reservation and presented themselves for check-in at the time stipulated by the carrier or no later than 45 minutes before the published departure time.[4]

---

1 Goran Petrović, 'Serbia' in Sean Gates (ed), *The Aviation Law Review* (8th edn, Gideon Roberton Law Business Research Ltd 2020).

2 Law on Obligations and Fundamentals of Property-Legal Relations in Air Transport ("Official Gazette of RS"), no. 87/2011 and 66/2015.

3 Reiterated in Article 3(7) and 8(1). See: Jelena Pejović and Mirjana Mladenović Paripović, 'Flight Delays, Flight Cancellations or Denial of Boarding – Rights of Passengers in the Republic of Serbia' (*ROKAS*, S.D) <https://rokas.com/wp-content/uploads/2024/07/Flight-delays-flight-cancellations-or-denial-of-boarding-rights-of-passengers-in-the-Republic-of-Serbia.pdf>.

4 Article 8(2)(1)(2).

DOI: 10.4324/9781003746164-54

Passengers travelling free of charge or at a reduced fare not publicly available are generally excluded from compensation and assistance rights, but those with tickets issued under frequent flyer or other commercial programmes are included.[5] Part two of the Law starts with provisions regarding the contract of carriage, which binds the airlines to perform the carriage of the passenger from the place of departure to final destination at the time provided for by the flight time-table.[6] Airlines must provide a ticket which represents the proof of the concluded contract.[7]

When an airline is expected to face a situation of overbooking, it must first ask for volunteers to give up their reservations in exchange for benefits and a choice of reimbursement or re-routing.[8] When there is an insufficient number of volunteers, the airline may deny boarding to passengers against their will. In such cases, these passengers are immediately entitled to compensation, assistance, and care.[9] Airlines can also deny boarding on reasonable grounds such as health, safety, or security reasons, or inadequate travel documentation.[10]

Scenario	Passenger Rights
Voluntary Denied Boarding (airline asks for volunteers)	Benefits + choice of reimbursement/re-routing.
Involuntary Denied Boarding (not enough volunteers)	Immediate compensation + assistance/care.

The same definition as under Regulation 261 is used for the term cancellation, namely the "non-operation of a flight which was previously planned and on which at least one place was reserved."[11] Under Article 10, passengers have the right to assistance and care alongside the right to compensation if the cancellation occurs less than two weeks before the scheduled departure.[12] Indeed, if the passenger was informed at least two weeks before the scheduled departure, they are not entitled to compensation.[13] If the passenger was informed between two weeks and seven days before departure and offered re-routing allowing the passenger to depart no more than two hours before scheduled departure and arrive at their final destination less than four hours after scheduled arrival, then

5 Article 8(2).
6 Article 5.
7 Article 6.
8 Article 9.
9 Article 9.
10 Article 3(38).
11 Article 3(22).
12 Article 10(3).
13 Article 10(3)(1).

no compensation is due.[14] When the passenger is informed less than seven days in advance and is offered re-routing allowing them to depart no more than one hour before scheduled departure and arrive at their final destination less than two hours after scheduled arrival, then compensation is not due either.[15] The burden of proof rests on the airline to demonstrate the passenger was indeed informed of the cancellation.[16]

When Cancelled	Compensation Due?
≥14 days before departure.	No.
7–14 days before departure.	No, if re-routing allows departure ≤2h earlier and arrival ≤4h later.
<7 days before departure.	No, if re-routing allows departure ≤1h earlier and arrival ≤2h later.
<14 days notice + no suitable re-routing.	Yes.

No compensation is due if the airline is able to demonstrate that the cancellation is attributable to extraordinary circumstances which could not have been avoided even if all reasonable measures had been taken.[17] The term "extraordinary circumstance" is loosely defined in the Law as

> situations in which the outcome of the decision concerning administration of air transport and in particular a certain aircraft on a certain day leads to longer delay, delay of aircraft overnight or cancellation of one or more flights of such aircraft, although such air carrier has undertaken all reasonable measures to avoid such delays or cancellations.[18]

The list of potential situations as found in Regulation 261 has not been included making it even more vague than the definition in the original Regulation.

When a flight is delayed, passengers are entitled to care if the delay reaches certain thresholds based on flight distance: two hours or more for flights of 1,500 km or less, three hours or more for intra-Community flights of more than 1,500 km and for all other flights between 1,500 km and 3,500 km, and four hours or more for all flights over 3,500 km.[19] If the delay is five hours or more, passengers have the right to reimbursement if they decide not to pursue the flight.[20]

14 Article 10(3)(2).
15 Article 10(3)(3).
16 Article 10(3).
17 Article 10(3).
18 Article 3(4).
19 Article 11(1).
20 Article 11(3)(3).

While Article 6 of the Regulation itself does not explicitly mention compensation for delays, the Serbian Law has been worded differently to include all disruptions.[21] Passengers are entitled to €250 converted in RSD for flights up to 1,500 km, €400 converted in RSD for flights between 1,500 and 3,500 km, and €600 converted in RSD for flights over 3,500 km.[22] The compensation can be reduced by 50% if the airline offers re-routing to the final destination with a new arrival time that does not exceed the scheduled arrival time of the original flight by two hours for flights of 1,500 km or less, three hours for flights between 1,500 km and 3,500 km, and four hours for flights over 3,500 km.[23] The distance is measured by the great circle route method.[24]

Flight Distance	**Standard Compensation**	**Reduced by 50% if Re-routing Arrives Within:**
≤1,500 km.	€250 converted in RSD.	≤2 hours of original arrival.
1,500–3,500 km.	€400 converted in RSD.	≤3 hours of original arrival.
>3,500 km.	€600 converted in RSD.	≤4 hours of original arrival.

The conversion must take into account the "middle exchange rate of the National Bank of Serbia on the day of the payment."[25]

Passengers can request a reimbursement of the full cost of the ticket for the part of the journey not undertaken or re-routing at the earliest opportunity under comparable transport conditions and re-routing at a later date.[26] In the event the passenger is re-routed to a different airport than originally booked, the airline must bear the cost of transferring the passenger from the alternative airport to the initial airport.[27]

The Law provides for passengers to be adequately cared for which includes meals and refreshments reasonable in relation to the waiting time; two free telephone calls, telex or fax messages, or emails; and hotel accommodation and transport between the airport and the accommodation if an overnight stay or a stay of longer than one night becomes necessary.[28] Special attention must be given to persons with reduced mobility and unaccompanied children.[29] Unlike many laws around the world, the Law

21 Article 12.
22 Article 12(1)–(3).
23 Article 12(2)(1)–(3).
24 Article 12.
25 Article 12.
26 Article 13(1)–(3).
27 Article 13.
28 Article 14(1)–(3).
29 Article 14.

does not provide a fixed threshold for when airlines must offer meals and refreshments.

Upgrading is allowed without additional payment from the passenger. Downgrading must result in a reimbursement of a percentage of the ticket price within seven days based on flight distance; 30% for flights of 1,500 km or less, 50% for intra-Community flights over 1,500 km and for all other flights between 1,500 km and 3,500 km, and 75% for all flights over 3,500 km.[30]

Airlines and tour operators must give priority to persons with reduced mobility and any persons accompanying them, as well as unaccompanied children, in terms of care and assistance.[31] Compared to the EU Regulation, the Serbian Law contains much more detailed provisions on the rights of persons with special needs in the event of denial of boarding, cancellation, or long delays.[32] The Law prohibits airlines from refusing to carry a passenger on the ground of disability if they have a valid reservation unless there are safety reasons or it is a physical impossibility due to aircraft limitations.[33] Refusal is allowed if it's necessary to meet applicable safety requirements established by ratified international agreements, national law, or the authority that issued the air operator's certificate (AOC) to the specific air carrier.[34] Refusal is also permitted if the physical characteristics of the aircraft itself – specifically its size or the dimensions of its doors – make the embarkation or carriage of the disabled person or person with reduced mobility physically impossible.[35] If a reservation is refused on either of the two permissible grounds, the carrier/agent/tour operator must make "reasonable efforts to propose an acceptable alternative to the person in question."[36] This signifies a duty to explore other feasible options rather than simply denying service outright. Air carriers and their agents are obliged to make publicly available, in accessible formats and at least the same languages as other passenger information, the safety rules they apply to the carriage of disabled persons and persons with reduced mobility. This includes any restrictions on their carriage or on mobility equipment due to aircraft size. This ensures transparency and allows passengers to be informed before booking.[37]

30 Article 15(1)–(3).
31 Article 16.
32 Articles 37–51.
33 Article 38.
34 Article 39(1).
35 Article 39(2).
36 Article 39.
37 Article 39.

Article 42 defines the responsibility of the airport managing body for providing assistance as found in Article 49.[38] This primary responsibility is conditional on the passenger having notified their assistance needs at least 48 hours before departure. Even if the 48-hour notification is not met, the airport managing body still has a duty to make "all reasonable efforts" to provide the necessary assistance. This is a crucial safety net for passengers who might not be aware of, or able to meet, the pre-notification deadline. The assistance provided must be, "as far as possible, appropriate to the particular needs of the individual passenger," emphasizing a tailored approach rather than a one-size-fits-all solution. Article 43 makes it clear that assistance must be given without additional charge to ensure accessibility. Both air carriers and airport managing bodies must ensure that all personnel, including subcontractors, who provide direct assistance to disabled persons and persons with reduced mobility have the necessary knowledge to meet diverse needs.[39] Any non-compliance could result in a fine between 100,000 and 400,000 RSD.[40]

Article 17 clarifies that the compensation provided for in the Law does not prevent passengers from seeking further compensation under national law, but the compensation paid may be deducted from any such further compensation. However, such right does not apply to passengers who have voluntarily surrendered their reservation. Carriers are under the obligation to fully inform the passengers of their rights in order for them to be able to effectively exercise their rights, according to Article 19.

The Law also expressly provides that passengers are entitled to have one hand baggage in the cabin at no additional charge. However, it is for the airlines to determine the size and weight of such luggage.[41] Airlines are responsible for any loss or damages to mobility aids.[42]

An airline can be fined ranging from 100,000 to 400,000 RSD (Serbian Dinars) if they are found to be in violation of key passenger protection provisions of the Law. Article 175 lists specific scenarios where an operating air carrier will be fined such as the failure to compensate and

38 Key areas of assistance:
- Arrival and Check-in.
- Pre-Flight Journey.
- Boarding and Onboard Transition.
- Disembarkation and Post-Flight Journey.
- Transit and Connections.
- Basic Needs: Assistance to Move to Toilet Facilities if Required.
- Mobility Equipment and Assistance Dogs.

39 Article 46.

40 Article 176.

41 Article 35.

42 Article 47.

assist,[43] the failure to inform about alternative,[44] failure to compensate for downgrading,[45] or failure to prioritize vulnerable passengers.[46]

Serbian air passenger rights law, as encapsulated in the "Law on Obligations and the Basics of Property Relations in Air Transport," demonstrates a high degree of formal alignment with the core principles of Regulation 261. This alignment is a direct consequence of Serbia's status as a signatory to the European Common Aviation Area (ECAA) Agreement, necessitating the transposition of the EU acquis. The Law faithfully transcribes the central tenets of the Regulation, establishing a harmonized regime that guarantees passengers departing from Serbian airports, and those on certain incoming flights, rights to compensation, assistance, and care in cases of denied boarding, cancellation, and lengthy delays that are substantively equivalent to those enjoyed within the European Union by largely mirroring the provisions of the Regulation.

Specific nuances in the domestic legislation exist. For instance, the Serbian legislator adopted an integrative approach, embedding the Regulation's provisions within a broader domestic framework that also incorporates elements of the Montreal Convention. The Law exhibits a degree of elaboration in certain areas. It explicitly clarifies that compensation is payable for qualifying delays, a point of historical judicial interpretation in the EU, thereby pre-empting ambiguity. Furthermore, it substantially expands upon the rights of persons with reduced mobility and disabled passengers, incorporating detailed obligations for carriers and airport managing bodies that surpass the Regulation's requirements in specificity, particularly regarding non-discrimination, transparency of safety rules, and the duty to provide assistance.

Conversely, the Serbian transposition introduces greater legal uncertainty than its EU counterpart. The most significant divergence lies in the definition of "extraordinary circumstances," which the Serbian Law frames in broader, more generic terms, omitting the illustrative list found in the Regulation. This vagueness may complicate the consistent application of this key exemption for carriers, potentially leading to increased litigation. Procedurally, the placement of the Law's scope within Article 8, rather than in introductory provisions, is a drafting peculiarity that does not affect substance but differs from common EU legislative practice.

In conclusion, the Serbian Law successfully establishes a comprehensive passenger rights regime that is fundamentally congruent with EU law,

43 Article 175(1)–(5).
44 Article 175(3).
45 Article 175(8).
46 Article 175(9).

ensuring a standardized level of protection. Its integrative nature and enhanced provisions for vulnerable passengers represent deliberate legislative choices that, in some respects, extend beyond the EU baseline. The principal point of divergence and potential weakness remains the less precise formulation of the “extraordinary circumstances” defence, which echoes the Regulation’s inherent complexities without its guiding examples. Overall, the framework provides a solid foundation for consumer protection, though its practical efficacy will inevitably depend on consistent enforcement and judicial interpretation, particularly regarding its more open-textured clauses.

Comparison with EU Regulation

Feature	**Law on Obligations and the Basics of Property Relations in Air Transport**	**EU Regulation 261/2004**
Delay Compensation	≥3h: €250–€600 in RSD.	≥3h: €250–€600 (by distance).
Cancellation Compensation	<14d notice: Refund or re-routing + €250–600 compensation (by distance).	<14d notice: Refund or re-routing + €250–600 compensation (by distance).
Denied Boarding Compensation	Volunteer first; €250–€600 in RSD if denied boarding.	Volunteer first; €250–€600 (by distance) if denied boarding.
Baggage Compensation	Not specified.	Not specified.

Bibliography

- Law on Obligations and the Basics of the Property Relations in Air Transport Published in the Official Gazette of the Republic of Serbia No 87/11 and 66/15 <https://cad.gov.rs/upload/regulativa/eng/Law%20on%20Obligations%20and%20the%20Basic%20of%20Property%20Relations%20in%20Air%20Transport.pdf> accessed 19 December 2025.
- Pejović, J. and Paripović, M. M. ‘Flight Delays, Flight Cancellations or Denial of Boarding–Rights of Passengers in the Republic of Serbia’ (*ROKAS*, S.D) <https://rokas.com/wp-content/uploads/2024/07/Flight-delays-flight-cancellations-or-denial-of-boarding-rights-of-passengers-in-the-Republic-of-Serbia.pdf> accessed 19 December 2025.
- Petrović, G., ‘Serbia’ in S. Gates (ed), *The Aviation Law Review* (8th edn, Gideon Roberton Law Business Research Ltd 2020).

II.44

Sierra Leone

Sierra Leone's passenger rights are primarily governed by the Consumer Protection Regulations, which form Part 20B of the Sierra Leone Civil Aviation Regulations, administered by the Sierra Leone Civil Aviation Authority (SLCAA).[1]

The Regulations apply to passengers departing from an airport within Sierra Leone on a domestic or international journey.[2] They also apply to passengers arriving in Sierra Leone from another country, unless they were already provided with benefits and assistance in that other country.[3] They also apply to passengers on foreign airlines with respect to the flight segments originating in Sierra Leone.[4] The rules cover scheduled flights, including packaged tours, for passengers with confirmed reservations who present themselves for check-in on time, no later than two hours before the published departure time.[5] They do not apply to passengers on entirely free or non-public discounted tickets but do apply to those using frequent flyer tickets.[6]

A passenger who fails to show up for their scheduled flight may be wait-listed on a later flight, subject to seat availability.[7] The regulations explicitly permit airlines to overbook a flight in anticipation of some passengers not showing up.[8]

In the event of an oversold flight, an airline must first seek volunteers to give up their seats before involuntarily denying boarding to any passenger.[9] The airline must clearly advise potential volunteers of their

1 Sierra Leone Civil Aviation Regulations, Part 20B-Consumer Protection Regulations, February 2024.
2 Article 3.1(a).
3 Article 3.1(b).
4 Article 3.1(c).
5 Article 3.2(a).
6 Article 3.3.
7 Article 4.1.
8 Article 4.2.
9 Article 5.1(b).

DOI: 10.4324/9781003746164-55

risk of being involuntarily bumped and the compensation they would be owed, as well as any restrictions on the volunteer offer.[10] Volunteers are to be compensated in accordance with the sections on compensation.[11] In the event an insufficient number of volunteers come forward, the airline may deny boarding to other passengers in accordance with its boarding priority procedure.[12] The airline must establish and file clear, non-discriminatory boarding priority procedures with the Authority. This procedure must minimize involuntary denied boarding and cannot unduly preference or disadvantage any passenger.[13] Factors that may be considered include passengers on urgent medical trips, time of check-in, fare paid, frequent-flyer status, and the needs of persons with reduced mobility or families (maximum two adults) with children under 5.[14] If passengers are involuntarily denied boarding, the airline must immediately provide compensation and assistance.[15]

For domestic flights, airlines must provide reasons for a delay within 30 minutes. After a two-hour delay, refreshments such as water, soft drinks and snacks,[16] and communication facilities must be offered; after three hours, passengers are entitled to reimbursement of their ticket;[17] and for delays between 10 PM and 4 AM or when the airport is closed, hotel accommodation and transport are required.[18] For international flights, compensation and communication are required for delays between two and four hours, meals and communication for delays over four hours, and hotel accommodation and transport when the new departure time is at least six hours later than originally announced.[19] Interestingly, for international flights there is no mentions of refreshments which might be included within the "meal" heading.

Type of Assistance/ Compensation	**Domestic Flights**	**International Flights**
Reason for Delay	After **30 minutes.**	Not specified.
Refreshments	After **2 hours.**	Not specified but could be within "meal."

(*Continued*)

10 Article 5.3(a).
11 Article 5.2.
12 Article 5.4.
13 Article 6.1.
14 Article 6.2.
15 Article 6.4.
16 Article 11.1(a).
17 In accordance with Article 10.
18 Article 7.1.1(a)–(c).
19 Article 7.1.2(a)–(c).

(Continued)

Type of Assistance/ Compensation	Domestic Flights	International Flights
Meal	Not explicitly listed separately.	After **4 hours.**
Communication (2 phone calls, SMS, emails)	After **2 hours.**	**2–4 hours.**
Reimbursement	After **3 hours.**	Not available.
Compensation (% of ticket price)	Not applicable for domestic delays.	**2–4 hours** (30% of ticket).
Hotel Accommodation and Transport	**Overnight delay** (10 –PM–4 AM) or **airport closure.**	**New departure is at least 6 hours** after the original time.

In the event of a cancellation, airlines must offer passengers care, reimbursement, or re-routing to their final destination.[20] For domestic flights, passengers have a right to compensation unless informed of the cancellation at least 24 hours before departure.[21] For international flights, the right to compensation exists unless passengers are informed at least seven days in advance, or are offered re-routing that does not significantly alter their travel schedule.[22] This means that the passenger was informed between three and seven days and offered re-routing allowing them to reach their final destination no more than four hours after the scheduled time of arrival.[23] The Regulations stipulate in paragraph iii again less than seven days and a re-routing allowing passengers to depart not more than one hour before the scheduled time of departure and to reach their final destination less than two hours after the scheduled time of arrival. However, that seems to directly contradict paragraph ii which regulates notice received between seven and three days by imposing a stricter obligation on airlines. It might be an error which should be read as when the notice of cancellation is given less than three days before scheduled time as in its current format. Paragraphs ii and iii are creating a contradiction that undermines the intended sliding scale of protection. The logic is that the more notice the passenger receives, the more leniency for the airline. A similar mistake was spotted in Nigeria.

20 Article 8.1(a) and (b).
21 Article 8.1(c).
22 Article 8.1(d)(i).
23 Article 8.1(d)(ii).

Notice Given by Airline	Permitted Change to Departure	Permitted Change to Arrival	Compensation Due?
7+ Days	Any alternative flight.	Any alternative flight.	No.
3 to 7 Days	Up to 2 hours earlier.	Up to 4 hours later.	No.
Less Than 7 Days	Up to 1 hour earlier.	Up to 2 hours later.	No.

An airline is not obliged to pay compensation if the cancellation was caused by extraordinary circumstances which could not have been avoided.[24] The term is vaguely defined in Article 2.1(r) as including "any mechanical, technical, operational, climatic, socio-political or any other conditions beyond the actual control of the party involved." Article 27 mentioned the defences to specific provisions of Article 20 (misleading information) some of which are not found in the text itself. Indeed, Article 20 only contains five paragraphs, yet Article 27 refers to 20.6 and 20.7. Moreover, the Article itself refers to denied boarding and cancellation which are not dealt with in Article 20. Interestingly, Article 27 stipulates that an airline can be relieved of its obligations to pay compensation for denied boarding or cancellation if it can prove that the incident was caused by extraordinary circumstances beyond its control, or by circumstances necessary for the safety or security of passengers or the aircraft. IS 27.1. (annexed to Part 20B) then lists the various elements which might be considered as extraordinary circumstances. The list can be grouped into several categories such as security, political and labour issues, weather and air traffic management, unexpected aircraft damage and technical defects. The most important nuance in this list is the fundamental legal distinction for technical defects; For any technical defect falling under points (8) through (11), which cover unforeseen physical damage to the aircraft or technical failure that result in a significant operational disruption, the Regulations automatically deem it an extraordinary circumstance, and no further investigation into the cause is required. However, this is not the case for defects categorized as last-minute or in-flight technical fault which are only considered an extraordinary circumstance if the airline can successfully prove that the specific component which failed had been properly maintained in strict accordance with the manufacturer's guidance.

24 Article 8.3.

Category	Specific Circumstances (from IS 27.1)	Key Details/Examples
Security, Political, and Labour Disruptions	(1) Political instability, riots, or military intervention. (2) Terrorist activity. (3) Strikes by airline employees or critical third parties.	Covers external civil unrest, security threats, and labour actions involving essential services like air traffic control or airport security.
Weather, Infrastructure, and Authority Directives	(4) Meteorological conditions incompatible with flight safety. (5) Airport or airspace closures. (6) Congestion or failure of airport/air traffic navigation infrastructure. (7) Any decision by an air traffic management or regulatory body.	Includes severe weather, infrastructure breakdowns, and mandatory orders from authorities that ground or re-route flights.
Unexpected Aircraft Damage and Specific Technical Events	(8) Damage to the aircraft structure. (9) A bird strike. (10) In-flight damage from the immediately preceding flight. (11) A technical defect causing an unscheduled diversion or return to departure airport.	These technical issues and damages are automatically considered extraordinary, with no need to prove maintenance.
Last-Minute and In-Flight Technical Defects	(12) A technical defect apparent immediately before departure or in-flight.	**Crucial Proviso:** This is only an extraordinary circumstance if the airline can prove the faulty component was properly maintained according to the manufacturer's guidance. The burden of proof is on the airline.

When compensation is due, passengers shall receive at least 25% of the ticket price for domestic flights and 30% for international flights.[25] This compensation may be reduced by 50% if the airline offers re-routing that

25 Article 9.1(a) and (b).

arrives very close to the original scheduled time, namely one hour for domestic flights and three hours for international flights.[26] If a passenger is downgraded, the airline must reimburse the price difference for the downgraded segment plus 30% of the ticket price for domestic flights and 50% for international flights.[27]

Airlines must give priority to persons with reduced mobility, their companions, unaccompanied minors, and families with young children. These groups are entitled to care in cases of denied boarding, cancellation, and delays.[28]

The Regulations also contain a provision allowing for misspelt names corrections free of charge up to 48 hours before the flight.[29] It also contains a provision on baggage rights which indicates that passengers have the right to have their baggage carried on the same flight.[30] If baggage is off-loaded for operational, safety, or security reasons, the airline must inform the passenger promptly, carry the baggage on the next available flight, and immediately tender compensation of LE 300 for domestic flights or $150 USD for international flights for the inconvenience.[31] If baggage is lost – after seven days for domestic flights and 21 days for international flights – or damaged, the passenger shall be compensated under the Sierra Leone Civil Aviation Authority Act 2023.[32] Checked baggage fees will be refunded if baggage is not delivered within 24 hours of flight arrival.[33]

Airlines must display a clearly visible notice at check-in informing passengers of their rights in case of denied boarding, cancellation, or delay and give a written notice setting out the procedures for compensation.[34] All airfare advertising must state the final, entire price to be paid, and airlines must file all advertisements with the Authority.[35] The Regulations are silent regarding any fines for non-compliance.

The Sierra Leone Regulations establish a robust foundation which distinguishes between domestic and international flights. A particular strength lies in its detailed and precise list of extraordinary circumstances in IS 27.1, which provides crucial legal clarity. Notably, the Sierra Leone law incorporates a sophisticated distinction for technical defects, explicitly

26 Article 9.2(a) and (b).
27 Article 12.2(a) and (b).
28 Article 13.
29 Article 16.
30 Article 18.1.
31 Article 18.2.1(a) and (b).
32 Article 18.3.
33 Article 18.4.
34 Article 17.
35 Article 20.

stating that a last-minute fault is only considered an extraordinary circumstance if the airline can prove the defective component was properly maintained. This provision effectively prevents airlines from using routine maintenance issues as a blanket excuse, a point often subject to litigation in other jurisdictions.

Despite these strengths, several key differences place the Sierra Leone Regulations as a less stringent and, in one critical area, a less coherent version of the EU model. The most glaring issue is a likely drafting error concerning the notice period for international flight cancellations. The regulation creates an internal contradiction by setting identical seven-day notice thresholds for two different tiers of obligation, thereby muddling the intended sliding scale of protection and creating legal uncertainty. In contrast, the EU regulation employs a clear and logical three-tiered system. However, the notice period is shorter than under the EU Regulation making it stricter on airlines.

Furthermore, the financial compensation mechanism in Sierra Leone is significantly less impactful. Compensation is calculated as a percentage of the ticket price, specifically 25% for domestic and 30% for international flights. This stands in sharp contrast to the EU's model, which mandates fixed amounts that are not tied to the fare paid, currently set at €250, €400, or €600 depending on flight distance. The EU's fixed-sum approach ensures a meaningful and standardized remedy for passengers, whereas the Sierra Leone model may result in very low payouts, reducing its deterrent effect on airlines.

Its lower compensation amounts and, most importantly, the critical ambiguity in its cancellation renders it a foundational but imperfect piece of legislation that would benefit from future clarification and strengthening to match the global standard set by its European counterpart.

Comparison with EU Regulation

Feature	Part 20B of the Sierra Leone Civil Aviation Regulations	EU Regulation 261/2004
Delay Compensation	No.	≥3h: €250–€600 (by distance).
Cancellation Compensation	<7d notice: Refund or re-routing + compensation.	<14d notice: Refund or re-routing + €250–600 compensation (by distance).
Denied Boarding Compensation	Volunteer first; 25% for domestic/30% for international flights if denied boarding.	Volunteer first; €250–€600 (by distance) if denied boarding.
Baggage Compensation	LE 300 for domestic flights or $150 USD for international flights for inconvenience.	Not specified.

Bibliography

- Sierra Leone Civil Aviation Regulations, Part 20B-Consumer Protection Regulations, February 2024 <https://slcaa.gov.sl/wp-content/uploads/2025/01/Part-20B-SLCAA-Consumer-Protection-Signed-and-Stamped-5-Feb-2024.pdf> accessed 19 December 2025.

II.45

South Africa

In South Africa, passengers are only protected against overbooking and overbooking through the Consumer Protection Act 68 of 2008 as amended (CPA). According to the CPA, suppliers or service providers are not permitted to accept payment for goods or services that do not exist, which means airlines are generally not authorized to overbook flights.[1] It can be wondered if this provision does not also apply to downgrading as it could be argued that airlines accepted payment for a service that does no longer exist.

In case of overbooking, the passenger is entitled to a refund of the amount paid plus interest at the prescribed rate.[2] In addition, airlines must compensate any costs directly incidental to the breach.[3] This means the transportation to the airport but also if the person spent the night at a hotel to catch the flight the next day. This compensation is not due if the denial of boarding was the result of a circumstance beyond the airline's control and the airline took reasonable steps to inform the passenger as soon as practicable.[4] The even would not be beyond the supplier's control "if the shortage results partially, completely, directly or indirectly from a failure on the part of the supplier to adequately and diligently carry out any ordinary or routine matter pertaining to the supplier's business."[5] The carrier also has a defence if they offer an alternative but comparable flight and the passenger unreasonably refused the offer.[6]

For delayed and cancelled flights, the ability to claim compensation largely depends on the specific conditions of carriage. If the passenger is flying into or out of South Africa, they might be able to claim compensation under the Montreal Convention for financial losses from

1 Article 47(2)(a).
2 Article 47(3)(a).
3 Article 47(3)(b).
4 Article 47(5)(a) and (b).
5 Article 47(6).
6 Article 47(4)(a) and (b)(ii).

DOI: 10.4324/9781003746164-56

flight disruptions. However, they will need to prove financial loss; the delay itself doesn't automatically grant a claim.

While the Consumer Protection Act, offers some protection for overbooked flights, these rights are hard to enforce.[7] Annex 6 of the Yamoussoukro Decision and its regulations are not really embodied in South African law. There are no fixed fines in case of non-compliance with the CPA.

South Africa's primary instrument, the Consumer Protection Act (CPA) of 2008, approaches air passenger rights not as a specialized regime of transport law but through the broader lens of consumer transactions. Its core prohibition against accepting payment for non-existent services effectively outlaws the practice of overbooking, a stance more stringent in principle than the EU's regulated tolerance of the practice followed by mandatory compensation. The CPA's remedy for such a breach – a refund plus interest and compensation for "costs directly incidental" to the disruption – provides a meaningful, if narrow, avenue for redress, covering expenses like accommodation and transport necessitated by the denial of boarding.

However, this foundation reveals significant limitations when contrasted with the European model. The South African framework lacks the automatic, standardized compensation for inconvenience that is the hallmark of Regulation 261, which provides fixed amounts for denied boarding, cancellations, and lengthy delays without the need to prove specific financial loss. In South Africa, outside the specific context of overbooking, recourse for delays and cancellations is largely dependent on individual airline conditions of carriage or the stringent requirements of the Montreal Convention, which demands proof of quantifiable damage. This places a considerable burden of enforcement on the passenger and creates a system of variable, rather than universal, protection.

Furthermore, while the CPA offers a substantive right, its procedural efficacy is hampered by the absence of prescribed fines for non-compliance and a general lack of dedicated enforcement mechanisms in the aviation sector. The potential extension of its logic to scenarios like downgrading remains untested and speculative. Crucially, regional instruments like the Yamoussoukro Decision have not been meaningfully embodied in domestic law, leaving a regulatory gap. Ultimately, South African law provides a foundational consumer safeguard against deliberate overbooking and its immediate consequences, rooted in the principle of

7 Kiasha Nagiah, 'Flight Delays: What Compensation Can You Claim?' (*Norton Rose Fulbright*) <https://www.nortonrosefulbright.com/en-za/knowledge/publications/2aa233f4/flight-delays-what-compensation-can-you-claim>.

contractual fairness. Yet, it falls short of establishing a comprehensive, self-executing air passenger rights regime. It defers to airline policies and the burden of proof in a manner that Regulation 261 deliberately seeks to overcome, resulting in a system where protection is more theoretical for many and invariably less predictable and uniform than that afforded to passengers within the European Union.

Comparison with EU Regulation

Feature	Consumer Protection Act (CPA) of 2008	EU Regulation 261/2004
Delay Compensation	Not specified.	≥3h: €250–€600 (by distance).
Cancellation Compensation	Not specified.	<14d notice: Refund or re-routing + €250–600 compensation (by distance).
Denied Boarding Compensation	Prohibited; refund + interest at the prescribed rate.	Volunteer first; €250–€600 (by distance) if denied boarding.
Baggage Compensation	Not specified.	Not specified.

Bibliography

- Consumer Protection Act 68 of 2008, Official Gazette 32186 of 24 April 2009, as amended in 2015 Government Gazette 38557 <https://www.saflii.org/za/legis/consol_act/cpa2008246.pdf> accessed 19 December 2025.
- Nagiah, K., 'Flight Delays: What Compensation Can You Claim?' (*Norton Rose Fulbright*) <https://www.nortonrosefulbright.com/en-za/knowledge/publications/2aa233f4/flight-delays-what-compensation-can-you-claim> accessed 19 December 2025.

II.46

Switzerland

Any disruption in Switzerland is regulated by the Air Passenger Rights Regulation which implements EU Regulation 261. Despite not being an EU member, Switzerland largely adheres to the Regulation for air travel. The Air Passenger Rights Regulation applies to all air travel departing from an airport within the European Union, Switzerland, Norway, and Iceland.[1] The Regulation also applies

> to travelers departing from a third country and whose destination airport is in the EU, Switzerland, Norway or Iceland if the flight is operated by an airline that has its principal place of business in the EU, Switzerland, Norway or Iceland.[2]

However, the Regulation does not apply to charter flights or certain other transport arrangements like freight. Passengers should also have presented themselves for check-in no later than 45 minutes before the published departure time.[3]

When an airline is expected to face a situation of overbooking, it must first ask for volunteers to give up their reservations in exchange for benefits and a choice of reimbursement or re-routing, in accordance with Article 8.[4] When there is an insufficient number of volunteers, the airline may deny boarding to passengers against their will. In such cases, these passengers are immediately entitled to compensation as per Article 7, assistance as per Article 8, and care as per Article 9.[5] Airlines can also deny boarding on reasonable grounds such as health, safety, or security reasons, or inadequate travel documentation.[6]

1 Federal Office of Civil Aviation, 'Air Passenger Rights' <https://www.bazl.admin.ch/en/airpassengerrights>.
2 Federal Office of Civil Aviation, 'Air Passenger Rights' <https://www.bazl.admin.ch/en/airpassengerrights >. Article 1 and 3(1) of the Regulation.
3 Article 3(2)(a).
4 Article 4(1).
5 Article 4(2) and (3).
6 Article 2(j).

DOI: 10.4324/9781003746164-57

Scenario	Passenger Rights
Voluntary Denied Boarding (airline asks for volunteers)	Benefits + choice of reimbursement/re-routing (Article 8).
Involuntary Denied Boarding (not enough volunteers)	Immediate compensation (Article 7) + assistance/care (Articles 8 and 9).

The term cancellation is not clearly defined by Article 2(1), which only refers to the "non-operation of a flight which was previously planned and on which at least one place was reserved." Under Article 5, passengers have the right to assistance and care alongside the right to compensation if the cancellation occurs less than 14 days before the scheduled departure.[7] Indeed, if the passenger was informed at least two weeks before the scheduled departure, they are not entitled to compensation.[8] If the passenger was informed between two weeks and seven days before departure and offered re-routing allowing the passenger to depart no more than two hours before scheduled departure and arrive at their final destination less than four hours after scheduled arrival, then no compensation is due.[9] When the passenger is informed less than seven days in advance and is offered re-routing allowing them to depart no more than one hour before scheduled departure and arrive at their final destination less than two hours after scheduled arrival, then compensation is not due either.[10] The burden of proof rests on the airline to demonstrate the passenger was indeed informed of the cancellation.[11]

When Cancelled	Compensation Due?
≥14 Days Before Departure	No.
7–14 Days Before Departure	No, if re-routing allows departure ≤2h earlier and arrival ≤4h later.
<7 Days Before Departure	No, if re-routing allows departure ≤1h earlier and arrival ≤2h later.
<14 Days Notice + No Suitable Re-routing	Yes.

No compensation is due if the airline is able to demonstrate that the cancellation is attributable to extraordinary circumstances which

7 Article 5(1)(a)–(c).
8 Article 5(1)(c)(i).
9 Article 5(1)(c)(ii).
10 Article 5(1)(c)(iii).
11 Article 5(4).

could not have been avoided even if all reasonable measures had been taken.[12] The term "extraordinary circumstance" is loosely defined in the Regulation, points 14 and 15 of the preamble, through a list of potential situations such as severe weather and air traffic control strikes outside the airline's control.

When a flight is delayed, passengers are entitled to care (as per Article 9) if the delay reaches certain thresholds based on flight distance: two hours or more for flights of 1,500 km or less, three hours or more for intra-Community flights of more than 1,500 km and for all other flights between 1,500 km and 3,500 km, and four hours or more for all flights not falling under (a) or (b) (i.e., over 3,500 km).[13] If the delay is five hours or more, passengers have the right to reimbursement (as per Article 8(1)(a)) if they decide not to pursue the flight.[14]

While Article 6 itself does not explicitly mention compensation, the European Court of Justice ruled in the *Sturgeon* case that passengers arriving at their final destination three hours or more late are entitled to compensation under Article 7, unless the delay was due to extraordinary circumstances. This effectively treats long delays like cancellations for compensation purposes. If the delay is attributable to extraordinary circumstances, the passengers are not entitled to payment of compensation. While the rule applies to Switzerland, the Federal Office of Civil Aviation (FOCA) makes it clear that "due to the lack of a legal basis, the FOCA is unable to fine an airline for failure to pay compensation in the event of a delay."[15]

The core article for financial compensation is Article 7 which establishes that passengers are entitled to €250 for flights up to 1,500 km, €400 for flights between 1,500 and 3,500 km, and €600 for flights over 3,500 km.[16] The compensation can be reduced by 50% if the airline offers re-routing to the final destination with a new arrival time that does not exceed the scheduled arrival time of the original flight by two hours for flights of 1,500 km or less, three hours for flights between 1,500 km and 3,500 km, and four hours for flights over 3,500 km.[17] The distance is measured by the great circle route method.[18]

12 Article 5(3).
13 Article 6(1).
14 Article 6(1)(iii).
15 Federal Office of Civil Aviation, 'Air Passenger Rights' <https://www.bazl.admin.ch/en/airpassengerrights>
16 Article 7(1).
17 Article 7(2).
18 Article 7(4).

Flight Distance	**Standard Compensation**	**Reduced by 50% if Re-routing Arrives Within:**
≤1,500 km.	€250.	≤2 hours of original arrival.
1,500–3,500 km.	€400.	≤3 hours of original arrival.
>3,500 km.	€600.	≤4 hours of original arrival.

In cases of denied boarding or cancellation (and delays of five hours or more), passengers must be offered the choice between reimbursement, re-routing at the earliest opportunity under comparable transport conditions, and re-routing at a later date.[19]

The Regulation provides for passengers to be adequately cared for, Article 9, unless such care would further delay the flight, preamble Point 18. When delays reach the thresholds in Article 6, or in cases of denied boarding or cancellation, passengers must be offered meals and refreshments in reasonable relation to the waiting time, two free telephone calls, telex or fax messages, or emails, and hotel accommodation and transport between the airport and the accommodation if an overnight stay or a stay of longer than one night becomes necessary.[20] Special attention must be given to persons with reduced mobility and unaccompanied children.[21] Unlike many laws around the world, the Regulation does not provide a fixed threshold for when airlines must offer meals and refreshments.

Upgrading is allowed without additional payment from the passenger. Downgrading must result in a reimbursement of a percentage of the ticket price within seven days based on flight distance: 30% for flights of 1,500 km or less, 50% for intra-Community flights over 1,500 km and for all other flights between 1,500 km and 3,500 km, and 75% for all flights over 3,500 km.[22]

Airlines and tour operators must give priority to persons with reduced mobility and any persons accompanying them, as well as unaccompanied children, in terms of care and assistance.[23] Article 12 clarifies that the compensation provided for in the Regulation does not prevent passengers from seeking further compensation (e.g., for damages beyond the standardized amounts) under national law, but the compensation paid under Regulation 261 may be deducted from any such further compensation. Carriers are under the obligation to fully inform the passengers of their

19 Article 8(1).
20 Article 9(1).
21 Article 9(3).
22 Article 10(2)(a)–(c).
23 Article 11.

rights in order for them to be able to effectively exercise their rights, Point 20 and Article 14.

While FOCA cannot directly enforce individual compensation claims, they can investigate and, if an infringement is found, initiate administrative proceedings against the airline, which can include fines. This means passengers, after complaining to the airline and the NEB, may still have to pursue their claim through courts or alternative dispute resolution mechanisms, which can be burdensome and time-consuming. There are no fixed sanctions in the Regulation, but Switzerland can impose sanctions which are "effective, proportionate and dissuasive."[24]

EU Regulation 261, which Switzerland has largely adopted, stands as a crucial piece of legislation in safeguarding air passenger rights, but it is not without its complexities and controversies. From a consumer perspective, its greatest strength lies in establishing a clear, standardized framework for compensation and assistance in cases of denied boarding, cancellations, and significant delays. However, the Regulation faces substantial criticisms, particularly from the airline industry, and has practical challenges in its implementation. One of the most contentious aspects is the interpretation of "extraordinary circumstances." Airlines frequently invoke this clause to avoid compensation, leading to disputes and a perception of airlines trying to shirk their responsibilities. While the ECJ has provided some clarification, it remains a "grey area" that often necessitates legal action or intervention by claims agencies. Enforcement is another significant weakness.

Comparison with EU Regulation

Feature	**Air Passenger Rights Regulation**	**EU Regulation 261/2004**
Delay Compensation	≥3h: €250–€600 (by distance).	≥3h: €250–€600 (by distance).
Cancellation Compensation	<14d notice: Refund or re-routing + €250–600 compensation (by distance).	<14d notice: Refund or re-routing + €250–600 compensation (by distance).
Denied Boarding Compensation	Volunteer first; €250–€600 (by distance) if denied boarding.	Volunteer first; €250–€600 (by distance) if denied boarding.
Baggage Compensation	Not specified.	Not specified.

24 Article 16(3).

Bibliography

- Federal Office of Civil Aviation, 'Air Passenger Rights' <https://www.bazl.admin.ch/en/airpassengerrights> accessed 19 December 2025.

II.47

Tanzania

The Civil Aviation Act (CAP.80) is the primary legislation in Tanzania that provides the legal framework for all civil aviation activities. Under this Act, the minister responsible for civil aviation through the Tanzania Civil Aviation Authority (TCAA) has the power to make various regulations to implement the provisions of the Act and ensure the safe, secure, and orderly development of civil aviation. The regulation primarily concerned with the protection of air passengers is the Civil Aviation (Carriage by Air) Regulations 2024 covering liability for death/injury, baggage, delays, cancellations, and denied boarding.[1] These regulations incorporate international standards, particularly those from the Montreal Convention, but also extend the protection afford to passengers. For instance, the Civil Aviation (Carriage by Air) Regulations 2024 contains an article dedicated to cancellation or re-routing.

The Civil Aviation (Carriage by Air) Regulations 2024 applies to domestic carriage performed by airlines within the Republic.[2] While not expressly stated, it can be safely assumed that it also applied to international carriage in circumstances where the Montreal Convention would have applied.[3] It does not apply to passengers travelling free of charge or at a reduced rate not available to the public.

Article 20 of the Civil Aviation (Carriage by Air) Regulations 2024 resembles the Montreal Convention provision, indicating that airlines are liable for damage occasioned by delay without providing any fixed compensation or calculation mechanism. The same exoneration of liability exists.[4] The limit of liability for delay is the equivalent in Tanzanian shillings of Special Drawing Rights 4,150.[5]

1 Civil Aviation (Carriage by Air) Regulations 2024, Government Notice No. 4 of 2024.
2 Article 2(1)(b).
3 Article 2(1)(a).
4 Article 20(2).
5 Article 30.

DOI: 10.4324/9781003746164-58

In the event of a cancellation, the passenger must be offered assistance, re-routing, and compensation "upon proof of loss or damages."[6] However, when the cancellation is the result of an "extraordinary circumstance," then the carrier is not liable.[7] The term is defined in Article 3 as including bad weather, strikes, political circumstances, natural disasters, bird strike, unruly or ill passenger, or delay caused by airport operations. This list is non-exhaustive as the definition reads as "may include."

Denial of boarding is dealt with in Article 22 and requires airlines to first find volunteers in exchange of benefits and care.[8] In case there are insufficient number of volunteers, the air carrier can deny boarding but must provide passengers with care and assistance and compensation upon proof of loss or damages.[9] However, denial of boarding is authorized when there are reasonable grounds such as health, safety, or security reasons or inadequate travel documentation or inability to prove the person is the one named[10] on the ticket but also if such action would prevent the infringement of any applicable law or the passenger has been refused entry into the country.[11] Article 23 redefines Article 3 by noting that the

> conduct, age, mental or physical state of the passenger is such that (i) it requires special assistance of the carrier; (ii) evidently violates principles of good conduct, in a manner which may raise serious objections of other passengers; or (iii) possesses a threat to himself, other passengers or someone else's property.[12]

Unruly passengers are also a reason to refuse carriage, as well as any refusal to submit to a security check.[13] The non-payment of the ticket is another reason as well as fraudulently acquired tickets, counterfeit, or tickets reported as lost or stolen.[14] The list of exceptions is very exhaustive and quite detailed. Similarly, airlines can escape liability if they prove that the damages were caused or contributed to by the passenger.[15] The major difference between the two articles is that Article 3 exempts airlines for liability for delays and cancellations while Article 23 allows airlines to refuse carriage.

---

6 Article 21(1)(a)–(c).
7 Article 21(3).
8 Article 22(2).
9 Article 22(3) and (4)(a) and (b).
10 Article 23(1)(k).
11 Article 3 in conjunction with Article 23(1)(b) and (i).
12 Article 23(1)(c).
13 Article 23(1)(d) and (e).
14 Article 23(1)(f) and (j).
15 Article 28.

Legal Ground	**Specific Scenarios**
Safety/Security	- Threat to flight safety (e.g., violence, hazardous items). - Refusal of security checks.
Legal Compliance	- Violation of laws in departure/destination countries. - Fake/altered travel documents
Passenger Conduct	- Unruly behaviour (disrupting others). - Mental/physical state risking safety.
Non-Compliance	- Ignoring crew instructions (e.g., seatbelt rules). - Refusing document checks.
Financial/Ticketing Issues	- Unpaid fares/taxes. - Fraudulent/lost/stolen tickets.
Documentation Failures	- Missing visas/passports. - Destroying documents mid-journey.
Prior Misconduct	- Repeat offenses (e.g., prior flight disruptions).

Comparison Table: Article 3 vs. Article 23

Aspect	**Article 3: Extraordinary Circumstances**	**Article 23: Refusal of Carriage**
Purpose	Exempts airlines from liability for delays/cancellations due to uncontrollable events.	Allows airlines to deny boarding for safety, security, or compliance reasons.
Key Triggers	- Natural disasters (weather, earthquakes). - Strikes (air sector). - Airport operational failures. - Unruly/ill passengers.	- Safety/security threats. - Invalid travel docs. - Unpaid fares/fraudulent tickets. - Passenger misconduct.
Who Controls It?	External factors (beyond airline's control).	Passenger actions/status (often within their control).
Effect on Passengers	No automatic compensation; must prove damages.	Immediate denial of boarding (no refund if justified).
Airline Obligation	Must prove the event was unforeseeable and unavoidable.	Must document reasons for refusal (e.g., safety risk, fraud).
Legal Flexibility	Broad, non-exhaustive list ("may include").	Exhaustive list (specific scenarios).

When a flight is cancelled or significantly delayed or the person is denied boarding, they have the choice between the right to reimbursement within seven days or re-routing under comparable transport condition – at the earliest opportunity or a later date.[16] If the passenger is at a connecting airport and the trip is no longer serving any purpose, they can opt for a full refund – even for the part already used – and request a return flight to their point of departure.[17]

The Regulations contain a right of care, however, there is no timeframe for when the provision starts applying. Passengers are entitled to meals and refreshment in relation to the waiting time, hotel accommodation for overnight stay, and transport to and from the accommodation.[18] The law does not contain a provision regarding communication but insists that airlines must give priority on the right of care to person with special needs.[19]

Scenario	Passenger Rights	Airline Obligations
Flight Delay	Compensation for damages (limit: SDR 4,150).	Liable for damages caused by delay.
Cancellation	Right to: - Reimbursement (7 days). - Re-routing. - Care (meals, lodging).	Offer assistance, re-routing, and compensation upon proof of loss.
Denied Boarding	Compensation upon proof of loss + care (if involuntary).	Seek volunteers first; provide care/compensation if forced denial.

In case of downgrading, the airline must reimburse the difference.[20] Airlines must give priority to passengers with special needs or reduced mobility as well as unaccompanied children and certified service dogs.[21] The liability for lost luggage is the equivalent in Tanzanian shillings of Special Drawing Rights 1,000 for each passenger unless the passenger has made, at the time when the checked baggage was handed over to the carrier, a special declaration of interest.[22]

The Regulation contains a provision on penalty for both natural and legal persons. A natural person will be liable to a fine of not less than the equivalent in Tanzanian shillings of 1,000 United States dollars or imprisonment for a term not less than 12 months or both.[23] For a legal person, the law does not lay a fixed penalty but mentions that the corporate body and any guilty managerial person would be prosecuted accordingly.[24]

16 Article 24.
17 Article 24(1).
18 Article 25(1).
19 Article 25(2).
20 Article 26(b).
21 Article 27.
22 Article 31(1).
23 Article 66(1).
24 Article 66(2).

Tanzania's Civil Aviation (Carriage by Air) Regulations, 2024, provide a robust legal framework for air passenger protection regarding delays, cancellations, and denied boarding. Tanzania's Regulations apply primarily to domestic flights, with implied coverage for international flights where the Montreal Convention would apply. In contrast, EU Regulation 261 explicitly governs all flights departing from EU airports and flights arriving in the EU on EU-based carriers. While the "reasonable measures" defence offers airlines a necessary shield against unforeseeable events, the Regulations place a significant onus on carriers to prioritize passenger welfare and handle disruptions with transparency and due diligence. However, the lack of automatic compensation and requirements for passenger to prove damages make it heavier on passengers. Although Tanzania's Civil Aviation (Carriage by Air) Regulations, 2024 provides for a right to care, it does not specify time triggers, creating ambiguity on when assistance begins. While Tanzania's 2024 Regulations align with global standards (e.g., Montreal Convention), they fall short of EU Regulation 261's pro-passenger rigor. The lack of automatic compensation, vague care rules, and broad airline exemptions make Tanzanian rights less predictable for travellers. However, Tanzania's framework is progressive for the region and could easily be strengthened.

Comparison with EU Regulation

Feature	**Tanzania Civil Aviation Regulations 2024**	**EU Regulation 261/2004**
Delay Compensation	No fixed compensation. Re-routing/refund + care (meals/hotel). Passenger must **prove damages** (max equivalent in Tanzanian shillings of Special Drawing Rights 4,150).	≥3h: €250–€600 (by distance).
Cancellation Compensation	No fixed compensation. Right to re-routing/refund + care (meals/hotel). Compensation only upon proof of loss.	<14d notice: Refund or re-routing + €250–600 compensation (by distance).
Denied Boarding Compensation	Volunteers first; re-routing/ refund + care. Compensation only upon proof of loss.	Volunteer first; €250–€600 (by distance) if denied boarding.
Baggage Compensation	Tanzanian shillings of Special Drawing Rights 1,000, unless special declaration.	Not specified.

Bibliography

- Civil Aviation (Carriage by Air) Regulations 2024, Government Notice No. 4 of 2024, published 5 January 2024 <https://tcaa.go.tz/ctrback/docs/AQRgV4HWMM9v20240205130150.pdf>.

II.48

Thailand

The Thai Passenger Protection Rights Regulation No. 101, also known as the Civil Aviation Board Announcement No. 101, establishes rules to protect air passengers in Thailand, particularly in cases of flight disruptions such as delays, cancellations, or denied boarding, in force in November 2025.[1] The Thai Regulation is modelled after the European Regulation and repeals the previous Announcement namely the 2010 Announcement.[2] While the 2010 Announcement has been described as "unquestionably inspired by the EU's approach to air passenger rights," Regulation No. 101 seems to depart slightly from its European heritage.[3] Although the definition of "reservation" in the EU and Thai Regulation is verbatim,[4] other definitions are no longer entirely identical such as denial of boarding.

Regulation No. 101 applies to flights departing from the Kingdom of Thailand operated by domestic or international airlines which hold a Thai Commercial Air Transport Operating License[5] and foreign air operators permitted under the Air Navigation Act B.E. 2497.[6] The inclusion of international scheduled flights is a welcomed addition compared to the 2010 Announcement which was only confined to domestic routes.[7] It also

1 Regulation of the Civil Aviation Board N° 101, Measures to Protect Passenger Rights on Domestic and International Scheduled Flights. Using the unofficial translation provided by the Civil Aviation authority of Thailand <https://www.caat.or.th/wp-content/uploads/2024/11/REG-of-CAB-No.-101-Measures-to-Protect-Passenger-Rights-on-Domestic-and-International-Scheduled-Flights1.pdf>.

2 Article 3 of the Regulation.

3 Lalin Kovudhikulrungsri, 'Limitation of Actions and Air Passenger Rights in Thailand: Importing the Law but Leaving Judicial Reasoning Behind' (2024) 49 Air and Space Law 95, 99.

4 Article 4.

5 Article 5(1).

6 Article 5(2).

7 Section 3.

DOI: 10.4324/9781003746164-59

brings the regime in line with the Charter Announcement of 2013 which regulates both chartered domestic and international flights.[8]

Unlike the European Regulation but similarly to other national laws, Regulation No. 101 also includes provisions implementing the Warsaw or Montreal Convention, such as compensation in case of death or bodily injury.[9] Similarly to Malaysian or Venezuelan law, the Regulation includes an article on the information which must be made available upon purchase of the ticket.[10] Article 8 contains a prohibition of automatic additional paid ancillary services.

Upgrading and downgrading are regulated by Article 9 and offer identical protection and compensation as found in Regulation 261. Article 9 establishes that involuntary upgrading should be free of charge for the passenger. Downgrading entitles the passenger to a reimbursement of the difference in fare as well as a compensation of 30% of the fare for flights with a distance of 1,500 km or less, 50% of the fare for flights with a distance greater than 1,500 km but not exceeding 3,500 km, and finally, 75% of the fare for flights with a distance greater than 3,500 km.[11]

Situation	**Carrier Obligation**
Seat in Higher Class Available	Upgrade passenger free of charge.
Downgrading	1) Refund of the difference between the original fare and the replacement fare + 2) Compensation based on the distance: a. <1,500 km = 30% of the fare. b. Between 1,500 km and 3,500 km = 50% of the fare. c. >3,500 km = 75% of the fare.

The Thai Regulation specifies which passengers are entitled to protection in Article 10: firstly, passengers who present themselves for check-in within the timeframe specified by the carrier or 45 minutes for domestic flights or one hour for international flights.[12] It also applies to passengers who have been transferred from a reserved flight to another and those whose reserved flight has been rescheduled by more than five hours from the original departure time.[13]

When passengers entitled to assistance pay for their food and beverage, communication facilities or accommodation, airlines should reimburse

8 Royal Gazette, Volume 130, Special part 90 Ngor, 22 on 30 July 2013.
9 Article 6.
10 Article 7.
11 Article 9(2)(a), (b) and (c).
12 Article 10(1)(a) and (b).
13 Article 10(2) and (3).

them.[14] Similarly to Nigeria, flight delays are divided into domestic and international flights delays. Article 11 is concerned with domestic flight delays and establishes that in the event of a delay exceeding two hours, passengers are entitled to food and beverages or food vouchers as well as free calls or emails.[15] Passengers can also decide not to proceed with the flight and received a reimbursement.[16] A delay exceeding three hours entitles passengers the same assistance (food, refreshment, and phone calls).[17] Additionally, passengers who do not wish to continue with the journey can request a refund or re-routing to the original destination or an alternative destination close to the original one.[18] If the re-routing results in a lower air fare, the carrier must reimburse the difference. Similarly, if the re-routing flight arrives at another airport than the original, airlines must bear the transport costs.[19] For domestic delays exceeding five hours, airlines must provide passengers with the same assistance but also compensation of 1,200 Baht.[20]

Delays on international flights are regulated by Article 12. While the protection in case of a delay exceeding two hours is identical for domestic flights,[21] Article 12 is silent regarding flight delays between two and five hours. Delays on international flights exceeding five hours result in an assistance obligation (refreshment and food, as well as phone calls) but also compensation of 1,500 Baht within 14 days from the date of the delay.[22] Passengers should also be provided accommodation as necessary. Passengers can always opt to cancel their trip, resulting in a right to reimbursement only.[23] Regulation No. 101 has departed from the provisions in the 2010 Announcement which entitled passengers suffering from a delay between five and six hours to compensation of THB 600 and delay exceeding six hours resulted in a right to compensation in the amount of THB 1,200.[24] Instead, the new Regulation increased the minimum delay time to delays exceeding ten hours on an international flight for passengers to be entitle to a right to compensation.

---

14 Article 10.
15 Article 11(1)(a) and (b).
16 Article 11(1)(c).
17 Article 11(2)(a) and (b).
18 Article 11(2)(c)(1) and (2).
19 Article 11(2)(c)(2).
20 Article 11(3) and (4).
21 Article 12(1)(a) and (b).
22 Article 12(2)(a), (b) and (c).
23 Article 12(2)(e).
24 Lalin Kovudhikulrungsri, 'Limitation of Actions and Air Passenger Rights in Thailand: Importing the Law but Leaving Judicial Reasoning Behind' (2024) 49 Air and Space Law 95, 100.

In case of a flight delay exceeding ten hours on an international flight, passengers must be provided with assistance but compensation in cash based on the distance of the flight: "a) 2,000 baht for flights with a distance of 1,500 kilometers or less; b) 3,500 baht for flights with a distance greater than 1,500 kilometers but not exceeding 3,500 kilometers; c) 4,500 baht for flights with a distance greater than 3,500 kilometers."[25] The passenger can also opt for a credit shell, travel voucher, or mileage which cannot have a lesser value than the cash compensation.[26] Accommodation and transport must be made available when necessary.[27] Passengers can also elect to cancel their flight which would result in reimbursement of the fare or re-routing.[28] As for domestic delays, re-routing would be on the next available flight, next day, or at the passenger's earliest convenience to the original destination or an alternative destination close to the original one.[29] Interestingly, under the Regulation a flight delayed by more than six or ten hours no longer equates to flight cancellation as was the case under the 2010 Announcement.

The Regulation also includes a provision on tarmac delay which grants more protections than those found in Article 11 and 12.[30] The term "tarmac delay" is not defined and Article 13 does not include any minimum delay. However, in light of the wording, it seems that the protection will start kicking in after two hours' delay. The additional protections are that passengers have the right to proper ventilation and access to the lavatory.[31] "In case where the passenger requires urgent medical assistance, the carrier shall facilitate and provide such medical assistance adequately and appropriately, to the best of their ability."[32] Finally, when the delay exceeds three hours, and there is no definite take-off time, the carrier shall allow the passenger to disembark from the aircraft.[33] This last obligation is also found in Saudi Arabia and Nigeria for instance.

Compensation and Assistance	**Domestic Flights**	**International Flights**	**Tarmac Delay**
Short Haul (≤2 hours)	No cash compensation.	No cash compensation.	?
Medium Haul (3–5 hours)	No cash compensation.	Nothing mentioned.	?

(Continued)

25 Article 12(3)(c)(1).
26 Article 12(3)(c)(2).
27 Article 12(3)(d).
28 Article 12(3)(e)(1) and (2).
29 Article 12(3)(e)(2).
30 Article 13.
31 Article 13(1).
32 Article 13(2).
33 Article 13(3).

(Continued)

Compensation and Assistance	Domestic Flights	International Flights	Tarmac Delay
Long Haul (>5 hours)	1,200 THB.	1,500 THB.	?
10-Hour Delay	Not mentioned.	Cash: • 2,000 Baht for flights ≤1,500 km • 3,500 Baht for flights >1,500 <3,500 km • 4,500 Baht for flights >3,500 km Equivalent in miles, voucher or credit shell	?
Refund Rights	If passenger cancels as of 2 hours.	If passenger cancels after 5 hours	Full refund or rebooking
Rebooking Rights	Only if delay >5 hrs.	Only if delay >10 hrs	Next available flight
Meals/Refreshments	2+ hours.	2 + hours	Immediately or after 2 hours unclear
Hotel Accommodation	Not hotel	If overnight delay	Not mentioned
Communication Access	2 free calls/emails	2 free calls/emails	Not mentioned

Denial of boarding is found in Article 14 of Regulation No. 101 and requires airlines to first seek volunteers in exchange of the benefit agreed between the passengers and the airline. They are also entitled to the same protection as available in the event of a cancellation. In case of an involuntary denial of boarding, passengers are entitled to immediate compensation and assistance as provided to passengers suffering from a cancelled flight.

Those rules seem to have been supplemented by Regulation No. 104 introduced at the end of 2024 and in force since 19 February 2025.[34] This relatively short Regulation lists in Article 4 the reasons an airline may deny boarding. The list includes reduced mobility passengers who fail to request special assistance service from the carrier in advance and the carrier, despite its every reasonable effort, was unable to arrange

34 Article 2 Regulation 104.

such services;[35] passengers without proper documentation;[36] passengers who are prohibited from entering or transiting through the country of destination;[37] a newborn passenger under 14 days of age;[38] a passenger under 5 years of age travelling alone;[39] and finally, pregnant passengers beyond the limits of pregnancy age specified in the condition of carriage of each carrier.[40] Unlike Uruguay, the Thai Civil Aviation Authority did not feel it was adequate to provide a clear rule on pregnant women leaving it to each carrier to decide. The interaction between Regulation No. 101 and 104 is not entirely clear.

Cancellation is dealt with in Article 15 which stipulates that airlines are required to supply passengers with meal and beverages and means of communication such as access to email or phone calls.[41] When the next flight's departure is more than one day later than the original departure, the passenger should be given accommodation and transport.[42] Compensation for domestic flight is 1,500 Baht to be provided immediately upon cancellation.[43] It is, however, unclear if such compensation requires a minimum distance as is found under compensation for international flight cancellations nor is it clear if the compensation diminishes when the notice is given ahead of time.

For international flights, the compensation will be based on the distance and equivalent to the one for international delays, namely compensation in cash based on the distance of the flight: "a) 2,000 baht for flights with a distance of 1,500 kilometers or less; b) 3,500 baht for flights with a distance greater than 1,500 kilometers but not exceeding 3,500 kilometers; c) 4,500 baht for flights with a distance greater than 3,500 kilometers."[44] Moreover, airlines must offer either a reimbursement or re-routing.

Compensation and Assistance	**International Flight Cancellation**	**Domestic Flight Delay**	**Denied Boarding (Overbooking)**
Short Haul (≤1,500 km)	2,000 THB.	1,500 THB (?).	2,000 THB.
Medium Haul (1,500-3,500 km)	3,500 THB.	1,500 THB (?).	3,500 THB.
Long Haul (>3,500 km)	4,500 THB.	1,500 THB.	4,500 THB.

(*Continued*)

35 Article 4(1) Regulation 104.
36 Article 4(2) Regulation 104.
37 Article 4(3) Regulation 104.
38 Article 4(4) Regulation 104.
39 Article 4(5) Regulation 104.
40 Article 4(6) Regulation 104.
41 Article 15(1)(a) and (b).
42 Article 15(1)(c).
43 Article 15(2)(a).
44 Article 15(2)(b) referring to Article 12(3)(c).

(Continued)

Compensation and Assistance	International Flight Cancellation	Domestic Flight Delay	Denied Boarding (Overbooking)
Refund Rights	Full refund or re-routing.	Full refund or re-routing.	Full refund or re-routing.
Rebooking Rights	Next available flight.	Only if delay >5 hrs.	Next available flight.
Meals/Refreshments	Immediately.	Immediately.	Immediately.
Hotel Accommodation	If overnight delay.	If overnight delay.	If needed.
Communication Access	2 free calls/emails.	2 free calls/ emails.	2 free calls/ emails.

The carrier will be exempted from their obligations to pay compensation under Article 15 when they have informed the passenger of the cancellation at least three days in advance for scheduled domestic flight or at least seven days in advance for scheduled international flights.[45] Such exemption also applies in the event the passenger has been informed less than three days in advance for domestic flights or seven days for international ones if the new flight – departing prior to or after the original date and time – arrives at the original destination no later than three hours prior or after the original date and time.[46] The final exclusion found in Article 16 is when the cancellation is caused by an extraordinary circumstance.[47]

Similarly, carriers are exempted of their obligation to pay compensation in case of delay – both domestic and international – when the delay is caused by an extraordinary circumstance.[48] The Thai Regulation defines "extraordinary circumstances" as "external events that are unforeseeable and unavoidable, even after the carrier has taken all reasonable measures to prevent them."[49] Without much information, it will be for the courts to determine what such event it might cover.

The Thai authority has also included a provision regarding tickets purchased through an agent which extends the reimbursement period to 60 days from the date on which the carrier or agent received the reimbursement form and all relevant documents.[50] The period of 60 days is much longer than the one afforded to airlines under Article 18 which is 14 days for cash reimbursement or 45 days for tickets bought through

45 Article 16(1).
46 Article 16(2).
47 Article 16(3).
48 Article 17.
49 Article 4.
50 Article 19.

a credit card.[51] For reimbursement in miles or travel voucher, the time is reduced to seven days. Similarly to Regulation 261, airlines are under the obligation to inform passengers of their rights.[52]

The sanctions which were included in the 2010 Announcements are no longer found in Regulation No. 101. This could be explained by the fact that there have been no penalties enforced.[53] Interestingly, Article 24 mentions that the carrier can comply with more favourable passenger right protection measures as long as they do not violate or infringe the Regulation. Such inclusion then begs the question as to what the consequences of a violation would be.

Thai Passenger Protection Rights Regulation No. 101 represents a significant modernization and expansion of Thailand's legal framework for air passenger rights, and a notable upgrade from its 2010 predecessor, particularly in downgrade protections and tarmac delay rules. While modelled after the European Union's Regulation 261, the Thai Regulation exhibits deliberate departures, creating a distinct hybrid that incorporates elements from other national systems and tailored provisions to its domestic context.

However, the core regimes for delays and cancellations demonstrate substantive divergence. Regulation No. 101 establishes notably higher thresholds for compensation eligibility, particularly for international flights. While EU Regulation 261 ties compensation to lengthy delays at arrival, the Thai Regulation requires a delay exceeding ten hours on an international flight before distance-based compensation is triggered. For delays between five and ten hours on international routes, a flat compensation of 1,500 THB applies, which is generally lower in monetary value than EU standards. The structure for domestic flights is entirely separate, featuring flat-rate compensation (e.g., 1,200 THB for delays over five hours, 1,500 THB for cancellations) without a distance-based calculation.

Both regimes share a nearly identical definition of "extraordinary circumstances" as a carrier exemption. A notable innovation in the Thai text is Article 13, which addresses tarmac delays by guaranteeing access to lavatories, ventilation, medical assistance, and the right to disembark after three hours if no definite take-off time is known, a provision not found in the EU Regulation but seen in other jurisdictions like Nigeria and Saudi Arabia.

51 Article 18(3)(a) and (b).

52 Article 20.

53 Ridha Aditya Nugraha and Lalin Kovudhikulrungsri, 'Aviation Legal Issues in Indonesia and Thailand: Towards Better Passenger's Rights in ASEAN' (2017) 7 Indonesia Law Review 23, 36.

The regulatory approach to enforcement also marks a contrast. Unlike EU Regulation 261, which is backed by member-state enforcement authorities, Regulation No. 101 reportedly omits the specific penalty provisions present in its 2010 predecessor, potentially relying on general administrative or consumer protection law for redress. This absence of dedicated sanctions within the text may impact the regulation's practical efficacy. Another distinctive feature is Regulation No. 101's interaction with the separate Regulation No. 104 (2025), which enumerates specific grounds for permitted denial of boarding (e.g., advanced pregnancy as per carrier policy, lack of documentation), creating a more prescriptive framework than the EU's more general approach.

In conclusion, Thai Regulation No. 101 is a comprehensive legislative step that synthesizes international models while asserting local priorities. It provides a clear baseline of passenger rights, expands protections into new areas like tarmac delays, and creates a unified system for all flights departing Thailand. Compared to EU Regulation 261, it offers a structurally similar but materially more moderate protection scheme, characterized by higher compensation thresholds, generally lower compensation amounts, and a more carrier-friendly set of exemption conditions.

Comparison with EU Regulation

Feature	**Thailand**	**EU Regulation 261/2004**
Delay Compensation	>5hrs: THB 1,200 domestic or 1,500 international >10hrs (international): THB 2,000–4,500 THB (by distance).	≥3h: €250–600 (by distance).
Cancellation Compensation	THB 2,000–4,500.	<14d notice: Refund or re-routing + €250–600 compensation (by distance).
Denied Boarding Compensation	Volunteers first; THB 2,000–4,500 (by distance).	Volunteer first; €250–€600 (by distance) if denied boarding.
Baggage Compensation	Not specified.	Not specified.

Bibliography

- Announcement of the Ministry of Transport on Protection of Passenger Rights Related to Charter Flight Services. B.E. 2556 (2013), Royal Gazette 130, Special part 90 Ngor, 22 on 30 July 2013.
- Regulation of the Civil Aviation Board N° 101, Measures to Protect Passenger Rights on Domestic and International Scheduled Flights. Using the Unofficial Translation Provided by the Civil Aviation Authority of Thailand

<https://www.caat.or.th/wp-content/uploads/2024/11/REG-of-CAB-No.-101-Measures-to-Protect-Passenger-Rights-on-Domestic-and-International-Scheduled-Flights1.pdf> accessed 22 December 2025.

- Aditya Nugraha, R. and Kovudhikulrungsri, L., 'Aviation Legal Issues in Indonesia and Thailand: Towards Better Passenger's Rights in ASEAN' (2017) 7 Indonesia Law Review 23.
- Kovudhikulrungsri, L., 'Limitation of Actions and Air Passenger Rights in Thailand: Importing the Law but Leaving Judicial Reasoning Behind' (2024) 49 Air & Space Law 95.

II.49

Trinidad and Tobago

The cornerstone of aviation consumer rights in Trinidad and Tobago regarding flight disruption is the Civil Aviation [(No. 17) Economic] Regulations 2016.[1] This comprehensive legislative framework establishes specific and enforceable passenger protections, administered under the authority of the Trinidad and Tobago Civil Aviation Authority (TTCAA). While the regulations incorporate several global best practices, their structure reveals a distinct prioritization of certain passenger rights over others, creating a nuanced landscape of consumer protection.

The regulations address flight disruptions primarily through Part V, which contains some general provisions, and Part VI on consumer protection which further defines any previous provisions. Regulation 39 forms the core of passenger entitlements during delays and cancellations. It stipulates that where a passenger flight is delayed, all confirmed passengers must be provided with a meal voucher valued at no less than 8 United States dollars for every three hours that pass beyond the scheduled departure time.[2] In more severe circumstances where a flight is cancelled or experiences a delay in excess of 12 hours, the airline's obligations expand significantly. Each confirmed passenger must be provided with suitable hotel accommodations, meals, and ground transportation to and from the hotel until their departure flight.[3] Furthermore, each confirmed passenger has the right to request a full refund. This refund covers all unused tickets, tickets for flights already taken that no longer serve any purpose in relation to the passenger's original travel plan, and, where applicable, a flight back to the original point of departure at the earliest

1 Regulations made by the Trinidad and Tobago Civil Aviation Authority with the approval of the minister under section 33 of the Civil Aviation Act and subject to negative resolution of the Parliament, The Civil Aviation (N°17) Economic] Regulations, 2016, Legal Notice N°182.
2 Regulation 39(1).
3 Regulation 39(2)(a).

DOI: 10.4324/9781003746164-60

opportunity.[4] A crucial consumer protection principle is embedded in the rules, stating that operators must uphold their own contracts of carriage and policies in instances where these are more beneficial to the passenger than the requirements of the Regulations or any other law in force in Trinidad and Tobago.[5]

Situation	**Type of Compensation/Right**	**Key Details**
All Delays	Meal Vouchers.	• **Trigger:** Every 3 hours beyond scheduled departure. • **Value:** No less than **USD $8.**
Cancellation or Delay >12 Hours	Full Assistance.	• Suitable **hotel accommodations, meals, and ground transport** to/from the hotel until departure.
Cancellation or Delay >12 Hours	Right to a Full Refund.	• Passenger can request a refund for: 1. All **unused tickets.** 2. Tickets for flights already taken that are now useless for the original plan. 3. A **flight back to the original point of departure.**

The Regulations focus heavily on the immediate care and well-being of passengers during disruptions. The primary financial compensation is the right to a full refund of the ticket price if the disruption is severe enough. Unlike regimes such as EU Regulation 261, there is no provision for automatic, fixed monetary compensation for the inconvenience or time loss resulting from a cancellation or delay. It is critical to note that, unlike the detailed and separate section for denied boarding, these provisions for delays and cancellations do not possess their own dedicated part or provision within the regulations. They are contained within a single, broad provision that mixes these care obligations with other unrelated licensing and advertising rules. This contrasts sharply with the detailed, standalone compensation structure explicitly defined for involuntarily denied boarding.

The Regulations govern advertising practices to ensure transparency. All advertisements must display the base fares or rates as well as all associated charges and fees.[6] Advertised routes must be presented exactly as granted.[7] Furthermore, all advertisements must include specific phrases

4 Regulation 39(2)(b)(i)–(iii).
5 Regulation 39(4).
6 Regulation 40(1).
7 Regulation 40(3).

indicating the status of the operator's authorization: Operations with a pending application must state "Subject to approval by the Trinidad and Tobago Civil Aviation Authority" while operations that have received a permit must include the phrase "This operation has been approved by the Trinidad and Tobago Civil Aviation Authority."[8]

Part VI (Regulations 46–54) establishes a detailed framework for consumer protection related to denied boarding and overbooking on both domestic and international commercial flights with segments originating or terminating in Trinidad and Tobago.[9] In the event of an oversold flight, an authorized carrier is obligated to ensure that the smallest practicable number of persons holding confirmed reservations are involuntarily denied boarding.[10] The carrier must first request volunteers for denied boarding before using any other boarding priority system.[11] When soliciting volunteers, the carrier must advise each passenger, at the time of solicitation, whether they are in danger of being involuntarily denied boarding and must inform them of the compensation the carrier is obligated to pay if they are involuntarily bumped.[12] If an insufficient number of volunteers come forward, the carrier may then deny boarding to other passengers according to its boarding priority rules.[13] When a carrier offers free or reduced-rate air transportation as compensation to volunteers, it must fully disclose all material restrictions, including administrative fees, advance purchase or capacity restrictions, and blackout dates, before the passenger decides to give up their confirmed space.[14] For the purposes of these regulations, any passenger who is denied boarding is considered to have been denied boarding involuntarily, even if that passenger accepts the denied boarding compensation.[15]

To minimize involuntary denials, every authorized carrier must establish and publish understandable Boarding Priority Rules for determination which must not give any undue preference or advantage to any particular person or subject any person to unjust prejudice.[16] Factors that may be included in these rules are a passenger's check-in time, having a pre-assigned seat, the fare paid, frequent-flyer status, and a passenger's disability or status as an unaccompanied minor.[17]

---

8 Regulation 40(4) and (5).
9 Regulation 46(a) and (b).
10 Regulation 47(1).
11 Regulation 47(2).
12 Regulation 47(3).
13 Regulation 47(3).
14 Regulation 47(4).
15 Regulation 47(5).
16 Regulation 48(1) and (3).
17 Regulation 48(4).

An airline must compensate eligible passengers on the day and at the place the denied boarding occurs, in the form of cash or an immediately negotiable cheque.[18] If alternate transportation is arranged that departs before the payment can be prepared, the tender must be made by mail or other means within 24 hours.[19] The compensation amounts are tiered based on the delay of the alternate transportation offered. For international flights, the compensation is calculated based on the delayed arrival time of the alternate transportation. No compensation is required if the alternate flight is planned to arrive at the passenger's destination within one hour of the original flight's planned arrival.[20] In other circumstances, compensation of 200% of the fare is required if the alternate flight arrives more than one hour but less than two hours after the original arrival time, and 400% of the fare is required if the alternate flight arrives more than two hours after the original arrival time or if no alternate transportation is offered.[21] Airlines may offer free or reduced-rate air transportation in lieu of cash or a cheque, provided the value of the transportation benefit is equal to or greater than the required payment, the passenger is fully informed of their right to decline the benefit and receive the payment, and all material restrictions on the use of the transportation are fully disclosed.[22] The compensation requirements also apply to passengers with "zero fare tickets," for whom the fare for calculation purposes is the lowest payment charged for a ticket in the same class of service on that flight.[23] This inclusion addresses the gap create by "zero fare" and ensures comprehensive consumer protection. In addition to the denied boarding compensation, a carrier must refund all unused ancillary fees for optional services paid by a passenger who is voluntarily or involuntarily denied boarding, though fees for services provided with the alternate transportation need not be refunded.[24]

Compensation Feature	Rule/Calculation Method
Compensation Tiers	• **0%:** Alternate flight arrives within **1 hour** of original time. • **200%:** Alternate flight arrives **1–2 hours** later. • **400%:** Alternate flight arrives **over 2 hours** later or no flight is offered.
"Zero Fare" Passengers	**Eligible** for compensation.

18 Regulation 49(1).
19 Regulation 49(2).
20 Regulation 50(1)(a).
21 Regulation 50(1)(b) and (c).
22 Regulation 50(2)(a)–(c).
23 Regulation 50(3).
24 Regulation 50(4).

Passengers are not eligible for denied boarding compensation if they do not comply fully with the carrier's contract of carriage or tariff provisions regarding ticketing, reconfirmation, check-in, and acceptability for transportation; are accommodated in a different section of the aircraft at no extra charge notwithstanding the downgrading refund; or if the airline arranges comparable transportation that is planned to arrive at the passenger's destination not later than one hour after the planned arrival time of the original flight.[25]

Failure to appropriately compensate eligible passengers for denied boarding constitutes an offence liable to a fine of 20,000 dollars for each passenger not duly compensated.[26] Failure to disclose the required notice on deliberate overbooking and boarding procedures constitutes an offence liable to a fine of 50,000 dollars for a first offence and 100,000 dollars for each subsequent offence.[27]

Part VII is dedicated to the passenger service plan, which must be clear, just, reasonable, and consistent with international agreements.[28] The contents of the plan must address several key subjects and comply with specific minimum standards. These include disclosing on the carrier's website, at the ticket counter, or during reservation calls that the lowest fare may be available elsewhere, notifying customers of known delays, cancellations, and diversions and delivering baggage on time, including making every reasonable effort to return mishandled baggage within 24 hours. The plan must also compensate passengers for reasonable expenses resulting from baggage delivery delays and reimburse any baggage fee if the bag is lost.[29] Furthermore, the Passenger Service Plan must allow reservations to be held without payment or cancelled without penalty for at least 24 hours if made one week or more before departure.[30]

The Regulations also contain a provision which is rarely found requiring airlines to designate an employee to monitor the effects of flight delays, cancellations, and lengthy tarmac delays. This employee must have input into decisions on which flights to cancel or delay.[31]

The Regulations require notification of delays, cancellations, and diversions within 20 minutes of the carrier becoming aware of a flight

25 Regulation 51.
26 Regulation 54(1).
27 Regulation 54(2).
28 Regulation 55(1).
29 Regulation 56.
30 Regulation 56(d).
31 Regulation 57(1).

status change.[32] This information must be provided in the boarding gate area, on the carrier's website, and via the telephone reservation system.[33] For customers who subscribe to flight status notification services, the carrier must deliver the notification by the passenger's chosen means within the same 20-minute timeframe.

Unlike Regulation 261, the Civil Aviation [(No. 17) Economic] Regulations 2016 contains a section dedicated to tarmac delays. Airlines are expected to adopt and adhere to a contingency plan.[34] For both domestic and international flights, an aircraft must not remain on the tarmac for more than one and a half hours without allowing passengers to deplane, unless the pilot-in-command determines a safety or security reason prevents it, or if air traffic control advises that deplaning would significantly disrupt airport operations.[35] For all flights, adequate food and potable water must be provided no later than one hour after the aircraft leaves the gate or touches down, unless safety or security concerns prohibit it.[36] Passengers must have access to operable lavatory facilities and adequate medical attention if needed.[37] Passengers must receive status updates every 20 minutes, including the reasons for the delay, and must be notified every 20 minutes after the scheduled departure time that they have the opportunity to deplane if the opportunity exists.[38] Carriers may amend their plan to decrease the time limits for tarmac delays, food and water provision, or notifications.[39] A carrier that contravenes its established contingency plan or fails to adhere to the minimum requirements is liable, on summary conviction, to a fine of 5,000 dollars per passenger on board for a first offence and 10,000 dollars per passenger for a subsequent offence.[40]

The Regulations are also silent about downgrading despite including that the difference in price must be refunded. It also does not contain any provision related to force majeure or extraordinary circumstances. While the Civil Aviation [(No. 17) Economic] Regulations 2016 is extremely well structured – with penalties after each type of offences – the provisions on delays and cancellations are underwhelming.

---

32 Regulation 58(1).
33 Regulation 58(2).
34 Regulation 60.
35 Regulation 61(a)(i) and (ii) and 61(b)(i) and (ii).
36 Regulation 61(c).
37 Regulation 61(d).
38 Regulation 61(e) and (f).
39 Regulation 62.
40 Regulation 64.

Offense/Violation	Penalty
Failure to Pay Denied Boarding Compensation	**$20,000 per passenger** not duly compensated.
Failure to Disclose Overbooking Notice	**First offence: $50,000.** **Subsequent offence: $100,000.**
Violation of Tarmac Delay Contingency Plan	**First offence: $5,000 per passenger** on board the aircraft. **Subsequent offence: $10,000 per passenger** on board the aircraft.

Civil Aviation [(No. 17) Economic] Regulations 2016 represents a sophisticated and comprehensive framework for aviation consumer protection. The law's principal strength lies in its extensive scope and its incorporation of several global best practices. It demonstrates a strong regulatory intent through its detailed and enforceable provisions for denied boarding, which include a fare-based, tiered compensation system, robust protections for volunteers, and the crucial inclusion of passengers holding zero fare tickets. Compared to the treatment of other disruptions, the Regulations, perhaps unintentionally, seem to signal a hierarchy of protected passenger inconveniences. Provisions for flight delays and cancellations are contained within Regulation 39, a single, broad provision nestled among unrelated rules on licensing and advertising in Part V and VI. This stands in stark contrast to the detailed, dedicated, and systematic treatment afforded to involuntary denied boarding, which occupies its own clearly defined section (Regulations 46–54). This architectural choice suggests that while denied boarding is viewed as a discrete event requiring a precise, compensatory response, delays and cancellations are treated more as operational failures meriting care and restitution but not necessarily compensation for inconvenience.

A notably proactive and rare feature is the requirement for airlines to designate an employee to monitor delays and have direct input into cancellation decisions, aiming to mitigate passenger inconvenience at its source. The Regulations also excel in their specific and stringent contingency plan for lengthy tarmac delays, which imposes a 90-minute deplaning limit for all flights, mandates the provision of food and water within one hour, and requires regular passenger updates, all backed by severe per-passenger fines that create a powerful deterrent against non-compliance.

However, the law possesses a significant and defining weakness in its approach to flight cancellations and delays. Philosophically, the Regulations emphasize immediate welfare and financial restitution over compensatory redress. There is no inherent recognition, as found in EU

261, that the disruption itself – the loss of time, missed connections, and spoiled plans – constitutes a harm worthy of standardized monetary compensation, irrespective of the ticket price. This creates a fundamental divergence in how passenger hardship is quantified and remedied and a major gap in consumer rights compared to passengers suffering from denied boarding. Additional shortcomings include the structurally underwhelming value of the mandated meal vouchers, a complete silence on compensation for involuntary downgrading beyond a fare difference refund, and a fragmented legal structure that buries delay and cancellation provisions within a general section, unlike the dedicated and detailed treatment given to denied boarding.

In conclusion, the Civil Aviation (No. 17) Economic Regulations 2016 is a law of two halves. Its provisions on denied boarding, tarmac delays, and transparency are world-class, featuring detailed processes, inclusive eligibility, and forceful penalties. It demonstrates a clear intent to regulate airline overbooking practices rigorously and to prevent egregious onboard stranding. Its principal shortcoming, however, is fundamental. By failing to establish a right to compensation for cancellations and long delays, it leaves a vast spectrum of passenger disruption under-protected relative to modern international standards.

Comparison with EU Regulation

Feature	**Civil Aviation [(No. 17) Economic] Regulations 2016**	**EU Regulation 261/2004**
Delay Compensation	No.	≥3h: €250–€600 (by distance).
Cancellation Notice	12 hours+ = refund.	<14d notice: Refund or re-routing + €250–600 compensation (by distance).
Denied Boarding	Volunteer first; 200% or 400% of the fare ticket.	Volunteer first; €250–€600 (by distance) if denied boarding.
Baggage Liability	Not specified.	Not specified.

Bibliography

- Regulations Made by the Trinidad and Tobago Civil Aviation Authority with the Approval of the Minister Under Section 33 of the Civil Aviation Act and Subject to Negative Resolution of the Parliament, The Civil Aviation (N°17) Economic] Regulations, 2016, Legal Notice N°182 <https://www.ttparliament.org/wp-content/uploads/2021/10/The-Civil-Aviation-No.-17-Economic-Regulations-2016.pdf> accessed 22 December 2025.

II.50

Türkiye

Passengers in Türkiye have enjoyed dedicated protections and rights in case of delays, denial of boarding, and cancellation since the Regulation on Air Passenger Rights (SHY-PASSENGER) of 2011 entered into force in January 2012.[1] The Regulation was adopted by the Turkish Directorate General of Civil Aviation (DGCA) in accordance with Article 143 of the Turkish Civil Aviation Law of 1983 and is largely adapted from Regulation 261.[2] In December 2024, the amendments of the SHY-PASSENGER, the Regulation on the Rights of Passengers Traveling by Air (SHY-YOLCU), entered into force.[3] Additionally, rights of passengers are also regulated by Circular on Passenger Rights Implementation Principles of 2015 and Circular on Passenger Rights Assessment and Implementation Principles of 2023 issued by the Directorate General of Civil Aviation.

The SHY-PASSENGER – and its amendment the SHY-YOLCU – apply to all Turkish carriers flying in and out of Türkiye, as well as non-Turkish carriers flying from Türkiye.[4] In other words, the Regulations do not apply to non-Turkish airlines arriving in Türkiye.

	Turkish Carrier	**Non-Turkish Carrier**
Flights Departing From Türkiye	Yes.	Yes.
Flights Arriving in Türkiye	Yes.	No.

In case of denial of boarding, airlines must first try to find volunteers and provide them with "benefits to be agreed on between the related

1 Article 21(1) SHY-PASSENGER.

2 Ali Yalcinkaya, 'Applicability of Turkish Air Passenger Rights Regulation Before German Courts' (*Lexology*, 27 July 2022) <https://www.lexology.com/library/detail.aspx?g=6014085f-c516-402e-b81b-7695a52edf6d>.

3 Regulation on Air Passenger Rights (SHY-PASSENGER) numbered 32748.

4 Article 2(1)(a) SHY-PASSENGER.

DOI: 10.4324/9781003746164-61

passenger and the air transport operator."[5] Additionally, those passengers are entitled to assistance as prescribed in Article 9. If the airline cannot find sufficient volunteers, then the airline can exercise its discretion in denying the boarding of some passengers.[6] Those passengers would be entitled to compensation, assistance, a refund, or re-routing depending on the passenger's preference.[7]

The Regulation 261 influence is very visible in Article 7 dedicated to flight delays which even keeps the initial currency – the euro – and requests airlines to convert it in Turkish lira. Indeed, the protection is divided in both length of delay and distance of the flight. Until the revision, delayed passengers were only entitled to assistance and a full refund of the ticket or an alternative flight for any delays over five hours. Following the enactment of SHY-YOLCU Regulation, delayed passengers are now also entitled to compensation for delays exceeding three hours due to technical and operational reasons.[8] Under the amendments, passengers on domestic flights will receive 100 euros in Turkish lira for delays, while international flight compensation will range from 250 to 600 euros in Turkish lira depending on the distance travelled and the duration of the delay.

If the flight is cancelled, passengers are entitled to a full refund of the ticket or an alternative flight to the final destination.[9] Additionally, the airline must provide assistance, including meals, refreshments, and, if necessary, accommodation.[10] Passengers also have the right to financial compensation which varies based on the flight distance and the moment they were informed of the cancellation.[11] For instance, passengers are entitled to compensation when they are not informed at least two weeks in advance or if they were informed between two weeks and seven days and they were not offered a route change allowing them to depart not more than two hours before the original departure time and arrive four hours after the original arrival time. No compensation is due when passengers are informed less than seven days in advance and not offered a route change allowing them to depart not more than one hour before the original departure time and arrive two hours after the original arrival time.[12]

5 Article 5(1) SHY-PASSENGER.
6 Article 5(2) SHY-PASSENGER.
7 Article 5(3) SHY-PASSENGER.
8 Article 2 SHY-YOLCU.
9 Article 6(1)(b) SHY-PASSENGER.
10 Article 6(1)(a) SHY-PASSENGER.
11 Article 6(2) in conjunction with Article 8(1).
12 Article 6(2)(1), (2) and (3) SHY-PASSENGER.

National flights entitle passengers to the equivalent of 100 euros in Turkish lira.[13] For international flights of up to 1,500 km, the compensation is the equivalent of 250 euros in Turkish lira. For flights between 1,500 and 3,500 km, the amount increases to the equivalent of 400 euros in Turkish lira and finally for international flights over 3,500 km, the compensation is 600 euros in Turkish lira.[14] This modification of Regulation 261 makes sense and should be considered by any country wanting to adapt the EU Regulation to their country's needs.

Situation	**Airlines Obligation**
Flights from a Turkish airport to a Turkish airport.	100 euros in Turkish lira.
International flights less than 1,500 km.	250 euros in Turkish lira.
International flights between 1,500 km and 3,500 km.	400 euros in Turkish lira.
International flights more than 3,500 km.	600 euros in Turkish lira.

The amount of compensation can be divided by two if passengers are offered an alternative flight which arrives at the final destination no later than two hours for flights of less than 1,500 km, three hours for flights between 1,500 and 3,500 km, and four hours for flights longer than 3,500 km.[15]

Situation	**Airlines Obligation**
Alternative International flights less than 1,500 km arriving within 2 hours of the original time.	125 euros in Turkish lira.
Alternative international flights between 1,500 km and 3,500 km arriving within 3 hours of the original time.	200 euros in Turkish lira.
Alternative international flights more than 3,500 km arriving within 4 hours of the original time.	300 euros in Turkish lira.

Unlike the EU Regulation, the Turkish Regulations do not include a specific provision excluding airline's liability. The Regulation only refers to force majeure in the context of cancellation – despite its amendments – which is defined in Article 4.[16] Force majeure includes "weather conditions

13 Article 8(1) SHY-PASSENGER.

14 Article 8(1)(a), (b), and (c) SHY-PASSENGER. Nigar Guliyeva, 'Evaluation of the Regulation Amending the Regulation on Air Passenger Rights (SHY-Passenger)' (*Aviation Law*, 12 December 2024) <https://kilinclaw.com.tr/en/passenger-rights-for-delayed-flights/> accessed 22 December 2025.

15 Article 8(3)(a), (b), and (c) SHY-PASSENGER.

16 Article 6(4) and 4(ğ) SHY-PASSENGER.

not suitable for performing the related flight," natural disasters, political instability, security risks, strikes, and unexpected flight safety deficiencies. The burden of proof lies with the airline.[17] This omission might result in some lawsuits.

Under Article 9, passengers can elect to request either a refund or an alternative route to their final destination or alternative route under similar transportation conditions at a later date.

Passengers are entitled to assistance in case of denial of boarding, delay, or cancellation. Article 10 stipulates that under any circumstance, passengers have the right to make two phone calls, faxes, or emails.[18] Any waiting time between two and three hours entitles the passengers to hot and cold beverages. Between three and five hours, they become entitled to breakfast or lunch. For any delay exceeding five hours, airlines must provide additional beverages and snacks.[19] Passengers might also have the right to accommodation at a hotel and transport "when necessary."[20]

The Turkish Regulations also contain a provision on upgrading and downgrading. Under Article 11, airlines cannot demand payment for any upgrades if the upgrade was not done at the passenger's request.[21] On the other hand, if a passenger is downgraded by the airline for any reason, the airlines must refund the difference between the ticket prices and pay compulsory compensation of 30%, 50%, or 75% depending on the flight distance.[22]

Passengers with restricted mobility or special needs are given priority in an event of disruption and are entitled to care "as soon as possible."[23] The Regulations also recognize the right of a passenger to claim compensation under other laws or from other responsible parties but the compensation under the Regulation might be deducted from any other amount.[24] The SHY-PASSENGER also includes a provision making it clear that airlines cannot exclude their liability through disclaimers.[25]

---

17 Article 6(5) SHY-PASSENGER.
18 Article 10(2) SHY-PASSENGER.
19 Article 10(1)(a)(1), (2) and (3) SHY-PASSENGER.
20 Article 10(1)(b) SHY-PASSENGER.
21 Article 11(1) SHY-PASSENGER.
22 Flight distance less than 1,500 km: 30% of the ticket value.
Flight distance 1,500 km to 3,500 km: 50% of the ticket value.
Flight distance of more than 3,500 km: 75% of the ticket value.
Article 11(2)(a), (b) and (c) SHY-PASSENGER.
23 Article 12(2) SHY-PASSENGER.
24 Article 13(1) SHY-PASSENGER.
25 Article 16(1) SHY-PASSENGER.

The Amendment Regulation also clarified the exchange rate to be applied by stipulating that it is the one on the "date the compensation is paid."[26]

The Turkish regime, principally embodied in the SHY-PASSENGER Regulation (2011) and its significant amendment, SHY-YOLCU (2024), stands as a deliberate and largely successful transplantation of the EU model into a distinct jurisdictional and economic context, offering strong protections. Structurally, the Turkish Regulation is a faithful adaptation of the EU blueprint. Its core pillars – the tiered compensation system for cancellations and long delays (pegged directly to the euro amounts of Regulation 261), the obligation of care (assistance), and the volunteer-first approach for denied boarding – create a familiar protective landscape for passengers departing Turkish airports. The 2024 amendments crucially aligned Türkiye with the EU standard by introducing compensation for qualifying long delays (exceeding three hours), closing a previously significant gap. Furthermore, the nuanced rules on compensation reduction by 50% when re-routing minimizes arrival delays, and the detailed provisions on downgrading directly reflect the intricacies of the European regulation.

However, critical divergences exist, highlighting Türkiye's sovereign adjustments and areas where legal clarity may be tested. The most fundamental jurisdictional difference is the principle of territorial departure: Protection extends to all carriers departing Türkiye but does not cover non-Turkish carriers arriving in Türkiye. This creates an asymmetrical scope compared to the EU's application to all carriers departing and arriving within its territory, a deliberate policy choice by Turkish legislators.

On substantive provisions, the treatment of force majeure presents a notable departure and a potential source of litigation. Unlike Regulation 261, which provides a specific list of extraordinary circumstances exempting carriers from compensation liability, the Turkish text references force majeure primarily in the context of cancellations. Its definition, encompassing "weather conditions not suitable for performing the related flight" alongside strikes and security risks, is arguably broader and more susceptible to carrier invocation than the EU's stricter interpretation. This omission of a generalized exemption clause for delays, coupled with a burden of proof resting on the airline, creates a passenger-favourable stance that may be contested in courts, requiring judicial refinement.

26 Dr. iur. Onur Ergönen and Can Kaleli, 'The Right to Compensation Granted to Airline Passengers in Cases of Cancellation Has Been Extended to Delays' <https://acarergonen.av.tr/media/2albxbco/ae-legal-alert-the-right-to-compensation-granted-to-airline-passengers-in-cases-of-cancellation-has-been-extended-to-delays.pdf>.

Operationally, the mechanism for currency conversion introduces a unique element of financial variability. While the compensation rights are defined in euro denominations, the obligation is to pay the equivalent in Turkish lira at the exchange rate prevailing on the date of payment, not the date of the disrupted flight. In an environment of potential currency volatility, this can lead to significant disparities in the real value of compensation received by passengers, a consideration absent from the static euro-denominated EU system.

In conclusion, Turkish air passenger rights law constitutes a robust and sophisticated regime that has effectively integrated the core acquis of Regulation 261. The 2024 amendments signify a commitment to maintaining high, European-standard protections. The framework's distinct characteristics – its departure-based scope, its broadly defined force majeure clause, and its dynamic currency conversion – are not flaws but rather intentional adaptations that reflect national legal and economic realities. For any jurisdiction contemplating a similar adoption of the EU model, the Turkish experience offers a compelling case study in both the benefits of harmonization and the necessity of contextual adaptation. The system's future stability will hinge on the consistent application and judicial interpretation of its more flexible provisions, particularly concerning liability exemptions. Nevertheless, it stands as a testament to the global influence of EU passenger rights principles and their successful transplantation into a major aviation market outside the European Union.

Comparison with EU Regulation

Feature	Türkiye SHY-YOLCU 2024	EU Regulation 261/2004
Delay Compensation	≥3h: €100–€600 in Turkish lira (by distance). €100 compensation in Turkish lira (domestic flights).	≥3h: €250–€600 (by distance).
Cancellation Notice	<14d notice: Refund or re-routing + €250–600 compensation (by distance).	<14d notice: Refund or re-routing + €250–600 compensation (by distance).
Denied Boarding	Volunteer first; €250–€600 in Turkish lira (by distance) if denied boarding.	Volunteer first; €250–€600 (by distance) if denied boarding.
Baggage Liability	Not specified.	Not specified.

Bibliography

- Regulation on Air Passenger Rights (SHY-PASSENGER) <https://web.shgm.gov.tr/doc4/shy-passenger.pdf> accessed 22 December 2025.

- Regulation on the Rights of Passengers Traveling by Air (SHY-YOLCU) Regulation Amending the Regulation on the Rights of Passengers Traveling by Air ("Amendment Regulation"), numbered 32748, Official Gazette on 10 December 2024 <https://www.mevzuat.gov.tr/File/GeneratePdf?mevzuatNo=15549&mevzuatTur=KurumVeKurulusYonetmeligi&mevzuatTertip=5> accessed 22 December 2025.
- Ergönen, Dr. iur. O. and Kaleli, C., 'The Right to Compensation Granted to Airline Passengers in Cases of Cancellation Has Been Extended to Delays' <https://acarergonen.av.tr/media/2albxbco/ae-legal-alert-the-right-to-compensation-granted-to-airline-passengers-in-cases-of-cancellation-has-been-extended-to-delays.pdf> accessed 22 December 2025.
- N Guliyeva, 'Evaluation of the Regulation Amending the Regulation on Air Passenger Rights (SHY- Passenger)' (*Aviation Law*, 12 December 2024) <https://kilinclaw.com.tr/en/passenger-rights-for-delayed-flights/> accessed 22 December 2025.
- A Yalcinkaya, 'Applicability of Turkish Air Passenger Rights Regulation Before German Courts' (*Lexology*, 27 July 2022) <https://www.lexology.com/library/detail.aspx?g=6014085f-c516-402e-b81b-7695a52edf6d> accessed 22 December 2025.

II.51

Ukraine

Ukraine's air passenger rights are primarily governed by the Aviation Rules of Ukraine "On Air Transportation and Rights of Passengers and Cargo" (often referred to in English as the "Aviation Rules of Ukraine" related to passenger rights) which repeats the protections found in Articles 103 to 107 of the Air Code. This comprehensive regulation, specified in Order of the Ministry of Infrastructure of Ukraine No. 1239 (N° 141/33112) of November 2018, as amended, notably in October 2021[1] and replacing the Order of the Ministry of Infrastructure of Ukraine No. 735 (N° 2219/22531) of November 2012.[2] The Aviation Rules of Ukraine mirror many provisions of EU Regulation 261.[3] Indeed, the Charter I paragraph 3 of the Aviation Rules stipulates that the Aviation Rules have been developed taking into account Regulation 261 as well as other European legislation and the Montreal Convention.

The Rules apply to flights to and from Ukraine, irrespective of the nationality of the carrier and irrespective of the flight being domestic or international.[4] Unlike the EU Regulation, the term "extraordinary circumstances" is defined within the list of definitions found in Section I paragraph 6. The definition also provides an open list of situations which could amount to "extraordinary circumstances" which includes "military action, civil commotion, sabotage, embargo, fire, flood or other natural disaster, explosion, action or inaction of government agencies, strikes, technical obstacles resulting from failures and malfunctions, malfunctions

1 The State Aviation Service of Ukraine, Order 1543 of 1 October 2021. On approval of Amendments to some Aviation Regulations of Ukraine. <https://zakon.rada.gov.ua/laws/show/z1427-21#n4> accessed 22 December 2025.

2 Article 3 of the State Aviation Service of Ukraine, Order 1239 of 26 November 2018. On approval of the Aviation Rules of Ukraine 'Rules of Air Transportation and Passenger and Baggage Handling' <https://zakon.rada.gov.ua/laws/show/z0141-19#Text> accessed 22 December 2025.

3 Anna Tsirat, *'Ukraine' in Sean Gates, the Aviation Law Review* (4th edn, Law Business Research Ltd 2016).

4 Section I(4) of the Rules, Section II(1).

DOI: 10.4324/9781003746164-62

of power supply systems, communications, equipment, software." Interestingly, the definition also stipulates that technical malfunctions are not extraordinary circumstances.

Feature	**Ukrainian Aviation Rules**	**EU Regulation 261/2004**	**Key Differences**
Legal Basis	Order of the Ministry of Infrastructure No. 1239 (2018, amended 2021).	EU Regulation (EC) No 261/2004.	Ukraine's rules are national decrees; the EU's are directly applicable across Member States.
Applicability	Applies to all flights **to/from Ukraine**, regardless of carrier nationality or flight type.	Applies to all flights **departing from the EU** or arriving in the EU on an EU carrier.	Ukraine covers all flights to/ from its territory; the EU is origin/ destination-based.
Extraordinary Circumstances	Defined explicitly (e.g., war, strikes, technical malfunctions). Technical failures **not** exempt.	Defined broadly; CJEU case law clarifies exemptions (e.g., *Sturgeon*).	Ukraine explicitly excludes technical malfunctions from exemptions; the EU leaves interpretation to courts.

The Rules are also more extensive than the EU Regulation on which it is based as it contains a chapter on the contract of carriage. Airlines might declare the ticket invalid if the ticket is damaged or altered by an unauthorized third party, the ticket was fraudulently acquired – through stolen or invalid credit card for instance, violation of the sequence of use of the flight coupons, or failure to pay the cost or invalid fare.[5] However, if the ticket is declared invalid due to a fault from the airline, then such ticket must be reissued.[6] Reissuance of a ticket due to damages attributable to the passenger is only permitted after the passenger signed an agreement to "reimburse the air carrier for losses in the amount of the cost of the original ticket that the air carrier has suffered or may suffer in connection with the use of the original ticket by a third party."[7] The airline is entitled to charge a fee for the reissuance. Tickets are valid for a year unless otherwise specified, which can be extended in some circumstances.[8]

5 Section II(1)(5).
6 Section II(1)(6).
7 Section II(2)(1).
8 Section II(4)(6). Circumstances Section II(5).

Airlines have the right to upgrade or downgrade a passenger. In the event of downgrading, the passenger must be informed as soon as possible and offer compensation in accordance with Chapter 5, Section XV.[9] When a passenger is placed in a lower class, they are entitled to a reimbursement of a percentage of the ticket price, based on flight distance: 30% for short-haul flights, 50% for medium-haul flights, and 75% for flights over 3,500 km.[10]

Section VI deals with air travel reservation and contains a provision on passenger data and their protection.[11] Section VII contains a part on service at the airport but also on board, requiring airlines to ensure the cabin is equipped for safety and maintains appropriate temperature, cleanliness, and functional equipment (lighting, fans, seatbelts). They also need to provide seats for passengers with children and make provisions for those on stretchers or with disabilities.[12] The law explicitly lists several services that must be provided free of charge: assistance with boarding/disembarking (finding seat, placing hand luggage), information and reference service (safety rules, emergency equipment, flight conditions, free/paid services), first aid, drinking water upon request, and use of restrooms. Airlines must inform passengers about these free services immediately after the flight begins.[13]

The Rules recognize different service classes: first, business, premium/comfort, and economy, with varying service standards based on carrier rules.[14] Specific quantities of first aid kits are mandated based on the number of passenger seats such as one unit for 0–99 seats, up to four units for 300+ seats.[15] Chapter 3 of Section VII is dedicated to the quality of the service based on the class. For instance, first and business class passengers must be served in separate cabins, with layout depending on aircraft type.[16] Premium class, defined as a class with higher service standards (meals, baggage allowance) than economy, equipped with seats provided for the economy class cabin and separated from the other class.[17] The economy class is located behind higher classes, with standard seating.[18] Strict adherence to product shelf life is required for catering services.[19] While

9 Section II(7)(4).
10 Section XV(5)(2).
11 Section VI(2)(3).
12 Section VII(2)(2).
13 Section VII(2)(4).
14 Section VII(2)(5).
15 Section VII(2)(8).
16 Section VII(3)(1).
17 Section VII(3)(2)–(3).
18 Section VII(3)(5).
19 Section VII(3)(6).

there is nothing ground breaking in those rules, it is rare to have them included within a piece of legislation. Similarly, in Chapter 4, there is a rule relating to flight attendant duties which stipulates that they must inform passengers about emergency equipment and safety instructions, inspect cabins, ensure proper baggage placement, enforce seatbelt use in turbulence, and check gangway installation.[20] Another provision is that the maximum number of persons cannot exceed available belted seats.[21] Those are common knowledge and sense but still have been added in the Rules.

Section VIII is dedicated to the carriage of passengers with certain needs, including those with reduced mobility, pregnant women, and children. Chapter 1 of this section affords similar protections as under Regulation 1107/2006, stipulates that airlines cannot refuse booking or boarding to disabled or reduced mobility passengers unless specific safety requirements – international law, Ukrainian law, or operator certificate rules – are violated, or if aircraft size physically prevents boarding/transport.[22] In those circumstances, airlines must offer acceptable alternative transportation.[23] Additionally, any denial of boarding based on the exemptions entitles the passenger to a refund or a re-routing but not to compensation.[24] Airport operators should ensure accessibility and that assistance is available.[25] Any request for assistance should be sent to the carrier at least 48 hours before departure. Airlines then transmit information to relevant airports within 36 hours. If it is not possible, any issue must be resolved promptly.[26] Carriage of guide dogs and other service animals is mandatory and free.[27] Up to two units of mobility equipment (including electric wheelchairs) must be transported, subject to notice and safety/space restrictions.[28] Medical certificates might be requested when the health of the passenger causes concerns and the carrier is not responsible for the deterioration of the health of the passenger.[29] Finally, assistance must be provided without degrading dignity, ensuring these passengers receive services provided to all, adapted to their needs and safety requirements.[30]

---

20 Section VII(4)(5).
21 Section VII(4)(3).
22 Section VIII(1)(1) and (2).
23 Section VIII(1)(2).
24 Section VIII(1)(3).
25 Section VIII(1)(6)–(7).
26 Section VIII(1)(10).
27 Section VIII(1)(13).
28 Section VIII(1)(21).
29 Section VIII(1)(25) and (26).
30 Section VIII(1)(32).

Ukraine took a similar approach to the transport of children as seen in Kazakhstan by setting minimum ages for children to be allowed as unaccompanied – 5 to 14 for domestic flights and 5 to 16 for international flights.[31] There is also an infant ratio; an adult can carry no more than two infants, one without a separate seat, the second with a separate paid seat.[32] This means that a parent of twins and an older child cannot travel on their own. For an infant, under 2, to seat on a different seat, they must be transported in a certified car seat, otherwise the airline may refuse the transport on the separate seat.[33] Pregnant women are accepted up to 35 weeks for single pregnancy or 32 weeks for multiple pregnancy based on the condition established by the carrier.[34] Unlike Kazakhstan, the Rules do not prohibit the transport of newborns in the first seven days after childbirth but recommend to avoid it.[35] The Ukrainian Rules go a step further than the EU legislations as there is no EU-wide rule on pregnant women or unaccompanied minors, instead relying on airlines' policies.

Section X provides clear grounds for an airline to refuse carriage or remove a passenger, and lays out detailed rules regarding checked and unchecked baggage. This section reiterates the reasons a passenger can be refused boarding in order to comply with legislation of the country of departure, destination, or transit or at the request of authorized state authorities of Ukraine.[36] In these cases, passengers are entitled to a forced refund as they are mandatory grounds for refusal.[37] Discretionary grounds are also listed and include the passenger's condition – both mental and physical; non-compliance with airline safety requirements; behavioural issues (aggressive behaviours); security refusal, if the passenger poses a danger to others or the aircraft; payment issues; document issues – damaged or lost identity documents, no valid entry document, or refusal to present documents; intoxication; repeated offenses; ticket irregularities – invalid ticket, starting the journey at a later stopover, ticket declared lost or stolen; other cases found in the Rules.[38] In those instances, the passengers are typically entitled to voluntary refund.[39]

The airline can withdraw or invalidate a ticket and refuse a refund if it was purchased from unauthorized source, lost, stolen, forged, the presenter cannot identify as the ticket holder, purchased with fake or

31 Section VIII(2)(4).
32 Section VIII(2)(7).
33 Section VIII(2)(7).
34 Section VIII(2)(9).
35 Section VIII(2)(10).
36 Section X(1).
37 Section X(5) in conjunction with Section XVIII, Chapter 2, Paragraphs 1 and 2.
38 Section X(2).
39 Section X(5) in conjunction with Section XVIII, Chapter 2, Paragraph 3.

stolen or invalid payment card, an incorrect fare applied, or not fully paid due to passenger's fault.[40]

Category	Details
Mandatory Grounds for Refusal	- Compliance with legislation (departure, destination, or transit country). - Request by authorized state authorities of Ukraine. **Passenger Entitlement:** Forced refund
Discretionary Grounds for Refusal	1. **Passenger's Condition:** Mental/physical state. 2. **Safety Non-compliance:** Failure to follow airline safety rules. 3. **Behavioural Issues:** Aggression, disturbance, or posing danger to others/aircraft. 4. **Security Refusal:** Denied by security protocols. 5. **Payment Issues:** Failure to pay applicable fares/ fees. 6. **Document Issues:** - Damaged/lost identity documents. - No valid entry documents. - Refusal to present documents. 7. **Intoxication:** Under influence of alcohol/drugs. 8. **Repeated Offenses:** Previous violations of airline rules. 9. **Ticket Irregularities:** - Invalid ticket. - Starting journey at a later stopover. - Ticket declared lost/stolen. 10. **Other Cases:** As specified in Aviation Rules. **Passenger Entitlement:** Voluntary refund (typically).

Baggage is found in Section XI and Section XII for specific categories of baggage including birds. Chapter 2 lays down the conditions for free baggage transportation and establishes in excess of the standard allowance that passengers can carry free of charge as hand luggage, regardless of the fare rules, child's food for flight, baby travel cot for under 1 year, stroller, folding wheelchair, and crutches and special equipment for disable person.[41] Airlines can expand the list and total weight of items transported free of charge.[42] Section XI also expressly mentions that the maximum capacity for liquids is 100 ml in one bottle and the total of those liquids cannot exceed 1.1 kg per person.[43]

40 Section X(3).
41 Section XI(2)(1).
42 Section XI(2)(2).
43 Section XI(10)(3).

Flight cancellations and delays are dealt with in Section XIV. Airlines are required to take all necessary measures to avoid delays.[44] Airlines must inform the passenger, unless the delay or cancellation is due to an extraordinary circumstance.[45] For other reasons, the airline or its sales agent must notify the passengers of delay or cancellation no later than three hours before the start of check-in.[46] The airline must enter delay/cancellation information into the ASB/GRS no later than eight hours before departure. If not, the airline is solely responsible for timely passenger notification. If a flight lands at an unscheduled airport due to extraordinary circumstances, transportation to the original destination airport is at the airline's expense.[47] The airline (or service agent/airport operator) must inform passengers about the estimated delay duration and expected departure time every 30 minutes, using available means at the departure airport.[48]

If a passenger incurs losses due to being late for a connecting flight booked on separate tickets, the issue of compensation by the delaying airline is handled through a claim's procedure, and not through automatically fixed compensation.[49] In many jurisdictions globally, airlines explicitly disclaim any responsibility for missed connections when passengers book separate, unlinked tickets (self-connecting flights). By providing a clear "claims procedure," Ukraine's law explicitly acknowledges that the delaying airline may still bear some responsibility for losses arising from a missed subsequent flight, even if on a separate ticket. This provides a legal avenue for recourse that might otherwise not exist.

Section XV, titled "The rights of passengers in case of denial of air carriage, cancellation or delay of flights," outlines compensation amounts for passengers of scheduled or charter flights when a flight is cancelled, denied boarding, or delayed and the departure is rescheduled; it closely mirrors the EU Regulation, namely 250 euros for flights up to 1,500 km in distance, 400 euros for flights ranging from 1,500 to 3,500 km, and 600 euros for flights exceeding 3,500 km.[50] The compensation amount is set in euros but to be paid in Ukrainian hryvnia, and the distance is defined

44 Section XIV(2).
45 Section XIV(3).
46 Section XIV(3).
47 Section XIV(3).
48 Section XIV(4).
49 Section XIV(6).
50 Section XV(2)(5) for denial of boarding, Section XV(3)(1). See: Case, 2/760/74/22, Solomyanskyi District Court of Kyiv, decided on 13 October 2022 about a 14-hour delay resulting in a 400 euro compensation. Case 22-ц/4805/1062/19, Zhytomyr Court of Appeal, decided on 13 June 2019 about a nine-hour delay.

through the great circle route distance method.[51] For passengers to be entitled to those rights, they must have a confirmed reservation and either be present for check-in on time – as stipulated by carrier rules or at least 45 minutes before departure if not specified – or have a flight that was already delayed/transferred by the carrier/charterer.[52]

Interestingly, the Ukrainian Aviation Rules have specific definitions for "performed" and "cancelled" flights which encompass some of the interpretations by the Court of Justice of the European Union. According to Chapter 2, Section XV, paragraph 7 a flight is considered "performed" "if its performance is transferred to another air carrier, which ensures the transportation of all passengers of the transferred flight on a specially organized flight." This is a clear and explicit definition. It means if the original airline cannot operate the flight but arranges for another airline to fly all passengers on a dedicated flight to their destination, the original flight is still considered "performed" for the purposes of compensation. A flight is considered as "cancelled," without the need for the carrier to formally declare the flight as cancelled, "if the departure is delayed by more than 48 hours." Regulation 261 does not have a provision that automatically reclassifies a delay of a specific duration as a cancellation. The definition of cancellation under EU 261 suggests a formal decision by the airline. While the CJEU has in a way offered some clarity in *Sturgeon* for compensation purposes, it has also blurred the line between long delays and cancellations. By including a fixed duration for a flight to directly qualify as cancelled, some of this layer of complication has been removed. Moreover, the law makes it clear that "A change of departure or arrival airport within the same administrative-territorial unit cannot be considered a flight cancellation."

Feature	**Ukrainian Aviation Rules**	**EU Regulation 261/2004**	**Key Differences**
Flight "Performed" if Transferred to Another Carrier	**Explicitly stated**: Yes, if another carrier transports all passengers on a specially organized flight.	**Implied**: Re-routing on another carrier fulfills the obligation. Compensation depends on final arrival delay (CJEU case law, e.g., *Air France v Folkerts*).	Ukraine explicitly defines "performed" for substitute carriers; the EU relies on case law.

(*Continued*)

51 Section XV(1)(4).
52 Section XV(1)(1).

(Continued)

Feature	Ukrainian Aviation Rules	EU Regulation 261/2004	Key Differences
Change of Airport Within Same Administrative Unit	**Explicitly stated**: "Cannot be considered a flight cancellation."	**Not explicitly stated**, but CJEU (*McDonagh v Ryanair*) rules that it may trigger delay compensation if arrival is delayed by 3+ hours.	Ukraine outright excludes it from cancellations; the EU treats it as a potential delay claim.
Delay Automatically Becomes "Cancellation"	**Explicitly stated**: A delay of **>48 hours at departure** reclassifies as cancellation.	**Not explicitly stated**, but CJEU (*Sturgeon*) treats **delays of 3+ hours at final destination** like cancellations for compensation.	Ukraine has a strict 48-hour rule at departure; the EU uses a 3-hour threshold at arrival.

As required in many countries, in case of denial of boarding, the airlines must first seek volunteers willing to give up their confirmed reservation in exchange for an agreed reward. In addition to the reward, volunteers must be offered a choice between reimbursement or re-routing to the final destination at the earliest opportunity or later in time at the passenger's request subject to seat availability.[53] Any ground transport from the denial airport to the alternative route's start airport, or from the alternative landing airport to the original destination, is at the airline's expense.[54] If insufficient volunteers, the airline can deny boarding against a passenger's will and compensate the passengers based on the distance of the flight, 250 euros for flights up to 1,500 km in distance, 400 euros for flights ranging from 1,500 to 3,500 km, and 600 euros for flights exceeding 3,500 km.[55] Compensation can be reduced by 50% if the airline offers re-routing with an alternative flight arriving within two hours for flights ≤1,500 km, three hours for flights >1,500 to 3,500 km, and four hours for flights >3,500 km.[56] Payment of fixed compensation does not exempt the airline from offering the choice of reimbursement/re-routing, as per

53 Section XV(2)(1) and (2).
54 Section XV(2)(3).
55 Section XV(2)(4) and (5).
56 Section XV(2)(6).

paragraph 2 of this chapter, and care/assistance as per Para 5 of Chapter 3 of this section.[57]

Requirement	Details
Volunteer Seek Process	Airlines must first seek volunteers willing to give up seats in exchange for: - **Agreed reward** (cash, vouchers, etc.). - **Choice between:** a) Reimbursement + return to origin (if applicable). b) Re-routing (earliest or later flight, subject to availability). - **Ground transport** between airports covered by airline.
Involuntary Denial (if no volunteers)	Passengers denied boarding against their will are entitled to **fixed compensation** based on flight distance: - **€250**: Flights ≤1,500 km. - **€400**: Flights >1,500 km to ≤3,500 km. - **€600**: Flights >3,500 km.
Compensation Reduction (50%)	Compensation may be **halved** if airline offers re-routing that arrives: - **€125: ≤2 hours** (for flights ≤1,500 km). - **€200: ≤3 hours** (for flights >1,500 km to ≤3,500 km). - **€300: ≤4 hours** (for flights >3,500 km).
Additional Rights	- **Care**: Meals, refreshments, phone calls, accommodation if needed. - **Refund/Re-routing**: If passenger refuses re-routing, full ticket refund + return flight (if applicable).

In case of cancellation, passengers must be offered re-routing or reimbursement as well as compensation unless they have been informed of the cancellation two weeks before scheduled departure, between two weeks and seven days before departure and offered re-routing allowing departure no more than two hours before scheduled time and arrival no more than four hours after scheduled time or less than seven days before departure and offered re-routing allowing departure no more than one hour before scheduled time and arrival no more than two hours after scheduled time.[58] Airlines must explain the reasons for cancellation or delay upon request.[59] As with Regulation 261, airlines are exempted from compensation if they can prove the cancellation was due to extraordinary circumstances or force majeure that could not have been avoided even

57 Section XV(2)(7).
58 Section XV(3)(1).
59 Section XV(3)(2).

with all reasonable measures.[60] Passengers are still entitled to care and assistance composed of meals and refreshments proportional to waiting time, hotel accommodation if an overnight stay is required, ground transfer, and two free phone calls, fax, telex, or email.[61]

Chapter 4 regulates delays and establishes that airlines must provide meals/refreshments and two free calls/messages for delays of two hours or more for flights ≤1,500 km, three hours or more for flights >1,500 to 3,500 km, and four hours or more for all other flights.[62] If the delayed flight is postponed to the next day, the airline must provide hotel rooms, meals, and airport-hotel transfers. For delays exceeding five hours, passengers must be offered the choice of reimbursement or re-routing.[63] Interestingly, the amendments of the law did not include a provision for compensation for long delays, despite courts granting such compensation.[64] The lack of provision is made even more complex as Chapter 5 of Section XXVI refers to the Montreal limits on liability for delay to the amount of 5,346 SDRs for each passenger, making it at best confusing.

Feature	**Ukrainian Aviation Rules**	**EU Regulation 261/2004**
Compensation Amounts	Identical to EU: €250 (≤1,500 km), €400 (1,500–3,500 km), €600 (>3,500 km). Paid in UAH.	Same tiered amounts (in EUR).
Compensation Reduction	50% reduction if re-routing arrives within: - 2h (≤1,500 km). - 3h (1,500–3,500 km). - 4h (>3,500 km).	Same reduction criteria.

The Ukraine's Aviation Rules go a step further than Regulation 261 by including a compensation for delayed baggage which is based on the need for basic necessities and capped at US$50.[65] Section XXVI is dedicated to the obligation of the carrier to compensate for damages, which is the implementation of the Montreal Convention.

Another interesting provision is found in Section XXV, Chapter 3, which allows airlines to reclaim from passengers any payment or deposit advance

60 Section XV(3)(3).
61 Section XV(3)(5).
62 Section XV(4)(1).
63 Section XV(4)(3).
64 See: Case, 2/760/74/22, Solomyanskyi District Court of Kyiv, decided on 13 October 2022 about a 14-hour delay resulting in a 400 euro compensation. Case 22-ц/4805/1062/19, Zhytomyr Court of Appeal, decided on 13 June 2019 about a nine-hour delay.
65 Section XVI(1).

due to non-compliance of the passenger with the legal requirements of the countries they are flying to, from, or through. The Aviation Rules do not contain any specific provision allowing the aviation authority to fine airlines for non-compliance with the Rules.

Ukraine's legal framework for air passenger rights is established through the Aviation Rules of Ukraine, specifically the Order of the Ministry of Infrastructure No. 1239 of November 2018, as amended, which offers a highly detailed and specific regulatory framework for air passenger services and rights. This regulation forms a comprehensive national regime that consciously aligns with and extends beyond the standards set by EU Regulation 261. While the Ukrainian law adopts the core principles of the EU regulation – such as compensation tiers for cancellations and denied boarding, care obligations during delays, and protections for passengers with reduced mobility – it goes significantly further into operational aspects of passenger service, cabin conditions, safety, and, notably, provides very granular and protective provisions for vulnerable passengers such as children and pregnant women. This level of detail, particularly concerning on-board service specifics and special categories of passengers, offers a more comprehensive regulatory scope than often found in compensation-focused regulations alone.

Regarding passenger protection, the Rules closely mirror the EU's tiered compensation system for denied boarding, cancellation, and certain cases of delay, using the same distance bands and monetary amounts (250, 400, and 600 euros, payable in hryvnia). The conditions for reducing compensation by 50% for re-routing are identical. Care obligations during delays – such as provisions for meals, communications, and accommodation – are also aligned. However, the Ukrainian framework introduces greater textual clarity in several contentious areas. It explicitly defines a flight as "performed" if all passengers are transported on a specially organized flight by another carrier, and it states that a change of airport within the same administrative-territorial unit does not constitute a cancellation. Most significantly, it establishes a bright-line rule that a departure delay exceeding 48 hours is automatically reclassified as a cancellation, providing a legal certainty that the EU regulation lacks, as the latter relies on CJEU jurisprudence to equate long delays to cancellations for compensation purposes.

The Rules also provide extensive, prescriptive regulations for specific passenger categories that go beyond EU norms. Protections for passengers with reduced mobility are aligned with EU Regulation 1107/2006. However, Ukraine sets detailed national rules for unaccompanied minors, specifying age ranges, and for infants, stipulating adult-to-infant ratios. It also establishes permissible travel timeframes for pregnant women, areas where the EU has no harmonized legislation, leaving policy to individual airlines. The provisions on baggage include a specific free allowance for essential items like child food and strollers and explicitly restate the 100 ml limit for liquids.

One progressive element addresses missed connections on separate tickets. While the Ukrainian Rules provide a clear claims procedure for passengers to seek compensation for losses from the delaying airline, the Rules rely on a claims process rather than fixed compensation, creating uncertainty for passengers. Conversely, a notable omission is the lack of an explicit administrative fine regime for carrier non-compliance within the Rules themselves, potentially leaving enforcement more reliant on passenger-initiated claims. The law's silence on compensation for long delays (despite court rulings granting it) also introduces inconsistency, especially when juxtaposed with references to Montreal Convention liability limits.

In conclusion, Ukraine's Aviation Rules construct a detailed and passenger-centric regulatory ecosystem that assimilates the core compensation and care principles of EU Regulation 261 while enhancing them with operational codifications and explicit definitions that pre-empt legal ambiguity. Its approach is often more prescriptive and broader in scope, particularly regarding in-flight services and vulnerable passenger categories. However, the absence of a defined penalty mechanism for airlines and the unresolved tension between the lack of a statutory delay compensation clause and existing court practice represent points of divergence and potential weakness compared to the more mature, if judicially dependent, EU system. The Ukrainian framework thus represents a distinct model: one that seeks certainty through legislative precision and comprehensiveness, building upon but not merely replicating its European inspiration.

Comparison with EU Regulation

Feature	Ukraine's Aviation Rules	EU Regulation 261/2004
Delay Compensation	≥3h: €250–€600 (by distance).	≥3h: €250–€600 (by distance).
Cancellation Rights	<14d notice: Refund or re-routing + €250–600 compensation (by distance).	<14d notice: Refund or re-routing + €250–600 compensation (by distance).
Overbooking	Volunteer first; €250–€600 (by distance) if denied boarding.	Volunteer first; €250–€600 (by distance) if denied boarding.
Baggage Compensation	US$50 for essential products then Montreal.	Not specified.

Bibliography

- The State Aviation Service of Ukraine, Order 1239 of 26 November 2018. On approval of the Aviation Rules of Ukraine "Rules of Air Transportation and Passenger and Baggage Handling" <https://zakon.rada.gov.ua/laws/show/z0141-19#Text> accessed 22 December 2025.
- The State Aviation Service of Ukraine, Order 1543 of 01 October 2021. On approval of Amendments to some Aviation Regulations of Ukraine <https://zakon.rada.gov.ua/laws/show/z1427-21#n4> accessed 22 December 2025.
- Case, 2/760/74/22, Solomyanskyi District Court of Kyiv, decided on 13 October 2022.
- Case 22-ц/4805/1062/19, Zhytomyr Court of Appeal, decided on 13 June 2019.
- Tsirat, A., 'Ukraine' in S. Gates (ed), *The Aviation Law Review* (4th edn, Law Business Research Ltd 2016).

II.52

United Arab Emirates

The United Arab Emirates (UAE) has introduced regulations to protect air passengers, outlined primarily in Chapter 5 of the Commercial Transactions Law[1] and the Passenger Welfare Program (CAR PWP)[2] issued by the General Civil Aviation Authority (GCAA). Federal Decree-Law No. 50/2022, referred to as the Commercial Transactions Law, includes provisions regarding the protection of air passengers' rights and outlines legal remedies available in the event of disputes or incidents during air transport which are mainly in line with the Montreal Convention.[3] The Passenger Welfare Program primarily focuses on the care and assistance that airlines must provide to passengers suffering from a denial of boarding, delay, or cancellation.[4]

The Passenger Welfare Program applies to airlines departing or arriving in the United Arab Emirates, UAE airport operators, and flights diverted to the UAE.[5] The CAR PWP only applies to flight disruptions occurring at UAE's airports.[6] This limitation was added in 2024 in order to clarify the scope of the CAR PWP. Like many regulations around the world, this law does not apply to passengers travelling free of charge or on reduced fares which are not available to the public.[7]

1 Federal Decree-Law No. 50/2022.

2 Civil Aviation Regulations Passenger Welfare Program (CAR PWP), issue 2. <https://www.gcaa.gov.ae/en/epublication/EPublications/Civil%20Aviation%20Regulations%20%28CARs%29/CAR%20III%20-%20GENERAL%20REGULATIONS/CAR-PWP%20-%20PASSENGER%20WELFARE%20PROGRAM%20-%20ISSUE%2002.pdf> accessed 22 December 2025.

3 Hassan Elhais, 'Legal Obligations of Airlines and the Rights of Passengers Under UAE Law' (*Chambers and Partners*, 29 June 2025) <https://chambers.com/articles/legal-obligations-of-airlines-and-the-rights-of-passengers-under-uae-law> accessed 22 December 2025.

4 PWP.A.002.

5 PWP.A.003.

6 GM1 to PWP.A.003.

7 GM1 to PWP.A.003.

DOI: 10.4324/9781003746164-63

For denial of boarding, the passenger must be offered a re-routing or return to their first point of departure as well as care such as refreshment, meals, or hotel accommodation, unless the passenger is voluntarily giving their seat or there are valid reasons such as health, safety, or incomplete documentation.[8] The airlines should first request volunteers to surrender their reservation in exchange of benefits before starting to deny boarding on other passengers.[9]

Flight delays in the UAE are covered by both the Passenger Welfare Program (CAR PWP) and the Commercial Transactions Law. They address different aspects of the airline's responsibilities. In the event of flight delays or damage to luggage or goods, Article 357 of the Commercial Transactions Law ensures that affected passengers are entitled to compensation for any inconvenience or loss suffered. The CAR PWP distinguishes between tarmac delay and delay at terminal. Delay at terminal of between one and three hours requires the airline to inform the passengers with up-to-date information.[10] Any delay of three to eight hours regardless of the distance of the flight entitles the passenger to up-to-date information, free meals, and refreshment commensurate with the waiting time, appropriate means of communication, and hotel accommodation, depending on the time of the day for passengers who have missed their connection and their next flight is after eight hours.[11] The article leaves room for interpretation such as what is meals or refreshment commensurate with the waiting time. When an anticipated delay exceeds eight hours, passengers must be provided with hotel accommodation, free meals and refreshment commensurate with the wait, appropriate means of communication, and transport between airport and hotel.[12]

In case of tarmac delay between one and three hours, passengers are only granted a right to up-to-date information. For delays of three to eight hours, passengers should be offered the opportunity to disembark as well as the same assistance as passengers suffering for the same length of delay at airport.[13] For tarmac delays of more than eight hours, the passengers must be disembarked from the aircraft and granted all the rights available to passengers suffering an eight-hour delay.[14]

8 PWP.B.002 and GM1 PWP.B.002.
9 GM2 PWP.B.002.
10 PWP.B.003(a).
11 PWP.B.003(b)(1)–(4).
12 PWP.B.003(c)(1)–(4).
13 PWP.B.004(b)(1)–(5).
14 PWP.B.004(c)(1)–(5).

Duration	Terminal Delay Requirements	Tarmac Delay Requirements
1–3 Hours	• Up-to-date flight information.	• Up-to-date flight information.
3–8 Hours	• Continuous flight updates. • Meals/refreshments matching wait time. • Communication access. • Hotel if next flight >8hrs (overnight).	• Opportunity to disembark if safe. • Same benefits as terminal delay (updates, meals, communication, hotel if applicable).
More Than 8 Hours	• Mandatory hotel accommodation. • Full meal service. • Airport-hotel transfers. • Communication access.	• Mandatory disembarkation. • All terminal delay benefits apply (hotel, meals, transport, communication).

The law also contains a specific provision on diversion. If your flight lands at an airport different from your planned destination, the airline is obligated to provide care including refreshments, meals, hotel accommodation, transport between the airport and the place of accommodation, and appropriate means of communication.[15] The provision of these items is in accordance with PWP.B.003 and PWP.B.004 (which would detail the specific triggers and timings for these, as we discussed previously, e.g., after a certain number of hours). Additionally, passengers must be offered the choice between a return flight to the first point of departure (if they wish to abandon their journey) or a re-routing to their final destination without any additional cost.[16]

Passengers are eligible for care and assistance if the flight is cancelled within 48 hours from the scheduled departure time.[17] CAR PWP requires airlines, regardless of whether the passenger has already checked in, to inform them of any cancelled flights at the earliest practicable time as well as offer care similar to diversions and delays.[18] The airline must carry the passenger and their baggage as soon as practicable on another flight where space is available. The validity period of their ticket must be extended to accommodate this new carriage if necessary.[19] Passengers must be given the option for either a return flight to the first point of departure or re-routing within a reasonable period of time, even if the flight is operated by a different carrier.[20] Subparagraphs 3 and 4 might seem a bit at odds

15 PWP.B.005(a).
16 PWP.B.005(b).
17 PWP.A.005.
18 PWP.B.006(a)(1) and (2).
19 PWP.B.006(a)(3).
20 PWP.B.006(a)(4).

with one another or repetitive, as paragraph 3 requires re-routing while paragraph 4 allows for a return flight. The requirements for cancellations apply to all transit flights and flights not originating from the city of residence/domicile of the passenger.[21] It is unclear from the wording of paragraph b whether the exact application of the provision might vary for flights originating from a passenger's home city, though general principles of care would still apply.

Airlines are required to implement mechanisms for periodic review of the implementation of the CAR PWP.[22] However, no fixed fines are introduced by the CAR PWP. The UAE system offers no standardized compensation, instead relying on case-by-case assessment under commercial law where passengers must prove damages according to Article 357 of the Commercial Transaction Law. This liability is often interpreted in line with the Montreal Convention of 1999, to which the UAE is a signatory. For instance, liability for baggage is capped at 500 Dirhams, unless higher amount is agreed.[23]

Neither the CAR PWP nor the Commercial Transactions Law contain special provisions for special needs passengers or passengers with disability. The CAR PWP is also missing a provision on downgrading; however, Article 329 of the Commercial Transaction Law provides for the reimbursement of the difference in price. The timeframe to bring a claim is two years.[24]

The regulatory framework for air passenger protection in the United Arab Emirates, as established by the General Civil Aviation Authority's Passenger Welfare Program and the Commercial Transactions Law, represents a significant and detailed codification of passenger rights. The UAE system is fundamentally centred on the principle of passenger welfare and care, mandating specific and escalating duties of assistance in the event of denied boarding, cancellations, or delays, with particular attention paid to the operational distinctions between tarmac and terminal delays. The scope of the CAR PWP is more restricted than Regulation 261 as it primarily covers flights to and from UAE airports. Its cancellation provisions explicitly extend to all transit flights and flights not originating from the passenger's city of residence/domicile. It focuses more on the location of the airport (UAE) rather than the airline's nationality in the same way as EU 261.

While the care and assistance is pretty similar, the EU regime triggers these obligations sooner (after two to four hours depending on flight

21 PWP.B.006(b).
22 AMC2 PWP.B.001(a).
23 Article 359 of Commercial Transaction Law.
24 Article 370 of Commercial Transaction Law.

distance versus the UAE's 3+ hour threshold). The CAR PWP primarily focuses on "care" and "welfare" provisions (meals, accommodation, re-routing) rather than direct, fixed cash compensation for delays which will be determined according to Article 357 based on proof of damages. The only reason to avoid compensation is if the flight cannot be operated due to force majeure or circumstances endangering lives or due to the health of the passenger.[25] Those terms should have been defined carefully in the laws as they are left to interpretation. However, it can be safely assumed that war risks, security risks and "act of God" will be regarded as force majeure.

The UAE framework, while robust in its operational welfare rules, does not contain specialized provisions for passengers with disabilities or for downgrading, points which are addressed within the broader EU regulation. Ultimately, both systems serve to protect passengers but do so through different legal instruments; the UAE provides a strong safety net of immediate care grounded in its territorial authority, whereas the EU combines similar care with a more assertive, harmonized financial compensation scheme, resulting in a potentially more potent deterrent against disruptions and a more uniform passenger experience across its jurisdiction.

Comparison with Regulation 261

Feature	UAE CAR PWP	EU Regulation 261
Delay Compensation	No fixed amounts.	≥3h delay: €250–€600 (by distance).
Cancellation Notice	<48 hours: Immediate info + full care + rebooking options.	<14d notice: Refund or re-routing + €250–600 compensation (by distance).
Denied Boarding	Volunteer first; full care + rebooking options.	Volunteer first; €250–600 (by distance) if denied boarding.
Baggage Liability	500 Dirhams per kg (unless higher amount is agreed).	Not mentioned.

Bibliography

- Federal Decree-Law No. 50/2022, Promulgating the Commercial Transaction Law. 3 October 2022 (corresponding to 7 Rabi Al-Awwal 1444 H), Official Gazette N°737 <https://uaelegislation.gov.ae/en/legislations/1610/download> accessed 22 December 2025.
- Civil Aviation Regulations Passenger Welfare Program (CAR PWP), issue 02 <https://www.gcaa.gov.ae/en/epublication/EPublications/Civil%20Aviation%20Regulations%20%28CARs%29/CAR%20III%20-%20GENERAL%20

25 Articles 322 and 323.

REGULATIONS/CAR-PWP%20-%20PASSENGER%20WELFARE%20 PROGRAM%20-%20ISSUE%2002.pdf> accessed 22 December 2025.

- Elhais, H., 'Legal Obligations of Airlines and the Rights of Passengers Under UAE Law' (*Chambers and Partners*, 29 June 2025) <https://chambers.com/articles/legal-obligations-of-airlines-and-the-rights-of-passengers-under-uae-law> accessed 22 December 2025.

II.53

United Kingdom

Passenger rights in the United Kingdom are governed by what is known as the UK261.[1] The UK Regulation 261 – pursuant to section 3 European Union (Withdrawal) Act 2018 and amended by The Air Passenger Rights and Air Travel Organisers' Licensing (Amendment) (EU Exit) Regulations 2019 (APR), which came into force in January 2021, largely mirrors the pre-Brexit EU Regulation 261. Regarding the applicable version, the Supreme Court also ruled by majority that any causes of action which had accrued prior to the IP completion day (namely 31 December 2020) would fall under Regulation 261 and not its amended version.[2]

With the status of assimilated law, UK Regulation 261 continues to apply to flights departing from an airport located in the UK, regardless of the airline's nationality[3] and flights departing from an airport outside the UK or the EU to an airport within the UK operated by UK or EU/EEA carriers or departing from the UK to the EU when the flight is operated by a UK carrier unless the passengers received benefits or compensation and were given assistance in that other country.[4] The Regulation also applies to connecting flights if they were booked as a single unit and departing from a country within the scope of the law, embodying the ruling in *Gahan/Buckley v Emirates*.[5]

1 Regulation (EC) No 261/2004 of the European Parliament and of the Council <https://www.legislation.gov.uk/eur/2004/261/contents>.

2 *Lipton and Another v BA Cityflyer* Ltd [2024] UKSC 24. See: Blue Elliott, 'Flight Compensation in "Extraordinary Circumstances": The Supreme Court Has Its Say' (*Farrer and Co*, 15 July 2024) <https://www.farrer.co.uk/news-and-insights/flight-compensation-in-extraordinary-circumstances-the-supreme-court-has-its-say/> accessed 22 December 2025.

3 *Varano v Air Canada* [2021] EWHC 1336 (QB).

4 Article 3(1)(a)(b).

5 Article 3A(a) and (b). [2017] EWCA Civ 1530.

So a flight that leaves the US to India via London Heathrow does not entitle the passenger to compensation. *Chelluri v Air India Ltd* [2021] EWCA Civ 1953. See: Jacob Turner, 'Court of Appeal Refuses to Expand Scope of Flight Delay Compensation' (*Fountain Court*, 21 December 2021) <https://fountaincourt.uk/2021/12/court-of-appeal-refuses-to-expand-scope-of-flight-delay-compensation/> accessed 22 December 2025.

DOI: 10.4324/9781003746164-64

Despite some broadening of the scope of the Regulation, the ruling of *Cathay Pacific* (pre-Brexit) would probably be the same as the flight was not operated by an English carrier.[6] However, the statement

> It seems to me, therefore, that the judge below was right to say that the regulation is only concerned with the individual flight components of any journey so that the flight to which the claimant says he was denied boarding, CX111, did not depart from the UK but from Hong Kong

would no longer be appropriate as English law now codifies the single-unit journey principle, making the "individual flight component" view obsolete for a single booking.

Flight Route	**UK Airline (UK261)**	**UK Airline (EC261)**	**EU Airline (UK261)**	**EU Airline (EC261)**	**Other Airlines (UK261)**	**Other Airlines (EC261)**
EU – EU	✓	✓	No	✓	No	✓
EU – UK	✓	✓	✓	✓	No	✓
EU – Third Country	✓	✓	No	✓	No	✓
UK – EU	✓	No	✓	✓	✓	No
UK – UK	✓	No	✓	No	✓	No
UK – Third Country	✓	No	✓	No	✓	No
Third Country – EU	✓	No	No	✓	No	No
Third Country – UK	✓	No	✓	No	No	No

UK Regulation 261 is essentially the UK's version of the European Union's Regulation 261 and the core protections for air passengers remain consistent.[7] However, the UK legislator, for clarity purposes, has enacted the Aviation (Consumers) (Amendment) Regulations 2023 (ACAR) to incorporate key principles established by the Court of Justice of the European Union (CJEU) into English law.[8] While there was some hope from some of the CJEU judgments to have been scrutinized by the Court of Appeal, it did not materialize and due to their codification it

6 *Sanghvi v Cathay Pacific Airways* [2012] 1 Lloyd's Rep 46.

7 Robert Lawson QC, 'Air Passenger Rights in the UK Post-Brexit: The Position So Far' (2021) 46 Air and Space Law 45.

8 George Leloudas, 'Resolving Airline Passenger Disputes by Alternative Dispute Resolution Methods an Appraisal of the UK System' in Baris Soyer (ed), *Commercial Disputes* (1st edn, Informa Law 2024).

seems quite unlikely for the UK to depart from the EU established regime, especially with the wording of Article 3(7) and (8). Article 3(7) also makes it clear that "an obligation to pay compensation or offer assistance in accordance with Articles 7 to 9 does not constitute a liability for damage occasioned by delay for the purposes of Article 19 of the Montreal Convention."

In cases where airlines overbook flights and consequently deny boarding to passengers holding valid tickets, airlines must first seek volunteers to give up their reservations in exchange for benefits (e.g., re-routing, refund) before denying boarding involuntarily.[9] Those volunteers are entitled to assistance.[10] If insufficient volunteers come forward, and passengers are denied boarding against their will, they are entitled to compensation, re-routing or refund, and care/assistance.[11] The compensation amount is structured based on distance, ranging from £220 for short flights to £520 for long-haul journeys.

Scenario	Passenger Rights
Voluntary Denial	Volunteers get benefits (re-routing/refund) + assistance.
Involuntary Denial	Compensation + re-routing/refund + care/assistance.
Compensation Amounts	- £220 (short flights). - £350 (medium flights). - £520 (long-haul flights).

When a flight is cancelled, the passenger must be offered assistance and re-routing.[12] Passengers are entitled to compensation unless they are informed of the cancellation in advance at least two weeks before departure.[13] Similarly no compensation is due if the passengers have been informed between two weeks and seven days before the scheduled time and are offered re-routing and the alternative departed no more than two hours before the scheduled time of departure and reached their final destination less than four hours after the scheduled time of arrival.[14] For cancellations with less than seven days' notice, this window narrows to one hour before the schedule time and reaching their final destination less than two hours later.[15] These strict timeframes ensure airlines make every effort to minimize disruption to passengers' travel plans. Moreover,

9 Article 4(1).
10 Article 4(1).
11 Article 4(2) and (3).
12 Article 5(1)(a).
13 Article 5(1)(c)(i).
14 Article 5(1)(c)(ii).
15 Article 5(1)(c)(iii).

airlines are also exempt from compensation if the cancellation is due to "extraordinary circumstances" that could not have been avoided even if all reasonable measures had been taken.[16]

Notice Period	Compensation Applicable?
≥14 Days	No.
7–14 Days	No, if re-routing departs ≤2 hrs earlier and arrives ≤4 hrs later.
<7 Days	Yes, unless re-routing departs ≤1 hr earlier and arrives ≤2 hrs later.
Any Time	Exempt if due to *extraordinary circumstances*.

Although the ACAR retains the extraordinary circumstances defence and applies the EU test established in *Wallentin-Hermann v Alitalia*[17] namely

> (a) that – (i) by their nature or origin are not inherent in the normal exercise of the activity of the air carrier, (ii) are beyond the actual control of the air carrier, and (iii) the air carrier has taken all reasonable measures in relation to but was unable to avoid.

While most of the EU case law are still relevant in the UK, the Supreme Court has had the opportunity to give its own interpretation of the extraordinary circumstance defence. The UK Supreme Court ruled that flight cancellation due to a sudden illness of the pilot does not qualify as an "extraordinary circumstance" under the Regulation.[18] In *Frederique Jager v easyJet Airline Limited*, the judge ruled that weather conditions affecting a previous flight cannot apply to a subsequent flight and the knock on delays are not covered by the extraordinary circumstance defence.[19] In *Dunbar*, the Scottish court clarified that

> however, there had to come a point where extraordinary circumstances ceased to exist, or at the very least, the longer between the circumstances causing the original delay coming to an end and the continuation of delays, the weaker the extraordinary circumstances exception had to be.[20]

Air traffic management decisions to suspend flights is an extraordinary circumstance.[21]

16 Article 5(3).
17 *C-549/07.*
18 *Lipton and Another v BA Cityflyer Ltd* [2024] UKSC 24.
19 Cheshire County Court, 16 September 2013, unreported but quoted in *Dunbar v easyJet Airline Co Ltd* [2015] ScotSC 70.
20 Paragraph 24.
21 *Blanche v Easyjet Airline Company Ltd* [2019] EWCA Civ 69.

Following the Court of Appeal's ruling in *Huzar v Jet2*, it is clear that the test for establishing a hidden manufacturing defect is narrower than under European law.[22] Judge Platts found:

> Against that background, I am persuaded that in this case the cause of delay or cancellation was the need to resolve the technical problem which had been identified. That being the case, in my judgment it does not matter how the technical problem was identified. Whether it was identified by routine maintenance (as was the case in *Wallentin*) or as a result of a warning light during flight (as in the present case) seems to me to be irrelevant. Equally and for that very reason the fact that it was unexpected and unforeseeable is also irrelevant. The reality is that once a technical problem is identified it is inherent in the normal activity of the air carrier to have to resolve that technical problem. Further, the resolution of the problem, as was demonstrated in this case, is entirely within the control of the carrier. On such an analysis the delay caused by the resolution of an unexpected, unforeseen and unforeseeable technical problem cannot be said to be an extraordinary circumstance given the *Wallentin* test. Air carriers have to encounter and deal with such circumstances as part of running an airline just as the owner of a car has to encounter and deal with unexpected and unforeseen breakdowns of his car.[23]

While the case of *Matkustaja A v Finnair Oyj*[24] relating to default with a brand-new aircraft is no longer binding in the UK, it could still be cited as "persuasive authority."

To ensure a smooth resolution of complaint – and potentially to avoid backlogs – the Civil Aviation Authority (CAA) has published a list of flights which it "would consider have been cancelled due to extraordinary circumstances."[25] While the list is non-exhaustive, it might be a way forward to avoid airlines receiving claims which would fall under "extraordinary circumstances." National authorities could review cancelled flights and provide an updates list to passengers.

In case of delay, a passenger has the right to assistance which varies based on flight distance, differentiating between short-haul (up to 1,500 km), medium-haul (between 1,500 km and 3,500 km), and long haul (exceeding 3,500 km). For short-haul, the delay must be of at least two hours, for medium-haul the delay must amount to three hours or more, and for long-haul delays must be of four hours or more. As with cancellation, airlines can escape liability by demonstrating that the situation was caused

22 Jeremias Prassl, 'EU Aviation Law Before the English Courts: Dawson, Huzar, and Regulation 261/2004' (2014) 39 Air and Space Law 365.

23 [2014] EWCA Civ 791, paragraphs 27 and 28.

24 *Case C-385/23 Finnair (Vice de conception du réservoir), ECLI:EU:C:2024:497.*

25 CAA, 'Am I Entitled to Compensation?' <https://www.caa.co.uk/passengers-and-public/resolving-travel-problems/delays-and-cancellations/making-a-claim/am-i-entitled-to-compensation/> accessed 20 February 2025.

by extraordinary circumstances. Since the *Sturgeon* ruling, passengers suffering a delay of more than three hours at their destination are entitled to compensation which has been added to the wording of Article 6.[26]

Flight Distance	Delay Threshold for Assistance	Compensation Amount	If Arrival Within
Short (≤1,500 km)	≥2 hours.	≥3 hours £220.	≤2 hours late => 50% reduction.
Medium (1,500–3,500 km)	≥3 hours.	≥4 hours £350.	≤3 hours late => 50% reduction.
Long (>3,500 km)	≥4 hours.	≥4 hours £520.	≤4 hours late => 50% reduction.
Exemption	If delay due to *extraordinary circumstances.*		

Article 7 provides that passengers will receive compensation of £220 for flights of up to 1,500 km, £350 for flights between 1,500 km and 3,500 km, and finally £520 for flights over 3,500 km.[27] However, the amount can be divided by 50% if the flights arrived within two hours for flights of up to 1,500 km, three hours for flights between 1,500 km and 3,500 km, and four hours for flights over 3,500 km.[28] This liability cannot be waived.[29]

The right to care and assistance is defined in Article 9 which includes meals and refreshments "in a reasonable relation to the waiting time"[30] which is not defined and leaves it quite vague, two free telephone calls, telex or fax messages, or emails,[31] hotel accommodation and transport between the airport and the hotel, if an overnight stay or a stay longer than planned becomes necessary.[32]

This regulation also covers downgrading and upgrading. If an airline places a passenger in a higher class than booked, it cannot request additional payment. When a passenger is placed in a lower class, they are entitled to a reimbursement of a percentage of the ticket price, based on flight distance: 30% for short-haul flights, 50% for medium-haul flights,

26 Article 6(3) inserted by The Aviation (Consumers) (Amendment) Regulations 2023 (S.I. 2023/1370), regs. 1(2) and 2(5).
27 Article 7(1)(a), (b) and (c).
28 Article 7(2)(a), (b) and (c).
29 Article 15(1).
30 Article 9(1)(a).
31 Article 9(2).
32 Article 9(1)(b) and (c).

and 75% for flights over 3,500 km.[33] The Court of Justice of the European Union interpreted the concept of price mentioned in Article 10(2) as

> price of the ticket to be taken into consideration for the purposes of determining the reimbursement owed to that passenger, where he is downgraded on a flight, is solely the price of the flight itself, to the exclusion of taxes and charges indicated on that ticket, as long as neither the requirement to pay those taxes and charges nor their amount depends on the class for which that ticket has been purchased.[34]

Article 11, mirroring the EU regulation, provides some protection to people with special needs or reduced mobility. People with special needs or reduced mobility must be offered priority boarding.[35] In cases of denied boarding, cancellation, and delays of any length, persons with reduced mobility and any persons accompanying them, as well as unaccompanied children, shall have the right to care in accordance with Article 9 as soon as possible.[36] Compared to other countries, it is one of the least protections offered which could be explained by the broad reach of the Equality Act 2010.

Like EU Regulation 261, airlines have an obligation to inform passengers of their rights through a legible notice.[37] Any passenger having been denied boarding or suffering a cancellation must receive a written notice setting out the rules for compensation.[38] The CAA was given the power to issue sanctions based on Part 8 Enterprise Act 2002 which was omitted by the Digital Markets, Competition and Consumer Act 2024 and can issue a fine of up to £5,000.[39]

One major difference is that the ACAR 2023 reaffirms the six-year limitation period (five for Scotland), as established in *Dawson v Thomson Airways Ltd*,[40] under section 9 of the Limitation Act 1980 for passengers to make compensation claims which is much longer than the two-year period under the Montreal Convention. That case also reiterated that obligations under the Regulation fall outside the scope of the Montreal Convention 1999.

33 Article 10(2)(a), (b) and (c).
34 Case C-255/15 *Steef Mennens v Emirates Direktion für Deutschland*, ECLI:EU:C:2016:472.
35 Article 11(1).
36 Article 11(2).
37 Article 14(1).
38 Article 14(2).
39 Coupled with Article 16 of the Regulation. *The Civil Aviation Authority v Ryanair DAC* [2022] EWCA Civ 76 <https://www.caa.co.uk/publication/download/14492#:~:text=robust%20and%20effective.-,Stages%20of%20Enforcement,we%20will%20deploy%20these%20tools>.
40 [2014] EWCA Civ 845.

In *Smyth v British Airways Plc & Anor*, the High Court made it clear that representative action intended to claim statutory damages under EU Regulation 261 did not meet the requirements of CPR 19.8, specifically the "same interest" requirement.[41] In 2022, the Supreme Court made it clear that solicitors can have equitable lien over compensation paid to passengers in order to deduct its fees.[42]

The post-Brexit landscape for air passenger rights in the United Kingdom is characterized by continuity tempered by a measured process of domestic legal assimilation. The governing instrument, commonly termed UK261, was born from the European Union (Withdrawal) Act 2018 and subsequent amendments, effectively transplanting the substantive provisions of EU Regulation 261 into UK law as retained EU law, now classified as "assimilated law." This transition was designed to provide stability, ensuring that the core entitlements to compensation and assistance in cases of denied boarding, cancellation, and long delay remained familiar to passengers and carriers alike. However, a comparative analysis with its progenitor, Regulation 261, reveals nuanced divergences in scope, application, and evolving judicial interpretation, marking the beginning of a distinct, albeit closely aligned, legal trajectory.

In terms of territorial and carrier applicability, UK261 has recalibrated the jurisdictional nexus. It applies principally to flights departing from UK airports on any airline, and to flights arriving into the UK on UK or EU/EEA carriers, where equivalent compensation has not already been provided in the departure country. This creates a symmetrical but distinct framework from Regulation 261, which continues to govern flights within, into, or from the EU. A significant clarification, codifying the principle from the *Gahan/Buckley v Emirates* ruling, is the explicit application to connecting flights booked as a single unit where the first leg departs from within the regulation's scope. This renders obsolete the pre-Brexit "individual flight component" analysis seen in cases like *Cathay Pacific*, demonstrating a legislative intent to protect the integrity of a contracted journey.

Substantively, the protections themselves – the tiered compensation amounts, the right to care and assistance, and the provisions on downgrading – remain directly equivalent. The UK legislator, through

41 *Smyth v British Airways Plc & Anor* [2024] EWHC 2173 (KB). See: Ian Denham, 'James Dawson v Thomson Airways Limited [2014] EWCA Civ 845, [2014] WLR (D) 279 – Case Note' (*Travellawyersblog*, 13 October 2014) <https://travellawyersblog.wordpress.com/2014/10/13/james-dawson-v-thomson-airways-limited-2014-ewca-civ-845-2014-wlr-d-279/> accessed 22 December 2025.

42 [2022] UKSC 8. See: Inês Afonso Mousinho, 'Bott & Co Solicitors Ltd v. Ryanair DAC' (2022) 47 Air and Space Law 515.

the Aviation (Consumers) (Amendment) Regulations 2023 (ACAR), has further entrenched this alignment by statutorily incorporating key principles established by the Court of Justice of the European Union (CJEU). Notably, ACAR codifies the *Sturgeon* principle that compensation is due for arrivals delayed by three hours or more, and clarifies that regulatory compensation is distinct from damages under the Montreal Convention. This deliberate incorporation suggests a policy choice to maintain harmony with the established EU regime, particularly evident in the retention of the *Wallentin-Hermann* test for "extraordinary circumstances." This defence, which exempts carriers from compensation for events not inherent in the normal exercise of their activity and beyond their control, remains a pivotal and contested boundary in both jurisdictions.

Nevertheless, the UK judiciary has begun to exercise its autonomy in interpreting this common framework. While pre-Brexit CJEU jurisprudence remains highly persuasive, UK courts are developing their own gloss on key concepts. The Supreme Court's ruling that sudden pilot illness does not constitute an extraordinary circumstance exemplifies a potentially stricter approach to the defence, narrowing its scope compared to some EU Member State applications. Similarly, in *Huzar v Jet2*, the Court of Appeal delineated a narrower interpretation for technical defects, concluding that the resolution of an unexpected technical problem is inherent in an airline's normal activity, regardless of how it was discovered. This stands in some contrast to the CJEU's approach in *Finnair*, highlighting an area where interpretative divergence may emerge, albeit from a shared foundational test.

Procedural and enforcement distinctions are also apparent. A major procedural advantage for claimants under UK261 is the reaffirmation of a six-year limitation period (five in Scotland) for bringing claims, as established in *Dawson*, which significantly exceeds the two-year period applicable under the Montreal Convention and commonly applied in many EU states. Enforcement powers reside with the Civil Aviation Authority (CAA), which can impose financial penalties, and the recent statutory affirmation of solicitors' equitable liens over recovered compensation shapes the litigation landscape. Furthermore, the UK approach to collective redress for these claims appears more restrictive following *Smyth*, where the High Court found representative actions unsuitable for such individualized statutory claims.

In conclusion, the UK regulation is best understood as a deliberate and largely faithful replication of the EU's passenger rights architecture, now operating within a separate legal orbit. The immediate post-Brexit strategy has been one of consolidation and clarity, through ACAR, rather than radical reform. The core substantive rights are identical, fostering continuity for consumers and operators. Yet, the seeds of divergence are present in the refined rules of application, the extended limitation period, and the emerging contours of domestic judicial interpretation, particularly regarding the bounds of "extraordinary circumstances." For now, the regimes run in parallel, with the UK statute reflecting its EU origins while gradually asserting its own jurisprudential identity within the broader framework of assimilated law.

Comparison with EU Regulation

Feature	UK261	EU Regulation 261/2004
Delay Compensation	≥3h: £220–£520 (by distance).	≥3h: €250–€600 (by distance).
Cancellation Notice	<14d notice: Refund or re-routing + compensation.	<14d notice: Refund or re-routing + €250–600 compensation (by distance).
Denied Boarding	Volunteer first; £220–£520 (by distance) if denied boarding.	Volunteer first; €250–€600 (by distance) if denied boarding.
Baggage Liability	Not specified.	Not specified.

Bibliography

Primary Sources

- The Aviation (Consumers) (Amendment) Regulations 2023 (S.I. 2023/1370).
- Regulation (EC) No 261/2004 of the European Parliament and of the Council <https://www.legislation.gov.uk/eur/2004/261/contents>.
- *Blanche v Easyjet Airline Company Ltd* [2019] EWCA Civ 69.
- *Bott & Co Solicitors v Ryanair DAC* [2022] UKSC 8.
- Case C-255/15 *Steef Mennens v Emirates Direktion für Deutschland*, ECLI:EU:C:2016:472.
- Case C-385/23 *Finnair (Vice de conception du réservoir)*, ECLI:EU:C:2024:497.
- Case C-549/07 *Friederike Wallentin-Hermann v Alitalia – Linee Aeree Italiane SpA*. ECLI:EU:C:2008:771.
- *Chelluri v Air India Ltd* [2021] EWCA Civ 1953.
- *The Civil Aviation Authority v Ryanair DAC* [2022] EWCA Civ 76.
- *Frederique Jager v easyJet Airline Limited* Cheshire County Court, 16 September 2013, unreported but quoted in *Dunbar v easyJet Airline Co Ltd* [2015] ScotSC 70.
- *Gahan/Buckley v Emirates* [2017] EWCA Civ 1530.
- *Huzar v Jet2* [2014] EWCA Civ 791.
- *James Dawson v Thomson Airways Limited* [2014] EWCA Civ 845.
- *Lipton and Another v BA Cityflyer Ltd* [2024] UKSC 24.
- *Sanghvi v Cathay Pacific Airways* [2012] 1 Lloyd's Rep 46.
- *Smyth v British Airways Plc & Anor* [2024] EWHC 2173 (KB).
- *Varano v Air Canada* [2021] EWHC 1336 (QB).

Secondary Sources

- CAA, 'Am I Entitled to Compensation?' <https://www.caa.co.uk/passengers-and-public/resolving-travel-problems/delays-and-cancellations/making-a-claim/am-i-entitled-to-compensation/> accessed 20 December 2025.
- Afonso Mousinho, I., 'Bott & Co Solicitors Ltd v. Ryanair DAC' (2022) 47 Air and Space Law 515.
- Denham, I., 'James Dawson v Thomson Airways Limited [2014] EWCA Civ 845, [2014] WLR (D) 279 – Case Note' (*Travellawyersblog*, 13 October 2014) <https://travellawyersblog.wordpress.com/2014/10/13/james-dawson-v-thomson-airways-limited-2014-ewca-civ-845-2014-wlr-d-279/> accessed 22 December 2025.
- Elliott, B., 'Flight Compensation in "Extraordinary Circumstances": The Supreme Court Has its Say' (*Farrer and Co*, 15 July 2024) <https://www.farrer.co.uk/news-and-insights/flight-compensation-in-extraordinary-circumstances-the-supreme-court-has-its-say/> accessed 22 December 2025.
- Lawson QC, R., 'Air Passenger Rights in the UK Post-Brexit: The Position So Far' (2021) 46 Air & Space Law 45.
- Leloudas, G., 'Resolving Airline Passenger Disputes by Alternative Dispute Resolution Methods an Appraisal of the UK System' in Baris Soyer (ed), *Commercial Disputes* (1st edn, Informa Law 2024).
- Prassl, J., 'EU Aviation Law before the English Courts: Dawson, Huzar, and Regulation 261/2004' (2014) 39 Air and Space Law 365.
- Turner, J., 'Court of Appeal Refuses to Expand Scope of Flight Delay Compensation' (*Fountain Court*, 21 December 2021) <https://fountaincourt.uk/2021/12/court-of-appeal-refuses-to-expand-scope-of-flight-delay-compensation/> accessed 22 December 2025.

II.54

United States

The rights of airline passengers in the United States (US) are found at three different levels: in federal law, regulatory provisions, and the policies adopted by individual airlines.[1] Currently, the US does not have any specific federal law for passenger rights, as found in the EU, despite "the quality of passenger service has deteriorated significantly since 1978."[2] After many unsuccessful attempts by federal legislators to regulate the issue of delays and cancellation,[3] the US has a piecemeal regime in place with some rights scattered in various pieces of legislation. For instance, the FAA Extension, Safety, and Security Act of 2016, signed into law in July 2016, included a few provisions relating to passenger rights and changed tarmac delay calculation.[4] The absence of comprehensive regulation in the United States leaves passengers subject to each air carrier's policies concerning the assistance or compensation available to them.[5] As Foote noted, "under U.S. law, air carriers may delay or cancel flights with basically no legal consequences."[6]

In response to increasing passenger dissatisfaction regarding flight cancellations and delays, the US Department of Transportation (DOT) published the so-called Enhancing Airline Passenger Protections rules

1 Rachel Y Tang, 'Airline Passenger Rights: The Federal Role in Aviation Consumer Protection' (2016) Congressional Research Service R43078 <https://sgp.fas.org/crs/misc/R43078.pdf>.

2 Timothy Ravich, *Introduction to Aviation Law* (Foundation Press 2020) 294.

3 Matthew Schoonover, 'Oversold, Delayed, Rescheduled: Airline Passenger Rights and Protections' (2011) 35 Washington University Journal of Law & Policy 519, 532.

4 P.L. 114-190.

5 M Tanner Giar, 'United States Air Passenger Rights: Grounded or Cleared for Take-Off?' (2024) 40 Arizona Journal of International and Comparative Law 516.

6 Hannah Foote, 'Delayed Flights and Delayed Rights: It Is Time for the United States to Follow the European Union's Lead and Enact More States to Follow the European Union's Lead and Enact More Regulations to Protect Airline Passengers Regulations to Protect Airline Passengers' (2023) 88 Journal of Air Law and Commerce 919, 929.

DOI: 10.4324/9781003746164-65

in 2009 as enhanced in 2011.[7] While the DOT rules offer protections to passengers, those are often situation specific instead of a more comprehensive regulation. For instance, a key provision is found under Section 49 of the US federal rule §41712, which broadly prohibits unfair and deceptive practices. A new rule on disclosure of prices up front which should have been applicable in April 2025 has been blocked by the U.S. Court of Appeals for the fifth circuit.[8] Currently, there are no specific laws providing for compensation in case of cancellation or for general delay, however, airlines may opt to provide a form of compensation to their passengers at their discretion.[9]

There have been multiple proposed Airline Passengers' Bill of Rights in the US, aiming to align US law with places like Europe and Canada by providing automatic compensation and rights for passengers during flight disruptions, including delays, cancellations, denied boarding, and lost luggage.[10] The latest to date was introduced in Senate in 2023, and could have brought the US system closer to the EU while better protecting passengers, by offering a fixed compensation and making the rules more accessible.[11] It would provide passengers suffering from a delay between one and four hours an automatic refund as well as an obligation to arrange alternative transport.[12] Passengers experiencing a delay superior to four hours would on top of the refund and re-routing be entitled to a cash compensation of $1,350 and a meal.[13] Any overnight delay would entitle the passenger to compensation for the cost of the hotel.[14] The proposal also covers unreasonable fees. It would also make it an unfair or deceptive practice to attribute a delay or cancellation to force majeure event unless it can be proven that such event took place.[15] However, so far, there has been no movement on this latest Bill.

---

7 DOT, 'Final Rule on Enhancing Airline Passenger Protections' (21 September 2012) <https://www.transportation.gov/airconsumer/final-rule-enhancing-airline-passenger-protections>.

8 *Airlines for America and others v Department of Transportation*, Case No. 24-60231.

9 See: Ruwantissa Abeyratne, *Is Air Law International: Perspectives from Practice and Global Regulation* (Ethics International Press 2025) 573.

10 See for example; S.3222 introduced in November 2021.

11 S.178 – Airline Passengers' Bill of Rights, 118th Congress (2023–2024). See: Noor Ain, 'Navigating Passenger Compensation: Implications for Airlines Navigating Passenger Compensation: Implications for Airlines and Consumers' (2024) 89 Journal of Air Law and Commerce 507, 517.

12 Section 103(1)(A) and (B).

13 Section 103(2)(A)–(D). Kris Van Cleave and Analisa Novak, 'Senators Push for "Passenger Bill of Rights" that Would Give Travelers at Least $1,350 if Bumped Due to Oversold Flight' *CBS News* (6 February 2023) <https://www.cbsnews.com/news/passenger-bill-of-rights-airline-delays-cancellations-baggage-seating-fees/>.

14 Section 103(3).

15 Section 104.

Proposed Airline Passengers' Bill of Rights (2023)

Scenario	Compensation
Delay 1–4 Hours	Automatic refund + alternative transport.
Delay >4 Hours	Refund + re-routing + **$1,350 cash** + meal.
Overnight Delay	Hotel cost coverage.
Force Majeure	Airlines must prove weather/security caused cancellation.

While no comprehensive Bill has been passed, some of these ideas were explored under the Biden administration. In 2024, the FAA Reauthorization Act of 2024[16] – named the Securing Growth and Robust Leadership in American Aviation Act – was introduced which contained some provisions on "passenger experience improvements." A key part of this Act is the implementation of the DOT automatic refund rule which was introduced in October 2024. The regulations mandate that airlines operating flights to, from, or within the United States must provide automatic refunds to passengers if their flights are cancelled or significantly changed for any reason – including bad weather, staffing, equipment, or air traffic control.[17] Such compensation is only available if alternative transportation or travel vouchers are not offered or are rejected by the passenger. That is the key condition; if an airline is able to book the passenger on another flight – on the same day or even the next – and the passenger accepts it, then the new rules do not apply.[18] But if the passenger refuses the rebooking, then he or she is entitled to the automatic full refund including taxes and fees, even on a nonrefundable ticket. This rule would have applied to both US and foreign airlines.

The Rule proposed to amend 14 CFR part 399 to add 14 CFR part 260 to define both cancelled flights and "significant change of flight itinerary."[19] Significant change would include flights which depart at least three hours late for domestic flights and six hours or more for international flights or arrive at least three hours late for domestic flights and six hours or more for international flights.[20] Significant change would also encompass departure from or arrival at a different airport than the one contracted

16 H.R. 3935.

17 Docket (DOT-OST-2022-0089) <https://www.federalregister.gov/documents/2024/04/26/2024-07177/refunds-and-other-consumer-protections>.

18 14 CFR part 260(1).

19 "Cancelled flight as a flight that was published in a carrier's Computer Reservation System (CRS) at the time of the ticket sale but not operated by the carrier."

20 14 CFR part 260(1) and (2).

for.[21] Similarly, if the itinerary is changed resulting in more connection points than originally purchased.[22] Downgrading is also considered a significant change.[23] Finally, if the plane is substituted resulting in some accessibility features being unavailable, it will fall under this category of significant change.[24] Passengers would have received an automatic compensation of $200–$300 for domestic delays of at least three hours, $375–$525 for six-hour delays, and $750–$775 for nine-hour delays.

Scenario	**Refund Eligibility**
Cancelled Flight	Full refund (including taxes/fees) if no alternative flight/voucher is offered **or** passenger rejects rebooking.
Significant Change (domestic flight)	- Departure/arrival ≥3 hours late. - Different airport. - Increased connections. - Downgrading. - Inaccessible substitute aircraft.
Significant Change (international flight)	- Departure/arrival ≥6 hours late. - Other criteria same as domestic.
Refund Process	Airlines must inform passengers of refund rights **before** offering vouchers/alternatives.

The Rule also provides from an amendment to 14 CFR parts 259 and 399 to require US and foreign airlines and ticket agents to inform consumers that they are entitled to a refund of the ticket before making an offer for alternative transportation or travel credits, vouchers, or other compensation in lieu of refunds. Airlines will also have an obligation to promptly inform passengers in case of delay or cancellation. There was some discussion regarding the amount of compensation with the DOT analysing the rules in Canada, Europe, and the UK.[25] However, in September 2025, the DOT announced its plan to withdraw the Rule as they were not consistent with the department priorities.[26]

21 14 CFR part 260(3). US Department of Transportation, 'Biden-Harris Administration Announces Final Rule Requiring Automatic Refunds of Airline Tickets and Ancillary Service Fees' (24 April 2024) <https://www.transportation.gov/briefing-room/biden-harris-administration-announces-final-rule-requiring-automatic-refunds-airline>.

22 14 CFR part 260(4).

23 14 CFR part 260(5).

24 14 CFR part 260(7).

25 Advanced notice of proposed rulemaking (ANPRM) Docket No. DOT-OST-2024-0062 <https://www.federalregister.gov/documents/2024/12/11/2024-28930/airline-passenger-rights>.

26 <https://www.reginfo.gov/public/do/eAgendaViewRule?pubId=202504&RIN=2105-AF20>.

At present, US laws do not mandate airlines to compensate for missed connections or delays or cancellations, nor do they require airlines to provide passengers with rebooking or reimbursement of expenses related to food or accommodation. Instead, it is left to the goodwill of airlines and the terms of their contracts of carriage resulting in compensation varying greatly between airlines.[27] For instance, all airlines provide a meal or meal voucher in case of controllable delays of over three hours or cancellation.[28] Most airlines, except for Frontier, provide for accommodation for overnight delays.[29] Similarly, they all provide for a rebooking at no additional costs on their next available flights. However, only a few airlines offer rebooking on alternative airlines.[30] None of the airlines provide for cash compensation for controllable delays of over three hours and only Alaska, Hawaiian, Jetblue, and Southwest offer a credit voucher. Only Alaska and Hawaiian offer frequent flyer miles for delays over three hours.[31]

Airlines with most comprehensive delay commitments

Commitment	AS	AA	DL	HA	B6
Rebook on Same Airline at No Cost	v	v	v	v	v
Rebook on Partner/Other Airline at No Cost (where agreement exists)	v	v	v	v	v
Meal/Voucher for Delay ≥3 Hours	v	v	v	v	v
Complimentary Hotel for Overnight Delay + Transport	v	v	v	v	v
Credit/Voucher for Delay ≥3 Hours	v	x	x	v	v
Frequent Flyer Miles for Delay ≥3 Hours	v	x	x	v	x

Note: v = yes; x = no

27 M. Tanner Giar, 'United States Air Passenger Rights: Grounded or Cleared for Take-off?' (2024) 40 Arizona Journal of International and Comparative Law 516.

28 See: DOT, 'Airline Cancellation and Delay Dashboard' <https://www.transportation.gov/airconsumer/airline-cancellation-delay-dashboard>.

29 Point 12 of Frontier's Customer Service Plan <https://www.flyfrontier.com/legal/customer-service-plan?mobile=true>.

30 Frontier, Southwest and Spirit do not offer such option. See: DOT, 'Airline Cancellation and Delay Dashboard' <https://www.transportation.gov/airconsumer/airline-cancellation-delay-dashboard>

31 See: DOT, 'Airline Cancellation and Delay Dashboard' <https://www.transportation.gov/airconsumer/airline-cancellation-delay-dashboard>.

For cancellation, airlines are not legally required to pay for additional expenses beyond providing a refund for the ticket price.[32] In fact, airlines' policies tend to offer exactly the same commitments as for controllable delays. While all airlines are willing to rebook passengers on their next available flight at no extra cost and a meal or voucher, none have committed to cash compensation. The same airlines – namely Alaska, Hawaiian, Jetblue, and Southwest – offer a credit voucher, and only Alaska and Hawaiian offer frequent flyer miles for cancellation resulting in a delay of over three hours.[33]

Commitments for controllable delays and cancellations[34]

Service Commitment Category	AS	G4	AA	DL	F9	HA	B6	WN	NK	UA
Rebooking (same carrier)	Yes	Yes	Yes	Yes	Yes	Yes	Yes	Yes	Yes	Yes
Rebooking (interline/partner)	Yes	No	Yes	Yes	No	Yes	Yes	No	No	Yes
Meal/Meal Vouchers	Yes	Yes	Yes	Yes	Yes	Yes	Yes	Yes	Yes	Yes
Complimentary Lodging	Yes	Yes	Yes	Yes	No	Yes	Yes	Yes	Yes	Yes
Monetary Compensation (cash)	No	No	No	No	No	No	No	No	No	No
Travel Credit/Vouchers	Yes	No	No	No	No	Yes	Yes	Yes	No	No

The only mandatory compensation in US law relates to denied boarding. While the practice of overbooking is not prohibited in itself, airlines must seek volunteers first, providing them with benefits.[35] If an insufficient number of volunteers come forward, the airline can involuntarily deny passengers. Passengers involuntarily denied boarding are entitled to compensation which varies depending on the extent of the passenger's subsequent delay, from 200% of the one-way ticket fare, with a maximum of $1,075 for delays of one to two hours, to 400% of the fare, with a maximum of $2,150 for late domestic arrival of over two hours or

32 Noor Ain, 'Navigating Passenger Compensation: Implications for Airlines Navigating Passenger Compensation: Implications for Airlines and Consumers' (2024) 89 Journal of Air Law and Commerce 507, 523.

33 See: DOT, 'Airline Cancellation and Delay Dashboard' <https://www.transportation.gov/airconsumer/airline-cancellation-delay-dashboard>.

34 AS: Alaska; G4: Allegiant; AA: American; DL: Delta; F9: Frontier; HA: Hawaiian; B6: JetBlue; WN: Southwest; NK: Spirit; UA: United.

35 14 CFR Part 250. See: M Schoonover, 'Oversold, Delayed, Rescheduled: Airline Passenger Rights and Protections', (2011) 35 Washington University Journal of Law & Policy 519–45.

four hours on international flights.[36] No compensation is due when the passenger arrives to their final destination within one hour of the originally scheduled arrival. In addition, paid services which are not available on the rebooked flight should be reimbursed. However, no compensation is due if the passenger does not comply with the contract of carriage, if the passenger is intoxicated or interferes with the duties of a flight crew member, engages in unruly behaviour or is "Having an offensive odour that is not caused by a disability or illness."[37] As of April 2021, passengers may not be involuntarily bumped once their "boarding pass has been collected or scanned and the passenger has boarded."[38]

Scenario	**Compensation**
Arrival ≤1 Hour Late	No compensation.
Arrival 1–2 Hours Late (domestic or international)	200% of one-way ticket price (max **$775**).
Domestic flight: Arrival **2+ hours late OR** airline fails to provide substitute travel	400% of one-way ticket price (max **$1,550**).
International flight: Arrival **4+ hours late OR** airline fails to provide substitute travel	400% of one-way ticket price (max **$1,550**).

Involuntarily denied boarding passengers are not eligible for compensation in case of aircraft change, weight and balance restrictions, downgrading, flights departing from a foreign location, and charter flights.[39] Compensation must be paid at the airport on the same day unless the substitute transportation leaves before the airline can pay the passenger, then the payment must be made within 24 hours.

There is no specific assistance or compensation for cancellation nor for general delay, however tarmac delays have their own very detailed provisions in 14 C.F.R.§ 259. The U.S. Department of Transportation imposes strict regulations, prohibiting airlines from keeping passengers

36 14 CFR Part 250.5(a)(2) and (3). DOT, 'Bumping & Oversales' (22 January 2025) <https://www.transportation.gov/individuals/aviation-consumer-protection/bumping-oversales#:~:text=Before%20an%20airline%20forces%20a,are%20willing%20to%20give%20up>.

37 14 CFR Part 250.6. DOT, 'Bumping & Oversales' (22 January 2025) <https://www.transportation.gov/individuals/aviation-consumer-protection/bumping-oversales#:~:text=Before%20an%20airline%20forces%20a,are%20willing%20to%20give%20up>.

38 14 CFR Parts 250 and 254 [Docket DOT-OST-2020-0251] <https://www.transportation.gov/sites/dot.gov/files/2021-01/Oversales%20and%20Domestic%20Baggage%20Final%20Rule.pdf>.

39 DOT, 'Bumping & Oversales' (22 January 2025) https://www.transportation.gov/individuals/aviation-consumer-protection/bumping-oversales#:~:text=Before%20an%20airline%20forces%20a,are%20willing%20to%20give%20up.

on the tarmac for more than three hours unless there is a safety or security issue or air traffic control deems that allowing the plane to move would disrupt airport operations.[40] For international flights, the limit is four hours.[41] Regardless of flight type, airlines must provide food and water within two hours of delay as well as functional lavatories and medical assistance when needed.[42] Passengers must also be informed of the status of the delay within 30 minutes and provide updates.[43] Whenever a suitable disembarkation point is available, carriers are required to promptly inform passengers on board that they have the opportunity to deplane.[44] Any failure could result in a fine up to $27,500 for each passenger on board the affected flight.[45] The DOT has, in fact, imposed fines on airlines not complying with the tarmac delay rule which requires airlines to return to the gate after three hours for national flights and four hours for international ones.[46] Tarmac delays – whether before take-off or after landing – do not typically require compensation for passengers on domestic flights.[47]

Scenario	Requirements
Domestic Flights	- Max 3-hour delay (exceptions: safety/ATC orders). - Food/water after 2 hours; functional lavatories/medical care.
International Flights	- Max 4-hour delay. - Same amenities as domestic.
Penalties	Fines up to **$27,500 per passenger** for violations.

The new DOT rule, effective in June 2024, requires airlines to refund baggage fees if checked bags arrive 12 hours or more late for domestic flights, starting from when the flight arrives at the gate. For international flights, refunds are required if baggage is delivered 15 to 30 hours late,

40 Based on the power conferred by Section 2308 of the FAA Extension, Safety, and Security Act of 2016. 14 C.F.R.§ 259.4 requires a contingency plan <https://www.ecfr.gov/current/title-14/chapter-II/subchapter-A/part-259> See: DOT 'Tarmac Delay Rule' (25 October 2019) <https://www.regulations.gov/document/DOT-OST-2019-0144-0001>.

41 14 C.F.R.§ 259.4 (c)(2).

42 14 C.F.R.§ 259.4 (c)(4) and (5).

43 14 C.F.R.§ 259.4 (c)(6).

44 14 C.F.R.§ 259.4 (c)(7).

45 David Goguen, 'Tarmac Delays and Airline Passenger Rights' (*NOLO*, 13 May 2024) <https://www.nolo.com/legal-encyclopedia/tarmac-delays-airline-passenger-rights-33011.html>.

46 Vincent Correia and Noura Rouissi, 'Global, Regional and National Air Passenger Rights – Does the Patchwork Work?' (2015) 40 Air and Space Law 123, 133.

47 M. Giar, 'United States Air Passenger Rights: Grounded or Cleared for Take-off?' (2024) 40 Arizona Journal of International and Comparative Law 516.

depending on flight duration.[48] However, it is not clear what the obligations of airlines are regarding essential expenses for delayed baggage.

The US also has a proposal to prohibit airlines from charging families extra to guarantee a child 13 or younger will sit next to a parent or adult travel partner.[49] The U.S. Department of Transportation has also announced a new regulation that increases protections for passengers with disabilities, including those who use wheelchairs.[50] The rule mandates airlines to provide safe and dignified assistance to passengers with disabilities, implement hands-on training for employees and contractors assisting these passengers and handling wheelchairs, and take specific actions to protect passengers when a wheelchair is damaged or delayed during transport. The rule contains varying implementation timelines ranging from 16 January 2025 to 17 June 2026 for training requirements.[51]

The United States' approach to air passenger rights diverges fundamentally from other national regimes such as European Union Regulation 261 or the APPR. In the United States, passenger rights derive from a fragmented legal and regulatory framework that combines limited federal statutes, DOT rules, and airline-specific contracts of carriage. This system does not mandate compensation for delays or cancellations, except in cases of involuntary denied boarding, where compensation is calculated as a percentage of the ticket price subject to statutory caps. It also offers significantly weaker protections across all key areas. Additional protections are narrowly tailored, such as tarmac delay limits and amenities during extended ground holds. Beyond these specific requirements, assistance such as meals, lodging, and alternate transportation remains largely discretionary and varies by carrier.

The most striking difference lies in compensation for flight disruptions. While the EU mandates automatic compensation for qualifying delays and cancellations, the US system provides no such guaranteed payments, instead limiting passenger recourse to refunds only when airlines fail to offer acceptable alternatives. This fundamental disparity creates a substantial gap in consumer protection, leaving American travellers without financial recourse and to the goodwill of airlines. For overbooking, the US employs a variable compensation model tied to ticket prices, with amounts ranging from 200% to 400% of the one-way fare but capped at $1,550–$2,150, while

48 14 CFR part 260(1)–(3).
<https://www.transportation.gov/briefing-room/biden-harris-administration-announces-final-rule-requiring-automatic-refunds-airline>.

49 Family Seating in Air Transportation, Docket DOT-OST-2024-0091.

50 14 CFR Part 382, Ensuring safe accommodation for air travellers with disabilities using wheelchairs, 17 December 2024.

51 §382.141.

the EU's fixed compensation structure ensures more predictability. Perhaps the most significant divergence appears in the area of passenger care during disruptions. The EU regulation mandates comprehensive assistance including meals, accommodations, and communication facilities for delays exceeding two to three hours, regardless of cause. In stark contrast, US law imposes no such general obligations, with its tarmac delay rules representing the only area where specific care requirements exist.

Enforcement mechanisms also differ markedly. In the EU, passengers may pursue claims directly through national enforcement bodies or civil courts, with airlines liable for compensation unless they demonstrate extraordinary circumstances. In the US, enforcement is primarily regulatory, conducted by the DOT through fines and corrective actions, while individual recourse is largely confined to contract law or airline goodwill gestures.

The proposed but unimplemented US Airline Passengers' Bill of Rights and the withdrawn 2024 DOT compensation rule reflect ongoing efforts to align American standards more closely with international models, including fixed compensation for lengthy delays. However, as of the current regulatory landscape, the US continues to rely on a hybrid model of limited federal oversight and carrier discretion, whereas the EU upholds a standardized, compensatory, and assistance-oriented regime.

In essence, EU Regulation 261 provides a more comprehensive and directly financially compensatory framework for flight disruptions that are within an airline's control, offering passengers a clearer path to fixed compensation for inconvenience. The US system, while providing essential consumer protections, places more emphasis on refunds for unfulfilled travel and relies more on airline-specific policies for compensation or care during delays and cancellations not caused by overbooking.

Comparison with EU Regulation

Category	**United States DOT Rules**	**EU Regulation 261/2004**
Flight Delay	- Refund only if ≥3h (domestic) or ≥6h (international). - No cash compensation.	≥3h: €250–€600 (by distance).
Cancellation	- Full refund if no alternative flight/ voucher accepted. - No cash compensation.	<14d notice: Refund or re-routing + €250–600 compensation (by distance).
Overbooking	- Compensation: 200%–400% of ticket price (max $1,550–$2,150). - No payout if rebooked ≤1h.	Volunteer first; €250–€600 (by distance) if denied boarding
Baggage Compensation	- Refund baggage fee if ≥12h late (domestic) or 15–30h (international). - Max $3,800 liability for loss.	Not specified.

Bibliography

Primary Sources

- Advanced notice of proposed rulemaking (ANPRM) Docket No. DOT-OST-2024-0062 <https://www.federalregister.gov/documents/2024/12/11/2024-28930/airline-passenger-rights> accessed 23 December 2025.
- *Airlines for America and others v Department of Transportation*, case No. 24-60231.
- Airline Passengers' Bill of Rights, 118th Congress (2023–2024).
- Code of Federal Regulations, Title 14. Chapter II, Subchapter A, Part 250 (14 CFR part 250).
- Docket (DOT-OST-2022-0089) <https://www.federalregister.gov/documents/2024/04/26/2024-07177/refunds-and-other-consumer-protections> accessed 23 December 2025.
- DOT, 'Airline Passenger Rights' 2105-AF20 (2025) <https://www.reginfo.gov/public/do/eAgendaViewRule?pubId=202504&RIN=2105-AF20> accessed 23 December 2025.
- Family Seating in Air Transportation, Docket DOT-OST-2024-0091 <https://www.transportation.gov/sites/dot.gov/files/2024-09/Family%20Seating%20in%20Air%20Transportation%20DOT-OST-2024-0091.pdf> accessed 23 December 2025.
- H.R. 3935- FAA Reauthorization Act of 2024 <https://www.congress.gov/bill/118th-congress/house-bill/3935> accessed 23 December 2025.
- H.R. 636- FAA Extension, Safety, and Security Act of 2016 <https://www.congress.gov/bill/114th-congress/house-bill/636/text> accessed 23 December 2025.
- Public Law 114-190, 15 July 2016 <https://www.congress.gov/114/plaws/publ190/PLAW-114publ190.pdf> accessed 23 December 2025.
- 14 CFR Parts 250 and 254 [Docket DOT–OST–2020–0251]- Implementing Certain Provisions of the tickets Act and Revisions to Denied Boarding Compensation and Domestic Baggage Liability Limits <https://www.transportation.gov/sites/dot.gov/files/2021-01/Oversales%20and%20Domestic%20Baggage%20Final%20Rule.pdf> accessed 23 December 2025.
- 14 CFR Part 382- nondiscrimination on the basis of disability in air travel <https://www.ecfr.gov/current/title-14/chapter-II/subchapter-D/part-382> accessed 23 December 2025.
- S.3222- Stop Shut-Offs During Shutdowns Act <https://www.congress.gov/bill/119th-congress/senate-bill/3222/all-actions> accessed 23 December 2025.

Secondary Sources

- Abeyratne, R., *Is Air Law International: Perspectives from Practice and Global Regulation* (Ethics International Press 2025).
- Ain, N., 'Navigating Passenger Compensation: Implications for Airlines Navigating Passenger Compensation: Implications for Airlines and Consumers' (2024) 89 Journal of Air Law and Commerce 507.
- Correia, V. and Rouissi, N. 'Global, Regional and National Air Passenger Rights – Does the Patchwork Work?' (2015) 40 Air and Space Law 123.

- DOT, 'Airline Cancellation and Delay Dashboard' <https://www.transportation.gov/airconsumer/airline-cancellation-delay-dashboard> accessed 23 December 2025.
- DOT, 'Biden-Harris Administration Announces Final Rule Requiring Automatic Refunds of Airline Tickets and Ancillary Service Fees' (24 April 2024) <https://www.transportation.gov/briefing-room/biden-harris-administration-announces-final-rule-requiring-automatic-refunds-airline> accessed 23 December 2025.
- DOT, 'Bumping & Oversales' (22 January 2025) <https://www.transportation.gov/individuals/aviation-consumer-protection/bumping-oversales#:~:text=Before%20an%20airline%20forces%20a,are%20willing%20to%20give%20up> accessed 23 December 2025.
- DOT, 'Final Rule on Enhancing Airline Passenger Protections' (21 September 2012) <https://www.transportation.gov/airconsumer/final-rule-enhancing-airline-passenger-protections> accessed 23 December 2025.
- DOT, 'Tarmac Delay Rule' (25 October 2019) <https://www.regulations.gov/document/DOT-OST-2019-0144-0001> accessed 23 December 2025.
- Foote, H., 'Delayed Flights and Delayed Rights: It Is Time for the United States to Follow the European Union's Lead and Enact More States to Follow the European Union's Lead and Enact More Regulations to Protect Airline Passengers Regulations to Protect Airline Passengers' (2023) 88 Journal of Air Law and Commerce 919.
- Frontier's Customer Service Plan <https://www.flyfrontier.com/legal/customer-service-plan?mobile=true> accessed 23 December 2025.
- Giar, M. T., 'United States Air Passenger Rights: Grounded or Cleared for Take-Off?' (2024) 40 Arizona Journal of International and Comparative Law 516.
- Goguen, D., 'Tarmac Delays and Airline Passenger Rights' (*NOLO*, 13 May 2024) <https://www.nolo.com/legal-encyclopedia/tarmac-delays-airline-passenger-rights-33011.html> accessed 23 December 2025.
- Ravich, T., *Introduction to Aviation Law* (Foundation Press 2020).
- Schoonover, M., 'Oversold, Delayed, Rescheduled: Airline Passenger Rights and Protections' (2011) 35 Washington University Journal of Law & Policy 519.
- Tang, R. Y., 'Airline Passenger Rights: The Federal Role in Aviation Consumer Protection' (2016) Congressional Research Service R43078 <https://sgp.fas.org/crs/misc/R43078.pdf> accessed 23 December 2025.
- US Department of Transportation, 'Biden-Harris Administration Announces Final Rule Requiring Automatic Refunds of Airline Tickets and Ancillary Service Fees' (24 April 2024) <https://www.transportation.gov/briefing-room/biden-harris-administration-announces-final-rule-requiring-automatic-refunds-airline> accessed 23 December 2025.
- Van Cleave, K. and Novak, A., 'Senators Push for "Passenger Bill of Rights" that Would Give Travelers at Least $1,350 if Bumped Due to Oversold Flight' *CBS News* (6 February 2023) <https://www.cbsnews.com/news/passenger-bill-of-rights-airline-delays-cancellations-baggage-seating-fees/> accessed 23 December 2025.

II.55

Uruguay

Uruguay has the *Cartilla de los Derechos del Usuario del Transporte Aéreo* which was initially introduced in 1997. It was not really extensive and was updated in 2024 by *Resolución Dinacia Nro 422/2024.*[1] It is a rather short document which mainly focuses on denial of boarding.

According to the *Resolución*, denied passengers have the right to re-routing and compensation – which is not precisely defined. Chapter I establishes that the compensation depends on the applicable norms and the place the overbooking occurred. If the delay exceeds four hours, passengers have the right to a meal and refreshment and when necessary, a hotel and transport. This assistance is also available if the delay results in the passengers losing their connection.

Passenger Rights	**Details**
Re-routing	No timeframe for the alternative flight (next one? within a day? a week?).
Compensation	Amount not specified; depends on "applicable norms" and location of overbooking.
Assistance for Delays >4hrs	Meal, refreshments, and (if needed) hotel + transport.
Exemptions	Not applicable for delays/cancellations due to **meteorological circumstances**.

It is not clear whether such protection also applies for delays in general or cancellations. Indeed, while the paragraph seems to only refer to denial of boarding, the last sentence of Chapter I stipulates that the previous paragraphs are not applicable in case of delay or cancellation due to meteorological circumstances.

1 *Direccion Nacional de Aviacion Civil e Infrastructura aeronautica, Resolucion N° 422-2024 <https://www.dinacia.gub.uy/sites/default/files/2024-12/_RESOLUCION_DINACIA_NRO_422-2024.pdf>.*

DOI: 10.4324/9781003746164-66

Chapter II relates to luggage but does not contain any specific provision for the destruction or damage of the latter. For loss of baggage, the *Resolución* lists the steps to be taken and that the passenger has the right for judicial redress of the damage caused by such loss.

The *Resolución* contains a specific provision regarding priority rule for children under 5 years old, elderly passengers over the age of 70, and passengers with reduced mobility.[2] This rule is similar to the one found in Brazil. It also requires pregnant women over six months of pregnancy to provide a medical authorization. Such provision aims to avoid potential conflict in carriers' different policies. Chapter III also regulates the transport of animals, allowing emotional support animals in the cabin.

Passenger Category	**Special Provisions**
Children <5, Elderly >70, Reduced Mobility	Priority boarding (similar to Brazil).
Pregnant Women (>6 months)	Must provide medical authorization.
Emotional Support Animals	Allowed in cabin.

Chapter V establishes a right to reimbursement for the part of the journey that was not used while Chapter VI regulates the liability limits in case of injury or death of the passenger or luggage. Yet again that provision is relatively short without many substantive rights provided. Finally, Chapter VII contains the minimum information that a carrier must share with a passenger such as which is the operating carrier.

The Uruguayan framework, the *Cartilla de los Derechos del Usuario del Transporte Aéreo*, represents a foundational but markedly minimalist approach to air passenger rights. Its primary orientation is the regulation of denied boarding, establishing core principles such as the right to re-routing, compensation, and basic assistance during lengthy delays. However, the Regulation's substantive content is characterized by significant gaps and ambiguities. Crucially, it omits fixed compensation amounts, leaving sums to undefined "applicable norms," does not mention its scope and remains silent on passenger rights in the event of cancellations not linked to overbooking. The *Cartilla*'s provisions on baggage are limited to loss, excluding damage or destruction. Unlike the other specific laws on the topic, it lacks essential legal definitions, particularly for force majeure, which invites legal uncertainty. The inclusion of specific rules for priority boarding and emotional support animals indicates a focus on particular operational and social aspects, yet this does not compensate for the overall lack of a comprehensive, rights-based structure. Uruguay's regulations

2 Chapter III.

are less comprehensive than Saudi or Brazilian frameworks for instance, prioritizing flexibility over passenger guarantees. In stark contrast, EU Regulation 261 establishes a detailed, prescriptive, and passenger-centric regime. It creates unambiguous, monetized rights triggered by specific circumstances.

The philosophical divergence between the two systems is profound. The Uruguayan model prioritizes regulatory flexibility and carrier discretion, resulting in a framework where guarantees are general and enforcement is likely deferred to individual legal action. The EU model, conversely, prioritizes legal certainty and robust passenger protection, shifting the balance of power toward the passenger through standardized, immediately actionable financial remedies. Consequently, while the Uruguayan resolution lays a preliminary groundwork for passenger rights, it does not establish the strong, self-executing protections that define the EU's regulatory approach. For passengers, the practical difference is between having a statement of principle (Uruguay) and possessing an enforceable claim with a predetermined value (EU). In summary, the 2024 Uruguayan update, while a positive step in affirming passenger rights, consolidates a model of minimal obligation.

Comparison with EU Regulation

Feature	Uruguay Resolution 422/2024	EU Regulation 261/2004
Delay Compensation	Only assistance. Compensation?	≥3h: €250–€600 (by distance).
Cancellation Rights	Compensation?	<14d notice: Refund or re-routing + €250–600 compensation (by distance).
Overbooking	Volunteers first; re-routing/refund + compensation.	Volunteer first; €250–€600 (by distance) if denied boarding.
Baggage Compensation	Not specified.	Not specified.

Bibliography

- Direccion Nacional de Aviacion Civil e Infrastructura aeronautica, Resolucion N° 422-2024 <https://www.dinacia.gub.uy/sites/default/files/2024-12/_RESOLUCION_DINACIA_NRO_422-2024.pdf>.

II.56

Venezuela

In 2009, Venezuela introduced rules on passenger rights which have been updated in 2016 and 2024. Also called General Conditions for Air Transport,[1] the *Providencia Administrativa* PRE-CJU-GDA-308–24 of 2024 repeals the previous regulation.[2] The scope of application of the General Conditions is quite large as they apply to both domestic and international scheduled and non-scheduled air transport services, irrespective of the nationality of the carrier, departing from or arriving in Venezuela – unless they enjoy more favourable compensation and assistance in the country of departure.[3] Those rules also cover free of charge transport operations when performed by a public air transport service operator.[4] Interestingly, according to the Conditions, successive flights are to be treated as a single operation when covered by a single contract of carriage in which case the de facto carrier's omission will be considered as omissions of the de jure carrier.[5] This approach differs from the solution adopted by the Court of Justice of the European Union in Emirates.[6]

The Conditions also apply to the information that public air transport service operators must provide to passengers before, during, and after the service is provided.[7] Similarly to the Argentinian or Malaysian law, the *Providencia Administrativa* contains a chapter dedicated on the formation

1 Despacho del Presidente, Providencia Administrativa PRE-CJU-353-09 (Instituto Nacional de Aeronáutica Civil, 14 December 2009); Providencia Administrativa PRE-CJU-GDA-398-16, published in the Gaceta Oficial N° 6.228 Extraordinario on 18 May 2016; Despacho del Presidente, Providencia Administrativa PRE-CJU-GDA-308-24, published in the Gaceta Oficial N° 43.000 on 5 November 2024.

2 Aurelio Fernandez Concheso, 'Nuevas Condiciones Generales de Transporte Aéreo' (21 April 2025) <https://aureliofernandezconcheso.com/es/nuevas-condiciones-generales-de-transporte-aereo/> accessed 22 December 2025.

3 Article 2(a).

4 Article 2(d).

5 Article 2(e).

6 Case C-173/07 *Emirates Airlines – Direktion für Deutschland v Schenkel*.

7 Article 2(h) in conjunction with Article 5.

DOI: 10.4324/9781003746164-67

of the contract and the information rights of the passenger. Chapter II also contains a provision on baggage policies which must contain the clear information accessible to passengers.[8] The rules made it clear that passengers must be treated with dignity and respect by airlines and their staff.[9] Interestingly, Article 7 expressly allows airlines to enact more beneficial compensation for passengers in relation to damages caused by destruction, loss, or damage to checked or hand luggage.

Chapter III is dedicated to the obligations and rights of passengers, as found in the Saudi Arabian Regulation. Article 9 establishes that passengers must arrive at least two hours in advance for domestic flights and three hours for international ones while Article 25 stipulates that the check-in area may only be closed one hour before the flight for domestic flights and two for international flight.[10] Article 12 requires passengers to ensure at all time "respect, courtesy, and compliance with the instructions imposed by current legislation." The article goes a step further by noting that

> Disturbance of public order by passengers may result in justifiable denial of boarding and the payment of penalties and price differences for flight rescheduling. If the passenger's conduct warrants it, the necessary security or enforcement measures and procedures will be applied to guarantee civil aviation safety and operational security. Unlawful conduct may result in civil, criminal, and administrative liability for the damages caused.[11]

Requirement	**Consequence of Violation**
Arrive 2hrs (domestic)/3hrs (international) before flight.	Denial of boarding (no refund).
Maintain "respect, courtesy, and compliance."	Denial of boarding + penalties + legal liability (civil/criminal).

The *Providencia Administrativa* contains a provision on the protection of personal data which can only be used to formalize a reservation or execute the contract. Airlines and any intermediaries have the obligation under that law to protect those data.[12] The General Conditions also

8 Article 6.

9 Article 10.

10 Article 25.

11 "La alteración del orden público por parte del pasajero, podrá ocasionar la denegación de embarque de manera justificada y el pago de penalidades y diferencias de precio por reprogramación de su vuelo. Si la conducta del Pasajero lo amerita, se aplicarán las medidas y procedimientos de seguridad o coerción necesarios para garantizar la seguridad de la aviación civil y la seguridad operacional. La conducta contraria a derecho podrá generar responsabilidad civil, penal y administrativa por los daños ocasionados."

12 Article 14.

enshrined a service quality obligation which requires airlines to man each of the airports they operate with personnel duly qualified and trained in the area of traffic and quality of service.[13] Moreover, those staff members who have direct contact with the public must be trained every 12 months or when changes occur in the norms.

Denial of boarding, cancellation, and delays are dealt in a similar manner as under the EU legislation and other national regimes by granting passengers the right to care and assistance, compensation and reimbursement. Overbooking of tickets is expressly and completely prohibited. As a result, airlines will be liable for any "immediate and indirect harmful consequences it caused to the passenger."[14] Denial of boarding is dealt with in Article 29 which entitles passengers to financial compensation as established in Article 30, paragraphs a, b, c, and d unless the situation falls within one of the eight exceptions listed: 1) an act or attempt which could compromises the protection of "passengers, crews, the public, ground personnel, aircraft, airports, and their facilities"; 2) unruly or insubordinate passengers; 3) intoxicated or under the influence passengers; 4) the passenger's in very poor health condition; 5) passengers who does not possess the valid documentation required to travel; 6) passengers late at check-in or for boarding; 7) the passenger who allegedly, by action or omission, violates national legislation; and 8) passengers with a forged or illegally purchased ticket. Except in case of an alleged violation of national legislation, the passenger is entitled to reschedule their trip once "the act that motivated the denial has ceased." Those passengers will have to bear the price differences and potential penalties.[15]

The rights in case of cancellation attributable to the carrier are found in Article 30 and require the airline to offer an alternative transportation or reimbursement to the affected passenger in accordance with Article 33.[16] The affected passengers are also entitled to assistance – as found in Article 34 – which must be commensurate with the waiting time.[17] Additionally, passengers are also entitled to compensation as stipulated in Article 32.[18] If the passenger affected by the cancellation has an all-inclusive package or a combined trip organized or marketed by the air operator, the latter must compensate and make the necessary arrangements for rescheduling,

13 Article 20.
14 Article 29.
15 Article 29.
16 Article 30(a).
17 Article 30(b).
18 Article 30(c).

payment of penalties, and corresponding price differences, on behalf of the passenger.[19]

Airlines are exempted from their obligation of assistance and compensation in case of cancellation when passengers have been notified 15 days in advance.[20] Similarly, the exemption applies if the passengers are informed less than 15 days but no less than 24 hours in advance and an alternative flight which allowed the passenger to reach the final destination.[21] Unlike the EU law and other national law, the *Providencia Administrativa* does not specify a time within which the new flight must depart or arrive. If the passenger cannot travel on the alternative flight, the carrier must provide another flight on the same route at the passenger's convenience without additional costs. In that instance, the passenger is entitled to compensation.[22] In the event that the flight cancellation is due to unforeseen circumstances or force majeure, the affected passenger will be exempt from paying penalties and fare changes, regardless of the date on which the contracted flight materializes.[23] The passenger can also request a refund without any penalty.[24] When a flight is cancelled due to an unforeseen event or force majeure and the passenger does not accept any of the alternatives proposed by the carrier, then the latter will be released of its obligation to assist or compensate.[25]

Notice Period	**Passenger Rights**
>15 Days	No compensation.
<15 Days but >24hrs	Alternative flight (no time limit specified) **or** refund + 25% compensation.
Force Majeure	No compensation; refund allowed without penalties.

The burden of proof regarding the date and time the passenger was informed of the flight cancellation rests with the airline operator. Likewise, the airline operator must keep passengers affected by the flight cancellation informed at all times.[26]

Delayed passengers are entitled to assistance depending on the waiting time.[27] The passenger in an all-inclusive package or a combined trip, even if not organized by the airline, is entitled to assistance and compensation

19 Article 30(d).
20 Article 30(e).
21 Article 30(f).
22 Article 30(g).
23 Article 30(h).
24 Article 30(i).
25 Article 30(j).
26 Article 30.
27 Article 31(a).

for damages caused by the delay.[28] When the delay is attributable to the carrier and the flight ends up being cancelled, passengers are entitled to refund or re-routing, assistances and compensation.[29] If the passenger is informed of the delay, and the flight is not considered cancelled under the General Conditions, and it is impossible for the passenger to travel at the new time, the airline is under the obligation to transfer the passenger to their final destination on the next flight and same route operated by the carrier or any other operator, subject to the acceptance of the passenger. The passenger will be entitled to assistance and compensation as established in Article 31 (b).[30] If the passenger does not accept any alternative or considers the trip is no longer justified, they will be entitled to reimbursement as found in section (a) of Article 33 as well as a compensation equivalent to 25% of the value of the ticket.[31] Article 31 (f) makes it clear that reimbursement for other services or package contracted through an agent or intermediary is not subject to the General Conditions. Passengers must be kept informed at all times.[32] The burden of proof is on the operating carrier.[33]

Airlines can escape their obligation to assist and their liability when the delay is caused by unforeseen circumstances or force majeure.[34] None of those two terms are defined in Article 3 of the General Conditions. Airlines face administrative investigation for any delay exceeding one hour which is attributable to the carrier.[35]

The right of compensation is found in Article 32 of the *Providencia Administrativa*. Unlike other jurisdictions, the Venezuelan legislator did not opt for a flat-rate compensation or one proportionate with the distance of the flight but instead the compensation is proportionate to the ticket price. Consequently, passengers are entitled to financial compensation equivalent to 25% the ticket price if the passenger did not start his or her journey. Otherwise, the 25% will be calculated on the value of the unexecuted segments.[36] This amount must be paid in the same currency in which the air ticket was purchased[37] and on the day of the event or no later than three days after.[38] Moreover, the General Conditions makes it clear

28 Article 31(b).
29 Article 31(c).
30 Article 31(d).
31 Article 31(e).
32 Article 31(h).
33 Article 31(j).
34 Article 31(i).
35 Article 31(k).
36 Article 32(a).
37 Article 32(b).
38 Article 32(c).

that the right of compensation does not cease and is independent of any alternative transport arrangements mandated by the law itself.[39] Finally, Article 32 (f) stipulates that passengers can resort to judicial proceedings in case the carrier fails to comply with its obligations.

Article 33 regulates the right to a refund and re-routing. It grants the right to a full refund in the same currency as the purchased ticket within seven days.[40] Airlines must provide passengers with a written payment commitment expressly indicating the agreed amount and the date of payment.[41] If the journey is no longer appropriate due to the delay or cancellation, the airline must offer a return flight to the point of departure on the next available flight without any additional cost to the passenger.[42] Any failure to comply with this provision allows the passenger to resort to judicial proceedings.[43] When passengers elect the re-routing and the city or region is served by more than one airport, the passengers must be re-routed to the same airport. If, due to unforeseen circumstance, unforeseeable event, or force majeure, the passenger is transferred to another airport, the air operator is obliged to transport the passenger and their luggage to the contracted destination airport.[44]

The *Providencia Administrativa* also stipulates that any advance flight by more than one hour entitles passengers to assistance and compensation – unless the passenger decides to cancel their trip which then would entitle them to a refund.[45]

	Assistance	**Compensation**	**Reimbursement or Re-routing**
Denial of Boarding	Yes.	Yes, 25% of the value of the ticket if not agreeing with alternative flights.	Yes, full refund.
Cancellation	Yes, if informed <15 days and no alternative flight.	Yes, if informed <15 days and no alternative flight. 25% of the value of the ticket.	Yes, full refund.

(*Continued*)

39 Article 32(e).

40 Article 33(a)(1). Passengers with package tour or all-inclusive packages are also covered- Article 33(a)(4).

41 Article 33(a)(2).

42 Article 33(a)(3).

43 Article 33(a)(5).

44 Article 33(c).

45 Article 36.

(Continued)

	Assistance	Compensation	Reimbursement or Re-routing
Delay	Yes.	Yes, 25% of the value of the ticket if not agreeing with alternative flights.	Full refund if not agreeing with alternative flights.
Flight Departure Advanced by More Than 1 Hour	Yes.	Yes.	Yes, if the passenger decides to cancel the journey.

The level of assistance is found in Article 34 and includes non-alcoholic beverages, snacks, and complete meals, depending on the waiting time.[46] After 30 minutes, passengers are entitled to constant hydration with non-alcoholic beverages. After two hours, the airline must provide snacks and beverages. Finally, any delay of more than four hours entitles passengers to a full meal – breakfast, lunch, or dinner, depending on the time – comprising of a portion of protein, carbohydrates, and vegetables.[47]

	30 minutes	2 hours	4 hours
Beverages	Yes.	Yes.	Yes.
Snacks	No.	Yes.	No.
Full Meal	No.	No.	Yes.

When airlines make use of vouchers, the value of the voucher must be commensurate with the food to be purchased.[48] Article 34 also stipulates that the food must be of quality, adequate nutritional value and hygiene.[49] The General Conditions goes a step further by noting that passengers with special dietary needs must notify the carrier, and the latter will ensure that assistance is provided for such needs.[50] Such inclusion might in fact open the door to abuse. Additionally, it does seem unfair airlines will need to cater to a need they might not have been aware of. The assistance must be provided in priority to persons with disabilities, special medical

46 Article 34(a)(1).
47 Article 34(e).
48 Article 34(a)(1)(ii).
49 Article 34(a)(1)(i).
50 Article 34(a)(1)(iii).

conditions, pregnant women, the elderly, children, adolescents, and their companions.[51]

When the flight is for reasons attributable to the air operator, the latter must offer accommodation to passengers in hotels of at least three stars "ensuring that they offer the conditions of quality, comfort, hygiene and personal safety established for this type of accommodation."[52] Additionally, airlines must guarantee safe and efficient transportation between the airport and the place of accommodation.[53] Passengers are also entitled to two phone calls, internet connection, and any other means of communication.[54] For passengers living at the place of departure, airlines must transfer them from the airport to their residence and back to the airport on the date and time of the new flight at no cost.[55]

The *Providencia Administrativa* establishes minimum rights for upgrading and downgrading.[56] Like other laws, airlines cannot charge for any involuntary upgrading.[57] In case of downgrading, the airline is liable to reimburse the difference in value of the ticket and pay a compensation of 25% of the value of the affected part of the ticket.[58]

Detailed rules for passengers with reduced mobility are also found in the Venezuelan law.[59] Article 41 recognizes an obligation of the airline operator to compensate the passenger with 30% of the value of the unused ticket. Passengers may reschedule the contracted flight but will be liable to pay any penalty established in addition to the difference in value of the ticket for the segment affected by the rescheduling.

Unlike the European Regulation but similarly to other national laws, the General Conditions also include provisions implementing the Warsaw or Montreal Convention, such as compensation in case of death or bodily injury.

Chapter VII is dedicated to detailed rules on luggage, such as baggage allowance, excess of luggage, transport of luggage or firearms. It includes the luggage allowance of 23 kg on domestic and international flights.[60] Passengers on business class on international flights will have an allowance up to three pieces of 23 kg while economic class could have up to two

51 Article 34(f).
52 Article 34(b).
53 Article 34(c).
54 Article 34(c).
55 Article 34(c).
56 Article 37.
57 Article 37(a).
58 Article 37(b).
59 Article 39.
60 Article 43(a) and b).

pieces.[61] Passengers have the right to a 10 kg hand luggage free of charge as long as the dimensions, characteristics, and content allow its transport in the aircraft cabin.[62] This rule does not apply to aircraft with a capacity of less than 30 seats.[63]

Chapter VIII relates to claims connected to the loss, damage, or destruction of a baggage. Article 54 stipulates that in case of loss, destruction, or damage to checked baggage, the airline operator shall be obligated to compensate the passenger with an amount equivalent to 17 Special Drawing Rights (SDR) per kilogram of gross weight of the baggage. Article 55 establishes that airlines are liable for any damages caused to the passenger due to the delay in the delivery of checked baggage at the final destination of the contracted flight. Airlines are under the obligation to immediately reimburse the passenger for the expenses incurred – evidenced by invoices or supporting documents – as a result of the delay in baggage delivery. Those expenses must be reasonable and proportionate – however, none of those terms are defined by the law and, therefore, open to interpretation. Moreover, the passenger has a right to compensation of 100 SDR.[64]

Issue	**Compensation**	**Notes**
Loss/Destruction	17 SDR/kg (checked); 1,000 SDR (carry-on).	Airlines exempt for passenger negligence/force majeure.
Delay	100 SDR + reasonable expenses (with invoices).	Must be "proportionate" (undefined).
Allowance	23 kg (domestic/ international); 10 kg hand luggage (excl. small aircraft).	Business class: 3 × 23 kg; economy: 2 × 23 kg.

In case of loss, destruction, or damage to carry-on baggage caused by reasons attributable to the airline, the latter must compensate the passenger with 1,000 SDR. In addition, carriers must also reimburse any emergency products or clothing brought by the passengers.[65] This obligation as well as the special declaration is very similar to what is found in Brazil. Airlines will be fully or partially exonerated from their liability if they can prove that the event that caused the damage or contributed to its occurrence was caused by the passenger's omission, negligence, incompetence,

61 Article 43(c)(1) and (2).
62 Article 43(d).
63 Article 43(f).
64 Article 56.
65 Article 57.

imprudence, or carelessness.[66] Similarly, when the damage was caused by an act of God or force majeure, or by a defect or flaw inherent in the baggage, airlines will be freed from their liability.

Article 60 stipulates,

> The Carrier or air operator may not benefit from the liability limits established in these General Conditions of Air Transport when it is proven that the damage, destruction, loss or delay of the baggage that gave rise to the passenger's claim originated or is the result of an action or omission of its employees, dependents, managers or intermediaries, with the intention of causing it or was the product of imprudence, negligence or non-compliance with established procedures or common logic.

This provision might give rise to many conflicts due to its vagueness.

For the General Conditions, connecting flights are considered as a single operation even if bought separately. The responsibility for checked baggage and carry-on baggage rests with the airline operator that operated the segment of the route on which the delay, loss, destruction, or damage occurred, unless one of them has assumed responsibility for the entire trip. Successive carriages are not considered as one operation and the airline responsible will be the one which operated the segment on which the delay, loss, destruction, or damage occurred.[67] The General Conditions also lay down the right of the carrier to seek reimbursement from any third party responsible for the damage or inconvenience suffered by the passenger.[68]

Chapter IX is dedicated to conciliation which is at the heart of the resolution of conflict between airlines and passengers. Conciliation is, however, not possible when the alleged violations reported stem from acts that endanger the life or health of persons or involve matters in which transactions are prohibited for reasons of public order.[69] Although the General Conditions are very extensive and cover most aspects in much detail, they do not include any rule on tarmac delay nor any set fines or sanctions for non-compliance with the rules.

Venezuela's current air passenger rights framework, established by the *Providencia Administrativa* PRE-CJU-GDA-308–24 (2024) and known as the General Conditions for Air Transport, represents a significant and detailed codification of passenger protections. This legislation, which repeals and updates prior regulations from 2009 and 2016, provides a robust legal structure that shares core principles with the European Union's Regulation 261 while exhibiting distinct characteristics tailored to its jurisdiction. The scope of the Venezuelan General Conditions is notably

66 Article 59.
67 Article 62.
68 Article 63.
69 Article 68.

broad, applying to all scheduled and non-scheduled flights, both domestic and international, departing from or arriving in Venezuela, irrespective of the carrier's nationality. This universal application is tempered only by a provision allowing for the application of more favourable rules from a passenger's country of departure. A distinctive feature is the treatment of successive flights under a single contract as a unified operation, an approach that diverges from the CJEU's interpretation in cases such as *Emirates*, reflecting a focus on the contractual relationship over operational segmentation.

In common with Regulation 261, the Venezuelan rules establish clear passenger rights in cases of denied boarding, flight cancellation, and delay, including entitlements to care, re-routing, refund, and compensation. The foundational philosophy aligns with the EU model in holding airlines accountable for operational disruptions within their control. However, the mechanisms and thresholds differ substantially. Most notably, Venezuela opts for a compensation model based on a percentage of the ticket price – 25% of the fare for the affected segment – rather than the fixed-distance-based amounts mandated by Regulation 261. This creates a variable compensation system directly tied to the cost of the ticket, which may lead to higher payouts for premium fares but less predictable and potentially lower compensation for discounted tickets compared to the EU's standardized sums.

The legislation is stringent in several areas. It imposes a complete prohibition on overbooking. The rules on assistance are highly prescriptive, specifying exact timelines and nutritional standards for the provision of food and drink, and mandating three-star hotel accommodation when necessary. These provisions, including prioritized care for vulnerable passengers and obligations to cater to special dietary needs upon notification, create a high standard of care that may exceed the requirements of many other regimes. However, the open-ended obligation to meet notified dietary needs, without clear limits, presents a potential operational challenge.

The framework also incorporates elements less common in passenger rights regulations, such as detailed chapters on contract formation, baggage, and data protection. Baggage liability rules are explicitly aligned with the Montreal Convention's SDR-based limits, and provisions on downgrading and services for persons with reduced mobility are included. A unique and potentially contentious feature is the integration of a conciliation process as a primary dispute resolution mechanism, except for matters involving public order or safety.

Nevertheless, certain gaps and ambiguities are apparent. The General Conditions lack specific rules governing extended tarmac delays, an area addressed in other jurisdictions. Key terms such as "unforeseen circumstances or force majeure" are not defined, which may lead to legal uncertainty in their application. The notice period for cancellations that triggers compensation – set at 15 days – is longer than the 14-day period in Regulation 261, and the law does not specify a required arrival time for an alternative flight offered for a cancelled service, merely that it must be on the same route. Furthermore, while the regulation outlines passenger rights in detail, it does not establish specific administrative fines or sanctions for airline non-compliance, potentially relying more heavily on judicial enforcement by passengers, as expressly permitted in the text.

In conclusion, Venezuela's 2024 General Conditions for Air Transport establish a comprehensive, passenger-centric legal framework that draws inspiration from international models like Regulation 261 but establishes its own identity. It is characterized by a broad scope, a ticket-price-based compensation model, a strict prohibition on overbooking, and highly detailed assistance obligations. The regulation demonstrates a clear intent to uphold passenger dignity and provide substantial protections. Its effectiveness in practice, however, will depend on consistent enforcement and the resolution of its inherent ambiguities, particularly around undefined key concepts and the absence of tarmac delay rules. When placed in a comparative context, the Venezuelan system can be seen as adopting a similarly protective ethos as the EU regime but through a distinct legal architecture that reflects its specific policy choices and legal tradition.

Comparison with EU Regulation

Feature	**Venezuela PRE-CJU-GDA-308–24 of 2024**	**EU Regulation 261/2004**
Delay Compensation	25% of ticket value.	≥3h: €250–600 (by distance).
Cancellation Rights	<15d notice: Re-routing or refund. no alternative flight → 25% of the value of the ticket.	<14d notice: Refund or re-routing + €250–600 compensation (by distance).
Overbooking	Volunteers first; re-routing/refund.	Volunteer first; €250–€600 (by distance) if denied boarding.
Baggage Compensation	17 SDR/kg (checked); 1,000 SDR (carry-on).	Not specified.

Bibliography

- Despacho del Presidente, Providencia Administrativa PRE-CJU-353-09 (Instituto Nacional de Aeronáutica Civil, 14 December 2009).
- Providencia Administrativa PRE-CJU-GDA-398-16, published in the Gaceta Oficial N° 6.228 Extraordinario on 18 May 2016.

- Despacho del Presidente, Providencia Administrativa PRE-CJU-GDA-308-24, published in the Gaceta Oficial N° 43.000 on 5 November 2024.
- Case C-173/07 *Emirates Airlines – Direktion für Deutschland v Schenkel.*
- Aurelio Fernandez Concheso, 'Nuevas Condiciones Generales de Transporte Aéreo' (21 April 2025) <https://aureliofernandezconcheso.com/es/nuevas-condiciones-generales-de-transporte-aereo/> accessed 22 December 2025.

II.57

Vietnam

Vietnam's air passenger rights are primarily governed by the Law on Civil Aviation 2006 as amended in 2014, 2023, and 2025[1] and several related circulars. Circular No. 14/2015/TT-BGTVT of 2015 of Ministry of Transport provides non-refundable fixed compensation for air passengers, which has been amended and supplemented with a number of articles by Circular No. 27/2017/TT-BGTVT of 2017, Circular No. 21/2020/TT-BGTVT of 2020, Circular No. 19/2023/TT-BGTVT of 2023, and Circular No. 44/2023/VBHN-BGTVT of 2023.[2] The Circulars are applicable to all flights departing from Vietnam for passengers with a confirmed reservation.[3] Under those laws, passengers are entitled to compensation in the event of denied boarding, a flight cancellation, or a delay of more than four hours provided that the cause of the disruption is within the airlines' control.[4] It is the first time a law makes it clear from the outset and first article the minimum time threshold as well as the need for the cause of the disruption to be the carrier's fault. These regulations ensure that passengers departing from Vietnam are entitled

1 Law No. 66/2006/QH11, as amended by Law No. 61/2014/QH13, and most recently in 2023.

2 <https://thuvienphapluat.vn/van-ban/EN/Giao-thong-Van-tai/Circular-19-2023-TT-BGTVT-amendment-of-Articles-under-Circulars-relating-to-air-transport/575086/tieng-anh.aspx>.

In December 2025, amendments to the Law on Civil Aviation were passed and will take effect from 1 July 2026. Those amendments will fully replace the existing Law. At the time of writing, the text was not yet available for Law No. 130/2025/QH15. But there is a consolidated text (Văn bản hợp nhất 102/VBHN-VPQH 2025) which will integrate the 2025 amendments with the original 2006/2014 laws accessible at <https://thuvienphapluat.vn/van-ban/Giao-thong-Van-tai/Van-ban-hop-nhat-102-VBHN-VPQH-2025-Luat-Hang-khong-dan-dung-Viet-Nam-672481.aspx>.

See: Minh Kiet, 'New Legal Framework for Aviation Development' (*VnEconomy*, 15 December 2025) <https://en.vneconomy.vn/new-legal-framework-for-aviation-development.htm>.

3 Article 1 Circular No. 14/2015/TT-BGTVT <https://www.malaysiaairlines.com/my/en/legal/vietnam-consumer-protection.html>.

4 Article 1 introduced by amendment through Circular No. 19/2023/TT-BGTVT of 2023.

DOI: 10.4324/9781003746164-68

to fixed compensation based on the guidelines provided in the circulars, irrespective of the airline's policies. The Circulars are based on the departure delay and not the arrival delay which might end up being less favourable for passengers. It seems that those Circulars will be replaced by the New Law on Civil Aviation since it mandates airlines to compensate passengers and provide meals, accommodation, and transport for delayed or cancelled flights.

The Circulars are quite short. After defining some key terms, Circular 14/2015/TT-BGTVT directly mentions the rules for compensation.[5] However, Article 3 does not include the amount of compensation which is found in Article 8. Instead, Article 3 mentions that the non-refundable compensation is due in the event of denial of boarding, flight cancellations and long delays – of more than four hours.[6] Article 4 Clause 1 redefines Article 3 Clause 1 by stipulating that compensation is due unless the situation falls within the exemption of Articles 5 to 7. The compensation does not affect other carrier obligations.[7] If a carrier is liable for civil damages, the fixed compensation can be deducted from that larger amount.[8] Article 10 of Circular 14/2015/TT-BGTVT as amended by Circular No. 19/2023/TT-BGTVT grants passengers the right to request non-refundable advance compensation if an airline fails to fulfil its compensation obligation on time. Indeed, the delay at departure might be within the four hours but result in a long delay at arrival.

The amount is influenced by the distance of the flight but also by whether the flight is a domestic or international flight.[9] The compensation only applies once, meaning that if a flight is delayed and later cancelled, passengers only can claim once. For domestic flights with a distance under 500 km, passengers are entitled to 200,000 Vietnamese Dong (VND), flights between 500 and 1,000 km result in a compensation of 300,000 VND, finally flights over 1,000 km must be compensated by 400,000 VND. For international flights, the minimum distance is 1,000 km which entitles passengers to $25, flights between 1,000 and 2,500 km to $50, flights between 2,500 km and 5,000 km to $80, and finally, flights above 5,000 km result in a compensation of $150. The compensation can be paid in cash, by bank transfer, or, with passenger agreement, through free tickets/vouchers or other services.[10]

5 Article 3.
6 Article 3(1) Circular No. 14/2015/TT-BGTVT.
7 Article 3(2) Circular No. 14/2015/TT-BGTVT.
8 Article 3(3) Circular No. 14/2015/TT-BGTVT.
9 Article 8 Circular No. 14/2015/TT-BGTVT.
10 Article 9.

Flight Type	Distance	Compensation
Domestic (VND)	Under 500 km.	200,000 VND.
	500 km–under 1,000 km.	300,000 VND.
	1,000 km or more.	400,000 VND.
International (USD)	Under 1,000 km.	$25.
	1,000 km–under 2,500 km.	$50.
	2,500 km–under 5,000 km.	$80.
	5,000 km or more.	$150.

Passengers are also entitled to care and assistance, starting after one hour for drinks, two hours for a full meal, and more than six hours and overnight delay for accommodation.[11] The Circulars do not mention entitlement to phone calls or internet access.[12]

Waiting Time	Services Provided
1 Hour to Less Than 2 Hours	Free drinks (water, soft drinks, etc.).
2 Hours to Less Than 6 Hours	Free **meals and drinks** (full meal service).
More Than 6 Hours	**Accommodation** (if overnight delay) + meals/drinks + transport to/from hotel (if needed).

Interestingly, the Civil Aviation Law of Vietnam contains a provision on denial of boarding[13] which has been supplemented by Circular 14/2015/TT-BGTVT and its amendments. A passenger will be considered as denied of boarding in case of early departure which has not been notified or with which the passenger does not agree.[14] Circular 19/2023/TT-BGTVT further clarifies the definition of "early departure" (15 minutes earlier than scheduled) and the airline's obligations in such cases, including refunds.[15] When a passenger is regarded as being denied boarding, they are entitled to a non-refundable advance compensation, re-routing, or rebooking on a different flight.[16] If the passenger refuses the re-routing/rebooking, they

11 Harley Miller, 'Passenger Rights in Case of Flight Delays 2025' (23 April 2025) <https://luatminhnguyen.com/en/enterprise/business-sectors/aviation/passenger-rights-in-case-of-flight-delays-2025/#:~:text=by%20Circular%20No.-,19%2F2023%2FTT%2DBGTVT),from%20the%20date%20of%20request>.
12 Article 4.
13 Article 146.
14 Clause 8 Article 8 Circular No. 19/2023/TT-BGTVT.
15 Clauses 7 and 8 Article 8 Circular No. 19/2023/TT-BGTVT.
16 Clause 6(a) and (b) Article 8 Circular No. 19/2023/TT-BGTVT.

are entitled to a full refund.[17] It is not clear however if the airlines have an obligation to first find volunteers before denying boarding.

Circular No. 19/2023/TT-BGTVT of 2023 clarified that a delayed flight is a flight whose actual departure time is 15 minutes later than the expected departure.[18] In such an event, if no fault of the passengers is found, the airline is obliged to provide and fully update the information for the passenger. Furthermore, the airline is required to issue an apology to affected passengers and cover expenses for food, accommodation, communication, and other costs directly associated with airport waiting times, in accordance with the regulations of carriage.[19] The airline must also uphold high standards of passenger service quality at the airport.

For flights delayed by two hours or more, the airline must adjust the passenger's itinerary, may transfer them to another flight, and must waive all change restrictions and surcharges.[20] For delays of five hours or more, passengers can choose between accepting these arrangements or requesting a refund for the full or unused ticket value at the airport or official offices.[21] In cases of significant delays, airlines must provide non-refundable advance compensation to affected passengers with confirmed tickets, as regulated by the Ministry of Transport.

While most of the definitions of key terms is quite standard, flight cancellation refers to the non-operation of a scheduled flight that has been published in the carrier's reservation system (CRS) within 24 hours prior to the scheduled departure time.[22] According to Article 147 Clause 2 of the Civil Aviation Law of Vietnam, passengers have the right to request the carrier to rearrange the itinerary or refund the unused ticket in the event the transport is not operated due to a fault of the carrier. If a passenger is not transported due to an airline's responsibility and the flight is cancelled without notifying the passenger in advance, the airline is required to provide compensation, in addition to fulfilling obligations similar to those for flight delays.[23]

However, the Circulars also contain very broad exemptions found in Articles 5, 6, and 7. Article 6 lists "objective reasons" for long delays and cancellations such as adverse weather and unsafe flight conditions, security risks, government decisions, passenger health emergencies,

17 Clause 6(c) Article 8 Circular No. 19/2023/TT-BGTVT.

18 Circular No. 19/2023/TT-BGTVT of 2023 including an Article 8(1).

19 Article 8 Clause 3 of Circular No. 14/2015/TT-BGTVT, Article 7 of Circular No. 36/2014/TT-BGTVT as amended and supplmented by Circular No. 19/2023/TT-BGTVT.

20 Clause 4(a) Article 8 Circular No. 19/2023/TT-BGTVT.

21 Clause 4(b) Article 8 Circular No. 19/2023/TT-BGTVT.

22 Article 2(4) Circular No. 14/2015/TT-BGTVT and Clause 5 of Article 8 Circular No. 19/2023/TT-BGTVT.

23 Clause 5 Article 8 Circular No. 19/2023/TT-BGTVT.

aircraft sabotage, armed conflict or political instability or strikes, insufficient infrastructure or air navigation services, technical problems after the captain signs for flight readiness, or other force majeure events. Those terms are quite vague requiring courts' interpretation such as "technical problems during aircraft operation," which can be a significant loophole for airlines. Moreover, compensation is not due if the passenger is re-routed and arrives within a specified timeframe: four hours for direct, six hours for connecting. Article 7 relates to passenger non-cooperation or proper notification. For instance, if the passenger did not register contact information or could not be reached or the passenger did not show up for check-in on time. Crucially, it also exempts compensation if the airline provides notice of delay/cancellation at least 24 hours prior. Exemptions also apply to passengers on free or heavily discounted tickets.

Category	Exemption Conditions
Objective Reasons (Article 6)	• Adverse weather conditions. • Security risks (terrorism, unruly passengers). • Government/airport decisions. • Medical emergencies. • Aircraft sabotage or armed conflict. • Strikes (staff, air traffic control). • Infrastructure/air navigation failures. • Technical defects after flight readiness. • Force majeure (natural disasters, pandemics, etc.).
Re-routing Policy	Passenger arrives within: • **4 hours** (direct flights). • **6 hours** (connecting flights).
Passenger-Related (Article 7)	• Passenger failed to provide contact info/could not be reached. • Passenger missed check-in/boarding. • Airline notified ≥24 hours before departure. • Free or heavily discounted tickets (unless otherwise specified).

Article 11 briefly states that passengers must provide sufficient and accurate contact information. Downgrading is not explicitly dealt with in the Circulars nor is tarmac delay.

All the amendments make it a very difficult law to read which might be now resolved with the new Law. As of July 2026, the amendments on the Law on Civil Aviation will be effective. The recently enacted legislation stipulates that carriers bear responsibility for ensuring the accuracy of delay and cancellation announcements but also to provide timely information regarding flight statuses, while the aviation authority is tasked with overseeing adherence to these regulations.

The amendments delineate specific circumstances under which passengers are eligible for refunds on unused tickets or services. When a disruption is attributable to the carrier and a passenger with a confirmed reservation experiences a delay, flight cancellation, or denied boarding, the carrier is obligated to offer an alternative itinerary or refund the unused portion of the ticket upon request, without imposing any additional charges.[24]

For passengers holding confirmed bookings who experience delays, cancellations, or denied boarding through no fault of their own, carriers must issue an apology, arrange meals, accommodation, and transportation, and cover all reasonable waiting-time expenses incurred at the airport. Furthermore, in case of disruption caused by the carrier, carriers are obligated to provide a non-refundable advance compensation payment in cash or as a voucher of equivalent value. If further compensation is awarded under civil liability provisions, this advance payment will be deducted from the final amount owed.

The revised legislation also clarifies passenger rights, including the entitlement to request an alternative itinerary or a refund if transportation is not provided due to the carrier's fault. Additionally, the law permits passengers to discontinue their journey at any airport or mandatory stopover, entitling them to a refund for the unused portion of their ticket or services, subject to allowable deductions.[25]

Vietnam's system is characterized by a hybrid legal structure. The overarching Law on Civil Aviation, most recently amended in 2025, sets forth broad passenger rights and carrier obligations. The operational specifics, however, are largely codified in subordinate instruments, primarily Circulars. This structure creates a clear, rule-based entitlement to fixed monetary compensation for denied boarding, cancellation, and long delays exceeding four hours, provided the disruption is within the airline's control. The compensation amounts are precisely defined, tiered by flight distance and domestic/international classification. This approach offers predictability and administrative simplicity. The framework also mandates a graduated scale of care and assistance – refreshments, meals, and accommodation – based on the duration of a delay and includes specific provisions for scenarios like early departure (denied boarding) and advance compensation payments.

24 Vietnam Today, 'New Law Enhances Passenger Protections for Cancelled Flights' (11 December 2025) <https://dtinews.dantri.com.vn/vietnam-today/new-law-enhances-passenger-protections-for-cancelled-flights-20251211150426791.htm>.

25 Vietnam Today, 'New Law Enhances Passenger Protections for Cancelled Flights' (11 December 2025) <https://dtinews.dantri.com.vn/vietnam-today/new-law-enhances-passenger-protections-for-cancelled-flights-20251211150426791.htm>.

However, critical distinctions emerge when this model is measured against the EU Regulation. First, the compensation trigger in Vietnam is based on the departure delay, whereas the EU employs the more passenger-centric arrival delay. This fundamental difference can significantly affect eligibility, as a nominal departure delay can result in a substantial arrival delay, a scenario where EU passengers would be protected but Vietnamese passengers might not be. Second, the fixed compensation amounts under the Vietnamese Circulars, while explicit, are generally modest in comparison to the tiers established under Regulation 261, which are higher and not differentiated between domestic and intra-EU flights.

Third, the scope of exemptions available to carriers presents a potential variance in practical application. Vietnam's Circulars enumerate a broad list of "objective reasons," including "technical problems during aircraft operation," which could be interpreted more expansively than the EU's stricter jurisprudence on "extraordinary circumstances." The EU's evolving case law has progressively narrowed this exemption, particularly regarding technical defects, often requiring airlines to demonstrate that the issue was not inherent in the normal exercise of their activity. The Vietnamese framework's inclusion of an exemption where re-routing achieves arrival within four or six hours, and where notice is given 24 hours prior to departure, also creates avenues for carrier relief that are either absent or structured differently in the EU model.

The 2025 amendments to the Law on Civil Aviation signify a purposeful step towards strengthening this framework. By codifying core obligations – such as the carrier's duty to provide care, compensation, and refunds in cases within its control – into the primary law, Vietnam is transitioning from a system heavily reliant on ministerial circulars to one with a firmer statutory foundation. This move aims to enhance legal certainty and elevate the stature of passenger rights. The amendments also introduce principles like carrier responsibility for accurate information and enhanced oversight by the aviation authority, aligning with broader trends in consumer protection governance.

In conclusion, Vietnam has established a functional and increasingly formalized system for air passenger rights. Its strengths lie in its clear, codified compensation tables and structured care obligations. Nevertheless, it emerges as a generally less protective regime in key operational dimensions: the use of departure delay as the primary metric, the comparatively lower value of fixed compensation, and the potentially wider latitude for airlines to invoke exemptions. The forthcoming implementation of the 2025 law from July 2026, along with its crucial guiding decrees, will determine whether this new statutory phase meaningfully narrows that gap by refining definitions, particularly of "carrier fault" and exemption categories, and by potentially recalibrating compensation levels to offer a more robust level of consumer redress.

Comparison with EU Regulation 261

Feature	Vietnam Circular 14/2015/ TT-BGTVT as Amended	EU Regulation 261/2004
Delay Compensation	• Domestic: 200K–400K VND (by distance). • International: $25–$150 (by distance).	≥3h: €250–€600 (by distance).
Cancellation Rights	<24 hours notice: Refund/ rebooking + compensation (if airline at fault).	<14d notice: Refund or re-routing + €250–600 compensation (by distance).
Overbooking	Refund/rebooking if denied boarding.	Volunteer first; €250–€600 (by distance) if denied boarding.
Baggage Compensation	Not specified.	Not specified.

Bibliography

- Law No. 66/2006/QH11, Vietnam Civil Aviation, 29 June 2006 <https://thuvienphapluat.vn/van-ban/EN/Giao-thong-Van-tai/Law-No-66-2006-QH11-of-June-29-2006-Vietnam-civil-aviation/80639/tieng-anh.aspx> accessed 29 December 2025.
- Law No. 61/2014/QH13, Law amending and supplementing a number of articles of the Vietnam Civil Aviation Law, 21 November 2014 <https://thuvienphapluat.vn/van-ban/EN/Giao-thong-Van-tai/Law-No-61-2014-QH13-amending-and-supplementing-a-number-of-articles-of-the-Vietnam-civil-aviation-Law/267271/tieng-anh.aspx> accessed 29 December 2025.
- Law No. 03/VBHN-VPQH, Law Vietnam Civil Aviation, 2 August 2023 <https://thuvienphapluat.vn/van-ban/Giao-thong-Van-tai/Integrated-document-03-VBHN-VPQH-2023-Law-Vietnam-Civil-Aviation-599642.aspx> accessed 29 December 2025.
- Law No. 2025/QH15.
- Consolidated text (Văn bản hợp nhất 102/VBHN-VPQH 2025) <https://thuvienphapluat.vn/van-ban/Giao-thong-Van-tai/Van-ban-hop-nhat-102-VBHN-VPQH-2025-Luat-Hang-khong-dan-dung-Viet-Nam-672481.aspx> accessed 29 December 2025.
- Circular No. 14/2015/TT-BGTVT, Circular on Non-Refundable Fixed Compensation in Air Passenger Transport, 27 April 2015 <https://thuvienphapluat.vn/van-ban/giao-thong-van-tai/circular-no-14-2015-tt-bgtvt-non-refundable-fixed-compensation-in-air-passenger-transport-275468.aspx> accessed 29 December 2025.

- Circular No. 36/2014/TT-BGTVT, Circular Providing for Quality of Passenger Services at the Airports, 29 August 2014 <https://thuvienphapluat.vn/van-ban/EN/Thuong-mai/Circular-No-36-2014-TT-BGTVT-providing-for-quality-of-passenger-services-at-the-airports/298892/tieng-anh.aspx> accessed 29 December 2025.
- Circular No. 19/2023/TT-BGTVT, Circular Amendment, Annulment of Articles Under Circulars Relating to Air Transport, 30 June 2023 <https://thuvienphapluat.vn/van-ban/EN/Giao-thong-Van-tai/Circular-19-2023-TT-BGTVT-amendment-of-Articles-under-Circulars-relating-to-air-transport/575086/tieng-anh.aspx> accessed 29 December 2025.
- Kiet, M., 'New Legal Framework for Aviation Development' (*VnEconomy*, 15 December 2025) <https://en.vneconomy.vn/new-legal-framework-for-aviation-development.htm> accessed 29 December 2025.
- Miller, H., 'Passenger Rgiths in Case of Flight Delays 2025' (23 April 2025) <https://luatminhnguyen.com/en/enterprise/business-sectors/aviation/passenger-rights-in-case-of-flight-delays-2025/#:~:text=by%20Circular%20No.-,19%2F2023%2FTT%2DBGTVT),from%20the%20date%20of%20request)> accessed 29 December 2025.
- Vietnam Today, 'New Law Enhances Passenger Protections for Cancelled Flights' (11 December 2025) <https://dtinews.dantri.com.vn/vietnam-today/new-law-enhances-passenger-protections-for-cancelled-flights-20251211150426791.htm> accessed 29 December 2025.

Conclusion

In recent years, a global trend has emerged: the proliferation of national and regional legislation designed to grant air passengers enhanced rights in cases of delay, cancellation, or denial of boarding. These initiatives aim to provide a higher standard of protection and certainty than that afforded by the global regimes of the 1929 Warsaw Convention or the 1999 Montreal Convention, which were originally designed to create a uniform legal regime but are silent on specific passenger entitlements. We are currently facing "the golden age of consumer protection,"[1] an era pioneered and led by the European Union with its Regulation 261.

The global landscape of air passenger rights regulation is defined by a powerful and paradoxical tension: the centrifugal force of European regulatory hegemony versus the centripetal pull of national diversification. The "Brussels Effect" of Regulation 261 is undeniable, in light of the number of countries which have copied or gotten inspired by that Regulation.[2] Its influence operates through multiple channels: considering the binding integration within the European Common Aviation Area (ECAA) and the Euro-Mediterranean Aviation Agreements (EMAA) frameworks to voluntary emulation by nations as geographically and culturally distant as the Philippines' Air Passenger Bill of Rights and Türkiye's SHY-PASSENGERS, the EU's model has become the global benchmark. Similarly, Kazakhstan has moved to strengthen passenger rights under its Civil Aviation Law, establishing carrier responsibilities that align with the EU's standardized triggers for liability but conferring much more protection to special needs passengers.

1 Vincent Correia, *Advanced Introduction to International Air Law* (Edward Elgard Publishing 2025) 102.
2 Anu Bradford, *The Brussels Effect: How the European Union Rules the World* (Oxford University Press 2020) 25–65.

DOI: 10.4324/9781003746164-69

Beyond direct emulation, the EU model establishes a powerful normative baseline that compels engagement. Indeed, even jurisdictions seeking to distinguish themselves have adopted the EU's core pillars such as standardized compensation, clear triggers for liability, and narrow "extraordinary circumstances" defences. For instance, Saudi Arabia's Executive Regulations and Oman's recent frameworks mirror the EU model but adapt them to regional economic priorities. Brazil offers hybrid models with ANAC *Resolución* 400 incorporating EU-inspired care and compensation but with distinct calculation methods. Similarly, the Nigerian Civil Aviation Regulations (Nig. CARs) Part 19 represents an adaptation of EU standards with a distinct compensation of 25% of the ticket price but a much more stringent standard than the EU regarding refreshments. This has created a de facto standard, ensuring a baseline of passenger protection across vast networks of air travel and establishing a powerful normative framework that new legislations are almost compelled to engage with, whether by adoption or reaction.

Alongside this regional dominance, a parallel and equally significant trend has been the proliferation of unique national initiatives. Countries such as Canada and Israel have crafted distinctive regulatory approaches that, while acknowledging the EU's precedent, tailor provisions to their specific legal and consumer landscapes, such as Canada's tiered compensation based on delay length and carrier size. The United States, with its prescriptive but narrow focus on lengthy tarmac delays and mandatory refunds, consciously rejects the EU's compensation model for cancellations, favouring a complaint-driven enforcement system that places a different burden on the passenger. Countries like China have taken a different approach but still ensure passengers have a right to care while Australia's prescriptive Consumer Law creates a strict, but non-automatic, right to care and remedies that depends heavily on judicial interpretation. Through the Civil Aviation Law (Ley de Aviación Civil), Mexico has introduced some of the most stringent refund policies globally, allowing passengers to cancel reservations within 24 hours of purchase for a full refund and requiring compensation of at least 25% of the ticket price for delays exceeding four hours.

This has resulted in a patchwork of protections where rights and carrier liabilities can vary dramatically depending on the departure point or the operating airline. While this diversity can foster innovation and allow for higher standards of protection in some cases, it also creates significant complexity and potential unfairness, undermining the Montreal Convention's foundational goal of uniformity. A passenger travelling from London to New York via a connection in Toronto may find their rights shifting three times in a single journey, creating a legal grey area where carrier liability depends more on geography, nationality,[3] or place the ticket was bought than on the nature of the service failure.

Regulation of passenger rights for delayed or cancelled flights is neither unique nor a recent global development. However, in the face of this complex interplay between regional hegemony and national diversification, the question arises whether the continued fragmentation of passenger rights is sustainable. The current landscape, characterized by overlapping and sometimes conflicting regional and national rules, renders compliance a labyrinthine challenge for airlines and creates legal uncertainty for passengers. This reality compellingly invites a renewed debate on the necessity of a dedicated international convention on passenger rights. While achieving global consensus among states with entrenched regimes like the US and EU would be a formidable undertaking, the alternative – an increasingly fragmented and contradictory regulatory environment – directly undermines the international effort to harmonize aviation law. A new multilateral instrument may be the most adequate solution to reconcile the legitimate demand for robust passenger protection with the aviation industry's critical need for legal uniformity and predictability.

3 Brazilian courts have a tendency to accept jurisdiction despite the case having little connection to Brazil.

INDEX

For Product Safety Concerns and Information please contact our EU
representative GPSR@taylorandfrancis.com
Taylor & Francis Verlag GmbH, Kaufingerstraße 24, 80331 München, Germany

www.ingramcontent.com/pod-product-compliance
Ingram Content Group UK Ltd.
Pitfield, Milton Keynes, MK11 3LW, UK
UKHW020156200926
475702UK00016B/2743
* 9 7 8 1 0 4 1 2 5 3 2 1 1 *